Computational Intelligence in Biomedical Internet of Medical Things

Scrivener Publishing
100 Cummings Center, Suite 541J
Beverly, MA 01915-6106

Publishers at Scrivener
Martin Scrivener (martin@scrivenerpublishing.com)
Phillip Carmical (pcarmical@scrivenerpublishing.com)

Computational Intelligence in Biomedical Internet of Medical Things

Edited by

Satya Prakash Yadav
Department of Computer Science and Engineering, Madan Mohan Malaviya University of Technology, Gorakhpur, U.P., India

Abhay Bansal
School of Computer Science Engineering and Technology, Bennett University, Greater Noida, UP, India

and

Victor Hugo C. de Albuquerque
Department of Teleinformatics Engineering, Federal University of Ceará, Brazil

Scrivener Publishing

WILEY

This edition first published 2026 by John Wiley & Sons, Inc., 111 River Street, Hoboken, NJ 07030, USA and Scrivener Publishing LLC, 100 Cummings Center, Suite 541J, Beverly, MA 01915, USA

For more information about Scrivener publications please visit www.scrivenerpublishing.com.

Wiley Global Headquarters
111 River Street, Hoboken, NJ 07030, USA

For details of our global editorial offices, customer services, and more information about Wiley products visit us at www.wiley.com.

The manufacturer's authorized representative according to the EU General Product Safety Regulation is Wiley-VCH GmbH, Boschstr. 12, 69469 Weinheim, Germany, e-mail: Product_Safety@wiley.com.

Library of Congress Cataloging-in-Publication Data

ISBN 978-1-394-38662-8

Cover image: Generated with AI using Adobe Firefly
Cover design by Russell Richardson

Set in size of 11pt and Minion Pro by Manila Typesetting Company, Makati, Philippines

Printed in the USA

10 9 8 7 6 5 4 3 2 1

Contents

Preface

This book fills a critical gap in the field of Computational Biomedical Intelligence by bringing together, in a single volume, the state-of-the-art in designing and implementing IoMT information systems—particularly in developing countries. It specifically addresses the challenge of transforming existing information systems into effective management support systems. The overarching goal is to improve the performance of health units by leveraging computational intelligence and IoMT technologies, ultimately leading to better health outcomes and more efficient healthcare delivery.

The rationale for this approach stems from a number of persistent issues in the primary biomedical systems of most developing countries. Traditional health unit-based computational systems often suffer from the same inefficiencies and disorganization that have long plagued data collection and utilization in peripheral health units, as previously discussed.

The book explores the latest trends and developments in Computational Intelligence within Biomedical IoMT, aiming to empower medical professionals, caregivers, and surgeons. It provides insights into diagnostics and treatment of chronic diseases and explains how various human physiological parameters—such as heart rate, blood sugar levels, blood pressure, temperature, and air quality—can be monitored using a range of sensors.

It further explores the growing role of IoMT in transforming the healthcare industry. The book demonstrates how medical instruments—scanners, robots, appliances, cameras, handhelds, wearables, and other devices—can be integrated with cloud-based software applications, analytics platforms, digital twins, databases, and AI models to enable intelligent behavior.

A key focus is healthcare data and the application of AI in interpreting sensor and device outputs. It illustrates how AI can generate realistic data from sample inputs and convert raw data into actionable knowledge, enabling real-time monitoring and intelligent diagnostics.

This book aims to integrate emerging technologies, novel research, and strategic approaches in Health Information Systems powered by computational intelligence. It is structured for exceptional readability and clear understanding, facilitating the adaptation of key concepts by a diverse audience that includes students, researchers, policymakers, healthcare managers, system designers, academicians, and practitioners engaged in Biomedical IoMT research and development.

We extend our sincere thanks to all who supported the creation of this book, especially Martin Scrivener and the team at Scrivener Publishing, for their guidance and dedicated efforts.

The Editors
November 2025

Part I

FOUNDATIONS AND FRAMEWORKS

1

Introduction to Computational Biomedical Intelligence

G. Padma Priya[1], Anima Nanda[2*], Nimisha Ghosh[3], E. Sakthivel[4], Devendra Parmar[5] and Rakesh Kumar Yadav[6]

[1]*Department of Chemistry and Biochemistry, Jain (Deemed-to-be University), Bangalore, Karnataka, India*
[2]*Department of Biomedical, Sathyabama Institute of Science and Technology, Chennai, Tamil Nadu, India*
[3]*Centre for Internet of Things, Siksha 'O' Anusandhan (Deemed to be University), Bhubaneswar, Odisha, India*
[4]*Department of Computer Science and Engineering, Presidency University, Bangalore, Karnataka, India*
[5]*Computer Science and Engineering, Parul Institute of Technology, Parul University, Vadodara, Gujarat, India*
[6]*Department of Computer Science, Maharishi School of Engineering & Technology, Maharishi University of Information Technology, Uttar Pradesh, India*

Abstract
Computational biomedical intelligence (CBI) is an interdisciplinary field that integrates artificial intelligence (AI), machine learning (ML), and computational tools to solve complex problems in healthcare, from disorder prognosis to personalized medicinal drugs. However, the scope of this study is limited to data availability, AI approach interpretability, and regulatory limitations in healthcare applications. The objective of this article is to discover the function of CBI in advancing precision medicine, improving early detection, and improving healthcare decision-making through AI-driven insights. This study examines various components,

**Corresponding author*: animananda.biomed@sathyabama.ac.in; ORCID: 0000-0003-3629-7937
G. Padma Priya: ORCID: 0000-0004911-1823
Nimisha Ghosh: ORCID: 0000-0002-0697-6368
Devendra Parmar: ORCID: 0000-0003-1114-693X
Rakesh Kumar Yadav: ORCID: 0000-0002-0151-4981

Satya Prakash Yadav, Abhay Bansal and Victor Hugo C. de Albuquerque (eds.) Computational Intelligence in Biomedical Internet of Medical Things, (3–16) © 2026 Scrivener Publishing LLC

which include AI applications in disease diagnosis, personalized medicinal drugs, drug discovery, and scientific imaging. It also explores demanding situations, including data privacy, model transparency, and healthcare. The advantages of medical practitioners and researchers lie in offering complete information on how CBI can transform healthcare, optimize patient outcomes, and inform future study directions.

Keywords: Computational biomedical intelligence, AI, machine learning, precision medicine

1.1 Introduction

The field of computational biomedical intelligence (CBI) is at the intersection of computer technology, artificial intelligence (AI), and biomedical sciences. It leverages computational tools, algorithms, and data evaluation strategies to address complex challenges in healthcare, biology, and medicine. The Internet of Medical Things (IoMT) is an aspect of the Internet-of-Things (IoT) technique that includes interconnected equipment for medicine for healthcare surveillance. The IoMT components, sometimes referred to as IoT for healthcare, integrate technology, interface detectors, and machine learning (ML)-based AI to allow individuals to have intervention-free monitoring of healthcare. The IoMT software connects patients to physicians' medical equipment, enabling remote data collection, processing, and transmission *via* a secure connection. The IoMT technology helps to cut unnecessary hospitalizations and associated medical costs by allowing remote monitoring of health metrics. The IoMT medical technology category includes portable, in-home individual health surveillance devices, as well as medical or point-of-care (POC) devices based on clinical systems [1]. The IoMT portable technology can also detect accidental tumbles in elderly persons. Injuries in the elderly are unavoidable, but conditions should be observed and managed to minimize long-term harm. The IoMT technologies that enable remote surveillance of indicators of health assist in lowering unnecessary hospital stays and associated medical costs [2].

Artificial intelligence and technological advances are transforming several industries, including healthcare. This is largely due to the potential benefits of AI technology for patients. Advancements in technology and financing have led to the widespread use of machinery in healthcare, including next-generation sequencing, computerized data collection and storage, diagnosis, and recommendations [3]. Advanced medical technology has extended to major start-ups globally, improving patient safety and longevity. Initially, advances in the health industry were driven by software and accessibility, which enabled digitization of formerly paper-based operations [4].

The term AI describes computer techniques that simulate human cognitive functions, for instance, deep learning (DL), cognition, involvement, flexibility, and perception. Certain systems can perform activities that often need the judgment and intelligence of individuals. These approaches are interdisciplinary and relevant to many domains, such as medical care and health [5]. Artificial intelligence has a big impact on the healthcare industry, with implementations spanning several phases. Artificial intelligence has a significant impact on pharmaceutical product development, including medication discovery and management. The AI technologies are utilized in discovering drugs, including screening and design [6]. Computational intelligence (CI) is an emerging topic at the forefront of bioinformatics and biomedical systems. To address the most difficult difficulties in disease knowledge and healthcare, cutting-edge CI combines biological disciplines. Bioinformatics has made significant advances in predicting the study of genetics, protein structures, and deciphering complex cell networks [7]. Computational biomedical intelligence is shown in Figure 1.1.

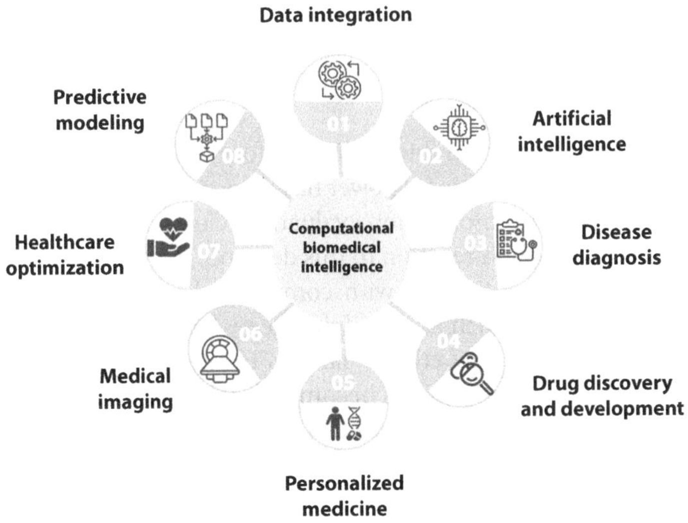

Figure 1.1 Computational biomedical intelligence. (Source: Own elaboration).

Data analysis, mathematical modeling, and simulations are included in using computational tools in biology, biotechnology, biomedical research, medical care, and medical procedures. These tools enable and benefit insight into complicated structures of biology and understanding the structural underpinnings of illness. The combination of biological science, bioinformatics, and computing methods is aimed at improving the understanding of biological processes and increasing the accuracy in healthcare decision-making [8]. The functions of ML in the biological materials' domain concentrate on the effects, problems, and future possibilities. It facilitates the creation of innovative systems for delivering drugs, biological frameworks, and surgical instruments; biological materials are essential to medicine. A thorough understanding of nanoparticles' characteristics is necessary due to the complex connection they have with biological tissues, functions, and interconnections.

Machine learning offers a way to advance this knowledge, as well as to develop and optimize the [9]. Nanoscience in healthcare provides important advances in diagnostic and therapeutic imaging, biosensing, tailored drug delivery structures, and so on. Artificial intelligence has the potential to expand applications in biomedical engineering by analyzing and interpreting biological information, accelerating drug development, and identifying selected tiny molecules or distinctive substances with predictive behavior [10].

1.2 Emergence of Computational Biomedical Intelligence

The rapid development of biomedical information, coupled with the advancements in computational power has necessitated the development of sophisticated tools for information evaluation. Computational biomedical intelligence emerged as a reaction to this demand, integrating AI, ML, and computational biology to cope with complicated biomedical challenges. Advanced technology, such as modifying genes, AI, and huge amounts of data, have introduced new ethical hazards to medical research, and the capacity to safeguard patients has become more insufficient [11]. The epidemic acted as an accelerator, and the broad adoption of remote medicine was accelerated to its highest point. As a result, the role of telemedicine in modern healthcare has increased, irrevocably transforming the landscape of medical practice. Telecommuting characterized using digital communication, as well as technology to deliver distant medical treatments, has been established for several decades [12].

Biosensor development is receiving a lot of interest in bioscience and healthcare because of its extensive usage in therapeutic sessions, healthcare, and food preparation. Biosensors are used for illness detection, diagnosis, therapy, patient health observations, and human health control [13]. The emergence of CBI is shown in Figure 1.2.

The area of medical services has entered the big data era due to significant advancements in medical technology and biomedical data expansion. In this environment, computerized medicine became a brand-new area. The multidisciplinary discipline of computing healthcare blends biology, arithmetic technology, and the domain of medicine to analyze large amounts of biological data with computers [14]. The IoMT consists of biological instruments and systems that interface with healthcare infrastructures to handle data [15]. The rising cost of medical care may impede corporate growth. Chronic problems are also becoming more prevalent, which is exacerbated by the global population's aging in diverse parts of the world. Indeed, there is a greater likelihood that the current population is more prone to chronic illnesses.

As a result, healthcare accessibility will inevitably become costly for most people. The IoMT has improved biopharmaceutical and healthcare processes while also allowing virtual patient treatment [16]. Machine learning and other strong computational technologies with great precision, accuracy, and robustness help with autonomous experimentation (AE). As demonstrated by the instance of INS018_055, it is a small-molecule inhibitor identified by *Insilico* medicine using an AI-driven approach.

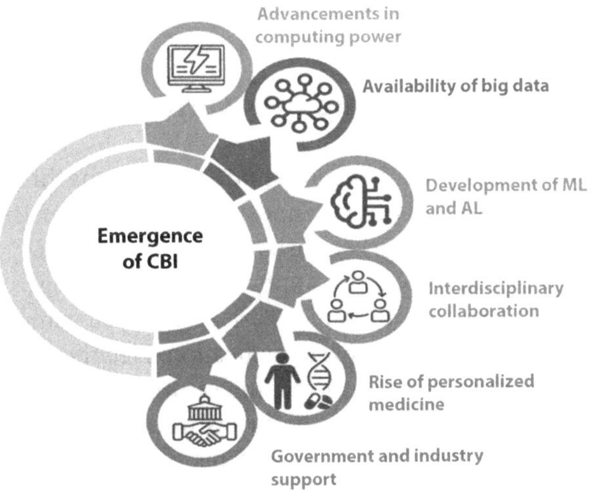

Figure 1.2 The emergence of CBI. (Source: Own elaboration).

These systems can do tasks that scientific researchers would require years to complete. Instead of manually reproducing tests and engaging in experimenting operations, AE applications create robust information and execute investigations not including the logistical and cognitive constraints that people face. Data consistency and ML-driven testing of hypotheses limit the likelihood of subjective interpretations of outcomes [17–19].

Autonomous experimentation is projected to possess a substantial influence on research in biomedicine due to its effectiveness in expediting discovery and rationalising the utilization of limited resources of material for research and development activities. The fields of chemistry and environmental sciences, biotechnology and drug development, and molecular system engineering, in particular, are fuelling an expanding pipeline of healthcare-related innovations and solutions [20, 21]. During that time, the rapid expansion of the biomedical industry was accountable for decentralized investments in research and development throughout the world, encouraging based on regional information competencies in developing countries. This change in geography and technology converted medical study and innovations in health operations into the integration area, combining diverse options in natural, scientific, technological, and quantitative techniques [22]. Strong human-computer partnerships and AI-driven durable experimenting frameworks for scientific inquiry and testing hypotheses signalled the transfer away from R&D that relies significantly on experimentation that mostly concentrated on small enhancements and thorough adapting of biotechnology to research in medicine and medical inventiveness, which quickly advanced toward the computerization of tasks in laboratories [23].

1.3 Applications Driving Innovation in Healthcare

Computational biomedical intelligence finds applications throughout multiple domains, including disease diagnosis, enhancing precision through image evaluation and biomarker discovery; drug discovery accelerates the identification of therapeutic compounds and the usage of computational simulations. Treatment regimens are customized using lifestyle and genetic data to inform individualized medication. Healthcare management improves aid allocation and choice-making in clinical settings.

Patient safety and privacy must be prioritized above anything else in the growth and implementation of AI systems, as it transforms healthcare interactions and ushers in an era of more tailored, efficient, and accessible care. There is a lot of excitement about the idea of personalized medicine. Since every individual has unique and variable characteristics at the molecular, psychological, cognitive, and ecological levels, customized healthcare is based on the notion that these characteristics may need illness therapies tailored to the individual. This notion has been partially validated by the strategy of advanced methods such as the field of imaging of proteome techniques, genome sequencing, and cellular health surveillance tools, which have demonstrated significant variation in illness processes across individuals [24]. Digital twins can help identify patterns and signs that may indicate the existence of illnesses or predict the chance of developing particular medical disorders, as well as the course of such diseases. However, the use of individual virtual twins raises moral questions about data ownership, informed permission, and the possibility to discriminate based on medical profiles. To overcome these obstacles and make sure that the search for cutting-edge medical solutions do not jeopardize patient rights and wellbeing, strong rules and regulations are desperately needed [25].

Health organizations need to overcome many challenges. Some of these challenges include a lack of understanding on the advantages and disadvantages of specific types of AI technological advances, unresolved plans for efficiently incorporating different AI applications into the healthcare organizations that are presently functioning to tackle the most urgent issues, a lack of personnel with the appropriate education for implementation, the unsuitability of AI technologies with obsolete systems, and a lack of accessibility to diverse and trustworthy data. An AI system also gathers important data from numerous patients to help in decision-making. Alerts for health risks and real-time deductions are used to predict medical outcomes [26].

1.4 Bridging Biomedical Complexity with Advanced Computing

Biomedical structures are inherently complex, characterized with the aid of substantial and heterogeneous records from genomic sequences, medical imaging, clinical records, and wearable devices. Computational intelligence offers a systematic way to uncover patterns, predict outcomes, and optimize remedies. For example, AI-driven diagnostics at present enable faster and accurate detection of diseases, such as cancer and cardiovascular conditions. Medical science has seen tremendous change in recent years, leading to ground-breaking discoveries that have transformed healthcare.

In addition to improving illness detection and treatment, these developments have raised the bar for patient care, giving people hope and promoting a higher quality of life [27]. The multidisciplinary area that is motivated by efforts to improve human health, studies, and attempts to utilize biomedical information, data, and understanding for scientific inquiry, resolution of issues, and choosing a course of action is known as biomedical informatics. Bioinformatics, a subset of biomedical informatics, should be distinguished from the former as it solely deals with data and information at the cellular and molecular level. Proteomics, transcriptomics, and genomics are only a few of the several subfields that make up bioinformatics. Additionally, biomedical informatics differs from closely related disciplines such as computer science, mathematics, statistics, and biological sciences since each has a unique focus and set of constraints [28].

1.5 Prospects and Challenges

Integrating advanced computational models with biomedical research holds the promise of revolutionizing healthcare. However, demanding situations, which include information privacy, interpretability of AI models, and the integration with existing clinical workflows, need to be addressed. As computational tools evolve, CBI is prepared to play a much greater pivotal role in advancing human health and well-being. The combination of engineering concepts and technology utilized for disease diagnosis, treatment, monitoring, and prevention is known as biomedical technologies. Science and engineering are always improving, and AI is keeping up with these developments. Artificial intelligence has advanced more quickly in recent years. It has the potential to completely transform human life. Recent developments in generative models should accelerate the development of biomedical devices [29, 30]. Every period of medical history has presented unique difficulties.

A growing population, rising life expectancy, and financial limitations are just a few of the numerous issues facing modern medicine. In addition, there is a concerning rise in cardiovascular, cancer, and neurological diseases, most of which are preventable with early diagnosis. However, a significant degree of specialization has been brought though the developments in several medical fields [31–34].

Medical decision assistance systems, or CDSSs, have evolved significantly over the past several years, providing doctors with the information required to make educated decisions about the treatment of patients. The CDSSs are currently a practical tool for improving patient experiences and reducing medical expenses [35, 36]. By offering evidence-based suggestions tailored to each patient, these systems use medical knowledge databases, electronic health records, and intricate methods like AI and ML to support physicians to make more precise choices in therapy. There are some obstacles despite its possible advantages associated with establishing CDSS. These are issues with data security, system integration, and clinician uptake. Despite the great potential of CDSS, recruitment and implementation remain challenging [37, 38]. Challenges of CBI are shown in Figure 1.3.

Based on heuristic and subject expertise, self-learning robots provide insights based on data for each examination or therapy, which the ultimate user, a doctor or lab assistant, may approve, disapprove, or modify. Laboratory end users' final choices are influenced by knowledge of (or prejudices against) AI. To state briefly, to help the healthcare industry, future healthcare practitioners will need to be proficient in ML, the computerization of huge data, and generated techniques [39].

The largest disparity is the paucity of biological sciences research on AI implementation. The biomedical science curriculum designer must consciously address this deficiency in scholarly and applied research on AI integration. Since biomedical research is expanding, educational approaches must be significantly modified to fill in the gaps in AI instruction. In addition to curriculum creation, professional mentoring, resources, and student desire to embrace the academic shift are necessary for the smooth incorporation of AI into the curriculum [40]. Numerous ethical questions are brought by the quick spread of AI technology in the

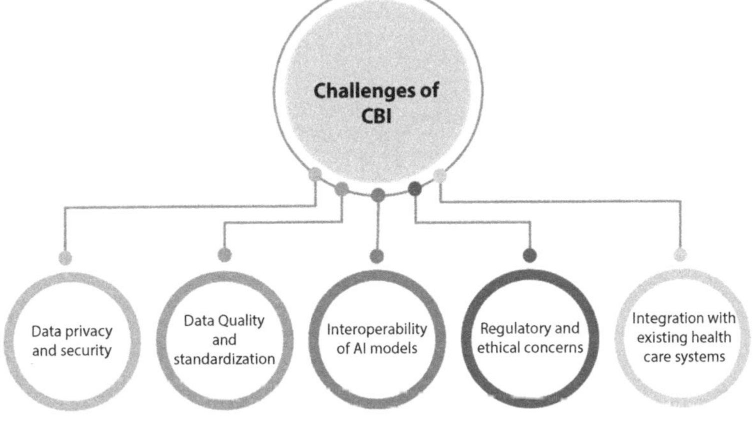

Figure 1.3 Challenges of CBI. (Source: Own elaboration).

medical field. These include striking a balance between duties to tissue and data donors and threats to freedom, autonomy, justice, privacy, and data security. Furthermore, more governmental oversight and the harmonization of international norms are necessary due to worries about how AI is traded against larger societal commitments, such as the unexpected influence of AI on public safety. Biomedical data science will have to contend with a number of significant ethical dilemmas in the future. The data used to develop AI tools needs to be examined more thoroughly. This involves a more comprehensive understanding of how bias is incorporated into the data-to-AI pipeline by those who gather and clean data, as well as those who decide which technologies should be prioritized. Other forms of bias that could call for nontechnical remedies are obscured by the present emphasis on prejudice as algorithmic fairness, despite the fact that it is a significant factor. Accordingly, further investigation is required on how prejudice is produced by AI users, as well as possible countermeasures [41]. Prospects of CBI are shown in Figure 1.4.

In biomedical innovation, data sharing is essential since it allows researchers to examine enormous volumes of data pertaining to human subjects. To exchange biological data, hospitals, businesses, and university labs create collaborative consortia. This culture is upheld by international norms and government regulations, which are based on cooperative initiatives like the project for the human genome [42].

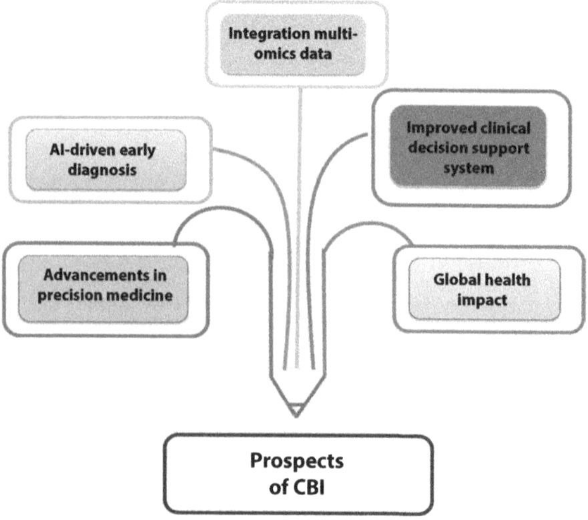

Figure 1.4 Prospects of CBI. (Source: Own elaboration).

1.6 Conclusion

Computational biomedical intelligence represents a transformative intersection of superior computing techniques and the biomedical field, presenting an immense ability to revolutionize healthcare and scientific studies. By harnessing the power of AI, ML, and information analytics, CBI provides more accurate disease diagnosis, personalized treatments, and efficient healthcare management. Its applications span across diverse domains consisting of drug discovery, sickness prevention, medical imaging, and predictive modelling, notably improving patient outcomes and quality of care. Additionally, CBI is set to integrate multi-omics data in the future, promoting more thorough methods for observing intricate biological systems. The role of AI in early detection and precision medication will continue to evolve, providing revolutionary solutions to longstanding healthcare challenges. Furthermore, CBI's capacity to optimize healthcare systems globally, particularly in low-resourced regions, presents an opportunity to address significant public health problems. Its success in healthcare faces demanding situations like data security, quality, and standardization. However, its capacity to improve care accessibility and quality is promising. As technology advances, CBI's role in biomedical sciences becomes critical, driving innovation in the healthcare landscape.

References

1. Górriz, J.M., *et al.*, Artificial Intelligence within the Interplay between Natural and Artificial Computation: Advances in Data Science, Trends and Applications. *Neurocomputing*, 410, 237–270, 2020, https://doi.org/10.1016/j.neucom.2020.05.078.
2. Manickam, P., *et al.*, Artificial Intelligence (AI) and the Internet of Medical Things (IoMT) Assisted Biomedical Systems for Intelligent Healthcare. *Biosensors*, 12, 8, 562, 2022, https://doi.org/10.3390/bios12080562.
3. Dzobo, K., *et al.*, Integrating Artificial and Human Intelligence: A Partnership for Responsible Innovation in Biomedical Engineering and Medicine. *OMICS: J. Integr. Biol.*, 24, 5, 247–263, 2020, https://doi.org/10.1089/omi.2019.0038.
4. Badnjević, A., Avdihodžić, H., Gurbeta Pokvić, L., Artificial intelligence in medical devices: Past, present and future. *Psychiatria Danubina*, 33, suppl 3, 101–106, 2021, https://hrcak.srce.hr/257613.
5. Secinaro, S., *et al.*, The Role of Artificial Intelligence in Healthcare: A Structured Literature Review. *BMC Med. Inf. Decis. Making*, 21, 1 23, 2021, https://doi.org/10.1186/s12911-021-01488-9.

6. Bhattamisra, S.K., *et al.*, Artificial Intelligence in Pharmaceutical and Healthcare Research. *Big Data Cognitive Computing*, 7, 1, 10, 2023, https://doi.org/10.3390/bdcc7010010.
7. Prabha, C., Future Perspective and Emerging Trends in Computational Intelligence, in: *Intelligent Data Analytics for Bioinformatics and Biomedical Systems*, pp. 381–396, 2024, https://doi.org/10.1002/9781394270910.ch16.
8. Leung, C.K., Biomedical Informatics: State of the Art, Challenges, and Opportunities. *BioMedInformatics*, 4, 1, 89–97, 2024, https://doi.org/10.3390/biomedinformatics4010006.
9. Suwardi, A., *et al.*, Machine Learning-Driven Biomaterials Evolution. *Adv. Mater.*, 34, 21, 2102703, 2022, https://doi.org/10.1002/adma.202102703.
10. Kasture, K. and Shende, P., Amalgamation of Artificial Intelligence with Nanoscience for Biomedical Applications. *Arch. Comput. Methods Eng.*, 30, 8, 4667–4685, 2023, https://doi.org/10.1007/s11831-023-09948-3.
11. Yijin, R,., *et al.*, Clinical translation of the assets of biomedical engineering–a retrospective analysis with looks to the future. *Expert Rev. Med. Dev.*, 16, 11, 913–922, 2019, https://doi.org/10.1080/17434440.2019.1685869.
12. Anglano, C., Canonico, M., Desimoni, F., Guazzone, M., Savarro, D., The HealthTracker System: App and Cloud-Based Wearable Multi-Sensor Device for Patients Health Tracking. *Appl. Sci.*, 14, 2, 887, 2024, https://doi.org/10.3390/app14020887.
13. Mohankumar, P., Ajayan, J., Mohanraj, T., Yasodharan, R., Recent Developments in Biosensors for Healthcare and Biomedical Applications: A Review. *Measurement*, 167, 108293, 2021, https://doi.org/10.1016/j.measurement.2020.108293.
14. Yang, S., Zhu, F., Ling, X., Liu, Q., Zhao, P., Intelligent Health Care: Applications of Deep Learning in Computational Medicine. *Front. Genet.*, 12, 607471, 2021, https://doi.org/10.3389/fgene.2021.607471.
15. Al-Turjman, F., Nawaz, M.H., Ulusar, U.D., Intelligence in the Internet of Medical Things Era: A Systematic Review of Current and Future Trends. *Comput. Commun.*, 150, 644–60, 2020, https://doi.org/10.1016/j.comcom.2019.12.030.
16. Anitha Kumari, K., Padmashani, R., Varsha, R., Upadhayay, V., Securing Internet of Medical Things (IoMT) Using Private Blockchain Network, in: *Principles of Internet of Things (IoT) Ecosystem:Insight Paradigm*, pp. 305–326, Springer, Cham, Switzerland, 2020, https://doi.org/10.1007/978-3-030-33596-0_12.
17. Stach, E., DeCost, B., Kusne, A.G., Hattrick-Simpers, J., Brown, K.A., Reyes, K.G., Schrier, J., Billinge, S., Buonassisi, T., Foster, I., Gomes, C.P., Autonomous Experimentation Systems for Materials Development: A Community Perspective. *Matter*, 4, 9, 2702–26, 2021, https://doi.org/10.1016/j.matt.2021.06.036.
18. Seifrid, M., Pollice, R., Aguilar-Granda, A., Morgan Chan, Z., Hotta, K., Ser, C.T., Vestfrid, J., Wu, T.C., Aspuru-Guzik, A., Autonomous Chemical

Experiments: Challenges and Perspectives on Establishing a Self-Driving Lab. *Acc. Chem. Res.*, 55, 17, 2454–66, 2022, https://doi.org/10.1021/acs.accounts.2c00220.
19. Ferguson, A.L. and Brown, K.A., Data-Driven Design and Autonomous Experimentation in Soft and Biological Materials Engineering. *Annu. Rev. Chem. Biomol. Eng.*, 13, 1, 25–44, 2022, https://doi.org/10.1146/annurev-chembioeng-092120-020803.
20. Abolhasani, M. and Kumacheva, E., The Rise of Self-Driving Labs in Chemical and Materials Sciences. *Nat. Synth.*, 2, 6, 483–92, 2023, https://doi.org/10.1038/s44160-022-00231-0.
21. da Silva, R.G. and Blasimme, A., From Lab to Society: Fostering Clinical Translation of Molecular Systems Engineering. *Bioeng. Transl. Med.*, 9, 1, e10564, 2024, https://doi.org/10.1002/btm2.10564.
22. Feng, Y.C., *et al.*, Taiwan Biobank: A Rich Biomedical Research Database of the Taiwanese Population. *Cell Genomics*, 2, 11, 2022, https://doi.org/10.1016/j.xgen.2022.100197.
23. Aspuru-Guzik, A., The Decade of Artificial Intelligence in Chemistry and Materials. *Digit. Discov.*, 2, 1, 10–11, 2023, https://doi.org/10.1039/D3DD90001K.
24. Goetz, L.H. and Schork, N.J., Personalized Medicine: Motivation, Challenges, and Progress. *Fertility Sterility*, 109, 6, 952–963, 2018, https://doi.org/10.1016/j.fertnstert.2018.05.006.
25. Vallée, A., Envisioning the Future of Personalized Medicine: Role and Realities of Digital Twins. *J. Med. Internet Res.*, 26, e50204, 2024, https://doi.org/10.2196/50204.
26. Haddad, A., *et al.*, Systematic review on ai-blockchain based e-healthcare records management systems. *IEEE Access*, 10, 94583–94615, 2022, 10.1109/ACCESS.2022.3201878.
27. Akhtar, Z.B., Exploring Biomedical Engineering (BME): Advances within Accelerated Computing and Regenerative Medicine for a Computational and Medical Science Perspective Exploration Analysis. *J. Emerg. Med. OA*, 2, 1, 1–23, 202, https://doi.org/10.33140/JEMOA.02.01.06.
28. Jarrahi, M.H., Artificial intelligence and the future of work: Human-AI symbiosis in organizational decision making. *Bus. Horiz.*, 61, 4, 577–586, 2018, https://doi.org/10.1016/j.bushor.2018.03.007.
29. Achiam, J., *et al.*, GPT-4 Technical Report, arXiv PreprintarXiv:2303.08774, https://doi.org/10.48550/arXiv.2303.08774, 2023.
30. Lee, P., Bubeck, S., Petro, J., Benefits, Limits, and Risks of GPT-4 as an AI Chatbot for Medicine. Reply. *New England J. Med.*, 388, 25, 2400, 2023, https://doi.org/10.1056/NEJMc2305286.
31. Lixi, L,., *et al.*, Nowcasting and forecasting global aging and cancer burden: analysis of data from the GLOBOCAN and Global Burden of Disease Study. *J. Natl. Cancer Center*, 4, 3, 223–232, 2024, https://doi.org/10.1016/j.jncc.2024.05.002.

32. Mensah, G.A., Roth, G.A., Fuster, V., The global burden of cardiovascular diseases and risk factors: 2020 and beyond. *J. Am. Coll. Cardiol.*, 74, 20, 2529–2532, 2019, https://doi.org/10.1016/j.jacc.2019.10.009.
33. GBD 2019 Mental Disorders Collaborators, Global, regional, and national burden of 12 mental disorders in 204 countries and territories, 1990–2019: a systematic analysis for the Global Burden of Disease Study 2019. *Lancet Psychiatry*, 9, 2, 137–150, 2022, https://doi.org/10.1016/S2215-0366(21)00395-3.
34. Marques, L., *et al.*, Advancing Precision Medicine: A Review of Innovative *In Silico* Approaches for Drug Development, Clinical Pharmacology, and Personalized Healthcare. *Pharmaceutics*, 16, 3, 332, 27 Feb. 2024, https://doi.org/10.3390/pharmaceutics16030332.
35. Kleppe, A., *et al.*, A Clinical Decision Support System Optimizing Adjuvant Chemotherapy for Colorectal Cancers by Integrating Deep Learning and Pathological Staging Markers: A Development and Validation Study. *Lancet Oncol.*, 23, 9, 1221–1232, 1 Sept. 2022, https://doi.org/10.1016/S1470-2045(22)00391-6.
36. Nagendran, M., *et al.*, Artificial Intelligence versus Clinicians: Systematic Review of Design, Reporting Standards, and Claims of Deep Learning Studies. *BMJ*, m689, 368, 25 Mar. 2020, https://doi.org/10.1136/bmj.m689.
37. Kwan, J.L., *et al.*, Computerized Clinical Decision Support Systems and Absolute Improvements in Care: A Meta-analysis of Controlled Clinical Trials. *BMJ*, 370, m3216, 17 Sept. 2020, https://doi.org/10.1136/bmj.m3216.
38. Lu, Y., Melnick, E.R., Krumholz, H.M., Clinical Decision Support in Cardiovascular Medicine. *BMJ*, 059818, 377, e069759, 25 May 2022, https://doi.org/10.1136/bmj-2020-059818.
39. Sapci, A.H. and Sapci, H.A., Artificial Intelligence Education and Tools for Medical and Health Informatics Students: Systematic Review. *JMIR Med. Educ.*, 6, 1, e19285, 30 June 2020, https://doi.org/10.2196/19285.
40. Sharma, A., *et al.*, Integrating Artificial Intelligence into Biomedical Science Curricula: Advancing Healthcare Education. *Clin. Pract.*, 14, 4, 1391–1403, 11 July 2024, https://doi.org/10.3390/clinpract14040112.
41. Federico, C.A. and Trotsyuk, A.A., Biomedical Data Science, Artificial Intelligence, and Ethics: Navigating Challenges in the Face of Explosive Growth. *Annu. Rev. Biomed. Data Sci.*, 7, 1, 1–14, Apr. 2024, https://doi.org/10.1146/annurev-biodatasci-102623-104553.
42. Cho, H., *et al.*, Privacy-Enhancing Technologies in Biomedical Data Science. *Annu. Rev. Biomed. Data Sci.*, 7, 1, 317–343, 23, Aug. 2024, https://doi.org/10.1146/annurev-biodatasci-120423-120107.

2

Fundamentals of Biomedical Data and Social Determinants

Girija Shankar Sahoo[1], D. Alex Anand[2*], Manoranjan Parhi[3], Abdul Khadar A.[4], Subbulakshmi Ganesan[5] and Swapnil M. Parikh[6]

[1]*Maharishi School of Engineering & Technology, Maharishi University of Information Technology, Uttar Pradesh, India*
[2]*Department of Biomedical, Sathyabama Institute of Science and Technology, Chennai, Tamil Nadu, India*
[3]*Department of Computer Science and Engineering, Siksha 'O' Anusandhan (Deemed to be University), Bhubaneswar, Odisha, India*
[4]*Department of Computer Science and Engineering, Presidency University, Bangalore, Karnataka, India*
[5]*Department of Chemistry and Biochemistry, Jain (Deemed-to-be University), Bangalore, Karnataka, India*
[6]*Computer Science and Engineering, Parul Institute of Technology, Parul University, Vadodara, Gujarat, India*

Abstract
Biomedical data and social determinants, such as socioeconomic status, education, environment, and healthcare access, collectively influence healthcare outcomes, disease progression, and health disparities. The objective of this review paper is to explore the foundational aspects of biomedical data and the role of social determinants in healthcare outcomes, aiming to understand their impact on health disparities and disease progression. Despite the available wealth of data, a significant limitation is the complexity and high dimensionality of biomedical and social determinant data, which often leads to issues in data quality, interpretability, and integration. To solve these issues, the study investigates the application

**Corresponding author*: alexanand.bioinfo@sathyabama.ac.in; ORCID: 0000-0002-5842-5365
Manoranjan Parhi: ORCID: 0000-0002-1625-6022
Subbulakshmi Ganesan: ORCID: 0000-0002-8345-116X
Swapnil M. Parikh: ORCID: 0000-0001-7831-6927

Satya Prakash Yadav, Abhay Bansal and Victor Hugo C. de Albuquerque (eds.) Computational Intelligence in Biomedical Internet of Medical Things, (17–34) © 2026 Scrivener Publishing LLC

of machine learning (ML) and deep learning (DL) models, which provide strong tools for data-driven insights and predictive modeling in this field. This review focuses on relevant datasets and discusses essential preprocessing steps, including data cleaning and normalization, necessary to ensure model robustness and accuracy. Results from various studies demonstrate that ML and DL approaches can enhance the predictive accuracy of health outcomes by effectively analyzing both biomedical and social determinant data. In conclusion, while challenges remain, this review highlights the potential of advanced computational models to bridge gaps in understanding and support decision-making in healthcare, paving the way for more equitable and personalized health interventions.

***Keywords*:** Biomedical data, machine learning (ML), deep learning (DL), social determinants

2.1 Introduction

Understanding population inequalities and health outcomes requires the combination of social determinants of health (SDOH) and biological data [1]. In biomedical data, huge amounts of health-related information include images, genetic data, lab findings, and clinical records. Such data provides diagnoses for the treatment and prediction of medical disorders [2]. The SDOH refers to social, economic, and ecological factors that affect people's health, including healthcare access, education, income, and local conditions [3]. This will be the dimension that reflects this holistic view of health: social and environmental factors can exert influence on medical results, in addition to biological ones [4]. The interaction among these factors is increasingly common with the fact that engagement by policymakers and healthcare providers in addressing causes of health inequalities is in addition to formulating better plans of intervention. This will allow more effective and targeted healthcare programs once people understand the relationship between bad communities and higher prevalence rates of chronic diseases like diabetes or hypertension [5]. In this case, biological data with SDOH poses a significant challenge: the completeness of data. Although today's advancements in wearable health technology allow collecting large amounts of biomedical data, this data is sometimes missing, inconsistent, or impossible to measure. Most social elements like community trust, family relationships, or mental health remain impossible to quantify using traditional assessment approaches [6]. Many of these social elements, such as family dynamics, mental health, and community trust, are subjectively biased and are difficult to measure using traditional data-gathering methods [7]. Privacy concerns are also raised by the extraction of personal social and biological data, which raises issues of data security and permission [8]. Furthermore, sophisticated models currently being created and evaluated for scalability are needed to apply these diverse datasets to healthcare procedures [9]. This review considers the interaction between biomedical data and social determinants in health outcomes and how machine learning (ML) and deep learning (DL) models can contribute to improving predictive accuracy in healthcare by addressing problems in biomedical data.

2.2 Methodology

This review focuses on an intense study of the existing literature on socio-economic determinants and biological data, focusing on studies that make use of ML and DL models to provide predictive healthcare insights. It includes fundamental steps, such as checking datasets and preparing techniques for data in modeling applications to assess their efficiency in dealing with complexity in data and enhancing predictions related to health outcomes. Figure 2.1 shows the methodological overview.

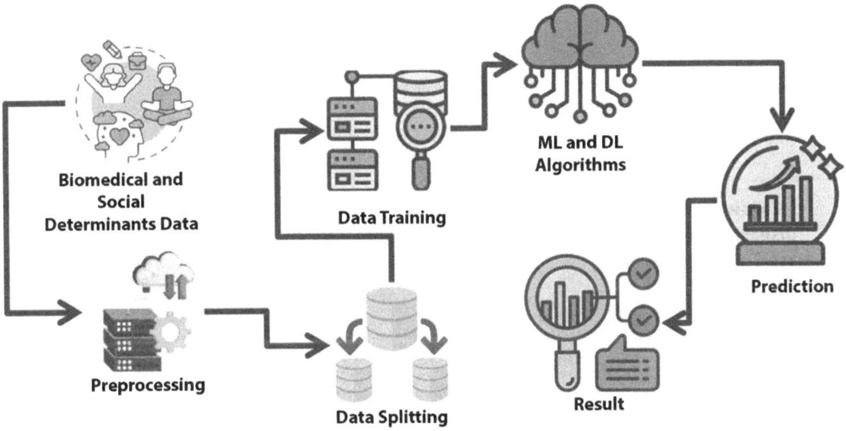

Figure 2.1 An overview of the methodology. (Source: Own elaboration).

2.2.1 Dataset

Two datasets were evaluated for this study [10]: the Heart Disease Cleveland (HDC) dataset, which was sourced from Kaggle. In particular [11], the Kaggle dataset on cardiovascular disease (CVD), which has 12 characteristics and 70,000 instances, was used. The target variable is the last characteristic among these eleven properties. The ML repository provided the heart failure prediction (HFP) dataset that used in this investigation [12]. This collection of data was created by combining previously available but unmerged information. The cardiovascular heart disease (CVHD) dataset [13] is taken from the Kaggle library. This dataset has 1000 subjects with 12 features. Figure 2.2 shows the CVD indicators.

- ➢ **Demographic factors (gender, age):** These aid in the identification of trends and patterns across numerous demographic groups that can throw light on whether there is influence based on age or gender in cardiovascular outcomes.
- ➢ **Biometric factors (height and weight):** The actual physical characteristics state whether the individual is fit or not. These are basic indicators in assessing the cardiovascular risk for the individual.

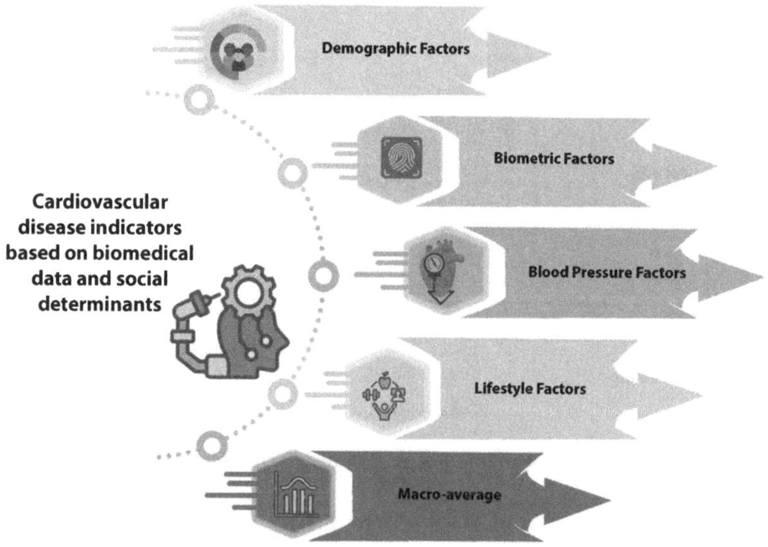

Figure 2.2 Cardiovascular disease indicators. (Source: Own elaboration).

- **Cholesterol and glucose levels [cholesterol, glucose (gluc)]:** Biochemical factors that indicate the status of metabolic health and are hence likely to immediately affect the risk of developing CVD.
- **Lifestyle factors [smoking, alcohol, physical activity (smoke, alco, active)]:** These lifestyle-related attributes affect an individual's health and play a major role in developing CVD.
- **Blood pressure factors [systolic blood pressure (ap_hi), diastolic blood pressure (ap_lo)]:** Clinical criteria have indicated blood pressure readings as crucial elements that are to be taken into account in cardiovascular health determination and, therefore, should be referred to in interpreting heart risk.
- **Clinical factors [target variable or (cardio)]:** The target variable in clinical factors is the outcome of interest, which is either the presence or absence of a condition and serves as a clinical factor that could directly correlate with the health status.

2.2.2 Preprocessing

The preprocessing technique can modify the HFP data to create a more dependable ML model [14]. Preprocessing enhances the correctness of the data by eliminating outliers, selecting characteristics, and filling in missing values, among other activities. The Kaggle CVD dataset was preprocessed [15] using one-hot encoding to transform binary categorical variables, including the target classification, into a format that ML algorithms can use. To standardize the data and guarantee equal contribution across features, all other numerical variables, such as blood glucose and cholesterol categories, were also scaled to a range of (0, 1). These preprocessing steps stabilize model training and enhance the performance of methods such as ensemble models, neural networks, and support vector machines (SVMs). Preliminary techniques were applied to the CVHD prediction dataset [16], including data cleaning, which corrects errors and eliminates noise; integration, which merges data from various sources to improve coherence and remove redundancy; transformation, which merges, normalizes, and removes data to make it consistent and comprehensible; and reduction, which separates complex data into training and testing sets to guarantee accurate model performance. When these procedures are used together, the data is guaranteed to be coherent, clean, and well-structured for ML.

Applications of data filtering from preprocessing techniques [17] have been used in the HDC dataset, eliminating any unnecessary information from data gathered from Kaggle. Categorical variables were encoded into a numerical format by generating dummy variables from the Pandas library using *get_dummies()* and handling missing values by using the *isnull()* method to look for any missing or trash entries. This set of steps prepares a dataset equipped for model training by cleaning it to ensure completeness and numerical format.

2.3 Models of Machine Learning and Deep Learning are Employed to Predict Cardiovascular Diseases

Random Forest (RF): It uses the DT-based grouping approach, and the number of distinct tree result categories determines the RF result category [18]. The RF classifier requires reliable medical data that was collected by medical sensors. As the Internet of Things (IoT) expands, robust wireless sensor network (WSN)-based data transfer technologies can safely and efficiently transport and store massive amounts of data [19]. A decision tree (DT) specifically chooses the most significant characteristics from pre-existing feature sets. On the contrary, RF takes the most effective features from the subsets after randomly selecting a subset from an anode set that is part of the basic decision trees. The RF performs well for certain high-dimensional samples and has high accuracy, making it suitable for usage in large datasets. Figure 2.3(a) shows the RF structure.

Decision Trees: It is a tree-like, decision-making approach that consists of three parts. There are three types of nodes in question: decision nodes, root

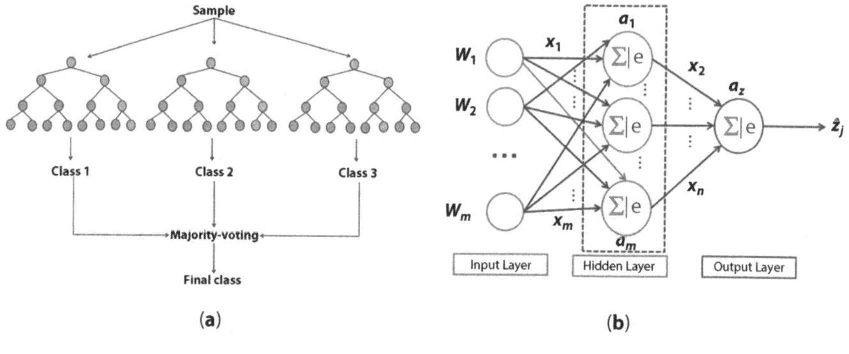

Figure 2.3 (a) Random forest structure; and (b) multi-layer perceptron structure. (Source: (a) https://www.geeksforgeeks.org/machine-learning/xgboost/ (b) https://www.mdpi.com/2075-4426/12/8/1208).

nodes, and leaf nodes [20]. The method separates the training dataset into several branches, which is separate from the others. The selection nodes offer the connection to the leaves, while the DT nodes supply the characteristics required to forecast the result. The dataset's properties are shown by the decision nodes and root nodes [21]. As a result, the DT algorithm generates several outcomes, from which the most effective is selected as the final result.

Support vector machine: It is a powerful technique for categorizing data by increasing the margin between positive and negative classifications [22]. These make SVM quite successful when data is linearly separable; however, when data is nonlinearly separable, the initial approach in SVM cannot be directly applied because kernel functions can convert the data into a space with more dimensions so that a decision boundary of this type could be found [23]. To classify patient data, the SVM classification algorithm uses a variety of features. In cases where the decision boundary is unclear, a Naïve Bayes method is employed to classify the data with the highest conditional probability, considering relevant factors to produce more accurate predictions [24].

Multi-layer perceptron (MLP): It is a complex neural network that receives numerical input and outputs numerical values as results. An input layer, one or more feature-extracting hidden layers, and an output layer that uses these structures to generate forecasts represent the characteristics of these networks [25]. Multiple hidden layers increase the depth of deep neural networks; however, this is done with a problem of vanishing gradients, which requires specially tailored algorithms. Selecting the amount of hidden layers and neurons to use requires extreme caution; in certain situations, cross-validation must be observed. An activation function is used in every neuron in the hidden and output layers. Common variants include sigmoid and ReLU: Sigmoid-the logistic function output falls between 0 and 1, and it has a very smooth gradient everywhere; ReLU just allows beneficial inputs to pass through while producing zero for any adverse input, hence, being able to computationally handle heavy hidden layers [26]. The outputs of the MLP depend on weights, biases, and inputs; training focuses on adjusting these parameters, so the MLP correctly predicts outcomes. Figure 2.3(b) shows the MLP structure.

Convolutional neural networks (CNN): These are advanced neural networks premised on three critical architectural concepts, namely: local receptive fields, shared weights, and sub-sampling of spatial or temporal channels for decreasing model complexity. The CNN layers consist of neural units that receive the extracted features from the previous layers, while CNNs are used for different kinds of data, including images, speech, and time-series signals, with each having its particular form of kernel formation. These 1D CNNs are especially beneficial for raw sequential data, like time series data [27]. Some examples are the Phonocardiogram and electroencephalogram. The model works well without the feature extraction process, which is a resource-hungry task. In the case of a 1D CNN, feature extraction is a sequence of convolutions. The operation of the first layer is defined by applying a convolutional kernel to the input, with feature maps being the result. The spatial features are extracted in the 2D CNN, using a kernel for multiple hidden layers. Its functions of each layer follow on from the convolutional operation on the output of previous neurons, with an activation function used to determine the final output [28].

2.4 Results

Experimental setup: TensorFlow/Keras is used for DL models, scikit-learn is used for ML models, and Pandas is used for data preparation in the experimental setup for ML and DL models in Python. GridSearchCV is used to tune hyperparameters. Performance measurements are used to train, validate, and assess models. Python 3.9, a CPU/GPU, 16GB of RAM, and programs like PyCharm and Jupyter Notebook are included in the setup.

The MLP and RF models' efficacy in forecasting several health indicators associated with CVD is shown in Table 2.1. The study evaluates how effectively two ML models, RF and MLP, classify health indicators according to a number of criteria. These indications include blood pressure readings (systolic and diastolic), biometric data like height and weight, and demographic characteristics like age and gender. Further examined were blood glucose levels, lifestyle variables (such as smoking, drinking, and exercising), and clinical characteristics associated with cardiovascular risk (target variable: cardio). According to the data, the MLP model performs better than the RF model on average in terms of F1 scores for all indicators, with the optimal results for both models coming from clinical aspects (cardio). Additionally, included are the macro-averaged F1 scores for MLP and RF, which show the overall performance of the model across all health metrics.

The performance of two models, MLP and RF, in annotating parameters linked to CVD from text input, is shown in Table 2.2. The models recognized health problems like high blood pressure and high cholesterol together with demographic information like age and gender in the initial entry. In this instance, the identical set of variables was annotated by the MLP and RF models: "male, age 65, hypertension, cholesterol."

Table 2.1 Comparing the effectiveness of the RF and MLP models in terms of social determinants-based CVD indicators.

Health indicator		**MLP F1 (±SD)**	**RF F1 (±SD)**
Demographic factors	Gender	0.815±0.022	0.805±0.021
	Age	0.810±0.021	0.800±0.022
Biometric factors	Height	0.820±0.021	0.810±0.020
	Weight	0.818±0.022	0.808±0.021
Blood pressure factors	Systolic (ap_hi)	0.835±0.023	0.823±0.023
	Diastolic (ap_lo)	0.833±0.024	0.835±0.021
Glucose levels		0.843±0.023	0.833±0.022
Lifestyle factors	Smoking	0.800±0.025	0.790±0.024
	Alcohol	0.795±0.024	0.785±0.023
	Physical Activity	0.803±0.026	0.793±0.025
Clinical factors: target variable (cardio)		0.860±0.023	0.850±0.022
Macro-average		0.820±0.022	0.810±0.022

Both models consistently categorized important health characteristics like "BMI, smoker, family history, heart disease" and "heart bypass, blocked arteries" in the following scenarios, where the input described lifestyle factors or clinical situations including body mass index (BMI), smoking, glucose levels, and heart bypass surgery. Both models are found to have pertinent parameters, such as "blood pressure, healthy weight" and "physical activity, balanced diet," whether the input contained a healthy lifestyle or well-maintained blood pressure. But there were minor variations in the annotations, especially when it came to the phrases that were included or left out. Despite these small variations, the two models comparably extracted the main health-related metrics.

Table 2.3 highlights the performance measures of several ML and DL models. Several performance patterns can be seen when comparing different ML models for categorization results related to health. Metrics including precision, area-under-the-curve (AUC), accuracy, Receiver Operating Characteristic – Area under Curve (ROC-AUC), recall, sensitivity, specificity, F1 score, and Matthews correlation coefficient (MCC) were assessed for several methods,

Table 2.2 Comparison of annotated labels by MLP and RF models for CVD-related text input.

Text input	Annotated labels	MLP	RF
The patient is a male 65-year-old who has a history of elevated cholesterol and hypertension.	Male, age 65, hypertension, high cholesterol	Male, hypertension, cholesterol	Male, hypertension, cholesterol
The patient's systolic blood pressure is 150 mmHg, and diastolic is 90 mmHg.	Systolic, diastolic, high blood pressure	Systolic, diastolic	Systolic, diastolic
The individual's glucose level is 140 mg/dL, and cholesterol levels are elevated.	Glucose level, cholesterol level, CVD risk	Glucose, cholesterol	Glucose, cholesterol
The individual does not smoke but consumes alcohol regularly and is physically active.	Non-smoker, alcohol, physical activity	Non-smoker, alcohol, active	Non-smoker, alcohol, active
The patient underwent a heart bypass surgery due to blocked coronary arteries.	Heart bypass surgery, blocked arteries	Heart bypass, blocked arteries	Heart bypass, blocked arteries

(*Continued*)

Table 2.2 Comparison of annotated labels by MLP and RF models for CVD-related text input. (*Continued*)

Text input	Annotated labels	MLP	RF
The patient has a 120/80 mmHg blood pressure reading and maintains a healthy weight.	Blood pressure, healthy weight	Blood pressure, healthy weight	Blood pressure, healthy weight
The individual is a 45-year-old female who monitors her cholesterol and glucose levels regularly.	Female, age 45, cholesterol, glucose	Female, age 45, cholesterol, glucose	Female, age 45, cholesterol, glucose
The patient's lifestyle includes daily physical activity and a balanced diet.	Physical activity, balanced diet	Physical activity, balanced diet	Physical activity, balanced diet
The individual has been diagnosed with hypertension and is currently taking medication.	Hypertension, medication	Hypertension, medication	Hypertension, medication
The patient has a body mass index (BMI) of 32, is a smoker, and has a family history of heart disease.	Body mass index, heart disease, smoker, family history	Body mass index, heart disease, smoker, family history	Body mass index, heart disease, smoker, family history

Table 2.3 Performance comparison of ML and DL models based on various metrics.

Methods	Accuracy (%)	Precision (%)	AUC (%)	Recall (%)	ROC-AUC (%)	F1 score (%)	Sensitivity	Specificity	MCC (%)
MLP-PSO [26]	84.6	80.8	84.8	88.3	-	84.4	-	-	-
LR [26]	81.3	90.9	80.8	68.1	-	77.9	-	-	-
RF [29]	88.65	90.03	-	88.03	92	88.02	-	-	-
SVM [30]	76	80	-	80	-	80	-	-	-
DT [31]	80	80.37	-	80	-	79.82	-	-	-
Traditional CNN [32]	81.97	84	-	81	-	83	-	-	-
CNN-LSTM [33]	74.15	81.82	-	72.04	73.95	76.62	72.04	77.11	48.41
MLP [34]	84.25	82.08	-	-	-	85.60	89.43	78.57	68.60
XGBoost [35]	94.80	88	90	86	-	84.60	-	-	-

including Multi-Layer Perceptron – Particle Swarm Optimization (MLP-PSO), Logistic Regression (LR), RF, SVM, DT, Traditional CNN, CNN-Long Short-Term Memory (LSTM), MLP, and XGBoost. RF, MLP, and XGBoost were exhibiting excellent scores on a variety of assessment parameters. Overall classification performance, including F1 scores, was adequate for MLP, whereas RF demonstrated remarkable precision and recall rates. The remarkable accuracy and AUC of XGBoost highlighted its promise in predicting applications. However, in contrast, other models, such as CNN-LSTM and SVM performed lower. This demonstrates how effectively RF, MLP, and XGBoost perform in predictive modeling connected with health. Figure 2.4 shows the accuracy outcomes of ML and DL models.

Both MLP and RF models performed well when ML models were compared for predicting CVD indicators; however, MLP's average F1 scores were higher across all health indicators. Although there were minor differences in the annotations, both algorithms reliably detected important health variables when annotating text inputs. MLP, RF, and XGBoost performed well in terms of precision, accuracy, and recall among the models that were examined. The highest predictive accuracy and AUC were shown by XGBoost, indicating its promise for predicting applications. In some healthcare applications, simpler models can perform better than more sophisticated ones, as seen by the decreased performance of models like CNN-LSTM and SVM.

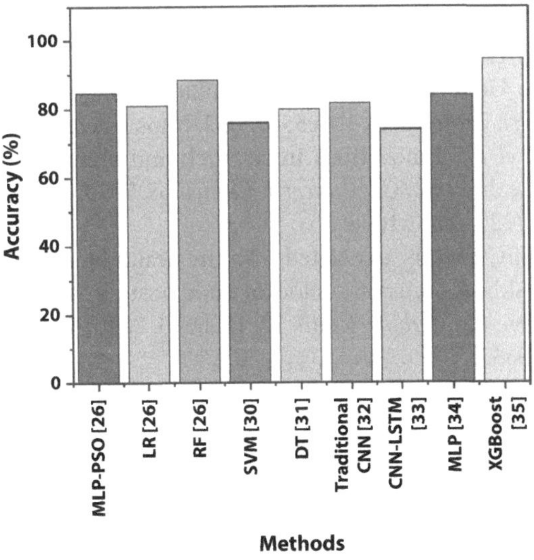

Figure 2.4 The accuracy outcomes of ML and DL models. (Source: Own elaboration).

2.5 Conclusion

This review underlines the translational power of ML and DL models to achieve a very high level of analysis of biomedical and social determinant data to improve health outcomes. Despite the difficulties in managing the high dimensionality and quality issues inherent in these datasets, there is strong optimism that ML and DL techniques could offer significant potential for improved predictive accuracy and the extraction of more meaningful data-driven insights. This type of model, by integrating biomedical data with social determinants, provides a pathway toward a more holistic understanding of health disparities and disease progression. Ultimately, this review highlights a strong potential to continue supportive advancements in new computational approaches and improved data preprocessing strategies for more equitable, personal, and effective health interventions. Steps would play a great role in reducing health disparities and improving healthcare delivery, thereby leading to a healthier and more inclusive society. High dimensionality, complexity, and difficulties integrating many datasets are the issues with the data, which result in a lack of interpretability and model resilience. Developing standardized methods for integrating diverse healthcare datasets and enhancing the existing DL and ML models to improve interpretability are recommended as the next steps.

References

1. Emeny, R.T., *et al.*, Inclusion of Social and Structural Determinants of Health to Advance Understanding of their Influence on the Biology of Chronic Disease. *Curr. Protocol.*, 2, 10, e556, 2022, https://doi.org/10.1002/cpz1.556.
2. Jim, H.SL., *et al.*, Innovations in research and clinical care using patient-generated health data. *CA Cancer J. Clinicians*, 70, 3, 182–199, 2020, https://doi.org/10.3322/caac.21608.
3. Cho, M., *et al.*, Factors associated with the health literacy on social determinants of health: A focus on socioeconomic position and work environment. *Int. J. Environ. Res. Public Health*, 17, 18, 6663, 2020, https://doi.org/10.3390/ijerph17186663.
4. Shantz, E. and Elliott, S.J., From social determinants to social epigenetics: Health geographies of chronic disease. *Health Place*, 69, 102561, 2021, https://doi.org/10.1016/j.healthplace.2021.102561.
5. Agurs-Collins, T., *et al.*, Perspective: Nutrition health disparities framework: a model to advance health equity. *Adv. Nutr.*, 15, 4, 100194, 2024, https://doi.org/10.1016/j.advnut.2024.100194.

6. Berg, K., *et al.*, Automating data collection methods in electronic health record systems: a Social Determinant of Health (SDOH) viewpoint. *Health Syst.*, 12, 4, 472–480, 2023, https://doi.org/10.1080/20476965.2022.2075796.
7. Jain, S., Pillai, P., Mathias, K., Opening up the 'black-box': what strategies do community mental health workers use to address the social dimensions of mental health? *Social Psychiatry Psychiatr. Epidemiol.*, 59, 3, 493–502, 2024, https://doi.org/10.1007/s00127-023-02582-1.
8. Thapa, C. and Camtepe, S., Precision health data: Requirements, challenges and existing techniques for data security and privacy. *Comput. Biol. Med.*, 129, 104130, 2021, https://doi.org/10.1016/j.compbiomed.2020.104130.
9. Rehman, A., Naz, S., Razzak, I., Leveraging big data analytics in healthcare enhancement: trends, challenges and opportunities. *Multimedia Syst.*, 28, 4, 1339–1371, 2022, https://doi.org/10.1007/s00530-020-00736-8.
10. Heart Disease Cleveland Dataset, https://www.kaggle.com/datasets/aavigan/cleveland-clinic-heart-disease-dataset.
11. Cardiovascular Disease dataset, https://www.kaggle.com/datasets/sulianova/cardiovascular-disease-dataset.
12. Heart Failure Prediction Dataset, https://www.kaggle.com/datasets/fedesoriano/heart-failure-prediction.
13. Cardiovascular Heart Disease dataset, https://www.kaggle.com/datasets/jocelyndumlao/cardiovascular-disease-dataset.
14. Rahmani, K., *et al.*, Early prediction of central line associated bloodstream infection using machine learning. *Am. J. Infect. Control*, 50, 4, 440–445, 2022, https://doi.org/10.1016/j.ajic.2021.08.017.
15. Hagan, R., Gillan, C.J., Mallett, F., Comparison of machine learning methods for the classification of cardiovascular disease. *Inf. Med. Unlocked*, 24, 1006065, 2021, https://doi.org/10.1016/j.imu.2021.100606.
16. Uddin, K.M.M., *et al.*, Machine learning-based approach to the diagnosis of cardiovascular vascular disease using a combined dataset. *Intelligence-Based Med.*, 7, 1001005, 2023, https://doi.org/10.1016/j.ibmed.2023.100100.
17. Bora, N., Gutta, S., Hadaegh, A., Using machine learning to predict heart disease, Diss., California State University San Marcos, 2021, DOI: 10.37394/23208.2022.19.1.
18. Guo, C., *et al.*, Recursion enhanced random forest with an improved linear model (RERF-ILM) for heart disease detection on the internet of medical things platform. *IEEE Access*, 8, 59247–592565, 2020, https://doi.org/10.1109/ACCESS.2020.2981159.
19. Sun, W., *et al.*, Prediction of cardiovascular diseases based on machine learning. *ASP Trans. Internet Things*, 1, 1, 30–35, 2021, https://doi.org/10.52810/TIOT.2021.100035.
20. Bai, Y., *et al.*, Construction of a non-mutually exclusive decision tree for medication recommendation of chronic heart failure. *Front. Pharmacol.*, 12, 7585735, 2022, https://doi.org/10.3389/fphar.2021.758573.

21. Charbuty, B. and Abdulazeez, A., Classification based on decision tree algorithm for machine learning. *J. Appl. Sci. Technol. Trends*, 2, 01, 20–28, 2021, https://doi.org/10.38094/jastt20165.
22. Balaha, H.M., *et al.*, A multi-variate heart disease optimization and recognition framework. *Neural Comput. Appl.*, 34, 18, 15907–15944, 2022, https://doi.org/10.1007/s00521-022-07241-1.
23. Punn, N.S. and Dewangan, D.K., Ensemble Meta-Learning using SVM for Improving Cardiovascular Disease Risk Prediction. *medRxiv*, 2024–05, 2024, https://doi.org/10.1101/2024.05.18.24307568.
24. Elsedimy, E.I., AboHashish, S.MM., Algarni, F., New cardiovascular disease prediction approach using support vector machine and quantum-behaved particle swarm optimization. *Multimed. Tools Appl.*, 83, 8, 23901–23928, 2024, https://doi.org/10.1007/s11042-023-16194-z.
25. Gunata, M., *et al.*, Estimation of Risk Factors Related to Heart Diseases With Multilayer Perceptron Model. *Med. Rec.*, 4, 2, 171–8, 2021, https://doi.org/10.37990/medr.1031866.
26. Al Bataineh, A. and Manacek, S., MLP-PSO hybrid algorithm for heart disease prediction. *J. Pers. Med.*, 12, 8, 1208, 2022, https://doi.org/10.3390/jpm12081208.
27. Sajja, T.K. and Kalluri, H.K., A Deep Learning Method for Prediction of Cardiovascular Disease Using Convolutional Neural Network. *Rev. d'Intelligence Artif.*, 34, 5, 601–606, 2020, https://doi.org/10.18280/ria.340510.
28. Shuvo, S.B., *et al.*, CardioXNet: A novel lightweight deep learning framework for cardiovascular disease classification using heart sound recordings. *IEEE Access*, 9, 36955–369675, 2021, https://doi.org/10.1109/ACCESS.2021.3063129.
29. Alqahtani, A., *et al.*, Cardiovascular disease detection using ensemble learning. *Comput. Intell. Neurosci.*, 2022, 1, 5267498, 2022, https://doi.org/10.1155/2022/5267498.
30. Ahmed, R., Bibi, M., Syed, S., Improving heart disease prediction accuracy using a hybrid machine learning approach: a comparative study of SVM and KNN algorithms. *Int. J. Comput. Inf. Manuf. (IJCIM)*, 3, 1, 49–54, 2023, https://doi.org/10.54489/ijcim.v3i1.223.
31. Shrivastava, P.K., Sharma, M., Kumar, A., HCBiLSTM: A hybrid model for predicting heart disease using CNN and BiLSTM algorithms. *Meas.: Sens.*, 25, 100657, 2023, https://doi.org/10.1016/j.measen.2022.100657.
32. Ram Kumar, R.P., *et al.*, Enhanced heart disease prediction through hybrid CNN-TLBO-GA optimization: a comparative study with conventional CNN and optimized CNN using FPO algorithm. *Cogent Eng.*, 11, 1, 2384657, 2024, https://doi.org/10.1080/23311916.2024.2384657.
33. Hossain, MM., *et al.*, Cardiovascular disease identification using a hybrid CNN-LSTM model with explainable AI. *Inf. Med. Unlocked*, 42, 1013705, 2023, https://doi.org/10.1016/j.imu.2023.101370.

34. Tiwari, A., Chugh, A., Sharma, A., Ensemble framework for cardiovascular disease prediction. *Comput. Biol. Med.*, 146, 105624, 2022, https://doi.org/10.1016/j.compbiomed.2022.105624.
35. Anjum, N., *et al.*, Improving Cardiovascular Disease Prediction through Comparative Analysis of Machine Learning Models. *J. Comput. Sci. Technol. Stud.*, 6, 2, 62–70, 2024, https://doi.org/10.32996/jcsts.2024.6.2.

3

The Impact of Biomedical Intelligence on Public Health

Smitha Madhavan[1], Malathi H.[2], Anjali R. Kumbar[3], Bethanney Janney J.[4*], Debahuti Mishra[5] and Ritesh Kumar[6]

[1]*Faculty of Nursing, Lincoln University College, Malaysia*
[2]*Department of Biotechnology and Genetics, Jain (Deemed-to-be University), Bangalore, Karnataka, India*
[3]*Department of Pharmacy, PES's Modern College of Pharmacy, Nigdi, Pune, India*
[4]*Department of Biomedical, Sathyabama Institute of Science and Technology, Chennai, Tamil Nadu, India*
[5]*Department of Computer Science and Engineering, Siksha 'O' Anusandhan (Deemed to be University), Bhubaneswar, Odisha, India*
[6]*Department of Computer Science, Maharishi School of Engineering & Technology, Maharishi University of Information Technology, Uttar Pradesh, India*

Abstract
The term biomedical intelligence describes the use of modern technology in the fields of public health, including artificial intelligence (AI), big data analytics, and predictive modeling. The study and practice of preserving and enhancing the health of individuals and their healthcare outcomes is known as public health. This employment involves recognizing, preventing, and treating infectious illnesses, promoting healthy lifestyles and studying injury and disease prevention. The study analyzes and comprehends complex medical data using machine learning (ML) and deep learning (DL) to assist predicted illness, treatment, and prevention in biomedical intelligence. The article examines the uses and present state of ML and DL, as well as the technological advancements and potential implications

**Corresponding author*: bethanneyjanney.biomed@sathyabama.ac.in; ORCID: 0000-0001-6367-1336
Malathi H.: ORCID: 0000-0001-6198-8428
Anjali R. Kumbar: ORCID: 0009-0003-5171-2999
Debahuti Mishra: ORCID: 0000-0002-6827-6121
Ritesh Kumar: ORCID: 0009-0008-6351-083X

Satya Prakash Yadav, Abhay Bansal and Victor Hugo C. de Albuquerque (eds.) Computational Intelligence in Biomedical Internet of Medical Things, (35–54) © 2026 Scrivener Publishing LLC

of these fields. To detect and predict illnesses before symptoms manifest, biomedical intelligence systems can find patterns in patient data, such as heart disease prediction, and skin cancer prediction. In biomedical intelligence, employing ML and DL technology provides substantial breakthroughs in early illness detection, diagnosis, and prevention, improving public health outcomes through data-driven insights and predictive modeling.

Keywords: Biomedical intelligence, public health, artificial intelligence (AI), machine learning (ML), disease prevention

3.1 Introduction

Public health places equivalent importance on the health of individuals and communities, as it focuses on the health of populations. By providing people and communities with information, tools, and opportunities to make sensible decisions, public health can enable them to take control of their health. The technological, epistemological, and geographic transfer of biological knowledge infrastructures globally has been facilitated for decades by computers, AI, ML, and other digital technologies. There is an interest in how science, technology, and innovation have impacted society. Researchers have looked at the historical and cultural processes in the social and humanities sciences [1]. New paths for biological knowledge are being made possible by introducing AI into scientific labs. In addition to the development, testing, and validation of expert knowledge, new AI tools will influence the design of health innovation problems and suggestions, including synthetic nanoparticle study, bioengineered devices, cancer vaccines, responsive biosystems, and molecular disease diagnostics [2]. An interdisciplinarity called biomedical engineering was developed by fusing engineering ideas with biology and medicine. Its goal is to create, develop, and apply innovative solutions to healthcare problems [3]. Medical equipment is essential to this field since it allows for accurate diagnosis, effective treatment, and improved patient monitoring.

A variety of mental health diseases that impact a person's emotions, thoughts, and behavior are included in mental illness, sometimes referred to as mental health disorders. Eating disorders, schizophrenia, depression, anxiety disorders, and addictive behaviors are examples of mental illnesses [4]. Furthermore, the areas of biomedicine and biomedical study generate a substantial amount of data, contributing to an overload of information and public health issues. Big data is designed to promote the use of innovative methods for the extraction of new data on a variety of topics and the analysis of huge amounts of publicly available datasets [5]. The process of scientific discovery from the lab bench to the patient's bedside is referred to as translational medicine, and it has the potential to influence medical practice and revolutionize healthcare globally. Other than aiding in the development of public health policies, scientific translation aims to translate evidence-based study to clinical applications, including novel treatments, medical equipment, tissue replacement implantable materials, and diagnostic instruments. The biological paradigm is flawed because it fails to include the impact of non-physical factors, such as the environment and psychological problems, on health. In many cases, focusing only on the biological model may make treatment more difficult for a patient [6]. Figure 3.1 shows the impact on public health.

Aim of the study: This article examines how biological intelligence systems can identify and diagnose diseases before symptoms develop. By identifying patterns in patient data, such as the prediction of skin cancer and heart disease, with help from ML and DL, and the technological advancements and potential implications of these fields.

Organization of the study: The following is the order of the following sections of this work. The related work is introduced in Section 3.2. Section 3.3 provides biomedical intelligence on public healthcare. Section 3.4 illustrates the findings metrics and the study discussion. Section 3.5 concludes the paper.

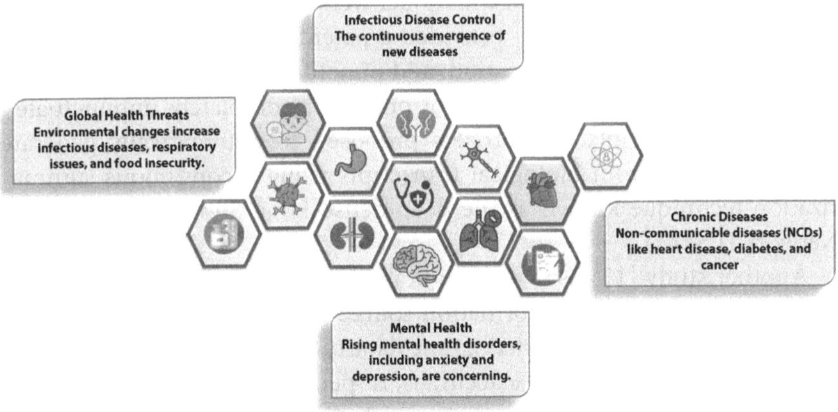

Figure 3.1 Challenges of public health. (Source: Own elaboration).

3.2 Related Works

The section on the several uses of biological intelligence in healthcare for illness prediction applications is organized as follows:

To automatically diagnose and identify cardiac arrhythmias, deep learning (DL) techniques must be employed [7]. The Massachusetts Institute of Technology - Beth Israel Hospital (MIT-BIH) arrhythmia database's waveforms were balanced for bias to develop a model. The electrocardiogram waveform accuracy in the MIT-BIH arrhythmia database was constructive. The paper [8] introduced a brand-new approach to illness identification. The study developed a system based on AI that retrieved different biological data from both homogeneous and dispersed sensors. To identify and diagnose illnesses, it investigated the relationships between various biological data using various DL architectures with ensemble learning and attention processes.

The suggested ML-based design approach [9] combined a Bayesian optimization method to enable the 3D printed ceramic scaffolds' time-dependent mechano-biological optimization at a relatively modest computer cost. The paper [10] proposed extending the Theory of Expected Information, which was used in several popular bioinformatics algorithms and data mining techniques, to Black Swan Event theorists to get around the difficulties associated with uncommon event analysis and sparse information.

In a study, a convolution neural network (CNN) approach [11] was applied to the International Skin Imaging Collaboration (ISIC) 2018 dataset to distinguish between the two primary tumor categories, malignant and benign. The outcomes of the model were similar to those of the pretrained model. A study [12] provided a patented method that combines subject modeling, phrase selection, and punctuation restorations to create more comprehensible summaries of poorly or completely unpunctuated discussion transcripts. Researchers proposed to automatically generate medical reports from biological transcripts using a continuous summarization technique known as the deep dense-Long Short Term Memory Network (LSTM).

Another study [13] used data on brain tumor genes from the Genomic Data Commons (GDC) information source and the University of Bonn's dataset. Using electroencephalogram data to diagnose epileptic seizures obtained 97.38% and 97.33% accuracy, respectively. Many applications of AI-enabled hydrogels in biomedicine, including drug administration, bioinks for improved production, tissue repair, and biosensors, were the main emphases [14] to provide a comprehensive and accessible overview of the subject. The traditional approaches of employing finite element analysis or mathematical equations to optimize wireless power transfer systems could be laborious and provide suboptimal designs. An article [15] provided a unique solution by using meta-heuristic and ML approaches to create and improve a compact, incredibly effective wireless power transfer receiving coil for use in biomedical applications.

3.3 Proposed Methods

The study introduces the impact of biomedical intelligence on public healthcare. Biomedical intelligence is consists of the use of AI and computational techniques to biomedical data (e.g., skin cancer, heart disease). Large volumes of medical data must be processed to produce insights, forecast the course of diseases, enhance treatment strategies, and increase system performance. Personalized treatment and preventative care are commonly provided by biomedical intelligence that frequently blends biological expertise with modern technology like ML and DL. The focus of public healthcare is opposed to individual health. Its goals are to prevent illness, improve wellness, and ensure that each person in a community has efficient, equitable, and accessible use of healthcare services. Public healthcare includes community-based and managerial initiatives, vaccination drives, public health education, sanitation, and disease surveillance to control and prevent health problems at the population level. The focus of public healthcare is on population health as opposed to individual health. Its goals are to prevent illness, improve wellness, and ensure that everyone has efficient, equitable, and accessible use of healthcare services, as shown in Figure 3.2.

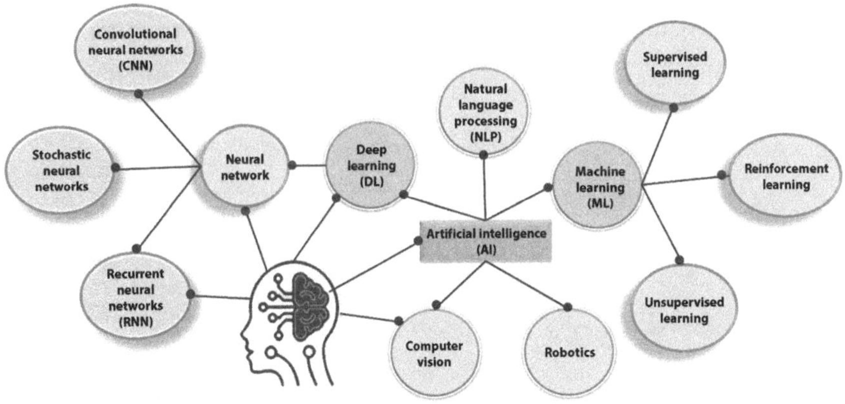

Figure 3.2 Application of biomedical intelligence. (Source: https://www.mdpi.com/2673-7426/2/4/49).

3.3.1 Data Collection

This section explains commonly used two disease (heart disease and skin cancer) datasets from open sources on the platform Kaggle. List out the two datasets for both diseases separately. The prediction process includes disease prediction data sources, data types including heart disease and skin cancer, prediction using ML and DL technologies, and finally suggesting the performance metrics, as below illustrated in Figure 3.3.

Heart disease datasets: Long Beach V., Cleveland, Hungary, and Switzerland are the four datasets that comprise this 1988 data collection. Only 14 of its 76 properties, including the predicted attribute, are utilized in all documented studies. The "target" field contains the patient's heart disease diagnosis. The disease is represented by a value of 1, and no disease by a value of 0 [16].

This dataset contains 11 factors that might be used to identify a potential cardiac condition, and it is a common occurrence associated with cardiovascular diseases. An ML model can greatly aid in the early detection and treatment of cardiac disease in individuals with, or at high risk for, the condition. Other previously accessible datasets that had not been joined were integrated to create this dataset. This is the biggest database of cardiac illness available for study purposes, including five heart datasets based on eleven common features. There were five datasets used in its curation. There were 1190 observations of all observations, 272 were duplicated. A total of 918 observations were included in the final dataset [17].

Skin cancer datasets: The existing collection of dermatoscopic images is small and lacks variety, which limits the ability to train neural networks for automated diagnosis of pigmented skin lesions. To solve this issue, the Human Against Machine (HAM) dataset with 10,000 training images

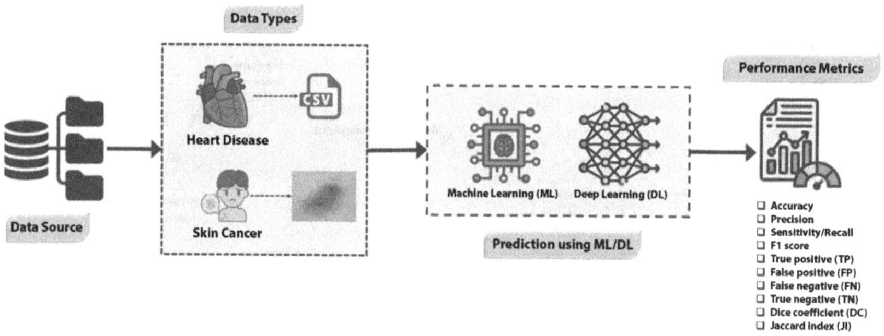

Figure 3.3 Methodology flow. (Source: Own elaboration).

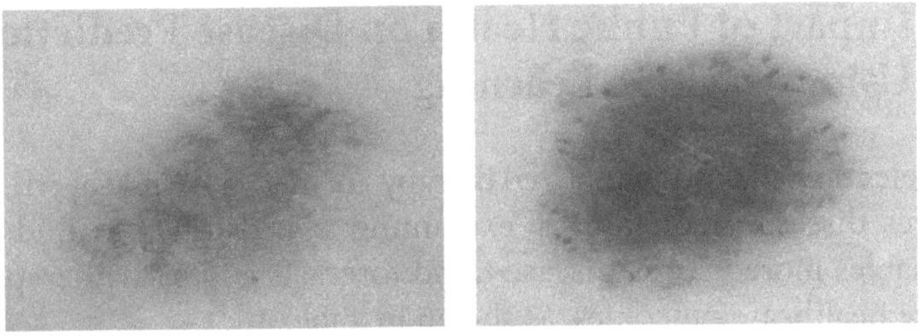

Figure 3.4 Dataset sample images of skin cancer MNIST: HAM10000. (Source: https://www.kaggle.com/datasets/kmader/skin-cancer-mnist-ham10000/?select=HAM10000_images_part_1).

(HAM10000 Human) is made publicly accessible. A study gathered and stored dermatoscopic images from a range of populations using a number of modalities. As a training set for ML applications in education, the final dataset contains 10,015 dermatoscopic images. The examples illustrate key diagnostic criteria in the study of colored lesions [18]. Figure 3.4 shows the sample images of skin cancer. MNIST: HAM10000.

The ISIC produced 2357 images of benign and malignant oncological conditions [19]. Every subgroup aside from melanomas and moles that are highly prevalent was split up into an equal number of images and categorized using the ISIC categorization.

3.4 Challenges the Biomedical Intelligence in Public Healthcare

The impact of biomedical intelligence on public healthcare in this section introduces disease prediction using ML and DL. Conventional heart disease diagnosis methods can be costly, computationally demanding, and produce inaccurate results. When sickness is rare, socioeconomic disparity can be a serious problem. As a result, models may function effectively for the dominant class but badly for the minority. Reliability and performance of ML models can be impacted by the quality or accessibility of datasets for testing and training. It is possible that many primary care physicians lack the knowledge necessary to recognize high-risk lesions. It is difficult to analyze dermoscopic images using DL models because of issues with noise filtering, image segmentation, and uneven image capture conditions. It might be challenging to identify skin lesions given differences in skin color for the challenges explored above using the technologies in ML and DL.

3.5 Impact of Public Health on Disease Prediction Using Machine Learning

Early detection and individualized therapy are made possible by ML, which improves disease prediction by examining vast datasets to find trends. This enables more precise disease trend forecasts and early therapies that enhance healthcare outcomes, as shown in Table 3.1.

3.6 Impact of Public Health in Disease Prediction Using Deep Learning

Initially, the majority of papers classified the skin lesion into two stages: melanoma and the first stage. This study mostly concentrated on an assessment based on differential sickness classification. An appropriate form of cancer is evaluated once melanoma or other cancers are diagnosed. Three major types of melanomas spread superficially: nodal melanoma, acral lentiginous, and lentigo malignant. Images of lesions were used to teach DL techniques to identify a particular kind. There are all shapes, locations, and lesion items concerning sizes and hues. The skin of superficial melanoma exhibits an odd line and a dark color, as shown in Table 3.2.

3.7 Result and Discussion

In the study, the impact of biomedical intelligence on public health briefly explains the evaluation metrics in the ML and DL approaches, and the study discussion is explained.

Evaluation metrics: The metrics calculate the number of misclassifications that ML and DL classifiers can produce and display their performance. Model performance is assessed using performance indicators, such as accuracy (Acc), precision (Pre), specificity (Spe), sensitivity/recall (Sen), dice coefficient (DC), F1-score, and Jaccard index (JI). The metrics listed below will demonstrate their impact on the suggested system, as following Equations 3.1 to 3.7.

True positive (TP): It predicts a positive outcome and expects the supplied input to be positive.
False positive (FP): It forecasts as positive despite the input predicted to be negative.

Table 3.1 Disease prediction using ML.

References	Dataset	Classification techniques	Findings
Heart disease prediction			
[20]	Cleveland Heart Disease dataset from the University of California Irvine	Machine learning techniques using k-nearest neighbor(KNN)	Acc- 87%, sen-73%, spe-86%, F1-score-77%, and ROC-88.5
[21]	University of California Irvine repository	Machine learning techniques using artificial neural network (NN)	Acc-92.30, pre-0.97, F1-score-0.92, ROC-0.92, recall-0.87,
[22]	Kaggle cardiovascular disease dataset	Random Forest (RF), and KNN, support vector machine (SVM), and KNN outputs are stacked, and logistic regression is used as the meta classifier	Acc-75.01% (Stacked model)
[23]	Cardiovascular disease dataset	Extreme gradient boosting (XGBoost)	Acc- 99.14%
[24]	Kaggle Cardiovascular Disease dataset	Multi-layer perceptron (MLP)	Acc- 87.28%, AUC-0.95
Skin cancer prediction			
[25]	ACS, HAM10000, PAD-UFES-20, and ISIC 2016	Anti-Coronavirus Optimized-Kernel Softplus Extreme Learning Machine (ACO-KSELM)	Acc-98.9%
[26]	International Skin Imaging Collaboration database	Random Forest	Acc-86.36%, Sen-95.00%

[Note: Sen-sensitivity, Acc-accuracy, Pre-precision, Spe-specificity].

Table 3.2 Disease prediction using DL.

References	Dataset	Classification techniques	Findings
Heart disease prediction			
[27]	Heart dataset from Cleveland	Logistic regression	Acc-96%
[28]	Cleveland and Hungarian datasets from the University of California Irvine	Bidirectional long short-term memory (Bi-LSTM)	Acc-98.86%, Pre-98.9%, Sen-98.8%, Spe-98.89%, F-Score-98.86%
[29]	Cardiovascular diseases	Back propagation neural network (BP-NN)	Sen- 97.85%, Spe-97.85%, pre-98.41%, recall-97.43%, acc-97.09%
[30]	Cleveland and Statlog datasets	GAN-Bi-LSTM, and generative adversarial network- one-dimensional CNN (GAN-1D-CNN),	Acc-99.1%, 99.3%, AUC-100%, Spe-99.2%, Sen-99.3%, F1-score-99.2%
[31]	University of California Irvine	DL-based modified DenseNet201 (MDenseNet201)	Acc-99.12%
Skin cancer prediction			
[32]	PH2, ISIC 2019	Convolutional neural network (CNN)	Sen- 100%, Pre-90.1%, acc-95%
[33]	ISIC data set	CNN+ regularize	Sen-94.3, Spec-93.2, Acc-97.6
[34]	Multiple dermis+ Der quest	Modified CNN	Sen-94.2%, Spec-94.5%, Acc-94.6

(*Continued*)

Table 3.2 Disease prediction using DL. (*Continued*)

References	Dataset	Classification techniques	Findings
[35]	Multiple	Fusion method (Alexnet+VGG 16)	Sen-99.3%, Spec-94.5%, Acc-94.6
[36]	PH2 dermoscopic images, ISIC 2017 dataset, and ISIC 2018 dataset, with numbers 2000 and 8695	Image segmentation using fuzzy logic and a modified DL model	Accelerate the detecting procedure without sacrificing the output's reliability

[Note: Sen-sensitivity, Acc-accuracy, Pre-precision, Spe-specificity].

False negative (FN): It anticipates a negative input and now makes a positive prediction.
True negative (TP): Both the expected and predicted outputs are negative for the given input.

Accuracy: It is defined as the proportion of correct forecasts to all predictions. When dealing with a balanced dataset, this measure is perfect. This metric's output might not accurately represent the model's performance in datasets with a majority class.

$$Ac = \frac{TP + TN}{Total\ samples} \tag{3.1}$$

Figure 3.5 shows the outcomes of the accuracy in ML methods in (a) heart disease prediction and (b) Skin cancer prediction. While (a) KNN obtains 87%, SVM at 75.01%, NN performs best with 92.30%, Similarly, the RF model had an accuracy of 86.36%, and the ACO-KSELM technique had the best accuracy at 98.9%.

Figure 3.6 shows the outcomes of accuracy in DL methods: (a) heart disease prediction; and (b) skin cancer prediction. The accuracy of MDenseNet201 is the greatest at 99.12%, with GAN-1D-CNN coming in second at 99.1%. With accuracies of 98.86% and 97.09%, respectively,

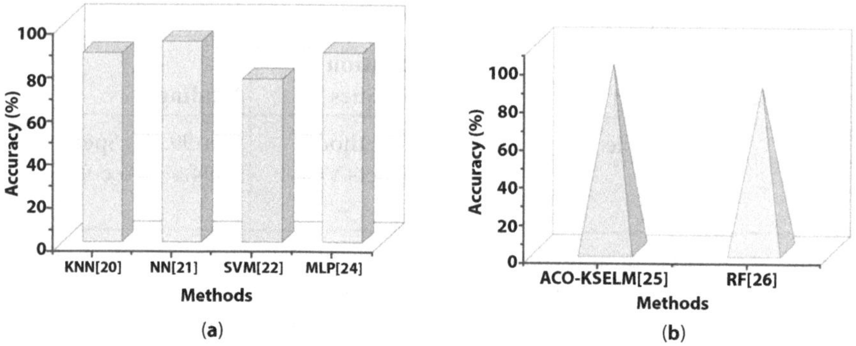

Figure 3.5 Outcomes of the accuracy in ML methods: (a) heart disease prediction; and (b) skin cancer prediction. (Source: Own elaboration).

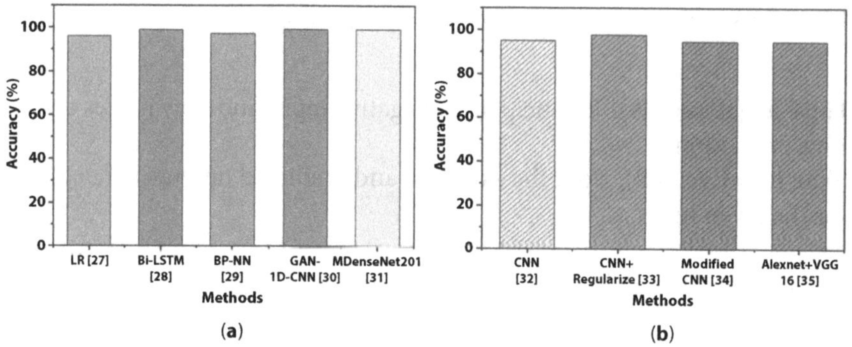

Figure 3.6 Outcomes of the accuracy in DL methods: (a) heart disease prediction; and (b) skin cancer prediction. (Source: Own elaboration).

other techniques like Bi-LSTM and BP-NN exhibit high accuracy. At 97.6%, CNN+ Regularize has the best accuracy for predicting skin cancer. While the improved CNN and the AlexNet+VGG16 combination both provide accuracies of 94.6%, CNN alone reaches 95%.

Precision: The accuracy of the ML model is one indicator of its capacity to determine the ratio of true positives among all projected positives. This statistic is useful when FPs are costly for model quality.

$$Precision = \frac{TP}{FP + TP} \tag{3.2}$$

Figure 3.7 shows the outcomes of the precision in ML methods for heart disease prediction; KNN achieves (87%), and NN offer (97%), respectively.

Figure 3.8 shows the outcomes of the precision in DL methods that show heart disease prediction. With the highest precision of 98.9%, the Bi-LSTM model is closely followed by the BP-NN model that has a precision of 98.41%.

Sensitivity/Recall: The precise segment lesions measurement. A metric used to determine how accurately an ML model finds the number of positives out of all real positives is called recall. This statistic is useful when the cost of FNs for model quality is high.

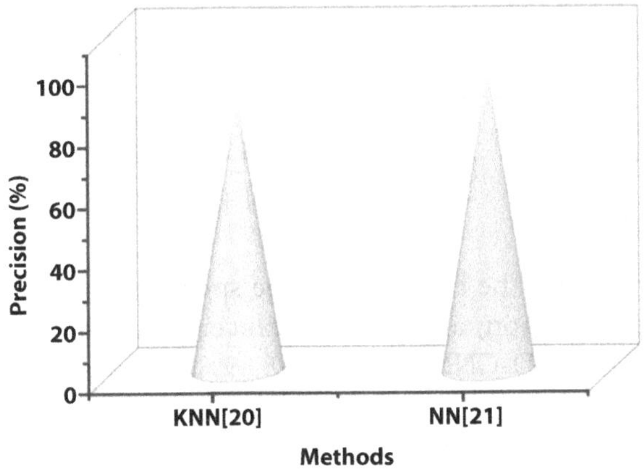

Figure 3.7 Outcomes of the precision in ML methods show heart disease prediction. (Source: Own elaboration).

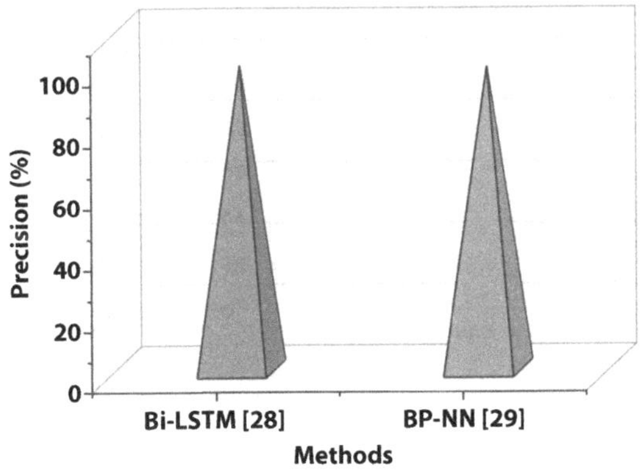

Figure 3.8 Outcomes of the precision in DL methods that show heart disease prediction. (Source: Own elaboration).

$$\text{Sensitivity/Recall} = \frac{\text{TP}}{\text{TP} + \text{FN}} \tag{3.3}$$

Figure 3.9 shows the outcomes of the sensitivity/recall in DL methods: (a) heart disease prediction; and (b) skin cancer prediction. The GAN-1D-CNN had the maximum recall (99.3%) in the prediction of heart disease (a), and CNN had the perfect recall (100%) in the prediction of skin cancer (b), though CNN+Regularize and modified CNN performed slightly higher.

Specificity: The TN rate is the probability of a negative test result if the subject of a medical examination to identify an illness scored negatively. Specificity is the capacity of a test to accurately identify people that are healthy and free of issues.

$$\text{Specificity} = \frac{\text{TN}}{\text{TN} + \text{FP}} \tag{3.4}$$

Figure 3.10 shows the outcomes of the specificity in DL methods: (a) heart disease prediction; and (b) skin cancer prediction. The Bi-LSTM, BP-NN, and GAN-1D-CNN obtained 98.89%, 97.85%, and 99.2% in the (a) prediction of heart disease (a). CNN+Regularize had 93.2%, modified CNN had 94.5%, and AlexNet+VGG16 had 94.5% for (b) skin cancer prediction.

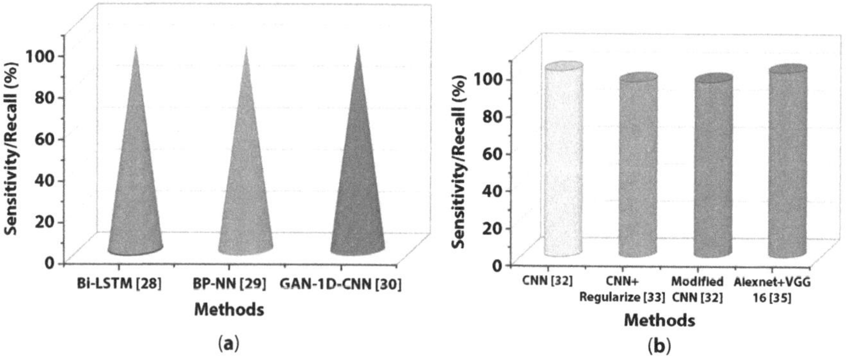

Figure 3.9 Outcomes of the sensitivity/recall in DL methods: (a) heart disease prediction; and (b) skin cancer prediction. (Source: Own elaboration).

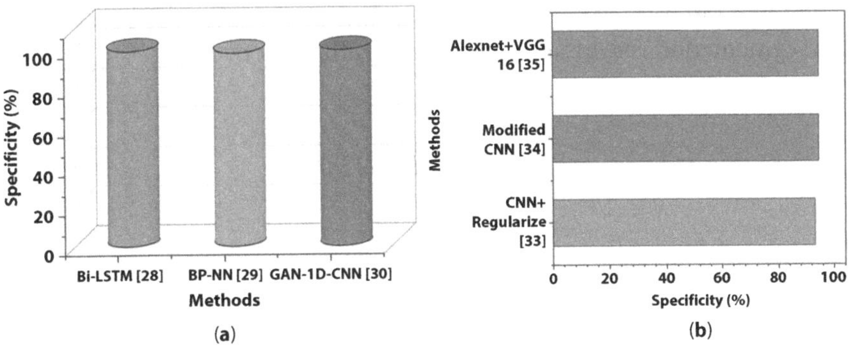

Figure 3.10 Outcomes of the specificity in DL methods: (a) heart disease prediction; and (b) skin cancer prediction. (Source: Own elaboration).

F1-score: It is the accuracy and memory harmonic mean. Accuracy and recall are modified to obtain the F1 Score. This score consequently accounts for both FP and FN. Although the F1-score is simpler to comprehend than accuracy, it is more useful, especially when the distribution of classes is unpredictable.

$$F1\ score = \frac{2 \times precision \times recall}{precision + recall} \tag{3.5}$$

Figure 3.11 shows the outcomes of the accuracy in ML methods the heart disease prediction. The F1-score attains ML methods such as KNN (77%), and NN (92%).

Figure 3.12 shows the outcomes of the accuracy in DL methods that show the heart disease prediction. With the highest precision o 98.9%, the Bi-LSTM model is closely followed by the BP-NN model that has a precision of 98.41%.

Dice coefficient: It is employed to quantify the segmented lesions and provide an explanation of the ground truth link.

$$DC = \frac{(2 \times TP)}{(2 \times TP) + FP + FN} \tag{3.6}$$

Jaccard index: A parameter called the JI is used to quantify how closely the segmentation results and the ground truth mask overlaps.

$$JI = \frac{TP}{TP + FN + FP} \tag{3.7}$$

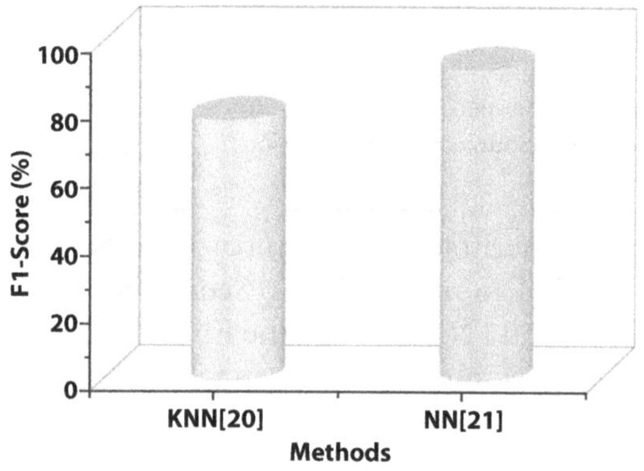

Figure 3.11 Outcomes of the F1-score in ML methods that show heart disease prediction. (Source: Own elaboration).

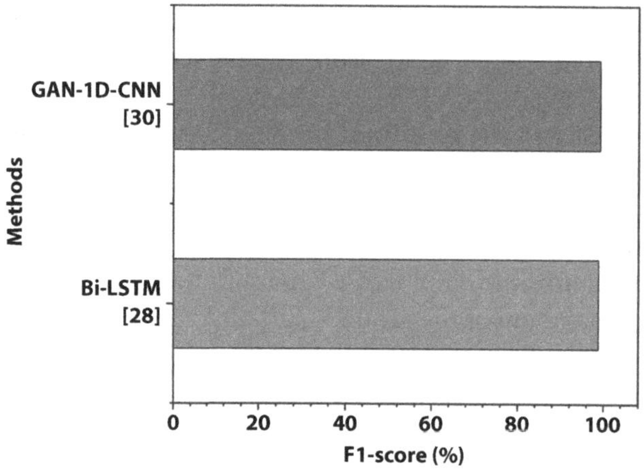

Figure 3.12 Outcomes of the F1-score in DL methods the heart disease prediction. (Source: Own elaboration).

3.8 Discussion

In the study, the efficiency impact of biomedical intelligence in enhancing public health outcomes is different and supports the earlier study. By monitoring epidemics, immunizing populations, and establishing safety regulations, public health aims to forecast heart disease and skin cancer and stop the spread of illness. Gender equality, school attendance, and life expectancy can all rise with access to clean drinking water. It advances population well-being by protecting it against environmental threats and ensuring access to high-quality medical care. A useful technique for estimating the risk of heart disease is ML, which analyzes a range of data, such as genetics, lifestyle variables, and medical records. Machine learning might improve the accuracy of risk assessment by spotting new risk indicators and trends that conventional approaches cannot detect. With the ultimate objective of creating an AI-powered gadget that can identify skin cancers in real time, DL-based algorithms help dermatologists diagnose skin malignancies quickly and accurately. In the discussion of several DL architectures for skin cancer detection, consideration is given to the application of DL algorithms for skin cancer categorization. An enhanced diagnostic system that can correctly diagnose many forms of skin cancer with superior specificity and sensitivity improvements has been created by combining a vast and diversified dataset, robust lesion segmentation, sophisticated DL methods, and optimization algorithms.

3.9 Conclusion

The study enhances biological intelligence's influence on healthcare using ML and DL methods. Predicting cardiac disease is essential for healthcare, since timely and precise detection of the condition can greatly enhance patient outcomes. By enabling individualized preventative methods, increasing treatment accuracy, and assisting early diagnosis, these technologies improve public health. To promote proactive treatment and potentially decrease the impact of chronic illnesses, medical intelligence systems find intricate patterns in medical information and provide early insights into problems like skin cancer and heart disease as symptoms develop. The study emphasizes how AI might be used to enhance human health outcomes while also pointing out the practical problems that must be fixed to optimize its application in healthcare. The biomedical model's drawback is that it excludes the impact of non-physical factors on health, including psychological problems and the environment. Future studies might concentrate on improving model accuracy in a variety of healthcare scenarios, increasing AI transparency, and developing ethical frameworks that ensure equitable and accurate public health results.

References

1. Ren, F., *et al.*, AlphaFold accelerates artificial intelligence powered drug discovery: efficient discovery of a novel CDK20 small molecule inhibitor. *Chem. Sci.*, 14, 6, 1443–1452, 2023, https://doi.org/10.1039/D2SC05709C.
2. da Silva, R.G.L., The advancement of artificial intelligence in biomedical study and health innovation: challenges and opportunities in emerging economies. *Glob. Health*, 20, 1, 44, 2024, https://doi.org/10.1186/s12992-024-01049-5.
3. Manickam, P., *et al.*, Artificial intelligence (AI) and internet of medical things (IoMT) assisted biomedical systems for intelligent healthcare. *Biosensors*, 12, 8, 562, 2022, https://doi.org/10.3390/bios12080562.
4. Adeli, E., Rekik, I., Park, S.H., Shen, D., Predictive intelligence in biomedical and health informatics. *IEEE J. Biomed. Health. Inf.*, *24*, 2, 333–335, 2020, https://doi.org/10.1109/JBHI.2019.2962852.
5. Bhatia, Paul, Acharjee, Ramachairy, Biosensors and their widespread impact on human health. *Sens. Int.*, *5*, 100257, 2024, https://doi.org/10.1016/j.sintl.2023.100257.
6. Duncan, D., *et al.*, Interdisciplinary K-12 Control Education in Biomedical and Public Health Applications. *IFAC-PapersOnLine*, 55, 17, 242–248, 2022, https://doi.org/10.1016/j.ifacol.2022.09.286.
7. Anand, R., *et al.*, An enhanced ResNet-50 deep learning model for arrhythmia detection using electrocardiogram biomedical indicators. *Evol. Syst.*, 15, 1, 83–97, 2024, https://doi.org/10.1007/s12530-023-09559-0.
8. Djenouri, Y., *et al.*, Artificial intelligence of medical things for disease detection using ensemble deep learning and attention mechanism. *Expert Syst.*, 41, 6, e13093, 2024, https://doi.org/10.1111/exsy.13093.
9. Wu, C., *et al.*, Machine learning-based design for additive manufacturing in biomedical engineering. *Int. J. Mech. Sci.*, 266, 108828, 2024, https://doi.org/10.1016/j.ijmecsci.2023.108828.
10. Robson, B. and Baek, O.K., Use of a theory of expected information for sparse data and adverse events in clinical trials and other biomedical studies. *Inf. Sci.*, 680, 121027, 2024, https://doi.org/10.1016/j.ins.2024.121027.
11. Gouda, W., *et al.*, Detection of skin cancer based on skin lesion images using deep learning. *Healthcare*, 10, 7, 1183, MDPI, 2022, MDPI, https://doi.org/10.3390/healthcare10071183.
12. Bedi, P.P.S., Bala, M., Sharma, K., Extractive text summarization for biomedical transcripts using deep dense LSTM-CNN framework. *Expert Syst.*, 41, 7, e13490, 2024, https://doi.org/10.1111/exsy.13490.

13. Das, A., *et al.*, Biomedical signal to image conversion and classification using flexible deep learning techniques. *Int. J. Bus. Intell. Data Min.*, 24, 2, 183–202, 2024, https://doi.org/10.1504/IJBIDM.2024.136439.
14. Li, Z., *et al.*, AI energized hydrogel design, optimization and application in biomedicine. *Mater. Today Bio*, 25, 101014, 2024, https://doi.org/10.1016/j.mtbio.2024.101014.
15. Bennia, F., Boudouda, A., Nafa, F., Optimal design of wireless power transfer coils for biomedical implants using machine learning and meta-heuristic algorithms. *Electr. Eng.*, 106, 5, 5869–5884, 2024, https://doi.org/10.1007/s00202-024-02345-4.
16. https://www.kaggle.com/datasets/johnsmith88/heart-disease-dataset.
17. https://www.kaggle.com/datasets/fedesoriano/heart-failure-prediction.
18. https://www.kaggle.com/datasets/kmader/skin-cancer-mnist-ham10000/data.
19. https://www.kaggle.com/datasets/nodoubttome/skin-cancer9-classesisic.
20. Srivastava, K. and Choubey, D.K., Heart disease prediction using machine learning and data mining. *Int. J. Recent Technol. Eng.*, 9, 1, 212–219, 2020, DOI:10.35940/ijrte.F9199.059120.
21. Jindal, H., *et al.*, Heart disease prediction using machine learning algorithms. *IOP Conf. Ser.: Mater. Sci. Eng.*, 1022, 1, 012072, 2021, https://doi.org/10.1088/1757-899X/1022/1/012072.
22. Shorewala, V., Early detection of coronary heart disease using ensemble techniques. *Inf. Med. Unlocked*, 26, 100655, 2021, https://doi.org/10.1016/j.imu.2021.100655.
23. Ogunpola, A., Saeed, F., Basurra, S., Albarrak, A.M., Qasem, S.N., Machine learning-based predictive models for detection of cardiovascular diseases. *Diagnostics*, 14, 2, 144, 2024, https://doi.org/10.3390/diagnostics14020144.
24. Bhatt, C.M., *et al.*, Effective heart disease prediction using machine learning techniques. *Algorithms*, 16, 2, 88, 2023, https://doi.org/10.3390/a16020088.
25. Liu, N., *et al.*, ACO-KELM: anti coronavirus optimized kernel-based softplus extreme learning machine for classification of skin cancer. *Expert Syst. Appl.*, 232, 1207195, 2023, https://doi.org/10.1016/j.eswa.2023.120719.
26. Bistroń, M. and Piotrowski, Z., Comparison of machine learning algorithms used for skin cancer diagnosis. *Appl. Sci.*, 12, 19, 9960, 2022, https://doi.org/10.3390/app12199960.
27. Subramani, S., *et al.*, Cardiovascular diseases prediction by machine learning incorporation with deep learning. *Front. Med.*, 10, 1150933, 2023, https://doi.org/10.3389/fmed.2023.1150933.
28. Nancy, A.A., *et al.*, Iot-cloud-based smart healthcare monitoring system for heart disease prediction via deep learning. *Electronics*, 11, 15, 2292, 2022, https://doi.org/10.3390/electronics11152292.
29. Vincent Paul, S.M., *et al.*, Intelligent framework for prediction of heart disease using deep learning. *Arabian J. Sci. Eng.*, 47, 2, 2159–2169, 2022, https://doi.org/10.1007/s13369-021-06058-9.

30. Sarra, R.R., *et al.*, A robust framework for data generative and heart disease prediction based on efficient deep learning models. *Diagnostics*, 12, 12, 2899, 2022, https://doi.org/10.3390/diagnostics12122899.
31. Mandava, M., MDensNet201-IDRSRNet: Efficient cardiovascular disease prediction system using hybrid deep learning. *Biomed. Signal Process. Control*, 93, 106147, 2024, https://doi.org/10.1016/j.bspc.2024.106147.
32. El-Khatib, H., Popescu, D., Ichim, L., Deep learning–based methods for automatic diagnosis of skin lesions. *Sensors*, 20, 6, 1753, 2020, https://doi.org/10.3390/s20061753.
33. Dorj, U.-O., *et al.*, The skin cancer classification using deep convolutional neural network. *Multimed. Tools Appl.*, 77, 9909–9924, 2018, https://doi.org/10.1007/s11042-018-5714-1.
34. Fuzzell, L.N., *et al.*, Cervical cancer screening in the United States: Challenges and potential solutions for underscreened groups. *Preventative Med.*, 144, 106400, 2021, https://doi.org/10.1016/j.ypmed.2020.106400.
35. Zhang, N., *et al.*, Skin cancer diagnosis based on optimized convolutional neural network. *Artif. Intell. Med.*, 102, 101756, 2020, https://doi.org/10.1016/j.artmed.2019.101756.
36. Singh, S.K., Abolghasemi, V., Anisi, M.H., Fuzzy logic with deep learning for detection of skin cancer. *Appl. Sciences*, 13, 15, 8927, 2023, https://doi.org/10.3390/app13158927.

4

Healthcare Data Integration and Management

Swaroop Mohanty[1], Piyali Roy Chowdhury[2], Renuka Jyothi S.[3], Satya Ranjan Das[4*] and Dhananjay Kumar Yadav[5]

[1]*C.V. Raman Global University, Odisha, India*
[2]*Management, Maulana Abul Kalam Azad University of Technology, Kolkata, India*
[3]*Department of Biotechnology and Genetics, Jain (Deemed-to-be University), Bangalore, Karnataka, India*
[4]*Department of Computer Science and Engineering, Siksha 'O' Anusandhan (Deemed to be University), Bhubaneswar, Odisha, India*
[5]*Maharishi School of Engineering & Technology, Maharishi University of Information Technology, Uttar Pradesh, India*

Abstract
Improving the ability, effectiveness, and availability of healthcare services requires a basic understanding of medical information, integration, and administration. With a focus on the difficulties and developments in handling enormous volumes of health data, this chapter examines the main tactics and tools used in the incorporation of healthcare data. The study discusses the significance of medical information interoperability, which guarantees smooth data transfers across various healthcare systems, improving treatment results and patient care. Additionally, the study covers electronic health records (EHRs) that could improve clinical operations and streamline administrative duties. This study looks at the importance of data privacy compliance, ensuring private patient information is shielded from unwanted access. Modern technologies revolutionize data management by providing new chances for safe, effective, and creative solutions including blockchain, machine learning (ML), and artificial intelligence (AI). As a result, the considerable emphasis on EHR shows that modern technologies can maximize operational efficiency. The necessity of extensive and flexible data integration platforms in contemporary medical facilities is emphasized in the review's conclusion.

**Corresponding author*: satyadas@soa.ac.in; ORCID: 0009-0009-5723-9665

Satya Prakash Yadav, Abhay Bansal and Victor Hugo C. de Albuquerque (eds.) Computational Intelligence in Biomedical Internet of Medical Things, (55–68) © 2026 Scrivener Publishing LLC

Keywords: Data integration, healthcare, management, electronic health records (EHR), interoperability

4.1 Introduction

Anticipatory, preventative, personalized, interactive, and online medicine would be the standard in the future of healthcare. Comprehensively deep and wide-ranging data and information must be accessible for study purposes, considering the level of care to support focused evaluation and therapy. Through every medical interaction, contributing to studies and study being utilized in real-time during clinical care to create a healthcare system that learns [1]. Conventional health information technology (IT) structures, such as personal health record (PHR) and electronic health record (EHR) networks, are built on unique designs to describe and maintain the data using various technological and semantic protocols. Each client-server system can employ a distinct database technique and language, and all are dependent on local software, hardware, and information storage [2]. There are more chances than ever before for small and big medical practices to create and execute patient-centered care delivery approaches because of recent advancements in e-healthcare. These advancements are based on the proactive dissemination of trustworthy and pertinent information over strong communication methods that enable a patient support system. Patient-centered care breaks down barriers that keep patients, as well as their families, out of the therapeutic setting. It is based on the bonds between patients, caregivers, and medical personnel [3]. Self-administration is much more practical because of the advancement and use of technology for communication and information in medicine. Many physicians have implemented EHR technologies. Patients employ portable medical equipment to focus on their physiological indicators. Patients are more involved in their medical treatment when self-monitoring and supervision approaches are used, which makes it easier to gather additional medical data [4]. Internet of Things (IoT)-based medical facilities offer applications and services. Additionally, the applications were separated into two groups: single-condition and double-condition applicants. The following is a list of all items. As a result, the majority of these apps and services require communication and interchange between different service mediums through integration [5]. The growing significance of huge quantities of data in biomedicine and healthcare, as well as the growing recognition of the potential of big data in technical and clinical studies, is shown by the term's expanding use in healthcare studies. Finding novel diagnoses and treatment tools that capture the complete complexity of illnesses is made feasible by the incorporation of such large, practical medical collections of information from electronic medical records, with information and specific biochemical and hormonal analyses [6]. Genomic medicine could be a large, interlinked field. Since it would be hard to cover all aspects of genomic medicine because of the field's rapid evolution, settled on a selection of specialties where the informatics issues are well understood for the intent. The goal of contemporary human genetics is to pinpoint the specific gene causing a hereditary illness. The fields of pharmacogenomics and pharmacogenomics aim to comprehend the role the genes or gene systems play in people's different responses to drug therapy [7]. The healthcare system is experiencing a big data conversion because of the rapid growth of data acquired through mobile devices, electronic medical records, and databases. The widely available data, which offers several advantages including a better quality of life, illness evaluation, therapy, and the operation of the healthcare system, requires a lot of information to be retrieved [8]. Large volume, variability, and speed are characteristics of the big data created in the medical field. Irregular data, a high number of parameters, and the requirement for actual time data analysis are some of the additional problems related to big healthcare data. These characteristics present several challenges for the collaboration, mining, and storage of data to support health-related studies [9]. Regulations and legislation about using big data in the medical field should be implemented to report these problems, along with the development of analytical methodologies that concentrate on the topic. From a patient's perspective, using big data exploration could improve care and cheapen expenses [10].

The main objective of the study is to investigate the methods and tools currently used in healthcare data management and integration, with a focus on improving operational effectiveness, confidentiality of information, and interoperability. The influence of cutting-edge technology like blockchain, artificial intelligence (AI), and machine learning (ML) on improving healthcare systems is also assessed.

4.2 Methodology

This study approach comprised an organized study of English-language publications on healthcare data management and integration that were released between 2019 and 2024. The selection of the studies was focused on their applicability to interoperability, technological breakthroughs, and healthcare data systems. Case studies, conference proceedings, or peer-reviewed

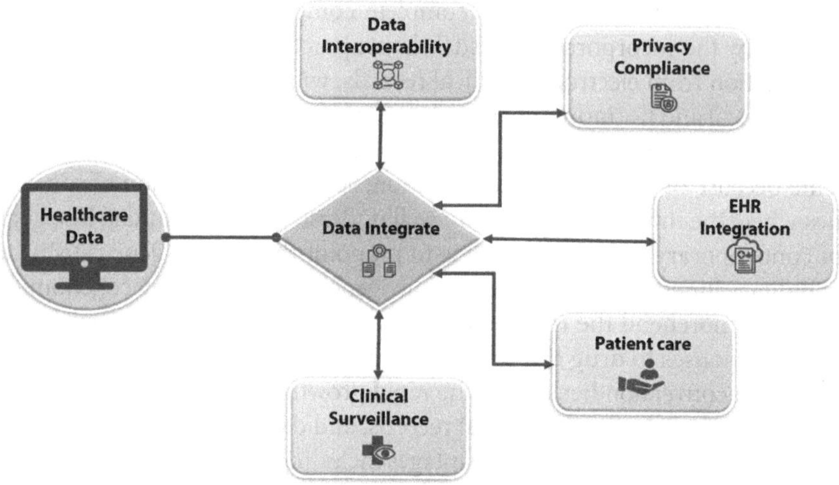

Figure 4.1 Data integration and management flow in the healthcare sector. (Source: Own elaboration).

journal studies offered significant new information about data integration techniques, practical applications, or advancements in healthcare technology that were included. Studies that lacked empirical data or well-defined procedures were not peer-reviewed nor dealt with unrelated subjects that were excluded after being vetted for quality. The publications were examined to find new developments, problems, and trends in the field. The schematic representations of the data integration flow are shown in Figure 4.1.

4.2.1 Selection Criteria

The search was initiated by studying English publications between the years of 2019 and 2024. This period was selected to encompass the latest developments and patterns in medical records integration, guaranteeing the incorporation of innovative approaches, technology, and procedures that have influenced the domain during the past decade. For this study, only papers satisfied these requirements and were relevant to the administration and integration of medical information.

4.2.1.1 Inclusion Criteria

- Studies published in the English language from 2019 until 2024.

- Studies about managing, integrating, or associated approaches to healthcare data.
- Studies on improvements in healthcare data systems' technology, methodology, or operations.
- Related scholarly works, proceedings of conferences, and subject to peer-reviewed publications.
- Papers that go into the use of data integration in healthcare environments, such as interoperability systems, EHRs, as well as health information exchange.
- Publications that offer intellectual frameworks, case studies, or actual data about the integration and administration of healthcare data.

4.2.1.2 *Exclusion Criteria*

- Publications before 2019 are excluded.
- Papers that are not in English or publications that do not provide enough information in English.
- Studies unrelated to the administration and integration of healthcare data.
- Publications that discuss healthcare-related subjects without discussing the management of data or integration strategies.
- Commentary, identification without peer reviewing or viewpoints.
- Investigations using imprecise methodology or inadequate data.
- Articles that do not include information about real-world uses or developments in medical data systems.

4.2.2 Challenges and Benefits of Healthcare Data Integration

Combining multiple types of information from various sources, such as patient portals, devices, EHRs, and telemedicine services into one unified framework is referred to as healthcare data integration. This integration allows healthcare providers to have a detailed and complete view of a person's health and therefore enables better decisions, personalized care, and better clinical outcomes. The inclusion of data across platforms and healthcare providers can reduce unnecessary services, identify the most effective treatments, improve processes in the healthcare service value chain, and increase output. Also, data integration helps in the management and study of health services. The analysis of how illness disseminates, forecasting public health interventions – invariably active surveillance of diseases, such as COVID-19 – becomes possible due to data integration across multiple clinics, hospitals, and health systems. It enables doctors to have the most current and complete information on the individual patients, which helps in decision-making and treatment planning. Connected data systems can reduce the risks of errors in medication prescriptions and prevent unnecessary repeat tests by allowing clinicians to view health records across multiple sites of care. Integrating data with a degree of seamlessness has its share of difficulties. This includes issues related to the security and privacy of the data, challenges in standardizing the data, and the vast volume of the data involved. It is hard to note that clinical data is mostly unstructured, thus the challenge of converting it into useful information. Many systems do not work adequately together because of legacy systems or incompatible formats. Despite these challenges, however, the relentless evolution of systems and processes to overcome such barriers is positive, making the convergence of healthcare IT a key focus area for further developments in healthcare.

4.3 Results

With an emphasis on administrative compliance, Table 4.1 displays studies covering healthcare-related topics. The investigations, which cover subjects including medical information interoperability, improving care for patients, cost savings, information security conformity, and health education resources integration, operated from 2019 to 2022. The majority of studies place a strong emphasis on following rules, highlighting how crucial

Table 4.1 Sampling of publications pertaining to healthcare and regulatory compliance.

References	Year	Target issue	Regulatory adherence
[11]	2022	Health data interoperability	Yes
[12]	2019	Patient carc and engagement	Yes
[13]	2020	Cost reduction in healthcare	No
[14]	2021	Data privacy compliance	Yes
[15]	2019	Electronic health record integration	Yes

it is for medical facilities to maintain standards. There could be an imbalance in giving priority to financial considerations because a study from 2020 on lowering expenses is the only study that does not comply with regulatory criteria. All things considered, the studies highlight the importance of balancing patient-centered care, creativity, and legal requirements in healthcare innovations.

Table 4.2 summarizes the studies on integrating data in medicine with a focus on different goals, along with integrating capabilities. Semantic and structural integration, as well as cutting-edge strategies like networked systems, bidirectional AI, and Internet of Health (IoH), are covered for secondary data usage. In the studies, which include topics such as information systems integration, personalized healthcare, and terminology mappings during COVID-19, run from 2019 to 2024. Semantic integration is the focus of most studies; however, structural approaches are being investigated. Although the use of unified information is not the primary goal, there are instances when regulatory compliance is evident, particularly in innovations such as clinical scoring software and healthcare data storage. The overall goal of these investigations is to simplify the administration and delivery of healthcare.

Table 4.3 provides a summary of studies on computing and integrating techniques used in medical care with an emphasis on different innovations and their results. The study covers topics, such as blockchain technology, AI/ML, semantic data integration, and application programming interface (API) and runs from 2019 to 2021. The results are noteworthy because they demonstrate the advantages of blockchain technology for reliability, information sharing, and independence; the integration of taxonomies and semantic data; and the use of APIs to discover new connections in patient survival. While new approaches in semantics seek to encourage innovative solutions in both business and academics, AI and ML are used to improve privacy and adherence in identity and access management systems.

The proportional values that indicate the importance of several healthcare-related measures are displayed in Figure 4.2. The significance of smooth data interchange in medical facilities is highlighted by the significant importance of medical information interoperability, which stands at 85%. With a 90% patient care rate, there is a clear emphasis on enhancing healthcare delivery. Eighty percent of healthcare costs are reduced, highlighting the importance of affordability and effectiveness. With a 92% rating, EHR incorporation is deemed essential to modernizing healthcare procedures. Finally, the importance of safeguarding patient information in medical facilities is shown by 88% data privacy adherence rate.

Table 4.2 An overview of healthcare data integration techniques.

References	Year	Data integration in healthcare	Objective	Utilization	Integration capability
[16]	2023	Yes	Examining the intricacies of terminologies, mappings, and annotations, especially in light of the COVID-19 epidemic.	No	Semantic
[17]	2019	Yes	The effects of AI on the administration of medical information and data.	No	Semantic
[18]	2022	Yes	Combination of new multimodal AI techniques with complementing data sources.	No	Structural
[19]	2024	Yes	Developments are used to improve healthcare systems by streamlining administration, making decisions, and data integrity.	No	Semantic
[20]	2024	Yes	The collaborative technical and content-related development of a distributed system for secondary utilization of medical information that can be accessed.	No	Structural
[21]	2021	Yes	The advancement of IS integration between medical providers and healthcare management merits support and encouragement.	No	Structural

(*Continued*)

Table 4.2 An overview of healthcare data integration techniques. (*Continued*)

References	Year	Data integration in healthcare	Objective	Utilization	Integration capability
[22]	2020	Yes	New healthcare data warehouse layout that builds on the reorganized extract–transform–load procedure.	Yes	Semantic
[23]	2022	Yes	The Pediatric Eosinophilic Esophagitis Symptom Score (PEESS™ v2.0's) is used in a forward-looking, interventional, regulated clinical setting.	No	Not mentioned
[24]	2019	Yes	Creating a clever method to integrate diverse knowledge and data sources in personalized healthcare.	No	Semantic
[25]	2023	Yes	The IoH is an approach to the issue that enables the IoH to prescribe drugs to an individual to avoid sharing patient data and granting the administrator accessibility to the drugs with the IoH's consent.	No	Not mentioned

Table 4.3 Technologies and software used in safety and medical study.

References	Integration	Utilization mentioned	Software used	Year of publication	Outcome
[26]	Application programming interfaces, consumer web portal profiles	No	Off-chain blockchain systems	2021	Free medical data by facilitating increased trust, sharing, and autonomy
[27]	Semantic data integration	No	Cloud, WiFi or mobile (3G/4G)	2021	Ontologies to integrate semantic data
[28]	Application programming interfaces	Yes	PrivGuard API	2019	Find novel relationships between patients and their survival duration.
[29]	Cybersecurity integration for data safety	Yes	Cybersecurity tools, encryption	2023	Enhanced safety of healthcare data, improved data security mechanisms.
[30]	Semantics	No	Web API, SPARQL Protocol and RDF (Resource Description Framework) Query Language (SPARQL) Micro-services	2019	New strategies are being used by industry and academic players to spread creative solutions.

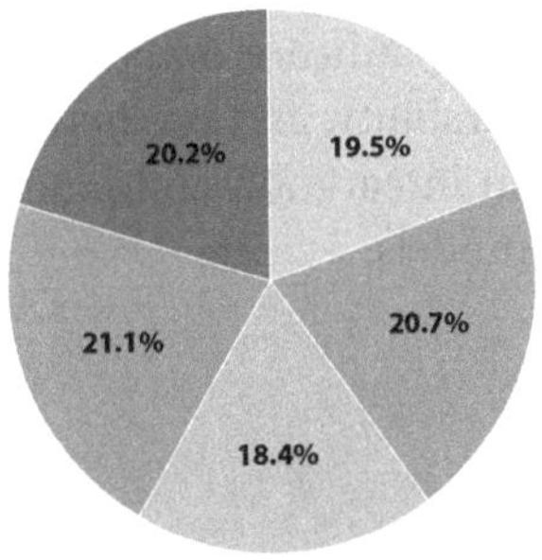

Metrics	Values (%)
Health Data Interoperability	85
Patient Care	90
Cost Reduction in Healthcare	80
Electronic Health Record Integration	92
Data Privacy Compliance	88

Figure 4.2 Display of category proportions in a pie chart. (Source: Own elaboration).

4.3.1 Discussion

The contemporary emphasis on electronic health record (EHR) integration (92%) and the limitation of costs in the healthcare sector (80%) point out the advent of modern technology as a tendency to enhance the effectiveness of operations and minimize the costs of healthcare. In addition, the study employing tools such as blockchain, AI, and APIs reveals the extent to which ingenious solutions in healthcare management, secure sharing of information, and abiding by the law can be made easier. The inclusion of ML model designs and ontologies and the development of semantic data integration shows that data management approaches are maturing and enhancing the patient experience, administrative efficiency, and even the overall robustness of the system. Collectively, these findings bring forward the importance of planning for healthcare data integration in relation to the medical and administrative objectives that need to be fulfilled.

4.4 Conclusion

Statistics and studies have shown that efficient integration and management of healthcare information are crucial in improving the medical system. Improvement of patient care satisfaction at 90%, adherence to data privacy policies at 88%, and health data interoperability at 85% indicate the need to easily exchange information to enhance the provision of healthcare and maintain the confidentiality of patient records. Tackling the cost issue (80%) and implementing EHR enrollment (92%) demonstrates laser-focused vision on how newer solutions can improve healthcare processes and reduce overheads. Moreover, the integration of autonomous and trustworthy systems using blockchain, along with AI technologies, APIs, and semantic data, synthesizes the transformation of healthcare information networks into a more innovative system for better healthcare output. To improve the precision of data, actual time interoperability, and predictive modeling, future studies in healthcare information integration and management could examine cutting-edge AI and ML models.

References

1. Prokosch, H.-U., *et al.*, Towards a national portal for medical research data (fdpg): Vision, status, and lessons learned, in: *Caring is sharing–Exploiting the value in data for health and innovation*, pp. 307–311, IOS Press, Amsterdam, Netherlands, 2023, https://doi.org/10.3233/SHTI230124.
2. Ranchal, R., *et al.*, Disrupting healthcare silos: Addressing data volume, velocity and variety with a cloud-native healthcare data ingestion service. *IEEE J. Biomed. Health. Inf.*, 24, 3182–3188, 2020, https://doi.org/10.1109/JBHI.2020.3001518.
3. Jayaratne, M., *et al.*, A data integration platform for patient-centered e-healthcare and clinical decision support. *Future Gener. Comput. Syst.*, 92, 996–1008, 2019, https://doi.org/10.1016/j.future.2018.07.061.
4. Peng, C., *et al.*, A literature review of current technologies on health data integration for patient-centered health management. *Health Inf. J.*, 26, 1926–1951, 2020, https://doi.org/10.1177/1460458219892387.
5. Balakrishna, S., Thirumaran, M., Solanki, V.K., IoT sensor data integration in healthcare using semantics and machine learning approaches, in: *A handbook of internet of things in biomedical and cyber physical system*, pp. 275–300, 2020, https://doi.org/10.1007/978-3-030-23983-1_11.
6. Dhayne, H., *et al.*, In search of big medical data integration solutions-a comprehensive survey. *IEEE Access*, 7, 91265–91290, 2019, https://doi.org/10.1109/ACCESS.2019.2927491.
7. Zitnik, M., *et al.*, Machine learning for integrating data in biology and medicine: Principles, practice, and opportunities. *Inf. Fusion*, 50, 71–91, 2019, https://doi.org/10.1016/j.inffus.2018.09.012.
8. Khanra, S., *et al.*, Big data analytics in healthcare: a systematic literature review. *Enterp. Inf. Syst.*, 14, 878–912, 2020, https://doi.org/10.1080/20479700.2018.1531606.
9. Hong, L., *et al.*, Big data in health care: Applications and challenges. *Data Inf. Manage.*, 2, 175–197, 2018, https://doi.org/10.2478/dim-2018-0014.
10. Shah, G., *et al.*, Panacea of challenges in real-world application of big data analytics in healthcare sector. *J. Data Inf. Manage.*, 1, 107–116, 2019, https://doi.org/10.1007/s42488-019-00010-1.

11. Yaqoob, I., *et al.*, Blockchain for healthcare data management: opportunities, challenges, and future recommendations. *Neural Comput. Appl.*, 34, 14, 11475–90, https://doi.org/10.1007/s00521-020-05519-w.
12. Dash, S., *et al.*, Big data in healthcare: management, analysis and future prospects. *J. Big Data*, 6, 1–25, 2019, https://doi.org/10.1186/s40537-019-0217-0.
13. Chen, P.-T., *et al.*, Big data management in healthcare: Adoption challenges and implications. *Int. J. Inf. Manage.*, 53, 102078, 2020, https://doi.org/10.1016/j.ijinfomgt.2020.102078.
14. Zaabar, B., *et al.*, HealthBlock: A secure blockchain-based healthcare data management system. *Comput. Netw.*, 200, 108500, 2021, https://doi.org/10.1016/j.comnet.2021.108500.
15. Kamble, S.S., *et al.*, A systematic perspective on the applications of big data analytics in healthcare management. *Int. J. Healthc. Manage.*, 12, 3226-240, 2019, https://doi.org/10.1080/20479700.2018.1531606.
16. Clunis, J., Enhancing health-care data integration via automated semantic mapping. *Electron. Lib.*, 41, 801–816, 2023, https://doi.org/10.1108/EL-06-2023-0142.
17. Stanfill, M.H., *et al.*, Health information management: implications of artificial intelligence on healthcare data and information management. *Yearb. Med. Inf.*, 28, 056–064, 2019, https://doi.org/10.1055/s-0039-1677913.
18. Boehm, K.M., *et al.*, Harnessing multimodal data integration to advance precision oncology. *Nat. Rev. Cancer*, 22, 114–126, 2022, https://doi.org/10.1038/s41568-021-00408-3.
19. Lopez, J., Innovations in Healthcare Information Management: AI, ML, and Master Data Integration Perspectives. *Int. J. Mach. Learn. Artif. Intell.*, 5, 1–10, 2024, https://jmlai.in/index.php/ijmlai/article/view/23.
20. Ogundipe, D.O., The impact of big data on healthcare product development: A theoretical and analytical review. *Int. Med. Sci. Res. J.*, 4, 341–360, 2024, https://doi.org/10.51594/imsrj.v4i3.932.
21. Wu, Z., *et al.*, Impact of information system integration on the healthcare management and medical services. *Int. J. Healthc. Manage.*, 14, 1348–1356, 2021, https://doi.org/10.1080/20479700.2020.1760015.
22. Gavrilov, G., *et al.*, Healthcare data warehouse system supporting cross-border interoperability. *Health Inf. J.*, 26, 1321–1332, 2020, https://doi.org/10.1177/1460458219876793.
23. Kuhn, B.R., *et al.*, Patient reported data integration for management of Eosinophilic Esophagitis. *Dis. Esophagus*, 35, doac012, 2022, https://doi.org/10.1 093/dote/doac012.
24. Khovrichev, M., *et al.*, Intelligent approach for heterogeneous data integration: Information processes analysis engine in clinical remote monitoring systems. *Procedia Comput. Sci.*, 156, 134–141, 2019, https://doi.org/10.1016/j.procs.2019.08.188.
25. Jeyaranjani, J., Prakash, K.G., *et al.*, Multi-Source Medical Data Integration and Mining for Healthcare Services, in: *2023 7th International Conference*

on Intelligent Computing and Control Systems (ICICCS), IEEE, pp. 1–5, 2023, https://doi.org/10.1109/ICIC CS56967.2023.10142755.
26. Miyachi, K. and Mackey, T.K., hOCBS: A privacy-preserving blockchain framework for healthcare data leveraging an on-chain and off-chain system design. *Inf. Process. Manage.*, 58, 3, 102535, 2021, https://doi.org/10.1016/j.ipm.2021.102535.
27. Daramola, O. and Moser, T., Towards Semantic Data Integration in Resource-Limited Settings for Decision Support on Gait-Related Diseases, in: *Advanced Concepts, Methods, and Applications in Semantic Computing*, pp. 236–256, IGI Global, 2021, https://doi.org/10.4018/978-1-7998-6697-8.ch012.
28. Samimi, H., Tešić, J., Ngu, A.H.H., Patient Centric Data Integration for Improved Diagnosis and Risk Prediction. *Heterogeneous Data Management, Polystores, and Analytics for Healthcare: VLDB 2019 Workshops, Poly and DMAH, Los Angeles, CA, USA, August 30, 2019, Revised Selected Papers 5*, Springer International Publishing, 2019, https://doi.org/10.1007/978-3-030-33752-0_13.
29. Data Security in Healthcare: Enhancing the Safety of Data with CyberSecurity, in: *2023 8th International Conference on Communication and Electronics Systems (ICCES)*, IEEE, 2023, https://doi.org/10.1109/ICCES57224.2023.10192596.
30. Beneventano, D. and Vincini, M., Foreword to the special issue: Semantics for big data integration. *Information*, 10, 2, 68, 2019, https://doi.org/10.3390/info10020068.

5

Ethics and Legal Issues in Computational Biomedical Intelligence

Mohitkumar Jagdishchandra Rathod[1], Neha Arora[2], Sindu Divakaran[3]*, Ankita Agarwal[4], Suhas Ballal[5] and Chinmaya Kumar Mohapatra[6]

[1]*Computer Science and Engineering, Parul Institute of Technology, Parul University, Vadodara, Gujarat, India*

[2]*Department of Computer Science and Engineering, Presidency University, Bangalore, Karnataka, India*

[3]*Department of Biomedical, Sathyabama Institute of Science and Technology, Chennai, Tamil Nadu, India*

[4]*Maharishi School of Engineering & Technology, Maharishi University of Information Technology, Uttar Pradesh, India*

[5]*Department of Chemistry and Biochemistry, Jain (Deemed-to-be University), Bangalore, Karnataka, India*

[6]*Department of Legal Studies, Siksha 'O' Anusandhan (Deemed to be University), Bhubaneswar, Odisha, India*

Abstract

The use of advanced computing capabilities in the biomedical field has changed how healthcare, diagnostics, and personalized medicines are practiced today. However, there are ethical problems about advances in science that occur in isolation; rather, they often come with strict measures to ensure fair and consistent utilization of technology. In this review, the focus is on ethical aspects, including data privacy, consent, discrimination by algorithms, and loss of autonomy over decision-making in the context of computational biomedicine. It also appears in the law concerning the ownership of personal data and the protection of innovations created through artificial intelligence (AI) in healthcare, including liability issues.

**Corresponding author*: sindudivakaran.biomed@sathyabama.ac.in; ORCID: https://orcid.org/0000-0002-8514-7559

Ankita Agarwal: ORCID: https://orcid.org/0000-0001-7539-8592

Suhas Ballal: ORCID: https://orcid.org/0000-0002-6041-8332

Chinmaya Kumar Mohapatra: ORCID: https://orcid.org/0000-0002-6243-3974

Satya Prakash Yadav, Abhay Bansal and Victor Hugo C. de Albuquerque (eds.) Computational Intelligence in Biomedical Internet of Medical Things, (69–92) © 2026 Scrivener Publishing LLC

Also, the review considers the importance of building interdisciplinary teams to practice responsible AI. It outlines the emerging directions of policy regulation, which seeks to prevent excessive social risks posed by innovations. By tackling all concerns brought up in this review, this research hopes to give an in-depth understanding of both the legal and ethical aspects of computational biomedicine that are likely to shape its future.

Keywords: Biomedical intelligence, ethical considerations, legal considerations, healthcare, laws and regulations

5.1 Introduction

The fast-paced development of information technology and biomedical intelligence presents immense potential for transforming healthcare and medical research, particularly in the fields of diagnosis, treatment, and disease control. Still, these are advancements that come with ethical issues and social problems [1]. The convergence of computational technology and the life sciences necessitates, among other things, the placing of ethical and legal restraining mechanisms to ensure such advances are not detrimental to civilization and the society [2]. Ethical ideology serves as the moral compass that has been employed in the formulation and the objectives of all biomedical computing machines. It emphasizes the importance of respect for human dignity, protection of the privacy of patients, and the welfare of individuals and societies at large [3]. Every improvement in biomedical intelligence, whether for diagnostics, personalized treatment, or healthcare optimization, must adhere to these principles to prevent harm and build trust. Ethical considerations assure the advancement and intent of this technology remain anchored in humanity's broader assurance of equity, justice, and respect for life.

The significance of legal frameworks can be overlooked about the trustworthiness and ethical management of biomedical information profiling. Rules and protocols provide the mechanism for conflict resolution and management between different parties, such as biomedical researchers, clinical staff, patients, and infections caused by medical technologies [4]. By defining the standards for data security, informed consent, and the responsible use of technology, the legal system creates a robust foundation for protecting individual rights while fostering innovation [5]. Additionally, the system assists and addresses the potential risks, such as data breaches, biased algorithms, and misuse of computational tools, thereby explaining unintended consequences in high-stakes healthcare environments.

Implementing artificial intelligence (AI) in biological sciences provides numerous benefits, but it also presents specific challenges that should be managed consistently. By implementing ethical values and rigorous legal mechanisms at all stages of development and deployment [6], society capitalizes on the entire potential of these advances to enhance wellness while respecting human dignity and societal values. Figure 5.1 ensures that computational biomedical intelligence progresses in a sustainable, equitable, and harmonious manner with the broader goals of humanity.

Ethics and law also mediate the conflicting interests of diverse stakeholders in computational biomedical intelligence. Patients, healthcare providers, researchers, and equipment companies have distinct requirements and concerns [7]. Table 5.1 depicts the ethical frameworks and legal policy, assisting stability in this wellbeing, ensuring fairness in decision-making, equitable access to technical benefits, and dependability in case of error.

Moreover, these frameworks promote transparency, encouraging public confidence in integrating computational intelligence into healthcare systems [8]. Researchers looked into the role of AI in biomedical research and medical creation, focusing on its effects, difficulties, and prospects in

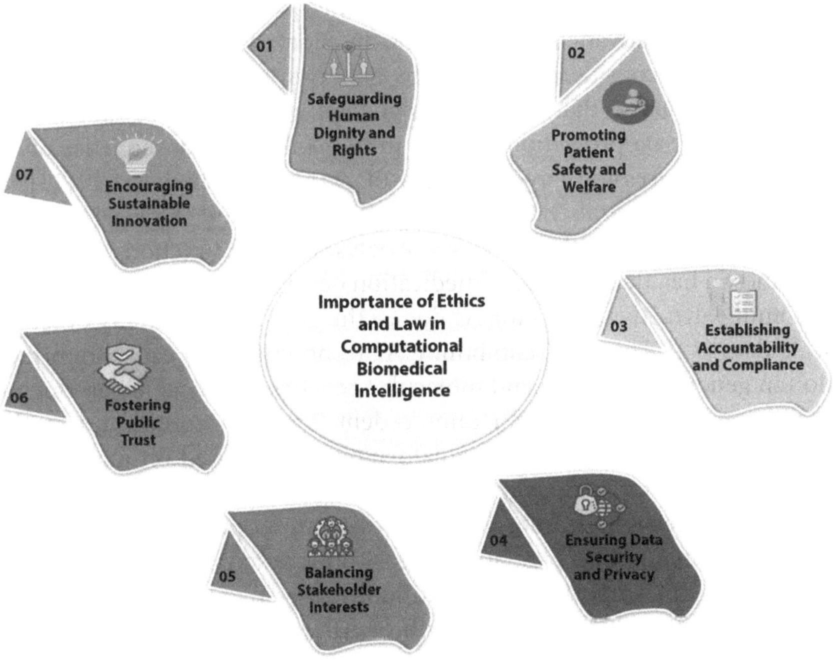

Figure 5.1 Importance of ethics and law in computational biomedical intelligence. (Source: Own elaboration).

Table 5.1 General framework of biomedical innovation.

Perspective	Evolution of biomedical innovation
Laws	Preservation of individual genes, biosecurity, and technological interests.
Ethics	Respect for the capacity to comprehend, scientific credibility, human rights, and the purposes of humanity and non-means.

developing nations [9]. It emphasized the potential for AI to co-produce global knowledge while also acknowledging the constraints that these countries confront due to low resources and financing. Decentralized AI infrastructures can assist in circumventing regional constraints and enable ethnically different, reasonable, and dependable AI expansion in health-related research and development.

Ethics and legislation in the advancement of biological science and technology is crucial [10]. It emphasized the need to limit scientific research behavior, preserve subjects' rights, and encourage healthy development. Ethics and legislation also encourage international collaboration and exchange, thus advancing global growth. Biomedical science and technology can be considered effective by adhering to ethical standards and legal regulations so that it promotes general wellness improvement. The necessity for data protection policies in biobanks as a consequence of AI algorithms processing large amounts of big data is emphasized [11]. It discussed the General Data Protection Regulation and the legal requirements for several health data types. Analyses on the functions of human genomes in health and disease, medication development, and medicine are becoming attractive topics for AI due to the growing availability of large-scale data [12]. However, combining AI techniques with causal information in genomic medicine and molecular genetics is critical for producing prediction information at an unprecedented rate. It contributes to the evolution of educational and regulatory policies focused on maximizing AI's advantages for society in genomics research and medicine. Although progress has been made, substantial issues continue, particularly regarding the confidentiality of information, algorithmic responsibility, and ethical quandaries. The importance of continuous assessments and adjustments to stay current with the rapid growth of AI and neural networks in biomedical engineering is required [13]. The results underscore the need for periodic reassessments to confirm the harmless application of biomedical engineering.

5.2 Description of Biomedical Technological Growth and Development

Biomedical technology is a systematic endeavor that seeks to combine biology, medicine, and biochemistry in the existing research, management, and the prediction of diseases such as diabetes, cancer, and heart disease, as described in Table 5.2. It transforms medicine and greatly impacts the ethics and laws of the culture of man.

These predictions can be identified and measured using the advanced remedies and avoidance of obstacles in biomedical innovation.

Table 5.2 Machine learning applications in healthcare predictions.

References	Objective	Method	Result
[14]	Summarize the current ML methods and use them for the processing, analysis, and synthesis of data from Internet of Things (IoT)-connected medical devices.	Application of IoT medical data.	Comparing various classifiers and predictors for the high-dimensional IoT healthcare data. The most appropriate methods must be selected based on the given dataset.
[15]	Propose an ML-based approach for classification and early-stage identification of diabetes, and IoT-based glucose monitoring.	Random Forest for classification, and ML models for predictive analysis.	It shows that the multilayer perceptron classified with accuracy (86.08%) than other classifiers in identifying patients with or without diabetes and long-short-term memory (87.26%) classified the patient with accuracy.

(*Continued*)

Table 5.2 Machine learning applications in healthcare predictions. (*Continued*)

References	Objective	Method	Result
[16]	It discovers explainable AI models within healthcare to allow customized decision-making and improved service delivery of medicines.	Analyzing different ML techniques for healthcare IoT data categorization and prediction.	Different ML algorithms exhibit varying performance and optimal methods could be chosen depending on the dataset.
[17]	Provide a comprehensive overview of ML applications in healthcare, focusing on disease diagnosis, health monitoring, and epidemic prediction.	The research has been classified into application areas of diagnosis, disease risk, vital health sign tracking, other discoveries in healthcare, and epidemic predictions.	These examples highlight the enormous potential of ML algorithms in healthcare, and thus encouraging further investigation into AI-based healthcare.
[18]	Examine the efficacy of ML methods for software defect prediction (SDP) and how it applies to datasets in the healthcare industry.	Implementation of ML models against seven datasets of software defect prediction.	Random Forest yields an overall average of 88.32%, the SVM is 87.99%, and the classification decision tree is 87.88%.

5.2.1 Advancement and Obstacles of Biomedical Innovation

There is still a great deal of interest in medical applications due to the emergence of new biomedical technologies including, but not limited to, gene editing, cell treatment, and AI. Gene editing offers the modification of specific target genes, which presents new possibilities in the field of medicine, research, and therapeutics. Cell therapy aims to restore function by repairing or replacing damaged cells, while AI including assisted diagnosis and personalized treatment has revolutionized healthcare delivery. Nevertheless, these technologies present contemporary legal and ethical issues [19]. The modification of genes brings together both benefits and fears into the preservation and exploitation of the human genetic material. Additionally, the application of these technologies denotes the possibility of infringing the rights of an individual either in terms of privacy or use of one's personal data. Such use of innovation, however, demands for a strong assessment of the potential ethical and legal implications. Many legal challenges such as those relating to IP, privacy, ethical evaluation, and legal liability pose major challenges to the safe, effective, and fair access to advanced biotechnology [20].

5.2.2 Identification and Aspects of Modern Biomedical Technologies

Advanced biomedical technologies are pivotal in biomedical research and clinical practice. It consists of processes like gene manipulation, cell management for therapeutic purposes, and AI. However, these technologies are effective in controlling diseases such as cancer and immunological diseases, pose risks, and pose ethical dilemmas [21]. While advanced biomedical technologies improve healthcare productivity and reduce costs, they also raise concerns about data privacy, information security, and ethics, prompting the development of identifying laws and regulations. Figure 5.2 depicts the overview of legal and ethical considerations in AI.

5.2.3 The Application of Ethical Principles in Biomedical Science and Technology

Ethics in biomedical science prioritizes individual autonomy, no harm, impartiality, safety, fair resource distribution, and social justice, addressing potential risks and resource scarcity. It is essential to encourage the field's robust and long-term growth. To uphold ethical standards and ensure that patients' rights and concerns are not infringed, research has to include ethical principles throughout its standards of practice. Furthermore, this raises awareness of biomedical research and technology, promoting fruitful cooperation between society and science [22]. To apply effective decisions and judgments when new ethical dilemmas arise, researchers require not just professional knowledge but also strong ethics and practical expertise.

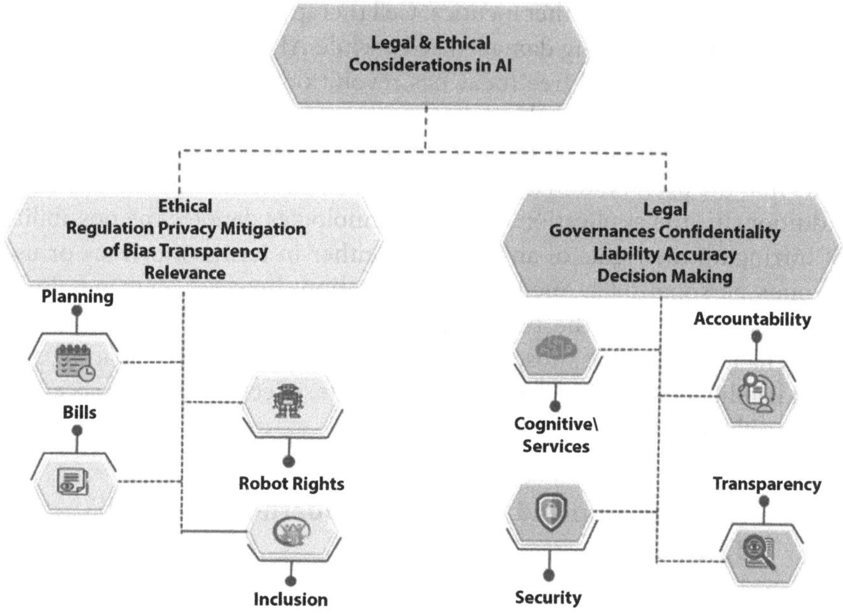

Figure 5.2 Overview of legal and ethical considerations in AI. (Source: https://www.frontiersin.org/journals/surgery/articles/10.3389/fsurg.2022.862322/full).

To support the sound advancement of biomedical and technological advances, participation is needed in the creation and enhancement of ethical standards.

The general population's interest and involvement with biomedical technology is growing, therefore, researchers have to concentrate on improving interaction, addressing skepticism, and attempting to attract community support. To establish science and technology as a solid social foundation for optimal growth, the public should also be actively involved in the oversight and administration of biomedical technology. The beneficial and long-term advancement of technological innovation is guaranteed by applying ethics in biomedical and technological fields [23].

5.3 Ethical Considerations in Computational Biomedical Intelligence

The argument around AI's legal classification and potential in healthcare is proceeding. Although there is a lot of promise in using AI in healthcare settings, there are also moral dilemmas. Four basic ethical concerns informed consent, safety, transparency, algorithmic fairness and biases, and data security should be addressed in order to apply AI in healthcare in a suitable manner. AI systems' legality is a delicate topic from a legal and political standpoint [24].

5.3.1 Ethical Perspective

To ensure ethical practices whenever dealing with sensitive patient data, medical decision-making, and individual lives, computational biological intelligence must prioritize principles. The challenges include protecting patient privacy, guaranteeing fairness and openness in AI systems, and preserving patient autonomy. Developers and practitioners must stress informed consent, impartial systems, and fair healthcare access while balancing technological improvements with patient rights and dignity. The goal is to assist individuals in positions of power and address ethical concerns about AI technologies in the health industry. The legal issues about AI algorithms raise the question of whether algorithms are above the law. AI must be responsible, fair, and accountable in high-risk situations. Transparency in information availability and understanding is critical. Machines that constantly learn and operate without clear limitations endanger the concept of accountability for employers or operators. The legal system that guards against moral violations and the society's values are both endangered by this divide. Because the extent of danger is unclear, everyone is held liable for any generated harm. Utilizing AI involves a risk that makes it challenging to hold people accountable or eliminate them for certain acts [25].

5.3.2 Ethical and Regulatory Considerations

The ethical consideration of patient privacy and data protection is fundamental in computational biomedical intelligence, as it directly impacts trust, autonomy, and the integrity of healthcare systems. This area involves the safeguarding of sensitive personal health information that is often processed, analyzed, and stored by advanced computational systems, integrating biomedical technology into ethics and regulations, which must be carefully considered in the healthcare industry. Maintaining patient independence, informed consent, and calculating personal medical category is crucial when balancing data-driven development with individual isolation. Preventing healthcare gaps requires addressing inequalities in obtaining biomedical-based treatment, particularly in underserved regions. Understanding the costs, risks, and limitations of biological treatments is necessary to enable patients and medical professionals to make informed decisions. This calls for an all-encompassing strategy to guarantee the secrecy and safety of biomedical information [26]. Legal structures are essential to the creation and application of biomedical technology as they guarantee adherence to data privacy laws and Food and Drug Administration rules. Risks have to be identified and reduced by pre- and post-market assessments. In biomedical growth, maintaining privacy by design entails incorporating privacy considerations into system design, implementing data minimization and anonymization strategies into practice, and giving patients alternatives for granularity approval [27].

To provide strong security and educate individuals through authorization processes and intuitive user experiences, biomedical expansion needs to set a high priority on privacy by architecture. Patient information is protected even in the event of unnecessary access to anonymity and elimination procedures, which improve isolation. Maintaining ethical integrity and compliance with laws requires a dynamic approach that changes with technology and continuous ethical planning. Figure 5.3 represents the features of AI biomedical ethical obstacles.

Biomedicals have the potential to revolutionize healthcare [28]. Long-term data of biological micro-electro-mechanical systems (BioMEMS) must be separated and preserved for improvements. The BioMEMS security can be enhanced while preserving accessibility by utilizing cryptographic keys, biometric verification, and multi-factor authentication. However, [29] combining these features necessitates careful analysis and managing the hurdles outlined in Table 5.3.

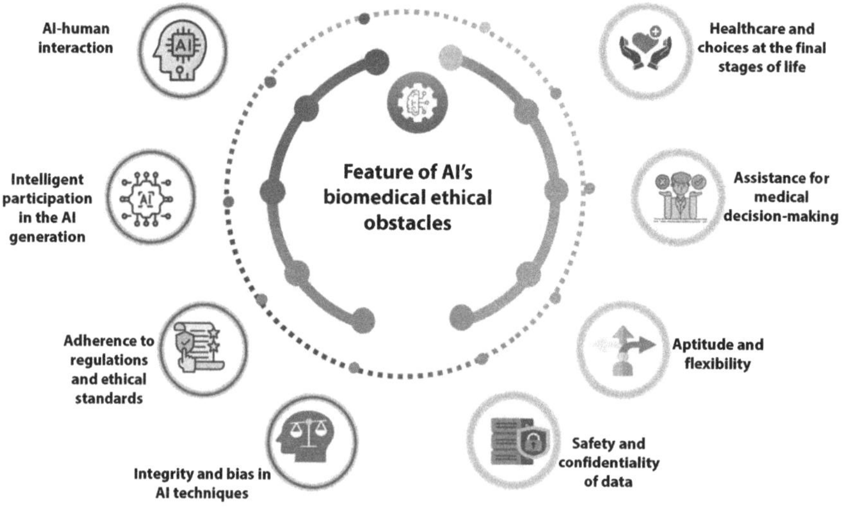

Figure 5.3 Aspects of biomedical ethical obstacles in AI.

Table 5.3 Characteristics of ethical considerations.

Features	**Challenges**	**Considerations**
Accessibility of biomedical sensors	To authenticate individuals, biometric identification entails collecting and preserving private biometric data. The integrity of this data is of primary significance because it cannot be altered, like a security code.	To prevent unauthorized access to biometric data, strong encryption, and information anonymization techniques must be implemented. Adherence to high regulatory standards is vital to protect patient privacy.
Implementation costs	Additional expenses for software development, hardware components, and maintenance can be incurred when combining multiple identities, biometric authentication, and cryptographic keys.	It is necessary to perform a cost-benefit evaluation to evaluate the trade-off between security improvements and related costs. The benefits and hazards of security measures should be balanced while making investments.
Interoperability and standardization	Considering systems and technology vary widely, it can be problematic to ensure compatibility and interoperability between various biomedical equipment and safety precautions.	Compatibility can be facilitated by using open standards for biometric data interchange and uniform security protocols. Establishing standard security frameworks through collaboration between industries can also make integration efforts easier.

(*Continued*)

Table 5.3 Characteristics of ethical considerations. (*Continued*)

Features	Challenges	Considerations
Accessibility and satisfaction with users	Biomedical equipment is frequently utilized by people with varied degrees of technical ability. Complicated safety precautions reduce usability and user acceptance.	Maintaining usability requires sensible design and intuitive interfaces. Cryptographic keys should be handled transparently, and biometric verification should be effortless and involve minimum work from users.

5.3.3 Principles of Biomedical Ethics in the Use of Artificial Intelligence in Medical Education

Health organizations have the technological capacity and competence to facilitate the incorporation of AI in medical training. It is critical to specify learning objectives and purposes, including methodological and ethical aspects. Artificial intelligence improves the classroom experience while maintaining human characteristics. Involving all important stakeholders, such as providers, regulators, medical bioethicists, and the decision-making procedures, ensure it is effective. Table 5.3 indicates that biomedical programs include AI in medical culture, emphasizing on the four fundamental values of biomedical ethics.

The four primary biomedical ethics concepts for healthcare organizations combined AI on biomedical training rather than just the overall morals of AI in medical care [30].

5.3.4 Self-Determination

Every individual includes intrinsic autonomy, which involves having the capacity to make moral decisions and logical conclusions. In medical bioethics, autonomy governs interactions between healthcare practitioners and patients, taking into consideration individual values and preferences. Though incorporating AI into health teaching raises important concerns among users and healthcare providers, emphasizing the importance of properly considering autonomy [31]. Table 5.4 shows the list of institutional policies adopted by selected Chinese universities, illustrating the shift from ideological education to career-oriented guidance. Artificial

Table 5.4 Fundamental principles of biomedical ethics.

Equality	Self-determination	Beneficence	Lack of malice
Assure equitable availability of AI technologies and capabilities.	Validate that AI algorithms are understandable and accessible.	Before utilizing AI programs, give thorough instruction.	Highlight the dangers of bias and prejudice and promote thinking critically when using AI.
Perform routine evaluations of the AI tools being utilized.	Incorporate AI models in the medical courses as an add-on.	To maximize their utilization in healthcare education, regularly monitor and reassess the effects of AI technologies.	Maintain surveillance for possible hazards and disadvantages related to AI applications or innovative application scenarios.
Verify that AI applications adapt to the various demands and perspectives of users.	Obtain an individual's informed approval.	Engage in extensive collaboration with all parties.	Provide facilities for validation that are not dependent upon AI.
An array of instructional data is utilized.	Encourage responsibility and obligation in the workplace.	Make assessments easily accessible.	Protect crucial data's safety and privacy.

intelligence's complexity and obscurity hinder critical decision-making and clinical judgment, reducing knowledgeable assessments of the appropriateness and accuracy of recommendations or diagnoses produced by AI [32]. Healthcare facilities, an understandable medical curriculum, informed user permission, and professional accountability allow participants to decide whether to use AI requests [33].

5.3.5 Equality

Medical institutions experience difficulty validating data sources, particularly for external vendor-developed AI technologies. Data-sharing agreements can be managed before installing AI applications. Furthermore, new laws and regulations governing data use can assist in alleviating this issue [34]. Artificial intelligence improvement is critical for establishing norms and upholding fair practices in medical teaching. An equitable and communal integrity structure must be developed to ensure AI incorporation in medical training is accessible and customized to users of different social classes, awareness levels, and interests. This can be efficient by providing financial support, financial aid, or assistance, designing AI applications that are accessible and adaptive, and using diverse training data [35]. Collaborations with diverse educational institutions enhance AI technology development and application, ensuring impartial and equitable instructional content through meticulous data assortment, curation, and continuous algorithm refinement [36].

5.3.6 Beneficence

In the field of biomedical ethics, the beneficent concept highlights the responsibility to encourage and safeguard humans' prosperity and mental health. In the framework of AI in healthcare, beneficial behavior is offering adequate AI application training before deployment to optimize benefits for all parties involved, including specialists, teachers, and learners. Artificial intelligence training in medical education encourages independence, fairness, and nonmaleficence by enabling informed decision-making, investigative equity, and the integration of AI effectively [37]. Training methods include tutorials, supervised sessions, and internet-based materials. Interface with learners, AI developers, and healthcare providers is crucial for effective deployment. Applications that use AI must be regularly assessed and optimized for maximizing benefits and minimizing disadvantages. Institutions can make data-driven decisions on how to enhance or change AI training to suit the learning objectives of both teachers and students by tracking and re-evaluating the effects of AI applications in the medical curriculum [38].

5.3.7 Lack of Malice

Non-maleficence, or the absence of malicious intent, highlights the importance of preventing damage and reducing any negative impacts.

Artificial intelligence algorithms in healthcare education are appropriately produced, confirmed, and experienced to deliver precise and trustworthy outcomes that never confound users or endanger patients. Before utilizing a model formed by AI, individuals deserve to be educated on the application's features, known potential threats, and biases, as required by each of the four ethical standards [39]. Artificial intelligence systems might perpetuate current medical injustices and prejudices when trained on biased or inadequate data, leading to discriminatory or inaccurate results and serious harm to particular patient populations. Healthcare organizations should clearly outline the limitations of AI applications, including potential risks from a lack of transparency and biased data. Medical data professionals, including physicians and educators, have an ethical obligation to identify bias and evaluate models and AI skills [40]. Artificial intelligence in medicine is a fast-expanding topic, with the potential to cause unhappiness and upheaval in medical organizations. However, it presents additional risks, including privacy and safety concerns, perceptual outcomes, and embedded biases. As a result, ethical rules should be frequently examined and changed to ensure AI's safety and effectiveness in medical applications.

5.4 Legal Considerations in Computational Biomedical Intelligence

Biomedical ethics are addressed by international law in terms of research ethics, protection of human genetic resources, and individual liberties. These regulations are important for biomedical technology advancement. In that regard, reinforcing the ethical review and monitoring is important whenever biomedical research is being conducted, aiming to observe and protect safety. It is necessary to enhance the ethical review system to mitigate abuse and other forms of crime portrayal from successful international experiences. Legal responsibilities governing participants in ethical biomedical research must be aligned with the international biomedical ethics treaties and codifications to offer justice in case of disputes. It is also important to ensure the clarity of human genetic resources protection. In this manner, it becomes possible to create an ethical and legal basis for conducting biomedical research, which encourages improvement of the practice of biomedical engineering practice [41]. Defining and learning from international biomedical ethical regulations is fundamental in the process of preventing the loss of genetic resources and damage to the subjects in research. These provisions aimed at defining the problems caused by abuse or damage and how this will be minimized, and instead of this, ethical review and supervision would be enhanced, legal responsibility attribution would be clear, and the protection of individuals would be enhanced. This ensures the development of biomedical technology adheres to moral and legal frameworks, protecting human genetic resources and participants' privacy.

5.4.1 Legal Control and Biomedical Moral Policy

Biomedical ethics regulations include steps that regulate biomedical research ethically, as well as short-term measures to control human gene resources. Although progress has been achieved in enhancing ethical assessment and oversight, there remains an inadequate protective perspective on technological advances, suggesting inadequate safeguards. The supervision of ethical review is quite effortless, focusing mostly on the evaluation of the applications, findings, and informed consent [42]. However, there are challenges with operational procedures and the formation of ethics committee standards and restrictions, as certain healthcare organizations concentrate largely on scientific research projects and are inadequate at executing particular ethical principles.

To enhance the quality of medical clinical trial research and safeguard subjects' rights, research institutions must establish a rigorous ethical review system. A policy framework outlining strict procedures for ethical review serves as a valuable reference. Strengthening the ethical review of medical research is crucial for formulating a robust clinical trial registration system. Legislation is strengthened to protect the rights of providers of human genetic resources, including genetic privacy, physical rights, and personal rights. Additionally, it is essential to ensure the rational use of biotechnology patents based on genetic resources. Establishing a clear management structure for overlapping genetic resource management and clarifying conditions for acquiring genetic resources, application, and approval procedures are also vital. Concerns about human genetic resource patents, such as ownership and information sharing, pose risks to biosecurity [43]. Tightening legislation is also important in the assurance of safety and progress in biotechnology, particularly in the aspects of ownership and information disclosure. In addition, engaging in the process of formulation of international biomedical ethics law and doing research on its world application, as well as enhancing and developing the domestic biomedical ethics law, is very important. Such an approach encourages biotechnology and its peaceful and secure application without compromising national interest and classified information.

5.4.2 Strategies for Legal Effects on the Advancement of Biomedical Technologies

The fast advancement of technology within the domains of biomedicine has contributed many advantages to the humane side; however, it also brought [44] many legal problems, which require extensive examination of these hindrances and their solutions.

Progress in novel biomedical technologies demands an integrated approach to the challenges posed by the law. It involves determining the acceptable ethical levels, establishing the limits of the research, and preventing exploitation. There should also be a legal framework that supports ethics review and control processes to help protect biomedical sciences and practice.

Developing systems is important for intellectual property rights to advance technology without encroaching on the creative interests of other people. Also, ensuring protection in the form of confidentiality is essential as most technologies in the biosciences are related to one's privacy, thereby protecting the individual's interests and rights.

Enhancing the effectiveness and efficiency of ethical review and monitoring is crucial for the prompt identification and response to any possible misuse of biotechnology, as well as ensuring the safety and effectiveness of conducting and applying biomedical research. Applying these strategies can make it easier and quicker to develop new technologies in biomedicine.

To understand the legal problems or the solutions associated with the invention of new biomedical technology, individuals must analyze the interplay of law and biomedical ethics. Improving the legal system, which includes intellectual property and privacy protection, improving ethical review and supervision, and addressing sources of legal liability, can effectively deal with these challenges and foster the growth of biomedical technologies.

5.5 Result

In this section, the ML models were evaluated using performance metrics such as the accuracy and overall average of various models. It is used to identify and enhance healthcare treatment.

- **Accuracy:** The accuracy of the model is the proportion of correct predictions out of total predictions calculated in Equation 5.1.

$$\frac{True\ Positive + True\ Negatives}{Total\ Predictions} \tag{5.1}$$

- **Overall average:** It is the mean of the accuracy values from different models.

$$Overall\ Average = \frac{1}{n}\sum_{i=1}^{n} Accuracy_i \tag{5.2}$$

Figure 5.4 shows the classification accuracy of two algorithms: diabetes prediction using the multilayer perceptron [15] and long-short-term memory (LSTM) [15]. The Deep Learning (DL) model LSTM reached the highest accuracy equal to 87.26%, while the multilayer perceptron classifier achieved a lower accuracy equal to 86.08%. These outcomes demonstrate adequate performance of both models for diabetic conditions classification, with LSTM having better performance.

Figure 5.5 summarizes the average performance of three ML techniques [18]: RF for software detect prediction (SDP), classification decision trees (CDT), and SVMs. It was found that RF (88.32%) had the highest overall average accuracy and was followed by the accuracy of SVM (87.99%) and CDT (87.88%). The findings presented here show that these models provide useful SDP and the accuracy of RF is better than that of the other types.

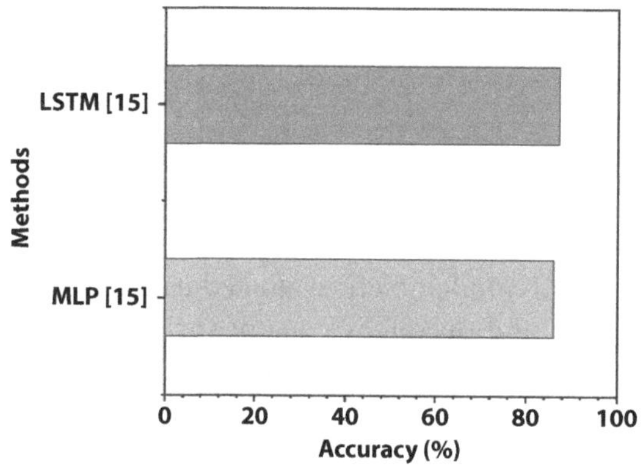

Figure 5.4 Classification level of accuracy in diabetics prediction.

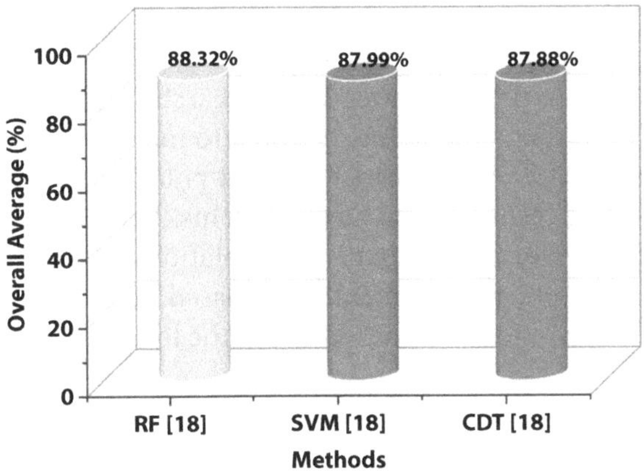

Figure 5.5 Models with software defect prediction.

5.6 Discussion

It demonstrates that the assessment of these models by accuracy and overall average metrics was useful in the healthcare and SDP. In diabetes classification, the models outperformed in demonstrating the competence of the recommended approach with healthcare data. In SDP, another model outperforms all the others, along with two more models performing nearly comparably. These results can emphasize how the implementation of ML approaches could be effective in preparing structured forms of data to improve medical therapy and software efficiency. The models that provided better results are indicative of their selective nature that could be most appropriate for the realization of higher accuracy and reliability of the forecasts within the corresponding fields of application.

5.7 Conclusion

While AI's application in healthcare and other fields has numerous advantages, it comes with important ethical and legal challenges. Some key ethical components that need to be tackled include data protection, public understanding, bias of algorithms, and the control of decision making, which needs to be addressed for justice and transparency. Additionally, it is necessary that existing laws on issues such as intellectual property, control of information, and liability evolve to accommodate new technologies to promote creativity but still hold individuals responsible for their actions.

To guarantee the fair application of AI in the healthcare industry, there is a requirement for adequate management of the diverse needs of the various stakeholders, such as patients, caregivers, research personnel, and technology developers, among others. It is essential to include various disciplines in the formulation of ethical principles and policies that protect society while encouraging technological advancements. Focusing on these problems will also preserve the effectiveness of solutions within the biomedical remedies, enabling the management of AI-based healthcare solutions and promoting a win-win for all stakeholders in the long run.

References

1. Akhtar, Z.B., *et al.*, Advancements within molecular engineering for regenerative medicine and biomedical applications an investigation analysis towards a computing retrospective. *J. Electron. Electromed. Eng. Med. Inf.*, 6, 1, 54–72, 2024. *J. Emerg. Med. OA*, 2, 1, 01–23, 2024, https://orcid.org/0009-0004-5498-6458.
2. Federico, C.A., Biomedical Data Science, Artificial Intelligence, and Ethics: Navigating Challenges in the Face of Explosive Growth. *Annu. Rev. Biomed. Data Sci.*, 7, 2024, https://doi.org/10.1146/annurev-biodatasci-102623-104553.
3. Ajiga, D., *et al.*, Navigating Ethical Considerations in Software Development and Deployment in Technological Giants. *Int. J. Ethics Res. Util.*, 7, 1, 2024, https://doi.org/10.53430/ijeru.2024.7.1.0033
4. Liu, Y., *et al.*, Bioinformatics: Advancing biomedical discovery and innovation in the era of big data and artificial intelligence. *Innov. Med.*, 1, 1, 100012, 2023, https://doi.org/10.59717/j.xinn-med.2023.100012.
5. Adekugbe, A.P., *et al.*, Navigating ethical challenges in data management for US program development: best practices and recommendations. *Int. J. Manage. Entrepreneurship Res.*, 6, 4, 1023–1033, 2024, https://doi.org/10.51594/ijmer.v6i4.982.
6. Aras Beger, G., How competing institutional logics affect corporate social responsibility benefits: The Mediating role of paradox mindset and multi-stakeholders. *J. Knowl. Econ.*, 15, 1, 1913–1951, 2024, https://doi.org/10.1007/s13132-023-01131-0.
7. Agu, E.E., *et al.*, Discussing ethical considerations and solutions for ensuring fairness in AI-driven financial services. *Int. J. Front. Res. Sci.*, 3, 2, 001–009, 2024. https://doi.org/10.56355/ijfrms.2024.3.2.0024.
8. Sheikhbahei, E., *et al.*, Harnessing the Power of Emerging Digital Technologies for improved Sustainability and Productivity in Biomedical Engineering and Neuroscience. *Sci. Hypotheses*, 1, 1, 2024, https://orcid.org/0000-0002-1252-9417.

9. da Silva, R.G.L., The advancement of artificial intelligence in biomedical research and health innovation: challenges and opportunities in emerging economies. *Glob. Health*, 20, 1, 44, 2024, https://doi.org/10.1186/s12992-024-01049-5.
10. Akhtar, Exploring Biomedical Engineering (BME): Advances within Accelerated Computing and Regenerative Medicine for a Computational and Medical Science Perspective Exploration Analysis. *J. Emerg. Med. OA*, 2, 1, 01–23, 2024, https://doi.org/10.33140/JEMOA.02.01.06.
11. Vidalis, T., Artificial intelligence in biomedicine: a legal insight. *BioTech*, 10, 3, 15, 2021, https://doi.org/10.3390/biotech10030015.
12. König, H., *et al.*, AI models and the future of genomic research and medicine: True sons of knowledge? Artificial intelligence needs to be integrated with causal conceptions in biomedicine to harness its societal benefits for the field. *BioEssays*, 43, 10, 2100025, 2021, https://doi.org/10.1002/bies.202100025.
13. Gulyamov, S.S., Legal Frameworks for the Integration of Artificial Intelligence, in: *International Conference on Nanotechnologies and Biomedical Engineering*, pp. 144–149, Springer Nature Switzerland, Cham, 2023, https://doi.org/10.1007/978-3-031-42782-4_16.
14. Aldahiri, A., Alrashed, B., Hussain, W., Trends in using IoT with machine learning in health prediction system. *Forecasting*, 3, 1, 181–206, 2021, https://doi.org/10.3390/forecast3010012.
15. Butt, U.M., *et al.*, Machine learning based diabetes classification and prediction for healthcare applications. *J. Healthc. Eng.*, 2021, 1, 9930985, 2021, https://doi.org/10.1155/2021/9930985.
16. Imrie, F., Davis, R., van der Schaar, M., Multiple stakeholders drive diverse interpretability requirements for machine learning in healthcare. *Nat. Mach. Intell.*, 5, 8, 824–829, 2023, https://doi.org/10.1038/s42256-023-00698-2.
17. Saleem, T.J. and Chishti, M.A., Exploring the applications of machine learning in healthcare. *Int. J. Sens. Wirel. Commun. Control*, 10, 4, 458–472, 2020, https://doi.org/10.2174/2210327910666191220103417.
18. Khan, B., *et al.*, Software defect prediction for healthcare big data: an empirical evaluation of machine learning techniques. *J. Healthc. Eng.*, 2021, 1, 8899263, 2021, https://doi.org/10.1155/2021/8899263.
19. da Silva, R.G.L., *et al.*, The Advancement of Artificial Intelligence in Biomedical Research and Health Innovation: Challenges and Opportunities in Emerging Economies. *Glob. Health*, 20, 1, 44, 2024. https://doi.org/10.1186/s12992-024-01049-5
20. Gonzalez-Moreno, M., *et al.*, Digital Technologies to Provide Humanization in the Education of the Healthcare Workforce: A Systematic Review. *Technologies*, 11, 4, 88, 2023, https://doi.org/10.3390/technologies11040088.
21. Jaime, F., *et al.*, Strengthening privacy and data security in biomedical microelectromechanical systems by IoT communication security and protection in smart healthcare. *Sensors*, 23, 21, 8944, 2023, https://doi.org/10.3390/s23218944.

22. Hirani, R., *et al.*, Artificial Intelligence and Healthcare: A Journey through History, Present Innovations, and Future Possibilities. *Life*, 14, 5, 557, 2024, https://doi.org/10.3390/life14050557.
23. Shin, D., The effects of explainability and causability on perception, trust, and acceptance: Implications for explainable AI. *Int. J. Hum.-Comput. Stud.*, 146, 102551, 2021, https://doi.org/10.1016/j.ijhcs.2020.102551.
24. Ryan, M., In AI we trust: ethics, artificial intelligence, and reliability. *Sci. Eng. Ethics*, 265, 2749–2767, 2020, https://doi.org/10.1007/s11948-020-00228-y.
25. Buruk, B., Ekmekci, P.E., Arda, B., A critical perspective on guidelines for responsible and trustworthy artificial intelligence. *Med. Health Care Philos.*, 23, 3, 387–399, 2020, https://doi.org/10.1007/s11019-020-09948-1.
26. ElHassan, B. T., and Arabi, A. A., Ethical Forethoughts on the Use of Artificial Intelligence in Medicine. *Int. J. Ethics Syst.*, 41, 1, 35–44, 2025, https://doi.org/10.1108/IJOES-08-2023-0190
27. Gerke, S., Minssen, T., *et al.*, Ethical and legal challenges of artificial intelligence-driven healthcare, in: *Artificial Intelligence in Healthcare*, pp. 295–336, Academic Press, 2020, https://doi.org/10.1016/B978-0-12-818438-7.00012-5.
28. Rodrigues, R., Legal and human rights issues of AI: Gaps, challenges and vulnerabilities. *J. Responsible Technol.*, 4, 100005, 2020, https://doi.org/10.1016/j.jrt.2020.100005.
29. Zaidan, A.M., The leading global health challenges in the artificial intelligence era. *Front. Public Health*, 11, 1328918, 2023, https://doi.org/10.3389/fpubh.2023.1328918.
30. Morley, J., *et al.*, The ethics of AI in health care: a mapping review. *Social Sci. Med.*, 260, 1131725, 2020, 10.1016/j.socscimed.2020.113172.
31. Busch, F., L., *et al.*, Biomedical ethical aspects towards the implementation of artificial intelligence in medical education. *Med. Sci. Educator*, 33, 4, 1007–1012, 2023, https://doi.org/10.1007/s40670-023-01815-x.
32. Schiff, D., Education for AI, not AI for education: The role of education and ethics in national AI policy strategies. *Int. J. Artif. Intell. Educ.*, 32, 3, 527–563, 2022, https://doi.org/10.1007/s40593-021-00270-2.
33. Durán, J.M., *et al.*, Who is afraid of black box algorithms? On the epistemological and ethical basis of trust in medical AI. *J. Med. Ethics*, 47, 5, 329–335, 2021, https://doi.org/10.1136/medethics-2020-106820.
34. Zhou, J., *et al.*, A survey on ethical principles of AI and implementations, in: *2020 IEEE Symposium Series on Computational Intelligence (SSCI)*, IEEE, pp. 3010–3017, 2020, https://doi.org/10.1109/SSCI47803.2020.9308437.
35. Murdoch, B., Privacy and artificial intelligence: challenges for protecting health information in a new era. *BMC Med. Ethics*, 22, 1-5, 2021, https://doi.org/10.1186/s12910-021-00687-3.
36. Esmaeilzadeh, P., *et al.*, Patients' perceptions toward human–artificial intelligence interaction in health care: experimental study. *J. Med. Internet Res.*, 23, 11, e25856, 2021, https://doi.org/10.2196/25856.

37. Pinski, M., *et al.*, AI knowledge: Improving AI delegation through human enablement, in: *Proceedings of the 2023 CHI Conference on Human Factors in Computing Systems*, pp. 1–17, 2023, https://doi.org/10.1145/3544548.3580794.
38. Farhud, D.D., *et al.*, Ethical issues of artificial intelligence in medicine and healthcare. *Iran. J. Public Health*, 50, 11, i, 2021, https://doi.org/10.18502/ijph.v50i11.7600.
39. Saheb, T., *et al.*, Mapping research strands of ethics of artificial intelligence in healthcare: a bibliometric and content analysis. *Comput. Biol. Med.*, 135, 1046605, 2021, https://doi.org/10.1016/j.compbiomed.2021.104660.
40. Zhang, J. and Zhang, Z.-M., Ethics and governance of trustworthy medical artificial intelligence. *BMC Med. Inf. Decis. Making*, 23, 1, 7, 2023, https://doi.org/10.1186/s12911-023-02103-9.
41. Martinez-Martin, N., Luo, Z., *et al.*, Ethical issues in using ambient intelligence in health-care settings. *Lancet Digit. Health*, 3, 2, e115–e123, 2021, 10.1016/S2589-7500(20)30275-2.
42. Bali, J., *et al.*, Artificial intelligence (AI) in healthcare and biomedical research: Why a strong computational/AI bioethics framework is required? *Indian J. Ophthalmol.*, 67, 1, 3–6, 2019, 10.4103/DLJO.DLJO_135_23.
43. Rasheed, K., *et al.*, Explainable, trustworthy, and ethical machine learning for healthcare: A survey. *Comput. Biol. Med.*, 149, 1060435, 2022, https://doi.org/10.1016/j.compbiomed.2022.106043.
44. Nebeker, C., *et al.*, Building the case for actionable ethics in digital health research supported by artificial intelligence. *BMC Med.*, 17, 1–75, 2019, https://doi.org/10.1186/s12916-019-1377-7.

Part II

ADVANCED ANALYTICAL TECHNIQUES

6

Bioinstrumentation and Medical Devices

Roopashree R.[1]*, Utpalkumar B. Patel[2], Krishnakumar Samikan[3], Joe Arun Raja[4], Preeti Naval[5] and Aneesh Wunnava[6]

[1]*Department of Chemistry and Biochemistry, Jain (Deemed-to-be University), Bangalore, Karnataka, India*
[2]*Computer Science and Engineering, Parul Institute of Technology, Parul University, Vadodara, Gujarat, India*
[3]*Department of Biomedical, Sathyabama Institute of Science and Technology, Chennai, Tamil Nadu, India*
[4]*Department of Computer Science and Engineering, Presidency University, Bangalore, Karnataka, India*
[5]*Maharishi School of Engineering & Technology, Maharishi University of Information Technology, Uttar Pradesh, India*
[6]*Department of Electronics & Communication Engineering, Siksha 'O' Anusandhan (Deemed to be University), Bhubaneswar, Odisha, India*

Abstract
The creative integration of computational intelligence (CI) into the Internet of Medical Things (IoMT) has led to significant bioinstrumentation breakthroughs, enhancing healthcare services, diagnostics, and patient monitoring. The application of artificial intelligence (AI), specifically deep learning (DL) and machine learning (ML), to the development of intelligent sensor networks for wearable technology, imaging diagnostics, and remote patient monitoring is covered. Patients' conditions can be continuously monitored by applications like IoMT-enabled devices and remote monitoring systems that depend on analyzing information in real-time. The limitations of security, regulatory compliance, and data quality, all of which necessitate proper data processing for patient safety, are explored. Because of the tendency toward edge computing, the future of CI in bioinstrumentation and medical devices is still bright. Monitoring

**Corresponding author*: r.roopashree@jainuniversity.ac.in; ORCID: 0000-0002-0382-6321
Utpalkumar B. Patel: ORCID: 0000-0002-2097-2216
Krishnakumar Samikan: ORCID: Https://Orcid.Org/0000-0002-3649-8969
Preeti Naval: ORCID: 0000-0003-2988 7082
Aneesh Wunnava: ORCID: 0000-0002-3869-1324

Satya Prakash Yadav, Abhay Bansal and Victor Hugo C. de Albuquerque (eds.) Computational Intelligence in Biomedical Internet of Medical Things, (95–110) © 2026 Scrivener Publishing LLC

equipment with 5G capability and diagnostic tools use DL algorithms. As it tackles the issues of ethics and integration, these advancements position CI-enhanced bioinstrumentation to transform early illness diagnosis and tailored healthcare.

Keywords: Computational intelligence, IoMT, bioinstrumentation, machine learning, deep learning, medical imaging, wearable technology, healthcare data security

6.1 Introduction

The Internet of Medical Things (IoMT) primary drivers of modern health care were bioinstrumentation and medical devices (MDs), which transformed the efficiency of patient processes for diagnosis, treatment, and control. Technology has grown at an amount never seen in scientific history in recent decades. Basic tools like measuring equipment have developed into complex, sophisticated, networked systems that could gather and analyze data immediately [1]. The use of electronics, sensors, and computational technologies for the measurement and tracking of physiological parameters that provide important insights into the body's health and operation is known as bioinstrumentation [2]. Electrocardiographs, electroencephalographs, blood pressure monitors, pulse oximeters, and other equipment are crucial for gathering data in real-time, which helps healthcare professionals make quick decisions [3]. Medical gadgets were crucial for therapeutic and life-supporting uses in addition to diagnostic ones. Examples include surgical instruments, implanted devices like insulin pumps and pacemakers, and imaging equipment like magnetic resonance imaging (MRI), computed tomography (CT) scans, and ultrasounds. This encompasses the precision, consistency, and dependability that human perception alone cannot supply, as well as the genius and usefulness of healthcare diagnostic and treatment equipment [4]. Therefore, bioinstrumentation combined with information technologies like the Internet of Things (IoT) and artificial intelligence (AI) have produced new technologies that include connected health systems and smart MDs. These had a chance to enhance patient outcomes, save costs, and extend accessibility to medicine because they could monitor in real-time, even from remote areas [5]. The advancements in bioinstrumentation and MDs increase possibilities in personalized medicine and minimally invasive treatment, as well as higher efficiency in healthcare. Yet the field comes along with challenges of data privacy, regulatory compliance, and system interoperability. All that demands continuous research and development in the highly evolving field [6]. Because diagnostic data for treatment and surveillance was mostly accurate, bioinstrumentation and medical equipment were vital to the health care system. Their applications have evolved from basic tools like blood pressure monitors to sophisticated imaging and implantable devices, all aimed at enhancing patient care [7]. Medical equipment was becoming intelligent, networked systems that could give analytics and present patient health observations thanks to the integration of AI and the IoT. More individualized healthcare, better treatment outcomes, and increased accessibility were made possible by the evolution. Nevertheless, data security and other problems, including device interoperability and regulatory compliance, still present difficulties [8]. With a focus on measurements, sensors, and signal processing, it examines the fundamental ideas of biomedical devices. Along with the categorization and use of instruments in clinical settings, important parts including transducers, electrodes, and amplifiers were covered. Notwithstanding its advantages, problems like electrical safety and quick technology advancements still exist [9].

Every lab activity leads students from the sensor level to data gathering and analysis at the computer, to measure a biophysical or biological parameter, blood pressure, temperature, heart rate, breathing rate, etc. It provides electrical circuits and various measuring setups that the authors experimented with while delivering undergraduate courses at their residence institute [10]. Biomedical engineering depends heavily on bioinstrumentation. To increase learning and engagement and prepare biomedical engineering students for careers in academia and industry, several techniques have been proposed with practical experiences throughout the curriculum. The application of challenge-based learning in a blended bioinstrumentation progress during the COVID-19 epidemic was discussed in the work [11]. The healthcare research community was becoming increasingly interested in the IoMT. In IoMT, MDs use the internet to collect critical health-related data. Patients are given extensive supportive information to help to navigate their recovery. However, due to a large number of MDs, device addresses could be altered by invaders, which provide a life-threatening risk to individuals with severe conditions, such as those with brain tumor illnesses [12]. Academic courses cover a wide range of medical equipment, from basic gloves to intricate artificial limbs. There was an educational method that has been developed to satisfy a variety of learning requirements. The MDs were chosen by the students and presented for group analysis. A learning taxonomy was reflected in the threefold presentation, which covered everything from fundamental ideas to critical evaluation and imaginative exhibitions [13]. The foundation of the contemporary healthcare system was made up of MDs. Assuming their meaning in monotonous health repetition, all facets of the manufacture, marketing, and use procedures must be delimited. A systematic based on evidence conformance evaluation of MDs in post-market surveillance (PMS) that depends on transparency of medical device measures may lead to higher dependability of MD performance and, consequently, greater accuracy of medical diagnosis and therapy. To establish a path toward MD, PMS harmonization addresses problems with MD PMS procedures [14]. Although MDs are essential health tools, little attention has been paid to affect the environment. To encourage sustainable choices, businesses all over the world were evaluating the complete life cycle of their products using technologies like eco-design and life cycle assessments. Research evaluates the conservational properties of MDs on polymers using life cycle assessments or eco-design. Despite the paucity of research on these techniques, their implementation could improve MDs' ecological responsibility [15].

The research will address the incorporation of computational intelligence (CI) techniques into MDs and bioinstrumentation. Some of these technologies' drawbacks and restrictions are discussed, as well as their potential to improve patient monitoring and diagnostic precision in the future.

6.2 Computational Intelligence Techniques in the Internet of Medical Things

Computational intelligence methods are used in the IoMT to enhance MDs and bioinstrumentation. These methods are dominated by CI-enchanted machine learning (ML), deep learning (DL), and edge computing, which have transformed healthcare through telemonitoring and intelligent, real-time diagnosis. Therefore, CI's ability to analyze complex data in a way that provides more accuracy in patient monitoring, early illness detection, and diagnostics leads to advancements in bioinstrumentation. Data security, legal restrictions, and significant implementation costs are some of the difficulties in incorporating this innovative technology into the current healthcare system. More innovation in the creation of medical equipment is anticipated in the future of CI, which will promote effective and individualized patient treatment. Figure 6.1 depicts the IoMT's architecture.

6.2.1 Using Computational Intelligence Techniques in Bioinstrumentation

6.2.1.1 The Role of Artificial Intelligence in Establishing a Smart Sensor Network

Research and the biomedical sector are becoming more interested in AI because of its ability to develop vast capacities of information, generate precise results, and regulate procedures for the best possible results.

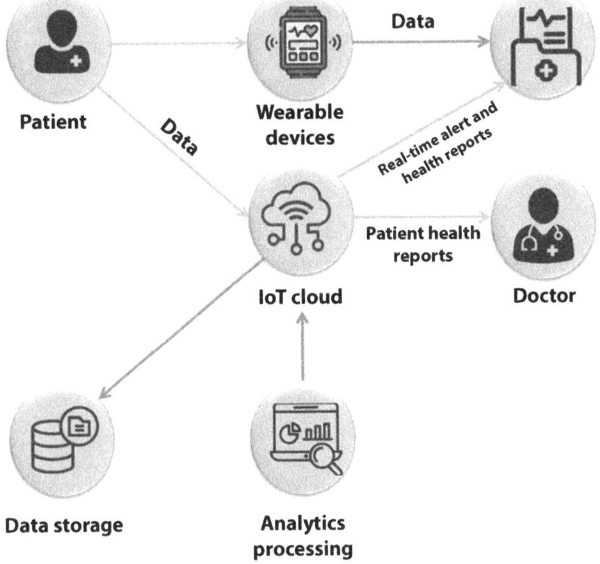

Figure 6.1 Internet of Medical Things architecture. (Source: Own elaboration).

Since machines are being employed to make decisions and forecast the long-term repercussions of diseases, AI is not new. With consideration for aspects like justice, explainability, accountability, reliability, and acceptance, algorithms and computers help with most everyday tasks in the current world. Intelligent tasks such as assisted surgery, medication discovery, knowledge-based learning, logical reasoning, and advanced imaging can be performed by AI. Several academics developed the idea of AI, which has drawn attention from researchers and the biomedical sector. Due to funding and computing capacity constraints, AI research stalled until the late 1990s. Businesses such as search engines, email service providers, and social network platforms were helped by AI models and plans in the mid-2000s. The current growth in AI can be attributed to advancements in CPU computing power and GPU calculations. Figure 6.2 illustrates the diagrammatic illustration of the relation between DL, ML, and AI [16].

Artificial intelligence techniques for generating predictions from patterns are ML. They fall into one of three categories: supervised, unsupervised, or reinforcement learning. Supervised learning is more accurate because it is trained on historical data. When input and output variables are related, like in weather forecasting, regression and classification techniques are employed. Classification algorithms divide output variables into true-false and yes-or-no categories. While unsupervised learning can find patterns in datasets even in the absence of accurate categorization or labelling, based on available data,

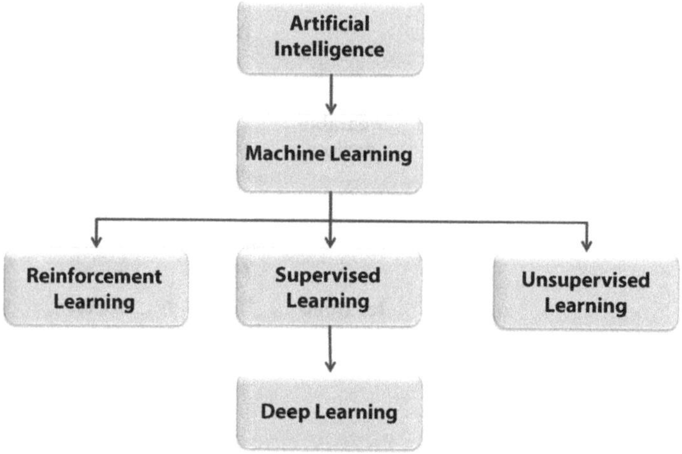

Figure 6.2 The diagrammatic illustration of the relation between DL, ML, and AI. (Source: https://electronics360.globalspec.com/article/19434/the-relationship-between-artificial-intelligence-and-machine-learning).

supervised learning can foresee results and resolve actual-life issues. When algorithms arrange data according to similarities and differences, become computationally multifaceted and lose precision. These processes fall into two categories: association and clustering. For product marketing, clustering algorithms arrange data according to commonalities, including consumer purchasing patterns. To recommend products, association algorithms look for patterns in variables, such as the shopping habits of specific customers. In reinforcement learning, desired outcomes are given positive values, while undesirable impacts are given negative ones. A subfield of machine learning called deep learning (DL) uses neural networks to mimic the behavior of humans. Recent developments in dispensation control and information analytics have made it possible for DL algorithms to watch, learn, and return to stimulating circumstances, despite the need for computer capacity. AI-model-predicted weather forecasts and email provider services are two examples.

6.2.2 Applications of CI Across Devices

6.2.2.1 Remote Patient Monitoring

Medical personnel in hospitals manually recorded symptoms and maintained a careful eye on patients' health. In hospitals, manually taking patients' vital signs was constrained by the clinical workload, staff hours, patient diagnosis, clinical leadership, national guidelines, and resource dependence. To compute the patients' vital signs, intrusive devices that required skin-to-skin contact were used for patient monitoring. The medical community was taken aback by technological advances in data transmission since it is possible to continuously monitor patients using non-invasive touching devices that do not derive into communication with their bodies. The traditional methods of keeping track of patient's health have been altered by breakthroughs, and patients can now be watched virtually from their homes, in patient-care hospitals, and in assisted-living communities. Figure 6.3 Displays the Patient monitoring architecture [17].

6.2.2.2 *IoMT-Enabled Devices*

Continuously patient monitoring can be achieved with the usage of an IoT-based immediate-time remote patient monitoring system, allowing medical personnel to attend to patients as needed and prevent unusual occurrences. There are three parts to the system's architecture. Section A displays electronic devices that patients can use to take their measurements; Section B, stores the collected data in cloud services for further analysis

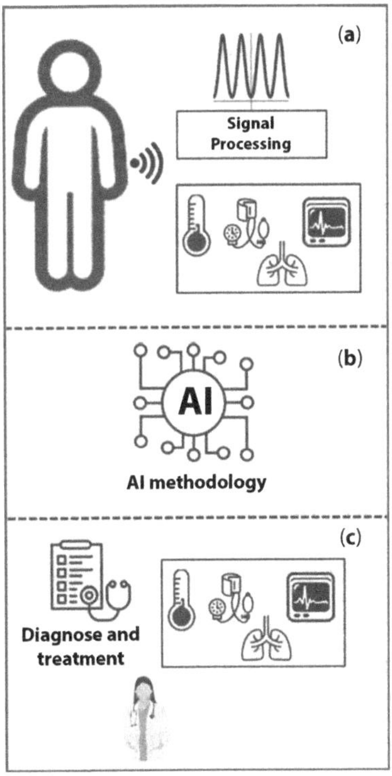

Figure 6.3 The patient monitoring architecture. (Source: Own elaboration).

using machine learning methods, and Section C, updates medical staff or healthcare professionals on any abnormal events. The wearable vital signs sensing technologies range from physiological measurements to gesture assessment and cardiac implantable devices. The system can be applied in numerous forms, such as t-shirts, chest straps, or adhesive patches.

6.2.3 Effective Use of CI to Enhance Bioinstrumentation and Medical Equipment

6.2.3.1 Deep Learning for Diagnostics

Advances in CI have also had a significant positive impact on radiology. With an accuracy on par with human experts, Google's DeepMind AI model analyses eye scans using deep learning to identify situations with age-related macular deterioration and diabetic retinopathy. By greatly cutting down on diagnosis time and facilitating prompt treatment, this approach assists radiologists in concentrating on urgent situations.

6.2.3.2 Remote Patient Monitoring with IoMT

IoMT solution that combines cloud computing and wearable technology, is another example of a successful implementation. The system notifies physicians of possible health declines by remotely collecting vital indicators from patients and analyzing those using CI algorithms. In addition to improving the quality of care and enabling patients to get monitoring from home, this strategy has been particularly successful in controlling chronic illnesses.

These illustrations show how CI applications in bioinstrumentation are revolutionizing healthcare by facilitating continuous patient monitoring, individualized treatment, and early identification, all of which lead to better outcomes for patients.

6.2.4 Utilizing CI in Medical Devices and Bioinstrumentation

6.2.4.1 Diagnostic Applications (Imaging Systems)

6.2.4.1.1 Machine Learning (ML)

The area of artificial intelligence is that learns from information and makes decisions automatically with minimal human involvement by using recognition of patterns. The most remarkable feature of a machine learning model is its capacity to self-adapt, acquire knowledge from previous calculations, and generate precise answers when used frequently to fresh inputs. The two main characteristics are (i) ML techniques that enable doctors to view medical pictures quickly through computer-aided design (CAD) and (ii) techniques for difficult jobs including segmenting brain tumor with MRI, breast cancer and mammograms, and CT scan segmentation. Traditional machine learning systems used current methods for every stage and worked on organized datasets, if any step was skipped, the applied technique failed. It is crucial to measure the excellence of the information that ML and DL algorithms employ. On the other hand, new algorithms modify data omissions according to algorithm robustness requirements. Figure 6.4 illustrates the approach taken by ML algorithms for identifying diseases and prognoses [18].

6.2.4.1.2 Deep Learning (DL)

Through improvements in methods for analyzing medical pictures, L models allow robots to attain accuracy. The tagged chest X-rays were used to diagnose cardiac disease.

Using data augmentation and TL, a cardiologist was able to extract features from images of heart failure. Using histopathological pictures and the ability to distinguish between positive and negative cancer images, an automatic feature selection method was created. A single-layer centroids network was used for learning without supervision, and Deep Neural Networks (DNN) and Principal Component Analysis (PCA) were used for

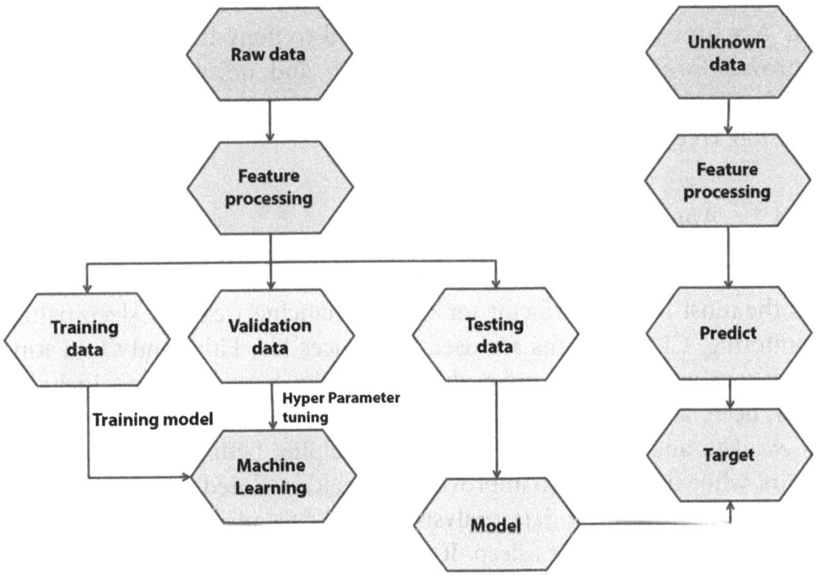

Figure 6.4 The approach taken by ML algorithms for identifying diseases and prognosis. (Source: Own elaboration).

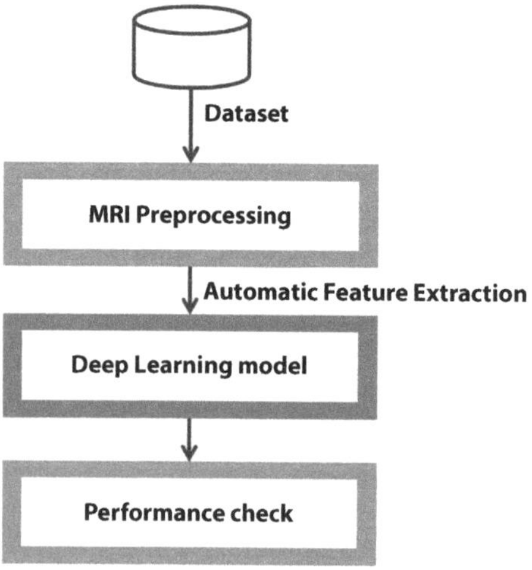

Figure 6.5 The procedure that DL algorithms utilize to predict and diagnose different diseases. (Source: Own elaboration).

the reduction of features. For effective data processing, feature extraction is automated by the DL model. The procedure that DL algorithms utilize to predict and diagnose different diseases is displayed in Figure 6.5.

Uses ML and DL techniques to develop medical images for improved forecast and accuracy. The images are segmented based on factors, essential and maximum features extracted, and refined for disease identification. Machine learning approaches are used to deny the descriptions for improved forecasts. After feature selection and noise removal, images are classified using classifiers like Support Vector Machine (SVM) and Decision Tree (DT) for disease classification.

6.2.4.2 Applications in Monitoring

6.2.4.2.1 The Role of CI in Wearable Sleep Pattern Monitoring

It is the most important factor for CI in enhancing wearable sleep pattern monitoring. CI algorithms are used by devices like Fitbit and Oura Ring, which continuously track and evaluate the various stages of sleep, including REM, deep, and light sleep. These wearables can show a user's sleep quality *via* data analytics and deep learning, helping better understand what occurs, while user sleep. To improve sleep health, tailored recommendations are developed based on data analysis. Sleep issues might range from sleep apnea to difficulty falling asleep. It offers positive input regarding optimal bedtimes, sleep lengths, and quality as well as ongoing live monitoring. More significantly, adaptive monitoring is made possible by the integration of CI, which gradually learns their sleep patterns and modifies the recommendations consequently. The final goal of CI-driven wearable technology is to authorize persons to take charge of their good sleeping habits, which will improve their overall health and lessen their reliance on sleep disorders.

6.2.5 Limitations and Difficulties

6.2.5.1 Ethical and Regulatory Concerns

Patient confidentiality and obedience to healthcare values are two moral and legal concerns with bioinstrumentation using CI techniques. Sensitive health data has a lot of room to be kept private, especially as cloud computing and Internet of Things-enabled gadgets become more commonplace. Strict adherence to laws such as HIPAA is necessary, as is intensive data protection. Maintaining safety standards is also necessary since malfunctioning equipment or incorrect diagnoses could cause injury. Rapid technology improvements make it difficult for regulatory organizations to keep up, necessitating ongoing revisions to safety procedures and moral standards to protect patient safety and data security.

6.2.5.2 Data Quality and Security Issues in IoMT Systems

In IoMT systems, data security and quality present serious issues as well as considerable hurdles. Inaccurate diagnoses and less-than-ideal therapy result from poor data quality, which might be caused by malfunctioning sensors, irregular data collection, or integration problems. Furthermore, IoMT devices are vulnerable to intrusions and illegal access because of the continuous transfer of private health information. For dependable patient care, data completeness, correctness, and consistency must be guaranteed. These implementations ought to incorporate privacy issues, encryption, access controls, and procedures for the safe transfer of data to safeguard patients' privacy. Only when integrity is preserved during information gathering, storage, and examination will the information be deemed complete.

6.2.5.3 Integration of CI with Existing Medical Infrastructure

The largest problem with traditional healthcare technologies is that might not be able to handle the sophisticated data analytics that the new AI systems can. Since it necessitates exchanging health information across platforms, associated privacy, and data security concerns also surface. To properly use such cutting-edge technologies, healthcare personnel need to receive training. Last but not least, the high implementation costs of CI solutions, regulatory body constraints, and ongoing upgrades make it challenging, to be widely accepted and integrated into modern medical practices.

6.2.6 Prospects and Patterns for the Future

6.2.6.1 Heavy Dependence on Edge Computing

IoMT's future is largely dependent on edge computing, which processes data locally on devices rather than sending it to central cloud servers. It significantly lessens bandwidth demand, improves real-time data analysis, and overcomes delays. For example, wearable health devices with edge computing capabilities can give real-time vitals analysis, including blood pressure, glucose levels, and ECG. This makes it possible to quickly identify irregularities and take action without having to wait for cloud processing. By reducing the quantity of private data sent over the internet, edge computing also improves data security by lowering possible cybersecurity threats.

6.2.6.2 5G-Connected Real-Time Monitoring Device

5G technology rollout promises to accelerate IoMT with high speed and low latency connections, which are needed to make real-time monitoring of patients feasible. With devices enabled through 5G, the continuous monitoring of patients in critical care or post-surgery recovery would not experience delays in data transmission. This is particularly useful for applications like remote monitoring of vital signs, whereby any lag in communication can have serious fallouts. High data rates would permit the deployment of much more complex medical sensors and devices capable of gathering enormous amounts of data and broadcasting in real-time, thus providing more accurate, real-time diagnoses.

6.2.6.3 Potential for Next-Generation Bioinstrumentation Devices Enhanced by CI

6.2.6.3.1 Superior Diagnostic Skills

Future bioinstrumentation devices will be able to identify complicated disorders even more precisely and early on thanks to the development of deep learning and AI algorithms. To diagnose illnesses and forecast will progress, these technologies will rely on massive datasets such as genetic, imaging, and wearable sensor data in real-time automated diagnostics. This will result in individualized diagnostic instruments that can recognize personal health hazards and serve as a preventative resource.

6.2.7 Artificial Intelligent (AI)-Based Diagnostic Applications

The applications of AI techniques to medical imaging and healthcare in IoT-enabled diagnostic devices are illustrated in Tables 6.1 and Figure 6.6. Several research investigations on diagnostic applications have different objectives, datasets, methods, and performance results.

Table 6.1 IoT-based diagnostic applications.

References	Objective	Dataset	Methodology	Results
[19]	Real-time detection of COVID-19 using Chest X-ray Images	COVID-19 Chest X-ray	IoT-based Deep Learning Framework	Accuracy:98.8%, Precision: 99%, Recall: 99%, F1-Score: 99%
[20]	Medical image analysis	Medical Imaging Dataset	Convolutional Neural Networks (CNN)	Accuracy: 95%, Precision: 94%, Recall: 92%, F1-Score: 93%
[21]	Early assessment of COVID-19	COVID-19 X-ray	IoT-based Deep Learning Framework	Accuracy: 97.5%, Precision: 96%, Recall: 94%, F1Score:95%
[22]	Automated COVID-19 diagnosis	COVID-19 X-ray Dataset	Ensemble Deep Learning + IoT	Accuracy: 98.3%, Precision: 0.97, Recall: 0.98, F1-Score: 0.98
[23]	Brain tumor detection in MRI	Brain MRI Dataset	Deep Convolutional Neural Networks (CNN)	Accuracy: 94.8%, Precision: 93%, Recall: 95%, F1-Score: 94%
[24]	Advanced patient monitoring and diagnosis	Healthcare Patient Monitoring Dataset	IoT-enabled Deep Learning Framework	Accuracy: 97.2%, Precision: 96%, Recall: 95%, F1-Score: 96%

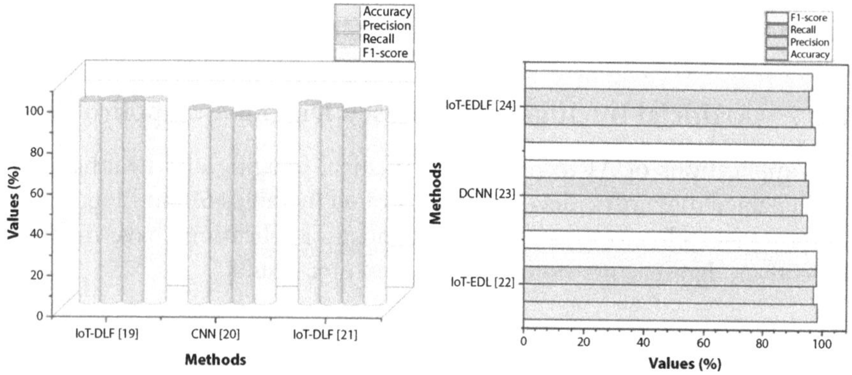

Figure 6.6 Evaluating the effectiveness of AI in IoT-based diagnostic applications.

6.3 Conclusion

Medical devices are becoming key components of health transformation due to advancements in bioinstrumentation, which enable more precise monitoring, diagnosis, and treatment. These technologies, which integrate with these devices to analyze data in real-time, forecast healthcare requirements, and provide customized healthcare results, include ML, AL, DL, and more. Caretakers may now closely monitor early disease detection and intervene when necessary thanks to advancements in wearable sensors, diagnostic imaging systems, and remote monitoring devices. The performance and data security of bioinstrumentation devices will be enhanced by cutting-edge technologies like IoMT, edge computing, and 5G connectivity, enabling real-time data transfer. The future of bioinstrumentation is promising, despite obstacles like data security, quality, and integration with existing systems, better health through individualized medicine could lead to a healthier outcome on a global scale. As long as research, innovation, and development are sustained, the healthcare system will remain intelligent and efficient.

References

1. Mishra, S. and Tyagi, A.K., The role of machine learning techniques in internet of things-based cloud applications. *Artif. Intell.-Based Internet Things Syst.*, 12, 7, 105–135, 2022, https://doi.org/10.1007/978-3-030-87059-1_4.

2. Jacob Rodrigues, M., Postolache, O., Cercas, F., Physiological and behavior monitoring systems for smart healthcare environments: A review. *Sensors*, 20, 8, 2186, 2020, http://dx.doi.org/10.3390/s20082186.
3. Silverio, A.A., *et al.*, An unobtrusive, wireless and wearable single-site blood pressure monitor based on an armband using electrocardiography (ECG) and reflectance Photoplethysmography (PPG) signal processing. *Electronics*, 12, 7, 1538, 2023, https://doi.org/10.3390/electronics12071538.
4. Ahmad, A., *et al.*, Ethical and clinical implications of AI integration in cardiovascular healthcare. *World J. Adv. Res. Rev.*, 23, .3, 2479–2501, 2024, https://doi.org/10.30574/wjarr.2024.23.3.2907.
5. Hemalatha, R.J., *et al.*, Biomedical instrument and automation: Automatic instrumentation in biomedical engineering, in: *Handbook of Data Science Approaches for Biomedical Engineering*, pp. 69–101, Academic Press, Cambridge, MA, 2020, https://doi.org/10.1016/B978-0-12-818318-2.00003-9.
6. Hazra, A., *et al.*, A comprehensive survey on interoperability for IIoT: Taxonomy, standards, and future directions. *ACM Comput. Surv. (CSUR)*, 55, 1, 1–35, 2021, https://doi.org/10.1145/3325097.
7. Krittanawong, C., *et al.*, Integration of novel monitoring devices with machine learning technology for scalable cardiovascular management. *Nat. Rev. Cardiol.*, 18, 2, 75–91, 2021, https://doi.org/10.1038/s41569-020-00445-9.
8. Alshamrani, M., IoT and artificial intelligence implementations for remote healthcare monitoring systems: A survey. *J. King Saud Univ. Comput. Inf. Sci.*, 34, 8, 4687–4701, 2022, https://doi.org/10.1016/j.jksuci.2021.06.005.
9. Josephson, C.J., *et al.*, Fundamentals of Biomedical Instrumentation (BMI): Principles and Application. *J. Adv. Biol. Biotechnol.*, 27, 9, 957–966, 2024, https://doi.org/10.9734/jabb/2024/v27i91367.
10. Fadzillah, N., Medical Devices and Technology Centre (MEDiTEC), 2023, https://doi.org/10.1201/9780429193989.
11. Santos-Díaz, A., *et al.*, Implementing a challenge-based learning experience in a bio instrumentation blended course. *BMC Med. Educ.*, 24, 1, 510, 2024, https://doi.org/10.1186/s12909-024-05462-7.
12. Khan, S.R., *et al.*, IoMT-based computational approach for detecting brain tumor. *Future Gener. Comput. Syst.*, 109, 360–3675, 2020, https://doi.org/10.1016/j.future.2020.03.054.
13. Uskoković, V., Teaching Medical Devices through Interactive Innovation: Challenges and Rewards. *Teach. Learn. Med.*, 1, 1–10, 2024, https://doi.org/10.1080/10401334.2024.2375223.
14. Badnjević, A., *et al.*, Post-market surveillance of medical devices: A review. *Technol. Health Care*, 30, 6, 1315–1329, 2022, DOI 10.3233/THC-220284.
15. Sousa, A.C., *et al.*, Assessment of the environmental impacts of medical devices: a review. *Environ. Dev. Sustain.*, 23, 9641–96665, 2021, https://doi.org/10.1007/s10668-020-01086-1.

16. Manickam, P., *et al.*, Artificial intelligence (AI) and Internet of medical things (IoMT) assisted biomedical systems for intelligent healthcare. *Biosensors*, 12, 8, 562, 2022, https://doi.org/10.3390/bios12080562.
17. Shaik, T., *et al.*, Remote patient monitoring using artificial intelligence: Current state, applications, and challenges. *Wiley Interdiscip. Rev.: Data Min. Knowl. Discov.*, 13, 2, e1485, 2023, DOI: 10.1002/widm.1485.
18. Rana, M. and Bhushan, M., Machine learning and deep learning approach for medical image analysis: diagnosis to detection. *Multimed. Tools Appl.*, 82, 17, 26731–26769, 2023, https://doi.org/10.1007/s11042-022-14305-w.
19. Karmakar, M., *et al.*, An IoT-Based Deep Learning Framework for Real-Time Detection of COVID-19 through Chest X-ray Images. *Computers*, 12, 1, 8, 2022, https://doi.org/10.3390/computers12010008.
20. Li, M., *et al.*, Medical image analysis using deep learning algorithms. *Front. Public Health*, 11, 12732535, 2023, https://doi.org/10.3389/fpubh.2023.1273253.
21. Ahmed, I., Ahmad, A., Jeon, G., An IoT-based deep learning framework for early assessment of COVID-19. *IEEE Internet Things J.*, 8, 21, 15855–15862, 2020, https://doi.org/10.1109/JIOT.2020.3034074.
22. Kini, A.S., *et al.*, Ensemble deep learning and internet of things-based automated COVID-19 diagnosis framework. *Contrast Media Mol. Imaging*, 2022, 1, 7377502, 2022, https://doi.org/10.1155/2022/7377502.
23. Siddique, M.A.B., *et al.*, Deep convolutional neural networks model-based brain tumor detection in brain MRI images. *2020 Fourth International Conference on I-SMAC (IoT in Social, Mobile, Analytics and Cloud)(I-SMAC)*, IEEE, 2020, https://doi.org/10.48550/arXiv.2010.11978.
24. Alharbe, N. and Almalki, M., IoT-enabled healthcare transformation leveraging deep learning for advanced patient monitoring and diagnosis. *Multimed. Tools Appl.*, 83, 1–14, 2024, https://doi.org/10.3390/computers12010008.

7

Biomedical Signal Processing for Community Health

Sheuli Sen[1], Santanu Kumar Sahoo[2], Rekha M.M.[3], Jemmy Christy H.[4*], Sumitra Menaria[5] and Pooja Shukla[6]

[1]Teerthakar Parshvnath College of Nursing, Teerthakar Mahaveer University, Uttar Pradesh, India
[2]Department of Electronics & Communication Engineering, Siksha 'O' Anusandhan (Deemed to be University), Bhubaneswar, Odisha, India
[3]Department of Chemistry and Biochemistry, Jain (Deemed-to-be University), Bangalore, Karnataka, India
[4]Department of Bioinformatics, Sathyabama Institute of Science and Technology, Chennai, Tamil Nadu, India
[5]Computer Science and Engineering, Parul Institute of Technology, Parul University, Vadodara, Gujarat, India,
[6]Maharishi School of Engineering & Technology, Maharishi University of Information Technology, Uttar Pradesh, India

Abstract
Biomedical signal processing entails the acquisition and preprocessing of physiological signals, followed by information retrieval to analyze signals for patterns and trends. Sources of biomedical signals are neural signals, cardiac rhythm, muscle movements, and normal activity signals. Research presents a novel framework, the White Shark Optimized Refined Random Forest (WSO-RRF), which leverages biomedical signal processing techniques to enhance community health monitoring and disease detection. White Shark Optimization (WSO) improves

**Corresponding author*: jemmychristy.bioinfo@sathyabama.ac.in; ORCID: 0000-0002-5538-4270
Sheuli Sen: ORCID: 0000-0002-0276-5918
Santanu Kumar Sahoo: ORCID: 0000-0001-8324-3101
Rekha M.M.: ORCID: 0000-0002-7371-6478
Sumitra Menaria: ORCID: 0000-0002-7155-9368
Pooja Shukla: ORCID: 0009-0005-0869-4793

Satya Prakash Yadav, Abhay Bansal and Victor Hugo C. de Albuquerque (eds.) Computational Intelligence in Biomedical Internet of Medical Things, (111–126) © 2026 Scrivener Publishing LLC

disease detection and community health monitoring by enhancing biomedical signal processing. The electrocardiogram signal data was gathered from the open-source Kaggle website. During the pre-processing phase, min-max scaling assists in converting biomedical signal data into a specified range, helping in noise minimization and improving the quality of subsequent analysis. Medical signals hold both temporal and frequency information that is crucial for analysis. The wavelet transform is used to extract multi-resolution features from medical signals. The research proposes a WSO-RRF model and shows the model's performance through various evaluation metrics. The WSO-RRF achieved the highest performance metrics with an accuracy of 94.6%, RMSE of 0.19, and MAE of 0.24. Biomedical signal processing offers an innovative strategy that can be harnessed to enhance community health. It directly impacts the healthcare sector by promoting early diagnosis, providing feedback, and making treatment per individual available worldwide.

***Keywords*:** Biomedical signal processing, White Shark Optimization (WSO), Dynamic Random Forest (DRF), community health monitoring, wavelet transform (WT), min-max scaling

7.1 Introduction

Biomedical signal processing refers to the techniques and methodologies used to analyze signals from the human body for example, electrocardiograms (ECGs), electroencephalograms (EEGs), and electromyograms [1]. A person's health and modern equipment for diagnosis, as well as monitoring, would therefore include these signals. Biomedical signal processing is a major milestone in improving community health, as it facilitates the exploration and comprehension of complex biological signals, which are vital to the improvement and capture of healthcare [2]. One of the major aspects is the identification of diseases at an earlier stage, with biomedical signals such as ECG and EEG being employed to look for abnormalities and predict whether physiological states progress to pathological ones or not [3]. As a result, there is no easy decline in health that occurs due to treatment that possibly cuts down any deficit of the diseases. It enhances the management of medical diseases for better precision and provided health monitoring using easily connected handheld devices [4]. These technologies are designed to universally monitor various physiological parameters including heart rate, oxygen levels, and general blood pressure while providing rapid medical attention and controlling certain health conditions such as diabetes, hypertension, and asthma [5]. The telemedicine and health care services, biomedical signal processing is a useful tool that helps integrate remote patients and clinical facilities. The signals are sent and received almost simultaneously improving the effectiveness of remote diagnosis and treatment and the level of health care in regions with a deficiency. The systems provide supporting evidence for public health provision through implementing syndrome surveillance, which is the collection and analysis of information from various groups of people to identify and monitor the existence and changes of certain diseases [6]. In the area of treatment processed biomedical signals assist biofeedback systems concerning physical rehabilitation or stress control and help augment the functionality of devices like neuroprosthetics. Biomedical signal processing is also of paramount importance in the emergency service, where it enables constant control of certain critical parameters and informs in case of emergencies [7]. Several challenges need resolution despite the possible benefits including noise in the signal acquisition, data security, and modularity. Community health status is bound to improve advances in machine learning (ML) and artificial intelligence (AI). Presently applied biomedical signal processing in healthcare is certain to improve with these developments making healthcare more predictable, preventive, and achievable [8]. Biomedical signal processing has limitations because of challenges including noise, the range of analysis of physiological signals, and the impossibility of processing. These problems can be solved *via* advanced signal preprocessing, standard data acquisition methods, and powerful algorithms providing accurate and extensible results. The research evaluates the WSO-RRF framework, which is aimed at enhancing disease detection and population health surveillance based on the principles of biomedical signal processing.

7.1.1 Contributions

- To present the WSO-RRF model improving disease detection and community health surveillance.
- To use Kaggle biomedical signal datasets after preprocessing with Min-max scaling to reduce noise and enhance accuracy.
- To Implement wavelet transform (WT) to retrieve time-frequency features of biomedical signals at multiple resolutions.
- Health monitoring to enhance the biomedical signal analysis through model performance optimization techniques using WSO.

Structure of the paper: The study is divided into phases. Phase 7.2 shows the literature reviews. Phase 7.3 outlines the methodology. Phases 7.4 and 7.5 include the results and discussion, and Phrase 7.6 shows the conclusion.

7.2 Literature Reviews

A functional neuro-imaging method called an EEG uses electric currents [9] to evaluate neural activity. Unlike other methods such as positron emission tomography, magnetoencephalogram, functional magnetic resonance imaging, and transcranial magnetic stimulation, it provides excellent temporal resolution, affordability, mobility, and non-invasiveness. The EEG signals can be utilized for tiredness detection, motor imagery monitoring, and neurological disease diagnosis. To produce realistic and labeled ECG data, the research presents three generative models based on deep learning (DL) [10]. The suggested WaveNet-based model employs convolutional layers and μ-law commanding transformation, whereas the spectrogram generative adversarial network (spectro GAN) and wavelet generative adversarial network (wavelet GAN) employ stationary WT and short-term Fourier transform. These models can provide ECG readings that are naturally continuous for more than 20 seconds and contain three distinct heartbeat types. The hyperglycemic patient [11] suggests a noninvasive blood glucose monitoring device that would allow for daily management at home. Smartphone photoplethysmography signals are used by the system to distinguish between warning, borderline, and normal levels. Gaussian functions, ML methods, a new algorithm, and a fitting-based sliding window approach are all used in the system. To evaluate mental effort during multitasking mental activities [12], two tasks are included in the dataset are estimated using a hybrid architecture that combines a deep neural network and the Grey Wolf Optimizer. The enhances the effectiveness and performance of operators. An effective feature extraction technique based on fuzzy wavelet packets (WP) is presented [13], and suggested signals were classified using a linear classifier, features were extracted using optimum WP decomposition, and the original signals were mapped to WP feature spaces using a WP transformation. To generate discriminative features with minimal variability by learning a double-sparse dictionary from particular data, researchers [14] suggested signal segment matrix is subjected to wavelet sparse principal component analysis. The approaches drastically reduce accuracy; the method obtains virtually perfect classification accuracy (99.7%) for long-term EEG recordings. An intelligent analysis of patient data, including biological data from imaging, blood pressure, temperature, ECG, and EEG, was essential to modern medicine. It [15] was difficult to extract pertinent information from this massive volume of data when processing and evaluating it in clinical settings included critical care and epilepsy care units. Healthcare administration systems can benefit from the expanding usage of biological signals in emerging nations. Researchers [16] suggested that the current infrastructure finds it difficult to offer high-end signal transfer capabilities. Using Hadoop-based systems and a four-layer model combined with the Fuzzy Interface System Algorithm, this research tackles the problem. Reference health data from many treatment facilities is used for data transfers.

7.3 Methodology

The framework begins with collecting biomedical signals and preprocessing using min-max scaling to normalize and reduce noise, followed by feature extraction using WT to capture time-frequency information. The WSO-RRF model is then trained on the processed data to enhance detection accuracy. Finally, the trained model is deployed for health monitoring, detecting anomalies, and enabling timely health interventions. The workflow of the entire framework is shown in Figure 7.1.

7.3.1 Data Collection

The signal data was gathered from the open-source Kaggle Website: https://www.kaggle.com/datasets/shayanfazeli/heartbeat. Two sets of cardiac signals from two popular datasets for heartbeat classification the Massachusetts Institute of Technology - Beth Israel Hospital (MIT-BIH) Arrhythmia collection and the Physikalisch-Technische Bundesanstalt

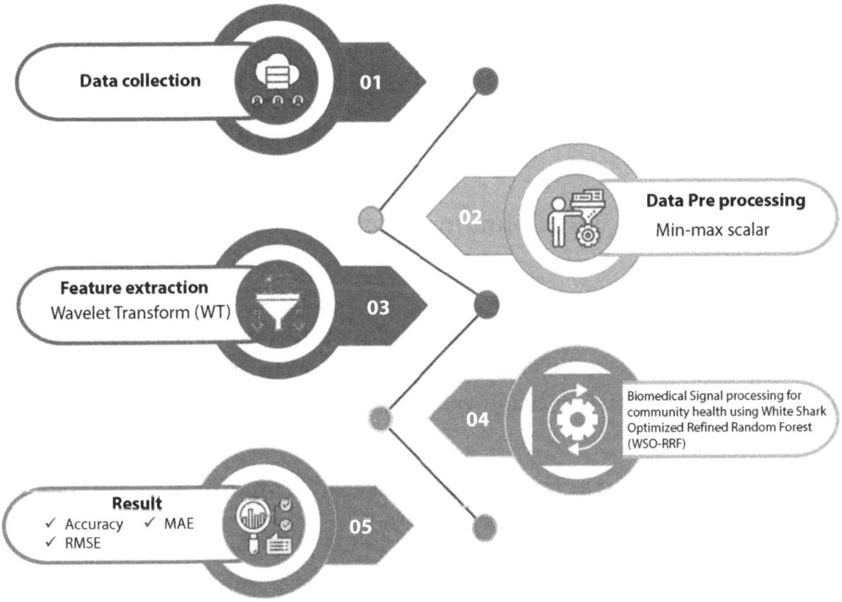

Figure 7.1 Proposed workflow. (Source: Own elaboration).

(PTB) Diagnostic ECG Database are included in this collection. This dataset has been used to rhythm classification and examine some of the transfer learning capabilities using advanced neural network architectures. Both normal and conditions involving arrhythmias and myocardial infarctions include signals that correspond to the heartbeat patterns on an ECG. This extracted and divided data segments each correspond to a beating heart.

7.3.2 Preprocessing Using Min-Max Scaler

Min-max scaler is particularly effective for normalizing biomedical signals, which often have varying amplitudes due to diverse physiological conditions. These normalization techniques ensure all signals are scaled in a uniform range (e.g., 0 to 1), enhancing the comparability of data and optimizing the performance of ML models. By eliminating biases caused by varying signal magnitudes. Min-Max Scaling facilitates the effective processing and analysis of biomedical signals in community health applications. Min-max scaling transforms each data point with Equation 7.1, showing how to scale a feature to a value between 0 and 1, with the least value mapping to 0 and the largest value mapping to 1. All intermediate values are scaled proportionately.

$$XScaled = \frac{x - x_{min}}{x_{max} - x_{min}} \tag{7.1}$$

Where,

$$x_{min} = \text{minimum value in } X \text{ Feature}$$

$$x_{max} = \text{minimum value in } X \text{ Feature}$$

This approach is essential in community health. Consistent signaling of biomedical signals like ECG is critical for accurate analysis, early disease detection, and effective decision-making.

7.3.3 Feature Extraction Using Wavelet Transform

Wavelet transform is particularly effective in the processing of non-stationary signals such as ECGs, which are widespread in biomedical applications. It allows performing the analysis at various levels, which makes it very suitable for the detection of features at different time-frequency scales. This is very important since the diagnosis and monitoring of community health require precision in feature detection. A time-frequency transformation is known as WT, which is the process of decomposing signal data into components known as subseries that represent different frequency ranges. Discrete wavelet transform (DWT) is a popular decomposition technique for finite duration time signals given by Equation 7.2.

$$DWT(n,m) = 2^{-n/2} \sum_{w=0}^{M-1} W(s)\psi^{*}\left(\frac{s-m2^{n}}{2^{n}}\right) \tag{7.2}$$

$\psi^{*}\left(\frac{s-m2^{n}}{2^{n}}\right)$ is the mother wavelet; * indicates the complex conjugate 2^{n} and $m2^{n}$, respectively, are the scaling factor and translation factor, signifying the frequency domain and time domain modification of the mother wavelet. Such transformations are fundamental to the recognition of biomedical signal features, so that the health events or disorders can be diagnosed accurately, improving society's health programs.

7.3.4 Biomedical Signal Processing for Community Health Using White Shark Optimized Refined Random Forest

The Refined Random Forest (RRF) focuses on achieving flawless classification, as well as having robust features. Thus, it is suitable in cure-seeking and public health surveillance activities. The WSO technique optimizes the model by hyperparameter tuning in addition to the WSO's optimization capabilities focused on model parameter tuning to avoid model underfitting or overfitting in biomedical signal analysis cases.

7.3.4.1 Refined Random Forest

Random Forest is a powerful ensemble approach to learning, which embodies excellent performance in dealing with high-dimensional biomedical signal data. As it can undertake both classification and regression, it is important for health condition diagnosis using biomedical signals. It performs well with noisy data, a characteristic that is typical in biomedical signal processing, while providing good generalization competency, which makes it amenable to early disease detection in population health settings. In signal processing of biomedical signals, the boosting technique changes the weight for each sample, depending on the corresponding error rate that is increasing for the misclassified samples and decreasing for the correctly classified ones. In the case of an RRF for analysis of biomedical signals, a single sub-forest is generated, and all sample weights are altered through that sub-forest; however, this alteration excludes the contribution of previous rounds. While constructing the RRF approach in synthesis of any signal processes, all constructed trees are treated as a new RRF for the second or n^{th} round of trees, combining boosting and bagging approaches to inter sample RRF better changes weight of each sample in the train set to be 1/N, N being the samples in total. Then, using the RRF technique, the first tree is produced, while all the samples' weights are adjusted. After that, the second tree is built up employing the bootstrap procedure, and all weights of the samples are updated with the help of the first and the second trees, forming a sub-forest. Subsequent sequences of additional trees are trained on this reweighted data for further improvement of the robustness of the model with regard to handling biomedical signals. The RRF proposes a novel approach towards feature selection. Random feature selection is applied; however, the number of characteristics at each node is randomly determined based on the average inherent information of each of the features. In the case of biological applications, this allows the model to focus on features that are important for signal interpretation, which enhances the overall diagnostic accuracy. Given the current forest's ability to predict the class of the sample, Bernard applied the following method to change the sample weight in Equation 7.3:

$$d(w,z) = \frac{1}{|g_{oob}|} \times \sum_{g_j \in g_{oob}} J(g_j(w) = z) \tag{7.3}$$

The output of the j classifier is represented by $g_j(w)$, the $g(w,\theta_j)$ equivalent symbol, where $w$is the input sample z is its actual class; and J is an instruction function. This mechanism always keeps the attention on difficult samples, while well-classified cases play a minor role in the training of the other trees. In the case of biomedical signal processing, this allows the model to improve its generalization across multiple community health datasets. The weight adjustment formula for a sample w is given by Equation 7.4:

$$X(d(w,z)) = 1 - d(w,z) \tag{7.4}$$

The instances are misclassified and are given larger weights, while instances are classified and given lower weights. In biomedical signal processing, this technique is adjusted further to deal with identified samples distinguishing correctly and incorrectly. The out-of-bag tree available in the current forest is used by the model to predict the class of the samples, paying particular attention to samples that are more uncertain in their prediction.

7.3.4.2 White Shark Optimization

White Shark Optimization, as a nature-inspired optimization technique, is effective for solving complex optimization problems, such as feature selection, parameter tuning, and improving the performance of ML models. These are critical tasks in biomedical signal processing, where precise feature extraction and classification are essential for monitoring and diagnosis. The unique characteristics of white sharks, including their remarkable hearing and sense of smell for foraging and navigation, have an impact on WSO to optimize biomedical data processing tasks.

7.3.4.2.1 Steps of the White Shark Optimization Algorithm in Biomedical Signal Processing

Speed in the direction of the prey after a white shark determines the location of its meal by analyzing the waves produced by the target's actions in Equation 7.5:

$$\delta_j(s+1) = v\left[\delta_j(s) + \rho_j.d_j(O_{Hbest}(s) - \rho_j(s)) + \rho_2.d_2(O_{jbest}(s) - \rho_j(s))\right] \tag{7.5}$$

The white shark command in the population of a size is formulated by the index $j(j = 1,2,...,m)$ in Equation 7.5s, m,t denotes speed, and o displays the j white sharks' current position vector. For biomedical signal processing, O_{best} displays the strategic standing vector that is high; O_{best} represents the current optimal position that has been reached thus far. Two random numbers between [0, 1] are $d_{1,}d_2, O_1, O_2$, and u are calculated using Equations 7.6, 7.7, and 7.8:

$$\rho_1 = \rho_{max} + (\rho_{max} - \rho_{min})f^{-(4s/s_{max})^2} \tag{7.6}$$

$$\rho_2 = \rho_{max} + (\rho_{max} - \rho_{min}) f^{-(4s/s_{max})^2} \tag{7.7}$$

$$v = \frac{2}{|2 - \tau - \sqrt{\tau^2 - 4\tau}\,|} ; \tau = 4.125 \tag{7.8}$$

White sharks move continuously in the direction of their ideal prey after detecting the target's scent, observing the prey's movement, or perhaps recognizing the waves the prey creates. In search for food, the prey either flees or escapes its location. Consequently, the white shark updated the position in Equation 7.9:

$$\begin{aligned} O_j(s+1) = \{O_j(s) \neg \oplus O_0 + ig.b + low.a; rand < n O_j(s) \\ + t_j(s)/e; rand \geq n \end{aligned} \tag{7.9}$$

The upper and lower bounds of the random search are denoted by high and low for biomedical signal space, g is the frequency of wave movement, and can be described as follows in Equation 7.10. In this case, a and b stand for a 1D binary vector.

$$n = \left(\left| b_0 + f^{\frac{s_{max}/2^{-s}}{b1}} \right| \right)^{-1} \tag{7.10}$$

Assume that the two constant parameters are b_0 and b_1. The motion in the direction of the White Sharking Equations 7.11 and 7.12:

$$n = \left(\left| b_0 + f^{\frac{s_{max}/2^{-s}}{b1}} \right| \right)^{-1} \tag{7.11}$$

$$O_j(s+1) = \{O_{Hbest}(s) + q_j.C.sgn(q_2 - 0.5); q_3 < T_t O_j(s); otherwise \tag{7.12}$$

Where C is the distance between the sharks and the targets, q_1, q_2, and q_3 are the random value ranges inside [0, 1]. This ensures precise convergence in identifying anomalies in biomedical signals. Fish school behaviors: Equation 7.13 was used to represent this phase.

$$O_j(s+1) = \frac{O_j(s) + O_j(s+1)}{2.rand} \tag{7.13}$$

The WSO-RRF model is an improved method for biomedical signal processing that employs the design of RRF and WSO techniques. Random Forest is efficient in the classification of biomedical signals, which are often complex in nature. The WSO optimizes the hyperparameters of the model and prevents data overfitting and underfitting. Such a strategy enhances the model's focus on generalizing and improving different health data performance. The WSO-RRF has a turn for community health monitoring for disease outbreaks prediction and control and brings more accuracy in disease predictors and health monitoring purposes. It helps with developing strategies aimed at improving people's health.

7.4 Results

Utilizing a PC with an Intel (R) Xeon (R) CPU, E5420, 2.5 GHz, and 8 GB of RAM, the simulations were conducted using MATLAB R2015a. The model of WSO-RRF enhances the efficiency of biomedical signal processing in community health by optimizing classification and feature extraction, ensuring adaptability to diverse biomedical signals. This advanced framework improves the accuracy of detecting community health anomalies, addressing the limitations of classical methods. The proposed WSO-RRF approach was compared with other methods, including DCNN-BiLSTM [17] and BiGridLSTM-CNN [18], to validate its superior performance.

7.4.1 Accuracy

Accuracy in biomedical signal processing refers to the proportion of correctly classified signals or detected health anomalies compared to the total number of signals analyzed. It measures the effectiveness of the model in correctly identifying patterns, trends, or diseases in the biomedical data. Table 7.1 and Figure 7.2 show the accuracy performance.

The accuracy for the proposed (WSO-RRF - 94.6%) outperforms existing systems, such as (DCNN-BiLSTM – 89.3%), respectively. Our suggested method is more effective than an existing method for biomedical signal processing for community health.

Table 7.1 Comparison of performance metrics for DCNN-BiLSTM and WSO-RRF models.

Methods	Accuracy (%)
DCNN-BiLSTM [17]	89.3
WSO-RRF [Proposed]	94.6

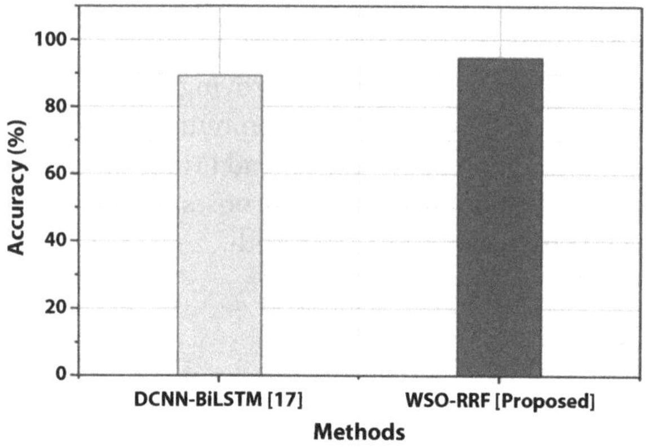

Figure 7.2 Accuracy performance. (Source: Own elaboration).

7.4.2 Root Mean Squared Error

Root mean squared error (RMSE) measures the standard deviation of the prediction error in biomedical signal processing, where residuals represent the difference between the predicted and actual signal values. It quantifies the spread of these errors, with a smaller RMSE, indicating a better fit between the model's predictions and the actual biomedical signals, thus reflecting higher accuracy in disease detection and health monitoring. Table 7.2 and Figure 7.3 show the RMSE performance.

Table 7.2 Overall outcome values RMSE.

Methods	RMSE
Bi-Grid LSTM-CNN [18]	0.25
WSO-RRF [Proposed]	0.19

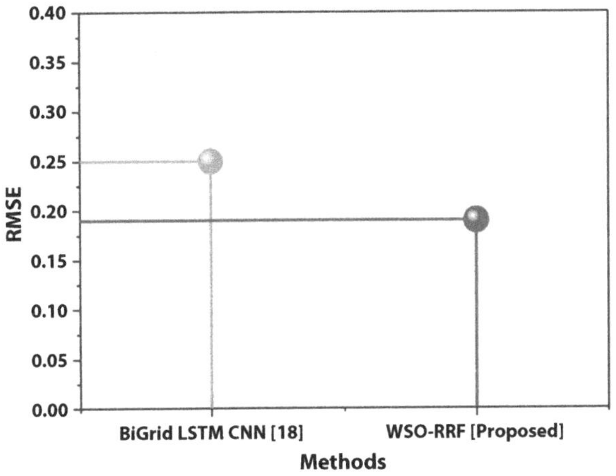

Figure 7.3 Root mean squared error performance. (Source: Own elaboration).

The RMSE for the proposed WSO-RRF – 0.19 outperforms the existing systems, such as Bi-Grid LSTM-CNN - 0.25, respectively. Our proposed method is better than an existing method for biomedical signal processing for community health.

7.4.3 Mean Absolute Error

In biomedical signal processing, the mean absolute error (MAE) is the average of the absolute differences between the expected and actual values. It serves as a gauge for the precision of anomaly detection and signal classification. Table 7.3 and Figure 7.4 show the MAE performance.

The MAE for the proposed WSO-RRF – 0.24 outperforms the existing systems, such as Bi-Grid LSTM-CNN –0.36, respectively. Our recommended method is superior to an existing method for biomedical signal processing for community health.

Table 7.3 Overall outcome values of the MAE.

Methods	MAE
Bi-Grid LSTM-CNN [18]	0.36
WSO-RRF [Proposed]	0.24

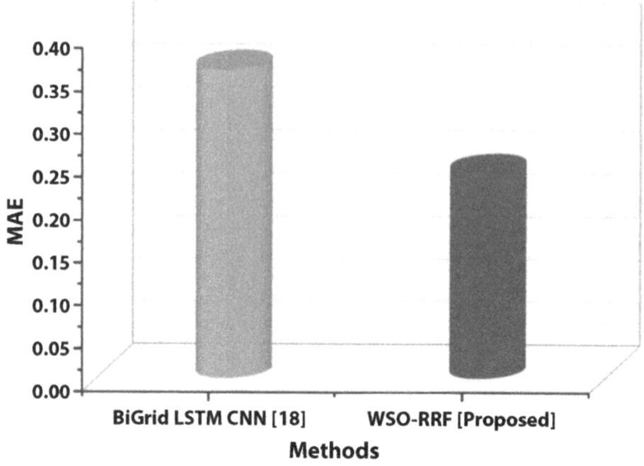

Figure 7.4 Mean absolute error performance. (Source: Own elaboration).

7.5 Discussion

The proposed WSO-RRF model addresses constraints of DCNN-BiLSTM and BiGridLSTM-CNN, such as high-power costs and difficulty in processing noisy biological signals. The WSO-RRF tries to perform two tasks; it enhances the process of selecting appropriate features and tunes model parameters, which assists in the fast and precise classification of signals. The WSO-RRF is more resilient to various input patterns than data-centric models such as DCNN-BiLSTM, which adapts well to inputs with simple data patterns. It also solves the problem of training data overfitting, which is likely to limit BiGridLSTM-CNN in low data scenarios. It makes WSO-RRF suitable in contemporaneous healthcare delivery systems for the monitoring and detection of diseases in the community.

7.6 Conclusion

In WSO-RRF, biomedical signal processing enhances the accuracy and specificity of health assessment and disease prognosis. Investigating the mechanisms of health issues at their earliest stages allows for the timely utilization of resources through analyzing physiological signals. Constant observation ensures that health status is reviewed regularly, which improves the effectiveness of managing such conditions. By using health profiles and needs to provide consumers with individualized care, the system is further improved. The potential for significant shifts in healthcare delivery systems due to the hybridization of technology and healthcare improves people's health. Performance parameters of accuracy (94.6%), RMSE (0.19), and MAE (0.24) were achieved by the WSO-RRF. According to currently available research, our method outperforms the alternative method for biomedical signal processing in community health. It challenges difficulties such as high noise levels, differences in the physiological signals that are captured, and temporal sensitivities in various locations. Future advancements increase the accuracy and scope of community health monitoring using wearable IoT devices, AI algorithms, and real-time visualizations.

References

1. Krishnan, S. and Athavale, Y., Trends in biomedical signal feature extraction. *Biomed. Signal Process. Control, 43*, 41–63, 2018, https://doi.org/10.1109/ISSPA.2012.6310458.
2. Lan, K., Fong, S., Liu, L.S., Wong, R.K., Dey, N., Millham, R.C., Wong, K.K., A clustering-based variable sub-window approach using particle swarm optimization for biomedical sensor data monitoring. *Enterp. Inf. Syst., 15*, 1, 15–35, 2021, https://doi.org/10.1080/17517575.2019.1597388.
3. Alakus, T.B., Gonen, M., Turkoglu, I., Database for an emotion recognition system based on EEG signals and various computer games–GAMEEMO. *Biomed. Signal Process. Control, 60*, 101951, 2020, https://doi.org/10.1016/j.bspc.2020.101951.
4. Tuncer, T., Dogan, S., Subasi, A., Surface EMG signal classification using ternary pattern and discrete wavelet transform-based feature extraction for hand movement recognition. *Biomed. Signal Process. Control, 58*, 101872, 2020, https://doi.org/10.1016/j.bspc.2020.101872.
5. Sharma, G., Parashar, A., Joshi, A.M., DepHNN: a novel hybrid neural network for electroencephalogram (EEG)-based screening of depression. *Biomed. Signal Process. Control, 66*, 102393, 2021, https://doi.org/10.1016/j.bspc.2020.102393.
6. AlHinai, N., Introduction to biomedical signal processing and artificial intelligence, in: *Biomedical Signal Processing and Artificial Intelligence in Healthcare*, pp. 1–28, Academic Press, Cambridge, MA, 2020, https://doi.org/10.1016/B978-0-12-818946-7.00001-9.
7. Kamble, A., Ghare, P.H., Kumar, V., Classifying phonological categories and imagined words from EEG signal, in: *Biomedical Signal Processing for Healthcare Applications*, pp. 93–121, CRC Press, Boca Raton, FL, 2021, https://doi.org/10.1201/9781003147817.
8. Londhe, A.N. and Atulkar, M., Semantic segmentation of ECG waves using hybrid channel-mix convolutional and bidirectional LSTM. *Biomed.*

Signal Process. Control, *63*, 102162, 2021, https://doi.org/10.1016/j.bspc.2020.102162.

9. Khosla, A., Khandnor, P., Chand, T., A comparative analysis of signal processing and classification methods for different applications based on EEG signals. *Biocybern. Biomed. Eng.*, *40*, 2, 649–690, 2020, https://doi.org/10.1016/j.bbe.2020.02.002.
10. Wulan, N., Wang, W., Sun, P., Wang, K., Xia, Y., Zhang, H., Generating electrocardiogram signals by deep learning. *Neurocomputing*, *404*, 122–136, 2020, https://doi.org/10.1016/j.neucom.2020.04.076.
11. Zhang, G., Mei, Z., Zhang, Y., Ma, X., Lo, B., Chen, D., Zhang, Y., A noninvasive blood glucose monitoring system based on smartphone PPG signal processing and machine learning. *IEEE Trans. Ind. Inf.*, *16*, 11, 7209–7218, 2020, https://doi.org/10.1109/TII.2020.2975222.
12. Chakladar, D.D., Dey, S., Roy, P.P., Dogra, D.P., EEG-based mental workload estimation using deep BLSTM-LSTM network and evolutionary algorithm. *Biomed. Signal Process. Control*, *60*, 101989, 2020, https://doi.org/10.1016/j.bspc.2020.101989.
13. Mukhopadhyay, A.K. and Samui, S., An experimental study on upper limb position invariant EMG signal classification based on deep neural network. *Biomed. Signal Process. Control*, *55*, 101669, 2020, https://doi.org/10.1016/j.bspc.2019.101669.
14. Njitacke, Z.T., Isaac, S.D., Nestor, T., Kengne, J., Window of multistability and its control in a simple 3D Hopfield neural network: application to biomedical image encryption. *Neural Comput. Appl.*, *33*, 6733–6752, 2021, https://doi.org/10.1016/j.bspc.2019.101669.
15. Karataş, F., Koyuncu, I., Tuna, M., Alçın, M., Avcioglu, E., Akgul, A., Design and implementation of arrhythmic ECG signals for biomedical engineering applications on FPGA. *Eur. Phys. J. Spec. Top.*, *231*, 5, 869–884, 2022, https://doi.org/10.1140/epjs/s11734-021-00334-3.
16. Selvarajan, S., Manoharan, H., Hasanin, T., Alsini, R., Uddin, M., Shorfuzzaman, M., Alsufyani, A., Biomedical signals for healthcare using Hadoop infrastructure with artificial intelligence and fuzzy logic interpretation. *Appl. Sci.*, *12*, 10, 5097, 2022, https://doi.org/10.3390/app12105097.
17. Hazra, D. and Byun, Y.C., SynSigGAN: Generative adversarial networks for synthetic biomedical signal generation. *Biology*, *9*, 12, 441, 2020, https://doi.org/10.3390/biology9120441.
18. Cheng, J., Zou, Q., Zhao, Y., ECG signal classification based on deep CNN and BiLSTM. *BMC Med. Inf. Decis. Making*, *21*, 1–12, 2021, https://doi.org/10.1186/s12911-021-01736-y.

8

Medical Image Processing and Analysis

Pallavi. M.[1]*, Sarbeswar Hota[2], Ankita Gandhi[3], Anbarasi Jebaselvi G. D.[4], G. Padma Priya[5] and Divyanshi Rajvanshi[6]

[1]Department of Computer Science and Engineering, Presidency University, Bangalore, Karnataka, India
[2]Department of Computer Application, Siksha 'O' Anusandhan (Deemed to be University), Bhubaneswar, Odisha, India
[3]Department of Computer Science & Engineering, Parul University, Vadodara, Gujarat, India
[4]Department of Electronics and Communication Engineering, Sathyabama Institute of Science and Technology, Chennai, Tamil Nadu, India
[5]Department of Chemistry and Biochemistry, Jain (Deemed-to-be University), Bangalore, Karnataka, India
[6]Maharishi School of Engineering & Technology, Maharishi University of Information Technology, Uttar Pradesh, India

Abstract
The effectiveness of disease identification and medical imaging technologies has completely transformed the healthcare sector. The capacity to identify and evaluate anomalies like neuronal tumors has become increasingly important in early detection and therapy planning due to the growing usage of diagnostic tools like magnetic resonance imaging (MRI). The purpose of the research is to investigate how sophisticated artificial intelligence (AI) models might improve the identification and categorization of brain cancers using medical imaging, particularly MRI scans. The brain tumor MRI image data was collected, and the denoising was used in the data preprocessing to overcome the medical image. The segmentation using k-means clustering and a convolutional neural network was utilized

**Corresponding author*: pallavim@presidencyuniversity.in
Sarbeswar Hota: ORCID: https://orcid.org/0009-0006-0921-8323
Ankita Gandhi: ORCID: https://orcid.org/0000-0002-3516-2187
Anbarasi Jebaselvi G. D.: ORCID: https://orcid.org/0000-0001-7792-6045
G. Padma Priya: ORCID: https://orcid.org/0000-0004911-1823
Divyanshi Rajvanshi: ORCID: https://orcid.org/0009-0004-6465-1846

Satya Prakash Yadav, Abhay Bansal and Victor Hugo C. de Albuquerque (eds.) Computational Intelligence in Biomedical Internet of Medical Things, (127–142) © 2026 Scrivener Publishing LLC

to extract specific MRI image analysis. The Enriched Whale Optimized Logistic Regression (EWO-LR) approach was used to detect brain tumors with MRI scans. The proposed EWO-LR approaches were higher than the existing method with the parameters of accuracy (98.98%), precision (98.45%), recall (97.12%), and F1-score (97.75%). By providing potential tools for healthcare practitioners to diagnose and plan appropriate therapies, these findings add to the expanding field of medical imagery analysis. Larger information sets, model understanding, and immediate-time medical applications should be the main topics of future studies for medical analysis.

Keywords: Medical image, convolutional neural network (CNN), enriched whale optimization (EWO), logistic regression (LR), healthcare technology

8.1 Introduction

In several approaches, medical imaging processing has expanded to incorporate image processing, recognition of patterns, image mining, and neural networks. One frequently used strategy that is used to provide a precise representation of the state is deep learning (DL). Diagnostic imaging has more options because those extensions of DL with medicine cover a wide range of topics, including individualized therapy recommendations, infection inspection, and cancer detection [1]. Utilizing cutting-edge computational methods to extract, improve, and interpret characteristics from the use of magnetic resonance imaging (MRI) is known as MRI-based healthcare image processing and evaluation. This procedure uses techniques, including division, feature collection, and categorization, to help detect anomalies like cancers. To provide accurate and effective healthcare services, models significantly maximize precision in diagnosis [2].

Computed graphic MRI, ultrasound imaging, magnetic resonance, and positron emission tomography are some of the frequently utilized kinds of imaging that have been produced. Additionally, increasingly complicated imaging methods have been created. The potential and necessity of creating computerized approaches to help radiologists analyze an MRI image and identification has been acknowledged as an important component of advancement and research with healthcare imaging, especially with the recent advancements in machine processing and mathematical methods [3]. Numerous studies showed that using computers for clinical image analysis was possible, because the work got little attention, probably because of the absence of processing power and high-quality digital MRI data. The disease only impacted a restricted number of people in its early stages. When most instances were resolved, it did not pose risks of such a vast magnitude. The virus is lethal for two main reasons: first, it is new and there are currently no vaccines for it; second, it is rapidly spread by either initial or subsequent contact with an infected person [4].

State agencies and government agencies worldwide have been forced to implement non-compromising confinement to enforce social distancing for the management of the sickness, as the number of instances newly notified every day continues to increase, rising at a rapid rate. To lower mortality rates, the general public in every nation has been made aware of the need to respond and seek treatment as soon as possible. This presumption, meanwhile, is very optimistic and might not hold in reality [5]. According to earlier research, the test error typically rises in direct proportion to the variation in distribution among the training and testing datasets. Medicinal imaging labeling is usually expensive, lengthy, and demanding, but includes the involvement of radiologists, doctors, and other specialists. Reusing models that were previously trained for a few related categories is an obvious strategy. These were the first initiatives to thoroughly examine domain adaptability techniques for multi-site, multiple modalities imaging information analysis [6]. The research objective is to employ sophisticated frameworks to increase the accuracy and efficiency of healthcare image processing for the detection of anomalies, such as brain tumors.

Organization of the research: The remaining parts are separated into multiple sections: Section 8.2 comprises the related work; Section 8.3 depicts the proposed methodology; Section 8.4 offers the results; Section 8.5 depicts the discussion, and Section 8.6 offers the conclusion.

8.2 Related Work

The category shift issue, which arises from disparate proportions between source data and destination data, typically plagues ML approaches used in computer-assisted analysis of medical images. Research [7] suggested the most recent developments in domain adaptation techniques for analyzing medical images. Additionally, they offer a concise overview of the standard medical image datasets that underpin ongoing studies on domain adaptability. Thanks to this assessment, researchers will be more qualified to comprehend the state, difficulties, and potential paths of the dynamic field of research. Imagery analysis due to the transformer architecture's outstanding performance in handling natural languages [8]. Several medical imaging analysis tasks, such as categorization, differentiation, detection, enrollment, manufacturing, and medical report creation, specifically offer a comprehensive and methodical overview of pertinent contemporary technological literature. They look at the uniqueness, advantages, and disadvantages of the various suggested approaches for each of these uses and create taxonomies that emphasize important characteristics and contributions.

On several medical detection tasks, methods using DL have proven to be highly successful and have even surpassed human experts in certain cases. However, the techniques' clinical application has been limited due to their black-box character. The goal of recent explication research [9] is to highlight the characteristics that most affect a model's choice. Most assessments of research in this field have concentrated on the need for rationales, ethics, and classifications. Research discusses the different methods, clinical implementation issues, and topics that need more investigation from the perspective of an ML researcher, who is creating a system for professional consumers. Medical diagnoses are revolutionized. Deep learning's diagnostic precision is unclear, nevertheless. The purpose [10] was to examine the predictive accuracy of when DL techniques for detecting disease in imaging studies from other specialties were considered. Presented were published studies that discussed how well DL algorithms detect pathology through imaging procedures. Measures related to research design, diagnostic accuracy, and reporting guidelines in the published works were the main results. There was significant variety in technique, language, and evaluation criteria, and there was a high degree of variability among the studies.

Artificial intelligence must not worsen nor spread healthcare inequities as it quickly surpasses human-level effectiveness in imaging applications. The research [11] included information from six global chest X-ray databases and spans three important medical imaging specialties: radiography, dermatology, and physician. Verified human demographic shortcuts are used by medical imaging AI to classify diseases. The research highlights important factors for AI clinical implementations across individuals and sites by establishing recommendations for MRI image processing models that preserve their abilities and fairness in installations outside of their original training environments. Large graphs with labels are necessary for the supervised development of DL networks. Getting such datasets for applications involving medical image processing is becoming more popular [12]. Recent research has demonstrated that label distortion can have a major effect on deep computational models' efficacy across a variety of image processing and ML settings. To mitigate the impact of various forms of label distortion on advanced models trained for healthcare image interpretation, techniques have been proposed.

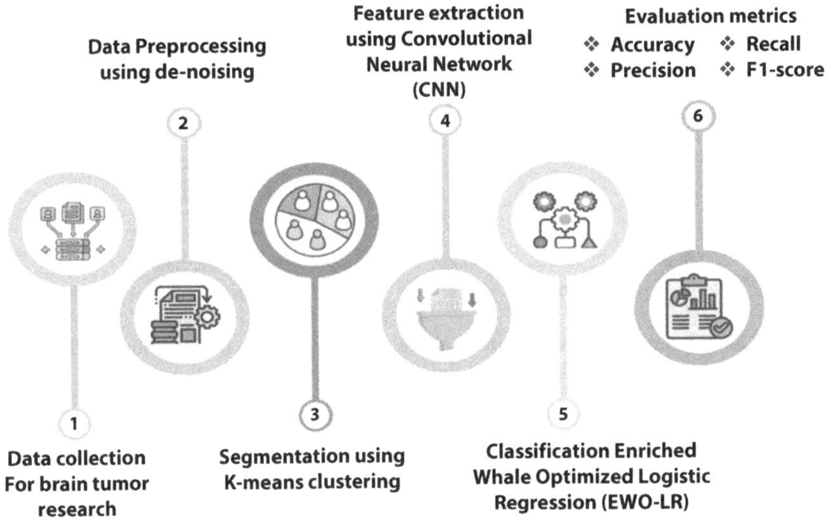

Figure 8.1 The methodology flow. (Source: Own elaboration).

8.3 Methodology

To understand and improve medical images, such as MRI scans, sophisticated computational techniques are applied as part of the approach for healthcare MRI image processing and evaluation. For a precise diagnosis, ML techniques are applied after pretreatment processes like eliminating noise and extraction of characteristics. Enhancing the effectiveness and precision of identifying anomalies, like brain tumors, is intended to enhance outcomes for patients and treatment plans, as shown in Figure 8.1.

8.3.1 Data Collection

The dataset was collected from the open source Kaggle websites: https://www.kaggle.com/datasets/mhantor/mri-based-brain-tumor-images, which consists of 400 MRIs and are arranged into a single folder called Brain Tumor Images. It has two subdivisions for each image type, Normal (170 MRI) and Tumor (230 MRI). These techniques use medical photos to identify and categorize human illnesses, as shown in Figure 8.2.

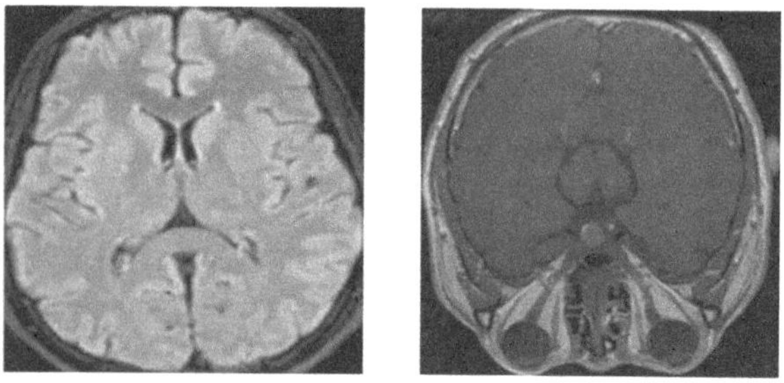

(a) Normal (b) Tumor

Figure 8.2 Difference between the normal brain and one with a tumor. (Source: https://www.kaggle.com/datasets/mhantor/mri-based-brain-tumor-images).

8.3.2 Data Preprocessing Using Denoising

There are many different applications for image denoising filters, such as information removal, radio space science, and medical images analysis. Each application has unique requirements. Finding lines, points, and edges essentially requires noise-free MRI images. Two general filters that are available in the realm of image preparation are smoothness and focusing. Images have high-frequency components. Smoothing techniques and filters play a crucial role in reducing those high vibrations. The sharing filters are used to improve or identify images edges by smoothing low-frequency images. Techniques for MRI image restoration and enhancement can be divided into two categories: frequency domain and territorial domain. Usually, this arrangement is made in response to an image's shifting Fourier conversion. Compared to the spatial category, noise evacuation in the audio frequency domain is confusing. Less time is required for spatially distributed noise expulsion. Algorithms for noise removal should protect the margins and provide a reasonable amount of noise removal.

8.3.3 Image Segmentation Using k-Means Clustering

A popular technique for dividing data into significant categories is grouping, which can be used to find connections or patterns in brain tumor MRI medical imaging. The k-means clustering technique, which separates a collection of medical images data into k-different clusters, according to comparison, has become one of the most often used clustering approaches. Each data point gets allocated to the region whose central point is farthest to it in the following step of the k-means approach, which first determines the k, the role of center points of all the information points, which constitute the exact middle of each grouping. A popular method for calculating how points close data are to center points is the Euclidean distance. This method is frequently used in healthcare settings for separating regions that are relevant in imaging techniques like MRI scans, allowing for continuous situation analysis and identification. To discover areas of significance like tumors or to find regions with aberrant tissue, medical MRI images can be divided into different groups based on similarity using clustering methods like k-means in medical processing of images and evaluation. The algorithm calculates each cluster's average when the initial categorization is complete. The Euclidean distance between the iteration and every data point (image pixel or region of attention) is calculated for every new centroid. The cluster whose geographic center optimizes the Euclidean distance is given the points back. To guarantee that each cluster has been identified by its member elements and their corresponding centroid, this repeated process is carried out until confluence. By reducing the distance between $w \times z$ images components and the associated centroids, $o(w,z)$ this technique can be used in medical imaging to segment areas such as tumors, tissues, or structures, facilitating the automated identification and analysis of a variety of disorders as denoted in Equations 8.1 and 8.2.

$$c = \left\| o(w,z) - d_l \right\| \tag{8.1}$$

$$d_l = \frac{1}{l} \sum\nolimits_{z \in d_l} \sum\nolimits_{w \in d_l} o(w,z) \tag{8.2}$$

K-means has certain disadvantages despite its significant benefit of being simple to use. The arbitrary choice of the starting centroid determines the level of quality of the final grouping results. Therefore, various initial centers will yield different results if the original centroid is picked at random. Thus, the first center will be packed with care to obtain the segmentation. When developing the K-means aggregation, the computational difficulty must be considered. The quantity of data items, clusters, and iterations all play a role.

8.3.4 Feature Extraction Using a Convolutional Neural Network

It serves as information allowing automated interpretation of medical imaging, including MRI examinations. The weights and biases of the clusters of the convolution are originally established before the CNN is programmed from beginning to end using gradient descent as the approach. The forward propagation is used with the set of targets to produce the output, P, during the training phase. The error, F, is computed by comparing the output with the fundamental truth labels, z. The distinction between the expected output and the labels themselves is used to calculate the accuracy given the sample collection of M images and d classifications. The CNN can learn and become more adept at identifying and categorizing anomalies, like growths or organ deviations, in medical MRI images by using this error to modify the weights as needed as denoted in Equation 8.3.

$$F^M = \frac{1}{2}\left\|z^M - P^M\right\|^2 = \frac{1}{2}\sum_{m=1}^{M}\sum_{l=1}^{d}(z_l^m - P_l^m)^2 \tag{8.3}$$

It evaluates the error value, F, to determine whether the representation has converged. The training phase is deemed finished if the error is substantially reduced, signifying that the prediction has converged. If not, the amount of correction required is computed using the final result's residual δ. The residual is calculated using an activated function e, such as the sigmoid function. The sigmoid functions convert the network's output into an estimate of the probability range, which is frequently employed in clinical image analysis tasks like binary detection. Through this iterative procedure, the CNN can enhance its ability to accurately identify medical diseases, such as tumors or abnormalities, in imaging studies by fine-tuning its default settings, as denoted in Equation 8.4.

$$\delta^K = \frac{\delta}{\delta z_m^K}\frac{1}{2}\left\|z^M - P^M\right\|^2 = -(z^M - P^M).e'(z^K) \tag{8.4}$$

After passing the remainders from the outcome degree to the initial layer, the residual in each layer is computed using Equation 8.3, where $\delta^{(k)}$ represents the kth layer's differential, as denoted in Equation 8.5.

$$\delta^{(k)} = \left(\left(X^{(k)}\right)^S \delta^{(k+1)}.e'(z^K)\right) \tag{8.5}$$

The development rate α is used to update individual layer's parameters and skew, as denoted in Equation 8.6.

$$X^{(k)} = X^{(k)} - \alpha \frac{\partial}{\partial X^{(k)}} F(\omega,a) = X^{(k)} - \alpha.\delta^{(k+1)}\left(b^{(k)}\right)^S$$

$$a_j^{(k)} = a_j^k - \alpha.\frac{\partial}{\partial X^{(k)}} F(\omega,a) = a_j^k - \alpha.\delta^{(k+1)} \tag{8.6}$$

The CNN follows the aforementioned procedure until it achieves the desired outcome. Additionally, throughout the training process, the CNN sends the characteristic vector to itself for confirmation. However, the CNN functions as a classifier throughout the evaluation stage, which is distinct from how it does during the training phase.

8.3.5 Medical Image Processing and Analysis Using Enriched Whale-Optimized Logistic Regression

Medical image processing and analysis utilizing Enriched Whale Optimized Logistic Regression (EWO-LR) integrates logistic regression (LR) for efficient identification with the capabilities of the Whale Optimization Algorithm (WOA) for choosing features and optimizing variables. By refining the features taken from medical images, the hybrid model improves accuracy and makes it possible to diagnose disorders like masses or injuries more accurately. Early identification and mechanized diagnosis of illnesses are made possible by LR's higher accuracy in classifying healthcare MRI images based on pertinent features, which is achieved by utilizing WOA's global search capacity.

8.3.5.1 Logistic Regression

Logistic regression is a popular statistical approach in medical analysis for categorizing medical images and identifying anomalies or illnesses. It offers a straightforward, efficient approach to binary categorization challenges by examining characteristics that have been retrieved from MRI images, facilitating computerized diagnosis, and making choices. The LR model is popular for its effective computing and strong medical picture classification capabilities. Logistic regression works especially well for applications like spotting anomalies in medical images, including tumors and abscesses. The following formula is used in the LR technique to determine a class's recommendation based on the features that were taken from healthcare images. Because of its computational capacity, the LR model is tuned to perform better, which makes it a useful tool for computerized medical evaluation and imaging-related decision-making, as denoted in Equation 8.7.

$$o\left(Z = spam\left|\overrightarrow{W}_j\right.\right) = \frac{exp(\overrightarrow{W}_j \cdot \vec{X})}{1 + exp(\overrightarrow{W}_j \cdot \vec{X})} = \frac{f^{\Sigma x_i W_{j,i}}}{1 + f^{\Sigma x_i W_{j,i}}} \tag{8.7}$$

Where $\overrightarrow{W}_j$ is the matching weight and $\overrightarrow{W}_j = \{W_{j,1}, W_{j,2}, \ldots, W_{j,m}\}$ is the vector representing the message's characteristics. The value of $(\overrightarrow{W}_j \cdot \vec{X})$ can be transformed from $-\infty$ $to + \infty$ to a possibility between 0 and 1 using Equation 8.1. If this likelihood exceeds a certain cutoff point, such as 0.5 in the research, the forecast is that the communication is junk; if not, it is forecasted that it is ham, as denoted in Equation 8.8.

$$x_i = x_i + (z_j - o) \times w_{ji} \times rate \tag{8.8}$$

Where z_j is the diamond judgment of w_j and rate is the educational rate or learning efficiency. To increase the precision of medical MRI image categorization, the system's efficacy in tasks like organ categorization, recognizing illnesses, and anomaly identification can be improved and its predictions refined by conditioning on these crucial samples, which would increase the overall accuracy of diagnosis.

8.3.5.2 Enriched Whale Optimized

By streamlining the feature identification and classification procedures in medical image and evaluation, the EWO improves upon the conventional Whale Optimization mechanism. This method increases the precision and effectiveness of identifying and diagnosing illnesses using intricate imaging data, including anomalies and tumors. The suggested method, EWO, is a hybrid strategy that improves the exploration compromise in medical MRI image processing and evaluation by integrating the EWO with the differential evolution modification operator. To maximize choosing and categorizing features in medical images, the primary user of EWO combines the alteration of the differential evolution with the elements of WOA, including surrounding prey, identifying prey, and circular position updates. To increase effectiveness on tasks like recognizing tumors and organ identification in medical images, the technique adjusts those involved during the exploratory stage when $rand < \lambda$. This is done by adjusting λ by Equation 8.9.

$$\lambda = 1 - \frac{s}{s_{max}} \tag{8.9}$$

The current generation is represented by the parameter λ, while the greatest amount of generations is indicated by s_{max}. The EWO's capacity for prospecting and mining is managed by the value of λ. Equation 8.8 states that λ decreases from $1 \text{ to } 0$ over time, permitting the algorithm to concentrate on exploring the first several generations, where it looks for the best characteristics over a wide area. As the generations, the emphasis turns to exploitation, improving the chosen features for exacting applications, such as organ differentiation, recognizing tumors, or illness categorization in medical imaging.

$$W_j(i) = \begin{cases} \delta_i + rndreal(0,1) \times (\mu_i - \delta_i) \; if \; W_j(i) < \delta_i \\ \mu_i - rndreal(0,1) \times (\mu_i - \delta_i) \; if \; W_j(i) < \mu_i \end{cases} \tag{8.10}$$

Specifically, the fitter position connecting parent W_j and descendant U_i is the first one established for i^{th} every person in the following generation. It is crucial to remember that boundary restrictions should be taken into account in solutions. The mending rule is used by Equation 8.10, if these restrictions are broken. The upper and lower bounds of the ith dimensional are denoted by δ_i and μ_i, accordingly. The jth component of the ith solution is denoted by $W_j(i)$. A selection of numbers from 0 and 1 is denoted by $rndreal(0,1)$.

8.4 Result

To effectively handle better quality of medical image datasets, the experimental setup for medical image transmission and analysis usually entails a system with Intel core 16–32 GB of RAM. In computationally challenging workflows, this guarantees seamless processing for jobs like separating features, segmentation, and categorization. Comparing the suggested method EWO-LR with existing approaches such as a support vector machine (SVM) [13] and the Visual Geometry Group 19-layer (VGG-19) [14] with

Table 8.1 Result of the accuracy, precision, recall, and F1-score.

Methods	Accuracy (%)	Precision (%)	Recall (%)	F1-score (%)
Support vector machine [13]	96.8	97.5	95.12	96.29
Visual Geometry Group 19-layer [14]	98.8	98.2	96.8	97.5
Enriched Whale Optimized Logistic Regression [Proposed]	98.98	98.45	97.12	97.75

the parameters of accuracy, precision, recall, and F1-score, as shown in Table 8.1.

Accuracy: The percentage of accurate diagnoses or deviations, like brain tumor identification, relative to the overall number of cases evaluated, is known as accuracy in healthcare MRI image processing and evaluation. It shows how well an algorithm or system minimizes misleading positives and negatives while accurately classifying images related to medicine. For healthcare, ensuring environments are accurate and dependable with healthcare decisions and high precision is essential. Table 8.1 and Figure 8.3 show the technique compared to traditional methods, such as SVM (96.8%) and VGG-19 (98.8%). The proposed method, EWO-LR, was 98.98% higher than the existing method.

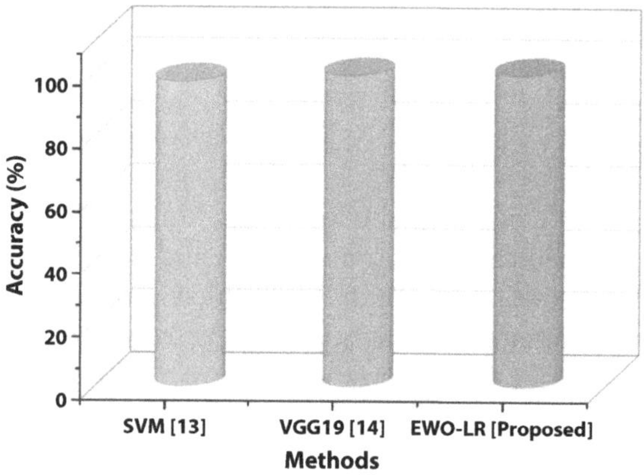

Figure 8.3 The outcome of the accuracy. (Source: Own elaboration).

Precision: The percentage of true beneficial tumor identifications among all cases the simulation identifies as positive is known as precision. It assesses how well the algorithm detects tumor locations without producing false positive results. Reduced incorrect categorization of non-tumor regions as tumors is a sign of high precision. Figure 8.4 and Table 8.1 illustrate the precision result. The proposal was EWO-LR (98.45%) scored higher than the existing methods, such as SVM (97.5%) and VGG-19 (98.2%).

Recall: The term recall describes a model's capacity to accurately recognize every pertinent incidence of a health issue, such as brain tumors in MRI images. It calculates the percentage of real positive cases, like tumors, that the program accurately detects. Precisely detecting essential situations is ensured by a higher recall, which denotes fewer incorrect results. Figure 8.5 and Table 8.1 illustrate the recall result. The proposal was EWO-LR (97.12%) scored higher than the existing methods, such as SVM (95.12%) and VGG-19 (96.8%).

8.4.1 F1-Score

A performance measure that strikes a balance between recall and accuracy is the F1-score. It is a single number that represents both exactness and the reliability of optimistic predictions, and recall, or the capacity to recognize all positive cases. The model successfully recognizes and categorizes pertinent clinical MRI images, such as recognizing brain tumors when the F1-score is high. Table 8.1 and Figure 8.6 show the technique compared

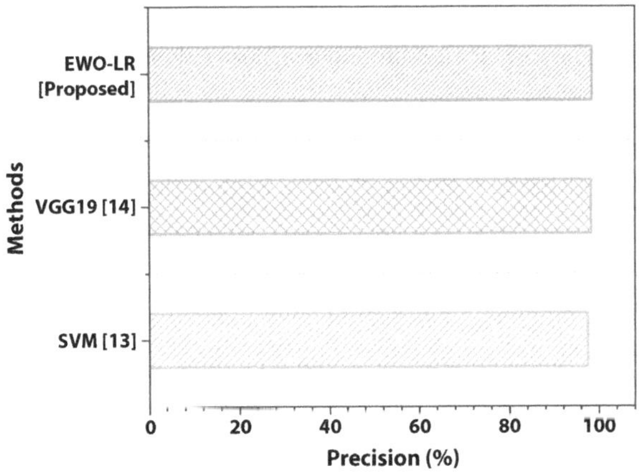

Figure 8.4 The outcome of the precision. (Source: Own elaboration).

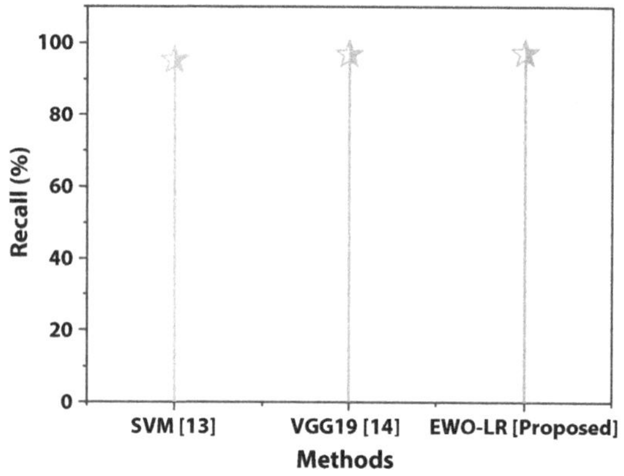

Figure 8.5 The outcome of the recall. (Source: Own elaboration).

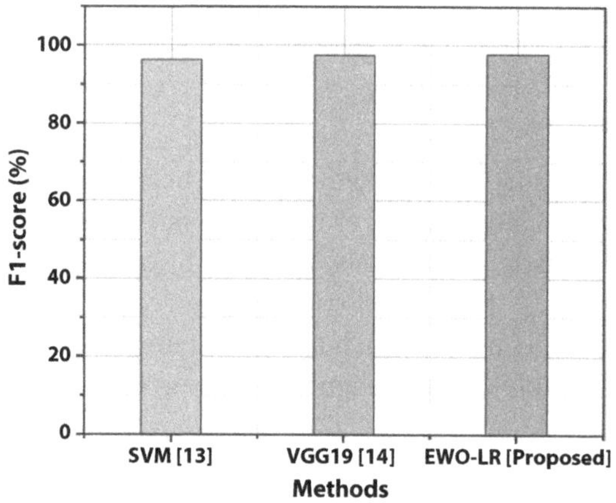

Figure 8.6 The outcome of the F1-score. (Source: Own elaboration).

to traditional methods, such as SVM (96.29%) and VGG-19 (97.5%). The proposed method EWO-LR was 97.75%, higher than the existing method.

8.5 Discussion

The medical MRI processing existing techniques like SVM and VGG-19 contain a limitation. Although SVM works well for linear separability, it has trouble with the high-dimensional, complicated datasets found in medical imaging, which frequently results in less than ideal accuracy and recall because it cannot identify complex patterns. The applicability of VGG-19 to a variety of medical image settings is limited by its computational complexity and propensity for overfitting, especially when working with smaller datasets, despite its sophisticated architecture and improved feature extraction capabilities. By utilizing an optimization-based logistic regression technique, which guarantees accurate feature selection and improved model generalization, the suggested EWO-LR overcomes these drawbacks. The EWO-LR is more suited for dependable and scalable clinical MRI image analysis because of its strong optimization framework, which manages complicated datasets and reduces overfitting.

8.6 Conclusion

The accuracy and effectiveness of early diagnosis and treatment planning have been greatly improved by medical image processing and examination, which has become a vital tool in contemporary healthcare. It makes it possible to precisely identify anomalies, such as brain tumors, in clinical imaging technologies, like CT and MRI scans, by using advanced algorithms like image preparation, removing features, and data mining. Incorporating potent models, such as CNNs and VGG 19, has demonstrated encouraging outcomes when automating and enhancing diagnostic procedures, giving medical practitioners important information for immediate action. Compared to the suggested method, EWO-LR was higher than the existing method with the parameters of accuracy (98.98%), precision (98.45%), recall (97.12%), and F1-score (97.75%). To process and analyze medical images in the future, algorithms must be progressively improved to handle bigger, more varied datasets, improve model accessibility, and lessen the dependence on black-box simulations. Diagnostic precision can be greatly increased by using heterogeneous data and investigating cutting-edge methods like explainable AI. Individualized and effective medical services will also be made possible by immediate analysis and implementation in clinical settings.

References

1. Pellico, J., *et al.*, Radiolabelling of nanomaterials for medical imaging and therapy. *Chem. Soc.*, 5, 3355–34235, 2021, https://doi.org/10.1039/D0CS00384K.

2. Chen, X., *et al.*, Recent advances and clinical applications of deep learning in medical image analysis. *Med. Image Anal.*, 79, 102444, 2022, https://doi.org/10.1016/j.media.2022.102444.
3. Chan, H.-P., *et al.*, Deep learning in medical image analysis, in: *Deep Learning in Medical Image Analysis: Challenges and Applications*, pp. 3–21, 2020, https://doi.org/10.1007/978-3-030-33128-3_1.
4. Ma, X., *et al.*, Understanding adversarial attacks on deep learning based medical image analysis systems. *Pattern Recognit.*, 110, 1073325, 2021, https://doi.org/10.1016/j.patcog.2020.107332.
5. Castiglioni, I., *et al.*, AI applications to medical images: From machine learning to deep learning. *Physica Med.*, 83, 9–245, 2021, https://doi.org/10.1016/j.ejmp.2021.02.006.
6. Kaissis, G., *et al.*, End-to-end privacy-preserving deep learning on multi-institutional medical imaging. *Nat. Mach. Intell.*, 3, 6, 473–484, 2021, https://doi.org/10.1038/s42256-021-00337-8.
7. Elhoseny, M., *et al.*, Hybrid optimization with cryptography encryption for medical image security in Internet of Things. *Neural Comput. Appl.*, 32, 10979–1099355, 2020, https://doi.org/10.1109/TNNLS.2020.2995319.
8. Mongan, J., *et al.*, Checklist for artificial intelligence in medical imaging (CLAIM): a guide for authors. *Radiol. Artif. Intell.*, 2, 2, e200029, 2020, https://doi.org/10.1148/ryai.2020200029.
9. Singh, A., *et al.*, Explainable deep learning models in medical image analysis. *J. Imaging*, 6, 525, 2020, https://doi.org/10.3390/jimaging6060052.
10. Aggarwal, R., *et al.*, Diagnostic accuracy of deep learning in medical imaging: a systematic review and meta-analysis. *npj Digit. Med.*, 4, 65, 2021, https://doi.org/10.1038/s41746-021-00438-z.
11. Yang, Y., *et al.*, The limits of fair medical imaging AI in real-world generalization. *Nat. Med.*, 30, 2838–2848, 2024, https://doi.org/10.1038/s41591-024-03113-4.
12. Karimi, D., *et al.*, Deep learning with noisy labels: Exploring techniques and remedies in medical image analysis. *Med. Image Anal.*, 65, 1017595, 2020, https://doi.org/10.1016/j.media.2020.101759.
13. Nanmaran, R., *et al.*, Investigating the role of image fusion in brain tumor classification models based on machine learning algorithm for personalized medicine, in: *Computational and Mathematical Methods in Medicine*, p. 7137524, 2022, https://doi.org/10.1155/2022/7137524.
14. Nagaraju, G., *et al.*, A Comparative Analysis of Advanced Machine Learning Techniques for Enhancing Brain Tumor Detection. *J. Electr. Syst.*, 20, 2s, 901–909, 2024, https://creativecommons.org/licenses/by/4.0/legalcode.

9

Genomic and Proteomic Data Analysis for Population Health

Roja Lakshmi Karri[1*], Anand Prakash[2], Suman Sau[3], Subbulakshmi Ganesan[4], Jayshree Nellore[5] and Shweta Singh[6]

[1]*MDS Oral Pathology, GSL Dental College & Hospital, Andhra Pradesh, India*
[2]*Department of Computer Science and Engineering, Presidency University, Bangalore, Karnataka, India*
[3]*Department of Computer Science and Information Technology, Siksha 'O' Anusandhan (Deemed to be University), Bhubaneswar, Odisha, India*
[4]*Department of Chemistry and Biochemistry, Jain (Deemed-to-be University), Bangalore, Karnataka, India*
[5]*Department of Biotechnology, Sathyabama Institute of Science and Technology, Chennai, Tamil Nadu, India*
[6]*Maharishi School of Engineering & Technology, Maharishi University of Information Technology, Uttar Pradesh, India*

Abstract
The integration of genomic and proteomic data is crucial for advancing the understanding of biological systems and improving healthcare outcomes. Genomics involves analyzing DNA sequences to uncover genetic variations, with the Human Genome Project providing key insights into human genetic variation, vital for understanding diseases and individual treatment responses. Proteomics focuses on protein structure and function, identifying biomarkers and therapeutic targets. New developments in throughput technology involving the acquisition of large amounts of genomic and proteomic data require the use of sophisticated management techniques. Differences between nucleic acid and protein databases highlight

**Corresponding author*: dr.rojalakshmi@gmail.com; ORCID: https://orcid.org/0000-0002-0264-9087?lang=en
Suman Sau: ORCID: 0009-0009-9362-347X
Subbulakshmi Ganesan: ORCID: 0000-0002-8345-116X
Jayshree Nellore: ORCID: https://orcid.org/0000-0002 2024-1093
Shweta Singh: ORCID: 0000-0001-54589269

Satya Prakash Yadav, Abhay Bansal and Victor Hugo C. de Albuquerque (eds.) Computational Intelligence in Biomedical Internet of Medical Things, (143–160) © 2026 Scrivener Publishing LLC

a requirement for specialized tools to handle unique aspects of their structure and function. Moreover, non-standard data, mostly unstructured, pose challenges in both integration and processing, including interpretation, thereby requiring advanced solutions for challenges in processing, interpreting, and maintaining metadata. Annotation and ontology are crucial for precise data representation, and integrating data from various related databases is vital for comprehensive analysis. The solutions to address these challenges necessitate a uniform set of data management solutions to handle complex queries, provide proper data synthesis, and maintain high-quality metadata, driving the further progress of personalized medicine and optimizing the interpretation and utility of genomic and proteomic data.

***Keywords*:** Proteomic, genomic, DNA, data, proteomic data

9.1 Introduction

Health refers to the general welfare of an individual, which encompasses a person's mental, social, and physical aspects; it includes the ability to function well and adapt to many challenges. Good health is maintained by the need for proper nutrition, regular physical activity, mental hardness, and preventive care [1]. This infrastructure is used for population health surveillance, healthcare delivery, health-related studies, and personal health management. Teleradiology and telemedicine services have made it more convenient for the rural and urban population to seek healthcare services. One can also utilize apps like Apple Health to manage their health [2]. Through treatments, policies, and the discovery of health inequities, it focuses on comprehending and enhancing community health. The study of an organism's whole collection of genes and how each gene works is known as genomics [3]. To comprehend genetic differences, transmission, and the ways genes affect characteristics, health, and illness, it entails examining the deoxyribonucleic acid (DNA) sequence. Genomics is crucial in fields like medicine, agriculture, and evolutionary biology, offering insights into personalized treatments, disease prevention, and genetic disorders [4]. Sequencing is one of the tools that genomics uses to unravel the devices of living organisms. Annotations and genome sequences are considered critical resource components of many genome-related projects, including different omics data analysis [5]. The development of next-generation sequencing (NGS) technology over the last few decades has made it possible to examine genomes in a high-throughput, cost-effective, and speedy manner [6]. Proteomics is defined as large-scale of proteins that have a significant and indispensable function in biological processes as performers of tasks in cells. Proteomics is a scientific method used to study individual protein components, their structures, location, activities, and properties to integrate and determine their contribution to biological life and disease [7]. In the proteome, researchers can uncover biomarkers for diseases, discover therapeutic targets, and gain insights into cellular mechanisms. Proteomics is a vital field for advancing personalized medicine and biotechnology [8]. The first high-throughput protein analysis was accomplished with protein array techniques that used prepackaged chips with predetermined protein detection [9]. In proteomics, the quantification of all protein identity and abundance in a sample allows for quicker, more accurate, sensitive, and efficient protein identification. Understanding how genetic and protein-based variables influence health outcomes in a variety of populations through the examination of genomic and proteomic data [10].

Genomic data reveals genetic variations linked to diseases, while proteomic data provides insights into how these variations manifest at the protein level, influencing biological processes [11]. This combined approach enhances the understanding of health disparities, disease prevention, and personalized treatments. Ultimately, genomic and proteomic data analysis in population health aims to improve overall well-being and inform public health policies [12]. The objective is to explore how genomic and proteomic data can be integrated to enhance understanding of population health. It is to identify biomarkers, disease mechanisms, and potential therapeutic targets for improving public health outcomes.

9.2 Methodology

This study combines genomic and proteomic data from a variety of populace health cohorts using advanced bioinformatics tools, data explanation, and ontology-based outlines to determine genetic difference and protein indicators connected with health results [13].

9.2.1 Genomes

The genome of an organism is the entire set of genetic code, represented in its cells. This genetic information is coded in nucleotides, consisting of four bases that represent cytosine, adenine, guanine, and thymine. The nucleotides are arranged in the shape of a double helix. Proteins are made from sequences of unique 20 amino acids, created into very complex 3D structures to perform key functions within the cell. However, the flow of genetic information in a cell is from DNA through RNA to protein [14]. To comprehend protein evolution, mechanistic knowledge is required, including precise models of transcription initiation and termination, as well as the role of the genome in transcription. Analyzing signal transduction pathways, along with creating models of alternative RNA splicing, is required, as well for understanding protein speciation. The task is currently challenging to predict precisely because the structure of a protein involves with intricate interactions. By comparing and reconstructing the sequences, the earliest stages of evolution are hereby revealed to solve the complexity of cellular activities, transcription, and translation [15]. Table 9.1 illustrates the database of genomes.

9.2.2 Proteomic

The characteristics of proteomics differ from more conventional approaches to protein study due to its comprehensiveness, scope, and philosophical attitude. Instead of thoroughly characterizing each component individually, protein identification utilizing mass spectrometric analysis can swiftly identify many proteins in each combination by comparing the observed patterns to those predicted in the genome. Structural proteomics is a branch of proteomics that focuses on 3D structures of proteins in data-driven projects rather than the details of a single protein [16].

9.2.3 Sequence of Important DNA

It is essential to accurately model the DNA double-stranded helix's 3D structure. It quickly became clear that the genetic data contained in DNA was discrete and limited. A complete understanding of the genetic information passed down from one generation to the next can be achieved by determining, or DNA sequencing, the precise configuration of the four centers in each organism's DNA strands. These bases form the foundation of the genetic code, which dictates the synthesis of proteins and regulates the biological functions within a cell. By deciphering the sequence of these bases, scientists can gain insights into the hereditary traits of organisms, understand genetic variations, and explore how these variations influence health, development, and disease [17]. The effective ways to use these augmented examples of genetic fragments are to figure out the DNA base arrangement and publish the full sequence of certain tiny viral genomes. The field of molecular genetics study was focused on identifying and separating certain genes of interest from the DNA of specific organisms [18].

9.3 Human Genome Project

Human sequencing did not start the Human Genome Project right away, as the National Study Council study had envisioned. Rather, the initiative

Table 9.1 Database of genomes.

Database	**Format**	**Size**
Nucleotide structure		
Nucleic acid database (NDB)	mmCIF and Protein Data Bank (PDB) format	NDB covers 3,557 Structures
Nucleotide databases		
Genbank	Abstract Syntax Notation 1 syntax (ASN.1)	GenBank covers the entries of 61,132,599
Family databases and protein domain, motif		
Prosite (ExPASy)	Prosite is an ASCII text file. That file can be read by a computer. Textual information is contained in Prosite.doc.	1,489 documentation entries
Blocks database	The Blocks database's data files are distributed as ASCII text files.	29,767 blocks, or 6,149 groups, are included in BLOCKS version 14.2
Interrelationship and protein structure databases		
Protein Data Bank	A variety of mmCIF data files	It contains 3,601 NMR restraint files, 27,984 structure factor files, and 45,506 molecular type files in total.
Structural classification of proteins (SCOP)	Hypertext documents that are tightly connected	There are 27,599 PDB entries

(*Continued*)

Table 9.1 Database of genomes. (*Continued*)

Database	Format	Size
Transcription factor databases		
Gene transcription factor database (TRANSFAC)	Flat folder format	9,621 factors included in TRANSFAC release 11.1.
Transcription regulatory regions database (TRRD)	Relational database	2,334 genes and 7,609 publications are included in the TRRD current release.
Specialized genomic databases		
MitoMap	ASN.1, Current: relational database.	Mitochondrial Genome: 16,569 nucleotides total per mitochondrion
Kyoto Encyclopedia of Genes and Genomes (KEGG)	Integration occurs at the level of data entries that are uniformly obtained through linkages across several databases.	56,987 pathways produced from 333 reference pathways.

aimed to construct infrastructure by means of various projects. Low-resolution maps of the human genome were created as part of these efforts, along with the investigation of alternate sequencing technologies and the modification of current technology to the easier task of sequencing smaller genomes of lab organisms [19].

Even the project's backers had rather different ideas about how to move forward. Many believed that the project would only become viable if entirely new sequencing techniques were developed that would be orders of magnitude quicker and less expensive than existing techniques [20]. This would reduce the amount of sequence required.

The human genetic map quickly became a framework, and it was much more detailed than expected. Circular DNA molecules, or vectors, were developed to convey ever-increasing volumes of DNA into bacteria and make it easier to physically map entire genomes. By adapting traditional

DNA sequencing techniques to highly automated machines, the world's capacity to sequence DNA has dramatically increased [7]. This led to the rapid production of the first bacterial genome, the first multicellular animal genome, and the first eukaryotic genome. Other issues were the difficulties in placing sequences of separate DNA fragments and then allocating each piece to a particular chromosomal site in the proper orientation and order. The change in approach was rejected following a heated discussion.

9.3.1 Human Genetic Variation

The analysis of DNA sequence variations is a key application of human genome data, which helps to understand individual differences and disease predispositions. As the human genome sequence has been published and genetic mapping advances, the identification of mutant genes responsible for genetic disorders has significantly increased. This progress enables more targeted approaches to diagnosing, preventing, and treating genetic diseases. Understanding these genetic variations holds the potential to revolutionize personalized medicine and improve human health [21].

Although creating new diagnostic tools has proven easier than using molecular insights to create alternative medicines, significant progress is being made. However, the increasing recognition that understanding the exact molecular structure of the genetic flaw or mutation can result in certain treatments that block the effects of the mutation indirectly is more hopeful [22].

These include the variations that underpin heritable variance across individuals for a vast array of characteristics, including skin and eye color. Additionally, genetically complex or multifactorial disorders arise from combinations of specific genetic variants within populations [23]. Comparative human genome sequencing is currently only being used by medical geneticists to characterize the common variants shared across groups and to comprehend the degree of genetic diversity.

To accomplish these goals, the scientific community will require freedom of operation, but there are worries that the numerous patents currently in place on genes and other parts of the human genome, together with the possibility of further ones, could hinder or even stop advancement [24]. Early-stage applications will probably be more negatively impacted.

9.3.2 The Significance of Protein Structure

A complete atomic description of the protein's 3D form can be obtained by computationally analyzing the diffraction pattern, or the spray of X-rays that emerges from the crystal [25]. Protein structures can be classified as first,

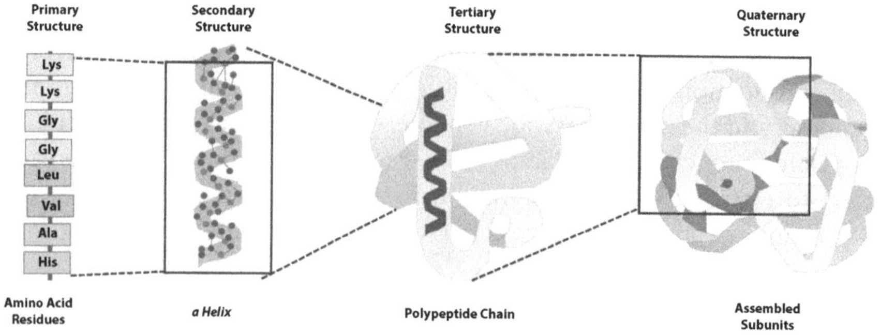

Figure 9.1 Types of protein structure. (Source: https://comis.med.uvm.edu/VIC/coursefiles/MD540/MD540-Protein_Organization_10400_574581210/Protein-org/Protein_Organization_print.html).

second, third, or quad. The series of amino acids connected by bonds called peptides, or polypeptide chains, is referred to as the main structure, which determines the protein's unique individuality. The secondary structure involves local folding into structures like beta sheets and alpha helices, stabilized by hydrogen bonds among amino acids. Quaternary structure is the 3D folding of the polypeptide chain into a specific shape, driven by interactions like hydrophobic interactions, ionic bonds, and disulfide bridges. The ability to design small-molecule medications to fit into protein regions that are responsible for biological functions is another significant practical benefit of understanding a protein's 3D structure [26]. Figure 9.1 shows the protein structure types.

9.3.3 Database

Numerous proteins offer valuable insights for researchers in cardiovascular medicine and other fields. This review provides an overview of various databases, focusing on their growth, content, and the differences between protein and nucleic acid database expansion [27]. It also explores the integration of proteomic and genomic databases. This integration enhances understanding of biological processes and aids in the development of targeted treatments.

9.3.4 Types of Databases

The distinction between the two main categories, protein and nucleic acid databases, is not entirely clear since there are numerous connections. Under the collaboration for the international nucleotide sequence database, a number of DNA sequence databases are arranged. It includes the

National Center for Biotechnology Information's base nucleotide library and the genetic data repository [28]. The Protein Information Resource (PIR), translation of DNA sequences in EMBL (TrEMBL), the PDB's 3D structures are examples of protein databases. The protein databases have grown at a more linear rate than the DNA databases.

9.3.5 Difference between Nucleic Acid and Protein Database

The most obvious tendency is growing disparity among the amount of information for proteins and DNA in addition to the remarkable surge in the amount of DNA order data that is publicly available. It is known that not every DNA sequence discovered will produce genes and, eventually, proteins [29]. The discrepancy between the number of putative genes and

Table 9.2 Database for nucleic acid and protein.

References	Type	Association	Explanations
[30]	Protein	Protein Data Bank	Global database of 3D macromolecular structure information
		ExPASy	An important source of information about proteins
[31]	Genomes	The Institute for Genome Study	Genome Sequencing Center
		Welcome Trust/ Medical Study Council	Genome Sequencing Center
[32]	Clustered ESTs	National Center for Biotechnology Information	A test method for automatically dividing GenBank sequences into a collection of gene-oriented clusters that are not duplicated
[33]	Peptide databases	-	Tools for using mass proteometry studies in conjunction with sequence database mining.

proteins and the amount of DNA sequence information will grow as more genomic sequence data becomes accessible. Table 9.2 shows the database of nucleic acid and protein.

Delineating the regions with features like exons and introns would be made easier with the help of annotation. There are multiple conceivable outputs from the analysis of the genetic sequence. The genomic segment might resemble a recognized gene that produces a certain protein. Even though this is the best result, given the amount of genes known, it is uncommon. Second, if the genomic fragment matches an expressed sequence tag, it provides details about some of the intron borders and possible open reading frames.

9.3.6 Developments in Throughput Technology

In addition to the importance of information databases, data is being sent at an ever-increasing pace due to the rapid advancement of technology. Although there has been a noticeable rise in throughput in the field of genomic sequencing, proteomics is also seeing significant advancements. Various technologies are also being investigated. Additionally, technologies that accelerate two-dimensional gel separation have been created. Some describe proteins by combining liquid chromatography and mass spectrometry. Figure 9.2 shows the genomic and proteomic data.

This method has the potential to improve protein analysis and throughput. Numerous modern technologies produce information such as the protein's fragment mass fingerprint or, in certain situations, the N-terminal amino acid sequence. A protein from a protein sequence database can be identified using these details [34]. The mass spectrometry community presently uses databases like PROWL that contain information about protein fragments.

9.4 Information Synthesis and Integration

It is an example of how proteomic and genomic data can be combined. The proteome databases are improved using anticipated genes, and annotated gene information from known putative protein identities can be determined from experimental data that provides primary sequence information, mass, and other factors regarding a particular protein.

These investigation spots are taken out of the gel, broken down, and then subjected to mass spectrometry analysis. Identifications are made by comparing protein remains from each location to a database of known protein remains [35]. Using metabolic pathway models, known proteins

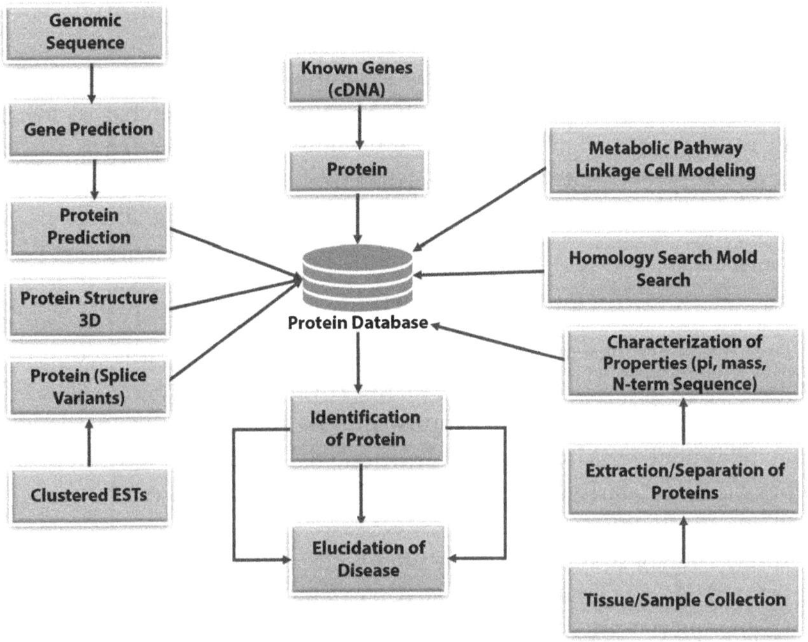

Figure 9.2 Incorporation of genomic and proteomic data. (Source: Own elaboration).

of interest might be mapped and their mechanisms of action clarified. By linking protein and gene information, it is possible to gain information on phenotypic or genetic markers that are useful for studying the disease process.

This information can be linked by using the internet wisely and by implementing program initiatives, such as the ones already mentioned. Technological developments are essential for analysis and boosting data throughput; the Internet and the World Wide Web (WWW) will remain vital for data distribution and resource connecting. Accurate databases of gene and protein knowledge combined with technological advancements will result in synergistic scientific progress.

9.4.1 Unstructured and Non-Standard Data

As demonstrated above, this data comprises sequence information for proteins, mRNA, DNA, and RNA. It is not apparent if each place in the sequence should be handled like a data item with surrounding information [36]. Current pattern search tools like BLAST and PSBLAST are used by scientists;

biological database management systems (DBMSs) must incorporate this feature.

In essence, chemical route databases are graphs with linkages that reflect various chemical reactions and events. Most traditional databases have little or no support for graph queries, especially recursive searches, and are difficult to express. Matrix-formatted data from microarray studies requires further processing for matrix operations, grouping, and classification.

9.4.2 Processing Complex Queries

The searches are typically complex, involving links and paths along connected data objects, as indicated in the features of biological data. The similarity between sequences, graphs, and 3D forms usually goes beyond what relational DBMSs and object-oriented DBMSs can query. In bioinformatics, similarity is a vague concept that depends on context and problem-specificity.

Today's database systems hardly offer recursive query processing, which is essential when graphical data is used, particularly in terms of paths. Graph matching queries are likewise extremely intricate and make use of homomorphism and isomorphism, among other features [37]. Subgraph matching looks for embedded subgraphs within a graph, while graph matching is often comparable to global sequence alignment. Another requirement for handling microarray or other data outputs is matrix multiplication.

9.4.3 Integration of Data from Various Related Databases

This highlighted the several databases that contain data on genes and proteins from living things, including humans. In the literature, specific species, such as E. coli, yeast, Creoleons, drosophila, or mice, have been extensively studied and reported [38]. The genomes of maize and rice have been the subject of extensive data collection in the botanical sector. With the current state of web link technology, it is impossible to obtain a comprehensive and consistent picture of the state of science on any one of these animals unless a scientist spends a significant amount of time using search engines and experiences the resulting frustration.

Although links and annotations allow biologists to navigate between databases, there are currently no standardized interfaces or data consolidation efforts in place that enable material to be accessible in an integrated manner by specific classification or context [39]. To serve a range of ambitious applications, as mentioned later, there is a great need to unify relevant heterogeneous data under a single standard border.

9.4.4 Needed Features vs Current Capabilities

Studies serve mostly as storage administrators, not making use of the sophisticated querying, transaction processing, concurrency control, and recovery features because biological databases are not meant for intensive transaction processing. The necessary subtyping and inheritance support is absent; for example, a gene mutation is subtyped into replacement, insertion, or deletion subtypes.

Subtyping and inheritance; for example, several of the aforementioned databases would require object-oriented DBMSs to handle complicated object structures. Using inheritance and encapsulation, it would be simple to identify characteristics, such as homologs, orthologs, and paralogs, and to capture the behavior of biological things [40]. For proteomic and genomic databases, the relational architecture is typically employed not because it is the most appropriate for the data but rather because of vendor support and the expected longevity of relational DBMSs in the market.

9.4.5 Key Areas of Focus for Data Management Study

The discussion above clarifies that solutions for managing biological data must be developed that go outside the capabilities of object-oriented and existing relational databases [41]. These solutions must be scalable and semantically capable enough to handle the features of biological information discussed in the previous section. Draw attention to the problems below. A few of these align with the previously mentioned.

9.4.6 Data Management Solutions

The objective is to provide more cost-effective and efficient techniques for identifying and classifying various genetic variations in each genome. It is particularly noteworthy since it will contribute to a better comprehension of genetic regulation. The focus has already started to move from gathering data to interpreting it, and it will only get bigger [42]. In the widely defined subject of bioinformatics, numerous public and private initiatives are currently focused on providing distributed data gathering, storage, and analysis, integrating data types, and providing consistent interfaces to complicated biological data sets. Reducing redundancy and improving quality through data curation requires cooperation to stop further chaos in the handling of raw data production and analysis [43].

9.4.7 Proteomic and Genomic Data Analysis

Proteomic and genomic data analysis have significantly contributed to the identification of disease-related biomarkers and genetic risk factors. The proteomic analysis focused on proteins related to diseases, though the genomic examination highlighted the detection of new illness associations and risk scores. The consequences of these educations provide critical insights into the advancement of precision medicine, with an increasing number of proteins and genes connected to illnesses being discovered each year. As seen in the data, the progress in both fields has been substantial, showing a dependable rise in the quantity of biomarkers, disease associations, and genomic loci studied, demonstrating the growing importance of these analyses in medical research. The discovery of novel biomarkers and genes offers potential for better investigative tools and more effective therapies. These results demonstrate the growing power of technologies in unravelling the complexities of human health and disease. Figure 9.3 displays proteomic data analysis results from 2020 to 2024. Figure 9.3 (a) signifies the total proteins analyzed; Figure 9.3 (b) diseases linked; and Figure 9.3 (c) denotes the number of new biomarkers discovered annually.

Figure 9.3 presents the proteomic data analysis results over five years, from 2020 to 2024. The number of proteins analyzed representation from 8,000 in 2020 to 25,000 in 2024, while the proteins linked to diseases increased significantly from 2,000 in 2020 to 10,000 in 2024. In relation to the new biomarkers discovered, the growth was notable, with 50 new biomarkers identified in 2020 and 200 by 2024. These results highlight the quickening progress in proteomics, with a greater number of proteins being examined and more biomarkers recognized each year.

Figure 9.4 highlights the steady growth in genomic study output over five years, with a marked growth in the total number of gene positions studied and

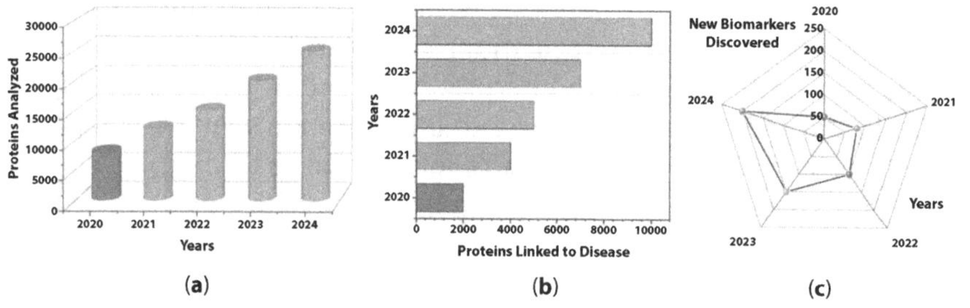

Figure 9.3 Proteomic data analysis results by year: (a) specifying total proteins, (b) diseases linked, and (c) the number of new biomarkers.

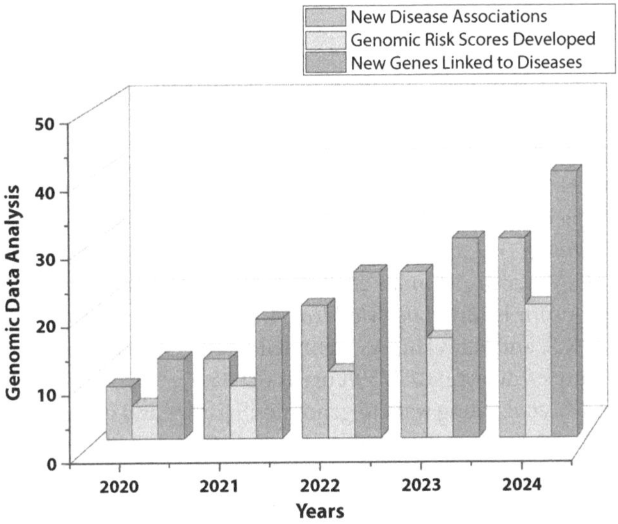

Figure 9.4 Genomic data analysis by year.

the discovery of new disease relations. By 2024, a total of 1,200 gene loci were studied, leading to the identification of 30 new disease associations and 40 new genes linked to diseases, underscoring the expanding depth of genomic study.

9.5 Conclusion

Genomics and proteomics advancements highlight the need for robust data management solutions to integrate diverse datasets, handle unstructured data, and support high-throughput technologies. Addressing these challenges will enable seamless synthesis and interpretation, driving meaningful biological discoveries. This review underlined the importance of genomic and proteomic progressions and highlighted the role of DNA sequencing, protein structure, and genetic variation in biological studies. Challenges persist in integrating diverse databases, managing unstructured data, and addressing metadata and query complexities, necessitating uniform data management solutions. Enhanced annotation, ontology, and synthesis capabilities are key to maximizing high-throughput technologies for seamless integration and influential discoveries. The future scope of this review includes further exploration of integrating genomic and proteomic data for personalized medicine. Additionally, advancing data management tools and improving sequencing technologies will enhance the understanding of complex biological systems.

References

1. Shao, T., *et al.*, Physical activity and nutritional influence on immune function: an important strategy to improve immunity and health status. *Front. Physiol.*, 12, 7513745, 2021, https://doi.org/10.3389/fphys.2021.751374.
2. Harahap, N.C., Handayani, P.W., Hidayanto, A.N., Functionalities and issues in the implementation of personal health records: systematic review. *J. Med. Internet Study*, 23, 7, e26236, 2021, https://doi.org/10.2196/26236.
3. Slavich, G.M., *et al.*, Human social genomics: Concepts, mechanisms, and implications for health. *Lifestyle Med.*, 4, 2, e75, 2023, 10.1002/lim2.75.
4. Vilhekar, R.S. and Rawekar, A., Artificial intelligence in genetics. *Cureus*, 16, 1, 2024, https://doi.org/10.7759/cureus.52035.
5. Giani, A.M., *et al.*, Long walk to genomics: History and current approaches to genome sequencing and assembly. *Comput. Struct. Biotechnol. J.*, 18, 9–195, 2020, https://doi.org/10.1016/j.csbj.2019.11.002.
6. Torrey, E.F., Did the human genome project affect study on Schizophrenia? *Psychiatry Study*, 333, 1156915, 2024, https://doi.org/10.1016/j.psychres.2023.115691.
7. Kwon, Y.W., *et al.*, Application of proteomics in cancer: recent trends and approaches for biomarkers discovery. *Front. Med.*, 8, 7473335, 2021, https://doi.org/10.3389/fmed.2021.747333.
8. Lill, J., *et al.*, Proteomics in the pharmaceutical and biotechnology industry: a look to the next decade. *Expert Rev. Proteomics*, 18, 7, 503–526, 2021, https://doi.org/10.1080/14789450.2021.1962300.
9. Javidanbardan, A., *et al.*, Microchromatography integrated with impedance sensor for bioprocess optimization: Experimental and numerical study of column efficiency for evaluation of scalability. *J. Chromatogr. A*, 1661, 4626785, 2022, https://doi.org/10.1016/j.chroma.2021.462678.
10. Carrasco-Zanini, J., *et al.*, Proteomic signatures improve risk prediction for common and rare diseases. *Nat. Med.*, 30, 9, 2489–2498, 2024, https://doi.org/10.1038/s41591-024-03142-z.
11. You, J., Guo, Y., *et al.*, Plasma proteomic profiles predict individual future health risk. *Nat. Commun.*, 14, 1, 7817, 2023, https://doi.org/10.1038/s41467-023-43575-7.
12. Pashayan, N., Antonis, C., *et al.*, Personalized early detection and prevention of breast cancer: ENVISION consensus statement. *Nat. Rev. Clin. Oncol.*, 17, 11, 687–705, 2020, https://doi.org/10.1038/s41571-020-0388-9.
13. Ogunjobi, T.T., *et al.*, Bioinformatics Applications in Chronic Diseases: A Comprehensive Review of Genomic, Transcriptomics, Proteomic, Metabolomics, and Machine Learning Approaches. *Medinformatics*, 2024, https://doi.org/10.47852/bonviewMEDIN42022335.
14. Huang, R. and Zhou, P.-K., DNA damage repair: historical perspectives, mechanistic pathways and clinical translation for targeted cancer therapy.

Signal Transduction Targeted Ther., 6, 1, 254, 2021, https://doi.org/10.1038/s41392-021-00648-7.

15. Wei, J., Chen, S., *et al.*, Protein–RNA interaction prediction with deep learning: structure matters. *Briefings Bioinf.*, 23, 1, bbab540, 2022, https://doi.org/10.1093/bib/bbab540.
16. Das, K. and Paital, B., Future call for policy making to speed up interdisciplinarity between natural and social sciences and humanities in countries such as India. *Heliyon*, 7, 3, 2021, https://doi.org/10.1016/j.heliyon.2021.e06484.
17. Warwick, T., *et al.*, A universal model of RNA. DNA: DNA triplex formation accurately predicts genome-wide RNA–DNA interactions. *Briefings Bioinf.*, 23, 6, bbac445, 2022, https://doi.org/10.1093/bib/bbac445.
18. Glick, B.R. and Patten, C.L., *Molecular biotechnology: principles and applications of recombinant DNA*, John Wiley & Sons, Hoboken, NJ, 2022, https://doi.org/10.1186/s43141-021-00231-1.
19. Bronkhorst, A.J., *et al.*, New perspectives on the importance of cell-free DNA biology. *Diagnostics*, 12, 9, 2147, 2022, https://doi.org/10.3390/diagnostics12092147.
20. Bostrom, N., Human genetic enhancements: a transhumanist perspective, in: *The ethics of sports technologies and human enhancement*, pp. 339–352, New York, NY: Routledge, 2020, https://doi.org/10.1093/nar/gkac689.
21. Dzobo, K., The role of natural products as sources of therapeutic agents for innovative drug discovery. *Compr. Pharmacol.*, 408, 2022.
22. Perrone, F., *et al.*, Emerging genetic complexity and rare genetic variants in neurodegenerative brain diseases. *Genome Med.*, 13, 1, 59, 2021. 44-53. 10.1126/science.abj6987.
23. Nurk, S., *et al.*, The complete sequence of a human genome. *Science*, 376, 6588, 44–53, 2022, https://doi.org/10.1016/B978-0-12-820472-6.00041-4.
24. Tsirelson, V.G. and Ozerov, R.P., *Electron density and bonding in crystals: Principles, theory, and X-ray diffraction experiments in solid state physics and chemistry*, CRC Press, Boca Raton, FL, 2020, https://doi.org/10.1186/s13073-021-00878-y.
25. Schauperl, M. and Denny, R.A., AI-based protein structure prediction in drug discovery: impacts and challenges. *J. Chem. Inf. Model.*, 62, 13, 3142–3156, 2022, https://doi.org/10.3390/membranes12020227.
26. Ramelot, T.A., *et al.*, Representing structures of the multiple conformational states of proteins. *Curr. Opin. Struct. Biol.*, 83, 1027035, 2023, https://doi.org/10.1021/acs.jcim.2c00026.
27. Zhu, Y., Ouyang, Z., *et al.*, New opportunities and challenges of natural products study: When target identification meets single-cell multiomics. *Acta Pharm. Sin. B*, 12, 11, 4011–4039, 2022, https://doi.org/10.1016/j.sbi.2023.102703.
28. Fang, Y., Liang, X., *et al.*, Mol-instructions: A large-scale biomolecular instruction dataset for large language models. *arXiv preprint arXiv:2306.08018*. https://doi.org/10.1016/j.apsb.2022.08.022, 2023.

29. Borowiec, M.L., *et al.*, White, Deep learning as a tool for ecology and evolution. *Methods Ecol. Evol.*, 13, 8, 1640–1660, 2022, 10.48550/ARXIV.2304.
30. Behzadi, P. and Gajdács, M., Worldwide Protein Data Bank (wwPDB): A virtual treasure for study in biotechnology. *Eur. J. Microbiol. Immunol.*, 11, 4, 77–86, 2022, 10.1111/2041-210X.13901.
31. Omenn, G.S., *et al.*, Progress identifying and analyzing the human proteome: 2021 metrics from the HUPO human proteome project. *J. Proteome Study*, 20, 12, 5227–5240, 2021, https://doi.org/10.1021/acs.jproteome.1c00590.
32. Alvarez, C.H. and Evans, C.R., Intersectional environmental justice and population health inequalities: A novel approach. *Social Sci. Med.*, 269, 1135595, 2021, https://doi.org/10.1016/j.socscimed.2020.113559.
33. Sarkizova, S., *et al.*, A large peptidome dataset improves HLA class I epitope prediction across most of the human population. *Nat. Biotechnol.*, 38, 2, 199–209, 2020, https://doi.org/10.1038/s41587-019-0322-9.
34. Pradhan, A.S. and Hiray, S.R., Application of Big Data Techniques for Efficient Web-Based Library Services Using Big Data: A Modern Approach, in: *Big Data Applications for Improving Library Services*, pp. 58–77, IGI Global, Hershey, PA, 2021, 10.4018/978-1-7998-3049-8.ch005.
35. Miller, R.M., *et al.*, Enhanced protein isoform characterization through long-read proteogenomics. *Genome Biol.*, 23, 1, 69, 2022, https://doi.org/10.1186/s13059-022-02624-y.
36. Nambiar, A. and Mundra, D., An overview of data warehouse and data lake in modern enterprise data management. *Big Data Cogn. Comput.*, 6, 4, 132, 2022, https://doi.org/10.3390/bdcc6040132.
37. Ferilli, S., Integration strategy and tool between formal ontology and graph database technology. *Electronics*, 10, 21, 2616, 2021, https://doi.org/10.3390/electronics10212616.
38. Camargo, A., *et al.*, RNAsamba: neural network-based assessment of the protein-coding potential of RNA sequences. *NAR Genomics Bioinf.*, 2, 1, lqz024, 2020, https://doi.org/10.1093/nargab/lqz024.
39. Liu, C., *et al.*, Computational network biology: data, models, and applications. *Phys. Rep.*, 846, 1–665, 2020, https://doi.org/10.1016/j.physrep.2019.12.004.
40. Blum, M., *et al.*, The InterPro protein families and domains database: 20 years on. *Nucleic Acids Study*, 49, D1, D344–D354, 2021, https://doi.org/10.1093/nar/gkaa977.
41. O'Leary, N.A., *et al.*, Exploring and retrieving sequence and metadata for species across the tree of life with NCBI Datasets. *Sci. Data*, 11, 1, 732, 2024, https://doi.org/10.1038/s41597-024-03571-y.
42. Banimfreg, B.H., A comprehensive review and conceptual framework for cloud computing adoption in bioinformatics. *Healthcare Anal.*, 3, 1001905, 2023, https://doi.org/10.1016/j.health.2023.100190.
43. Diwan, G.D., *et al.*, Next generation protein structure predictions and genetic variant interpretation. *J. Mol. Biol.*, 433, 20, 167180, 2021, https://doi.org/10.1016/j.jmb.2021.167180.

10

Telemedicine and Remote Monitoring

Sheuli Sen[1]*, Girija Shankar Sahoo[2], Anjali R. Kumbhar[3], Sibun Parida[4], Aranganathan A.[5] and Malathi H.[6]

[1]*Teerthakar Parshvnath College of Nursing, Teerthakar Mahaveer University, Uttar Pradesh, India*
[2]*Maharishi School of Engineering & Technology, Maharishi University of Information Technology, Uttar Pradesh, India*
[3]*PES's Modern College of Pharmacy Nigdi Pune, Pune, India*
[4]*Department of Computer Science and Information Technology, Siksha 'O' Anusandhan (Deemed to be University), Bhubaneswar, Odisha, India*
[5]*Department of Electronics and Communication Engineering, Sathyabama Institute of Science and Technology, Chennai, Tamil Nadu, India*
[6]*Department of Biotechnology and Genetics, Jain (Deemed-to-be University), Bangalore, Karnataka, India*

Abstract
In the medical field, telemedicine and remote monitoring (RM) have become revolutionary tools that enhance the availability of health services and decrease the requirement for personal visits. Using wearable technology and internet-based apps, RM enables the feasibility to continually track critical biological indicators, leading to prompt action and effective management of long-term illnesses like diabetes, respiratory problems, and cardiovascular conditions. It highlights how well RM operates to enhance patient health by facilitating rapid treatment and saving the expense of long-term care. It focuses on detecting cardiac diseases in machine learning (ML), analyzing enormous amounts of data, and forecasting the development of the disease, yielding more accurate and personalized therapies. Integrating ML models into RM systems promotes diagnostic accuracy with

**Corresponding author*: sheulisen100@gmail.com; ORCID: 0000-0002-0276-5918
Girija Shankar Sahoo: ORCID: 0000-0001-5512-1441
Anjali R. Kumbhar: ORCID: 0009-0003-5171-2999
Sibun Parida: ORCID: 0000-0002-0624-9718
Aranganathan A.: ORCID: https://orcid.org/0000-0002-5986-6031
Malathi H.: ORCID: 0000-0001-6198-8428

Satya Prakash Yadav, Abhay Bansal and Victor Hugo C. de Albuquerque (eds.) Computational Intelligence in Biomedical Internet of Medical Things, (161–176) © 2026 Scrivener Publishing LLC

beneficial results in cardiac care, where prompt detection can have an important effect on the survival of patients. It explores the role of RM in modern cardiac care and its potential to revolutionize disease management through ML technologies.

Keywords: Health monitoring, machine learning, telemedicine, treatment

10.1 Introduction

The usage of telemedicine services to cut down on in-person and routine clinic visits has increased dramatically in recent years, protecting both individual and financial resources [1]. In addition, telemedicine assists with medical professionals' shortfalls and local medical facilities by allowing efficient transitions to treatment from any region [2]. Several unique issues can be solved or resolved with its assistance. It was created to effectively enhance emergency access to healthcare services [3]. The healthcare system's missing requirements could be addressed through telemedicine technology, typically known as remote monitoring (RM) [4]. One of the finest possibilities for distance concerns is the RM of patients' systems [5]. It also uses electronic devices to monitor important physiological changes in humans, facilitating rapid actions in medical solutions [6]. Implementing telemedicine and remote tracking technology using internet-based applications and messaging services can decrease the monetary burden associated with persistent diseases and improve treatment outcomes [7]. Early therapeutic decisions and more active approaches to therapy could prevent patient loss and deaths by employing telehealth devices to autonomously monitor for variables associated with disease prediction in residential and community settings [8]. Integrating RM theories into action while motivating professionals to implement proactive treatments will act as a valuable instrument that can deliver improved outcomes [9]. Advances in trending technologies that use telemedicine and RM for revolutionizing the medical field and enhancing satisfaction among patients with beneficial gains [10]. The RM is an important key element for tracking the patients continuously, which is displayed in Figure 10.1 and is more beneficial, particularly in chronic diseases such as cardiac disease.

It aims to integrate ML techniques with RM to monitor cardiac diseases and offer early detection. It utilizes two public source databases to train and test the ML method. The ML method combined with RM enables earlier risk assessments in cardiac disorders and significantly improves the findings of people who are affected by heart diseases.

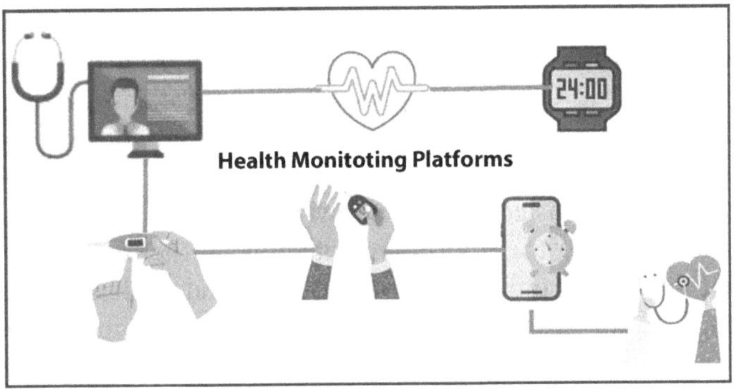

Figure 10.1 Environmental setting of the health monitoring system. (Source: https://integrio.net/blog/patient-health-monitoring-platforms).

The structured as follows: Section 10.2 offers the associated papers in the domain of cardiac illness detection, while Section 10.3 focuses on the methodology used, comprising the multiple ML models and their presentation for identifying disease across different data types. Section 10.4 offers the experimental results and performance evaluations, and Section 10.5 completes the process with discussions on its implementation and possible future suggestions.

10.2 Related Works

The ML model with RM highly influences the prediction and analysis of cardiac diseases and covid-19 diseases are explained below.

To evaluate [11] how the RM impacted the standard lifestyle and medical results of individuals undergoing automated dialysis therapy. It examined two groups of patients undergoing automated peritoneal dialysis using an observational technique. The participant demographic was tracked for six months. Experimental outcomes proved that RM was related to developed clinical outcomes, especially in patients with increased concurrent conditions and better acceptance and fulfillment with care. The RM impacted real-time clinical feedback and population-level screening when the COVID-19 pandemic was assessed [12]. It monitored a sizable participant group utilizing a technique based on observation, collecting data regarding physical characteristics and abnormalities. The delivered outcomes showed that RM assisted healthcare authorities and medical professionals in regulating the global epidemic by enabling efficient information acquisition, promoting quick measures, and enhancing outcomes for patients.

The practicality of a mobile phone-built RM strategy was developed to offer continuous care for individuals with recovery from Parkinson's disease throughout the COVID-19 pandemic [13]. Patients were asked to employ an application for their smartphones at least two times a week to monitor their jogging, thumping, shaking, recollection, and cognitive abilities. The results emphasized the economic technique of mobile-based RM. Additionally, it forced the importance of spotting the issues for the successful setting of environments related to practical applications. Remote monitoring [14] for heart failure was developed to enhance patient safety by providing constant, current information for recommending therapy. To increase the precision of predicting expanding cardiac failure, multiparameter strategies that integrate multiple physiological indicators have been examined. Overall, findings showed that the approach uses wearable and implantable tools to rapidly act on clinical concerns.

A model was developed [15] with the help of electronic devices to improve the treatment of cardiac failure. It evaluated the clinical influence of RM versus general care across the participants involved, with a concentration on medical operation, death rates, and confinement rates. The outcomes show that the RM improved clinical activity for people who suffer from cardiac diseases with atrial fibrillation, along with a superior amount of treatment for individuals with chronic or severe heart problems. Telemedicine for cardiovascular failure was implemented [16] to address the requirement for seamless tracking and immediate action. Telemedical technologies were employed to perform data analysis and interpretation using required parameters. By permitting aggressive healthcare and early detection of worsened conditions, the approach established improved findings for the patient monitoring system.

A practical, harmless, and remote solution was developed to track the fetal and parental heartbeats [17]. The approach utilized electromagnetic and acoustic technology was used to gather information and digital restoration of cardiovascular records. The data was efficiently transferred for processing in the data center. The findings demonstrated that the proposed approach was perfect in maternal and heart rate evaluations and showed a significant relationship with traditional cardiotocography. A cardiovascular condition forecasting framework [18] was proposed to efficiently process and evaluate massive quantities of sensor information. To identify correlations or produce forecasts, the information was analyzed using models based on ML or robust analytics, and its accuracy was evaluated. The model efficiently examined huge quantities of gathered and sensed information that yielded more precise heart disease predictions. The result helped to spot the most necessary characteristics and verified the model's capacity to reliably predict the probability of coronary disease.

Tracking the diagnosis of cardiac conditions was built to investigate existing hardware-software RM structures, with a focus on utilizing the electrocardiogram [19]. It is important to improve medical facilities and more operational sickness management, as long as uninterrupted monitoring aids patient recovery and expands the use of medical telemetry equipment. The result demonstrated a 30% increase in identification effectiveness; the suggested approach significantly improved atrial monitoring, promoted sufferers' psychological health, minimized patient disruption, and reduced the demand for medical professionals. A model was developed to investigate the performance of cardiac pacemakers [20] for RM. The Bluetooth low-energy model was developed in the suggested approach, along with the app-based transformation of sensational records. It was tested in multiple phases. The experimental findings showed that the app-based transmission had greater achievement rates across the associations coordinated by gender, tool type, and age in all three phases.

10.3 Methodology

This section describes the application of ML technologies to enhance and predict cardiovascular disease (CVD) management, which is tested on two open sources. These sources offer a strong foundation for evaluating distinct ML algorithms and comprise vital physiological parameters. It attempts to develop the concert outcome of heart disease prediction by consuming various ML techniques. This investigation facilitates the rapid detection and specific treatment strategy for different people concerned with cardiac conditions. Such advances promote the overall advancement of medical technology in CVD management and surveillance, as illustrated in Figure 10.2.

10.3.1 Dataset Collection

This part offers an in-depth discussion of two frequently utilized open-source dataset on heart diseases on the Kaggle database website. Employing these two datasets in heart disease monitoring assists in the development of telemedicine services that provide proactively engaged, customized therapy, and improves outcomes for people who have cardiovascular disorders. The datasets, such as University of California, Irvine (UCI) heart disease data and CVD_Vital_Signs are considered.

University of California, Irvine heart disease data [21]: This type of dataset is multidimensional, which relates to the supply or use of several

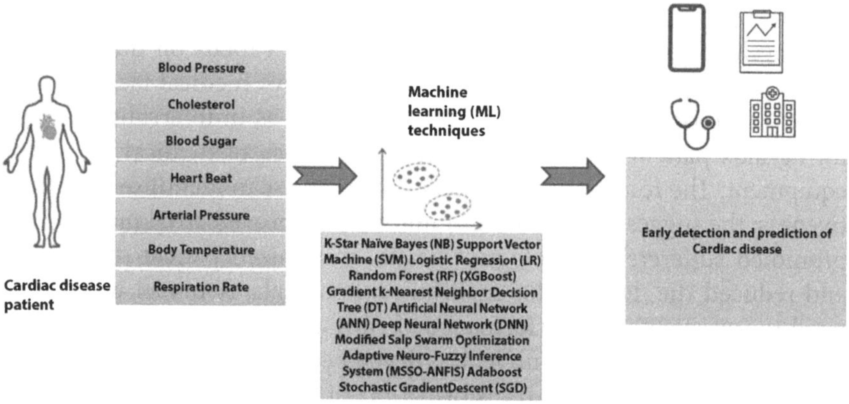

Figure 10.2 Methodology flow. (Source: Own elaboration).

different quantitative or mathematical components in a multidimensional numerical information process. Gender, age, kind of chest pain, blood pressure, circulating cholesterol, fasting plasma glucose, and electrocardiogram values are all included in this measure. The number of major vessels, exercise-induced angina, the maximal heart rate reached, the slope of the peak exercise ST segment, and the ST depression caused by activity are compared to rest. Although the database contains 76 characteristics, only 14 are used in all reported inquiries. Forecasting whether a patient has heart disease based on their characteristics is one of the primary duties of this dataset. Another is the trial assignment for determining the patient while obtaining additional insights from the data set that could help further understand the issue.

CVD_Vital_Signs [22]: The critical requirement for improving the detection and management of CVD, a major global cause of death is prompted. Correctly predicting and recognizing CVD in its earliest phases remains extremely challenging, despite improvements in medical knowledge. A combination of ML and deep learning (DL) approaches to investigate vital signs linked to CVD, such as heartbeat, arterial pressure, body temperature, oxygen saturation, and respiration rate, this investigation seeks to deal with this challenge. The data collection helps to identify the model with the greatest accuracy by assessing the efficacy of multiple ML and DL models. The multilevel predictive model demonstrated its capacity to attain extremely precise rates, which offers promising possibilities for strengthening CVD diagnosis and leadership methods. Overall, it emphasizes the revolutionary possibilities of AI approaches to healthcare and contributes to the increasing collection of information in the discipline of CVD prediction.

10.3.2 Remote Monitoring Using ML

Machine learning techniques enhance the forecasting of cardiac diseases by analyzing huge datasets to identify patterns, resulting in prompt identification and specific treatment. As illustrated by Table 10.1, utilizing these models enables accurate forecasts of the illness, which enables immediate actions and customized treatments that optimize outcomes for patients.

10.4 Experimental Results

The existing study uses multiple ML classifications to evaluate the recommended hybrid system for decision support for cardiac disease identification and describes detailed information about the performance metrics.

10.4.1 Performance Metrics

The heart disease detection approach performance metrics typically comprise multiple parameters to estimate the model's overall performance. The following metrics will show how it affects the systemthathasbeen suggested, asshown by Equations 10.1 to 10.9.

True negative (TN): For the specified input parameters, expected and expressed outcomes are negative.

False negative (FN): It forecasts a positive result after forecasting an unsuccessful source.

True positive (TP): It evaluates the correct data provided and projects a positive outcome.

False positive (FP): Although the input received is projected to be negative, it is predicted as a positive number.

Accuracy: The complete exactness of the model is evaluated. It provides the number of actual findings in the given dataset, including positives and negatives. A significant rate of accuracy implies that the model can reliably predict whether heart disease will exist or not, almost all the time.

$$accuracy = \frac{TN + TP}{TP + FP + TN + FN} \quad (10.1)$$

Precision: It offers the percentage of cardiac disease cases that were proven true. This is essential, especially when expensive surgical procedures might arise from incorrect findings, such as a diagnosis of heart disease when none exists.

Table 10.1 Heart disease prediction using ML.

References	Dataset	Used techniques	Outcomes
[23]	Heart disease dataset	Lightweight block encryption technique based on the K-star classification method in ML	acc - 95%, rec- 93.5%, pre- 94.5%, and f1-score- 93.99%.
[24]	Cleveland heart disease dataset	Support vector machine (SVM), logistic regression (LR), Random Forest (RF), and Naïve Bayes (NB),	acc- 86.60%, sen- 84.14%, spe- 89.02%, pre-88.46% and f1-score 86.25 %
[25]	Cleveland and Statlog	NB, SVM and Gradientboost (XGBoost)	pre- 97.1%, acc-95.9%, f1-score- 95.35 %, and rec- 94.67%
[26]	UCI Heart Disease dataset	k-Nearest Neighbor (KNN), LR, SVM, and XGBoost	AUC- 96%, pre-95.83 %, acc- 85.96% rec- 76.67% and mean - 81.68%
[27]	UCI Heart Disease dataset	RF-SVM	acc-91.4 %
[28]	CVD_Vital_ Signs dataset	Naïve Bayes, artificial neural networks (ANN), Decision Trees (DT), deep neural networks (DNN), SVM, and RF	Root mean square error (RMSE) - 0.0659, MAE- 0.0660, acc- 93.40 %, rec- 90.70, pre- 45.89
[29]	Pima Indian Diabetes database	SVM	Spe- 79 %, acc-83.20 % and sen- 87.20 %,

(*Continued*)

Table 10.1 Heart disease prediction using ML. (*Continued*)

References	Dataset	Used techniques	Outcomes
[30]	UCI Heart Disease dataset CVD_Vital_Signs dataset	Modified Salp Swarm Optimization Adaptive Neuro-Fuzzy Inference System (MSSO-ANFIS)	sen- 97.89 %, spe- 97.8 %, err- 0.55%, pre- 96.59 %, f1-score- 98.59 %, acc- 99.45 %
[31]	Heart Disease dataset	Support vector machine, Adaboost, KNN, NB, stochastic gradient descent (SGD), and DT	acc- 99.703 %
[32]	UCI Heart Disease dataset	k-Nearest Neighbor, DT, NB, SVM, RF	acc- 98.6 %. AUC – 98.5 %, pre- 98%, f1-score – 98.2%, rec- 98.5 %

Note: acc - accuracy, sen - sensitivity, rec - recall, spe - specificity, err - error, pre - precision, AUC - area under the curve.

$$precision = \frac{TP}{FP + TP} \tag{10.2}$$

Recall (Sensitivity): The model capacity to precisely identify the persons with heart problems is calculated. A stronger recall decreases inaccurate results, or undetected heart-related scenarios, which is essential for quickly identifying and avoiding detrimental effects.

$$recall = \frac{TP}{FN + TN} \tag{10.3}$$

F1-score: The balance of the two measurements of precision-recall characteristics is estimated. It produces one rating value, which demonstrates the accuracy of positive case forecasts, as well as its capacity to collect all factual positive incidences.

$$F1-score = 2 * \frac{precision * recall}{Precision + recall} \tag{10.4}$$

Area under the curve (AUC): It relates to the receiver operating characteristic (ROC) curve's area. It offers an in-depth evaluation of the system's ability to identify individuals with and without cardiac disease. Improved categorizing efficiency is represented by a larger AUC.

$$AUC = \int_0^1 ROC\ curve \tag{10.5}$$

Mean: The model's overall efficiency for forecasting coronary heart disease over multiple iterations is demonstrated by its mean rating of performance across every point of data.

$$mean = \frac{Total\ values}{total\ numbers} \tag{10.6}$$

Specificity: Specificity, commonly recognized as the actual unfavorable rate, assesses the number of potential individuals in good health without heart disease that the model precisely identifies. The model's capacity to differentiate between people who do not have heart disease. Greater specificity minimizes the possibility of misleading occurrences by suggesting that the model succeeds in correctly recognizing healthy people.

$$specificty = \frac{TN}{FP + TN} \tag{10.7}$$

Root mean square error (RMSE): The model's displayed risk of heart disease and the RMSE are used to compare real results. It provides an idea of the typical prediction error for every sample. A lower RMSE in CVD projection indicates the model calculated with the actual diagnosis, which aids healthcare providers in making intelligent decisions.

$$RMSE = \sqrt{\frac{1}{n}\sum_{i=1}^{N}(y_i - x_i)^2} \tag{10.8}$$

Mean absolute error (MAE): The variations between the projected and observed findings are denoted as MAE. It helps to make the average forecasting error simpler to read through, eliminating enormous mistakes. The forecasts made by the model tend to be closer to the actual results whenever the MAE is lower. Figures 10.3 – 10.7 display the outcomes of existing methods for all metrics (accuracy, precision, recall, f1-score, and specificity).

$$MAE = \frac{1}{n}\sum_{i=1}^{n}(y_i - \hat{y}_i) \tag{10.9}$$

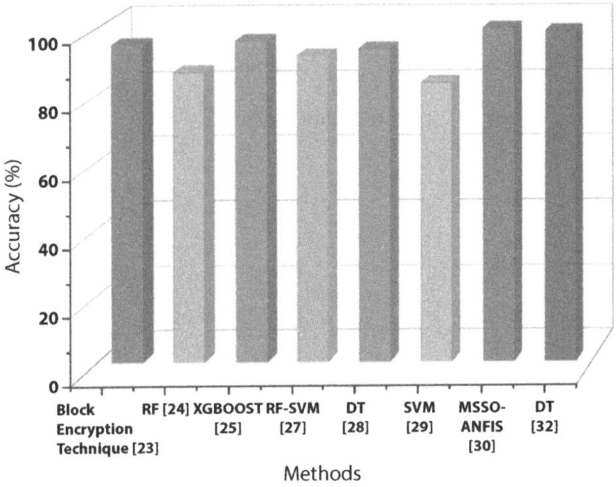

Figure 10.3 Outcome of the accuracy for existing methods.

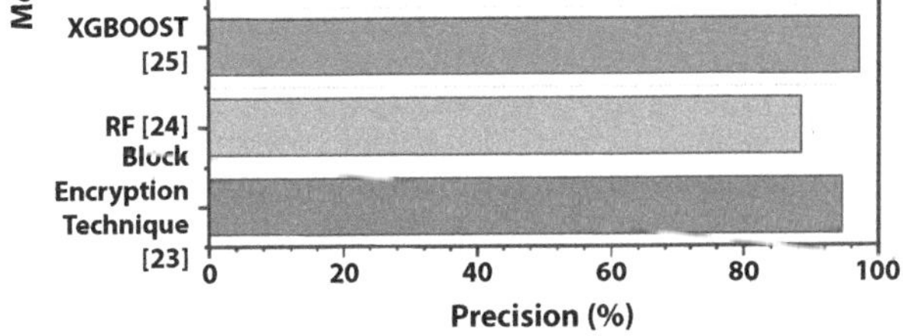

Figure 10.4 Outcome of the precision for existing methods.

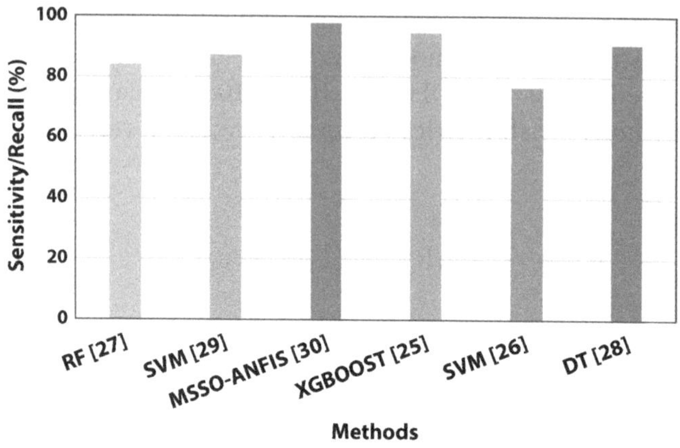

Figure 10.5 Outcome of recall for existing methods.

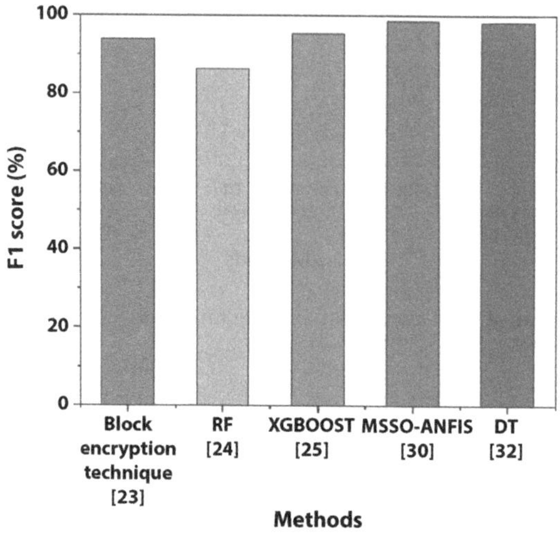

Figure 10.6 Outcome of the F1-score for existing methods.

10.5 Discussion

Significant advancements in the medical field have been made achievable by telemedicine and RM, particularly for the chronic illnesses of cardiac disease detection and treatment. These technologies facilitated seamless tracking, leading to proactive therapy. Particularly, in the field of cardiology, ML was growing rapidly as an important telemedicine tool. By evaluating

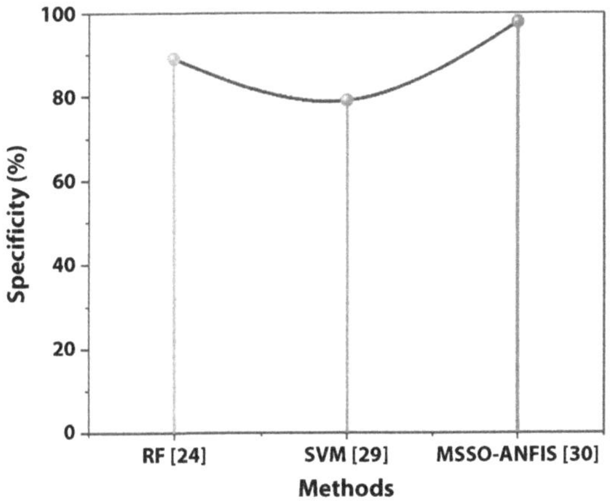

Figure 10.7 Outcome of the specificity for existing methods.

large datasets to identify early disease metrics, forecast courses, and offer tailored treatment plans, integrating ML with RM improved cardiac care. This enabled faster measures, lowered hospitalization prices, and enhanced diagnostic accuracy. Existing methods for heart disease prediction were estimated and employ a variety of ML techniques, each demonstrating different levels of accuracy and performance metrics. Conventional techniques, such as NB, SVM, and LR, were common and offered reasonable reliability, usually ranging between 85% and 90%. With a rate of accuracy above 90%, improved approaches such as ensemble methods and hybrid models yielded superior results. Methods that comprise optimization algorithms with adaptive systems delivered a superior performance of above 95%. In addition to increasing the accuracy of predictions, these kinds of models also make it faster to find minor forms in large datasets, resulting in more efficient detection and greater customization. Incorporating higher-level algorithms continue to challenge the boundaries of cardiac disease prediction as technology expands, delivering more reliable and timely treatments.

10.6 Conclusion

The existing study emphasizes that ML strategies could enhance healthcare results, particularly concerning the detection and management of cardiac conditions. Early and accurate forecasting of heart disease could significantly improve clinical results, permitting robust treatment strategies for medical professionals. It made use of important datasets, which include the CVD_Vital_Signs and UCI heart disease databases, which provided essential information on many kinds of symptoms and medical factors associated with cardiovascular disorders. Such databases assist the development of ML models that identify the abnormalities and offer notifications in advance, helping to prevent and manage the disease condition. Pharmacological technology has tremendous potential for changing the detection and management of persistent conditions like cardiovascular disorders as they progress faster. Also, it concentrated on the requirement for large model reliability and transparency in the implementation of the ML method. However, the availability of the data in the RM system and the dependability of the internet connectivity are inconsistent, which can affect the trustworthiness of the model. Further studies can be conducted to employ the pre-processing techniques to handle the inconsistent data and develop a cost-effective, user-friendly system that can operate on limited resources.

References

1. Aberer, F., *et al.*, Application of telemedicine in diabetes care: the time is now. *Diabetes Ther.*, 12, 3, 629–639, 2021, https://doi.org/10.1007/s13300-020-00996-7.
2. Stoltzfus, M., Kaur, A., Chawla, A., *et al.*, The role of telemedicine in healthcare: an overview and update. *Egypt. J. Intern. Med.*, 35, 1, 1–5, 2023, https://doi.org/10.1186/s43162-023-00234-z.
3. Latifi, R., *et al.*, Perspective on COVID-19: finally, telemedicine at center stage. *Telemed. e-Health*, 26, 9, 1106–1109, 2020, DOI: 10.1089/tmj.2020.0132.
4. Bekfani, T., *et al.*, A current and future outlook on upcoming technologies in remote monitoring of patients with heart failure. *Eur. J. Heart Fail.*, 23, 1, 175–185, 2021, https://doi.org/10.1002/ejhf.2033.
5. Alshammari, and Hamoud, H., The internet of things healthcare monitoring system based on MQTT protocol. *Alex. Eng. J.*, 69, 275–287, 2023, https://doi.org/10.1016/j.aej.2023.01.065.
6. Mirjalali, S., *et al.*, Wearable sensors for remote health monitoring: potential applications for early diagnosis of Covid-19. *Adv. Mater. Technol.*, 7, 1, 2100545, 2022, https://doi.org/10.1002/admt.202100545.
7. George, L.A., *et al.*, Remote monitoring and telemedicine in IBD: are we there yet? *Curr. Gastroenterol. Rep.*, 22, 1–6, 2020, https://doi.org/10.1007/s11894-020-0751-0.
8. Lukas, H., *et al.*, Emerging telemedicine tools for remote COVID-19 diagnosis, monitoring, and management. *ACS Nano*, 14, 12, 16180–16193, 2020, https://dx.doi.org/10.1021/acsnano.0c08494.

9. Imberti, J.F., *et al.*, Remote monitoring and telemedicine in heart failure: implementation and benefits. *Curr. Cardiol. Rep.*, 23, 1–11, 2021, https://doi.org/10.1007/s11886-021-01487-2.
10. Jeddi N., and Adam M., Remote patient monitoring using artificial intelligence, in: *Artificial Intelligence in Healthcare*, pp. 203–234, Academic Press, Cambridge, MA, 2020, https://doi.org/10.1016/B978-0-12-818438-7.00009-5.
11. Manani, M., *et al.*, Remote monitoring in peritoneal dialysis: benefits on clinical outcomes and on quality of life. *J. Nephrol.*, 33, 1301–1308, 2020, https://doi.org/10.1007/s40620-020-00812-2.
12. Watson, *et al.*, The value of remote monitoring for the COVID-19 pandemic. *Telemed. e-Health*, 26, 9, 1110–1112, 2020, DOI: 10.1089/tmj.2020.0134.
13. Motolese, *et al.*, Parkinson's disease remote patient monitoring during the COVID-19 lockdown. *Front. Neurol.*, 11, 567413, 2020, doi: 10.3389/fneur.2020.567413.
14. Ali, *et al.*, Remote physiologic monitoring for heart failure. *Curr. Cardiol. Rep.*, 22, 1–10, 2020, https://doi.org/10.1007/s11886-020-01309-x.
15. Zakeri, *et al.*, Impact of remote monitoring on clinical outcomes for patients with heart failure and atrial fibrillation: results from the REM-HF trial. *Eur. J. Heart Fail.*, 22, 3, 543–553, 2020, https://doi.org/10.1002/ejhf.1709.
16. Bertagnin, *et al.*, Remote monitoring for heart failure management during COVID-19 pandemic. *IJC Heart Vasc.*, 32, 100724, 2021, https://doi.org/10.1016/j.ijcha.2021.100724.
17. Mhajna, *et al.*, Wireless, remote solution for home fetal and maternal heart rate monitoring. *Am. J. Obstet. Gynecol. MFM*, 2, 2, 100101, 2020, https://doi.org/10.1016/j.ajogmf.2020.100101.
18. Babu, *et al.*, Remote health patient monitoring system for early detection of heart disease. *Int. J. Grid High Perform. Comput. (IJGHPC)*, 13, 2, 118–130, 2021, DOI: 10.4018/IJGHPC.2021040107.
19. Magrupov, *et al.*, A Medical Hardware-Software System for Remote Monitoring of Heart Diseases. *Proceedings of Higher Educational Institutions of Russia. Radioelectronics*, 24, 2, 78–86, 2021, https://doi.org/10.32603/1993-8985-2021-24-2-78-86.
20. Tarakji, *et al.*, Performance of first pacemaker to use smart device app for remote monitoring. *Heart Rhythm O2*, 2, 5, 463–471, 2021, https://doi.org/10.1016/j.hroo.2021.07.008.
21. https://www.kaggle.com/datasets/redwankarimsony/heart-disease-data.
22. https://www.kaggle.com/datasets/chidozieuzoegwu/cvd-vital-signs.
23. Akhbarifar, *et al.*, A secure remote health monitoring model for early disease diagnosis in cloud-based IoT environment. *Pers. Ubiquitous Comput.*, 27, 3, 697–713, 2023, https://doi.org/10.1007/s00779-020-01475-3.
24. Rani, *et al.*, A decision support system for heart disease prediction based upon machine learning. *J. Reliab. Intell. Environ.*, 7, 3, 263–275, 2021, https://doi.org/10.1007/s40860-021-00133-6.

25. Nagavelli, *et al.*, Machine Learning Technology-Based Heart Disease Detection Models. *J. Healthc. Eng.*, 2022, 1, 7351061, 2022, https://doi.org/10.1155/2022/7351061.
26. Desai, *et al.*, HealthCloud: A system for monitoring health status of heart patients using machine learning and cloud computing. *Internet Things*, 17, 100485, 2022, DOI:10.1016/j.iot.2021.100485.
27. Katarya, *et al.*, Machine learning techniques for heart disease prediction: a comparative study and analysis. *Health Technol.*, 11, 1, 87–97, 2021, https://doi.org/10.1007/s12553-020-00505-7.
28. Hemalatha, D., *et al.*, Machine learning techniques for heart disease prediction. *J. Cardiovasc. Dis. Study*, 12, 1, 93–96, 2021, DOI:10.31838/jcdr.2021.12.01.05.
29. Ramesh, *et al.*, A remote healthcare monitoring framework for diabetes prediction using machine learning. *Healthc. Technol. Lett.*, 8, 3, 45–57, 2021, https://doi.org/10.1049/htl2.12010.
30. Khan, *et al.*, A healthcare monitoring system for the diagnosis of heart disease in the IoMT cloud environment using MSSO-ANFIS. *IEEE Access*, 8, 122259–122269, 2020, DOI: 10.1109/ACCESS.2020.3006424.
31. Almustafa, *et al.*, Prediction of heart disease and classifiers' sensitivity analysis. *BMC Bioinf.*, 21, 1–18, 2020, https://doi.org/10.1186/s12859-020-03626-y.
32. Gao, *et al.*, Improving the accuracy for analyzing heart disease prediction based on the ensemble method. *Complexity*, 2021, 1, 6663455, 2021, https://doi.org/10.1155/2021/6663455.

11

Machine Learning and Artificial Intelligence in Biomedical Applications

Deepti Pandey[1]*, Indraah Kolandaisamy[2], Visvesvaran C.[3], Renuka Jyothi S.[4], Suraya Mubeen[5] and Prabhat Kumar Sahu[6]

[1]Sloan School of Management, Massachusetts Institute of Management, Cambridge, United States of America
[2]BBA, School of Business Management, Universiti Utara Malaysia, Sintok, Kedah Darul Aman, Malaysia
[3]Sri Krishna College of Engineering and Technology, Coimbatore (Autonomous - Affiliated to Anna University Chennai), Coimbatore, Tamil Nadu, India
[4]Department of Biotechnology and Genetics, Jain (Deemed-to-be University), Bangalore, Karnataka, India
[5]Department of ECE, CMR Technical Campus, Telangana, Hyderabad, India
[6]Department of Computer Science and Information Technology, Siksha 'O' Anusandhan (Deemed to be University), Bhubaneswar, Odisha, India

Abstract

Machine learning (ML) and artificial intelligence (AI) are transforming biomedical research by improving diagnostic accuracy, optimizing treatment plans, and supporting modified patient care. This review inspects the addition of ML and AI in healthcare, concentrating on their applications in medical imaging, disease diagnosis, patient monitoring, and drug discovery. These AI-driven methods examine complex biomedical data, such as magnetic resonance imaging (MRI) and computed tomography (CT) scans, to detect early-stage diseases like cancer and neurological disorders, allowing timely and exact interventions. Furthermore,

**Corresponding author*: deepti0180@gmail.com; ORCID: https://orcid.org/0000-0001-9058-9354
Visvesvaran C.: ORCID: https://orcid.org/0000-0001-6116-6037
Renuka Jyothi S.: ORCID: https://orcid.org/0000-0003-3248-337X
Suraya Mubeen: ORCID: https://orcid.org/0000-0001-7800-9644
Prabhat Kumar Sahu: ORCID: https://orcid.org/0000-0002-0460-9783

Satya Prakash Yadav, Abhay Bansal and Victor Hugo C. de Albuquerque (eds.) Computational Intelligence in Biomedical Internet of Medical Things, (177–196) © 2026 Scrivener Publishing LLC

modified medicine is proceeding as AI adapts actions to patient-specific needs, refining consequences for chronic situations, and reducing treatment side effects. Wearable devices powered by AI provide real-time monitoring, allowing clinicians to track patient health unceasingly and adjust care as needed. While AI offers considerable assistance, the study also addresses limits related to data security, model interpretability, and ethical considerations in medical practice. Future instructions highlight the need for interdisciplinary teamwork and improved frameworks for data treatment, transparency, and equality. Overall, this review underscores the potential of ML and AI to drive innovations in healthcare, moving toward a future of precision medicine and enhanced patient outcomes.

Keywords: Machine learning (ML), artificial intelligence (AI), biomedical applications, personalized medicine, diagnostic accuracy, patient monitoring

11.1 Introduction

Incorporating artificial intelligence (AI) and machine learning (ML) through biomedical settings has substantially improved the healthcare scene, proposing transformative methods to treatment, diagnosis, and individualized treatment [1]. These innovations affect large volumes of medical and biological information to enhance decision-making, precision, and patient outcomes [2]. Employing powerful methods, ML and AI can evaluate composite datasets from several sources like medicinal imaging, genomic information, and electronic health (e-health) records, recognizing patterns and tendencies that can otherwise go unnoticed [3]. In medicinal imaging, AI-driven tools have been established to be invaluable in detecting delicate aberrations in scans, including computed tomography (CT) scans, X-radiation (X-rays), and magnetic resonance imaging (MRIs) [4]. These processes can help healthcare professionals identify circumstances more rapidly and with superior accuracy, reducing the probability of human inaccuracy [5]. Correspondingly, in genomics, the ML algorithm examines genetic data to expose insights into disease exposure, treatment reactions, and modified treatments, generating a substantial move toward accuracy medicine [6]. Moreover, as for diagnostics, ML and AI have helped enhance drug detection and treatments. Through evaluating large datasets, these technologies can recognize probable drug applicants, conduct medical trials, and forecast patient replies, serving to decrease the duration and cost involved in bringing novel treatments to the market [7]. Although their transformation is probable, the use of AI and ML in biomedicine similarly offers trials linked to data confidentiality, procedure transparency, and bias in model forecasts [8]. These problems

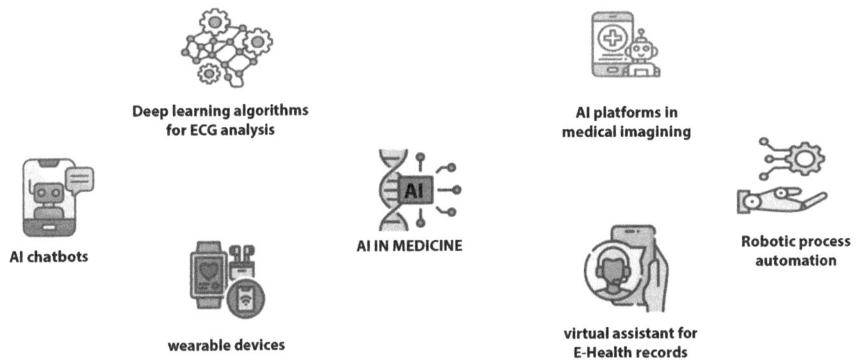

Figure 11.1 Artificial intelligence applications transforming modern healthcare and medicine. (Source: Own elaboration).

need cautious consideration to safeguard moral and dependable usage of technologies in healthcare settings. However, the continuing improvements in AI and ML are transforming biomedical applications, proposing further assistance to both clinicians and patients in the healthcare environment [9].

Figure 11.1 illustrates various AI roles in medicine, and ML and AI in biomedical applications. These include deep learning (DL) for electrocardiogram (ECG) analysis to detect cardiac abnormalities, AI platforms in medical imaging for identifying conditions through scans, and wearable devices for real-time health monitoring. Additional applications like robotic process automation improve operational efficiency, AI chatbots support patient interaction, and virtual assistants for e-health records aid in managing patient data [10]. Each component demonstrates AI's transformative role in healthcare diagnostics, patient management, and data processing.

11.2 Levels of Artificial Intelligence Applications Across Biomedical Subfields

There are three primary ways that ML is being used in medical applications: (1) as computer-aided diagnosis to assist doctors in making an early, successful diagnosis that is more coherent and less contradictory; (2) to improve the medical treatment of patients with more individualized treatments; and (3) to enhance human welfare, examining how social behaviors and illness transmissions relate to environmental elements, for instance, or put together a brain-machine connection for wheelchair control [11].

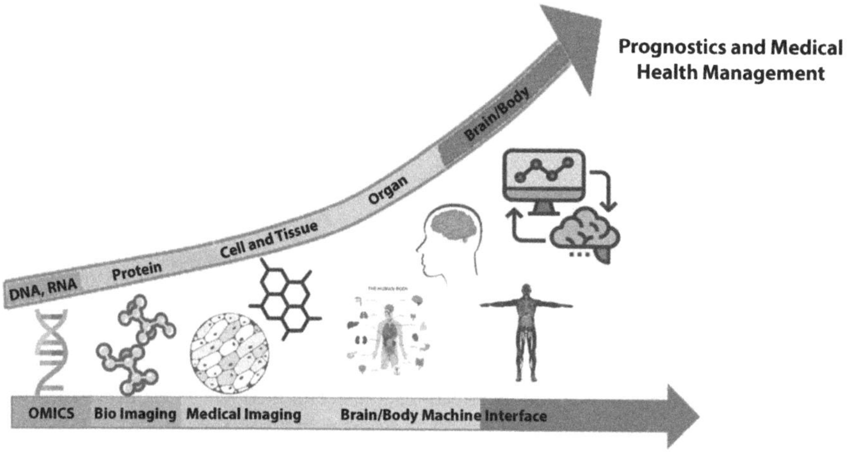

Figure 11.2 Levels of biomedical subgroups. (Source: https://www.mdpi.com/2076-3417/9/8/1526).

To accomplish these three goals, the biomedical discipline is divided into a number of subfields, as displayed in Figure 11.2.

Omics: DNA/RNA sequencing, protein interactions, and structure forecasting constitute the fields of genetics and proteomics.

Bioimaging: The investigation of biological cells and tissue using immunohistochemistry or histopathological image analysis. The analysis of human organs by MRI, X-rays, etc. is medical imaging. Investigating the brain-body technology interface involves examining several bio signals, including EEGs, to decode the interface. Public and medical health management is the study of massive medical data to create and improve healthcare choices for the welfare of mankind.

11.3 Artificial Intelligence-Based Medical Imaging

Medical imaging technology can benefit greatly from AI, which is based on bioinformatics-based systems and computational replicas. Any aberrant cellular development and biological alterations within a human body are able to be identified by it [12]. Artificial intelligence-assisted medical imaging technology is crucial to radiology, but it also significantly affects neuroradiography and medical connection image. Artificial intelligence has a wide range of exciting uses including data storage, data mining, interpreting pictures and classification, and numerous more. AI is expected to significantly aid radiotherapists in attractive analysis specificity because of its comprehensive application in biomedical imaging technology. Without radiology, medical care would not be full, mainly when it arises to cancer and it's aftereffects. Compared to other medical specialists, radiotherapists are required to possess the most digital knowledge. It are constantly at the forefront of embracing digital data about medical imaging. Compared with other conventional methods, AI has an increased sensitive rate and might detect aberrant findings at first glance [13]. Naturally, radiologists should be the primary communicators with patients whose outcomes are presence taken by AI. Although AI will never completely replace radiography at this time, the demand for radiologists is gradually declining due to AI's increased efficiency in interpreting pictures. Experienced radiologists who concentrate on technology are essential for creating distinctive formulas that analyze large amounts of data accurately and precisely. Following extensive experimental study, AI-based algorithms are able to identify certain patterns that reveal details about the anomalous results. While AI-based schemes extract all visible and invisible picture elements to produce more accurate results, conventional computer aid detection (CAD) organizations can regulate whether image elements are current and Figure 11.3 presented the medical imaging.

11.3.1 Cardiovascular Health

Machine learning is practical to assess ECG reports, cardiac MRIs, and CT scans, classifying irregularities in heart structure and function [14]. These models contributed to the early discovery of situations like heart failure, valve failure, and coronary artery disease. Artificial intelligence algorithms deliver exact second thoughts to cardiologists by measuring blood flow

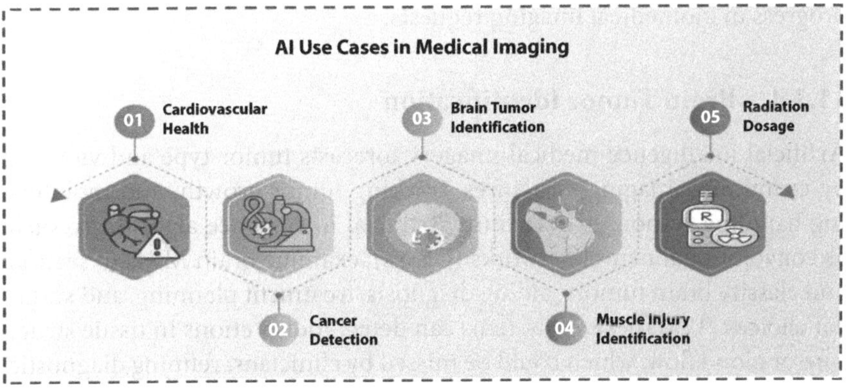

Figure 11.3 Artificial intelligence in medical imaging. Source: https://www.bacancytechnology.com/blog/ai-in-medical-imaging).

and blockages in coronary arteries, and supervisory choices on actions such as bypass surgery. Furthermore, AI tracks variations in heart function over time, secondary to the organization of chronic heart conditions and enhancing the presentation of next-generation innovators, artificial hearts, and ventricular assist devices.

11.3.2 Neurological Condition

Machine learning and AI are used to detect neurological conditions such as stroke, dementia, and multiple sclerosis by examining MRI and CT scans. Artificial intelligence algorithms recognized delicate brain structural irregularities that could be ignored by clinicians, allowing an earlier diagnosis and intervention. Additionally [15], AI contributions in examining brain action designs during functional MRI (fMRI) scans help identify neurological disorders and in personalized treatment preparation, a key request in biomedical imaging.

11.3.3 Cancer Detection

Machine learning and AI algorithms are functional to investigate mammograms, CT scans, and other imaging modalities for the early discovery of suspicious lesions and tumors. These AI models can distinguish between benign and malignant tumors, reducing unnecessary biopsies and minimizing patient nervousness associated with false positives [16]. Moreover, AI can classify high-risk cancers that could involve more violent treatments and flag possibly missed cancers, thus refining analytic accuracy. By enhancing early detection and minimizing false negatives, AI contributes significantly to more precise and effective cancer analysis, which is vital to progress in biomedical imaging requests.

11.3.4 Brain Tumor Identification

Artificial intelligence medical imagery forecasts tumor type and violence by examining imaging structures, tracking tumor growth, and monitoring handling responses over time. Artificial intelligence algorithms, such as convolutional neural networks (CNNs), examine brain MRIs to section and classify brain tumors, aiding diagnosis, treatment planning, and surgical choices [17]. These AI systems can detect indiscretions in tissue structure or blood flow, which could be missed by clinicians, refining diagnostic accuracy and providing precise sizes for action preparation.

11.3.5 Muscle Injury Identification

Artificial intelligence algorithms are practical to assess MRIs and sonography scans to notice muscle tears, strains, and irritation, offering a data-driven method to diagnose muscle injuries. Compared to traditional methods that rely on scientific inspection and patient response, AI reduces subjectivity and analytic errors by analyzing imaging data [18]. Moreover, AI analyzes movement patterns through video or motion-tracking data to classify indiscretions that could lead athletes to injuries. Wearable sensors, mechanical by AI, could quickly assess real-time drive data, alerting athletes to injury risks. Furthermore, AI tracks the curative process post-injury, safeguarding more accurate and timely retrieval assessments.

11.3.6 Radiation Dosage

Artificial intelligence enhances radiotherapy by making 3D models of tumors and nearby tissues, minimizing damage to vital organs; it examines scans and medical images to tailor radiation plans precisely to each patient's needs [19]. It can adjust radiation dosages in real-time, accounting for variations like tumor shrinkage during treatment, ensuring optimal results. By fine-tuning radiation doses, AI decreases side effects related to radiation therapy, refining patient results and enhancing their quality of life through the action process and in the long term. This modified method demonstrates AI's role in biomedical requests.

11.4 Different Diagnosis Using Machine Learning and Artificial Intelligence

Artificial intelligence can greatly advance differential diagnosis by assessing patient data and giving physicians a list of potential diagnoses. Probabilistic density curves are a useful tool for AI models to approximate the probability of an event. Machine learning algorithms like Bayesian networks often employ this policy, which calculates a prospective delivery based on prior explanations and updates it when new data becomes accessible. The possibility of an event built on a set of standards is intended using decision trees. By first training the network on a substantial dataset of inputs and their connected outputs, then using the system to estimate the likelihood of a new input, artificial neural networks (ANN) can also be used to estimate prospects [20]. The network's production coating can be set up to make a probabilistic delivery across all possible consequences. Using these approaches and procedures, AI can inspect enduring data by counting test results, e-health records, and medical images, to find trends and irregularities that might point to an exact disease or disorder. This can assist medical specialists in assessing a wider variety of likely diagnoses and locating uncommon diseases that could be difficult to identify. The ANN models that employ enduring data can be used to classify affected roles into separate risk collections for the diseases to which they are vulnerable. One such ANN was developed to forecast pancreatic cancer with a competence of 80.7% and an accuracy of 80.7% based exclusively on separate health records [21]. The advanced ANN was also accomplished to categorize persons into groups with low, middle, and increased cancer risk to offer more specific information and risk management. It has been recognized that a different population-based ML model can reliably predict a female's 5-year risk of emerging endometrial cancer using only her health record, without the need for aggressive testing and imaging. Artificial intelligence integrates diverse biomedical data sources, such as e-health records, medical images, patient vitals, medical literature, and genomic data, to improve diagnostic accuracy and efficiency [22]. Figure 11.4 presents a diagnosis using ML and AI. These systems' procedures show complex data to classify patterns and insights that support a precise diagnosis and personalized treatment. Aligning with the title ML and AI in biomedical applications, this figure validates that AI-driven analysis converts large volumes of medical data

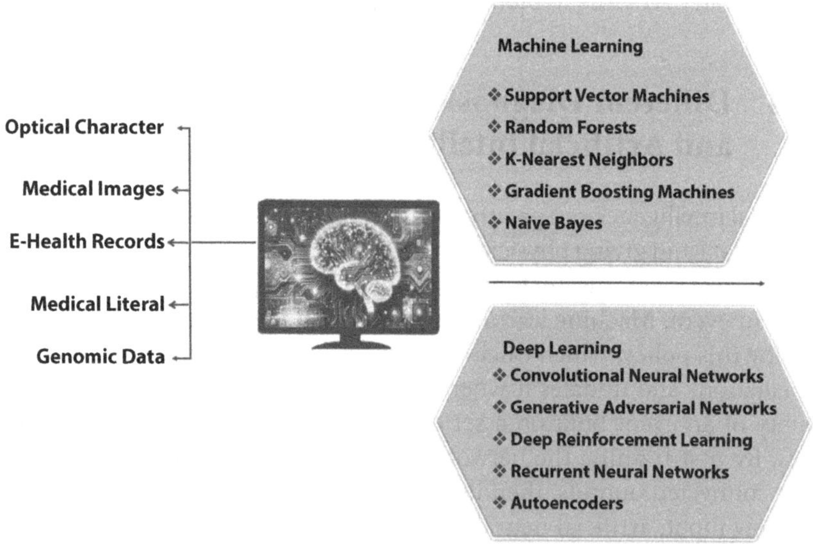

Figure 11.4 Artificial intelligence integrating biomedical data for a precise diagnosis. (Source: Own elaboration).

into actionable insights, transforming diagnostics and endorsing advanced healthcare explanations.

11.5 Performance Evaluation of Machine Learning and Deep Learning Methods in Biomedical Application

Table 11.1 highlights key ML systems used in biomedical applications, concentrating on support vector machines (SVMs), Random Forests (RF), k-Nearest Neighbors (kNN), gradient boosting machines (GBM), and Naïve Bayes. These approaches are widely used for responsibilities such as disease prediction, clinical data classification, and risk assessment due to their elasticity and lower computational stresses associated with DL methods. The system has distinct advantages, like RF's robustness to overfitting and SVM's high performance on small datasets, but it also has current tests. For example, some models need wide hyperparameter changes, while others could struggle with high-dimensional information. This table suggests an overview of these methods' donations and limits in organized biomedical statistics investigation.

The chart in Figure 11.5 delivers a scoring-based impression of key ML methods in biomedical requests, with GBM and RF scoring highest for their robust performance on large datasets in disease forecasting and clinical decision-making. The SVM, effective for small datasets with high dimensionality, plays a critical role in organizational tasks. Meanwhile, kNN, however modest and explainable, is limited to high-dimensional requests, while Naïve Bayes remains valuable for basic text organization. Each technique's assets and limits are allied with separate biomedical information requirements. Figure 11.6 determines the comparison outcomes of ML models.

Table 11.2 disguises advanced AI algorithms such as deep reinforcement learning (DRL), autoencoders, generative adversarial networks (GANs), recurrent neural networks (RNNs), and CNNs. These approaches excel in handling complex and unstructured biomedical data, like medical images, time-series patient monitoring data, and genomic sequences. Convolutional neural networks, for example, are involved in medical imaging analysis, while GANs help generate synthetic data for rare disease studies. However, these models typically demand wide computational power and large labeled datasets. Individual procedures contribute to the improvement of AI in medicine, mainly in areas like modified treatment

Table 11.1 Comparison of ML and AI algorithms used in biomedical applications.

Artificial intelligence algorithms	Applications in medical sciences	Significance	Drawbacks	Results
Support vector machine [23]	Disease classification, biomarker discovery, medical image analysis (e.g., cancer diagnosis)	• High accuracy in small, high-dimensional datasets • Effective in binary classification tasks	• Not well-suited for large datasets • Requires careful tuning of hyperparameters	The SVM model in this study demonstrated a strong performance with 87.52% balanced accuracy, 87.62% recall, 86.89% precision, and an F1-score of 87.25%, supporting reliability.
Random Forests [24]	Patient risk prediction, clinical data analysis, cancer diagnosis	• Handles large datasets well • Robust to overfitting • Can be used for classification and regression	• Less interpretable than some methods • Could require large computational resources	The RF model achieved 87% accuracy, 53.7% recall, 96.9% precision, 83.8% specificity, 65.7% sensitivity, and a 0.791 F1-score, indicating robust predictive capability.

(Continued)

Table 11.1 Comparison of ML and AI algorithms used in biomedical applications. (*Continued*)

Artificial intelligence algorithms	Applications in medical sciences	Significance	Drawbacks	Results
k-Nearest Neighbors [25, 36]	Disease prediction, medical record classification, similarity-based diagnosis	• Simple and intuitive • No model training required (lazy learning)	• Computationally expensive during prediction • Poor performance with high-dimensional data	The kNN model achieved 83.9% accuracy, 87.8% average classification accuracy, and a global classification accuracy of 79.0%, reflecting solid classification performance.
Gradient boosting machines [26]	Predicting patient outcomes, drug response prediction, survival analysis	• High predictive accuracy • Robust to outliers • Flexible (can be applied to both regression and classification)	• Prone to overfitting with improper tuning • Can be computationally expensive	Not mentioned
Naïve Bayes classifier [27, 36]	Text classification in e-health records, basic disease classification	• Simple and fast • Works well with small datasets and categorical data • Probabilistic interpretation	• Assumes feature independence (which is often violated) • Less effective with complex relationships	Naïve Bayes achieved 67.7% accuracy, 71.6% average classification accuracy, and 35.5% global classification accuracy.

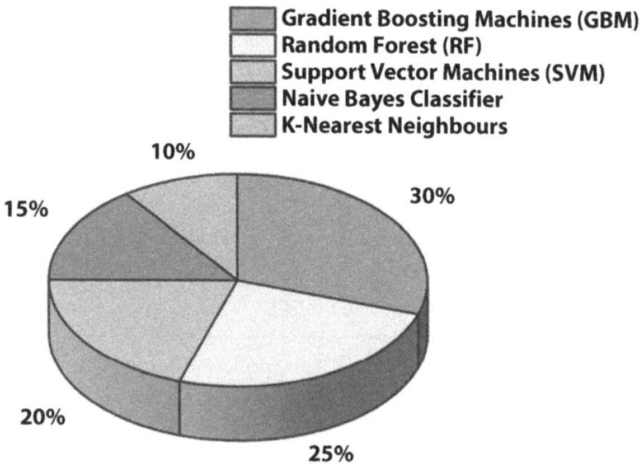

Figure 11.5 Machine learning and AI algorithms used in biomedical applications. (Source: Own elaboration).

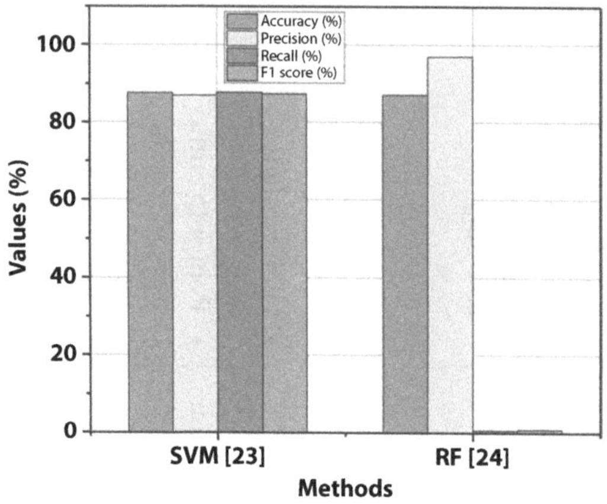

Figure 11.6 Comparison outcomes of ML techniques.

preparation, anomaly discovery, and drug discovery; however, it also has training and reserve tests.

The chart in Figure 11.7 offers an organized breakdown of practical DL methods in biomedical studies, with CNNs important in medical imaging tasks, RNNs outclassing in time-series patient monitoring, and GANs attracting synthetic data generation. While autoencoders and DRL are more particular, all contribute exclusively to medical diagnostics and optimization. Figure 11.8 illustrates the comparison results of RNN and autoencoders.

Table 11.2 Comparison of DL and AI algorithms used in biomedical applications.

Artificial intelligence algorithms	Applications in medical sciences	Significance	Drawbacks	Results
Convolutional neural networks [28]	Medical image analysis (e.g., tumor detection, organ segmentation, MRI, CT scans)	• High accuracy in image-based tasks • Automatic feature extraction • Suitable for large datasets	• Requires large labeled datasets • Computationally expensive (requires GPUs)	The CNN model achieved accuracy scores of 98.87%, 85.75%, and 99.1%, demonstrating high reliability across various test conditions.
Recurrent neural networks [29]	Time-series analysis (e.g., ECG signals, patient monitoring, genomic sequences)	• Good for sequence data • Captures temporal dependencies • Suitable for sequential patient data	• Struggles with long-term dependencies (vanishing gradient problem) • Computationally intensive	The RNN model attained a detection F1-score of 0.94, disambiguation precision of 91%, and total determination F1-score of 0.88.

(*Continued*)

Table 11.2 Comparison of DL and AI algorithms used in biomedical applications. (*Continued*)

Artificial intelligence algorithms	Applications in medical sciences	Significance	Drawbacks	Results
Autoencoders [30]	Dimensionality reduction, anomaly detection, medical image denoising, data compression	• Unsupervised learning • Effective for anomaly detection • Reduces noise in data	• Requires large datasets for training • Limited by the complexity of the model architecture	The Autoencoders model achieved an accuracy of 96.66%, an AUC of 99.46%, and an F1 score of 96.33%, indicating high performance.
Generative adversarial networks [31]	Medical image synthesis, data augmentation for rare diseases, drug discovery	• Can generate synthetic medical data • Useful for augmenting small or imbalanced datasets	• Difficult to train • Risk of generating unrealistic data if not properly trained	The GAN model achieved 0.79 accuracy, 0.76 recall, 119.34 seconds of processing time, and 0.97 precision, reflecting an efficient performance in classification tasks
Deep reinforcement learning [32]	Personalized treatment planning, drug discovery, optimizing clinical trials	• Learns optimal strategies for decision-making • Can be used for personalized medicine	• Requires significant computational power • Requires large, structured datasets for training	Not mentioned

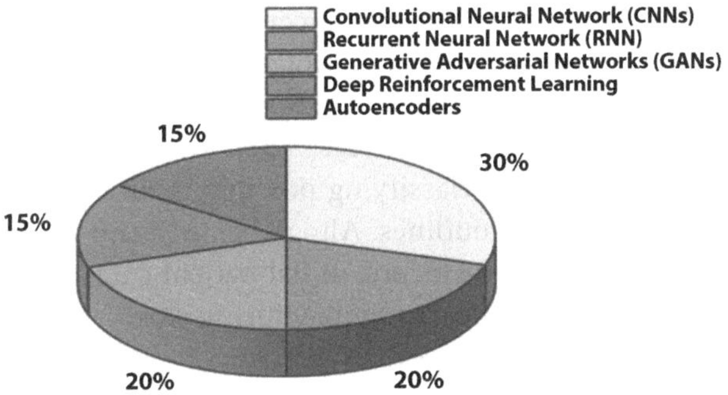

Figure 11.7 Machine leaning and AI algorithms used in biomedical applications. (Source: Own elaboration).

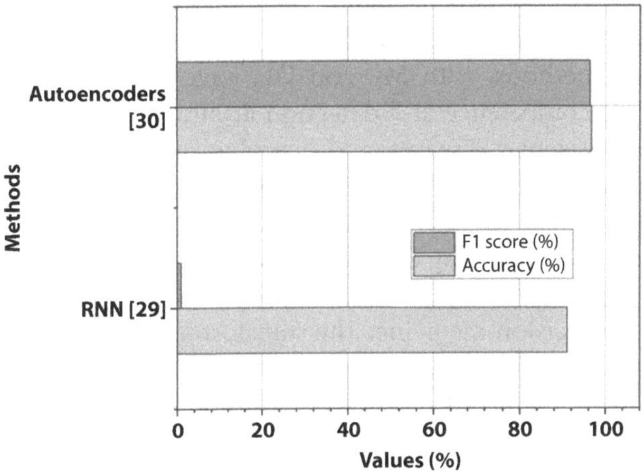

Figure 11.8 Comparison results of RNN and autoencoders.

11.6 Transformative Impact of Artificial Intelligence in Healthcare

Machine learning and AI transform biomedical research by bringing transformative progress across disease discovery, action preparation, and enduring monitoring. In diagnostics, AI imitations examine multifaceted imaging information from CT, MRI, and X-rays, allowing initial and precise detection of conditions such as cancer, cardiovascular disease, and neurological disorders. This competence allows for earlier intervention and better action consequences [33]. In modified medicine, AI adapts treatments by examining congenital and patient-specific data, devising action plans for conditions such as cancer, diabetes, and cardiovascular disorders. Moreover, wearing devices motorized by AI unceasingly monitor vital signs, providing real-time health information that clinicians use to make timely changes in patient care [34]. Artificial intelligence also quickens drug detection by classifying possible mixtures and envisaging their effectiveness and care outlines. Altogether, ML and AI in biomedical applications decrease analytic errors, initial patient care, and provision of clinicians, moving the healthcare manufacturing closer to attaining exactness in drugs and better consequences [35, 36].

11.7 Conclusion

Artificial intelligence can be found in numerous biomedical subfields, chiefly in medical imaging and ML applications. These AI-driven medical imaging methods, with ML and DL, have transformed diagnostics by enhancing competence and detection accuracy of conditions such as cancer, cardiovascular diseases, and neurological disorders. These developments have earlier discovery and modified action plans, which are vital for healthier patient results. Artificial intelligence research is spread outside diagnostics, supporting decision-making processes, enhancing action strategies, and predicting disease development, eventually easing the transition to precision medicine. The transformative role of AI in healthcare is increasingly evident, driving invention and competence in clinical practices. As AI endures to evolve, its addition into biomedical research promises to redesign healthcare, refining analytic competencies, reducing human error, and improving general patient care, paving the way for a future with more precise and personalized healthcare solutions. The limitation of the study is ensuring data security, model interpretability, and ethical considerations, which are vital for safe and accountable AI adoption in healthcare. Future research could focus on attractive AI model transparency, personalized treatment processes, and developing secure, ethical outlines for broader AI combination in biomedical research.

References

1. Cesarelli, G., *et al.*, Machine Learning for Biomedical Applications. *Bioengineering*, 11, 8, 790, 2024, https://doi.org/10.3390/bioengineering11080790.

2. Zhou, J., *et al.*, High-throughput microfluidic systems accelerated by artificial intelligence for biomedical applications. *Lab Chip*, 24, 5, 1307–1326, 2024, https://doi.org/10.1039/D3LC01012K.
3. Zhou, X., *et al.*, Editorial Deep Learning-Empowered Big Data Analytics in Biomedical Applications and Digital Healthcare. *IEEE/ACM Trans. Comput. Biol. Bioinf.*, 21, 4, 516–520, 2024, https://doi.org/10.1109/TCBB.2024.3371808.
4. Zhang, H., *et al.*, Recent advances in mass spectrometry imaging combined with artificial intelligence for spatially clarifying molecular profiles: Toward biomedical applications. *TrAC, Trends Anal. Chem.*, 178, 117834, 2024, https://doi.org/10.1016/j.trac.2024.117834.
5. Anjikar, A., *et al.*, Deep Learning in Biomedical Applications of Raman Spectroscopy, in: *Biomedical Imaging: Advances in Artificial Intelligence and Machine Learning*, pp. 209–247, Springer Nature Singapore, Singapore, 2024, https://doi.org/10.1007/978-981-97-5345-1_9.
6. Selvam, P., Kumar, M., *et al.*, Current updates on involvement of artificial intelligence and machine learning in semen analysis. *Medicina*, 60, 2, 279, 2024, https://doi.org/10.3390/medicina60020279.
7. Yi, Y., An, H.-W., Wang, H., Intelligent biomaterialomics: molecular design, manufacturing, and biomedical applications. *Adv. Mater.*, 36, 22, 2305099, 2024, https://doi.org/10.1002/adma.202305099.
8. Mishra, Y.K., Kaushik, A., Singh, A., Introduction to Advanced materials for sensing and biomedical applications. *Mater. Adv.*, 5, 16, 6346–6350, 2024, https://doi.org/10.1039/D4MA90092H.
9. Polce, E.M. and Kunze, K.N., A guide for the application of statistics in biomedical study concerning machine learning and artificial intelligence. *Arthrosc.: J. Arthrosc. Relat. Surg.*, 39, 2, 151–158, 2023, https://doi.org/10.1016/j.arthro.2022.04.016.
10. Mudhulu, S., *et al.*, Trends in graphene-based e-skin and artificial intelligence for biomedical applications—a review. *IEEE Sens. J.*, 23, 17, 18963–18976, 2023, https://doi.org/10.1109/JSEN.2023.3294297.
11. Kasture, K. and Shende, P., Amalgamation of artificial intelligence with nanoscience for biomedical applications. *Arch. Comput. Methods Eng.*, 30, 8, 4667–4685, 2023, https://doi.org/10.1007/s11831-023-09948-3.
12. Boulogeorgos, AAA., *et al.*, Machine learning in nano-scale biomedical engineering. *IEEE Trans. Mol. Biol. Multi-Scale Commun.*, 7, 1, 10–39, 2020, https://doi.org/10.1016/j.knosys.2023.110937.
13. Mentis, A.-F.A., *et al.*, Applications of artificial intelligence–machine learning for detection of stress: a critical overview. *Mol. Psychiatry*, 29, 6, 1882–1894, 2024, https://doi.org/10.1038/s41380-023-02047-6.
14. He, Z., *et al.*, The Importance of AI Algorithm Combined With Tunable LCST Smart Polymers in Biomedical Applications. *Front. Comput. Intell. Syst.*, 6, 3, 92–95, 2023, https://doi.org/10.54097/d30EoLHw.

15. Singh, J., *et al.*, Artificial intelligence in use of ZrO_2 material in biomedical science. *J. Electrochem. Sci. Eng.*, 13, 1, 83–97, 2023, https://doi.org/10.5599/jese.1498.
16. Rathore, A.S., *et al.*, Artificial intelligence and machine learning applications in biopharmaceutical manufacturing. *Trends Biotechnol.*, 41, 4, 497–510, 2023, https://doi.org/10.12665/j144.carroll.
17. Ma, X., *et al.*, Advances in integration, wearable applications, and artificial intelligence of biomedical microfluidics systems. *Micromachines*, 14, 5, 972, 2023, https://doi.org/10.3390/mi14050972.
18. Ong, X.-R., Chen, A.X., *et al.*, Nanocellulose: Recent advances toward biomedical applications. *Small Sci.*, 3, 2, 2200076, 2023, https://doi.org/10.1002/smsc.202200076.
19. Wang, C., *et al.*, Artificial intelligence enhanced sensors-enabling technologies to next-generation healthcare and biomedical platform. *Bioelectron. Med.*, 9, 1, 17, 2023, https://doi.org/10.1186/s42234-023-00118-1.
20. Sharma, P., Utilizing Explainable Artificial Intelligence to Address Deep Learning in Biomedical Domain, in: *Medical Data Analysis and Processing Using Explainable Artificial Intelligence*, pp. 19–38, CRC Press, Springer, Cham, Switzerland, 2023, https://doi.org/10.1007/s41324-022-00494-x.
21. Goel, A., *et al.*, The role of artificial neural network and machine learning in utilizing spatial information. *Spatial Inf. Study*, 31, 3, 275–285, 2023, https://doi.org/10.1007/s10462-023-10561-w.
22. Cascarano, A., *et al.*, Machine and deep learning for longitudinal biomedical data: a review of methods and applications. *Artif. Intell. Rev.*, 56, Suppl 2, 1711–1771, 2023, https://doi.org/10.1016/j.nbt.2023.02.001.
23. Mateo, J., Rius-Peris, J.M., *et al.*, Extreme gradient boosting machine learning method for predicting medical treatment in patients with acute bronchiolitis. *Biocybern. Biomed. Eng.*, 41, 2, 792–801, 2021, https://doi.org/10.1016/j.jbi.2023.104389.
24. Saeedbakhsh, S., Sattari, M., *et al.*, Diagnosis of coronary artery disease based on machine learning algorithms support vector machine, artificial neural network, and random forest. *Adv. Biomed. Study*, 12, 1, 51, 2023, https://doi.org/10.1111/exsy.13093.
25. Tanveer, M., *et al.*, Comprehensive review on twin support vector machines. *Ann. Oper. Study*, 339, 3, 1223–1268, 2024, https://doi.org/10.1080/00032719.2022.2094391.
26. Kumar, S. and Veer, K., Evaluation of Current Trends in Biomedical Applications Using Soft Computing. *Curr. Bioinf.*, 18, 9, 693–714, 2023, https://doi.org/10.1007/s10439-024-03459-3.
27. Guo, K., *et al.*, Artificial intelligence-driven biomedical genomics. *Knowl.-Based Syst.*, 279, 110937, 2023, https://doi.org/10.4018/978-1-6684-6937-8.ch017.

28. Pradhan, A.K., Das, K., Mishra, D., Chithaluru, P., Optimizing CNN-LSTM hybrid classifier using HCA for biomedical image classification. *Expert Syst.*, 40, 5, e13235, 2023, https://doi.org/10.1016/B978-0-12-820604-1.00010-8.
29. Magge, A., *et al.*, Bi-directional recurrent neural network models for geographic location extraction in biomedical literature, in: *Biocomputing 2019: Proceedings of the Pacific Symposium*, pp. 100–111, 2018, https://doi.org/10.1016/B978-0-323-85796-3.00011-1.
30. Gille, C., *et al.*, Semi-supervised classification using a supervised autoencoder for biomedical applications. *arXiv preprint arXiv:2208.10315.* https://doi.org/10.1016/j.inffus.2023.101945, 2022.
31. Hazra, D. and Byun, Y.-C., SynSigGAN: Generative adversarial networks for synthetic biomedical signal generation. *Biology*, 9, 12, 441, 2020, https://doi.org/10.5944/ried.27.1.37491.
32. Nawaz, A., *et al.*, Ensemble of Autoencoders for Anomaly Detection in Biomedical Data: A Narrative Review. *IEEE Access*, 12, 17273–17289, 2024, https://doi.org/10.59717/j.xinn-med.2023.100012.
33. Liu, Y., *et al.*, Bioinformatics: Advancing biomedical discovery and innovation in the era of big data and artificial intelligence. *Innov. Med.*, 1, 1, 100012, 2023, https://doi.org/10.59717/j.xinn-med.2023.100012.
34. Aslam, F., Advancing Intelligence: Unveiling the power of advanced machine learning algorithms for real-world applications. *J. Eng. Study Rep.*, 25, 7, 159–165, 2023, https://doi.org/10.9734/jerr/2023/v25i7949.
35. Miller, L.E., *et al.*, Recent trend in artificial intelligence-assisted biomedical publishing: a quantitative bibliometric analysis. *Cureus*, 15, 5, 2023, https://doi.org/10.7759/cureus.39224.
36. Mahfouz, M.A., *et al.*, EKNN: Ensemble classifier incorporating connectivity and density into kNN with application to cancer diagnosis. *Artif. Intell. Med.*, 111, 1019855, 2021, https://doi.org/10.1016/j.artmed.2020.101985.

12

The Internet of Medical Things in Chronic Disease Management

Ravindra Pandey[1], Shaktijeet Mohapatra[2], Suhas Ballal[3], Ritesh Kumar[4], Raesa Razeen[5] and Bavanilatha M.[6]*

[1]*Department of Management, Hult International Business School, Cambridge, United States*
[2]*Centre for Internet of Things, Siksha 'O' Anusandhan (Deemed to be University), Bhubaneswar, Odisha, India*
[3]*Department of Chemistry and Biochemistry, Jain (Deemed-to-be University), Bangalore, Karnataka, India*
[4]*Maharishi School of Engineering & Technology, Maharishi University of Information Technology, Uttar Pradesh, India*
[5]*Department of Computer Science and Engineering, Presidency University, Bangalore, Karnataka, India*
[6]*Department of Biotechnology, Sathyabama Institute of Science and Technology, Chennai, Tamil Nadu, India*

Abstract
The focus of this research is optimizing the Internet of Medical Things (IoMT) in the application to disease management of chronic conditions carried out using machine learning (ML) methods. The uses, benefits, and difficulties of using IoMT to manage long-term chronic disease problems are researched. An IoMT data-based chronic disease management (CDM) system for illness management is used to incorporate observation of various situations. A fine-tuned butterfly-optimized Random Forest (FBO-RF) integrates data from IoMT devices, enabling timely adjustments to treatment plans and reducing healthcare inefficiencies.

**Corresponding author*: bavanilatha.biotech@sathyabama.ac.in; ORCID: https://orcid.org/0000-0003-0663-5640
Ravindra Pandey: ORCID: https://orcid.org/0000-0002-1137-8506
Shaktijeet Mohapatra: ORCID: https://orcid.org/0000-0003-4713-3719
Suhas Ballal: ORCID: https://orcid.org/0000-0002-6041-8332
Ritesh Kumar: ORCID: https://orcid.org/0009-0008-6351-083X

Satya Prakash Yadav, Abhay Bansal and Victor Hugo C. de Albuquerque (eds.) Computational Intelligence in Biomedical Internet of Medical Things, (197–212) © 2026 Scrivener Publishing LLC

Data preprocessing is performed using min-max normalization, while feature extraction is conducted with principal component analysis (PCA). The proposed method is implemented using Python software. Experimental results demonstrate that the suggested approach outperforms existing methods in terms of accuracy (98%), recall (99.12%), F1 score (97.85%), and precision (95%). These results highlight how the IoMT has the potential to revolutionize the treatment of chronic illnesses and individualized medical care.

Keywords: Chronic disease management (CDM), machine learning (ML), Internet of Medical Things (IoMT), personalized healthcare, principal component analysis (PCA)

12.1 Introduction

The Internet of Things (IoT) is critical for sustainable healthcare delivery; it offers a wide range of options to improve healthcare quality while lowering costs. The IoT, which is made up of networked smart devices like smartphones and sensors, allows for constant communication for efficient service provision [1]. It transforms conventional healthcare by providing enduring care, precise prognoses, distribution of regional health strategies, monitoring of treatment compliance, individualized treatment plans, and insightful data, which helps manage chronic conditions [2]. The World Health Organization predicts that the prevalence of chronic illnesses will rise until 2030, especially in emerging nations. The IoT's potential to provide affordable healthcare solutions is crucial. There is a detailed overview of IoT applications for managing chronic diseases [3]. It highlights the IoT's role in tackling infrastructure, security, and technology issues to improve global health systems by outlining procedures, presenting findings, and discussing outcomes. The IoMT has revolutionized the treatment of chronic illnesses by utilizing digital technologies and connecting devices to improve patient outcomes, lower healthcare costs, and improve healthcare delivery [4]. By integrating wearable technology, cloud computing platforms, mobile applications, and remote monitoring tools, the IoMT allows patients with chronic illnesses like diabetes, hypertension, and heart disease to continuously and in real-time measure critical health parameters. This approach allows healthcare providers to proactively monitor patients outside traditional clinical settings, identifying potential health issues early and facilitating timely intervention [5]. Further, the IoMT will empower patients with personalized insights, reminders, and guidance on patient-owned health management. On the professional healthcare side, the IoMT enables healthcare professionals to make better decisions based on data analysis and gives an in-depth view of a patient's health pattern, which can lead to more precise diagnoses and treatment, tailoring adjustments [6]. It also integrates the IoMT into the management of chronic diseases, which further extends and expands the relationship between patients and their care providers and maintains a preventive care approach by alleviating the burden of chronic diseases on the healthcare systems of the world [7]. Leaving aside the major issues concerning data privacy, security, and interoperability of devices, the IoMT has been moving at a lightning pace, an area holding huge potential for redesigning the management of chronic diseases and changing the care to be offered to the patient of the future in the digital health revolution [8–10]. This research aims to identify how technologies in the IoMT can benefit patient outcomes, improve adherence to treatment through better compliance, and provide proactive interventions in healthcare, as well as address data security, privacy, and interoperability issues in healthcare.

12.1.1 Contributions of this Research

- Research explores the potential of the IoMT in enhancing remote monitoring for chronic disease management (CDM), enabling the tracking of patient health data and early detection of potential health issues.
- Research investigates how the IoMT can provide personalized health insights and care plans, enabling chronic condition patients to manage their health independently, enhance treatment adherence, and receive tailored support.
- This research explores the role of IoMT in improving CDM by enhancing healthcare providers' decision-making processes, improving patient outcomes, optimizing treatment plan, and increasing diagnosis accuracy.

Section 12.2 discusses related literature. Section 12.3 offers the suggested technique. Section 12.4 presents the results. Section 12.5 discusses the findings, and Section 12.6 presents the research's conclusion.

12.2 Related Works

The important themes in the literature are identified, followed by a list of technologies currently in use through the latent Dirichlet allocation algorithm and structural coding. Diabetes Mellitus and cardiovascular disease rank first and second, respectively, according to the findings on the best IoT implementation in emerging nations [11]. A novel forecast model for coronary artery disease that smoothly combines the IoMT and artificial intelligence (AI) [12]. The method increases the precision and effectiveness of heart disease prediction by utilizing cutting-edge approaches, particularly TabNet in combination with catBoost. The impact and potential mediating functions of several dietary variables on inflammation were investigated in the current article. New results show that standardized dietary patterns, eating behaviors, Chrono-nutrition aspects, food components, bioactive molecules, macro- and micronutrients, and culinary ingredients are all examples of nutritional substances that can impact inflamed processes [13]. The AI [14] in CDM is a platform that integrates AI, knowledge graphs, big data, and the IoT to provide an optimal solution from the standpoint of therapy and resource utilization. A care-aiding telemonitoring service is used by patients and clinicians; the service is seen to be impactful. The doctors are aware of the program's deployment in their organizations. A mixed method technique for evaluation was used in a sizable multi-site home telemonitoring trial [15]. The AI in CDM is a platform that integrates AI, knowledge graphs, big data, and the IoT to provide an optimal solution from the standpoint of therapy and resource utilization. Patients and hospital customers were included in the system, along with data storage and analytical tools for AI-based decision assistance [16]. Managing chronic illnesses in outpatient settings is done to evaluate how well instructional films improve patient anxiety, consultation satisfaction, and decision-making. Before a consultation, practitioners use mobile smart devices with an internet connection to create videos on patient education effectively, saving time and resources for opportunistic delivery [17]. Patients' illness management practices are affected by the internet to get health-related information and how perceived online information trustworthiness functions as a mediating factor. To demonstrate how perceived online information trustworthiness acts as a mediator [18]. An initial proof of concept was used to assess how well patient safety and medical device management worked. When implementing the IoMT system in a hospital setting, several needs should be taken into account [19]. A location spoofing detection method for IoMT networks is proposed. The suggested method detects spoofing utilizing the received signal strength and obtains delay times from anchor nodes. The long short-term memory algorithm enhances and qualitatively transforms the detection. The system's performance is assessed using both synthetic and real-world datasets.

12.3 Methodology

The methods included a fine-tuned butterfly-optimized Random Forest (FBO-RF) model to analyze data from IoMT devices, specifically aiming at CDM. Initially, data collected from IoMT devices is pre-processed using min-max normalization to scale the features, ensuring consistency across different devices. Principal component analysis (PCA) is applied for feature extraction, reducing data dimensionality and highlighting the most significant features for effective disease prediction and monitoring. The FBO-RF model to select optimal parameters for improved performance depicts the method flow, as shown in Figure 12.1.

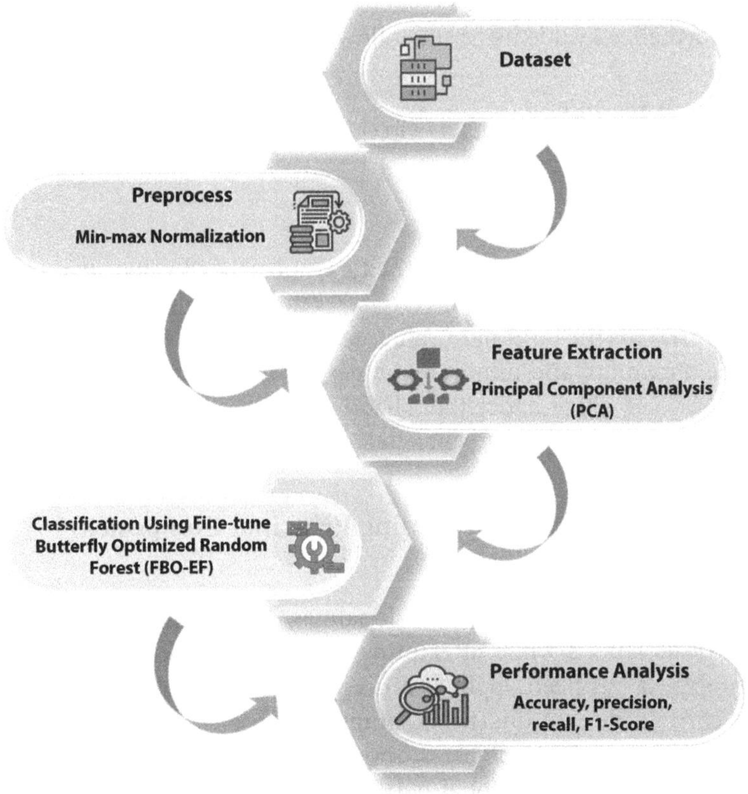

Figure 12.1 The flow of the proposed method. (Source: Own elaboration).

12.3.1 Data Collection

In an IoMT system, chronic disease data is collected through continuous monitoring across several conditions and captures health metrics from wearable devices, which help to improve treatment plans and practical management of chronic conditions.

12.3.2 Preprocessing Using Min-Max Normalization

Min-max normalization is a widely used approach in data preprocessing for CDM. In this approach, each feature's values are scaled down to fit with a predefined interval, typically [0, 1], facilitating consistent data analysis and modeling. By applying min-max normalization, the intrinsic relationships between values in CDM data are preserved, allowing for better interpretability and model accuracy. Each value in the feature is transformed into a normalized value using the following Equation 12.1:

$$u' = \frac{u - min_B}{max_B - min_B}(new\_max_B - new\_min_B) + new\_min_B \tag{12.1}$$

In this equation, u' represents the new normalized value, u represents the original value of the feature, max_B represents the maximum value, min_B represents the minimum value, and new min_B and new max_B represent the maximum and minimum values for the new range. This normalization process will enhance the reliability of the experimental results and facilitate the comparison of beneficial fields like CDM.

12.3.3 Feature Extraction Using Principal Component Analysis

The technique reduces the dimensionality of data by lowering the number of observations while attempting to preserve as much information as possible. It has been applied in diverse industries, for example, managing chronic disease due to its simplicity, ease of application, and no restrictive assumptions subject to modification. The primary objective of PCA is to map n-dimensional data into a k-dimensional feature space (where $k < n$), thereby creating a set of new principal components. The primary components provide a sufficient representation of the data in the reduced-dimensional space while capturing the highest directions of variance. In CDM, PCA can shorten data analysis by creating redundancy in patient records and monitoring parameters while identifying the key patterns to support proper diagnosis and treatment planning. The covariance matrix Σ of the data X in Equation 12.2:

$$\Sigma = \frac{1}{n-1} W^S W \tag{12.2}$$

The covariance matrix Σ is decomposed into its eigenvectors (principal components) v_i and eigenvalues λ_i: where λ_i represents the eigenvalue corresponding to the eigenvector v_i Equation 12.3:

$$\Sigma u_j = \lambda_j u_j \tag{12.3}$$

The new feature space is formed by projecting the data onto the principal components. The k-dimensional feature space is represented by the matrix W_k, which consists of the first k eigenvectors: where X_k is the transformed data in the reduced k-dimensional space Equation (12.4):

$$W_l = W.X_l \tag{12.4}$$

Thus, PCA reduces the dimensionality of the dataset while maintaining the original variance as possible by selecting the eigenvectors with the largest eigenvalues.

12.3.4 Fine-Tuned Butterfly-Optimized Random Forest

The FBO-RF model is a hybrid ML model that combines the complementary strengths of the Random Forest (RF) and the FBO in feature selection and parameter tuning. In CDM, this model leverages the best decision trees with the RF, benefiting from the global search capability of FBO. This synergy enhances accuracy, generalization, and performance, enabling the model to handle complex datasets effectively and efficiently. Such improvements make FBO-RF well-suited for classification and regression tasks, particularly valuable in chronic disease management applications where precise predictions are essential for patient outcomes and resource optimization.

12.3.5 Random Forest

Random Forest is increasingly applied in CDM and other related fields because of its robustness and versatility when handling tough and high-dimensional data sets. Research presents findings on sensitivity toward sample size, the number of variables, responsiveness toward different method parameters, and sensitivity concerning the presence of correlated variables in identifying RF variable importance scores. In essence, RF is the creation of a forest that is a component of the decision tree. Its accuracy is significantly higher than that of many other ML methods, particularly when dealing with large datasets that have a wide range of variables. It is frequently trained using the bagging strategy, which selects each tree randomly from the training set. This means that the younger trees are not dependent on the older ones. The model aggregates as predicted by the decision tree. Applying the bagging model has made RF more important in lowering decision tree variance and data over-fitting. Additionally, one prevalent treatment in RF architecture is addressing missing data.

The quantity of classification trees is combined with the RF classifier. The classification result is calculated using Equation 12.5.

$$D(s) = \underset{O}{max}\ F_s \sum_{j=1}^{L} (d_j(S) = O) \tag{12.5}$$

Let S be the initial dataset's training set S and L and L show the subsets from the S dataset. The program automatically produces, for every subset L decision tree using a random vector as an aid. $D(s)$ represents the outcome of the categorization, whereas $d_j(S)$ indicates the outcome of the classification of the jth decision tree. However, several RF hyper-parameters are being employed to either speed up the procedure or improve the model's prediction abilities. This approach can be applied to CDM, where the model's predictive power is crucial for identifying and classifying patterns related to various chronic conditions in Equation 12.6.

$$j(s) = 1 - e_1^2 - e_0^2(3) \tag{12.6}$$

The Gini impurity is computed using Equation 12.7, where each node, represented by s, is equivalent to any node in an RF and decision tree. The Gini impurity helps to determine the optimal split by providing an estimation of entropy. Additionally, e_i in Equation 12.8 represents the fraction of m_i samples relative to the total number of samples, with $i = 0,\ 1$ indicating the respective classes.

$$e_i = \frac{m_i}{m} \tag{12.7}$$

It can reduce δj by dividing and distributing the goods to two distinct sub-notes $(s_o \& s_r)$ based on a threshold for the variable Θ. This process is illustrated in Equation 12.8.

$$\delta j(s) = j(s) - e_o j(s_o) - e_r j(s_r) \tag{12.8}$$

After that, a thorough search is carried out using every value of Θ, which can be derived from the overall thresholds of the node. Following this, the reductions in Gini impurity values for all variables are recorded separately using Equation 12.9.

$$J_H(\Theta) = \Sigma_q \Sigma_r \delta j_\Theta(s, S) \tag{12.9}$$

The information gain indicates how often the feature Θ is chosen when there is a divide and its importance with the classifier for the specific problem addressed.

12.3.6 Fine-Tuned Butterfly Optimization

The main mechanism for achieving the trade-off between exploration and exploitation in this framework is the inertia weight. The algorithm's capacity is to explore previously undiscovered areas is closely correlated with its inertia weight. In this proposed research, the collective application of inertia weight and global exploration in the Fine-tuned Bee Optimization (FBO) algorithm enhances the methodology's exploration capabilities. This approach is particularly beneficial in CDM, where identifying optimal intervention pathways requires balancing new treatment explorations with known, effective methods. The symbol for the adjustment factor is s. As a result, the algorithm becomes more efficient. The natural exponent inertia weight iteration update in Equations 12.10, 12.11, and 12.12 as follows:

$$x(s) = x_{min} + (x_{max} - x_{min}).f^{-\left(\frac{\frac{s}{MAXITER}}{10}\right)} \tag{12.10}$$

x_{max} – Maximum weight value, x_{min} – minimum weightvalue, M -maximum number of iterations

$$w_j^{s+1} = x(s) * \alpha * w_j^s + (q^2 \times h^* - w_j^s) \times e_j \tag{12.11}$$

$$\alpha = \frac{T_{max}}{s^2} \tag{12.12}$$

Where T_{max} – max walk step in the FBO-RF model, the FBO helps explore and identify the best parameter combinations for the RF, such as the number of trees, maximum depth, and feature selection, allowing the model to perform more accurately and efficiently on complex datasets. The fine-tuning process leverages the butterfly algorithm's balanced exploitation and exploration capabilities, which mimic the natural foraging behaviors of butterflies. This approach ensures that the model avoids local optima and achieves improved predictive power and generalization in various application areas, including classification, regression, and anomaly detection tasks.

12.4 Results

Using an FBO-RF model, the research suggests optimizing for the IoMT in CDM using the Intel Xeon E3-1230v5 CPU, NVIDIA Quadro K420 graphics card, 16 GB DDR4 RAM, and 1TB SSD storage power system. Regarding this, the suggested approach is compared to convolutional neural networks (CNN) and k-Nearest Neighbors (KNN) [19] in terms of four important performance parameters: accuracy, F1 score, precision, and recall, as shown in Table 12.1.

Table 12.1 Outcomes of metrics.

Methods	Accuracy (%)	Precision (%)	Recall (%)	F1 score (%)
Convolutional neural networks and k-Nearest Neighbors [19]	96	93	99	97
Fine-tuned butterfly-optimized Random Forest [Proposed]	98	95	99.12	97.85

Accuracy: The primary performance metric in the CDM is the precision of the prediction models used for monitoring and diagnosing these conditions. Figure 12.2 depicts the outcomes of accuracy. It has been demonstrated to indicate the percentage of accurate predictions, also known as true positives, and true negatives among all the predictions made to ascertain if a patient has a chronic illness or not.

The accuracy of the FBO-RF method achieved 98%, which is compared with the existing methods of CNN and KNN [19] attained 96%. It explains how the suggested methodology performs better than the current methods.

Precision: Precision is an important measure of how good a predictive model does in classifying a patient's outcome or treatment response in CDM. Figure 12.3 depicts the outcomes of precision. Precision quantifies

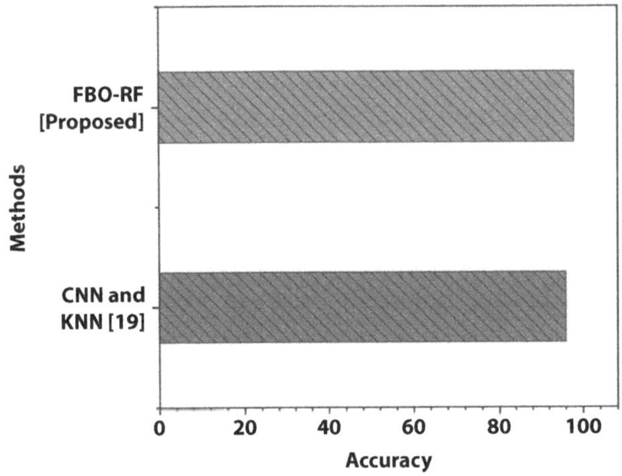

Figure 12.2 Analysis of accuracy. (Source: Own elaboration).

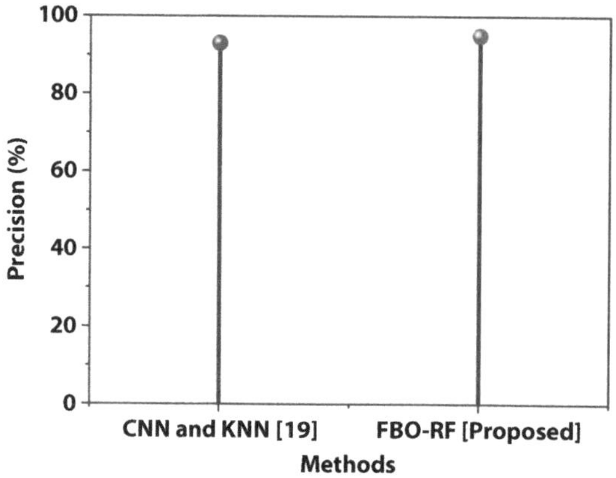

Figure 12.3 Analysis of precision. (Source: Own elaboration).

the positive predictive values, which calculate the number of true positives, defined as the instances in which the predicted outcome is correct, such as effectiveness or efficient treatment response, to the total count of both true and false positives, that is, incorrectly assigned positive outcomes.

The precision of the FBO-RF method achieved 95%, compared with the existing methods of CNN and KNN [19], which attained 93%. It explains how the suggested methodology performs better than the current methods.

Recall: In CDM, one important measure in classifying models that identify patients needing specific interventions or monitoring is recall. The model's recall quantifies its capacity to accurately detect instances in which the ailment or risk factor is present. Figure 12.4 depicts the outcomes of recall. This implies identifying the patients at risk of complications or who require a specific type of treatment.

The recall of the FBO-RF method achieved 99.12%, which is compared with the existing methods of CNN and KNN [19] that attained 99%. It explains how the suggested methodology performs better than the current methods.

F1 score: The F1 score is a single performance indicator for the classification model, particularly effective when the class distribution is unbalanced. It represents the harmonic mean of precision and recall. It will balance the false positives and negatives. Figure 12.5 depicts the outcomes of the F1 score. When it comes to managing chronic diseases, the F1 score can be very essential in evaluating the accuracy of the models that predict

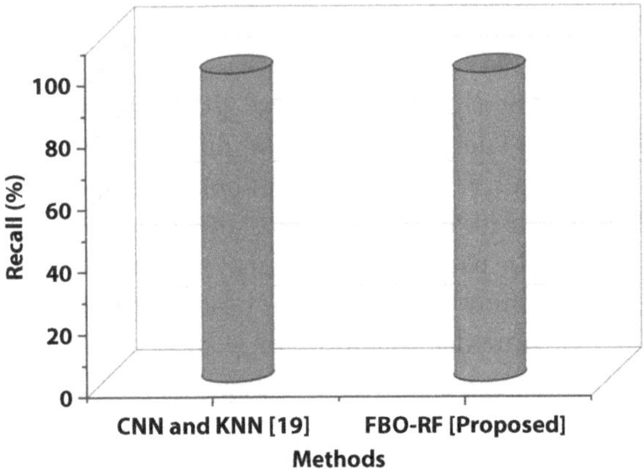

Figure 12.4 Analysis of recall. (Source: Own elaboration).

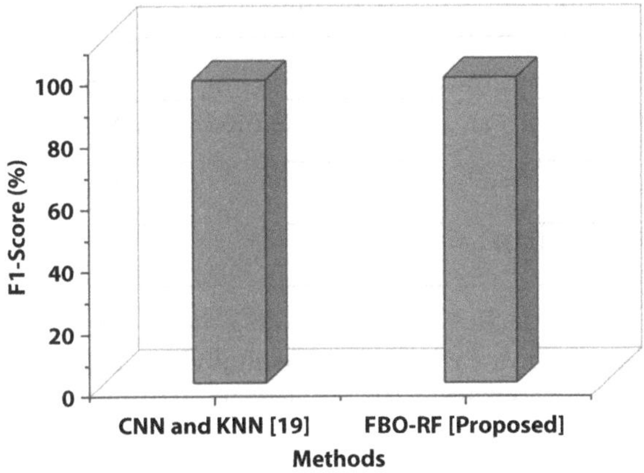

Figure 12.5 Analysis of the F1 score. (Source: Own elaboration).

the outcomes of patients, which aid in the betterment of health-care interventions considering both positive and negative signs of health.

The F1 score of the FBO-RF method achieved 97.85%, which is compared with the existing methods of CNN and KNN [19] that attained 97%. It explains how the suggested methodology performs better than the current methods.

12.5 Discussion

The CNN and KNN algorithms face several challenges, particularly in handling high-dimensional data and interpretability issues. Convolutional neural networks often require large datasets and high computational resources, while the KNN is sensitive to noisy data and less effective for complex, non-linear patterns. The use of a finer butterfly-optimized model to enhance the RF model would show greater accuracy, recall, F1 score, and precision, how effectively real-time data could be processed to provide personalized care. This potential new route into harnessing the IoMT and advanced algorithms for ML promises to make a better future by reducing inefficiencies in health services and potential hospital visits, thereby adding to patient outcomes. Privacy of data and device interoperability issues have to be sorted before this would become more widely adopted. The proposed FBO-RF method addresses these limitations by enhancing feature selection and reducing dimensionality, which streamlines data processing and improves model efficiency. The RF component introduces robustness against noise, while feature-based optimization reduces computational costs, providing a more accurate, scalable, and interpretable model solution.

12.6 Conclusion

Advanced ML approaches from the IoMT have the potential to completely transform CDM. By lowering hospital visits and increasing patient outcomes, the proposed FBO-RF for service integration with health service providers will develop more proactive and individualized treatment plans. The proposed approach significantly outperforms existing methods, achieving an accuracy of 98%, a recall of 99.12%, an F1 score of 97.85%, and a precision of 95%. This work forms a better foundation for the promising future of IoMT in solving the complexity of CDM towards a streamlined, personalized, and timely intervention in medical practice.

12.6.1 Limitations and Future Research

The IoMT systems depend on a wide range of devices, specifications, and data formats, which can make it difficult to guarantee device integration and platform consistency. Some future directions include evaluating the long-term performance and impact of the approach and taking into consideration CDM over time through assessments of patient adherence and lifestyle changes.

References

1. Hui, *et al.*, Distinguishing between smartphones and IoT devices *via* network traffic. *IEEE Internet Things J.*, 9, 2, 1182–1196, 2021, doi: 10.1109/JIOT.2021.3078879.
2. Adewole, *et al.*, Cloud-based IoMT framework for cardiovascular disease prediction and diagnosis in personalized E-health care, in: *Intelligent IoT Systems in Personalized Healthcare*, pp. 105–145, Academic Press, Cambridge, MA, 2021, https://doi.org/10.1016/B978-0-12-821187-8.00005-8.
3. Javed, *et al.*, Internet of Medical Things (IoMT) Enabled Intelligent System for Chronic Disease Prediction Using Deep Machine Learning in Healthcare 5.0. *J. Comput. Biomed. Inf.*, 7, 02, 2024, DOI: 10.56979.
4. Wang, X. and Song, Y., Edge-assisted IoMT-based smart-home monitoring system for the elderly with chronic diseases. *IEEE Sens. Lett.*, 7, 2, 1–4, 2023, doi: 10.1109/LSENS.2023.3240670.
5. Nigar, *et al.*, IoMT meets machine learning: From edge to cloud chronic diseases diagnosis system. *J. Healthc. Eng.*, 2023, 1, 9995292, 2023, https://doi.org/10.1155/2023/9995292.
6. Saha, J. and Sen, R., IoT vs IoMT—A comparative research based on knowledge among medical professionals. *Int. J. Multidiscip. Educ. Res.*, 13, 99–109, 2024, http://ijmer.in.doi./2024/13.5.13.
7. Shafiq, *et al.*, Advances in IoMT for Healthcare Systems. *Sensors*, 24, 1, 10, 2023, https://doi.org/10.3390/s24010010.
8. Mathkor, *et al.*, Multirole of the internet of medical things (IoMT) in biomedical systems for managing smart healthcare systems: An overview of current and future innovative trends. *J. Infect. Public Health*, 17, 4, 559–572, 2024, https://doi.org/10.1016/j.jiph.2024.01.013.
9. Wright, A., *et al.*, The invisible epidemic: neglected chronic disease management during COVID-19. *J. Gen. Internal Med.*, 35, 2816–28175, 2020, https://doi.org/10.1007/s11606-020-06025-4.
10. Dwivedi, *et al.*, Potential of Internet of Medical Things (IoMT) applications in building a smart healthcare system: A systematic review. *J. Oral Biol. Craniofac. Res.*, 12, 2, 302–318, 2022, https://doi.org/10.1016/j.jobcr.2021.11.010.
11. Ramos-Lopez, *et al.*, The role of nutrition on meta-inflammation: insights and potential targets in communicable and chronic disease management. *Curr. Obes. Rep.*, 11, 4, 305–335, 2022, https://doi.org/10.1007/s13679-022-00490-0.
12. Baseer, *et al.*, Healthcare diagnostics with an adaptive deep learning model integrated with the Internet of medical Things (IoMT) for predicting heart disease. *Biomed. Signal Process. Control*, 92, 105988, 2024, https://doi.org/10.1016/j.bspc.2024.105988.

13. Li, *et al.*, Home telemonitoring for chronic disease management: Perceptions of users and factors influencing adoption. *Health Inf. J.*, 27, 1, 1460458221997893, 2021, https://doi.org/10.1177/1460458221997893.
14. Yu, *et al.*, Improving chronic disease management for children with knowledge graphs and artificial intelligence. *Expert Syst. Appl.*, 201, 117026, 2022, https://doi.org/10.1016/j.eswa.2022.117026.
15. Kovoor, *et al.*, Clinician-created educational video resources for shared decision-making in the outpatient management of chronic disease: development and evaluation research. *J. Med. Internet Res.*, 23, 10, e26732, 2021, doi: 10.2196/26732.
16. Soroya, *et al.*, Impact of health-related internet use on disease management behavior of chronic patients: Mediating role of perceived credibility of online information. *Inf. Dev.*, 40, 3, 478–488, 2024, https://doi.org/10.1177/02666669221144622.
17. Kim, *et al.*, Application of an Internet of Medical Things (IoMT) to Communications in a Hospital Environment. *Appl. Sci.*, 12, 23, 12042, 2022, https://doi.org/10.3390/app122312042.
18. Jafarian, *et al.*, A qualitative spoofing detection system based on LSTMs for IoMT, in: *2023 14th International Conference on Information and Knowledge Technology (IKT)*, IEEE, pp. 98–102, 2023, doi: 10.1109/IKT62039.2023.10433044.
19. Alanazi, R., Identification and prediction of chronic diseases using machine learning approach. *J. Healthc. Eng.*, 2022, 1, 2826127, 2022, https://doi.org/10.1155/2022/2826127.

13

Wearable Technologies in Internet of Medical Things Biomedical Intelligence

Ramesh B. Darla[1]*, Biswaranjan Swain[2], Roopashree R.[3], Amreen Khanum D.[4], Trapty Agarwal[5] and Barani Selvaraj[6]

[1]Technology & Quality, Cisco Systems, India
[2]Centre for Internet of Things, Siksha 'O' Anusandhan (Deemed to be University), Bhubaneswar, Odisha, India
[3]Department of Chemistry and Biochemistry, Jain (Deemed-to-be University), Bangalore, Karnataka, India
[4]Department of Computer Science and Engineering, Presidency University, Bangalore, Karnataka, India
[5]Maharishi School of Engineering & Technology, Maharishi University of Information Technology, Uttar Pradesh, India
[6]Department of Electronics and Communication Engineering, Sathyabama Institute of Science and Technology, Chennai, Tamil Nadu, India

Abstract

The Internet of Medical Things (IoMT) has transformed the medical industry by allowing patients to be tracked using wearable devices. Current methods often struggle with issues such as high dimensionality, noise, and inefficiency in prediction accuracy, particularly in critical healthcare scenarios where decision-making speed and accuracy are crucial. This research addresses these issues by introducing the Intelligent Dwarf Mongoose fine-tuned Resilient LightGBM (IDM-RLGBM), to improve the accuracy and efficiency of classification in wearable IoMT devices. The IDM-RLGBM approach integrates the Intelligent Dwarf Mongoose algorithm (IDM), a powerful nature-inspired optimization technique, with the Resilient

**Corresponding author*: chiralaramesh@gmail.com; ORCID: https://orcid.org/0000-0002-7429-5425
Biswaranjan Swain: ORCID: https://orcid.org/0000-0002-2560-8755
Roopashree R.: ORCID: https://orcid.org/0000-0002-0382-6321
Trapty Agarwal: ORCID: https://orcid.org/0009-0007-4081-4999
Barani Selvaraj: ORCID: https://orcid.org/0000-0001-6323-4611

Satya Prakash Yadav, Abhay Bansal and Victor Hugo C. de Albuquerque (eds.) Computational Intelligence in Biomedical Internet of Medical Things, (213–228) © 2026 Scrivener Publishing LLC

LightGBM, an efficient gradient boosting framework. The IDM is used to fine-tune the hyperparameters of LightGBM to enhance its robustness and predictive power. The data collected from the ECG signal were preprocessed using min-max normalization to adjust the range of values. The features were then extracted through discrete wavelet transform (DWT) to identify significant time-frequency characteristics. The IDM-RLGBM model demonstrated superior results compared to conventional machine learning methods in terms of classified precision, F1 score, accuracy, and recall. This innovative IDM-RLGBM strategy offers a flexible and robust solution for wearable IoMT, significantly improving the accuracy of the electrocardiogram (ECG) signal analysis and facilitating effective, real-time detection of cardiovascular disease (CVD).

***Keywords*:** IoMT, wearable device, cardiovascular disease (CVD), ECG signal, IDM-RLGBM

13.1 Introduction

The Internet of Medical Things (IoMT) is a category of the Internet of Things (IoT) that connects medical equipment for healthcare monitoring. The IoMT software integrates patients and physicians *via* medical equipment, enabling remote data collection and transmission over secure networks [1]. With an increasing number of wearable technologies, conventional communication networks designed principally for human-centered applications face substantial issues, such as excessive latency, inadequate processing power, and short battery life [2]. Despite several groundbreaking findings that have made this technique extremely accurate and contextual in healthcare, it is unable to handle the complexity of many conditions, including diabetes and heart disease [3]. A system based on the cloud is essential for foreseeing the mortal progression of cardiovascular disease (CVD), especially in the IoMT era. While there has been improvement in predicting CVD over the past two decades, individualized diagnosis remains a significant problem [4].

Innovative healthcare delivery is a new multidisciplinary field that encompasses the collection, processing, transference, storage, retrieval, and use of biological and health data. The core of connected health, also known as p-health realization, is comprised of wearable technology, communications, and applications [5]. The fast development of wearable technology in the IoMT brings tremendous innovation to biomedical applications. These wearables can potentially detect early warning signs of chronic diseases or acute medical events *via* real-time monitoring and analytics [6]. Wearable devices, thus, promote not only a precautionary attitude toward health but also rapid response times in the event of potentially life-threatening incidents [7].

Wearable technology has a very significant role in remote patient monitoring, particularly for a patient who is located in a rural or underserved area of the country where there is a lack of healthcare facilities [8]. Devices in the IoMT send real-time data to healthcare providers, who can assess a patient's condition without necessarily needing the patient to come into a clinic or hospital. This has been particularly useful during events like the COVID-19 pandemic, where it became necessary for as many people as possible to avoid in-person healthcare interactions [9]. The capability for remote, secure monitoring of patients, whether after surgery or during a pandemic, means at least the most critical medical data is available to help maintain continuity of care for the patients [10]. The objective of this research is to improve the accuracy and efficiency of IoMT wearable devices in detecting CVDs by proposing an Intelligent Dwarf Mongoose fine-tuned Resilient LightGBM (IDM-RLGBM) model that combines the Intelligent Dwarf Mongoose (IDM) optimization algorithm with the Resilient LightGBM (RLGBM) for enhanced classification.

The organization of the research is divided into the following sections: Section 13.2 describes the literature review article on wearable devices in IoMT biomedical. Section 12.3 provides a methodology to clarify a proposed method process. The performance of the evaluated result is shown in Section 12.4. Finally, Section 12.5 discusses the overall research conclusion.

13.2 Related Articles

A long short-term memory (LSTM) neural network technique could be used in research [11] to improve the identification of medical equipment errors. To achieve the best performance, the dropout layer and hyperbolic tangent activation function were integrated. The suggested model attained 96% accuracy, with strong recall and assessment parameters (95%, 94.5%, and 97%), providing efficacy in forecasting anomalies and assuring healthcare equipment dependability.

Deep learning (DL) and cyber-physical systems are investigated to improve predictive analytics for the IoMT in the research [12]. The method included analyzing large datasets generated by IoMT sensors that used DL techniques, such as recurrent neural networks (RNN) and convolutional neural networks (CNN). The findings illustrated DL's usefulness in extracting significant insights, facilitating efficient decision-making, and addressing the IoMT's dependability and security issues.

Precise, individual-centric forecasting algorithms were used to handle type 1 diabetic mellitus using wearable technology and ML [13]. Using a collection of biological variables from 40 type 1 diabetic mellitus patients, it used the Random Forest approach to forecast blood sugar levels. The models demonstrated great accuracy and latency.

Creating an IoMT system for the early detection of respiratory disorders utilizing radiofrequency sensors and software-defined radio technologies was the objective of the research [14]. For categorization, a DL framework was used, which was compared to typical machine learning (ML) models. The finding shows that DL outperforms traditional models and attained over 98% accuracy in detecting respiratory problems by successfully capturing temporal patterns.

To measure blood glucose levels and create digital biomarkers for tracking diabetes mellitus, the research [15] intended to investigate the use of non-invasive wearable devices combined with ML algorithms. The approach entails relationships between glycemic health markers and data gathered from wearable devices. The finding shows the promise of wearable devices in the treatment of diabetes but indicates the need for additional accuracy validation.

The article's purpose is to investigate the use of ML in IoT networks enabled by healthcare, namely for illness diagnosis and patient status monitoring [16]. An ML-enabled IoT model was created for cloud-based biomedical applications as a component of the process. The findings show that incorporating ML into IoT systems improves the accuracy of illness diagnosis, expedites decision-making, and lowers false positives in the medical field.

To enhance EEG-based schizophrenia detection using a schizophrenia hybrid neural network, a hybrid DL model that combines CNN for extraction of features and LSTM for classified in the research [17]. The model beat CNN, LSTM, and ML structures, with a 99.9% accuracy throughout the two datasets. It also performed well with fewer electrodes and enabled IoMT-based smart healthcare and remote monitoring applications.

An artificial intelligent-powered IoMT telemedicine system for e-healthcare was offered to collect patient data through wearable sensor devices, transmitting and storing the data in an IoMT cloud repository by research [18]. A hybrid ResNet 18 and GoogleNet classifier was used to make abnormal/normal predictions, and notifications were given to healthcare providers as needed. The suggested system's efficiency was validated by performance analysis.

To enhance early-stage mental health diagnosis, particularly for schizophrenia, by combined wearable IoMT devices with a unique Deep CNN with a separated attention device was an objective of the research [19]. The approach consists of novel imputation, sliding window sampling, and the Synthetic Minority Over-sampling Technique (SMOTE) for class balance. The method reached 94% accuracy utilizing 24-hour actigraphy data, provided a non-invasive, objective option for actual-time mental health care.

To improve cardiac illness detection by combining the modified deep CNN with the Bag-of-Visual-Words method for enhanced feature selection of the paper [20]. The strategy involved gathering cardiac data using IoT devices and utilizing modified deep CNN for categorization. The results demonstrated an important increase in accuracy (98.77%) and precision (98.1%), indicating that the model was useful in predicting heart illnesses.

13.3 Methodology

The proposed method IDM-RLGBM is classified for CVD-detected wearable IoMT biomedical devices. The data was collected from the electrocardiogram (ECG) signal. Preprocessing utilized min-max normalization was used to scale the data. Discrete wavelet transforms (DWT) are used for feature extraction, which decomposes the ECG signal into frequency components. Figure 13.1 illustrates the flow chart of the proposed research.

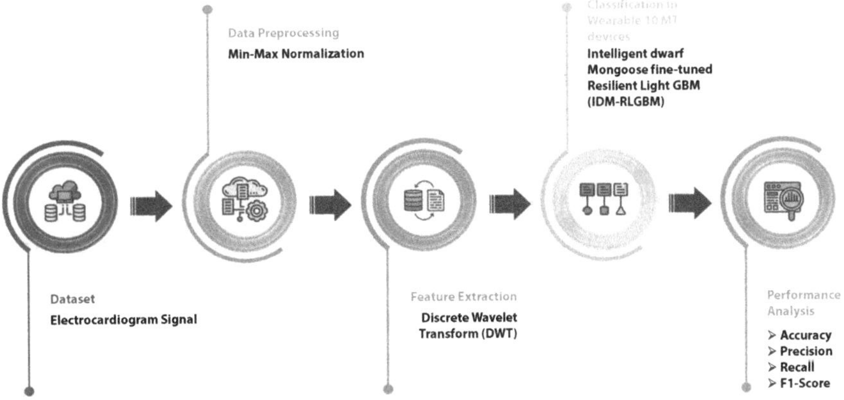

Figure 13.1 Basic concept of proposed research framework. (Source: Own elaboration).

13.3.1 Data Collection

The MIT-BIH Arrhythmia record contains 48 half-hour sections of two-channel ambulant ECG information from 47 distinct individuals, which the BIH Arrhythmia Lab investigated from 1975 to 1979. Twenty databases were selected randomly from 4024-hour ambulant ECG data collected from a mixed sample of hospital stay patients (roughly 60%) and day patients (about 40%). The other 25 databases were preferred from the same collection to contain fewer frequent but medically important dysrhythmias that could not be overrepresented in a small, randomized sample. The databases were made across a 10-mV range at 360 specimens per sec per channel, with an 11-bit resolution.

The dataset is available online: https://www.kaggle.com/datasets/mondejar/mitbih-database.

13.3.2 Preprocessing

Normalization is the process of converting a signal with input; for this example, an ECG is into a distribution of the numbers within the [0, 1] range. In this case, the min-max normalization approach is employed, which is a popular pre-processing method for ECG data. $Z[m]$ is the new magnitude for time-step n, $w[m]$ is the previous amplitude, minimum value for $w[m]$ of min, along with maximum value for $w[m]$ of max. This method employs in Equation 13.1 as follows.

$$Y[m] = \frac{w(m) - min}{max - min} \tag{13.1}$$

The outcomes of the models that utilized normalization after running the models on the datasets are without any preparation.

13.3.3 Feature Extraction

The ECG signal is analyzed using DWT for feature extraction. The DWT decomposes the signal into different frequency components such as approximation and detail coefficients at different scales, thereby capturing low- and high-frequency information. The multi-resolution analysis is constructed using filtration banks using the DWT, which has a comparatively short calculation time. Low pass and high pass filters are the two kinds of filters used in DWT. Fifty percent of the bandwidth of the entering signal is the cut-off frequency for both low pass and high pass filters. The analysis of wavelets combines down sampling and filtration. This results in a two-fold down-sampling of the signal. The first wavelet transform level is the result of down-sampling the original signal after it has been processed *via* the two filters. At most $[log_2 N]$, where N is the signal length, is a decomposition stage. Although the rebuilding stage similarly uses two filters, this down-sampling step is swapped to perform up-sampling, which up-samples by a factor of two and includes zeros in the up-sampling procedure. Here is a definition of the rebuilding Equation 13.2:

$$dB_j[l] = \sum_{-\infty}^{\infty} (dC_{j+1}[l]h[-m+2l] + dB_{j+1}[l]g[-m+2l]) \quad (13.2)$$

The estimated value factors are dB_j, whereas the detail values are dC_j.

13.3.4 Intelligent Dwarf Mongoose Fine-Tuned Resilient LightGBM

The IDM-RLGBM model could enhance performance in wearable IoMT device classification because of current demands in healthcare applications, where much more reliable real-time data analysis is required in this research. The nature-inspired optimization algorithm IDM is applied to tune the hyperparameters of the RLGBM, one of the most efficient gradient boosting frameworks, characterized by its swiftness and accuracy. Considering IDM as the fine-tuning strategy, this model enhances the predictive power and robustness of the RLGBM model, thereby contributing to solving challenges related to IoMT wearable devices regarding noise, large datasets, and high-performance classification in CVD monitoring. This makes health predictions more accurate and decision-making in medical diagnostics improved.

13.3.5 Resilient LightGBM

Resilient LightGBM serves as the basic classification model due to its efficiency and capability to handle large datasets with effectiveness. A wearable IoMT device generates a great quantity of data, which is processed and classified using a gradient-boosting framework called RLGBM. It is highly predictive, with high speed, and thus best suited for CVD monitoring applications in real-time, where fast and accurate classification is highly essential for timely decision-making in healthcare. LightGBM is a quick, efficient, and accurate implementation of gradient-boosting decision trees for tasks like classification. The classical classifier cannot identify data sample classes due to its failure to address class imbalance issues. To address the issue, RLGBM's loss function is modified with the L2 regular term, and specific sample categories have a greater weight. Employing one-sided gradient collection in LightGBM improves detection accuracy on unbalanced datasets. The enhancements are as follows in Equation 13.3:

The enhanced the function of loss in the sth trees is

$$L = \frac{1}{m}\left(\sum_{j=1}^{m} \alpha_j L\left(z_j, E_{s-1}(w_j)\right) + \frac{\lambda}{2} \|b\| \frac{2}{2} \right) \tag{13.3}$$

$$\alpha_j = \begin{cases} 1, z_j = 0 \\ d, z_j = 1 \end{cases} \tag{13.4}$$

In this Equation (13.4), α_j is the category's weight value, $L\left(z_j, E_{s-1}(w_j)\right)$ is the initial loss function, λ is the standardization value, and $z_j = 0$ *and* 1 indicate ordinary and minority sample labels, respectively. d corresponds to the sample percentage.

13.3.6 Intelligent Dwarf Mongoose

The optimization of IDM fine-tuned the hyperparameters of the RLGBM model, which improves the general performance of the model. The IDM algorithm can ensure better accuracy and robustness in the model's predictions. The efficiency of RLGBM was enhanced by IDM by optimizing critical settings that eventually provided more reliable classification results for wearable IoMT devices. It presents a novel IDM utilizing an alpha-directed learning strategy to address various mathematics benchmark functions and technological difficulties. The proposed solution includes improved LS to boost search abilities, with partial guidance from the revised alpha. The lth individual's (mongoose) is located in the cth dimension at repetition j. A random number between 0 and 1 is used to provide unpredictability to the searching process. *peep*, a metric that indicates the vocalization effect of the alpha female, which directs the direction of foraging. The general population of individuals in overall amount denotes M_{CN}. The number of babysitters in the group demonstrates Bst. Dim is several decision variables related to the optimization task. Consequently, the following

Equation 13.5 is an improvement to the location of each obtaining solution throughout the search space.

$$C_{l,c}(j+1) = \begin{cases} bestCN_c(j) + rand(0,1) \times \left(C_{l,c}(j) - C_{Q,c}(j)\right) & if\ rand < DO \\ C_{l,c}(j) + rand\ (0,1) \times peep & else \\ l = 1{:}\ M_{CN} - Bst, c = 1{:}\ Dim & \end{cases} \quad (13.5)$$

In this Equation 13.5, $bestCN_c$ is the location of the seeking individual with the highest fitness rating, $C_{Q,c}$ is a randomly selected person from the CN population, and DO is the probability of making a decision. To balance the improved exploit properties stated in Equation 13.5 with the investigative features offered, DO is set at 50%. While the investigative searching characteristics are maintained and acquired utilizing the conventional approach concurrently, the mistreatment features are significant and robust when using the structure.

13.4 Result and Discussion

A double Intel Pentium E5-2600 CPU running at 2.4 GHz, 64 GB of RAM, and the Keras Python library are used for the experiment. The performance evaluation for IDM-RLGBM classification due to CVD detects wearable techniques in IoMT biomedical. The results assessed in various traditional methods, such as Adaptive Hoeffding Tree (AHT) (Elbasi, and Zreikat, 2023) and Random Forest (Mulani et al., 2024) determine in different parameters, precision, recall, accuracy, and F1 score. The receiver operating characteristic area under the curve (ROC-AUC) plot of the IDM-RLGBM model is presented in Figure 13.2, showing its high capability of correctly classifying ECG signals. An AUC of 95% therefore informs that the model has a strong discriminative power in the detection of CVD. It reflects how effective the model IDM-RLGBM was in addressing the complexities of the ECG data and enhancing real-time CVD.

The proportion of every circumstance in the sample was correctly classified (both positive and negative). Figure 13.3 shows accuracy values. The accuracy of the IDM-RLGBM model (97%) is higher, compared with traditional approaches like AHT (95.67%) and RF (92%). High dimensionality and noisy ECG data may generate difficulties in recognizing cardiac events,

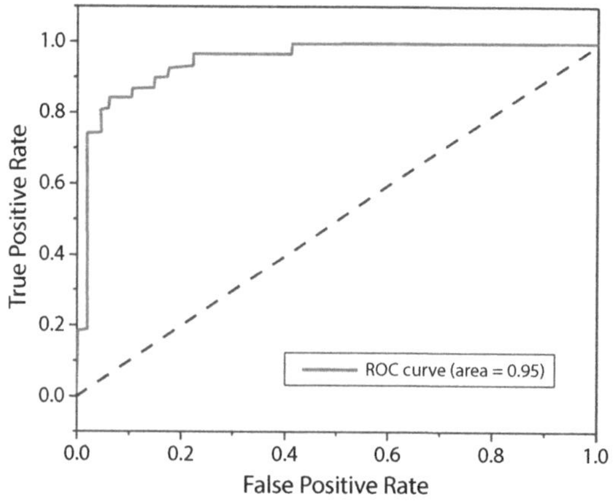

Figure 13.2 The ROU-AUC curve for the proposed IDM-RLGBM method. (Source: Own elaboration).

resulting in lower accuracy. The suggested method IDM-RLGBM is more effective for the classification of ECG signals due to CVD.

The ratio of true positive predictions among all instances is predicted as positive. Classic models like AHT is at 85.4% and RF is at 92% due to the less powerful optimization technique resulting in more false positives in the critical instances of CVD. Figure 13.4 shows precision values. The IDM-RLGBM achieved a much higher precision of 94% because its hyperparameter tuning with IDM resulted in minimized numbers of false

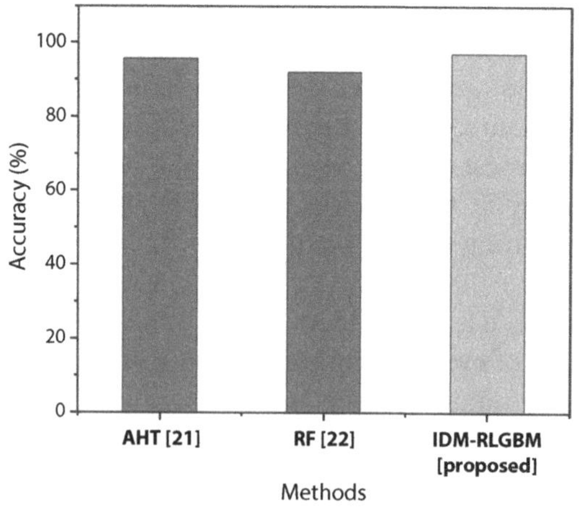

Figure 13.3 Comparison accuracy values of various traditional models vs. the proposed method. (Source: Own elaboration).

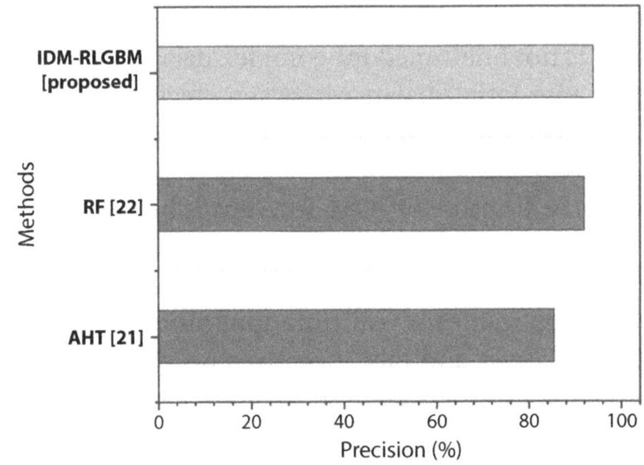

Figure 13.4 Comparison of precision values of various traditional models vs. the proposed method. (Source: Own elaboration).

positive predictions, making this model more applicable for a wide circle of medical procedures since a false positive might result in unnecessary treatment or intervention.

The ratio of true positive predictions concerning the overall actual positive instances are present within the dataset. Figure 13.5 demonstrates the recall values. Recall has been improved in the proposed model IDM-RLGBM, 96%, thus identifying actual positive CVD arrhythmias, which is very important to detect any cardiac events. Compared to the traditional

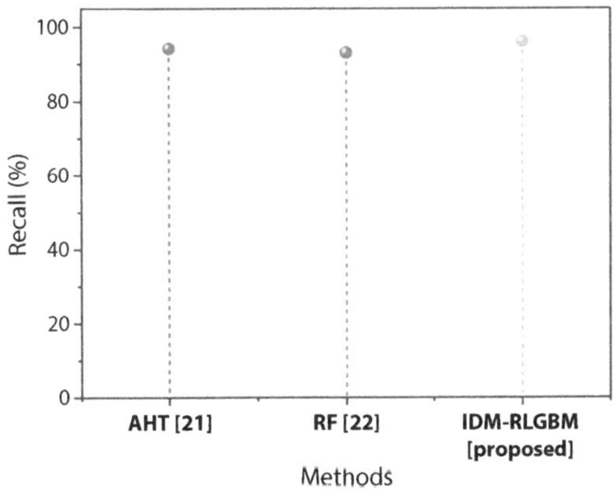

Figure 13.5 Comparison recall values of various traditional models vs. proposed method. (Source: Own elaboration).

approaches of AHT at 94.1% and RF at 93%, a lower recall might occur when the model is not fine-tuned for complex data like ECG signals.

It provides an appropriate balance between precision and recall through calculating the harmonized average of the two. It has been particularly useful in cases involving imbalanced datasets. Figure 13.6 illustrates the F1-score values. The F1 score of IDM-RLGBM is higher at 95% compared to conventional methods, such as AHT at 89.1% and RF at 92.5%, balancing the two important metrics of precision and recall very effectively. This makes the model applicable for real-time applications in medical domains since both false positives and false negatives need to be minimized. The performance comparison between the suggested approach and the traditional approach is shown in Table 13.1.

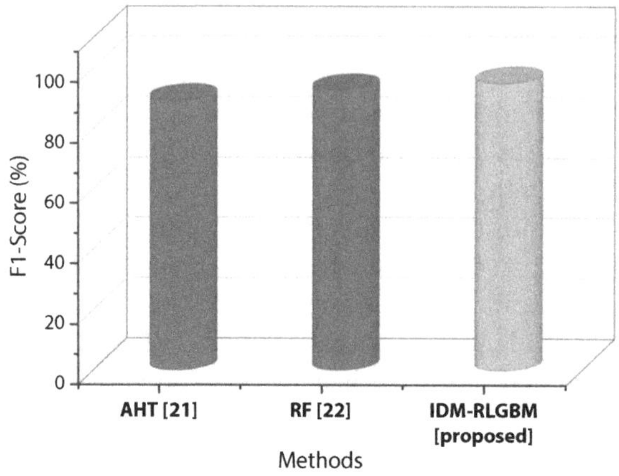

Figure 13.6 Comparison of F1-score values of various traditional models vs. the proposed method. (Source: Own elaboration).

Table 13.1 Model performance comparison based on proposed method with traditional models.

Methods	Accuracy (%)	Precision (%)	Recall (%)	F1 score (%)
Adaptive Hoeffding Tree [21]	95.67	85.4	94.1	89.1
Random Forest [22]	92	92	93	92.5
Intelligent Dwarf Mongoose fine-tuned Resilient LightGBM [proposed]	97	94	96	95

13.4.1 Discussion

Wearable technology within biomedical systems has made IoMT detection of CVD possible with continuous health monitoring through the analysis of real-time data, thus improving diagnosis and early intervention. Traditional methods of detection, AHT, and RF were the most applied wearable IoMT applications for CVD detection. These methods exhibit several limitations. The AHT [21] suffers from the problem of high-dimensional data, reducing its flexibility in both dynamic feature selection and capturing complex nonlinear patterns highly relevant for accurate cardiovascular monitoring. However, RF [22] works well for balanced datasets but overfits noisy, unbalanced wearable data and is memory-intensive, seriously affecting its running performance on resource-constrained wearable devices. Both methods also lack serious interpretability, which is much needed for any healthcare application that needs transparent diagnostic insights. A new approach is the enhancement of the detection of CVD using IoMT wearable technology through an innovative IDM-RLGBM method. It considers feature selection, detects complex patterns with gradient boosting, and handles large data in a big dataset for real-time monitoring. The proposed technique prevents overfitting, is more interpretable, and thus is clearer in healthcare applications due to memory efficiency for wearable devices with limited computational resources.

13.5 Conclusion

The IoMT significantly changed healthcare because it made continuous patient monitoring possible through wearables. The research has focused on improving the efficiency and effectiveness of CVD detection on IoMT wearable devices. The specific design and assessment that the research aimed for is the IDM-RLGBM. This hybrid approach has been designed to improve the performance of wearable IoMT-based classification tasks. The ECG signals were used for the dataset, which is used in the detection of CVD. Min-max normalization was done to change the scale of ECG signal values so that the model processes this information more effectively. Feature extraction was achieved using the DWT, a procedure that decomposes ECG signals into time-frequency components. The IDM-RLGBM model outperformed the classical ML methods. It performed better than these traditional models in terms of classified recall (96%), F1 score (95%), accuracy (97%), and precision (94%). The research performed on the IDM-RLGBM model that was successful in showing a significant improvement in the results for CVD detection using IoMT wearable devices.

13.5.1 Limitation and Future Scope

Wearable technologies in the IoMT facilitate real-time health monitoring, hence much enhanced patient care. On the contrary, cons include data privacy, integration with pre-existing healthcare systems, and sensor inaccuracy. The future development could be geared toward improvement in data security, sensor accuracy, seamless integration with artificial intelligence for personalized healthcare, and early disease diagnosis.

References

1. Manickam, P., *et al.*, Artificial intelligence (AI) and internet of medical things (IoMT) assisted biomedical systems for intelligent healthcare. *Biosensors*, 12, 8, 562, 2022, https://doi.org/10.3390/bios12080562.
2. Adewole, K.S., *et al.*, Cloud-based IoMT framework for cardiovascular disease prediction and diagnosis in personalized E-health care, in: *Intelligent IoT systems in personalized health care*, pp. 105–145, Academic Press, Cambridge, MA, 2021, https://doi.org/10.1016/B978-0-12-821187-8.00005-8.
3. Bajeh, A.O., *et al.*, Application of computational intelligence models in IoMT big data for heart disease diagnosis in personalized health care, in: *Intelligent IoT systems in personalized health care*, pp. 177–206, Academic Press, Cambridge,MA,2021,https://doi.org/10.1016/B978-0-12-821187-8.00007-1.
4. Verma, D., *et al.*, Internet of things (IoT) in nano-integrated wearable biosensor devices for healthcare applications. *Biosens. Bioelectron.: X*, 11, 1001535, 2022, https://doi.org/10.1016/j.biosx.2022.100153.
5. Ajakwe, S.O., *et al.*, Key wearable device technologies parameters for innovative healthcare delivery in B5G network: A review. *IEEE Access*, 10, 49956–499745, 2022, https://doi.org/10.1109/ACCESS.2022.3173643.
6. Guo, Y., *et al.*, A review of wearable and unobtrusive sensing technologies for chronic disease management. *Comput. Biol. Med.*, 129, 1041635, 2021, https://doi.org/10.1016/j.compbiomed.2020.104163.
7. Yang, Z., *et al.*, Evaluation of smart response systems for city emergencies and novel UV-oriented solution for integration, resilience, inclusiveness and sustainability. *2020 5th International Conference on Universal Village (UV)*, IEEE, 2020, https://doi.org/10.1109/UV50937.2020.9426215.
8. Tariq, M.U., Advanced wearable medical devices and their role in transformative remote health monitoring, in: *Transformative Approaches to Patient Literacy and Healthcare Innovation*, pp. 308–326, IGI Global, Hershey, PA, 2024, https://doi.org/10.4018/979-8-3693-3661-8.ch015.
9. Sola, P.P.B., Santos, M.A., Oliveira-Cardoso, EA., Emotional Suffering After the COVID-19 Pandemic: Grieving the Loss of Family Members in Brazil.

Int. J. Environ. Res. Public Health, 21, 11, 1398, 2024, https://doi.org/10.3390/ijerph21111398.
10. Ekvitayavetchanukul, P., *et al.*, Revolutionizing Healthcare: Telemedicine and Remote Diagnostics in the Era of Digital Health, in: *Healthcare Industry Assessment: Analyzing Risks, Security, and Reliability*, pp. 255–277, Springer Nature Switzerland, Cham, 2024, https://doi.org/10.1007/978-3-031-65434-3_11.
11. Moein, T., *et al.*, Optimizing the performance reliability of diagnostic equipment and wearable sensors and medical devices in IoMT. *Int. J. Nonlinear Anal. Appl.*, 16, 1, 75–88, 2024, https://doi.org/10.22075/ijnaa.2023.30810.4503.
12. Yousuff, M., *et al.*, Deep Learning Interpretation of Biomedical Data in IoMT and Cyber-Physical Systems, in: *Cyber-Physical Systems for Industrial Transformation*, pp. 235–258, CRC Press, Boca Raton, FL, 2023, https://doi.org/10.1201/9781003262527-13.
13. Rodríguez-Rodríguez, I., Campo-Valera, M., Rodríguez, J.-V., Forecasting glycaemia for type 1 diabetes mellitus patients by means of IoMT devices. *Internet Things*, 24, 1009455, 2023, https://doi.org/10.1016/j.iot.2023.100945.
14. AbuAli, N., *et al.*, Software defined radio frequency sensing framework for Internet of Medical Things. *Inf. Fusion*, 103, 1021065, 2024, https://doi.org/10.1016/j.inffus.2023.102106.
15. Ahmed, A., *et al.*, Performance of artificial intelligence models in estimating blood glucose level among diabetic patients using non-invasive wearable device data. *Comput. Methods Programs Biomed. Update*, 3, 1000945, 2023, https://doi.org/10.1016/j.cmpbup.2023.100094.
16. Kuppusamy, P., Palanivel, N., Suresh Joseph, K., A machine learning-enabled Internet of Things model for cloud-based biomedical applications, in: *Internet of Things Enabled Machine Learning for Biomedical Applications*, pp. 341–366, CRC Press, Boca Raton, FL, 2024, 10.1201/9781003487647-18.
17. Sharma, G. and Joshi, A.M., Novel eeg based schizophrenia detection with iomt framework for smart healthcare. *arXiv preprint arXiv:2111.11298*. https://doi.org/10.48550/arXiv.2111.11298, 2021.
18. Dahan, F., *et al.*, A smart IoMT based architecture for E-healthcare patient monitoring system using artificial intelligence algorithms. *Front. Physiol.*, 14, 11259525, 2023, https://doi.org/10.3389/fphys.2023.1125952.
19. Misgar, M.M. and Bhatia, M.P.S., Utilizing deep convolutional neural architecture with attention mechanism for objective diagnosis of schizophrenia using wearable IoMT devices. *Multimed. Tools Appl.*, 83, 13, 39601–39620, 2024, https://doi.org/10.1007/s11042-023-17119-6.
20. Arunachalam, N., Rukmani Devi, S., Meikandan, M., IoT Wearable Medical Device for Heart Disease Recognition Based Ml and Dl: A Bovw Based MDCNN Classification Approach. *2024 International Conference on Intelligent Algorithms for Computational Intelligence Systems (IACIS)*, IEEE, 2024, https://doi.org/10.1109/IACIS61494.2024.10721749.

21. Elbasi, E. and Zreikat, A.I., Heart Disease Classification for Early Diagnosis based on Adaptive Hoeffding Tree Algorithm in IoMT Data. *Int. Arab J. Inf. Technol.*, 20, 1, 38–48, 2023, https://doi.org/10.34028/iajit/20/1/5.
22. Mulani, A.O., *et al.*, ML-powered Internet of Medical Things (MLIoMT) Structure for Heart Disease Prediction. *J. Pharmacol. Pharmacother.*, 16, 1, 38–45, 2024, https://doi.org/10.1177/0976500X241281490.

Part III

SYSTEMS AND APPLICATIONS

14

Health Informatics and Community Decision Support Systems

Sheuli Sen[1], S. Jayashree[2*], Sudhanshu Shekhar Bisoyi[3], Rekha M.M.[4], Raesa Razeen[5] and Ankita Agarwal[6]

[1]*Teerthakar Parshvnath College of Nursing, Teerthanker Mahaveer University, Uttar Pradesh, India*
[2]*Department of Biotechnology, Sathyabama Institute of Science and Technology, Chennai, Tamil Nadu, India*
[3]*Department of Computer Science and Information Technology, Siksha 'O' Anusandhan (Deemed to be University), Bhubaneswar, Odisha, India*
[4]*Department of Chemistry and Biochemistry, Jain (Deemed-to-be University), Bangalore, Karnataka, India*
[5]*Department of Computer Science and Engineering, Presidency University, Bangalore, Karnataka, India*
[6]*Maharishi School of Engineering & Technology, Maharishi University of Information Technology, Uttar Pradesh, India*

Abstract

Health informatics and community decision support systems are vital in enhancing healthcare delivery and decision-making processes by integrating information technology with healthcare services. This review examines the evolution of applications and challenges associated with healthcare. The study aims to provide an in-depth understanding of how these systems are transforming the healthcare environment through better data management, decision support, and patient outcomes. By examining numerous implementations, including electronic health records (EHR), telemedicine, and predictive analytics, the review discovers how these technologies help healthcare professionals and improve patient care.

**Corresponding author*: jayashree.biotech@sathyabama.ac.in; ORCID: 0000-0002-2192-2237
Sheuli Sen: ORCID: 0000-0002-0276-5918
Sudhanshu Shekhar Bisoyi: ORCID: 0000-0002-7688-7379
Rekha M.M.: ORCID: 0000-0002-7371-6478
Ankita Agarwal: ORCID: 0000-0001-7539-8592

Satya Prakash Yadav, Abhay Bansal and Victor Hugo C. de Albuquerque (eds.) Computational Intelligence in Biomedical Internet of Medical Things, (231–250) © 2026 Scrivener Publishing LLC

The review discusses the major obstacles to the widespread use of health informatics, including interoperability problems, privacy concerns, data security, and the crucial requirement for sufficient resources and training. The study's findings highlight the significance of community decision support systems and health informatics in the healthcare system's transformation, encouraging ongoing innovation and interdisciplinary collaboration to optimize the potential to improve community health management and healthcare outcomes.

***Keywords*:** Electronic health records (EHR), clinical decision support systems (CDSS), health informatics, patient outcomes

14.1 Introduction

Health informatics developed into an innovative area of concern dealing with healthcare and information technology, and enhancing the collection, management, and use of health information. Nowadays, it seems that the use of EHR, telemedicine, health wearables, big health data, and health informatics has significantly changed the way health information is accessed and used by healthcare providers, patients, and the entire community [1]. Clinical decision support systems (CDSS) are debatably the most critical aspect of this domain. These programs employ health information technology to enhance health-related decision-making in a community. Such systems not only assist the caregivers but also involve the public in healthcare management, which expands the realms of healthcare beyond the conventional medical practice [2]. Paper-based records served as the primary means of documenting and storing patient information in the past. The transition of the healthcare industry into the computerized age and the demand for more reliable and better access to data gave emergence to health informatics. Health informatics includes diverse applications and systems that aim to capture, maintain, interpret, and communicate health information [3]. Electronic health records (EHR) are usually one of the main tools used by healthcare providers. However, health informatics includes more than EHRs and encompasses a wide range of digital health tools such as mobile health apps, telehealth services, and clinical support tools [4]. Collectively, these tools serve to bridge gaps in care, reduce costs, and enhance patient outcomes. Clinical decision support systems are considered to assist community stakeholders, including public health officials, community leaders, and residents in making informed decisions about community health requirements [5]. Through data analysis, this technology offers valuable data that empowers populations to promote wellness and public health. Clinical decision support systems intend to enhance individual healthcare-seeking behaviors in connection to population public health management by enabling people to take charge of patient health [6]. Clinical decision support systems examine the distribution of cases of chronic illness across populations and connect it to factors including socioeconomic status, healthcare access, and environmental factors. Using this data, community organizations or public health experts develop focused interventions like screening initiatives, awareness-raising campaigns, or improvements to hospitals nearby [7]. Figure 14.1 represents the framework for health informatics decision support systems.

This model also provides the participation of medical doctors, local authorities, and the local population in the improvement of community health [8]. The potential of automated healthcare frameworks carries out and ensures the appropriate use of an intervention has been acknowledged by the health sector. The application of systems in the therapeutic setting and intervention could be considered a component of a practical insight that necessitates an understanding of the business, barriers, and capabilities of the framework [9]. Furthermore, adding a suitable model to the qualitative decision analysis gives these ideas structure. It also suggests that the most important treatments are the ones that are easy to implement and have reduced chances of misuse [10]. The main objective of health informatics and community decision support systems is to improve healthcare delivery and community well-being by utilizing data analysis, and

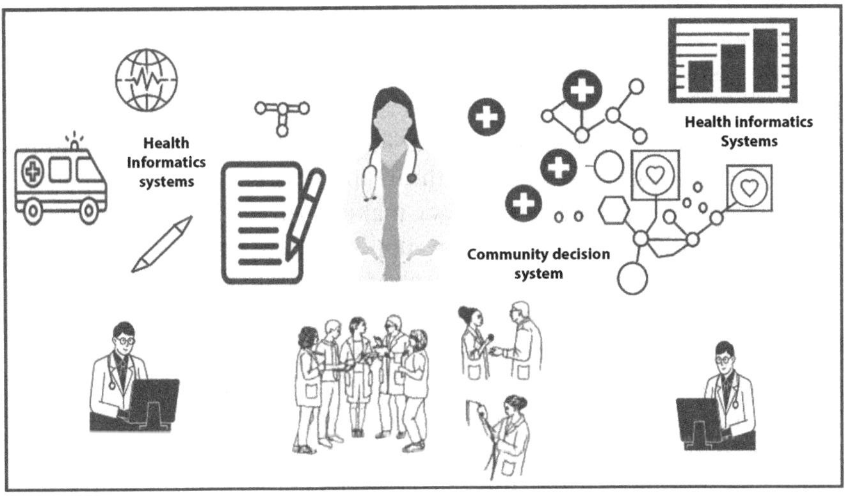

Figure 14.1 Framework for health informatics' decision support systems. (Source: Own elaboration).

decision-making tools to enhance informed choices, optimize resource allocation, and ensure better health outcomes.

The work is organized into the following sections: Section 14.2 briefly describes methodology flow; Section 14.3 explains healthcare informatics; Section 14.4 demonstrates the clinical decision support system framework; Section 14.5 explains the telemedicine framework; Section 14.6 explains the telehealth framework, and Section 14.7 concludes the study.

14.2 Methodology

This review examines patient-centered care through healthcare informatics by analyzing the roles of CDSS, telehealth, and telemedicine. A comprehensive synthesis of literature explores their implementation, effectiveness, and impact on improving patient outcomes.

14.3 Patient-Centered Care through Healthcare Informatics

The healthcare sector currently generates an extensive amount of data across various domains. It includes patient-related information stored in medical records, health insurance details, and data derived from clinical trial outcomes [11]. A significant quantity of information is collected from laboratory results, patient feedback, and data associated with health and therapeutic devices. The sector generates data related to pharmaceutical research, as well as medical imagery, which encompasses images, videos, graphics, and audio recordings. Furthermore, data concerning healthcare strategies, policies, and organizational frameworks also contribute to the vast data ecosystem within the healthcare industry [12]. An EHR system is used to capture and store patient data, making it accessible across different healthcare settings. Clinical decision support systems offer evidence-based alerts and suggestions to healthcare providers while healthcare providers care for patients [13]. By identifying possible problems, including medication interactions, allergies, or departures from clinical recommendations, CDSS assists in better decision-making through the analysis of patient data. Healthcare organizations exchange patient data between various systems and providers with health information exchange systems. It ensures that medical professionals have a thorough understanding of the patient's medical history, improves care coordination, and reduces the need for duplicate

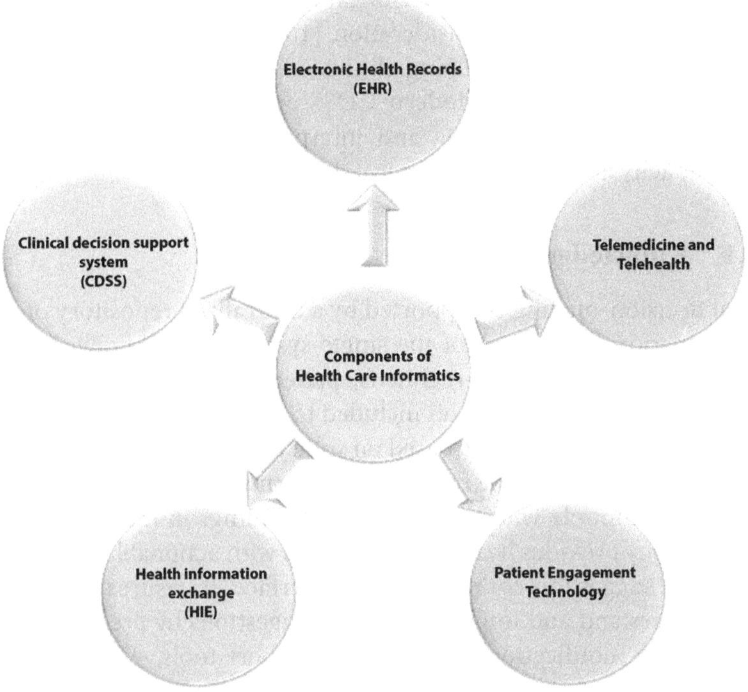

Figure 14.2 Key variables of healthcare informatics. (Source: Own elaboration).

testing [14]. Telehealth systems support access to healthcare, especially in rural or underserved areas. These technologies enable remote healthcare services, such as video consultations remote monitoring of chronic conditions, and e-prescribing [15]. Technologies for patient engagement are wearable technology, patient portals, and mobile applications of technologies that empower individuals to participate in patients' healthcare. Patients can communicate with providers, view patient medical information, and track patient health metrics using these technologies. Figure 14.2 depicts the key variables of healthcare informatics.

14.4 Clinical Decision Support Systems Framework

Clinical decision support systems enhance healthcare delivery by providing clinicians with valuable clinical knowledge, patient records, and other health-related material to improve decision-making. Clinical decision support systems include software that assists clinicians by matching patients' exclusive characteristics with the clinical knowledge base and offers personalized assessments for consideration [16]. This system is commonly used at the point of care, helping clinicians combine clinician expertise with the system's insights. Modern CDSS are evolving to advance data analysis techniques, processing and interpreting complex data beyond human capacity and enhancing clinical decisions [17].

14.4.1 Knowledge Base

Clinical decision-making is supported by a centralized repository of medical information that is part of the single system CDSS knowledge base. Clinical guidelines, therapy regimens, patient management techniques, and diagnostic algorithms are all included to guarantee that medical practitioners are given suggestions based on solid evidence [18]. To ensure that physicians have access to the most recent information, the knowledge base is updated commonly with the most recent findings in medical research. The technology provides healthcare providers with actionable information through the suggestion communication interface. It ensures that doctors quickly understand and implement these suggestions by presenting them through alerts, notifications, or decision-support tools. A single system

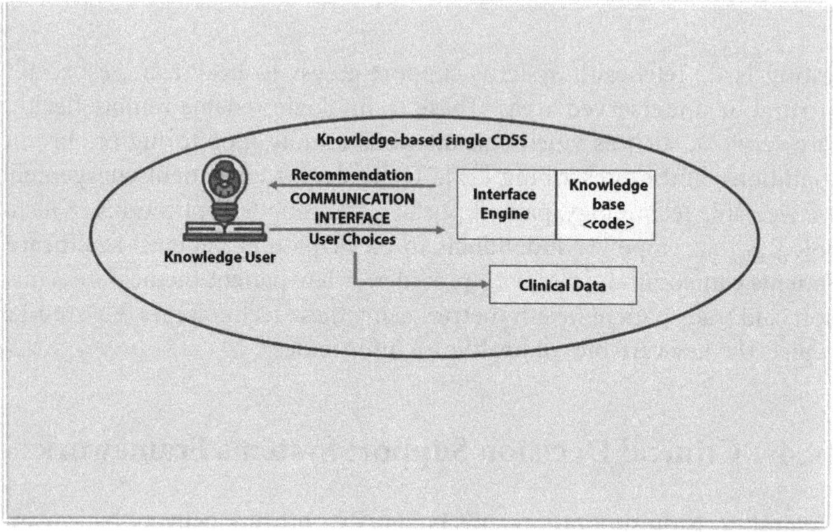

Figure 14.3 Knowledge-based CDSS. (Source: https://www.nature.com/articles/s41746-020-0221-y) .

setup ensures consistency and dependability across the clinical workflow while holding all patient data and medical knowledge in one location, allowing for easy access, efficient decision-making, and better patient care [19]. Figure 14.3 shows the knowledge-based CDSS.

14.5 Telemedicine Framework

A telemedicine framework is a methodical strategy that can use telecommunications technology to provide healthcare remotely [20]. Using electronic health communication, remote patient monitoring, and virtual consultations, healthcare specialists analyze patients from a distance, increasing patient access and delivery efficiency [21]. The functionality and design of telemedicine frameworks fluctuate to the needs of patients, healthcare systems, and healthcare practitioners. It involves three main stages: data acquisition, transmission, and interaction. Data acquisition is the process by which patient data, such as vital signs, medical history, or images, is gathered through wearable devices and mobile apps. Transmission data is securely transmitted through mobile networks to healthcare professionals using encryption protocols to ensure confidentiality. Telecommunication systems are used by providers to provide asynchronous and real-time care delivery for consultations, diagnosis, and treatment planning through video conferences, texting, or e-prescriptions. Figure 14.4 shows the framework of telemedicine.

Figure 14.4 Framework of telemedicine. (Source: https://www.appsrhino.com/blogs/what-is-the-importance-of-telemedicine-in-healthcare).

14.6 Telehealth Framework

A telehealth framework is a structured model for delivering healthcare services and information remotely through digital and telecommunication technologies, encompassing clinical care, education, and monitoring to enhance accessibility and efficiency [22] to improve healthcare delivery by leveraging technology to provide remote care support and patient outcomes. It ensures that patients and healthcare professionals communicate by applying internet-enabled devices from any location. To protect privacy, data and communications are transmitted through encrypted channels [23]. It integrates with EHR to facilitate the smooth exchange of information. Real-time and asynchronous care enables delayed evaluations of medical data and prompt consultations and increases responses to crises expanding healthcare requirements. Figure 14.5 shows the framework of telehealth.

Tables 14.1 and 14.2 show the various CDSS task categories of EHR data utilized in the decision-making process. It addresses topics such as illness prevention and diagnosis, referral channels, pharmaceutical and non-pharmacological care, and how clinical choices are influenced by demographic, diagnostic, medication, observation, laboratory, and manually input data.

The literature review highlights numerous AI based CDSS, accentuating the evolution, challenges and findings. It includes limited public information, integration issues, and the essential need for enhanced model accessibility. It demonstrates AI potential in enhancing diagnostics, treatment

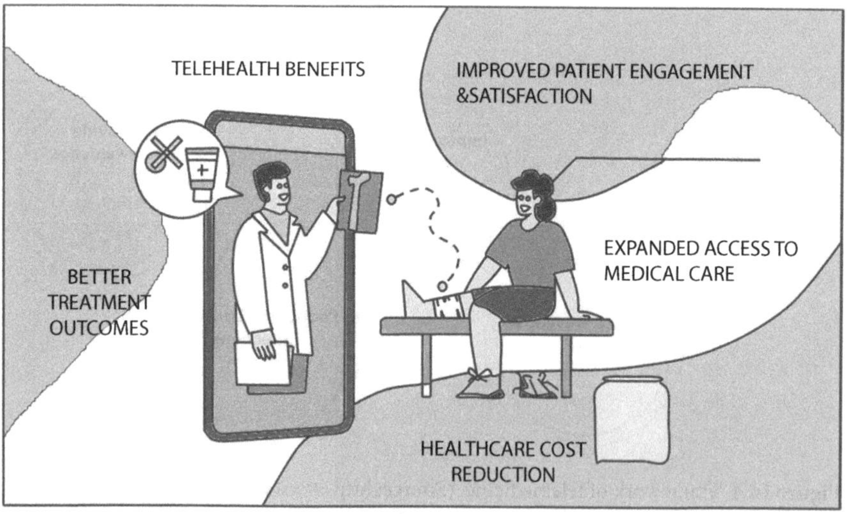

Figure 14.5 Framework of telehealth. (Source: https://www.scnsoft.com/healthcare/telemedicine-pros-cons).

Table 14.1 Descriptions and cases of CDSS classifications [24].

Clinical decision support systems' clinical task addressed	Descriptions and examples
Preventive and diagnostic	Activities about disease detection, determining disease likelihood (e.g., cardiovascular risk screening), and providing diagnoses (e.g., verifying a diagnosis of hypertension).
Pathway	Referrals for diagnostic procedures (e.g., blood tests), specialist consultations, and other care pathway actions.
Pharmacological	Tasks related to prescribing, adjusting medication doses, and modifying other pharmacological treatments.
Nonpharmacological management	Activities centered on lifestyle changes (e.g., dietary and exercise advice), patient education (e.g., through patient dashboards), and other non-pharmacological therapies (e.g., smoking cessation programs).

Table 14.2 Explanations and examples of EHR data types used [24].

Electronic health records data types used	Definition and/or examples
Enumeration	Basic personal information, including demographics like age and sex.
Diagnosis	Verification of existing diagnoses in the EHR, including setting off alarms for diseases like atrial fibrillation.
Medication	Information on medications within the EHR is used for generating decision support.
Observation	Structured data related to clinical observations within the EHR, like systolic blood pressure or body mass index measurements.
Lab	Urine albumin-creatinine ratios and structured laboratory result data are stored in the EHR.
Manual input	Manual entry of more data, such as family history or depression scale results, into the EHR to aid clinical decision-making.

plans, and patient consequences, though adoption and usability remain important challenges (Table 14.3).

The main objective of health informatics and community decision support systems is to improve healthcare delivery and community well-being

Table 14.3 Literature review summary considering various types of artificial intelligence (AI)-based CDSS.

References	Main purpose	Research gap	Findings
[25]	It explored the evolution of explainable AI in CDSS and identified challenges.	The research gap lies in the lack of public datasets and comprehensive evaluations.	The results emphasize the necessity of improving explainable AI's usefulness for medical professionals and striking a balance between explainability and model performance.
[26]	To develop and validate an advanced AI-CDSS for predicting breast cancer recurrence using machine learning.	Existing models for predicting breast cancer recurrence are limited in prediction accuracy and accessibility, enhanced pre-processing, model development, and user accessibility.	The AI-CDSS tool demonstrated effectiveness in personalized treatment planning and involving patients in clinical decisions.
[27]	The review explored the potential of CDSS in ophthalmology to improve diagnostic accuracy, treatment plans, and patient management.	Limited integration of CDSS in ophthalmic practice, with challenges in data integration, user adoption, and regulatory approval.	The CDSS applications in diagnosing retinal diseases, glaucoma, and diabetic retinopathy show promise, but significant barriers hinder widespread use.

(*Continued*)

Table 14.3 Literature review summary considering various types of artificial intelligence (AI)-based CDSS. (*Continued*)

References	Main purpose	Research gap	Findings
[28]	Study explored how AI-empowered AI-CDSS are used, designed, and evaluated, focusing on clinician perceptions.	The research gap lies in understanding human, social, and contextual factors influencing AI-CDSS adoption.	Findings highlight six key challenges, including technical limitations, workflow misalignment, and usability issues, which hinder effective implementation.
[29]	Research explored AI's transformative role in CDSS, focusing on these applications in healthcare decision-making.	The research gap lies in addressing challenges such as AI interpretability and bias.	Findings emphasize AI's potential in enhancing diagnostics, treatment, and patient outcomes, with recommendations for improved adoption.
[30]	The study aimed to explore trends in the application of AI in diagnosing and treating oral and maxillofacial pathologies, focusing on its role in assisting pathologists and clinicians.	The gap addressed is the limited research synthesizing AI applications specifically for oral and maxillofacial pathology, particularly in diagnosis and treatment prediction.	The study found that AI, particularly in predictive modeling, has been effective in diagnosing progression, recurrence, and risk assessment for oral cancer.

by utilizing data analysis, and decision-making tools to enhance informed choices, optimize resource allocation, and ensure better health outcomes. Health informatics and community decision support systems require a Python setup on Windows utilizing libraries like Pandas, NumPy for analysis and databases for data storage and decision-making simulations. Table 14.4 and Figures 14.6 to 14.9 show the performance measures of several ML models. Numerous performance patterns are seen when comparing different ML models for categorization results related to CDSS. Metrics including precision, accuracy, recall, and F1 score, were assessed for several methods, including HTM+LSTM [31], RF [32], Stacking [33], and XGB

[34], which exhibited excellent scores on a variety of assessment parameters. The stacking method outperforms the other models in terms of all metrics with accuracy, precision, recall, and F1 score. It exceeds Hierarchical Temporal Memory + Long Short-Term Memory (HTM+LSTM), Random Forest (RF), and Extreme Gradient Boosting (XGB) in each category, displaying the most balanced and high-performing results.

Challenges and barriers in AI Integration: The adoption of AI in health informatics presents great opportunities to improve healthcare. However, the process is hindered by distinct challenges such as data privacy issues, inadequate infrastructure, and the digital division. Data privacy is especially important, where methods for collecting and storing data are less

Table 14.4 Evaluation of ML methods.

Methods	Accuracy (%)	Precision (%)	Recall (%)	F1-score (%)
HTM+LSTM [31]	89.5	76.2	91.2	73.3
RF [32]	92	94	88	91
Stacking [33]	98.42	98.42	98.42	98.42
XGB [34]	91	93	95	94

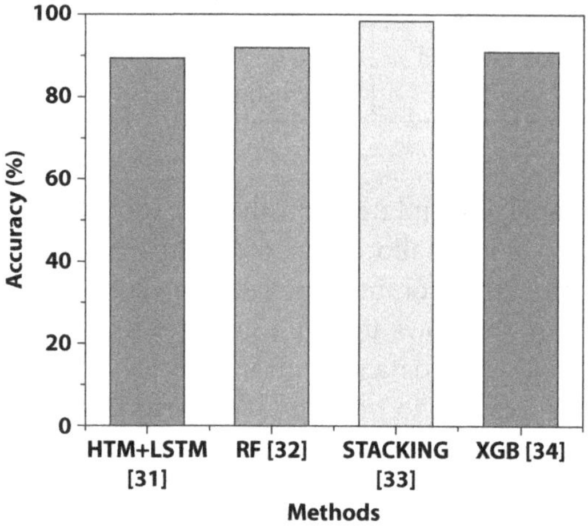

Figure 14.6 Result of accuracy.

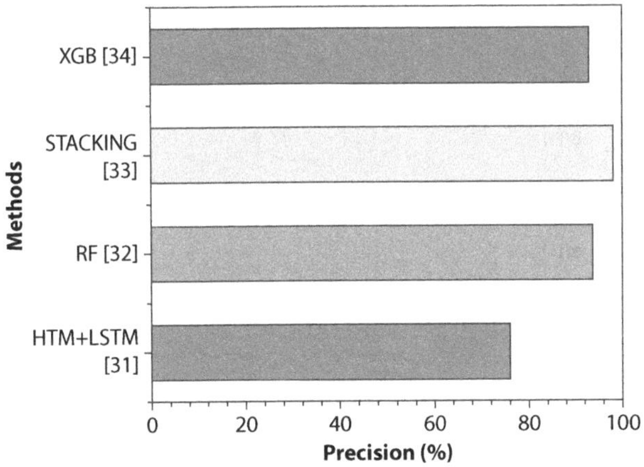

Figure 14.7 Outcome of precision.

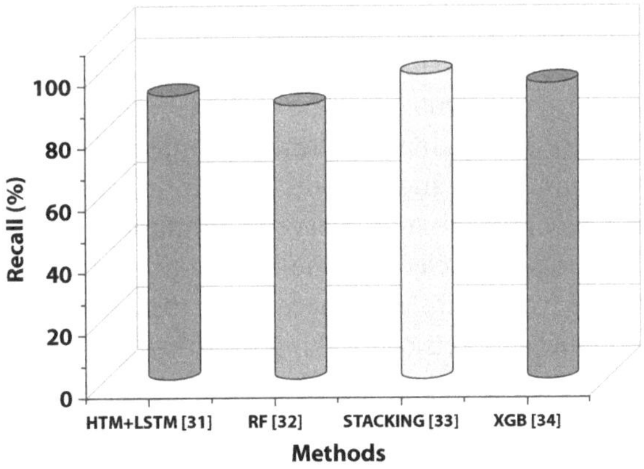

Figure 14.8 Outcome of recall.

secure than those in affluent countries [35]. Leveraging AI in health informatics requires handling vast amounts of sensitive patient data, which heightens concerns about breaches and unauthorized access. Table 14.5 summarizes the influence of telemedicine services on the healthcare industry in the context of blockchain technology, along with suggestions and limitations.

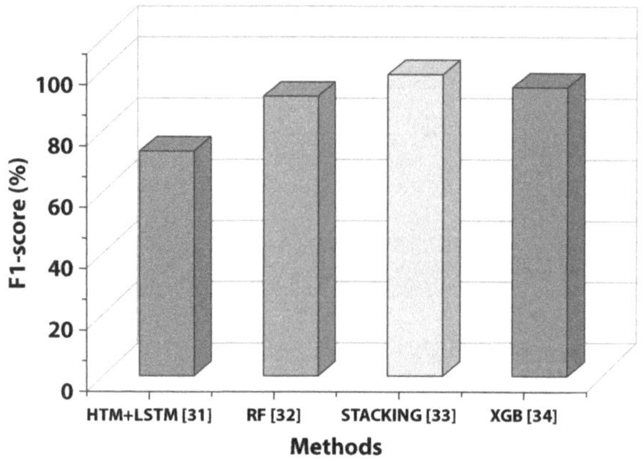

Figure 14.9 Result of the F1-score.

14.7 Conclusion

Health informatics is vital for improved patient care and health outcomes by integrating patient data and expert knowledge. Telemedicine and telehealth have revolutionized healthcare delivery, enabling remote consultations, monitoring, and chronic disease management, enhancing accessibility and efficiency in underserved communities. The development of CDSS frameworks and telemedicine has significantly improved health outcomes, making healthcare more accessible, timely, and efficient. These systems promote better decision-making, personalized care, and reduced medical errors. The integration of AI abilities achieved greater precision in diagnosis and treatment. Future research will focus on enhancing interoperability, patient privacy, and expanding telemedicine access, especially in rural areas, for equitable healthcare delivery.

Table 14.5 Impacts of telemedicine services enhanced by blockchain.

References	Aspect	Impact of telemedicine	Blockchain contribution	Suggestions	Limitations
[36]	**Data security**	Ensures secure patient-doctor communication.	Blockchain offers immutable and transparent records, reducing data breaches.	Develop standardized security protocols and adopt smart contracts for data sharing.	High energy consumption of blockchain networks could limit scalability.
[37]	**Patient privacy**	Maintains confidentiality in remote consultations.	Enables decentralized data storage with controlled access for better privacy management.	Implement privacy-focused cryptographic techniques.	Regulatory challenges could arise due to differing privacy laws across regions.
[38]	**Access to services**	Provides healthcare access in remote or underserved areas.	Blockchain improves supply chain tracking for medical equipment delivery in such areas.	Expand internet and blockchain infrastructure in rural regions.	Limited internet access and digital literacy in rural areas hinder adoption.
[39]	**Data interoperability**	Facilitates seamless data sharing among healthcare providers.	Blockchain enables standardized and interoperable data exchange across platforms.	Create universal blockchain protocols for healthcare interoperability.	Lack of standardization and integration with existing systems could delay progress.

References

1. Laing, S. and Mercer, J., Improved preventive care clinical decision-making efficiency: leveraging a point-of-care clinical decision support system. *BMC Med. Inf. Decis. Making*, 21, 1–85, 2021, https://doi.org/10.1186/s12911-021-01675-8.
2. Chen, W., O'Bryan, C.M., *et al.*, Barriers and enablers to implementing and using clinical decision support systems for chronic diseases: a qualitative systematic review and meta-aggregation. *Implement. Sci. Commun.*, 1, 815, 2022, https://doi.org/10.1186/s43058-022-00326-x.
3. Lewkowicz, D., Wohlbrandt, A., *et al.*, Economic impact of clinical decision support interventions based on electronic health records. *BMC Health Serv. Res.*, 20, 1–125, 2020, https://doi.org/10.1186/s12913-020-05688-3.
4. Stipelman, C., *et al.*, Electronic health record-integrated clinical decision support for clinicians serving populations facing health care disparities: literature review. *Yearb. Med. Inf.*, 31, 01, 184–198, 2022, https://doi.org/10.1055/s-0042-1742518.
5. Mengting, G., *et al.*, Measures of success of computerized clinical decision support systems: An overview of systematic reviews. *Health Policy Technol.*, 10, 1, 196–208, 2021, https://doi.org/10.1016/j.hlpt.2020.11.001.
6. Kawamoto, K. and McDonald, C.J., Designing, conducting, and reporting clinical decision support studies: recommendations and call to action. *Ann. Internal Med.*, 172, 11_Supplement, S101–S109, 2020, https://doi.org/10.7326/M19-0875.
7. Kouri, A., *et al.*, Do providers use computerized clinical decision support systems? A systematic review and meta-regression of clinical decision support uptake. *Implement. Sci.*, 17, 1, 21, 2022, https://doi.org/10.1186/s13012-022-01199-3.
8. White, N., *et al.*, Evaluating the costs and consequences of computerized clinical decision support systems in hospitals: a scoping review and recommendations for future practice. *J. Am. Med. Inf. Assoc.*, 30, 6, 1205–1218, 2023, https://doi.org/10.1093/jamia/ocad040.
9. Mahmoud, A.S., *et al.*, The impact of the implementation of a clinical decision support system on the quality of healthcare services in a primary care setting. *J. Fam. Med. Primary Care*, 9, 12, 6078–6084, 2020, https://doi.org/10.4103/jfmpc.jfmpc_1728_20.
10. Mebrahtu, T., *et al.*, Effects of computerised clinical decision support systems (CDSS) on nursing and allied health professional performance and patient outcomes: a systematic review of experimental and observational studies. *BMJ Open*, 11, 12, e053886, 2021, https://doi.org/10.1136/bmjopen-2021-053886.
11. Rezaie, J., *et al.*, A review on exosomes application in clinical trials: perspective, questions, and challenges. *Cell Commun. Signaling*, 20, 1, 145, 2022, https://doi.org/10.1186/s12964-022-00959-4.

12. McCarthy, N., *et al.*, Enterprise imaging and big data: A review from a medical physics perspective. *Physica Med.*, 83, 206–2205, 2021, https://doi.org/10.1016/j.ejmp.2021.04.004.
13. Olakotan, O.O. and Yusof, M.M., The appropriateness of clinical decision support systems alerts in supporting clinical workflows: a systematic review. *Health Inf. J.*, 27, 2, 14604582211007536, 2021, https://doi.org/10.1177/14604582211007536.
14. Feldman, S., *et al.*, Impact of provider prior use of HIE on system complexity, performance, patient care, quality and system concerns. *Inf. Syst. Front.*, 24, 1, 121–131, 2022, https://doi.org/10.1007/s10796-020-10064-x.
15. Tolu-Akinnawo, O., *et al.*, Telemedicine in cardiology: enhancing access to care and improving patient outcomes. *Cureus*, 16, 6, 2024, https://doi.org/10.7759/cureus.62852.
16. Gershov, S., *et al.*, Towards an autonomous clinical decision support system. *Eng. Appl. Artif. Intell.*, 127, 1072155, 2024, https://doi.org/10.1016/j.engappai.2023.107215.
17. Suganthi, and Kalaiselvi, Decision Support System in Healthcare Monitoring, in: *Artificial Intelligence-Based System Models in Healthcare*, pp. 55–78, 2024, https://doi.org/10.1002/9781394242528.ch3.
18. Farmaki, A., *et al.*, Will Precision Medicine Meet Digital Health? A Systematic Review of Pharmacogenomics Clinical Decision Support Systems Used in Clinical Practice. *OMICS: J. Integr. Biol.*, 28, 9, 442–460, 2024, https://doi.org/10.1089/omi.2024.0131.
19. Toh, Z.A., *et al.*, Clinical Decision Support System Used in Spinal Disorders: Scoping Review. *J. Med. Internet Res.*, 26, e539515, 2024, https://doi.org/10.2196/53951.
20. Kho, J., *et al.*, A systematic scoping review of change management practices used for telemedicine service implementations. *BMC Health Serv. Res.*, 20, 1–165, 2020, https://doi.org/10.1186/s12913-020-05657-w.
21. Vijayan, V., *et al.*, Review of wearable devices and data collection considerations for connected health. *Sensors*, 21, 16, 5589, 2021, https://doi.org/10.3390/s21165589.
22. Morelli, S., *et al.*, Optimizing Telehealth: Leveraging Key Performance Indicators for Enhanced TeleHealth and Digital Healthcare Outcomes (Telemechron Study). *Healthcare*, 12, 13, 1319, MDPI, 2024, https://doi.org/10.3390/healthcare12131319.
23. Anawade, P., *et al.*, A Comprehensive Review on Exploring the Impact of Telemedicine on Healthcare Accessibility. *Cureus*, 16, 3, 2024, https://doi.org/10.7759/cureus.55996.
24. Chen, W., *et al.*, Design, effectiveness, and economic outcomes of contemporary chronic disease clinical decision support systems: a systematic review and meta-analysis. *J. Am. Med. Inf. Assoc.*, 29, 10, 1757–1772, 2022, https://doi.org/10.1093/jamia/ocac110.

25. Aziz, N., *et al.*, Explainable AI in Healthcare: Systematic Review of Clinical Decision Support Systems, medRxiv, 2024, 2024-08, https://doi.org/10.1101/2024.08.10.24311735.
26. Lin, T.-H., *et al.*, An Advanced Machine Learning Model for a Web-Based Artificial Intelligence–Based Clinical Decision Support System Application: Model Development and Validation Study. *J. Med. Internet Res.*, 26, e560225, 2024, https://doi.org/10.2196/56022.
27. Shariati, M.M. and Darvish, A., Clinical Decision Support Systems in Ophthalmology: A Systematic Search and a Narrative Review. *Appl. Med. Inf.*, 46, 3, 2024, https://ami.info.umfcluj.ro/index.php/AMI/article/view/1065.
28. Wang, L., *et al.*, Human-centered design and evaluation of AI-empowered clinical decision support systems: a systematic review. *Front. Comput. Sci.*, 5, 11872995, 2023, https://doi.org/10.3389/fcomp.2023.1187299.
29. Elhaddad, M. and Hamam, S., AI-Driven clinical decision support systems: an ongoing pursuit of potential. *Cureus*, 16, 4, 2024, https://doi.org/10.7759/cureus.57728.
30. Abdul, N.S., *et al.*, Applications of artificial intelligence in the field of oral and maxillofacial pathology: a systematic review and meta-analysis. *BMC Oral Health*, 24, 1, 122, 2024, https://doi.org/10.1186/s12903-023-03533-7.
31. El-Ganainy, N.O., *et al.*, A new real time clinical decision support system using machine learning for critical care units. *IEEE Access*, 8, 185676–185687, 2020, https://doi.org/10.1109/ACCESS.2020.3030031.
32. Kang, I.-A., *et al.*, DCP: prediction of dental caries using machine learning in personalized medicine. *Appl. Sci.*, 12, 6, 3043, 2022, https://doi.org/10.3390/app12063043.
33. Alabdulhafith, M., Saleh, H., *et al.*, A clinical decision support system for edge/cloud ICU readmission model based on particle swarm optimization, ensemble machine learning, and explainable artificial intelligence. *IEEE Access*, 11, 100604–1006215, 2023, https://doi.org/10.1109/ACCESS.2023.3312343.
34. Zhang, A.Y., *et al.*, Development of a radiology decision support system for the classification of MRI brain scans, in: *2018 IEEE/ACM 5th International Conference on Big Data Computing Applications and Technologies (BDCAT)*, IEEE, pp. 107–115, 2018, https://doi.org/10.1109/BDCAT.2018.00021.
35. Balogun, O.D., *et al.*, Integrating ai into health informatics for enhanced public health in Africa: a comprehensive review. *Int. Med. Sci. Res. J.*, 3, 3, 127–144, 2023, https://doi.org/10.51594/imsrj.v3i3.643.
36. Abugabah, A., Nizamuddin, N., Alzubi, A.A., Decentralized telemedicine framework for a smart healthcare ecosystem. *IEEE Access*, 8, 166575–1665885, 2020, https://doi.org/10.1109/ACCESS.2020.3021823.
37. Ritunga, I., Claramita, *et al.*, Challenges and recommendations in the implementation of audiovisual telemedicine communication: a systematic review. *Korean J. Med. Educ.*, 36, 3, 315, 2024, https://doi.org/10.3946/kjme.2024.305.

38. Amri, S. and Sihotang, J., Impact of Poverty Reduction Programs on Healthcare Access in Remote Ar-eas: Fostering Community Development for Sustainable Health. *Law Econ.*, 17, 3, 170–185, 2023, https://doi.org/10.35335/laweco.v17i3.43.
39. Rasel, M.D., Bommu, R., *et al.*, Ensuring Data Security in Interoperable EHR Systems: Exploring Blockchain Solutions for Healthcare Integration. *Int. J. Adv. Eng. Technol. Innov.*, 1, 01, 212–232, 2023, https://ijaeti.com/index.

15

Healthcare Data Acquisition and Management

G. Padma Priya[1], Indumathi S.M.[2*], Rahul Priyadarshi[3], Brijesh Vala[4], Preeti Naval[5] and Kumari K.[6]

[1]*Department of Chemistry and Biochemistry, Jain (Deemed-to-be University), Bangalore, Karnataka, India*
[2]*Department of Biotechnology, Sathyabama Institute of Science and Technology, Chennai, Tamil Nadu, India*
[3]*Centre for Internet of Things, Siksha 'O' Anusandhan (Deemed to be University), Bhubaneswar, Odisha, India*
[4]*Department of Computer Science & Engineering, Parul University, Vadodara, Gujarat, India*
[5]*Maharishi School of Engineering & Technology, Maharishi University of Information Technology, Uttar Pradesh, India*
[6]*Department of Information Science, Presidency University, Bangalore, Karnataka, India*

Abstract
The field of healthcare is increasingly reliant on data-driven insights, as data acquisition and management are critical in improving patient outcomes, streamlining operations, and supporting informed decision-making. The study aims to provide a comprehensive framework for efficient healthcare data acquisition and management, focusing on structured processes to handle large volumes of complex healthcare data. A six-step healthcare data management framework has been introduced. It includes data acquisition, data preprocessing, data storage, data management, data analytics, data visualization, and reporting. Each step in this

**Corresponding author*: indumathi.biotech@sathyabama.ac.in; ORCID: 0000-0003-0854-0733
G. Padma Priya: ORCID: 0000-0004911-1823
Rahul Priyadarshi: ORCID: 0000-0001-5725-9812
Brijesh Vala: ORCID: 0000-0001-7094-7871
Preeti Naval: ORCID: 0000-0003-2988-7082

Satya Prakash Yadav, Abhay Bansal and Victor Hugo C. de Albuquerque (eds.) Computational Intelligence in Biomedical Internet of Medical Things, (251–266) © 2026 Scrivener Publishing LLC

framework ensures data accuracy, security, and accessibility across various stages of the data lifecycle, ultimately allowing for more robust and insightful data analytics. Data acquisition captures data from diverse sources Preprocessing refines it for consistency Storage ensures secure and organized retention; management facilitates data integration and accessibility. Advanced analytics provides insights, while visualization and reporting make these findings accessible to stakeholders. The entire potential of healthcare companies' data can be connected through this organized method, improving operational efficiency and care delivery. By implementing this framework, healthcare institutions can better respond to emerging challenges, adapt to technological advancements, and foster a data-driven culture that enhances patient outcomes and operational success.

***Keywords*:** Healthcare, data preprocessing, data acquisition, data management, data analytics, data storage, data visualization, reporting

15.1 Introduction

Modern healthcare relies completely on data collection and analytics to enhance the outcomes of treatment, patient care, and operational efficiency [1]. Wearable technologies, medical imaging, electronic health record (EHR) information, diagnostics, and patient-reported outcomes each generate an enormous quantity of data [2]. Data can be used by healthcare providers to make informed assumptions, alter treatment regimens, or track patients' outcomes in real-time [3]. Healthcare becomes more efficient in diagnosing a specific ailment, forecasting certain illnesses, and planning and using assets of various technological leads, such as big data analytics, artificial intelligence (AI), and machine learning (ML) [4]. Moreover, the administrative procedures can be improved, the number of errors may decrease, and an overall increase in the quality of treating the patients can be guaranteed with the use of healthcare data management systems [5]. Even though healthcare data collection and management have tremendous potential, there are a number of barriers and limitations. One is the interoperability of systems across so many platforms [6]. Particularly in multihospital environments, healthcare information can come in different forms, which makes it difficult to communicate and integrate effectively among healthcare agencies [7]. Lack of standard interchange standards can lead to errors in patient data, redundant testing, and fragmented treatment [8]. Moreover, due to the sensitive nature of healthcare information, privacy and security remain the major issues [9]. It becomes complicated to preserve information from multiple interfaces and systems, and multiple devices and platforms contribute to the complexity of regulatory compliance even though it is essential [10]. The patient's information is also unsafe from cyber threats such as hacking and data leakage [11]. There is another limitation, which is the voluminous amount of data that is produced. Healthcare data can be analyzed and useful insights drawn from it, considering its complexity and large volume [12]. There is an issue frequently with the data itself, which can be brought on by improper training or data entry problems [13]. Furthermore, emerging healthcare companies could find that different types of sophisticated healthcare data management systems are too expensive and difficult to handle [14]. Finally, a lack of work to appropriately evaluate and understand the massive data volumes typical of healthcare practice partially offsets the potential advantages of data analysis in clinical practice [15]. With an emphasis on standardized procedures to manage massive amounts of intricate healthcare data, the study seeks to offer a thorough foundation for effective healthcare data collection and administration.

15.2 Healthcare Data Framework

It can transform how healthcare providers leverage cultured technology to gain insights from clinical and other data sources, leading to accurate assessments through a six-step process: acquisition, preprocessing, storage,

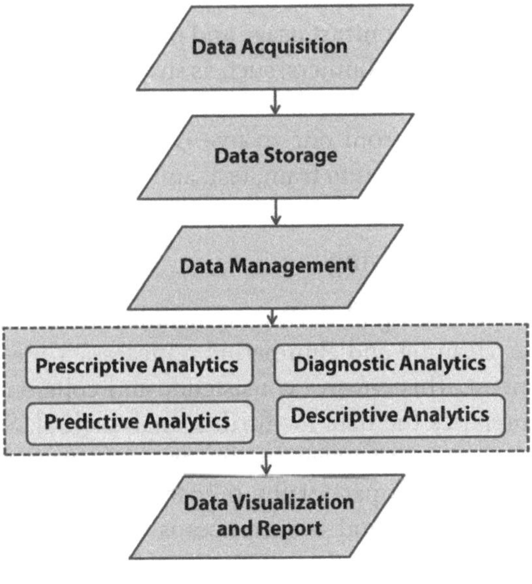

Figure 15.1 Healthcare framework. (Source: Own elaboration).

management, analytics, visualization, and reporting. Figure 15.1 shows the healthcare framework.

15.2.1 Data Acquisition

Healthcare data acquisition is the systematic collection of health data from many sources, such as medical patient inputs, imaging, and EHRs, to assist medical treatment and decision-making. The EHR datasets were used from Kaggle [16]. This software provides important information, including overall hospitalization admissions, the mean duration of inpatient stays, and a breakdown of medical conditions that lead to hospital admissions. Healthcare providers efficiently use resources and develop patient care plans based on more information obtained from knowledge of patient demographics, use of hospital units, and outcome of discharge. Clinical datasets [17], which are frequently obtained from websites like Kaggle, include comprehensive information from electronic medical records (EMRs), such as lab results, diagnoses, treatments, and demographics. Although EMRs are frequently accessible by internal persons, qualifying studies can be accessed through collaborative networks and archives, which simplify cohort identification and promote clinical study. A varied collection of medical pictures for analysis and AI-based model training is provided by the medical imaging dataset, which was acquired *via* Kaggle and divided into two categories: computed tomography (CT) images and chest X-rays. The CT scan dataset [18] is intended to evaluate patterns in CT image data regarding contrast usage and patient age to classify wrongly classified images or identify outliers, such as suspicious cases or equipment issues. The X-ray dataset [19], which includes 5,863 chest X-ray pictures (JPEG) of children ages from one to five is categorized as normal, and pneumonia and is arranged into train, test, and validation folders.

15.2.2 Data Preprocessing

The preliminary processing of EHR data includes standardizing the document structure, cleaning and eliminating unnecessary material, and formatting the content. This ensures consistency and coherence in the next processes and prepares the data for further analysis [20]. Stop words are eliminated, verbs are lemmatized to the present tense, and words are stemmed to root forms as part of the preparation of EMRs [21]. A dictionary of common terms and occurrences is created using Gensim. To recognize medical subjects, the latent Dirichlet allocation model is trained using key terms and term frequency-inverse document frequency scores.

Electronic medical records are subsequently categorized into relevant medical centers using this insight. In medical imaging, preprocessing transformations are crucial for maintaining spatial and intensity consistency between training examples, especially for CT scan pictures [22]. To ensure uniform spatial connections, voxel positions are aligned across pictures by spatial pretreatment. Commonly employed methods include reorientation, which aligns pictures to a consistent orientation, and resampling, which standardizes voxel spacing to be isotropic. Intensity normalization, which is crucial for maximizing model performance, entails standardization or scaling (e.g., PyTorch standardization or min-max scaling). Computed tomography scan histogram standardization accounts for differences in intensity distributions from various scanners or sequences, and only pertinent voxels are included in normalizing calculations using a binary mask. By ensuring consistency in the spatial and intensity dimensions, these preprocessing techniques enhance the simulation results. The preprocessing of chest X-ray images [23] involves converting digital imaging and communications in medicine or JPEG formats to NumPy arrays and downsampling to 256×256. By integrating lung segmentation with the lung balance contrast enhancement method, pixel values are adjusted based on the identified lung area. If segmentation is unsuccessful, a heuristic examines the lung region and, if necessary, applies BCET without doing particular lung processing. The uniformity method and Gamma correction are used, using values selected from previous studies and the Albumentations library. These procedures guarantee consistency for additional analysis and improve image quality.

15.2.3 Data Storage

All information could be maintained locally at the hospital or on a cloud server. For long-term preservation or real-time monitoring and evaluation, collected information can be stored in a data warehouse, data lake, or data mart [24]. Data has been preserved safely and accessible from a variety of locations, such as hospitals, pharmacies, emergency vehicles, and laboratories. Patient data can be gathered using the cloud's backend storage mechanisms by the data ingestion module or directly exchanged with the data connection module (such as HTTP or REST API requests). An effective and sizable storage platform is required as the amount of data in the healthcare sector increases. Cloud computing is the most promising technology because of its enormous capacity. Clouds offer the flexibility and power to access data, increase awareness, expedite the creation of scalable analytics solutions, and provide revenue. Cloud computing is a potent

Table 15.1 The healthcare data storage platform.

Storage type	Google	Microsoft	Amazon
Object storage	Google Cloud Storage, Cloud SQL	Azure Storage Blob Storage, Data Lake Store, Account	Amazon S3, Amazon Glacier
File storage	Google Cloud Filestore	Azure Files	Amazon Elastic File System
Block storage	Cloud Datastore, Firestore, Bigtable, BigQuery, Cloud Spanner	Table Storage, SQL Database, Persistent Disk, Azure Cosmos DB	Amazon Elastic Block Store, Amazon RDS, MariaDB, PostgreSQL, Oracle, SQL Server, DynamoDB

and exciting technology that can store vast amounts of data and carry out complicated, large-scale computations [25]. It eliminates the requirement for expensive computer gear, software, and specialized space. Table 15.1 shows the storage platforms of the healthcare system.

15.2.4 Data Management

It is the procedure for gathering, maintaining, organizing, and preserving data to ensure its accessibility, security, and quality [26]. It uses procedures like data governance, security, and privacy to satisfy legal requirements and facilitate effective decision-making. Figure 15.2 displays the data management process.

- **Data governance:** It refers to every stage of data administration in its lifetime with accuracy, security, and compliance with applicable laws [27]. Preserving the quality, integrity, and responsible usage of data mandates established procedures for owning, responsibility, and stewardship of data.
- **Data protection:** Encryption and authentication shield private patient information from unintentional access and changes, preserving its confidentiality and integrity throughout time [28].

Figure 15.2 Data management process in healthcare. (Source: Own elaboration).

- **Data security:** Firewalls are mandatory to secure networks, apart from two-factor authentication, to ensure comprehensive vulnerability assessment and audits are conducted [29].
- **Data privacy:** In the healthcare sector, protecting patient and medical information means making sure that only authorized individuals can access and utilize it for the right reasons [30]. It contains rules and policies that control consent, protect patient privacy, and restrict access to personal information.
- **Data minimization:** By limiting access to data through access only to relevant information, aggregating only needed information reduces the possible leakage of exposure and maintains the confidentiality of the patient [31].
- **Data de-identification:** Anonymization of personal information and de-identification using encryption or differential privacy preserves privacy while allowing extracts of insightful information to be derived from the medical data [32].

15.2.5 Data Analytics

In the healthcare industry, data analytics is the process of finding hidden patterns, unknown connections, patient preferences, and other relevant information that could assist with decision-making by sifting through massive and diverse datasets [33]. A variety of analytical techniques are used in healthcare data analytics to improve decision-making within the industry [34]. Table 15.2 shows the process of data analytics.

- ➢ Descriptive analytics examine historical healthcare data to identify patterns and evaluate how various factors affect patient outcomes.
- ➢ Diagnostic analytics examine historical data to determine the underlying causes of problems, helping to understand why particular occurrences or results occur.
- ➢ Using probabilistic models, predictive analytics forecast future patterns by utilizing both historical and real-time data.
- ➢ Lastly, prescriptive analytics help healthcare providers receive optimal results by providing practical suggestions on the most effective course of action, extending past simple predictions.

The healthcare data analytics tools and support for various medical imaging modalities and functionalities are included in Table 15.3. Numerous imaging modalities, such as MRI, CT-Scan, PET, and fMRI, are supported by tools like VTK, ITK, FSL, and SPM. They all share the goal of improving registration, segmentation, and visualization capabilities. Additionally, these programs provide strong graphical user interfaces for user-friendliness, guaranteeing compatibility with many medical imaging platforms, and some even allow more complex features like reconstruction and simulation. Clinical decision-making is much enhanced and healthcare data administration is streamlined with the help of such extensive tool assistance.

Table 15.2 Process of data analytics.

Healthcare data	**Data analytics platform**	**Data analytics**	**Result of data analytics**
	• Data capture • Data preparation • Data processing	• Data analytics algorithm • Data mining • ML	

Table 15.3 Healthcare data analytic tools.

Healthcare data analytic tools	VTK	ITK	FSL	SPM	ITK-snap	ANTS	GIMIAS
Supported image formats							
MRI	✓	✓	✓	✓	✓	✓	✓
Mammogram		✓					
X-ray	✓	✓					
CT-Scan	✓	✓			✓	✓	✓
PET	✓	✓	✓	✓			✓
EEG		✓					
fMRI	✓	✓	✓	✓		✓	✓
Graphical User Interface	✓	✓	✓	✓	✓		✓
Ultrasound	✓	✓			✓	✓	
Operations							
Reconstruction	✓	✓					✓
Segmentation	✓	✓	✓	✓	✓	✓	✓
Registration	✓	✓	✓	✓	✓	✓	✓
Generic	✓	✓			✓		
Visualization	✓	✓	✓	✓	✓	✓	✓
Simulation							✓

Note:

- *ITK - Insight Segmentation and Registration Toolkit*
- *SPM - Statistical Parametric Mapping*
- *ANTS - Advanced Normalization Tools*
- *FSL - FMRIB Software Library*
- *GIMIAS - Graphical Interface for Medical Image Analysis and Simulation*
- *VTK - Visualization Toolkit*

15.2.6 Data Visualization

To better comprehend complex information and make better decisions, data visualization involves displaying the analytical findings of healthcare data graphically or pictorially [35]. It could be applied to comprehend relationships and patterns in the data. Figure 15.3 shows how various publishing categories are distributed yearly between 2015 and 2023. The colorful bars reflect different publishing categories. With a peak in 2022, the data shows a notable rise in publishing activity starting in 2019.

The presented healthcare data framework emphasizes how important data collection, preparation, administration, storage, analytics, and visualization are to changing healthcare procedures. Healthcare professionals can make better decisions, allocate resources more effectively, and improve patient care by utilizing a variety of data sources, including EHRs and medical imaging. Preprocessing methods like segmentation and normalization ensure the consistency and quality of information, which is essential for precise analytics and decision-making. Incorporating data analytics technologies with data visualization helps identify patterns and provides actionable insights for better clinical results, which eventually improves the efficacy and effectiveness of healthcare.

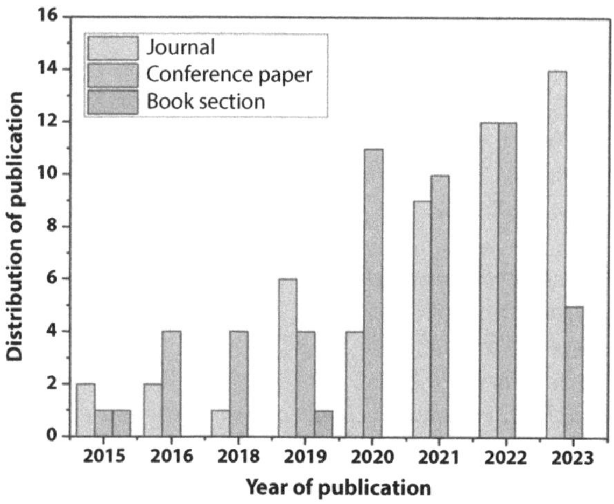

Figure 15.3 Results of data visualization. (Source: Own elaboration).

15.3 Assessment of Healthcare Data

Healthcare data management assessment involves checking gathering, storing, and analyzing healthcare information for accuracy, security, and accessibility. It deals with improving the quality of data, streamlining workflow, and ensuring regulatory standards. Better management leads to enhanced decision-making, support of patient care, and innovation in healthcare services. For the evaluation of healthcare data management, the methods used are the gradient boosting machine (GBM) [36], artificial neural networks [36], extreme gradient boosting [36], support vector machines [36], LightGBM [36], and convolutional neural networks [37].

15.3.1 Accuracy

In healthcare data management, accuracy is the correctness and dependability of the data that is gathered, saved, and processed. To aid decision-making and appropriate patient care, reliable data ensures that the patient's information in records, diagnoses, and treatment plans is current, accurate, and error-free. Figure 15.4 below presents the accuracy parameters.

Figure 15.4 presents the computation time of several authentication and verification systems for health data exchange with the increasing

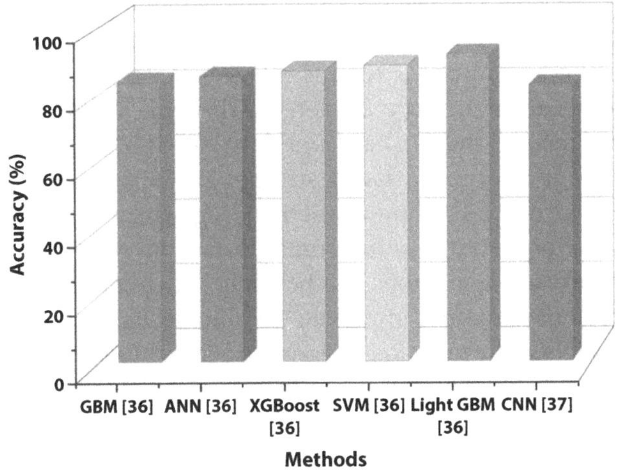

Figure 15.4 Accuracy parameters.

number of verifiers. The longest-computed program was the GBM [36], which had a high resource usage. The artificial neural network [36] and extreme gradient boosting [36] performed average. It had linear scalability, but its efficiency was lower compared to GBM. In contrast, the support vector machine [36] performed better in terms of efficiency and scalability, with the best result in terms of computation time. The LightGBM [36] technique also outperformed other techniques in verifier count while achieving smooth performance at minimal computation cost. Further, the convolutional neural network [37] model became quite promising, as it showed relatively fast times for computation and scalability; this illustrated its potential to be used comparatively effectively and practically in the safe management systems of healthcare data.

15.4 Conclusion

The six-step healthcare data management framework proposed by this study provides a structured and comprehensive approach to handling the complexities of healthcare data. By emphasizing acquisition, preprocessing, storage, management, analytics, and visualization of healthcare data, the entire framework assures health institutions that the critical steps of maintaining data at all stages of the lifecycle data are accurate, secure, and accessible. This would increase the efficiency of the healthcare services but at the same time enable data-driven decision-making that improves significantly patient outcomes. With an evolving healthcare industry, such a structure brings an organization's power to utilize its data better, enable it to adapt to technological changes, overcome emergent challenges, and foster a continuous improvement culture in care and operational performance delivery. Although it is an all-encompassing strategy, this structure could be prohibitively expensive and technically demanding, which would be problematic for smaller organizations. Integrating data from several sources while adhering to privacy regulations can be challenging and time-consuming. Future developments could improve real-time decision-making by using AI-driven insights, streamlining integration across healthcare systems, and improving data interoperability. The effectiveness of healthcare data management could be further increased by increasing the framework's flexibility to new data kinds and technological advancements.

References

1. Al-Jaroodi, J., Mohamed, N., Abukhousa, E., Health 4.0: on the way to realizing the healthcare of the future. *IEEE Access*, 8, 211189–2112105, 2020, https://doi.org/10.1109/ACCESS.2020.3038858.
2. Khatiwada, P., *et al.*, Patient-Generated Health Data (PGHD): Understanding, Requirements, Challenges, and Existing Techniques for Data Security and Privacy. *J. Pers. Med.*, 14, 3, 282, 2024, https://doi.org/10.3390/jpm14030282.
3. Udegbe, F. C., *et al.*, Real-time data integration in diagnostic devices for predictive modeling of infectious disease outbreaks. *Comput. Sci. IT Res. J.*, 4, 3, 525–545, 2023, https://doi.org/10.51594/csitrj.v4i3.1502
4. Paramesha, M., LiladharRane, N., Rane, J., Big data analytics, artificial intelligence, machine learning, internet of things, and blockchain for enhanced business intelligence. *Partn. Univers. Multidiscip. Res. J.*, 1, 2, 110–133, 2024, https://doi.org/10.5281/zenodo.12827323.
5. Yaqoob, I., *et al.*, Blockchain for healthcare data management: opportunities, challenges, and future recommendations, in: *Neural Computing and Applications*, pp. 1–16, 2022, https://doi.org/10.1007/s00521-020-05519-w.
6. Avula, R., Addressing barriers in data collection, transmission, and security to optimize data availability in healthcare systems for improved clinical decision-making and analytics. *Appl. Res. Artif. Intell. Cloud Comput.*, 4, 1, 78–93, 2021, https://orcid.org/0009-0006-8476-8544.
7. Oktaviani, N. and Permana, R., Healthcare Data Architectures: Advanced Frameworks for Accurate Analytics and Strategic Decision Support. *Int. J. Human-Centered Emerg. Technol.*, 11, 10, 1–20, 2021, https://scicadence.com/index.php/IJHET/issue/view/22.
8. Avula, R., Overcoming data silos in healthcare with strategies for enhancing integration and interoperability to improve clinical and operational efficiency. *J. Adv. Anal. Healthc. Manage.*, 4, 10, 26–44, 2020, https://orcid.org/0009-0006-8476-8544.
9. Keshta, I. and Odeh, A., Security and privacy of electronic health records: Concerns and challenges. *Egypt. Inf. J.*, 22, 2, 177–183, 2021, https://doi.org/10.1016/j.eij.2020.07.003.
10. Miryala, N.K. and Gupta, D., Data Security Challenges and Industry Trends. *IJARCCE Int. J. Adv. Res. Comput. Commun. Eng.*, 11, 11, 300–309, 2022, https://doi.org/10.1016/j.compbiomed.2020.104130.
11. Argaw, S.T., *et al.*, Cybersecurity of Hospitals: discussing the challenges and working towards mitigating the risks. *BMC Med. Inf. Decis. Making*, 20, 1–105, 2020, https://doi.org/10.1186/s12911-020-01161-7.
12. Singhania, K. and Reddy, A., Improving preventative care and health outcomes for patients with chronic diseases using big data-driven insights and predictive modeling. *Int. J. Appl. Health Care Anal.*, 9, 2, 1–14, 2024, https://norislab.com/index.php/IJAHA/issue/view/22.

13. Munappy, A.R., *et al.*, Data management for production quality deep learning models: Challenges and solutions. *J. Syst. Softw.*, 191, 1113595, 2022, https://doi.org/10.1016/j.jss.2022.111359.
14. Haleem, A., *et al.*, Telemedicine for healthcare: Capabilities, features, barriers, and applications. *Sens. Int.*, 2, 1001175, 2021, https://doi.org/10.1016/j.sintl.2021.100117.
15. Galetsi, P., Katsaliaki, K., Kumar, S., Big data analytics in health sector: Theoretical framework, techniques and prospects. *Int. J. Inf. Manage.*, 50, 206–2165, 2020, https://doi.org/10.1016/j.ijinfomgt.2019.05.003.
16. Electronic Health Record (EHR) Dataset: https://www.kaggle.com/datasets/anuchhetry/electronic-health-record.
17. Clinical Dataset: https://www.kaggle.com/datasets/imtkaggleteam/clinical-dataset.
18. CT Medical Images dataset: https://www.kaggle.com/datasets/kmader/siim-medical-images.
19. X-ray dataset: https://www.kaggle.com/datasets/paultimothymooney/chest-xray-pneumonia/data.
20. Nova, K., Generative AI in healthcare: advancements in electronic health records, facilitating medical languages, and personalized patient care. *J. Adv. Anal. Healthc. Manage.*, 7, 1, 115–131, 2023, https://research.tensorgate.org/index.php/JAAHM/article/view/43.
21. Memarzadeh, H., *et al.*, A study into patient similarity through representation learning from medical records. *Knowl. Inf. Syst.*, 64, 3293–3324, 12, 2022, https://doi.org/10.1007/s10115-022-01740-2.
22. Pérez-García, F., Sparks, R., Ourselin, S., TorchIO: a Python library for efficient loading, preprocessing, augmentation and patch-based sampling of medical images in deep learning. *Comput. Methods Programs Biomed.*, 208, 1062365, 2021, https://doi.org/10.1016/j.cmpb.2021.106236.
23. Chokchaithanakul, W., Punyabukkana, P., Chuangsuwanich, E., Adaptive image preprocessing and augmentation for tuberculosis screening on out-of-domain chest X-Ray dataset. *IEEE Access*, 10, 132144–1321525, 2022, https://doi.org/10.1109/ACCESS.2022.3229591.
24. Zeydan, E., Arslan, S.S., Liyanage, M., Managing Distributed Machine Learning Lifecycle for Healthcare Data in the Cloud. *IEEE Access*, 12, 115750–115774, 2024, https://doi.org/10.1109/ACCESS.2024.3443520.
25. Sha, M., Mohemmed, Rahamathulla, M.P., Cloud-based Healthcare data management Framework. *KSII Trans. Internet Inf. Syst. (TIIS)*, 14, 3, 1014–1025, 2020, https://doi.org/10.3837/tiis.2020.03.006.
26. Abbas, A., *et al.*, Blockchain-assisted secured data management framework for health information analysis based on Internet of Medical Things. *Pers. Ubiquitous Comput.*, 28, 1, 59–72, 2024, https://doi.org/10.1007/s00779-021-01583-8.

27. Janssen, M., *et al.*, Data governance: Organizing data for trustworthy Artificial Intelligence. *Gov. Inf. Q*, 37, 3, 101493, 2020, https://doi.org/10.1016/j.giq.2020.101493.
28. Suneetha, T. and Bhagwan, J., A Secure Framework For Enhancing Data Privacy And Access Control In Healthcare Cloud Management Systems. *Educ. Adm. Theory Pract.*, 30, 5, 13341–13349, 2024, https://doi.org/10.53555/kuey.v30i5.5783.
29. Miracle, N.O., The Importance of Network Security in Protecting Sensitive Data and Information. *Int. J. Res. Innov. Appl. Sci.*, 9, 6, 259–270, 2024, https://doi.org/10.51584/IJRIAS.2024.906024.
30. McGraw, D. and Mandl, K.D., Privacy protections to encourage use of health-relevant digital data in a learning health system. *npj Digit. Med.*, 4, 1, 2, 2021, https://doi.org/10.1038/s41746-020-00362-8.
31. Semantha, F.H., *et al.*, A conceptual framework to ensure privacy in patient record management system. *IEEE Access*, 9, 165667–1656895, 2021, https://doi.org/10.1109/ACCESS.2021.3134873.
32. Alabdullah, B., Novel reversible text data de-identification techniques based on native data structures, Diss. University of Sussex, 2022, https://hdl.handle.net/10779/uos.23489594.v1.
33. Razzak, M.I., Imran, M., Xu, G., Big data analytics for preventive medicine. *Neural Comput. Appl.*, 32, 9, 4417–4451, 2020, https://doi.org/10.1007/s00521-019-04095-y.
34. Roy, D., *et al.*, A complete overview of analytics techniques: descriptive, predictive, and prescriptive, in: *Decision Intelligence Analytics and the Implementation of Strategic Business Management*, pp. 15–30, 2022, https://doi.org/10.1007/978-3-030-82763-2_2.
35. Liu, H., *et al.*, Health care data analysis and visualization using interactive data exploration for sportsperson 2022. *Sci. China Inf. Sci.*, 65, 6, 162101, 2022, https://doi.org/10.1007/s11432-021-3412-9.
36. Golec, *et al.*, HealthFaaS: Ai-based smart healthcare system for heart patients using serverless computing. *IEEE Internet Things J.*, 10, 21, 18469–18476, 2023, https://doi.org/10.1109/JIOT.2023.3277500.
37. Lv, Z., Zengchen, *et al.*, Deep learning-based smart predictive evaluation for interactive multimedia-enabled smart healthcare. *ACM Trans. Multimed. Comput. Commun. Appl. (TOMM)*, 18, 1s, 1–20, 2022, https://doi.org/10.1145/3468506.

16

Telemedicine and Remote Health Monitoring for Underserved Communities

Sheuli Sen[1], Subbulakshmi Ganesan[2], Rohini Chavan[3*], Deepak Dasaratha Rao[4], Binayak Pand[5] and Ayesha Taranum[6]

[1]*Department of Pediatric Nursing, Teerthakar Parshvnath College of Nursing, Teerthanker Mahaveer University, Uttar Pradesh, India*
[2]*Department of Chemistry and Biochemistry, Jain (Deemed-to-be University), Bangalore, Karnataka, India*
[3]*Department of Pharmacy Practice, PES's Modern College of Pharmacy, Nigdi, Pune, India*
[4]*Department of AI and Data Science, Indian Institute of Technology, Patna, India*
[5]*Department of Computer Science and Engineering, Siksha 'O' Anusandhan (Deemed to be University), Bhubaneswar, Odisha, India*
[6]*Department of Computer Science and Engineering, Presidency University, Bangalore, Karnataka, India*

Abstract
Telemedicine and remote health monitoring have emerged as transformative solutions to address healthcare disparities in underserved communities. These communities often face significant barriers, including limited access to medical facilities, high costs, and geographic isolation. Telemedicine leverages technology to connect patients with healthcare providers, while remote health monitoring devices enable real-time tracking of chronic conditions, reducing the need for frequent hospital visits. The study explores the benefits of telemedicine, such as improved accessibility, cost-effectiveness, and enhanced healthcare outcomes. It examines the technological infrastructure required, including mobile health applications, wearable devices, and internet connectivity, while highlighting challenges like

**Corresponding author*: drrohinichavan33@gmail.com; ORCID: 0000-0002-0276-5918
Subbulakshmi Ganesan: ORCID: 0000-0002-8345-116X
Rohini Chavan: ORCID: 0009-0007-4249-2962
Deepak Dasaratha Rao: ORCID: 0000-0001-5959-3136
Binayak Pand: ORCID: 0000-0001-6027-3148

Satya Prakash Yadav, Abhay Bansal and Victor Hugo C. de Albuquerque (eds.) Computational Intelligence in Biomedical Internet of Medical Things, (267–284) © 2026 Scrivener Publishing LLC

technological illiteracy, cultural barriers, and data privacy concerns. Despite its promise, implementing telemedicine in underserved communities encounters barriers such as technological illiteracy, cultural resistance, inadequate infrastructure, and concerns over data privacy. Its potential is successfully demonstrated, highlighting the importance of community engagement and tailored approaches. Advances in 5G connectivity, artificial intelligence, and policy support are driving the scalability of telemedicine, fostering personalized care and widespread adoption. The study explores the current state, benefits, barriers, and future directions of telemedicine in underserved areas. It emphasizes the need for collaborative efforts among governments, healthcare providers, and technology developers to create inclusive healthcare solutions. Telemedicine represents a vital step toward equitable healthcare, promoting urban and rural revitalization through enhanced access to medical care and better health outcomes.

***Keywords*:** Telemedicine, remote health monitoring, community, healthcare infrastructure, digital health accessibility, continuous support, underserved populations

16.1 Introduction

Telemedicine and remote health monitoring (RHM) have become essential healthcare delivery models required in areas with rare access to healthcare infrastructure [1]. All of these technologies have the capability of modifying challenges of facility and healthcare provider infrequency, and high costs, which are challenges to efficient healthcare facilities for many patients [2]. Specifically, rural and low-income populations, the elderly, and minorities have limited access to healthcare services because of the insufficient density of physicians and healthcare resources. Telemedicine is the practice of using telecommunications and digital information technologies to deliver clinical services remotely and acting as a link, ensuring that these communities can access medical care at the right time without requiring an appointment [3]. Remote health monitoring is a subcategory of telemedicine, focusing on constant or intermittent tracking of a patient's health parameters, including heartbeat, blood pressure, glucose levels, and others, by a patient into a wearable device or smartphone application [4]. It can be applied in the management of patients' health conditions, provide timely intervention, and stop the growth of a disease. Telemedicine's effect, particularly in combined conjunction with RHM, has revolutionized health outcomes [5].

These technologies not only improve hospitalization rates and emergency department visits through preventive care and chronic disease management but also enable early intervention, especially for low-resource patients who may not receive standard care [6]. For example, telemedicine enables patients to schedule a virtual consultation with a specialist, removing the difficulty and cost of travel in remote areas where access to specialized treatment may be several hours away by automobile [7]. Also, remote monitoring may improve patient involvement and compliance with recommended medical treatments due to constant timely health status updates and declared self-management behaviors [8].

Apart from its clinical impacts, telemedicine has huge capabilities of saving on costs for both the patient and the healthcare systems [9]. Since it eliminates the need for travel, hospitalization, and face-to-face physician attendance, it can additionally help deal with the financial pressure that may drive people away from seeking treatment [10]. But as is obvious, there are issues such as the accessibility of technology, availability of broadband internet connection, and protection of information gathered. A number of communities have limited access to the internet and digital devices, and many have privacy concerns regarding personal health information [11]. Telemedicine and RMH serve as incredibly positive ideas that might transform the healthcare systems related to minority groups [12]. Through sustained investment in the infrastructure and technology, and commitment to policy reforms, these innovations can reduce health imbalances, enhance population health and promote equity and inclusiveness in healthcare delivery across the globe [13]. Figure 16.1 shows the following methods for telemedicine and RMH for underserved communities.

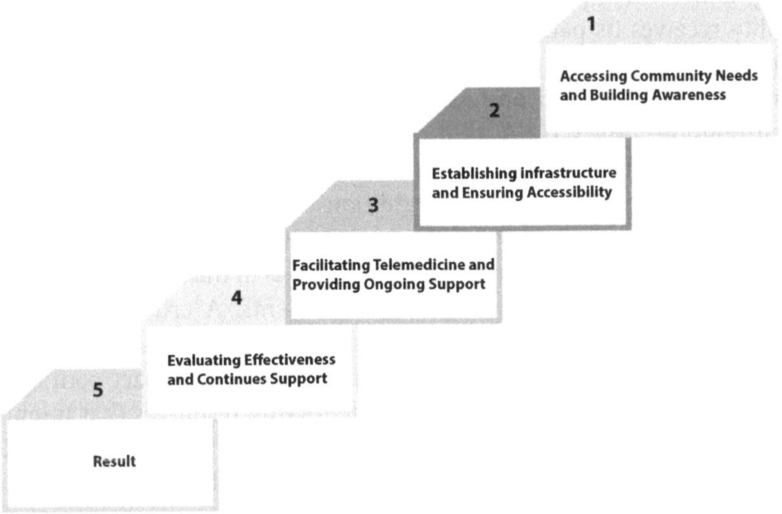

Figure 16.1 Features for telemedicine and RMH for underserved communities. (Source: Own elaboration).

16.2 Accessing Community Needs and Building Awareness

Apart from mandating financial aid for all tax-exempt hospitals, the Affordable Care Act (ACA) also mandated regular community health needs (CHNA) assessments. One new Internal Revenue Code provision that was added to the ACA is the CHNA [14]. It mandates that nonprofit hospitals evaluate the health status of the local community every three years and provide a strategy to address the issues. Since the evaluation is the responsibility of each hospital facility, healthcare requirements assessment must be institution-specific, in contrast to community benefits expenditure, which might be recorded at an organizational level across all locations. In addition to being "widely available to the public," assessments must be followed by yearly "implementation strategies" that the hospital has "adopted" with the aim of "meeting the community health requirements identified *via* the needs assessment."

16.2.1 Community Input Required

More information about the minimal components of the CHNA procedure can be found in the community input required (IRS) implementing regulations for CHNAs [15]. A hospital must identify the community; it serves in an assessment so that it does not leave out low-income, minority, or medically underserved populations that reside in the areas where the hospital facility receives its patients due to their need for financial aid or dependence on public insurance. In addition to considering community members' and public health professionals' opinions, a hospital must "solicit" their opinions. The CHNA itself needs to be a documented report that is publicly accessible and fully accepted by the hospital. The IRS requires the hospital to take into account, in addition to the need for medical treatment, the needs for the development or maintenance of health conditions in specific segments of the community as well as in the community at large when assessing community health requirements. A crucial part of this includes preventing disease, making sure people eat enough, or tackling social, behavioral, and environmental problems that impact community health. Prioritizing requirements and identifying resources that might be able to address them are both necessary. This means that the IRS considers socioeconomic determinants of health in addition to healthcare services when defining the needs assessment process [16].

16.2.2 Building Awareness

Hospitals are required to provide an implementation strategy in addition to their health needs assessment. Possibly the most important step in the needs assessment procedure is scheduling. Although implementation methods serve as a blueprint for the needs that the hospital could not focus on, as well as the resources that the hospital may commit to or seek in advancing their needs assessment, the IRS does not need to be made public, unlike needs assessments [17].

16.3 Establishing Infrastructure and Ensuring Accessibility

Many stakeholders use healthcare data for a variety of reasons, and these data are complex. There are three main ways to view healthcare data: the public health or community aspect, the individual perspectives or personal health aspect, and the health provider's aspect [18]. A foundation for the communication and information infrastructure of the healthcare industry will be built using these four essential elements:

- ➢ Electronic health records (EHRs)
- ➢ Personal health of records (PHRs)
- ➢ Electronic medical records systems (EMRSs)
- ➢ Features for exchanging information

16.3.1 Electronic Medical Records System

Information systems were created and implemented to manage healthcare data effectively and enhance healthcare quality and safety due to their volume and complexity. Many of the EMRSs in use today are the result of these innovative efforts. Clinical practice processes including scheduling care providers, gathering clinical notes, and recording administrative tasks like billing and scheduling are all automated by an EMRS [19]. These administrative and clinical tasks result in the creation of a patient's EMR. It was exclusive to that system and frequently remains within the particular EMRS that produced it. In such instances, only that particular EMRS can understand exactly what the EMR represents.

16.3.2 Electronic Health Record

The term "EHR" refers to all electronic information on a person that is needed to achieve and improve their health or well-being [20]. An EMR is fully included in an EHR, which is a superset of it. To achieve this goal, an EHR may gather data from several sources of personal information, as well as from various EMRSs throughout the healthcare system. The EHR has a constant meaning since it exists independently of any specific EMRS, as shown in Figure 16.2.

16.3.3 Personal Health of Records

A personal computerized collection of data is referred to as a PHR [21]. Personal medication progress and adjustment records for the patient, as well as electronic copies of their doctors' information, may be included in the PHR. Patients may also choose which details to disclose to their healthcare plan or providers. The capabilities and content of various records and record platforms frequently overlap significantly. Differences in ownership and purpose should also be taken into consideration.

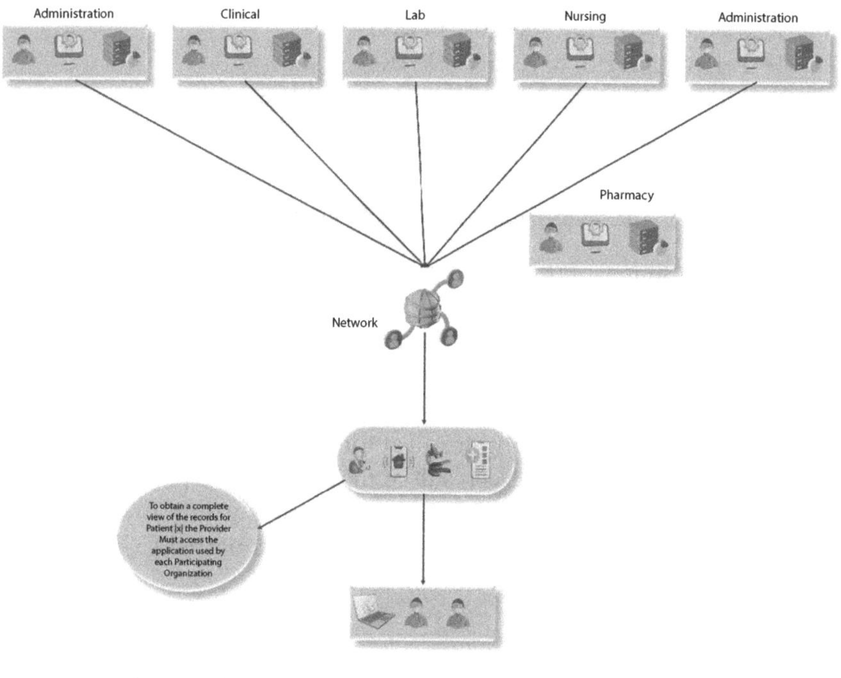

Figure 16.2 Electronic health record structure. (Source: Own elaboration).

16.3.4 Data Interchange Capabilities

A data exchange starts with a tool like a central client record or its equivalent function to identify the information that belongs to a particular individual [22]. It is possible to display information at one site that was collected from another location or to aggregate certain information, such as test findings or prescribed drugs, into a centralized database that can observe from any location. While the latter needs agreement on new technical standards for information exchange, as well as the deployment of communication and terminology standards, the former is relatively simple. In either situation, a system is required to permit access to data by an individual data location other than the source. Therefore, such a service involves as much common language, governance, and trust as it requires technology.

16.4 Implementing Remote Health Monitoring and Device Distribution

Remote health monitoring is a technology-driven strategy that enables medical professionals to keep an eye on patients away from conventional clinical settings. It stands as a customized patient care route in which health information about a person is gathered and provided to medical specialists at a different location [23]. For instance, to facilitate ongoing observation without requiring regular office visits, a diabetic patient may utilize a device to constantly record and transmit blood sugar readings to their healthcare physician. The use of RHM includes a variety of approaches and strategies that have transformed patient care, going beyond simple data collection. Vital indicators such as oxygen saturation, heart rate, and blood pressure can be measured *via* biometric sensors that are attached to the human body and communicated to healthcare providers. This ongoing monitoring can aid in the early identification of increasing problems in patients with chronic heart failure, allowing for timely management, as shown in Figure 16.3.

Direct patient-provider communication is made possible by telecommunications solutions like video conferencing. Virtual visits with therapists can help patients receive physical recovery following surgery by guiding them through exercises, monitoring their progress, and modifying treatments as necessary [24]. Remote health monitoring's predictive modeling and software algorithms aid in identifying patient patterns and can notify healthcare providers of possible issues. For instance, a heart

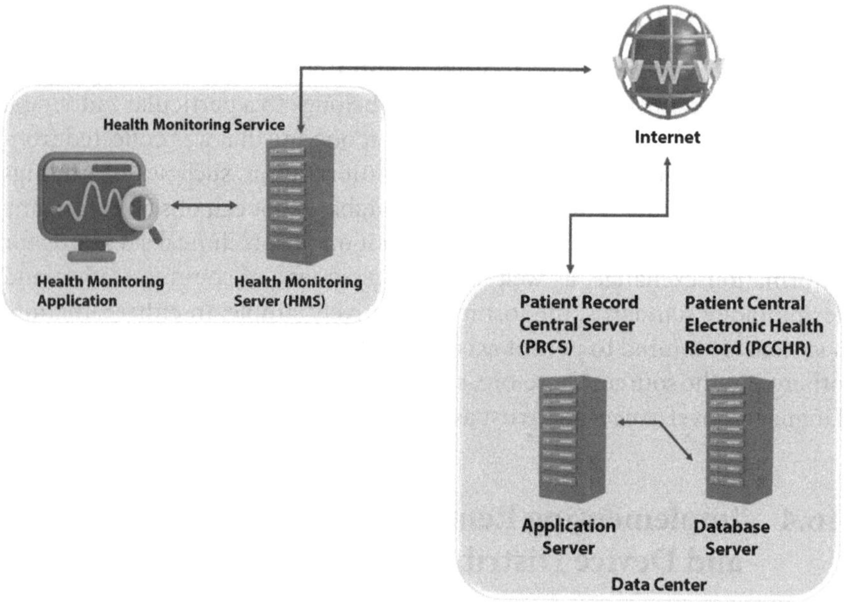

Figure 16.3 Remote health monitoring structure. (Source: https://www.sciencedirect.com/science/article/pii/S1319157821001385).

rhythm abnormality identified by monitoring could alert the cardiology team, allowing for prompt action and potentially preventing serious consequences.

The growth of RHM is not without difficulties, though. It takes technical know-how to integrate different technologies and procedures, and it can lead to inequalities in access to treatment, especially for older or less wealthy communities. Since any breaches could result in serious privacy violations, ethical questions surrounding data security and privacy are crucial. Furthermore, remote monitoring cannot completely replace the human touch that distinguishes traditional healthcare encounters. Healthcare professionals constantly struggle to balance between technology, empathy, and patient relationships.

The multidimensional strategy known as RHM combines technology, individualized treatment, and a novel approach to healthcare delivery [25]. It produces a comprehensive healthcare experience that goes beyond the clinic's boundaries by utilizing hardware, software, and creative approaches. Despite the particular difficulties it presents, there is no denying its potential to revolutionize healthcare. Remote health monitoring is a step toward a future in which healthcare is a continuous collaboration, informed by technology and driven by an unrelenting dedication to patient well-being, rather than occasional intervention.

16.5 Facilitating Telemedicine and Providing Ongoing Support

A service connected to health that uses electronic information technologies and telecommunications is called telemedicine. It encompasses the full range of products developed to assist patients, physicians, and other medical professionals. Among its numerous uses are remote management, online patient meetings, telehealth nursing, and virtual healthcare rehabilitation, both physically and mentally [26].

Telemedicine is making excellent healthcare services easier to obtain [27]. Additionally, clients can use videoconferencing apps to interact with the best medical professionals, and consultations may take place online. Improving care for patients and reducing the time doctors spend in rural places raises the requirements for the medical profession.

16.5.1 Telemedicine is Necessary for the Healthcare System

Because of the demand for better care and the growing expense of medical treatments, several clinics were looking at the advantages of telemedicine. The advantages of improved communication in telehealth are also applicable to conversations between doctors. To share their knowledge and provide better medical care, telehealth can assist physicians in setting up support networks. Telemedicine is the technique of delivering medical treatment online, usually through video chat. There are several ways in which this technology may help both people and medical professionals. Telemedicine can complement and improve the patient's experience overall, despite ongoing technical challenges and critics.

16.5.2 Telemedicine's Features and Capabilities When Integrated into a Healthcare Management System

The idea of telemedicine and related services is at present widely accepted and has been shown to benefit society [28]. Particularly for the healthcare industry, Figure 16.4 illustrates the range of services and amenities provided by the telemedicine concept. In the end, this methodology supports the healthcare and medical treatment field by offering care in critical and

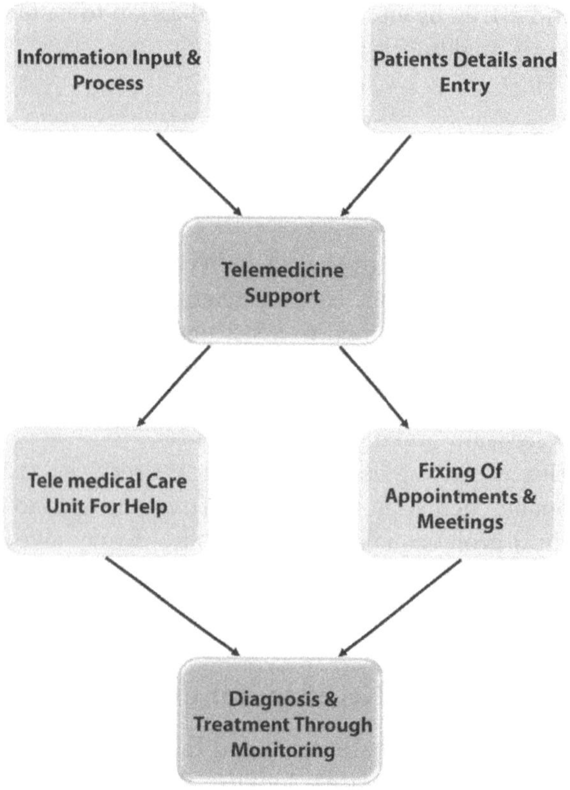

Figure 16.4 Telemedicine features and characteristics. (Source: https://www.researchgate.net/figure/Work-flow-treatment-process-through-telemedicine-support_fig2_353431866).

severe instances, remote services, prescription compliance, chronic health management, etc. Furthermore, certain telewearables give individuals personalized updates on their health and healing process. Since telemedicine is a cutting-edge information technology, many people call it innovative and disruptive. Therefore, to treat a patient who resides far away, telemedicine utilizes a range of electronic communication methods, such as teleconferences and picture-sharing, including patients' remote monitoring [29].

Features must learn a new file management technique and create improved IT support mechanisms. For instance, when primary care physicians have questions concerning the condition or course of therapy, a virtual meeting encourages them to consult with experts. The doctor sends X-rays or other photos, medical results, history, and exam reports to the specialist for assessment [30]. The specialist can respond electronically and schedule a video conference with the specialist. These online consultations can reduce wait times for expert opinions, save redundant travel, and address the issue of unnecessary in-person referrals to specialists. Telemedicine procedures are more useful when a physician can visit a patient, diagnose an illness, and record the visit.

16.5.3 Providing Ongoing Support

Telemedicine equipment has more immersive communication applications because of virtual reality (VR) technology [31]. The VR technology allowed doctors and complete surgical teams to observe a 3D display throughout operations. Physicians and especially surgeons might use video conferences to perform surgery on patients who are hundreds of kilometers away. This facilitates virtual communication and collaboration between medical professionals on various continents regarding difficult and urgent cases. The healthcare infrastructure may use VR to reproduce patient data and online conferencing to facilitate doctor-patient participation.

16.6 Evaluating Effectiveness and Continuing Support

Real-world applications highlight the evaluation of telemedicine and RHM, demonstrating how technology goes beyond theory to become a vital tool in patient care [32]. Imagine being a resident of a remote community with limited accessibility to quality healthcare. Local clinics can presently communicate with specialty hospitals located kilometers away through telehealth. A patient with a rare neurological condition would obtain professional care without having to travel because of telehealth consultations, a practice that has been duplicated in numerous remote areas across the globe.

The use of RHM in managing chronic diseases is another significant reason. The quality of life for those with diseases like diabetes or congestive heart failure has significantly improved. Healthcare professionals receive continuous data from monitoring equipment customized to their needs, allowing prompt interventions and treatment plan modifications [33]. Remote health monitoring's usefulness is demonstrated by the success histories of patients who were able to better manage their diseases with remote guidance. The potential of telehealth is also apparent in the treatment of mental health issues. Due to virtual therapy sessions, psychologists can currently reach patients who might not otherwise be able or wish to undergo treatment [34].

16.7 Result

Table 16.1 outlines key machine learning models applied in telemedicine and remote health monitoring, focusing on Long-short-term memory (LSTM) [37], Convolutional Neural Network-Long-Short Term Memory (CNN-LSTM) [35], Decision Trees (DT) [36], Bidirectional Long Short-Term Memory (BiLSTM) [38], and Advanced-spatial-vector-based Random Forest (ASV-RF) [39]. These models are employed for tasks such as disease prediction, trend analysis, and chronic care management. The benefits are enhanced decision-making and predictive capabilities. However, each model has distinct limitations. For instance, some face challenges with data privacy, computational requirements, and infrastructure costs, while others

Table 16.1 Comparison of machine learning used in telemedicine and RHM.

ML algorithm	Applications in medical sciences	Significant	Drawbacks	Result
Combine CNN-LSTM [35]	The RHM integrates the Internet-of-Things devices for continuous health assessment, trend analysis, and early disease detection.	It achieves high accuracy in improving trend identification and anomaly detection in health data.	Data obtained from the model is of low quality, compatibility issues with the user's device, high computational power, and restricted applicability of results for other patients might be an issue.	By combining CNN and LSTM, the accuracy reached 97.23%, which will improve health monitoring, trend analysis, and yearly disease detection.
DT [36]	Telemedicine, emergency, Internet of Things, smart chronic care, and ML.	Advantages include better decision-making, improved triage, and better support for patients with chronic illnesses.	Reliability of sensors, algorithm constraints, privacy issues, and the expenses on infrastructure.	The DT model was achieved, indicating higher accuracy and robust predictive capability.

(*Continued*)

Table 16.1 Comparison of machine learning used in telemedicine and RHM. (*Continued*)

ML algorithm	Applications in medical sciences	Significant	Drawbacks	Result
LSTM [37]	Telemedicine remote monitoring and predictive analytics: how to improve healthcare.	It increases the rates of efficiency and precision in disease forecasting.	There are significant issues in telemedicine such as data privacy, data security, and data interpretation.	An LSTM-based system attains an overall accuracy of 98.51% on efficiently identifying multiple diseases.
BiLSTM [38]	Telemedicine optimization, intelligent routing, multiple language support, and custom consultation pathways.	Enhances efficiency, addresses the issue of missing data, allows for parallel/ sequential consultation and degree of flexibility.	Data quality and generalization, overfitting, time complexity, and language barrier problems.	An LSTM-based system attains an overall accuracy of 65.2%, precision of 42.1%, f1-score of 35.8%, and recall of 35.6% on efficiently identifying multiple diseases.
ASV-RF [39]	Use of smart tracking technologies in improving the management of diabetic patients.	Solutions such as better diagnostics, workflow optimization, decreased costs, and better health for patients.	Some of the general challenges include data security concerns, infrastructure reliance, and high implementation costs.	ASV-RF achieved 99.8% accuracy, 99.6% precision, 99.1% sensitivity, 98.1% specificity, recall 99.9%, and f1-score 98.8%.

struggle with overfitting or handling complex, high-dimensional data. This table provides an overview of the strengths and challenges associated with each method in healthcare applications. Figure 16.5 represents the comparison of the ML technique.

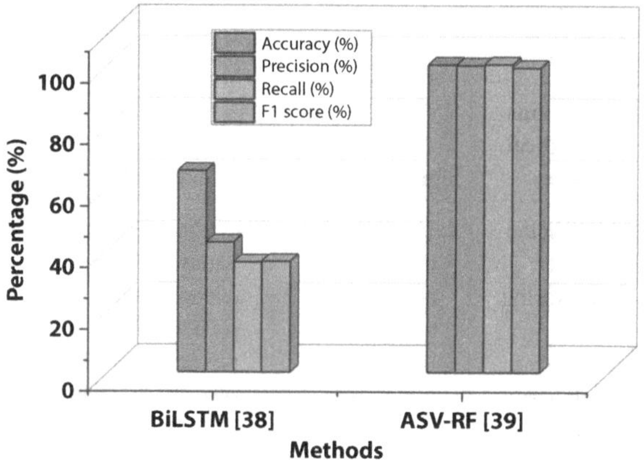

Figure 16.5 Outcomes of ML techniques.

16.8 Conclusion

Telemedicine and remote health monitoring are effective interventions, especially in identifying and reducing disparities in healthcare for underserved populations and improving healthcare delivery and outcomes. However, internet-based innovations such as social media and e-commerce encounter some barriers, including the technological barrier, the cultural barrier, the physical infrastructure barrier, and the data privacy barrier, which restrict their usage in organizations. Integrating electronic records, including EMRs, EHRs, PHRs, and overall strong data interchange standards, has laid a good track for complex healthcare data management. The above advancements enhance the coordination of stakeholders in care provision, enabling healthcare givers to provide individual and timely care. However, there are indeed issues like security, accessibility, and the integration of technology with interpersonal communication. Machine learning models such as CNN-LSTM and BiLSTM are used in telemedicine and RHM applications for predictive analysis and decision-making purposes. Despite these, there are challenges such as costs of computation and data complications. Other challenges include a lack of computer literacy, cultural barriers, and inadequate and inappropriate information technology infrastructure. Future directions include increasing people's technological competence, improving infrastructure, and adopting new technologies such as artificial intelligence and 5G, with a focus on individual patient care, making healthcare equal for everyone, as well as developing and integrating community-based health intervention strategies.

References

1. Kalasin, S. and Surareungchai, W., Challenges of emerging wearable sensors for remote monitoring toward telemedicine healthcare. *Anal. Chem.*, 95, 3, 1773–1784, 2023, https://doi.org/10.1021/acs.analchem.2c02642.
2. Yaqoob, I., *et al.*, Blockchain for healthcare data management: opportunities, challenges, and future recommendations. *Neural Comput. Appl.*, 34, 14, 11475–11490, 2022, https://doi.org/10.1007/s00521-020-05519-w.
3. Lyles, C.R., Wachter, R.M., Sarkar, U., Focusing on digital health equity. *Jama*, 326, 18, 1795–1796, 2021, https://doi.org/10.1001/jama.2021.18459.
4. Malviya, R. and Goyal, P., *Remote patient monitoring: a computational perspective in Healthcare*, CRC Press, Boca Raton, FL, 2023, https://doi.org/10.1201/9781032627991.
5. Alqahtany, A.S., *et al.*, Advancements in Telemedicine: Transforming Healthcare Delivery and Enhancing Access for Providers and Patients Alike. *Int. J. Health Sci.*, 6, S10, 1771–1785, 2022, https://dx.doi.org/10.53730/ijhs.v6nS10.15103.
6. Hardy, R., *et al.*, Social determinants of health needs and pediatric health care use. *J. Pediatr.*, 238, 275–2815, 2021, https://doi.org/10.1016/j.jpeds.2021.07.056.
7. Gulati, R., Digital Health and Technological Interventions. *Eng OA*, 2, 2, 01–05, 2024, http://dx.doi.org/10.21742/ijaner.2023.8.2.04.
8. Annis, T., *et al.*, Rapid implementation of a COVID-19 remote patient monitoring program. *J. Am. Med. Inf. Assoc.*, 27, 8, 1326–1330, 2020, https://doi.org/10.1093/jamia/ocaa097.
9. Rodler, S., *et al.*, The impact of telemedicine in reducing the carbon footprint in health care: a systematic review and cumulative analysis of 68 million clinical consultations. *Eur. Urol. Focus*, 9, 6, 873–887, 2023, https://doi.org/10.1016/j.euf.2023.11.013.
10. Grant, P., The Virtual Clinic, in: *The Virtual Hospital*, pp. 39–53, Springer Nature Switzerland, Cham, 2024, https://doi.org/10.1007/978-3-031-69944-3_4.
11. Spanakis, P., *et al.*, Use of the internet and digital devices among people with severe mental ill health during the COVID-19 pandemic restrictions. *Front. Psychiatry*, 12, 7327355, 2021, https://doi.org/10.3389/fpsyt.2021.732735.
12. Alanazi, H. and Daim, T., Health technology diffusion: Case of remote patient monitoring (RPM) for the care of senior population. *Technol. Soc.*, 66, 1016625, 2021, https://doi.org/10.1016/j.techsoc.2021.101662.
13. Essien, U.R., Dusetzina, S.B., Gellad, W.F., A policy prescription for reducing health disparities—achieving pharmacoequity. *Jama*, 326, 18, 1793–1794, 2021, https://doi:10.1001/jama.2021.17764.
14. Ingole, B.S., Ramineni, V., Krishnappa, M.S., Jayaram, V., AI-driven innovation in medicaid: enhancing access, cost efficiency, and population health management. *arXiv preprint arXiv:2410.21284*, 2024, https://doi.org/10.48550/arXiv.2410.21284.

15. Stabler, H.S. and Begun, J.W., Do nonprofit hospitals evaluate their community benefit activities? *J. Public Health Manage. Pract.*, 28, 1, E219–E225, 2022, https://doi:10.1097/PHH.0000000000001270.
16. Ebi, K.L., *et al.*, Extreme weather and climate change: population health and health system implications. *Annu. Rev. Public Health*, 42, 1, 293–315, 2021, https://doi.org/10.1146/annurev-publhealth-012420-105026.
17. Brooks, S.C., *et al.*, Optimizing outcomes after out-of-hospital cardiac arrest with innovative approaches to public-access defibrillation: a scientific statement from the International Liaison Committee on Resuscitation. *Circulation*, 145, 13, e776–e801, 2022, https:///doi/full/10.1161/CIR.0000000000001013.
18. Phuong, T., Nhung, Hoang, P.V., Dang, T.M., Huyen, T.N.T., Thi, T.N., Improving hospital's quality of service in Vietnam: the patient satisfaction evaluation in multiple health facilities. *Hosp. Top.*, 101, 2, 73–83, 2023, https://doi.org/10.1080/00185868.2021.1969871.
19. Wongtangman, K., *et al.*, The effect of a bundle intervention for ambulatory otorhinolaryngology procedures on same-day case cancellation rate and associated costs. *Anaesthesia*, 79, 6, 593–602, 2024, https://doi.org/10.1111/anae.16247.
20. Zhang, X. and Saltman, R., Impact of electronic health record interoperability on telehealth service outcomes. *JMIR Med. Inf.*, 10, 1, e31837, 2022, https://doi.org/10.2196/31837.
21. Kamarudin, D., Safie, N., Sallehudin, H., Electronic Personal Health Record Assessment Methodology: A Review. *Int. J. Adv. Comput. Sci. Appl.*, 13, 7, 375–383, 2022, https://DOI:10.14569/IJACSA.2022.0130747.
22. Chen, Z., *et al.*, A blockchain-based preserving and sharing system for medical data privacy. *Future Gener. Comput. Syst.*, 124, 338–3505, 2021, https://doi.org/10.1016/j.future.2021.05.023.
23. Al-Jaroodi, J., Mohamed, N., Abukhousa, E., Health 4.0: on the way to realizing the healthcare of the future. *IEEE Access*, 8, 211189–2112105, 2020, https://doi.org/10.1109/ACCESS.2020.3038858.
24. Aashima, M.N. and Sharma, R., A review of patient satisfaction and experience with telemedicine: a virtual solution during and beyond COVID-19 pandemic. *Telemed. e-Health*, 27, 12, 1325–1331, 2021, https://doi.org/10.1089/tmj.2020.0570.
25. LeBaron, V., Challenges and opportunities in designing and deploying remote health monitoring technology for older adults with cancer. *Innov. Aging*, 6, 6, igac057, 2022, https://doi.org/10.1093/geroni/igac057.
26. Haleem, A., *et al.*, Telemedicine for healthcare: Capabilities, features, barriers, and applications. *Sens. Int.*, 2, 1001175, 2021, https://doi.org/10.1016/j.sintl.2021.100117.
27. Gao, J., *et al.*, Telemedicine is becoming an increasingly popular way to resolve the unequal distribution of healthcare resources: evidence from China. *Front. Public Health*, 10, 9163035, 2022, https://doi.org/10.3389/fpubh.2022.916303.

28. Omboni, S., *et al.*, The worldwide impact of telemedicine during COVID-19: current evidence and recommendations for the future. *Connected Health*, 1, 75, 2022, https://doi.org/10.20517/ch.2021.03.
29. Parikh, R.B., *et al.*, Clinician perspectives on machine learning prognostic algorithms in the routine care of patients with cancer: a qualitative study. *Support. Care Cancer*, 30, 5, 4363–4372, 2022, https://doi.org/10.1007/s00520-021-06774-w.
30. Bull, C., *et al.*, 'I knew I'd be taken care of': Exploring patient experiences in the Emergency Department. *J. Adv. Nurs.*, 78, 10, 3330–3344, 2022.
31. Almousa, O., *et al.*, Virtual reality technology and remote digital application for tele-simulation and global medical education: an innovative hybrid system for clinical training. *Simul. Gaming*, 52, 5, 614–634, 2021, https://doi.org/10.1177/10468781211008258.
32. Yadav, L. and Ambhaikar, A., IOHT based Tele-Healthcare Support System for Feasibility and performance analysis. *J. Electr. Syst.*, 20, 3s, 844–850, 2024, https://doi.org/10.52783/jes.1382.
33. Cancela, J., *et al.*, Digital health in the era of personalized healthcare: opportunities and challenges for bringing study and patient care to a new level. *Digit. Health*, 7–31, 2021, https://doi.org/10.1016/B978-0-12-820077-3.00002-X.
34. Buckman, J.E.J., *et al.*, The barriers, benefits and training needs of clinicians delivering psychological therapy via video. *Behav. Cognit. Psychother.*, 49, 6, 696–720, 2021, https://doi.org/10.1017/S1352465821000187.
35. Mathivanan, S.K., *et al.*, A comprehensive health assessment approach using ensemble deep learning model for remote patient monitoring with IoT. *Sci. Rep.*, 14, 1, 15661, 2024, https://doi.org/10.1038/s41598-024-66427-w.
36. Kadum, S.Y., *et al.*, Machine learning-based telemedicine framework to prioritize remote patients with multi-chronic diseases for emergency healthcare services. *Netw. Model. Anal. Health Inf. Bioinf.*, 12, 1, 11, 2023, https://doi.org/10.1007/s13721-022-00407-w.
37. Unnithan, D.R. and Jeba, J.R., A novel framework for multiple disease prediction in telemedicine systems using deep learning. *Automatika*, 65, 3, 763–777, 2024, https://doi.org/10.1080/00051144.2024.2301889.
38. Alomari, A., Faris, H., Castillo, P.A., Specialty detection in the context of telemedicine in a highly imbalanced multi-class distribution. *PLoS One*, 18, 11, e0290581, 2023, https://doi.org/10.1371/journal.pone.0290581.
39. Menon, S.P., *et al.*, An intelligent diabetic patient tracking system based on machine learning for E-health applications. *Sensors*, 23, 6, 3004, 2023, https://doi.org/10.3390/s23063004.

17

Personalized Medicine and Computational Approaches

Dheeraj Kumar Singh[1], Sampath A. K.[2], Balasankar Karavadi[3]*, Malathi H.[4], Sarita Mahapatra[5] and Pooja Shukla[6]

[1]*Department of Information Technology, Parul University, Vadodara, Gujarat, India*

[2]*Department of Computer Science and Engineering, Presidency University, Bangalore, Karnataka, India*

[3]*Department of Bioinformatics, Sathyabama Institute of Science and Technology, Chennai, Tamil Nadu, India*

[4]*Department of Biotechnology and Genetics, JAIN (Deemed-to-be University), Bangalore, Karnataka, India*

[5]*Department of Computer Application, Siksha 'O' Anusandhan (Deemed to be University), Bhubaneswar, Odisha, India*

[6]*Maharishi School of Engineering & Technology, Maharishi University of Information Technology, Uttar Pradesh, India*

Abstract

Personalized medicine (PM) is a medical model that uses genetic, molecular, and lifestyle patterns of patients for prescribing relevant therapies or treatment strategies. The supplementation of diagnostics and treatments with computational tools in omics technologies helps to accurately diagnose diseases and determine combinations of treatments. In this frame, PM is investigated in this work by using a focused approach based on the analysis of the biomedical Internet of Medical Things (IoMT), the computational and bioinformatics, multi-omics framework, and the diagnostic and treatment PM strategies. The IoMT devices improve data gathering for individual patient's information to pave the way for individualized care.

**Corresponding author*: balasankar.bioinfo@sathyabama.ac.in; ORCID: 0000-0001-6520-0327
Dheeraj Kumar Singh: ORCID: 0000-0001-5071-3306
Malathi H.: ORCID: 0000-0001-6198-8428
Sarita Mahapatra: ORCID: 0009-0004-6374-8005
Pooja Shukla: ORCID: 0009-0005-0869-4793

Satya Prakash Yadav, Abhay Bansal and Victor Hugo C. de Albuquerque (eds.) Computational Intelligence in Biomedical Internet of Medical Things, (285–304) © 2026 Scrivener Publishing LLC

In computational methodologies, the presented machine learning (ML) and deep learning (DL) algorithms show a significant enhancement in accuracy for patient prognosis, diagnosing diseases, and treatment regimens. The utilization of these methods demonstrates effectiveness, especially in PM applications; while in more complicated high dimensional datasets, DL has displayed improvements over prior work. Molecular diagnosis and treatments, as well as diagnosis at the genomic and proteomic level, are made possible by bioinformatics and multi-omics analysis. This paper focuses on the diseases for which PM can be effective, including cancers, cardiovascular diseases, and neurological diseases, in which targeted interventions are most effective. Clinical decision support systems (CDSS) assist the practitioners to make correct decision-making based on the patient data provided. A comparison of computational approaches in PM studies shows accurate results to support the use of their ML and DL techniques.

Keywords: Personalized medicine (PM), computational approaches, machine learning (ML), artificial intelligence (AI), deep learning (DL)

17.1 Introduction

Personalized medicine (PM), also known as precision medicine, is a model shift within healthcare by individualizing medical treatment according to each patient's molecular variation. This aligns itself with people's variability over a lifetime along hereditary lines, diet and environment, vulnerability to diseases, people's progression, and response to treatment. Most traditional treatments tend to be standardized, and these methods do not benefit most patients. Personalized medicine also wants to enhance healthcare by considering individual characteristics. Customized medicine is due to the advancement of artificial intelligence (AI) in terms of machine learning (ML) and deep learning (DL) [1]. Machine learning, a sub-discipline of AI, plays a significant role in enhancing PM by its capability to analyze and make meaning out of disparate and intricate datasets. In addition to patient data, ML can identify possible trends and patterns related to patients' genotypes, clinical history, life experience, and other factors not recognizable by traditional analysis. In this branch of treatment, such algorithms provide support in grouping patients according to the potential of a specific disease to occur, estimating individual reactions to certain treatments, and tailoring treatments to achieve the best result and least harm. Deep learning is a kind of AI that shows a remarkable power to conclude meaningful trends out of large datasets. In customized medicine, DL techniques can handle massive data, including genomics data, medical images, as well as medical records, in search of abnormal characteristics that are likely to cause unique outcomes [2]. Figure 17.1 shows the structure of PM.

Genomic profiling, pharmacogenomics, and other omics approaches are required in PM, along with computational tools such as bioinformatics, ML, and systems biology to analyze large-scale biological data. These approaches allow healthcare providers to look for complex patterns in patients' genetic, molecular, and clinical data, resulting in an improved diagnosis of diseases and prognosis of patients, as well as identifying the appropriate therapy treatment [3]. For example, using ML, one can predict biomarkers that are linked genetically to particular diseases or individual clinical responses to treatment, whereas systems biology can offer a clue to the interactions between various biological components. Namely, the combination of personalization techniques and computational tools can be leveraged to substantially innovate existing areas of medicine including oncology and cardiology along with the field of pharmacogenomics. For example, by using computational models, clinicians can predict the possible reaction of a cancer patient undergoing therapy based on his/her new genomic pattern, which enhances the therapeutic result while reducing side effects [4]. The deployment of such systems poses some challenges, such as data security for dedicated computational facilities. As computational methods continue to progress, it is clear that PM, a key paradigm

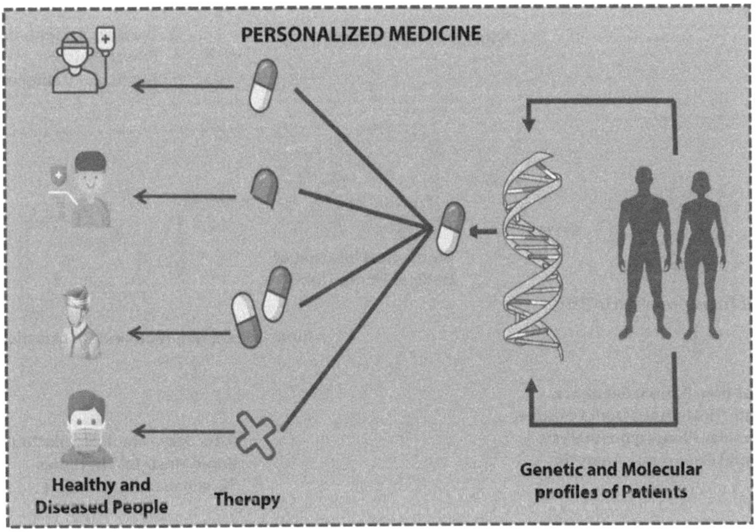

Figure 17.1 Personalized medicine structure. (Source: Own elaboration).

for the delivery of healthcare in the future, has a strong chance of becoming more patient-centered, effective, and precisely focused [5]. To improve the accuracy of PM by expanding the diagnosis of important diseases and improving treatment outcomes, this work focuses on reviewing the potential of sophisticated computational approaches, bioinformatics, and the Internet of Medical Things (IoMT). Additionally, it aims to discuss the reduction in accuracy outcomes with respect to the various methods for computation to analyze the comparative impact on PM.

17.2 Biomedical Internet of Medical Things

Historically, PM programs have failed to incorporate patients' experiences and therapeutic results in real-time along with everyday circumstances. The emergence of remote patient monitoring like smart sensors, wireless communication, AI, and IoMTs is altering the PM study and application environment. Digital change is poised to intensify PM and system science on numerous fronts, including deep real-time characterization with

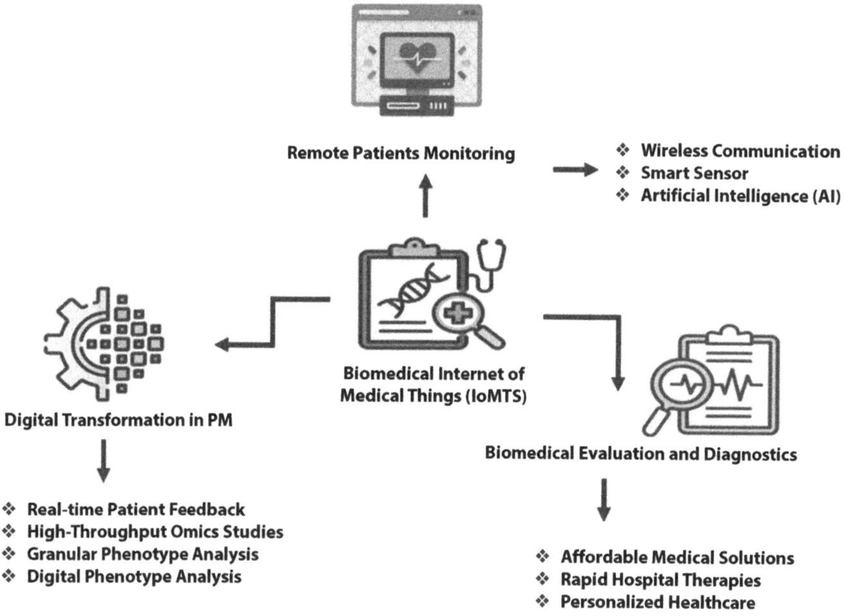

Figure 17.2 Biomedical IoMTs in PM. (Source: Own elaboration).

patient feedback, high-throughput collaboration investigations into omics and extremely granular phenotype variation, and digital clinical experiments, among others. It includes a conceptualized architecture for offering retrieval methods to extract details from patient files *via* sensors for biomedical evaluation and diagnostics toward a variety of conditions to enable to deliver affordable medical solutions, rapid hospital therapies, and PM, as shown in Figure 17.2 [6].

17.3 Computational Approaches in Personalized Medicine

17.3.1 Machine Learning in Personalized Medicine

Machine learning in PM leverages processes to analyze complex datasets and provide individualized healthcare solutions. Methods like support vector machines (SVMs), gradient boosting machines (GBM), decision trees (DTs), k-nearest neighbors (K-NN), and random forests (RFs) are used to predict patient outcomes, identify biomarkers, and tailor treatments. These models help in diagnosing diseases, assessing risks, and determining the most effective therapies based on a patient's unique genetic and clinical data. With advancements in AI, ML continues to revolutionize personalized approaches to medicine, making treatments more precise and effective [7]. Table 17.1 provides the ML approaches in PM.

17.3.2 Deep Learning in Personalized Medicine

Deep learning in PM utilizes advanced neural networks to analyze complex and large-scale data, such as genomic sequences, medical imaging, and patient records. Techniques like convolutional neural networks (CNNs), recurrent neural networks (RNNs), autoencoders (AE), generative adversarial networks (GANs), and deep reinforcement learning (DRL) are employed for image analysis, while RNNs handle sequential data to predict disease progression. Autoencoders and GANs support data generation and feature extraction, enhancing model performance. Deep reinforcement learning is also being integrated to optimize treatment plans, offering more dynamic and individualized care based on patient-specific data. Deep learning's capacity to manage complex information transforms PM [13]. Table 17.2 provides the DL approaches in PM.

Table 17.1 Machine learning approaches for PM.

Study	Objective	Methods	Significance	Limitation	Findings
[8]	To develop AI models to predict patient readmissions and tailor treatments.	RF, GBM, SVM	High accuracy, effective prediction in healthcare data	Limited to specific datasets; could not generalize	Random forest achieved 85.4% accuracy; GBM, 83.7%; SVM, 81.2%
[9]	Improve brain tumor classification accuracy using fused images from MRI and SPECT.	Contrast limited adaptive histogram equalization, discrete cosine transform-based fusion, SVM, KNN, Decision Tree	Enhanced classifier performance using fused images	Dependent on high-quality fused images; could be resource-intensive	SVM achieved accuracy at 96.8%, precision at 95%, recall at 94%, specificity at 93%, F1-score at 91%
[10]	Classify triple negative vs. non-triple negative breast cancer using gene expression data.	SVM, KNN, Naïve Bayes, DTs	Useful for precision medicine in aggressive cancer types	Moderate accuracy; limited by available gene expression data	SVM-RFE accuracy at 73%
[11]	Develop advanced ML model Stacked multi-Kernel SVM RF to improve diabetes detection accuracy.	Stacked multi-Kernel SVM RF	Improved diagnostic precision, leverages complementary model strengths	Moderate accuracy; could require more diverse data for improvement	Accuracy at 73.37%, recall at 71.62%, precision at 70.13%, F1-score at 71.34%
[12]	Identify chemotherapeutic sensitivity/resistance for MM patients using proteomic data.	Linear regression, RFs, SVM, data-balancing techniques	Potential for personalized treatment, data-balancing improves analysis	Small cohort size; limited generalizability	Accuracy at 81%

Table 17.2 Deep learning approaches for PM.

Study	Objective	Methods	Significance	Limitation	Results (numerical achievements)
[14]	Predict phenotypes of genomic samples based on microbial taxonomic abundance profile.	CNN	High accuracy, feasible for classification	Requires large datasets, could be computationally intensive	Accuracy: 99.47% (based on 1967 samples, three phenotypes)
[15]	Predict medication dosage for Parkinson's Disease patients.	RNN, long short-term memory, gated recurrent unit	Utilizes patient history for informed decision-making and accurate predictions	Complex model requires long-term patient data	Long short-term memory: mean squared error (levodopa: 0.009, dopamine agonists: 0.003), R-squared (levodopa: 0.514, dopamine agonists: 0.711)
[16]	Develop an AE-based system for biometric recognition using electrocardiogram (ECG) data.	AE	Efficient, personalized, low memory overhead, fast training	Relies on quality ECG data; could be less accurate with noisy data	Ninety percent identification accuracy with 500 heartbeat samples in five minutes
[17]	Apply deep reinforcement learning (DRL) to medical image segmentation and classification.	DRL	High accuracy in disease detection, effective in real-world applications	Require significant computational resources and training data	Deep deterministic policy gradient achieved 97% accuracy in Alzheimer's disease detection
[18]	Improve automatic sleep scoring using personalized data augmentation.	GAN	High accuracy, reduces manual effort, personalized approach	Needs specialized data augmentation for each individual	Average Accuracy: 95.74%, standard deviation: 3.78%, 8.08% improvement over general classifier

17.4 Bioinformatics and Multi-Omics in Personalized Medicine

Bioinformatics serves an important part in PM by enabling the analysis of complex biological data, such as genomic sequences, protein structures, and metabolic pathways. It combines massive volumes of information from several resources, like genomes, transcriptomics, proteome, and clinical data, to identify biomarkers, predict disease risks, and personalize treatments. Data integration ensures that these different data types work together seamlessly, creating comprehensive patient profiles. Advanced computational tools and algorithms are used to process and interpret this data, allowing for a better understanding of disease mechanisms and more accurate, individualized healthcare solutions. The combination of multi-omics information is critical in creating specific treatments and enhancing results for patients [19].

Many medications and vaccinations tend not to provide an optimal response to the overall population. Personalized medicine provides an extensive approach to personalized medical treatment. This is essential for enhancing early illness detection and therapy on an individual basis. Each person's pre- or post-disease medical, genetic, and ecological data is not distinct. Genome-wide association research assisted in identifying genes associated with severe adverse medication responses. In the last decade, biochemical research has achieved major improvements in personalized healthcare. Single nucleotide polymorphisms (SNPs) have emerged as the principal driver of human variation in genes, and SNPs serve as an invaluable tool for generating complex genomic features. A large number of DNA variants have been identified that are associated with diseases and characteristics. By combining this hereditary association with phenotypic and pharmaceutical reactions, tailored medicine can tailor therapy to each patient's unique genetics. Even if the whole genome sequence is currently unemployed in medical environments, there are several instances of PM in usage nowadays. Figure 17.3 depicts the various stages of PM construction, accordingly [20].

Personalized medicine is necessary to profit by combining genomic data with standard physiological testing using various high-volume approaches. Over the preceding decade, improvements in device affectability, rapidity, precision, and capacity have been accompanied by the advancement of innovations, such as varied response observation [21]. Such incidents and operations presently enable both top-to-bottom transparency, paving the way towards a clinical analytical area. In addition, the establishment

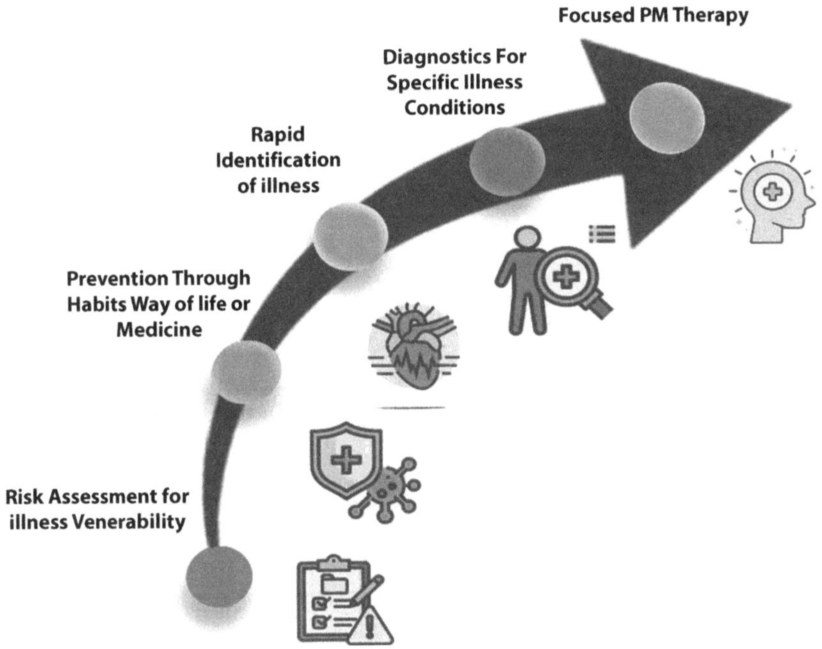

Figure 17.3 Stages of PM structure. (Source: https://sci-hub.se/https://doi.org/10.1007/978-981-33-6191-1_1).

of extensive data banks and the advancement of incredible *in silico* procedures are enabling feasible data mining. This has enabled interactome analyses, allowing for identifiable evidence of important flagging routes leading to possible novel therapeutic goals. Regardless of considering this, it was estimated that less than 20% of protein interaction in humans, excluding changing, tissue- or infection-specific connections, can be identified [22].

Medical oncology represents a significant utilization of PM because the actual processes of carcinogenesis and the prognosis frequently remain unknown. Multi-omics techniques are frequently used for methodically investigating the genesis of cancer at various biological stages, with an emphasis on multi-parameter systematical modeling. In multi-omic studies, SNPs, identified through genome-wide association studies, are used to explore genetic variations that influence complex traits and diseases by integrating genomic data with other omic layers (e.g., transcriptomics, proteomics). This approach helps uncover the genetic basis of disease susceptibility and response to treatments. Cancer, for instance, is a complicated, whole-body infection characterized by various irregularities in the amounts of DNA, RNA, and other components such as proteins. The frequently utilized data formats for multi-omics modeling are provided in Figure 17.4 [23].

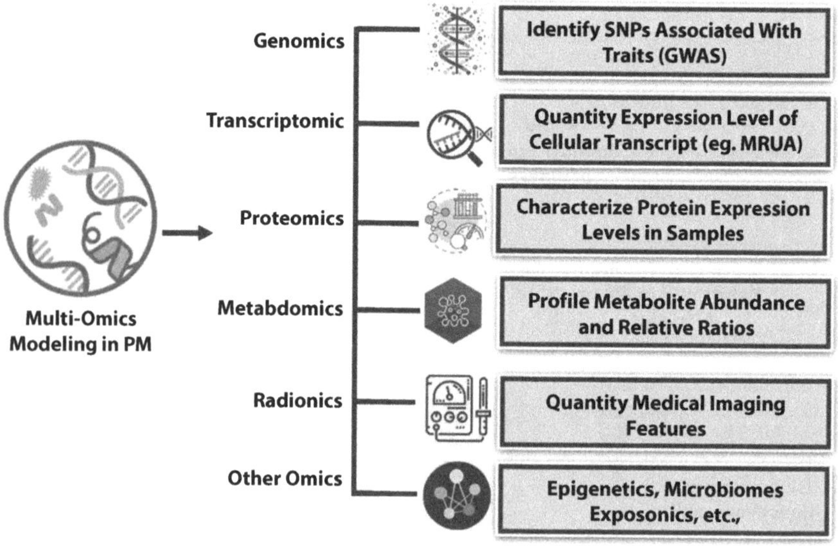

Figure 17.4 Multi-omics modeling. (Source: Own elaboration).

17.5 Diagnosis and Treatment in Personalized Medicine

Personalized diagnosis is based on individual data concerning diagnostic procedures to enhance the efficiency and timeliness of a diagnosis. Targeted therapy, in turn, means the development of specific therapy approaches with due account of a patient's genes, clinical conditions, and lifestyle to get the best results. Clinical decision support systems (CDSS) are useful in the process by providing support to the decision-making process of various healthcare givers through evidence retrieved from system databases and statistical models [24].

17.5.1 Personalized Diagnosis

Artificial intelligence-powered medical devices are changing how physicians examine disease diagnosis and treatment. These applications use ML algorithms and complex statistical analysis to handle and evaluate large volumes of healthcare data, such as images, genetic data, and medical records. Incorporating AI in diagnostics improves the rate and reliability of recognizing medical issues, frequently outperforming traditional methods. These AI-powered tools improve outcomes for patients through the capacity for faster and more exact diagnostics, especially in immediate disorders like cancer and heart disease. The effect of AI on diagnosis is visible in a variety of medical domains, such as images, pathologists, and preliminary detection of diseases [25]. In clinical imaging, AI systems evaluate medical images like X-rays, MRIs, and CT scanning with amazing precision, often discovering anomalies that human eyes could overlook. Artificial intelligence algorithms help pathologists examine tissue samples and accurately detect malignant cells. Furthermore, the combination of multiple datasets, such as genetic, medical, and behavioral data, is critical for successful customized treatment. However, ensuring seamless data transfer across several medical facilities and technologies is a huge technical issue. It depicts sophisticated AI applications in medical studies, including human structure, genomics, and organ-specific data, which enable tailored medicines and specific therapies [26].

17.5.2 Personalized Treatment

Personalized treatments are tailored to a person's specific genetic, molecular, and clinical description, improving effectiveness and decreasing adverse reactions. This strategy involves targeted medications, which target particular genetic abnormalities or biomarkers, to guarantee treatments have a direct influence on the patient's health. Pharmacogenomics, which examines how genetics affect drug reactions, permits precise medicine selection and dosage modifications [27]. Breast cancer is a major global health issue affecting women, with 30% of occurrences being HER2-positive and associated with decreased survival. Targeted medicines such as trastuzumab deruxtecan (T-DXd), trastuzumab, pertuzumab, and T-DM1 changed therapies for HER2-positive metastatic breast cancer (MBC). Though these medicines have enhanced MBC treatment and patient satisfaction, tolerance could arise, lowering efficacy. Personalized treatments according to cancer features provide optimism regarding improved responses and longer-term consequences [28].

17.5.3 Clinical Decision Support Systems

Clinical decision support systems are technological devices intended to aid medical professionals with making medical choices by delivering relevant expertise and patient-specific data. Such systems have grown greatly over time, with AI serving a critical role in improving system capabilities, especially for PM [29]. Artificial intelligence manages these issues by utilizing effective algorithms capable of learning from and adapting to novel data.

This allows AI-powered CDSS to make more accurate and timely suggestions to doctors. Another key benefit driven by AI-powered CDSS was its compatibility with different technologies and organizations. As technology evolves, AI-powered CDSS will probably become more essential in assisting physicians deliver individualized treatment to patients [30].

17.6 Major Disease in Personalized Medicine

The role of PM in treating common and major illnesses includes cancer, cardiovascular diseases, and neurological problems. This refers to patient-specific treatments that are effective when based on environmental, molecular, and genetic factors. There is interest in individualized care and early intervention, as well as therapies for these important diseases [31]. Figure 17.5 represents the major disease in PM.

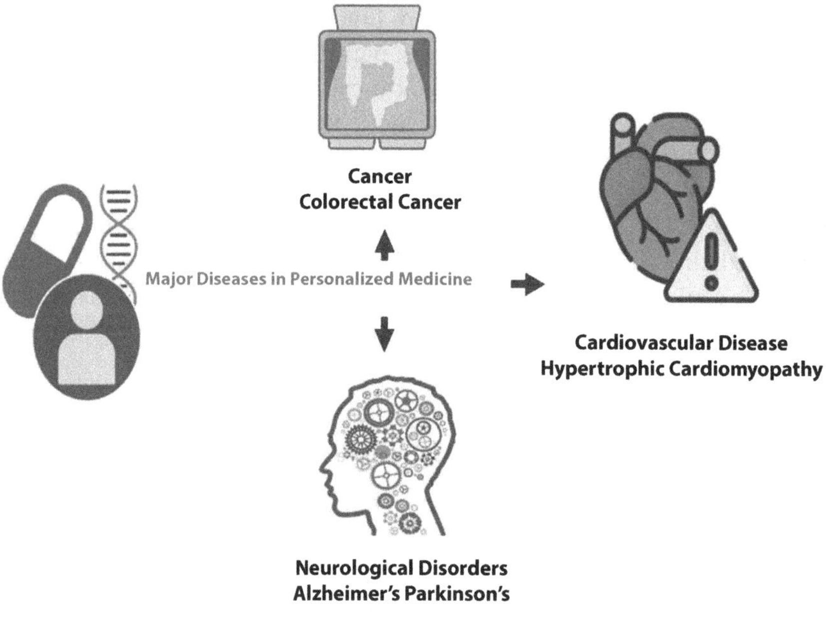

Figure 17.5 Major diseases in PM. (Source: Own elaboration).

17.6.1 Cancer

Colorectal cancer (CRC) accounts for around 10% of all cancers and is the second biggest cause of cancer-related fatalities. In about 20% of individuals, the initial clinical sign is a metastatic CRC. Furthermore, up to 50% of those with localized illness might get metastasis. Proper clinical care of these individuals remains a difficult medical problem. Numerous initiatives have been undertaken to reveal the molecular architecture of metastatic CRCs. It has led to the discovery of various druggable tumor molecule targets, to design customized therapy for all patients [32].

Artificial intelligence is quickly changing cancer studies and personalized therapeutic care. The accessibility of high-dimensional databases, combined with breakthroughs in powerful computers and new DL structures, has resulted in a proliferation of AI applications in numerous areas of oncology study. Such uses include cancer identification and classification, genetic characterization of cancers and microenvironments, drug development and recycling, and patient treatment forecasting [33].

17.6.2 Cardiovascular Diseases

Heart diseases were characterized in 1980 as cardiac muscle illnesses with an unknown origin. However, with greater awareness of genetic causes and pathology, particularly in hypertrophic cardiomyopathy (HCM), these are currently described as myocardial illnesses linked with cardiac failure. In the absence of additional unloading factors like aortic valve obstruction or high blood pressure, HCM is defined as left and/or right cardiac hypertrophy that is typically asymmetric and affects the septum between the ventricles. Hypertrophic cardiomyopathy progresses gradually and has substantially distinct clinical histories, ranging from a near-normal lifespan without signs to sudden cardiac deaths in adolescence. It is expected to affect one out of every 500 people. Around 60% of HCM patients possess a family background that indicates a dominant autosomal gene. Defects in genes that encode myocardial elements, including the sarcomere, contribute to 40–60% of HCM instances [34].

Clinical science advancements have transformed cardiac wellness and diseases using big data and digital health records. This large pool of medical and biological information has caused a change in emphasis from data gathering to optimum and usable data processing and analysis. The obstacle for big data is to harness treatments for personalized genetics and phenotypes, which are the basis of PM. Pursuing these objectives could help cardiovascular care, especially in light of declining advancements in common conditions such as heart failure, and the increasing spectrum of previously unidentified comorbidity associated with cardiovascular disorders [35].

17.6.3 Neurological Disorders

Many animal illness models have already been produced to explore the molecular mechanisms of neurological conditions and generate novel therapeutics. However, the absence of analogous human models has reduced success rates. A variety of crucial challenges remain unanswered, including the high price of generating animal models, moral issues, and the lack of likeness to illness in humans. Over 90% of medications fail in the end phase of an individual's clinical study because of inadequate initial testing and appraisal of molecules [36].

Personalized medicine techniques in neurology and mental health could offer screening remedies, implement time-sensitive detection/diagnosis, and adjust therapies to someone's specific clinical-genetic-biological traits and risk factors. Regardless of clinical manifestations, neurological and mental disorders are highly heterogeneous in terms of genetics and pathophysiology. Conventional medical models have emphasized the late-stage correlated characteristics of many disorders, with little regard for the fundamental genetics. Improvements in modeling diseases and methodological innovation paved the path for the creation of PM, a well-established concept in oncology that is gaining traction in various medical disciplines [37].

17.7 Computational Approaches and Accuracy Outcomes in Personalized Medicine Studies

In Table 17.3 and Figure 17.6, the PM studies employ various computational approaches to enhance predictive accuracy for patient-specific outcomes. Techniques like RF, GBM, and SVM demonstrate strong performance in patient re-admission prediction, with accuracies of 85.4%, 83.7%, and 81.2%, respectively [8]. Support vector machines, widely used in PM for tasks such as brain tumor classification, achieve an impressive 96.8% accuracy [9], while SVM reaches 73% in breast cancer subtype

Table 17.3 Computational approaches in PM studies and accuracy.

Personalized medicine studies	Computational approaches	Accuracy outcome (%)
[8]	RF	85.4
[8]	GBM	83.7
[8]	SVM	81.2
[9]	SVM	96.8
[10]	SVM	73
[11]	SVM	73.37
[11]	RF	73.37
[12]	RF	81
[12]	SVM	81
[12]	LR	81
[14]	CNN	99.47
[16]	AE	90
[17]	DRL	97
[18]	GAN	95.74

classification [10]. The SVM ensemble model for diabetes detection yields 73.37% accuracy, indicating potential in diagnostic precision [11]. Further, RF, SVM, and Linear Regression models attain 81% accuracy in predicting chemotherapeutic responses for multiple myeloma [12].

Advanced models such as CNN show a remarkable 99.47% accuracy in microbiome-based disease prediction [14], while AE achieves 90% in ECG-based identity recognition [16]. The DRL algorithms and GANs offer high accuracy (97% and 95.74%, respectively) in applications like Alzheimer's detection and sleep scoring [17, 18]. These computational approaches significantly advance PM studies by enabling precise, patient-centered predictions.

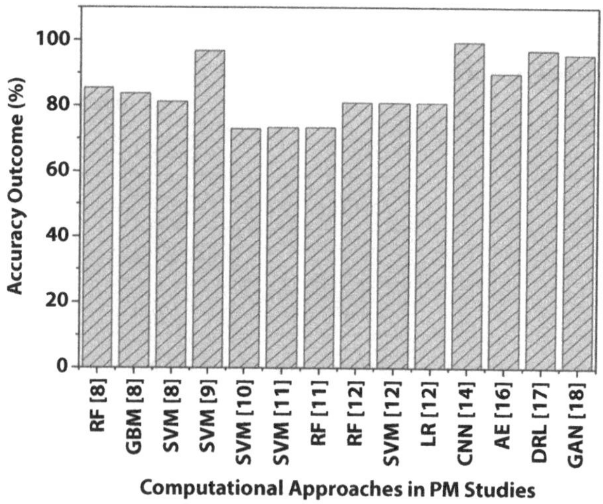

Figure 17.6 Computational approaches in PM studies and accuracy. (Source: Own elaboration).

17.8 Discussions

The use of AI, ML, and IoMT in PM is a potential model with a set of questions regarding the use of sensitive health information for all parties involved. The PM approaches with AI tend to introduce new forms of biases; for example, the models utilized under ML or DL could be trained with a set of non-heterogeneous data to provide a bias-driven prediction. This results in disparities that create variations in healthcare and affect those who are marginalized in society. Erasing such prejudices demands clear model creation and utilizing the demographic information of patients and other communities to achieve the same level of prediction accuracy. In addition, there is an accountability issue introduced by Clinical Decision Support Systems (CDSS) in PM with the use of AI. Any decisions made using the help of AI must be carefully reviewed and confirmed by healthcare practitioners to avoid overspending based on the wrong results produced by AI. Personalized medicine continues to be a relatively new area, and its regulations remain a growing concern as governments and healthcare organizations struggle to adjust to the increasingly fast-growing technological world. Innovation must be harmonized with explicit testing, validation, and compliance requirements for regulated AI and IoMT applications that address patient wellbeing globally. Therefore, future work as a multi-disciplinary team composed of technologists, physicians, policymakers, and ethicists responsible for regulating novel technologies that underlie the practice of personalized medicine must adequately balance the protection of a patient's interests on one hand and encourage further technological innovation on the other hand.

17.9 Summary and Future Directions

The use of biomedical IoMT, AI, ML, DL, and bioinformatics has revolutionized the delivery of PM, making healthcare delivery in real-time, data-based, and more personalized than ever. Improvements in methods and modeling, as well as the fusion of omics data, have created fresh opportunities to diagnose, prognose, and treat diseases at new levels of accuracy. Omics data analysis, imaging, and real-time tracking combined with complex algorithms have helped PM avoid the 'one size fits all' model, providing better customized/personalized medicine based on inhabitants' genetics and clinical characteristics. There is an expectation for future advancements in the domain of PM to focus on the improvement of data aggregation and compatibility of the information across various healthcare settings to gain complete patient information. Sustainable and objective creation of AI algorithms will be critical to increase the possibilities and non-discriminatory potential for patients of personalized medicine. This will similarly be complemented by progress in secure data-sharing frameworks and privacy-preserving AI as part of eradicating privacy challenges. Consistent funding for training more clinicians in using AI and data analysis for care management will enable PM to become a part of standard healthcare practice, hence enhancing healthcare.

References

1. Yang, S., Zhu, F., Ling, X., Liu, Q., Zhao, P., Intelligent health care: Applications of deep learning in computational medicine. *Front. Genet.*, 12, 607471, 2021, https://doi.org/10.3389/fgene.2021.607471.
2. Ingber, D.E., Human Organs-on-Chips for Disease Modelling, Drug Development and Personalized Medicine. *Nat. Rev. Genet.*, 23, 8, 467–491, 2022, https://doi.org/10.1038/s41576-022-00466-9.
3. Matthay, M.A., Arabi, Y.M., *et al.*, Phenotypes and Personalized Medicine in the Acute Respiratory Distress Syndrome. *Intensive Care Med.*, 46, 2136–21525, 2020, https://doi.org/10.1007/s00134-020-06296-9.

4. Mendhe, D., Dogra, A., *et al.*, AI-Enabled Data-Driven Approaches for Personalized Medicine and Healthcare Analytics, in: *2024 Ninth International Conference on Science Technology Engineering and Mathematics (ICONSTEM)*, IEEE, pp. 1–5, 2024, https://doi.org/10.1109/ICONSTEM60960.2024.10568722.
5. Singh, M.P., Rai, S., *et al.*, Molecular Subtypes of Colorectal Cancer: An Emerging Therapeutic Opportunity for Personalized Medicine. *Genes Dis.*, 8, 2, 133–145, 2021, https://doi.org/10.1016/j.gendis.2019.10.013.
6. Lin, B. and Wu, S., Digital Transformation in Personalized Medicine with Artificial Intelligence and the Internet of Medical Things. *OMICS: J. Integr. Biol.*, 26, 2, 77–81, 2022, https://doi.org/10.1089/omi.2021.0037.
7. Chen, X., AI in Healthcare: Revolutionizing Diagnosis and Treatment through Machine Learning. *MZ J. Artif. Intell.*, 1, 2, 1–18, 2024, https://mzjournal.com/index.php/MZJAI/article/view/259.
8. Udegbe, F.C., Ebulue, O.R., Ebulue, C.C., Ekesiobi, C.S., AI's impact on personalized medicine: Tailoring treatments for improved health outcomes. *Eng. Sci. Technol. J.*, 5, 4, 1386–1394, 2024, https://doi.org/10.51594/estj.v5i4.1040.
9. Nanmaran, R., Srimathi, S., *et al.*, Investigating the Role of Image Fusion in Brain Tumor Classification Models Based on Machine Learning Algorithm for Personalized Medicine. *Comput. Math. Methods Med.*, 2022, 71375245, 2022, https://doi.org/10.1155/2022/7137524.
10. Wu, J. and Hicks, C., Breast Cancer Type Classification Using Machine Learning. *J. Pers. Med.*, 11, 2, 61, 2021, https://doi.org/10.3390/jpm11020061.
11. Reza, Md.S., Hafsha, U., Amin, R., Yasmin, R., Ruhi, S., Improving SVM performance for type II diabetes prediction with an improved non-linear kernel: Insights from the PIMA dataset. *Comput. Methods Programs Biomed. Update*, 4, 100118, 2023, https://doi.org/10.1016/j.cmpbup.2023.100118.
12. Katsenou, A., O'Farrell, R., *et al.*, Using Proteomics Data to Identify Personalized Treatments in Multiple Myeloma: A Machine Learning Approach. *Int. J. Mol. Sci.*, 24, 21, 15570, 2023, https://doi.org/10.3390/ijms242115570.
13. Shirazi, A.Z., Fornaciari, E., Gomez, G.A., Deep Learning in Precision Medicine, in: *Artificial Intelligence in Precision Health*, pp. 61–90, Academic Press, Cambridge, MA, 2020, https://doi.org/10.1016/B978-0-12-817133-2.00003-3.
14. Reiman, D., Metwally, A., Dai, Y., Using Convolutional Neural Networks to Explore the Microbiome, in: *2017 39th Annual International Conference of the IEEE Engineering in Medicine and Biology Society (EMBC)*, IEEE, pp. 4269–4272, 2017, https://doi.org/10.1109/EMBC.2017.8037799.
15. Riasi, A., Delrobaei, M., Salari, M., A Decision Support System Based on Recurrent Neural Networks to Predict Medication Dosage for Patients with Parkinson's Disease. *Sci. Rep.*, 14, 1, 8424, 2024, https://doi.org/10.1038/s41598-024-59179-0.

16. Sun, L., Zhong, Z., Qu, Z., Xiong, N., PerAE: An Effective Personalized AutoEncoder for ECG-Based Biometric in Augmented Reality System. *IEEE J. Biomed. Health. Inf.*, 26, 6, 2435–2446, 2022, https://doi.org/10.1109/JBHI.2022.3145999.
17. Rajendran, P.S., A Comparative Study on Reinforcement Learning in Disease Prediction on Medical Data, in: *2024 International Conference on Advances in Data Engineering and Intelligent Computing Systems (ADICS)*, IEEE, pp. 1–7, 2024, https://doi.org/10.1109/ADICS58448.2024.10533525.
18. Kuo, C.E., Lu, T.H., *et al.*, Towards Precision Sleep Medicine: Self-Attention GAN as an Innovative Data Augmentation Technique for Developing Personalized Automatic Sleep Scoring Classification. *Comput. Biol. Med.*, 148, 1058285, 2022, https://doi.org/10.1016/j.compbiomed.2022.105828.
19. Field, M.A., Bioinformatic Challenges Detecting Genetic Variation in Precision Medicine Programs. *Front. Med.*, 9, 8066965, 2022, https://doi.org/10.3389/fmed.2022.806696.
20. Sunil Krishnan, G., Joshi, A., Kaushik, V., Bioinformatics in Personalized Medicine. *Adv. Bioinf.*, 303–315, 2021, https://doi.org/10.1007/978-981-33-6191-1_15.
21. Hu, C. and Jia, W., Multi-Omics Profiling: The Way Toward Precision Medicine in Metabolic Diseases. *J. Mol. Cell Biol.*, 13, 8, 576–593, 2021, https://doi.org/10.1093/jmcb/mjab051.
22. Morello, G., Salomone, S., D'Agata, V., Conforti, F.L., Cavallaro, S., From Multi-Omics Approaches to Precision Medicine in Amyotrophic Lateral Sclerosis. *Front. Neurosci.*, 14, 5777555, 2020, https://doi.org/10.3389fnins.2020.577755.
23. Reska, D., Czajkowski, M., *et al.*, Integration of Solutions and Services for Multi-Omics Data Analysis Towards Personalized Medicine. *Biocybern. Biomed. Eng.*, 41, 4, 1646–1663, 2021, https://doi.org/10.1016/j.bbe.2021.10.005.
24. Yan, J., Liu, Z., *et al.*, Diagnosis and Treatment of Breast Cancer in the Precision Medicine Era. 53–61, 2020, https://doi.org/10.1007/978-1-0716-0904-0_5.
25. Boehm, K.M., Khosravi, P., *et al.*, Harnessing Multimodal Data Integration to Advance Precision Oncology. *Nat. Rev. Cancer*, 22, 2, 114–126, 2022, https://doi.org/10.1038/s41568-021-00408-3.
26. Zeb, S., Nizamullah, F.N.U., Abbasi, N., Fahad, M., AI in healthcare: revolutionizing diagnosis and therapy. *Int. J. Multi. Sci. Arts*, 3, 3, 118–128, 2024, https://doi.org/10.47709/ijmdsa.v3i3.4546.
27. Akil, A.A.S., Yassin, E., *et al.*, Diagnosis and Treatment of Type 1 Diabetes at the Dawn of the Personalized Medicine Era. *J. Transl. Med.*, 19, 1, 137, 2021, https://doi.org/10.1186/s12967-021-02778-6.
28. Passaro, A., Al Bakir, M., *et al.*, Cancer Biomarkers: Emerging Trends and Clinical Implications for Personalized Treatment. *Cell*, 187, 7, 1617–1635, 2024, https://doi.org/10.1016/j.cell.2024.02.041.
29. Pandey, P., Chaudhary, R., *et al.*, Personalized Treatment Approach for HER2-Positive Metastatic Breast Cancer. *Med. Oncol.*, 41, 11, 252, 2024, https://doi.org/10.1007/s12032-024-02504-4.

30. Sanchez, R., AI-Powered Clinical Decision Support Systems for Precision Medicine: Developing AI-Powered Systems to Provide Clinicians with Decision Support Tailored to Individual Patient Characteristics. *J. Bioinf. Artif. Intell.*, 4, 2, 70–79, 2024, https://biotechjournal.org/index.php/jbai/article/view/84.
31. Bature, J.T., Eruaga, M.A., Itua, E.O., Integrating pharmacogenomic testing into personalized medicine practices in the USA: Implications for medication quality control and therapeutic efficacy. *GSC Biol. Pharm. Sci.*, 26, 3, 019–026, 2024. 10.30574/gscbps.2024.26.3.0081.
32. Ciardiello, F., Ciardiello, *et al.*, Clinical Management of Metastatic Colorectal Cancer in the Era of Precision Medicine. *CA: Cancer J. Clin.*, 72, 4, 372–401, 2022, https://doi.org/10.3322/caac.21728.
33. Bhinder, B., Gilvary, C., Madhukar, N.S., Elemento, O., Artificial Intelligence in Cancer Research and Precision Medicine. *Cancer Discov.*, 11, 4, 900–915, 2021, https://doi.org/10.1158/2159-8290.CD-21-0090.
34. Tada, H., Fujino, N., *et al.*, Personalized Medicine for Cardiovascular Diseases. *J. Hum. Genet.*, 66, 1, 67–74, 2021, https://doi.org/10.1038/s10038-020-0818-7.
35. Leopold, J.A., Maron, B.A., Loscalzo, J., The Application of Big Data to Cardiovascular Disease: Paths to Precision Medicine. *J. Clin. Invest.*, 130, 1, 29–38, 2020, https://doi.org/10.1172/JCI129203.
36. Pandey, S., Jirásko, M., *et al.*, iPSCs in Neurodegenerative Disorders: A Unique Platform for Clinical Research and Personalized Medicine. *J. Pers. Med.*, 12, 9, 1485, 2022, https://doi.org/10.3390/jpm12091485.
37. Hampel, H., Gao, P., *et al.*, The Foundation and Architecture of Precision Medicine in Neurology and Psychiatry. *Trends Neurosci.*, 46, 3, 176–198, 2023, https://doi.org/10.1016/j.tins.2022.12.004.

18

Internet of Medical Things and Social Health

Divyanshi Rajvanshi[1], Sumitra Menaria[2], Rajan Thangamani[3], Roselin Jenifer D.[4]*, Renuka Jyothi S.[5] and Alakananda Tripathy[6]

[1]Maharishi School of Engineering & Technology, Maharishi University of Information Technology, Uttar Pradesh, India
[2]Department of Computer Science & Engineering, Parul University, Vadodara, Gujarat, India
[3]Department of Computer Science and Engineering, Presidency University, Bangalore, Karnataka, India
[4]Department of Bioinformatics, Sathyabama Institute of Science and Technology, Chennai, Tamil Nadu, India
[5]Department of Biotechnology and Genetics, Jain (Deemed-to-be University), Bangalore, Karnataka, India
[6]Centre for Artificial Intelligence and Machine Learning, Siksha 'O' Anusandhan (Deemed to be University), Bhubaneswar, Odisha, India

Abstract
The review examines the incorporation of the Internet of Medical Things (IoMT) in the system of healthcare, emphasizing its role in enhancing patient monitoring and enhancing healthcare outcomes. The IoMT engages with associated medical devices and sensors to gather real-time health data, which is then transmitted and analyzed to provide actionable insights. A layered approach will be used to explore the architecture of IoMT systems, which work together to facilitate data collection, transmission, storage, and analysis. Key phases in handling IoMT data, such as data cleaning, normalization, and feature extraction, are also discussed, with a focus on improving the quality and consistency of data for predictive modeling.

**Corresponding author*: roselinjenifer.d.bte@sathyabama.ac.in; ORCID: 0000-0002-1792-4184
Divyanshi Rajvanshi: ORCID: 0009-0004-6465-1846
Sumitra Menaria: ORCID: 0000-0002-7155-9368
Renuka Jyothi S.: ORCID: 0000-0003-3248-337X
Alakananda Tripathy: ORCID: 0000-0002-0671-4333

Satya Prakash Yadav, Abhay Bansal and Victor Hugo C. de Albuquerque (eds.) Computational Intelligence in Biomedical Internet of Medical Things, (305–324) © 2026 Scrivener Publishing LLC

Additionally, it examines the function of artificial intelligence (AI) techniques in IoMT systems, highlighting their role in enabling early diagnosis, personalized treatment, and continuous health monitoring. Various existing research demonstrate how IoMT and AI models are applied in predicting and managing conditions such as heart disease, diabetes, and knee osteoarthritis. The results of these applications are evaluated using various performance metrics to evaluate the efficiency of IoMT-driven solutions in healthcare. The findings underscore the transformative possibility of the IoMT in transforming healthcare, enhancing disease detection, developing patient outcomes, and enabling smarter, more efficient healthcare delivery.

Keywords: IoMT, artificial intelligence (AI), healthcare monitoring, IoMT layers

18.1 Introduction

The Internet of Things (IoT) is a system of substantial items that connect more than the internet, with about 10 billion linked nodes and an estimated expansion of 22 billion by 2025. It aims to optimize data replacement and store it on a protected cloud server for shared communication [1]. Numerous frameworks have been developed to deal with real-time patient forecasts, analyses, and tracking in response to the growing need of adopting IoT in the healthcare industry. A subdomain of the IoT, the Internet of Medical Things (IoMT) gathers and analyzes data for medication development and healthcare [2]. It is a developing approach that keeps up with change, fosters technology developments, and addresses healthcare challenges. However, the effective use of IoMT data in the medical field is still difficult [3]. Smart cities, vehicle communications, cloud computing, smart campuses, smart ecosystems, smart agriculture, mobile communications, and healthcare are a few of the domains where the IoT finds application. These sensor-equipped gadgets are made for healthcare in a variety of locations, such as homes, clinics, hospitals, and communities. The IoMT technology involves tracking hospitalized patients, monitoring medication intake and effect, portable health devices, virtual care for chronic conditions, and information sharing with caregivers. It lessens the strain on health systems and saves physicians and patients time and effort. The IoMT's swift development and application allow frameworks to remotely diagnose and treat illnesses, as well as assess patients' health timely, securely, and accurately [4] The IoMT was sparked by new technological developments that are gaining global attention and becoming available for tracking, predicting, diagnosing, and avoiding the appearance of infectious diseases [5]. The IoMT is a utilization of the foundational ideas, concepts, methods, and tools of a widely accepted internet-based approach, especially for the medical and healthcare domains and industries. Linking the different medical services and the accessible medical facilities through internet-based gadgets requires a workable network of services [6]. Using wireless sensor networks (WSNs) and wireless devices, which are in charge of detecting human health factors including heart rate, body temperature, blood sugar, and respiratory activities, the IoMT facilitates healthcare contributors to continuously monitor a patient's condition. To make judgments on further or urgent remedial action, the medical center receives and stores real-time sensed data [7]. One of the most significant prerequisites for IoMT systems' success is security. Eleven security standards are present to ensure data integrity, availability, confidentiality, authenticity, and non-repudiation [8]. The IoMT, the convergence of medical devices and their subsequent submission, uses network technology to link the healthcare and pharmaceutical industries. Linking them *via* popular internet-based gadgets makes healthcare resources and services more convenient, particularly in rural and distant locations where access to basic healthcare services is still a major challenge [9]. The age of ubiquitous computing in health information systems is a result of the aging population and the quick advancement of wireless communication, sensor networks, embedded systems, and mobile computing. As a result, wearable technology and other applications for delivering new health services have grown in popularity. The idea of IoMT was born out of the IoT, which gives commonplace devices access to computers and the internet. By increasing patients' self-awareness of their health and reducing the need for medical professionals to intervene, IoMT-based platforms empower individuals. Interoperability and privacy issues are brought on by the variety of IoMT components. As a result, a ubiquitous healthcare platform must be adaptable enough to manage various ideas, including IoMT solutions in a compatible setting and creating data storage, processing, and dissemination [10]. The purpose is to examine the integration of the IoMT in healthcare systems, emphasizing its potential to enhance patient monitoring, improve disease diagnosis, and enable personalized treatment. By leveraging AI-driven analytics and addressing data processing challenges, it aims to showcase IoMT's transformative impact on healthcare delivery and outcomes.

The remaining parts of this review are divided into 7 sections: Section 18.2: IoMT architecture; Section 18.3: methodology; Section 18.4: healthcare monitoring *via* AI; Section 18.5: results; Section 18.6: discussion; finally, Section 18.7: conclusion.

18.2 The Internet-of-Medical-Things Architecture

The IoMT systems offer support for a range of medical ailments, including smartwatches for better healthcare experiences and implanted devices for illnesses like heart disorders. The internet of wearable devices (IoWDs) and implantable medical devices (IMDs) are the two subcategories of the IoMT systems. Implantable medical devices are implanted devices, like pacemakers for cardiac issues, that replace, maintain, or improve biological components. In contrast, IoWDs are wearable gadgets that people wear to track biometrics like heart rate to enhance general health. Although smartwatches are a common type of IoWD, layers are unlikely to return IMDs in vital situations because of their limits in sensor accuracy and battery life. Four layers usually make up the current IoMT systems, with IMD interacting with gateways like the Medtronic peacemaker [1]. The layers are explained in Table 18.1. The architecture of the IoMT layers was illustrated in Figure 18.1.

Table 18.1 The IoMT layer and its function.

Layers	Function
Sensor/perception layer (PL)	• Made up of a number of minute sensors that are damaged or entrenched and gather the biometric data of patients. • The second layer receives the data utilizing wireless etiquette like Bluetooth, and Wi-Fi.
Gateway layer (GL)	• The IoMT sensors limit data storage and processing, leading to unprocessed data in the second layer. Specialized devices perform preprocessing tasks and send data to the cloud *via* the internet.
Cloud layer (CL)	• It retrieves the data from the gateway for safe access, investigation, and storage. • Data processing may be part of the analysis to identify any alteration in patients' health and show them to the patients or doctors for additional action.
Visualization/action layer (AL)	• It displays data to physicians and patients may keep an eye on their health. • In addition, it comprises the actions the physician recommends based on the patient's medical condition. • It includes writing prescriptions or changing the dose of different medications.

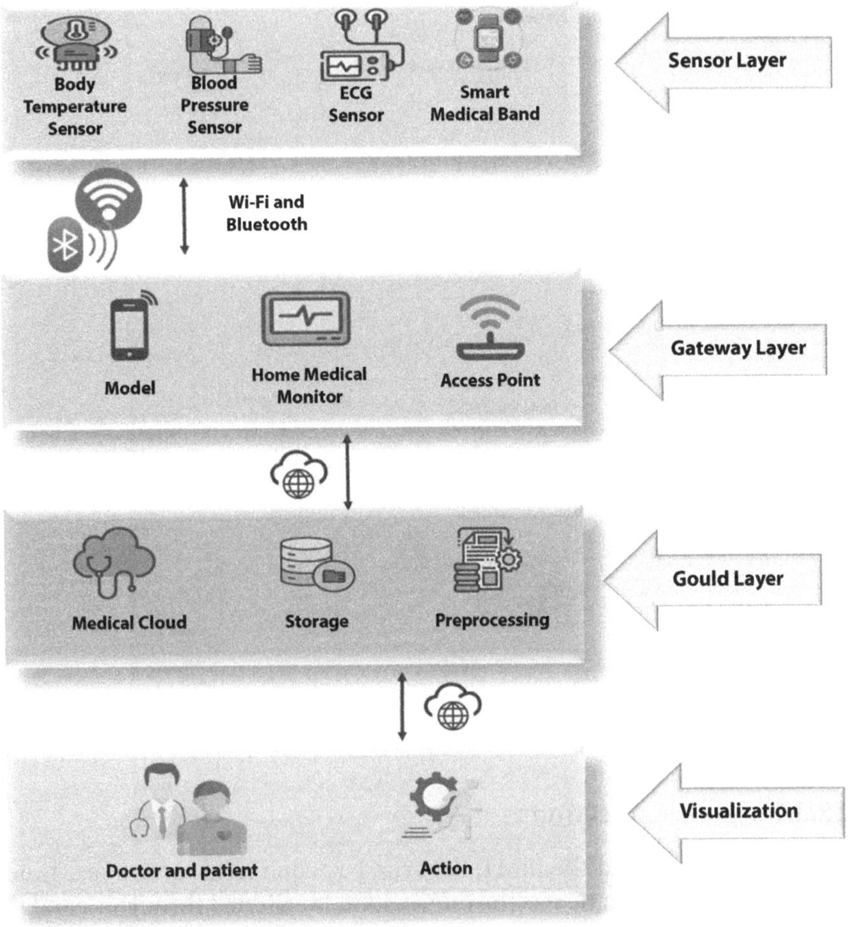

Figure 18.1 Architecture of the IoMT. (Source: https://www.researchgate.net/figure/oMT-system-architecture_fig1_347489306).

18.3 Methodology

The methodology section revolves around data collection from IoMT devices, preprocessing techniques, feature extraction, and integrating AI models with healthcare monitoring and the prediction of diseases. This section demonstrates the efficiency of the proposed system through various research and datasets used to improve patient care and predictive capabilities. Figure 18.2 illustrates the overall flow.

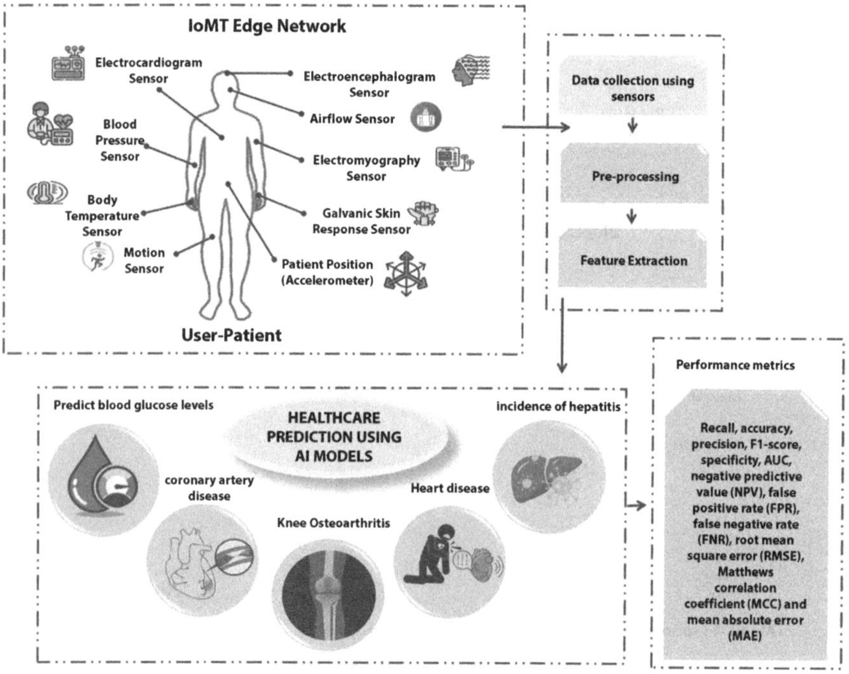

Figure 18.2 Flow of the use of the IoMT in predicting healthcare. (Source: Own elaboration).

18.3.1 Data Collection

Using IoT devices and the IoMT, data can be acquired to receive real-time health metrics from patients. The information is collected through wearable sensors, remote monitoring tools, and smart implants. These devices collect significant amounts of data on different health parameters, such as heart rate, blood pressure, glucose levels, and actual physical action. In most cases, the current open public dataset facilitates research work and analysis based on its findings. For example, the IoMT Alert dataset can be accessed from Kaggle [11] and contains artificial alerts concerning health metrics and emergencies such as heart rate (bpm), SpO2 level (%), systolic blood pressure (mmHg), body temperature (°C), diastolic blood pressure (mmHg), fall detection, predicted disease, data accuracy (%), Heart Rate Alert, SpO2 Level Alert, Blood Pressure Alert, and Temperature Alert. This will further allow researchers to examine trends, detect possible health issues, and construct predictive models. These datasets can be used to construct advanced analytics solutions for healthcare providers and researchers to enhance the care of patients, detect anomalies, and enrich predictive ability across systems of the IoMT.

18.3.2 Pre-Processing

It is one of the most significant requirements before applying the algorithms for accurate analysis and modeling of IoMT data. In the process, cleaning, normalization, transformation, range adjustment, and feature extraction have to be carried out to ensure quality and consistency.

- Data cleaning: The process of cleaning data involves the removal of noise, outliers, and irrelevant data; otherwise, analysis results may get distorted [12].
- Normalization and scaling: The purpose is to bring data within a defined scale to compare cross-unit or cross-magnitude. For example, z-score normalization [13] converts data into the numeral of standard deviations where each data point is from the average; it scales the information to have an average of 0 with a standard deviation of 1. It helps to deal with multiple measurement ranges found in IoMT datasets.

Pre-processing is intended to ensure that data provided by the IoMT is optimized for additional processing and, in turn, the reliability of approaching drawn from the data, as well as the effectiveness of the predictive models.

18.3.3 Feature Extraction

It is a crucial step in the overall process of preparing IoMT data for analysis. It isolates the most relevant features from the vast data at hand. This step reduces the dimensionality complexity of the original dataset and leads to considering only those attributes that provide relevant insight for proper analysis or model training. Feature extraction includes, but is not limited to, strategy dimensionality reduction [14] algorithms, for example, PCA [15]. For instance, in a dataset containing heart rate data from wearable sensors, feature extraction could involve calculating the mean heart rate, detecting irregularities like arrhythmias, or identifying fluctuations over time. In other cases, more advanced techniques like frequency-domain analysis or wavelet transformations [16] might be used to take out features associated with signal patterns. It helps in dropping the dimensionality of the dataset, improving computational efficiency, and ensuring that the most relevant information is used in subsequent analysis or ML models. This step even advances model performance as it enhances the most influential features by reducing processing time and contributes more to accuracy in results, hence more reliable results in health monitoring and decision-making.

18.4 Healthcare Monitoring Using Artificial Intelligence

In Table 18.2, various existing research using the IoMT and AI in healthcare monitoring and disease prediction have been summarized. It includes objectives, datasets applied, integration types of IoMT, AI models applied, evaluation metrics utilized, and specific healthcare applications. It presents how the integration of IoMT and AI may facilitate real-time data collection and investigation toward enhancing patient monitoring, early diagnosis, and personalized treatment. Each entry discusses various health applications and metrics associated with them, describing how the IoMT and AI can develop healthcare outcomes for many medical conditions.

In Table 18.2, a health application represents the transformative potential of IoMT data, as in monitoring and managing diverse types of health conditions. The IoMT devices assist in real-time data collection using wearable sensors and health-monitoring devices: from predicting diseases to personalized patient care supported by the AI model in performing early diagnosis, remote monitoring of patients, and targeted treatment. Some predict incidences of hepatitis, heart disease, and knee osteoarthritis by applying advanced AI techniques like DeepFM, MSSO-ANFIS, and ResNet-18. Additionally, the IoMT transforms elderly care, glucose monitoring in diabetes, and posture recognition with advanced diagnostic efficiency and health outcomes. These applications show how vital the IoMT is in advancing smart healthcare systems and PM.

18.5 Result

The performance of the model in predicting healthcare outcomes was evaluated using a range of metrics. These parameters provide an all-rounded test of the model to define its efficiency in correct diagnosis of health condition, less false predictions, and guaranteed output. The results can shows that the devised model can employ the potential of IoMT data along with the prowess of AI capabilities to issue early diagnosis, induce customized treatments, and devise advance patient tracking, thus realizing potential applications in improving healthcare. True positive (TP): Cases correctly

Table 18.2 State of the arts using the IoMT and AI in healthcare monitoring.

References	Objective	Dataset	IoMT integration	AI model	Metrics
[17]	Predict the incidence of hepatitis	2020 AI challenge disease prediction dataset	Health sensors for real-time data collection	Improved DeepFM	Area Under Curve (AUC) (86.05)
[18]	Improve posture recognition using errorless data fusion	Health organization case study	Wearable sensors for posture detection	RF	Accuracy, Error rate (0.03)
[19]	Predict heart disease with MSSO-ANFIS	Heart disease clinical dataset (BP, cholesterol, etc.)	Wearable devices for heart rate and health monitoring	Modified Salp Swarm Optimization (MSSO) - Adaptive Neuro-Fuzzy Inference System (ANFIS)	Accuracy (99.45%), Precision (96.54%), specificity (97.88%), sensitivity (97.89%), F1-Score (98.79%), Error rate (0.55%)
[20]	Combine IoMT and AI for coronary artery disease prediction	Patient heart data (ECG, BP, Heart Rate)	Wearable devices for continuous monitoring (ECG, heart rate, BP)	TabNet + CatBoost	Accuracy, precision, recall, f1-score

(Continued)

Table 18.2 State of the arts using the IoMT and AI in healthcare monitoring. (*Continued*)

References	Objective	Dataset	IoMT integration	AI model	Metrics
[21]	Monitor elderly healthcare using a smart healthcare model	IoMT elderly health datasets (Vital signs, Physical activity)	Wearable devices (Vital sign sensors)	ANN	Precision, recall (93.4%), f1-score, accuracy (93.6%), ROC values, specificity (93.7%)
[22]	Propose a new smart healthcare system using IoMT	Breast Cancer Wisconsin (Diagnostic) Data Set, Heart Disease Dataset (Comprehensive), Pima Indians Diabetes Database (PIMA), Parkinson's Disease Classification Data Set	Wearable sensors (health monitoring)	Improved Recurrent Neural Network (I-RNN) Optimized with Modified Vulture Satiation-based African Vultures Optimization Algorithm(MVS-AVOA)	Sensitivity (94.11%), Accuracy (94.03%), specificity (93.93%), F1-Score, precision (94.56%), FNR, FPR, NPV, FDR, MCC

(*Continued*)

Table 18.2 State of the arts using the IoMT and AI in healthcare monitoring. (*Continued*)

References	Objective	Dataset	IoMT integration	AI model	Metrics
[23]	Predict Knee Osteoarthritis (KOA) using X-ray images and deep learning	Knee X-ray Image Dataset	Wearables for real-time health data (e.g., gait sensors)	Transfer Learning, ResNet-18	Accuracy (98.26%), precision (98.76%), recall (98.94%), Specificity (97.67), F1-score (98.85%)
[24]	Heart disease Prediction	Cleveland dataset, echocardiogram image dataset	Wearable medical sensors for continuous monitoring (heart rate, ECG)	HLDA-MALO, hybrid faster R-CNN with SE-ResNet-101	F1-score (99.02%), Accuracy (99.15%), precision (98.06%), specificity (96.32%), recall (98.95 %)
[25]	Predict blood glucose levels and detect hypoglycemia in type 1 diabetes (T1D) patients	OhioT1DM dataset, ABC4Ddataset and ARISES dataset	Wearable device with low-power chip for Bluetooth and edge computing, CGM sensors	Attention-based evidential recurrent neural network	RMSE, mean absolute error, accuracy, MCC (0.70 ± 0.09), (0.68 ± 0.09), (0.70±0.12) for 3 different datasets, respectively

Note: Factorization Machine (FM), hybrid linear discriminant analysis with the modified ant lion optimization (HLDA-MALO), artificial neural network (ANN).

classified as positive in the classification task, where the method correctly identifies the existence of a condition. False positives (FP): Incorrect prediction by the model that an optimistic result actually exists for cases without the condition. False negatives (FN): Non-actual positive cases missed. True negatives (TN): Cases correctly classified as negative by the model as ruling out those without the condition. These are the basic metrics by which the accuracy and reliability of a model can be evaluated.

✓ **Accuracy:** The percentage of all predictions that were accurate, including both TP and TP. It shows how effective a model is overall (Equation 18.1).

$$Accuracy = \frac{TP+TN}{Totalsamples} \tag{18.1}$$

✓ **Precision:** The proportion of actual positive results to all expected positive results. It illustrates how well the model can steer clear of the FP (Equation 18.2).

$$Precision = \frac{TP}{FP+TP} \tag{18.2}$$

✓ **Specificity/TNR:** The proportion of actual negatives to TN. It assesses how well the framework can detect negative instances (Equation 18.3).

$$\frac{Specificity}{TNR} = \frac{TN}{TN+FP} \tag{18.3}$$

✓ **Sensitivity/recall/TPR:** The proportion of actual positives to TP. It demonstrates that the model can accurately detect every positive scenario (Equation 18.4).

$$\frac{\frac{\text{Sensitivity}}{\text{Recall}}}{\text{TPR}} = \frac{\text{TP}}{\text{TP+FN}} \tag{18.4}$$

✓ **F1-Score:** A single indicator of a model's reliability on positive cases is the harmonic average of recall and precision. It is mainly attributed to conditions when the allocation of classes is not homogeneous (Equation 18.5).

$$F1\ score = \frac{2 \times precision \times recall}{precision + recall} \tag{18.5}$$

✓ **False positive rate (FPR):** According to Equation 18.6, the ratio of negative occurrences that are mistakenly categorized as positive (FP) to all TN events is known as the FPR (Equation 18.6)

$$FPR = \frac{FP}{FP + TN} \tag{18.6}$$

✓ **False negative rate (FNR):** The percentage of positive outcomes that result in negative test results (Equation 18.7).

$$FNR = \frac{FN}{FN + TP} \tag{18.7}$$

✓ **Negative predictive value (NPV):** The percentage of all those who tested negative who were TN. It displays the likelihood that an unfavorable test outcome is accurate (Equation 18.8).

$$NPV = \frac{TN}{TN + FN} \tag{18.8}$$

✓ **False discovery rate (FDR):** The FDR is a technique for visualizing the rate of errors in screening when performing numerous comparisons (Equation 18.9).

$$FDR = \frac{FP}{FP + TP} \tag{18.9}$$

- ✓ **Area under the curve (AUC):** It calculates the capability of a method to differentiate among classes, with a superior AUC representing better performance.
- ✓ **Matthews correlation coefficient (MCC):** Gauge of how well testing is done in binary categories (Equation 18.10).

$$MCC = \frac{TN \times TP - FN \times FP}{\sqrt{(TP+FN)(TP+FP)(TN+FP)(TN+FN)}} \tag{18.10}$$

- ✓ **Root mean square error (RMSE):** A measure of mean extent of errors in predictions, providing insight into the model's prediction accuracy (Equation 18.11).

$$RMSE = \sqrt{\frac{1}{m}\sum_{j=1}^{m}(Predictedvalue_j - Actualvalue_j} \tag{18.11}$$

- ✓ **Mean absolute error (MAE):** The accuracy of continual forecasts is demonstrated by the mean absolute variance between projected and actual values (Equation 18.12).

$$MAE = \frac{1}{m}\sum_{j=1}^{m}|Predictedvalue_j - Actualvalue_j| \tag{18.12}$$

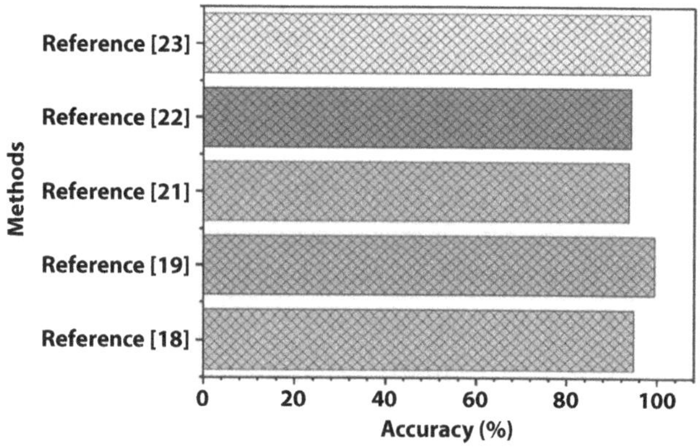

Figure 18.3 Contrast of various models with accuracy parameter.

These metrics together offer a detailed consideration of the performance of the existing model, highlighting potency and weaknesses in classification and prediction tasks. Figures 18.3–18.5 demonstrate the outcomes of existing research with an above parameter.

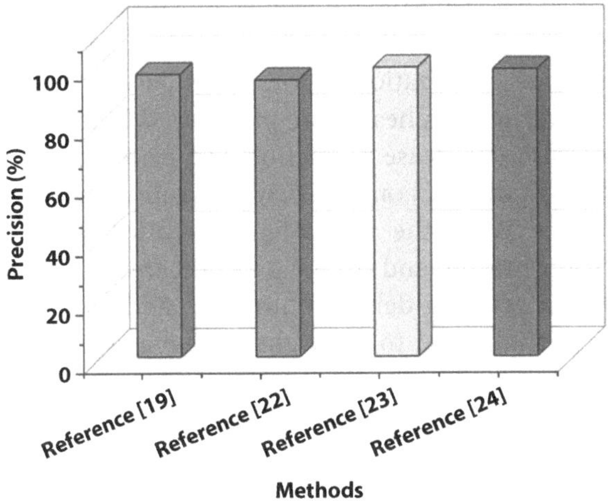

Figure 18.4 Precision comparison of models.

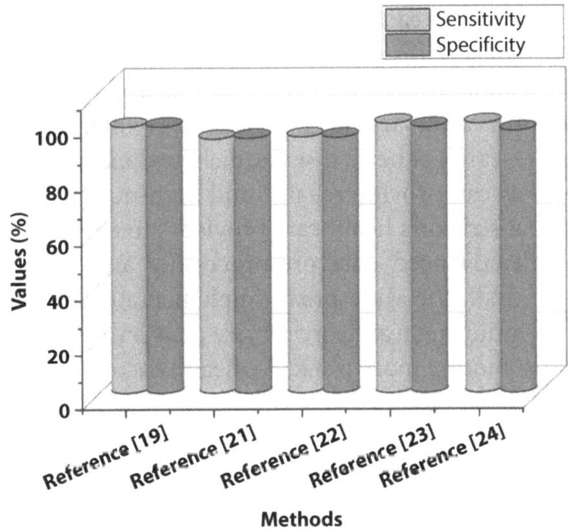

Figure 18.5 Evaluation of various methods with the parameters of specificity and sensitivity.

18.6 Discussion

The IoMT is transforming healthcare by enabling real-time, continuous monitoring and improving the quality of care through personalized treatments. By integrating wearables, implanted devices, and IoMT systems, healthcare providers can distantly check patients' health, recognize early warning signs, and intervene proactively, leading to better health outcomes. The four-layer architecture of the IoMT comprising the sensor/perception, gateway, cloud, and visualization/action layers ensures the seamless flow of data from the device to a healthcare provider. While the IoMT systems hold much promise in disease prediction and patient care optimization, there are hotbeds of disputes on data privacy, security issues, and interoperability of devices. While the AI combined with IoMT further enhances real-time decision-making and personal healthcare, the questions remain to be answered in grueling debates and issues addressed before a widespread adoption might lead to the right outcomes in enhancing patient services.

18.7 Conclusion

Integrating IoMT into healthcare introduces the most significant improvement in patient monitoring and disease management. Using a networked connection of various devices, the IoMT allows real-time aggregation and analysis of health data for early diagnosis and personalization in treatment. This architecture of IoMT systems has a PL, GL, CL and AL that ensure efficient data transmission, storage, and analysis. This integration of IoMT with AI has improved the accuracy of healthcare interventions based on several existing research of heart disease, diabetes, and knee osteoarthritis. The IoMT systems can provide reliable and high-quality data for predictive modeling that supports healthcare providers to compose an informed decision through advanced data pre-processing and feature extraction techniques. All in all, the widespread implementation of IoMT systems promises to revolutionize healthcare service delivery by advancing patient outcomes and promoting more proactive health management.

Limitation: The existing architectures and technologies of IoMT cannot predict the fast integration of the IoMT and AI. Another constraint is that the output of IoMT systems varies because of various factors such as device accuracy, data security, and variation in patient health conditions.

Future work: Future research could be in the development of stronger and more scalable IoMT systems to address these challenges with emphasis on data accuracy, security protocol improvement, and novel AI technologies along with more personalized healthcare solutions. Further, it can also be done on long-term collapse of the IoMT on patient outcomes and healthcare systems, as well.

References

1. Alam, *et al.*, Blockchain-based solutions supporting reliable healthcare for fog computing and Internet of medical things (IoMT) integration. *Sustainability*, 14, 22, 15312, 2022, https://doi.org/10.3390/su142215312.
2. Adewole, *et al.*, Cloud-based IoMT framework for cardiovascular disease prediction and diagnosis in personalized E-health care, in: *Intelligent IoT systems in personalized health care*, pp. 105–145, Academic Press, Cambridge, MA, 2021, https://doi.org/10.1016/B978-0-12-821187-8.00005-8.
3. Zamanifar, A., Remote patient monitoring: health status detection and prediction in IoT-based health care, in: *IoT in healthcare and ambient assisted living*, pp. 89–102, 2021, https://doi.org/10.1007/978-981-15-9897-5_5.
4. Bibi, *et al.*, IoMT-based automated detection and classification of leukemia using deep learning. *J. Healthc. Eng.*, 2020, 1, 6648574, 2020, https://doi.org/10.1155/2020/6648574.
5. Awotunde, *et al.*, AiIoMT: IoMT-based system-enabled artificial intelligence for enhanced smart healthcare systems, in: *Machine learning for critical Internet of Medical Things: applications and use cases*, pp. 229–254, 2022, https://doi.org/10.1007/978-3-030-80928-7_10.
6. Singh, R.P., Javaid, M., Haleem, A., Vaishya, R., Ali, S., Internet of Medical Things (IoMT) for orthopaedic in COVID-19 pandemic: Roles, challenges, and applications. *J. Clin. Orthop. Trauma*, 11, 4, 713–717, 2020, https://doi.org/10.1016/j.jcot.2020.05.011.
7. Osman, R.A., Internet of Medical Things (IoMT) optimization for healthcare: A deep learning-based interference avoidance model. *Comput. Netw.*, 248, 110491, 2024, https://doi.org/10.1016/j.comnet.2024.110491.
8. Ghubaish, *et al.*, Recent advances in the internet-of-medical-things (IoMT) systems security. *IEEE Internet Things J.*, 8, 11, 8707–8718, 2020, https://doi.org/10.1109/JIOT.2020.3045653.
9. Siddiqui, M.F., IoMT potential impact in COVID-19: combating a pandemic with innovation, in: *Computational intelligence methods in COVID-19: surveillance, prevention, prediction and diagnosis*, pp. 349 361, 2021, https://doi.org/10.1007/978-981-15-8534-0_18.

10. Rubí, S., J.N., Gondim, L., P.R., IoMT platform for pervasive healthcare data aggregation, processing, and sharing based on OneM2M and OpenEHR. *Sensors*, 19, 19, 4283, 2019, https://doi.org/10.3390/s19194283.
11. https://www.kaggle.com/datasets/prokashbarmancu/iomt-alert
12. Balhareth, G. and Ilyas, M., Optimized Intrusion Detection for IoMT Networks with Tree-Based Machine Learning and Filter-Based Feature Selection. *Sensors*, 24, 17, 5712, 2024, https://doi.org/10.3390/s24175712.
13. Wang, *et al.*, Anomaly prediction of CT equipment based on IoMT data. *BMC Med. Inf. Decis. Making*, 23, 1, 166, 2023, https://doi.org/10.1186/s12911-023-02267-4.
14. Swarna Priya, R.M., Maddikunta, P.K.R., Parimala, M., Koppu, S., Gadekallu, T.R., Chowdhary, C.L., Alazab, M., An effective feature engineering for DNN using hybrid PCA-GWO for intrusion detection in IoMT architecture. *Comput. Commun.*, 160, 139–149, 2020, https://doi.org/10.1016/j.comcom.2020.05.048.
15. Khelili, *et al.*, IoMT-fog-cloud based architecture for Covid-19 detection. *Biomed. Signal Process. Control*, 76, 103715, 2022, https://doi.org/10.1016/j.bspc.2022.103715.
16. Khafaga, *et al.*, Compression of Bio-Signals Using Block-Based Haar Wavelet Transform and COVIDOA for IoMT Systems. *Bioengineering*, 10, 4, 406, 2023, https://doi.org/10.3390/bioengineering10040406.
17. Yu, Z., Amin, S.U., Alhussein, M., Lv, Z., Research on disease prediction based on improved DeepFM and IoMT. *IEEE Access*, 9, 39043–39054, 2021, https://doi.org/10.1109/ACCESS.2021.3062687.
18. Ghazal, T.M., Hasan, M.K., Abdullah, S.N.H., Abubakkar, K.A., Afifi, M.A.M., IoMT-enabled fusion-based model to predict posture for smart healthcare systems. *Comput. Mater. Contin.*, 71, 2, 2579–2597, 2022, https://doi.org/10.32604/cmc.2022.019706.
19. Khan, M.A. and Algarni, F., A healthcare monitoring system for the diagnosis of heart disease in the IoMT cloud environment using MSSO-ANFIS. *IEEE Access*, 8, 122259–122269, 2020, https://doi.org/10.1109/ACCESS.2020.3006424.
20. Baseer, *et al.*, Healthcare diagnostics with an adaptive deep learning model integrated with the Internet of medical Things (IoMT) for predicting heart disease. *Biomed. Signal Process. Control*, 92, 105988, 2024, https://doi.org/10.1016/j.bspc.2024.105988.
21. Khan, *et al.*, An IoMT-Enabled Smart Healthcare Model to Monitor Elderly People Using Machine Learning Technique. *Comput. Intell. Neurosci.*, 1, 2487759, 20212021, https://doi.org/10.1155/2021/2487759.
22. Akhtar, *et al.*, IoMT-based smart healthcare monitoring system using adaptive wavelet entropy deep feature fusion and improved RNN. *Multimed. Tools Appl.*, 82, 11, 17353–17390, 2023, https://doi.org/10.1007/s11042-022-13934-5.

23. Javed, *et al.*, Internet of Medical Things (IoMT) Enabled Intelligent System for Chronic Disease Prediction Using Deep Machine Learning in Healthcare 5.0. *J. Comput. Biomed. Inf.*, 7, 02, 2710–1606, 2024, https://doi.org/10.56979/702/2024.
24. Manimurugan, *et al.*, Two-stage classification model for the prediction of heart disease using IoMT and artificial intelligence. *Sensors*, 22, 2, 476, 2022, https://doi.org/10.3390/s22020476.
25. Zhu, T., *et al.*, IoMT-enabled real-time blood glucose prediction with deep learning and edge computing. *IEEE Internet Things J.*, 10, 5, 3706–3719, 2022, https://doi.org/10.1109/JIOT.2022.3143375.

Part IV

INNOVATIONS AND FUTURE DIRECTIONS

19

Bioinformatics Algorithms and Tools

Suhas Ballal[1], Pooja Shukla[2], Hetal Bhaidasna[3], Riyazulla Rahman J.[4], Y. Swarna Latha[5]* and Abhilash Pati[6]

[1]Department of Chemistry and Biochemistry, Jain (Deemed-to-be University), Bangalore, Karnataka, India
[2]Maharishi School of Engineering & Technology, Maharishi University of Information Technology, Uttar Pradesh, India
[3]Department of Computer Engineering, Parul University, Vadodara, Gujarat, India
[4]Department of Information Science, Presidency University, Bangalore, Karnataka, India
[5]Department of Biotechnology, Sathyabama Institute of Science and Technology, Chennai, Tamil Nadu, India
[6]Department of Computer Science and Engineering, Siksha 'O' Anusandhan (Deemed to be University), Bhubaneswar, Odisha, India

Abstract

Bioinformatics algorithms and tools are essential components in modern biological research that make it possible to analyze the enormous volumes of biological data produced by high throughput technologies. Their resources work for innovations in genetics, disease mechanisms, and evolutionary biology by making it possible to align, assess, predict, and depict biological sequences, structures, and functions. The review aims to present a detailed account of the developments in bioinformatics algorithms and tools with respect to genomics, proteomics, and systems biology. Algorithms of bioinformatics, such as the basic local alignment search tool (BLAST) and dynamic programming Smith-Waterman pairwise sequence alignments, which are designed to find similarities between DNA, RNA, or protein sequences for phylogenetic relationships among organisms, are fundamental to bioinformatics. Machine learning (ML) is a bioinformatics method

**Corresponding author*: swarnalatha.biotech@sathyabama.ac.in; ORCID: 0000-0002-3632-4678
Suhas Ballal: ORCID: 0000-0002-6041-8332
Pooja Shukla: ORCID: 0009-0005-0869-4793
Hetal Bhaidasna: ORCID: 0000-0002-0043-3573
Abhilash Pati: ORCID: 0000-0002-3418-4202

Satya Prakash Yadav, Abhay Bansal and Victor Hugo C. de Albuquerque (eds.) Computational Intelligence in Biomedical Internet of Medical Things, (327–344) © 2026 Scrivener Publishing LLC

that produces predictions based on significant biological databases, such as gene expression data and disease risk factors. The coupling of biological understanding to bioinformatics algorithms and tools has expanded their usefulness in performing an in-depth analysis of the operations of proteins and the regulation of genes' aetiology of diseases. This review exemplifies the increasing demand and impact of computational methods in current biological research, which is also engineering new therapeutic approaches, personalized medicine, and drug development. The bioinformatics algorithms and tools are enhanced at their sharpest methods, creating ever-new possibilities for biological discovery. By evaluating the prevailing trends and determining the literature, this review helps researchers and practitioners to use computational techniques to advance life sciences.

Keywords: Bioinformatics, sequencing, genomics, proteomic, machine learning, phylogenetics, visualization

19.1 Introduction

Bioinformatics is the computational of biological and molecular data, such as protein structures and DNA sequences, including the collection, storage, organization, analysis, and interpretation of biomolecular data that utilize computer science, engineering, and mathematics [1]. It employs a variety of methods and tools, for example, databases, software, and algorithms to extract useful information from large amounts of data. Bioinformatics is also a key component of genomics, proteomics, and other omics investigations. It supports the understanding of biological systems, the prediction of gene functions, and the determination of possible therapeutic targets in personalized medicine [2]. A wide range of scientific and medical fields have benefited from the use of bioinformatics, as drug development and agricultural biotechnology are leveraged for disease research and evolutionary investigations. By processing an enormous amount of biological data using databases, algorithms, and computational tools, bioinformatics enables scientists to make well-informed conclusions based on computer analysis rather than laborious research [3]. The history of bioinformatics seems to go back to the early days of molecular biology [4]. The need for computational tools to organize and analyze increasing volumes of information became apparent in the era of sequencing technologies such as Sanger and high-throughput sequencing [5]. Due to significant advancements in databases and software, bioinformatics has become a skill capable of handling the rapidly increasing amount of data generated in genomics and related areas [6]. The bioinformatics discipline of enhanced bioinformatics focuses on molecular reducing interactions and functional structural modelling of proteins [7]. Similarly, bioinformatics has a close relation to systems biology, which manifests itself as an approach to understanding complex biological systems in depth. Systems biology entails building computerized models to study biological complexes such as interacting metabolic and gene regulatory networks. Using bioinformatics techniques, biological activities are generated, relationships are established and how cellular systems would function under different conditions is also forecasted [8]. Since it enables researchers to simulate how certain therapies impact a patient's distinct biological composition, this holistic approach is essential for the development of personalized medicine. Figure 19.1 shows the framework of bioinformatics.

Computation is used to comprehend biological processes and analyze biological data, particularly in increasing large-scale data, computational biology, and bioinformatics. The main aim of bioinformatics algorithms and tools is to develop computational methods to analyze biological data, enabling and comprehending intricate biological systems enhancing data

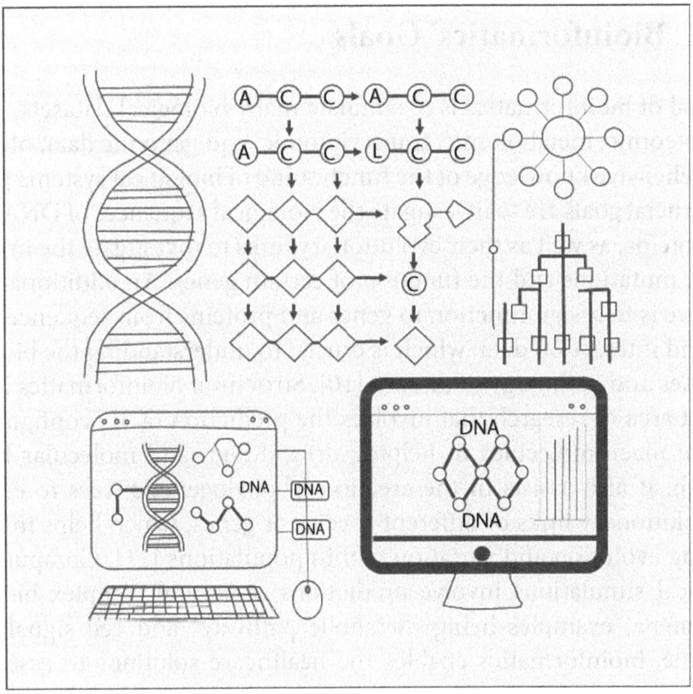

Figure 19.1 Framework of bioinformatics. (Source: Own elaboration).

interpretation, and supporting applications in genomics, proteomics, and systems biology.

The work organization is structured as follows: Section 19.2 describes the methodology; Section 19.3 explains bioinformatics' goals; Section 19.4 explains the biological sequence examination; Section 19.5 explains basic local alignment search tool (BLAST); Section 19.6 describes a comprehensive genome-to-proteome examination; Section 19.7 explains gene expression and functional examination; Section 19.8 describes challenges and future directions, and Section 19.9 concludes the study.

19.2 Methodology

This review examines the bioinformatics approaches to analyze biological sequences through pairwise alignment and BLAST. Comprehensive genome-to-proteome analysis and gene expression studies are conducted to examine functional relationships, allowing detailed insights into molecular mechanisms and biological interactions.

19.3 Bioinformatics' Goals

The goal of bioinformatics is to simulate many biological datasets, including proteomic, metabolomic, transcriptomic, and genomic data, offering a comprehensive knowledge of the functioning of biological systems [9]. The most crucial goals are to investigate the biological sequences of DNA, RNA, and proteins, as well as their evolutionary links to investigate the impact of genetic mutations and the function of certain genes. An additional prime objective is to assign function to genes and proteins from sequence, structure, and interaction data, which is crucial to understanding the biological processes and pathology of disease [10]. Structural bioinformatics is a significant area of research that involves the prediction of 3D configurations of large macromolecules in helping drug design and molecular biology research. It also assists in the creation of phylogenetic trees to establish the evolutionary links of different species or genes, which helps in understanding evolution and variation within populations [11]. Computational biological simulations involve predictions of several complex biological phenomena, examples being metabolic pathways and cell signaling. In medicine, bioinformatics enables the healthcare solutions to assess data on patients and focus on their genetics, environment, and lifestyle for the

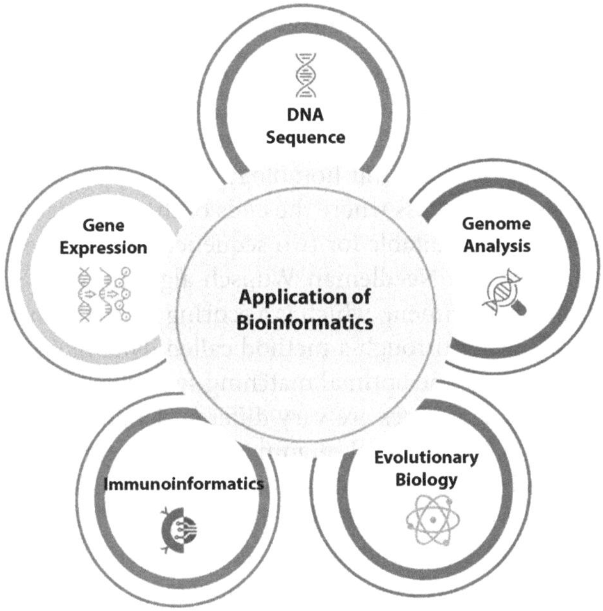

Figure 19.2 Applications of bioinformatics. (Source: https://link.springer.com/chapter/10.1007/978-981-33-6191-1_1).

best treatments. It is also important in pharmacology. For instance, the drug design processes, computerized methods are employed to search for new molecules that possess activity against the biological target of interest data [12]. Figure 19.2 shows the applications of bioinformatics.

19.4 Biological Sequence Examination

Sequence examination is a crucial bioinformatics technique that involves comparing nucleotide DNA, RNA, amino acid peptide, or protein sequences to identify shared patterns [13]. This method provides perceptions of evolutionary connections between species, genes, and organisms, as well as predictions about protein functions and structures [14]. Protein alignment is another key for bioinformatics technique, identifying conserved amino acids across different protein structures [15]. The method calculates the cost for aligning sequences to minimize differences and achieve the most accurate result. The goal is to obtain the best possible alignment, reflecting evolutionary and functional relationships between sequences.

19.4.1 Pairwise Sequence Alignment

Pairwise sequence alignment is a technique used in the comparison of two biological sequences to find the nearest optimal alignment of their identities and variations. This is useful for purposes like understanding phylogeny and functional or structural homology between the sequences [16]. Global alignment is a process where the ends of the sequences are aligned, and all the residues are suitable for two sequences that are comparable in lengths and similar. The Needleman-Wunsch algorithm is a widely used approach for global alignment, which is a scoring matrix, constructed and filled in a specific order through a method called dynamic programming. Local alignment locates the optimal matching segments of two sequences, especially when the sequences are very different lengths or only partially share similarities [17]. The local alignment is done through the Smith-Waterman method like dynamic programming scores, the regions allow the score to drop to zero for regions of non-similar biomolecules. This allows the finding of short and simple sequences containing regions of high similarity and long regions of low or no similarity. Since local alignment has the potential of finding a conserved protein motif over a larger protein, it also serves to focus on specific areas of the sequence important for functional activities [18].

19.4.2 Multiple Sequence Alignment

It involves matching three or more biological sequences to find common conserved areas. Finding functional motifs, structural resemblances, or evolutionary links among sequences, requires this kind of alignment [19]. When two sequences are compared pairwise, the multiple sequence alignment (MSA) assists in identifying patterns and functional areas that are not apparent. The MSA aligns three or more biological sequences of DNA, RNA, or protein to analyze the structural or functional patterns while determining conserved sections and deducing evolutionary links [20]. The MSA requires an enormous amount of computing power, since it aligns each pattern quickly, unlike pairwise alignment. Tools such as ClustalW and MAFFT use progressive and iterative refining strategies, whereas T-Coffee enhances accuracy by combining findings from many approaches. Phylogenetic tree building, conserved domain identification, and genetic diversity investigations extensively use the MSA [21].

19.5 Basic Local Alignment Search Tool

A bioinformatics technique called BLAST compares biological sequences to a database of sequences, which includes DNA, RNA, and proteins [22]. This method highlights areas of commonality and achieves the best possible scores of alignments for the sequences that are matched. BLAST is based on the Smith-Waterman local sequence alignment algorithm and adopts the k-tuple optimization technique to enhance the speed of the search [23]. The primary building blocks such as amino acids and nucleic acids, which are arranged in fixed lengths k-tuple of three intended for proteins and 11 for nucleotides. This encourages the specificity in the search, which almost raises the accuracy, thus making it efficient to use for sequence analysis tools such as BLAST [24]. The tool is capable of such functionalities in both DNA and protein sequences. Table 19.1 shows the overview of the best available MSA programs.

Table 19.1 Overview of the best available MSA programs [25].

Program	Advantages	Cautions
CLUSTALW	*Less memory-intensive than other applications*	*Less scalable and precise than contemporary substitutes*
DIALIGN	*Tries to differentiate among non-alignable and alignable regions*	*Less accurate than CLUSTALW in global benchmark tests*
MAFFT, MUSCLE	*Superior to CLUSTALW in speed and accuracy; offers a decent trade-off between computational cost and precision*	*Options for faster performance with lower accuracy for high-throughput use; for large datasets*
PROBCONS	*Achieves the highest accuracy in several benchmark evaluations*	*High computational time and memory requirements for large alignment tasks*
T-COFFEE	*Provides high accuracy and incorporates multiple types of information*	*High computational time and memory usage, especially for large datasets*

19.6 Comprehensive Genome-to-Proteome Examines

DNA sequencing makes it possible for genome-wide investigations, which transform molecular biology by offering comprehensive perceptions into genetic data. These methods enable thorough investigations of gene expression, protein activities, and their roles in cellular processes by bridging the gap between genomics and proteomics [26]. This change creates new opportunities for medication discovery and personalized treatment. The understanding of structural and functional genomics' underlying genetics of several disorders has significantly increased along with the genomics discipline. Furthermore, it enables the development of omics concepts transcriptomic, genomic, and metabolomic that offer fresh perspectives on all living things, including how various organisms use genetics and molecular biology to survive and procreate in both healthy and diseased conditions, as well as their population networks and environmental changes [27]. Next-generation sequencing (NGS) is a high-throughput technique for precisely and rapidly sequencing DNA and RNA. It provides a plethora of genetic information by enabling the quick sequencing of whole transcriptomes, exomes, or genomes. Next-generation sequencing has transformed genomics by making it possible to do extensive research at a fraction of the time and expense needed for conventional sequencing techniques. In bioinformatics, the three main principles are genome, transcriptome, and proteome.

- **Genome:** NGS has made genome sequencing more affordable, leading to numerous published genomes. However, the assembly software has difficulties assembling whole accurate genome sequences due to the small read length (150–300 bp) generated by such techniques. In addition, the growing amount of sequencing data generates computational difficulties requiring robust bioinformatics tools [28]. Scientists are creating new algorithms to increase the precision and effectiveness of genome assembly, including utilizing long-read sequencing methods to acquire around the drawbacks of short reads, using AI to automate analysis, forecast gene functions, and spot trends in massive datasets. Bioinformatics is also branching out into functional genomics, epigenomics, and metagenomics. A deeper understanding of genetic information is made possible by bioinformatics, which is crucial for developing personalized medicine, disease research, and ecological studies as sequencing technology advances.

- **Transcriptomic:** The goal of transcriptomics is to comprehend gene expression, regulation, and functional functions in a variety of biological processes by examining the entire collection of RNA transcripts generated by the genome under certain circumstances. Traditional methods like quantitative polymerase chain reaction and DNA microarrays have limitations, such as limited scalability and sensitivity [29]. Next-generation sequencing particularly RNA-sequence, overcomes these challenges by providing high-throughput, unbiased global gene expression analysis, detecting novel transcripts and offering deeper insights into gene regulation and cellular processes.
- **Proteomics:** The identification, measurement, and characterization of every cell protein are necessary for comprehending cellular physiology [30]. Protein structure, function, connections, and dynamics in space and time are examined systematically because of proteomics, which has rapidly expanded.

Table 19.2 and Figure 19.3 show the accuracy and precision of several ML models. Table 19.3 and Figure 19.4 show the recall and F1-score of several ML models. Numerous performance patterns are seen when comparing different ML models for categorization results related to bioinformatics. Metrics including precision, accuracy, recall, and F1 score, were assessed for several methods such as Random Forest (RF), gradient boosting classifier (GBC), k-nearest neighbor (KNN), and extreme gradient

Table 19.2 Assessment of ML methods using accuracy and precision.

Methods	Accuracy (%)	Precision (%)
RF [31]	91	88
GBC [32]	89	89
KNN [33]	98.6	98.5
XGBoost [34]	95	95

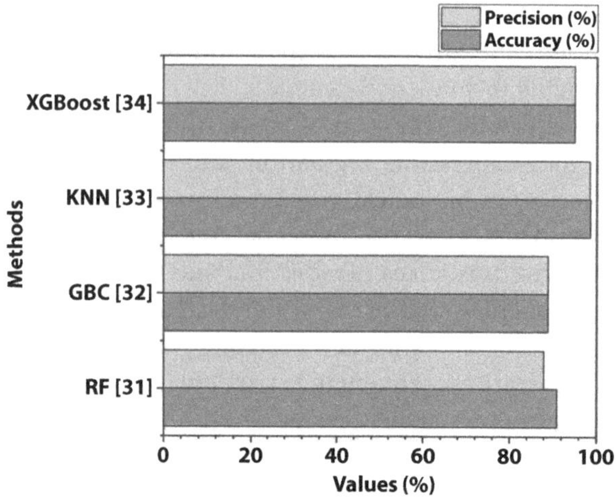

Figure 19.3 Graphical representation of accuracy and precision in ML models.

Table 19.3 Assessment of ML methods using recall and F1-score.

Methods	Recall (%)	F1-score (%)
RF [31]	89	88
GBC [32]	89	89
KNN [33]	98.6	98.4
XGBoost [34]	95	95

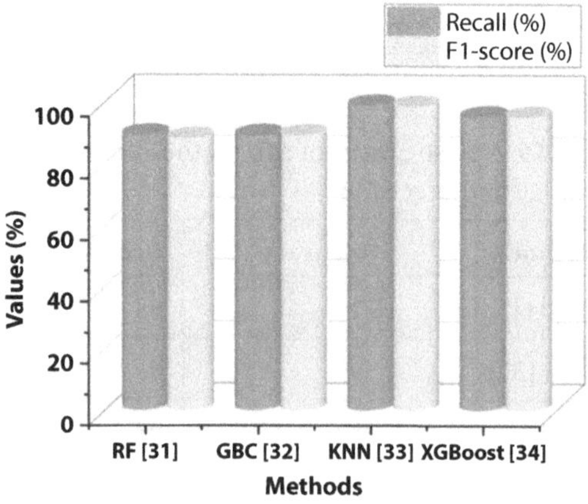

Figure 19.4 Graphical representation of recall and F1 score in ML models.

boosting (XGBoost), which were exhibiting excellent scores on a variety of assessment parameters. The KNN method shows the highest accuracy (98.6%), recall (98.6%), precision (98.5%), and F1-score (98.4%), outperforming the other methods in all evaluation metrics, indicating superior classification performance.

The literature review emphasizes the development, difficulties, and discoveries of various AI-based bioinformatics. Integration problems, a lack of public knowledge, and the imperative need for improved model accessibility are the key challenges as represented in Table 19.4.

Table 19.4 Literature review summary considering various types of AI-based bioinformatics.

References	Main purpose	Research gap	Findings
[35]	This review explored the prediction accuracy and integration of AI bioinformatics.	Limited reviews focus on AI's role in ocular biofluid analysis, particularly regarding the integration of AI with bioinformatics tools.	Supervised AI predicts disease status with high accuracy, and bioinformatics translates complex biomarker data, improving diagnostics and personalized treatments.
[36]	To clarify fundamental AI/ML concepts, provide examples of their applications, and offer perspectives on their effective integration into pharmaceutical research and development.	Artificial intelligence/ ML in the pharmaceutical industry amid the jargon and hype.	Artificial intelligence/ML has revolutionized pharmaceutical research and development, particularly in clinical trial design and analysis, boosting efficiency through automation and predictability.

(Continued)

Table 19.4 Literature review summary considering various types of AI-based bioinformatics. (*Continued*)

References	Main purpose	Research gap	Findings
[37]	To evaluate deep learning (DL) applications in medical and bioinformatics, categorizing the most effective DL techniques and their effectiveness in resolving medical and bioinformatics issues.	There was need to explore DL solutions' potential in improving healthcare outcomes.	Deep learning techniques showed effectiveness in medical diagnostics, treatment recommendations, and drug discovery, although challenges like adaptability, scalability, and data complexity remain.

19.7 Gene Expression and Functional Examination

Transcribing genetic information from DNA into RNA and converting it into proteins is known as gene expression. Understanding gene expression data in bioinformatics entails how genes are triggered or inhibited in different contexts, whether during development, illness or in reaction to environmental changes [38]. Functional investigations go beyond this by pathway enrichment or gene ontology analysis to connect gene activity to phenotypic features, pathways, and molecular functions. Managing massive datasets, finding trends, and forecasting gene function uses algorithms, databases, and computer models. Bioinformatics makes these procedures potential and advances the understanding of genetics, disease mechanisms, and personalized treatment. Gene expression and functional examination tools are essential for understanding how genes influence cellular function. Techniques such as reverse transcription polymerase chain reaction and quantitative polymerase chain reaction are widely used to measure RNA expression levels, providing perceptions of gene activity [39].

19.8 Challenges and Future Directions

Table 19.5 shows the challenges, future directions, and summary of key issues in bioinformatics, algorithms, and tools. It highlights scalability, computational power, data privacy, AI integration, and cost challenges, suggesting solutions like optimized algorithms and cloud computing.

Table 19.5 Challenges and future directions for bioinformatics algorithms and tools.

Reference	Category	Challenges	Future directions
[40]	Scalability	Handling the exponential growth of biological data.	Develop algorithms optimized for parallel computing and distributed systems.
	Computational power	High computational demands for large-scale analyses (e.g., NGS, proteomics).	Leverage cloud computing, GPU acceleration, and quantum computing to reduce processing time.
[41]	Data privacy	Genomic data privacy faces challenges in safeguarding sensitive personal information, ensuring consent, and preventing unauthorized access or misuse.	Implement secure and federated learning models to protect sensitive data.
	Artificial intelligence integration	Limited explainability and bias in ML models.	Develop interpretable AI models and integrate domain knowledge for informed predictions.

19.9 Conclusion

Bioinformatics is an essential field that combines several biological data types, such as metabolomic data, to offer a comprehension of biological systems. Among the bioinformatics algorithms, sequence alignment algorithms evaluate the DNA, RNA, and amino acid sequences, to establish their evolutionary relationship and measure their similarity. Bioinformatics tools utilize predictive modeling and also process big biological data concerning gene expression patterns or risk factors of diseases. Incorporating bioinformatics tools and algorithms has resulted in a greater comprehension of biological processes, offering priceless insights into the molecular causes of illnesses, protein activities, and gene control. The importance of computational techniques in contemporary biology is shown by these developments, which also continue to spur breakthroughs in biotechnology, drug discovery, and personalized medicine. Future directions in the field will focus on optimizing algorithms for scalability, leveraging cloud computing and AI for faster analysis, and ensuring secure data management.

References

1. Yuan, Q., *et al.*, AlphaFold2-aware protein–DNA binding site prediction using graph transformer. *Briefings Bioinf.*, *23*, bbab564, 2022, https://doi.org/10.1093/bib/bbab564.
2. Ndagi, U., *et al.*, Antibiotic resistance: bioinformatics-based understanding as a functional strategy for drug design. *RSC Adv.*, 10, 18451–18468, 31, 2020, https://doi.org/10.1039/D0RA01484B.
3. Naithani, U., *et al.*, Integrative computational approaches for discovery and evaluation of lead compound for drug design. *Front. Drug Discov.*, *4*, 1362456, 2024, https://doi.org/10.3389/fddsv.2024.1362456.
4. Lakshmi, and Ramyachitra, Review about bioinformatics, databases, sequence alignment, docking, and drug discovery, in: *Statistical modelling and machine learning principles for bioinformatics techniques, tools, and applications*, pp. 11–23, 2020, https://doi.org/10.1007/978-981-15-2445-5_2.
5. Larson, N.B., *et al.*, A clinician's guide to bioinformatics for next-generation sequencing. *J. Thorac. Oncol.*, *18*, 2, 143–157, 2023, https://doi.org/10.1016/j.jtho.2022.11.006.
6. Alosaimi, S., *et al.*, A broad survey of DNA sequence data simulation tools. *Briefings Funct. Genomics*, *19*, 1, 49–59, 2020, https://doi.org/10.1093/bfgp/elz033.

7. Sharaf, A., *et al.*, Establishing African genomics and bioinformatics programs through annual regional workshops. *Nat. Genet.*, *56*, 8, 1556–1565, 2024, https://doi.org/10.1038/s41588-024-01807-6.
8. Clark, A., *et al.*, A Comprehensive Review of Bioinformatics Tools for Genomic Biomarker Discovery Driving Precision Oncology. *Genes*, *15*, 8, 1036, 2024, https://doi.org/10.3390/genes15081036.
9. Prayogo, F.A., *et al.*, Metagenomic applications in exploration and development of novel enzymes from nature: a review. *J. Genet. Eng. Biotechnol.*, 18, 1–10, 2020, https://doi.org/10.1186/s43141-020-00043-9.
10. Wang, G., *et al.*, Dynamic alternative DNA structures in biology and disease. *Nat. Rev. Genet.*, *24*, 4, 211–2345, 2023, https://doi.org/10.1038/s41576-022-00539-9.
11. Gayathiri, E., *et al.*, Computational approaches for modeling and structural design of biological systems: A comprehensive review, in: *Progress in Biophys. Mol. Biol.*, vol. 185, pp. 17–32, Academic Press, 2023, https://doi.org/10.1016/j.pbiomolbio.2023.08.002.
12. Poroikov, Computer-aided drug design: From discovery of novel pharmaceutical agents to systems pharmacology. *Biochem. (Moscow) Suppl. Ser. B: Biomed. Chem.*, *14*, 3, 216–227, 2020, https://doi.org/10.1134/S1990750820030117.
13. Payne, A., *et al.*, *In situ* genome sequencing resolves DNA sequence and structure in intact biological samples. *Science*, *371*, 6532eaay3446, 2021, https://doi.org/10.1126/science.aay3446.
14. Eguchi, H., *et al.*, Applying metagenomic analysis using nanopore sequencer (MinION) for precision medicine in bacterial keratoconjunctivitis: comprehensive validation of molecular biological and conventional examinations. *Int. J. Mol. Sci.*, *24*, 3, 26115, 2023, https://doi.org/10.3390/ijms24032611.
15. Stoler, N. and Anton, N., Sequencing error profiles of Illumina sequencing instruments. *NAR Genomics Bioinf.*, *3*, 1, lqab019, 2021, https://doi.org/10.1093/nargab/lqab019.
16. Gabler, F., Nam, S.-Z., *et al.*, Protein sequence analysis using the MPI bioinformatics toolkit. *Curr. Protoc. Bioinf.*, 72, 1, e108, 2020, https://doi.org/10.1002/cpbi.108.
17. Hamamsy, T., *et al.*, Protein remote homology detection and structural alignment using deep learning. *Nat. Biotechnol.*, 42, 6, 975–985, 2024, https://doi.org/10.1038/s41587-023-01917-2.
18. Edgar, R.C., *et al.*, Petabase-scale sequence alignment catalyses viral discovery. *Nature*, *602*, 7895, 142–1475, 2022, https://doi.org/10.1038/s41586-021-04332-2.
19. Amorim, A.R., *et al.*, Metaheuristics for multiple sequence alignment: A systematic review. *Comput. Biol. Chem.*, *91*, 107563, 2021, https://doi.org/10.1016/j.compbiolchem.2021.107563.
20. Du, Y., *et al.*, Multiple Sequence Alignment Based on Indicator-Based Multi-Objective Evolutionary Algorithm, in: *2024 4th International Conference on*

Consumer Electronics and Computer Engineering (ICCECE), IEEE, pp. 239–242, 2024, https://doi.org/10.1109/ICCECE61317.2024.10504249.

21. Gong, C., *et al.*, Aligning speakers: Evaluating and visualizing text-based diarization using efficient multiple sequence alignment (extended version). *arXiv preprint* arXiv:2309.07677, https://doi.org/10.48550/arXiv.2309.07677, 2023.
22. Chaabane, L., *et al.*, An enhanced cooperative method to solve multiple-sequence alignment problem. *Int. J. Data Min. Model. Manage.*, *13*, 1–2, 1–16, 2021, https://doi.org/10.1504/IJDMMM.2021.112907.
23. Sharma, N., *et al.*, ToxinPred2: an improved method for predicting toxicity of proteins. *Briefings Bioinf.*, *23*, 5, bbac174, 2022, https://doi.org/10.1093/bib/bbac174.
24. Tiwari, R., *et al.*, Performance Analysis of DNA Sequence Alignment using FPGA's Tools. *Int. Res. J. Innov. Eng. Technol.*, 4, 10, 20, 2020, https://doi.org/10.47001/IRJIET/2020.410004.
25. McWhite, C., *et al.*, Leveraging protein language models for accurate multiple sequence alignments. *Genome Res.*, 33, 7, 1145–1153, 2023, https://www.genome.org/cgi/doi/10.1101/gr.277675.123.
26. Jakobson, C., *et al.*, A genome-to-proteome atlas charts natural variants controlling proteome diversity and forecasts their fitness effects. *bioRxiv*, 2024-10, 2024, https://doi.org/10.1101/2024.10.18.619054.
27. Satam, H., *et al.*, Next-generation sequencing technology: current trends and advancements. *Biology*, 12, 7, 997, 2023, https://doi.org/10.3390/biology12070997.
28. Athanasopoulou, K., *et al.*, Third-generation sequencing: the spearhead towards the radical transformation of modern genomics. *Life*, 12, 1, 30, 2021, https://doi.org/10.3390/life12010030.
29. Mitra, D., *et al.*, Evolution of Bioinformatics and its impact on modern bio-science in the twenty-first century: Special attention to pharmacology, plant science and drug discovery. *Comput. Toxicol.*, 24, 1002485, 2022, https://doi.org/10.1016/j.comtox.2022.100248.
30. Sies, H., *et al.*, Defining roles of specific reactive oxygen species (ROS) in cell biology and physiology. *Nat. Rev. Mol. Cell Biol.*, 23, 7, 499–515, 2022, https://doi.org/10.1038/s41580-022-00456-z.
31. Ravi, T., Yadav, A.P., *et al.*, Machine Learning In Bioinformatics: Disease Prediction Models. *Nanotechnol. Percept.*, 279–290, 2024, https://doi.org/10.62441/nano-ntp.v20iS14.17.
32. Nasim, S., *et al.*, A novel approach for polycystic ovary syndrome prediction using machine learning in bioinformatics. *IEEE Access*, 10, 97610–976245, 2022, https://doi.org/10.1109/ACCESS.2022.3205587.
33. Alshayeji, M.H. and Sindhu, S.C.B., Viral genome prediction from raw human DNA sequence samples by combining natural language processing and machine learning techniques. *Expert Syst. Appl.*, 218, 1196415, 2023, https://doi.org/10.1016/j.eswa.2023.119641.

34. Sami, A., *et al.*, MAC-ErrorReads: machine learning-assisted classifier for filtering erroneous NGS reads. *BMC Bioinf.*, 25, 1, 61, 2024, https://doi.org/10.1186/s12859-024-05681-1.
35. Pucchio, A., Saffire, H., *et al.*, Applications of artificial intelligence and bioinformatics methodologies in the analysis of ocular biofluid markers: a scoping review. *Graefe's Arch. Clin. Exp. Ophthalmol.*, 262, 4, 1041–1091, 2024, https://doi.org/10.1007/s00417-023-06100-6.
36. Alam, S., *et al.*, Artificial intelligence and machine learning in bioinformatics, in: *Advances in Bioinformatics*, pp. 321–345, Springer Nature Singapore, Singapore, 2024, https://doi.org/10.1007/978-981-99-8401-5_16.
37. Amiri, Z., Heidari, A., *et al.*, The deep learning applications in IoT-based bio-and medical informatics: a systematic literature review. *Neural Comput. Appl.*, 36, 11, 5757–5797, 2024, https://doi.org/10.1007/s00521-023-09366-3.
38. Del Val, C., *et al.*, Gene expression networks regulated by human personality. *Mol. Psychiatry*, 29, 7, 2241–2260, *London: Springer Nature*, 2024, https://doi.org/10.1007/978-981-99-8401-5_16.
39. Dai, Y., *et al.*, Unbiased RNA-Seq-driven identification and validation of reference genes for quantitative RT-PCR analyses of pooled cancer exosomes. *BMC Genomics*, 22, 1–135, 2021, https://doi.org/10.1186/s12864-020-07318-y.
40. Zainab, O.A., *et al.*, Utilization of big data analytics to identify population health trends and optimize healthcare delivery system efficiency. *World J. Adv. Res. Res.*, 24, 1, 2159–2176, 2024, https://doi.org/10.30574/wjarr.2024.24.1.3198.
41. Nasarian, E., *et al.*, Designing interpretable ML system to enhance trust in healthcare: A systematic review to proposed responsible clinician-AI-collaboration framework. *Inf. Fusion*, 108, 102412, Oxford: Elsevier, 2024, https://doi.org/10.1016/j.inffus.2024.102412.

20

Biomedical Data Acquisition and Management

Praveen Priyaranjan Nayak[1]*, Roopashree R.[2], Deeksha Choudhary[3], Jay Gandhi[4], Asif Mohamed H. B.[5] and Poonguzhali S.[6]

[1]*Department of Electronics & Communication Engineering, Siksha 'O' Anusandhan (Deemed to be University), Bhubaneswar, Odisha, India*
[2]*Department of Chemistry and Biochemistry, Jain (Deemed-to-be University), Bangalore, Karnataka, India*
[3]*Maharishi School of Engineering & Technology, Maharishi University of Information Technology, Uttar Pradesh, India*
[4]*Department of Computer Science & Engineering, Parul University, Vadodara, Gujarat, India*
[5]*Department of Computer Science and Engineering, Presidency University, Bangalore, Karnataka, India*
[6]*Department of Electronics and Communication Engineering, Sathyabama Institute of Science and Technology, Chennai, Tamil Nadu, India*

Abstract
The Internet of Medical Things (IoMT) refers to a network community of connected gadgets and sensors that collect and share well-being information in real-time to assist medical doctors and healthcare providers and improve affected patient care. The IoMT devices like wearables and clever scientific systems acquire raw data, including heart rate, blood stress, and glucose levels, which require pre-processing and metadata annotation for effective integration and evaluation. Healthcare professionals can benefit from information control, which involves processing and organizing data from devices. Information control enters through effect when the reality of these devices has to be processed and organized in a way that is helpful to

**Corresponding author*: praveennayak@soa.ac.in; ORCID: 0000-0003-1726-1605
Roopashree R.: ORCID: 0000-0002-0382-6321
Deeksha Choudhary: ORCID: 0009-0001-8298-6082
Jay Gandhi: ORCID: 0000-0002-1998-4180
Poonguzhali S.: ORCID: https://orcid.org/0000-0003-2147-788X

Satya Prakash Yadav, Abhay Bansal and Victor Hugo C. de Albuquerque (eds.) Computational Intelligence in Biomedical Internet of Medical Things, (345–364) © 2026 Scrivener Publishing LLC

medical professionals. The data ought to be saved in secure databases, and privacy and security are vital to guard sensitive patient information, which is done through encryption and access manipulation systems. The gathered information is frequently analyzed using advanced technology like machine learning and artificial intelligence. These innovative technologies assist doctors in discovering styles inside the records, predicting fitness issues, and enhancing diagnoses. Artificial intelligence analyzes large quantities of data to assist in discovering diseases early, improving the probability of successful treatment. With the usage of the IoMT, healthcare companies monitor patients remotely, offer personalized treatment, and make better decisions primarily based on the data gathered. This technology not only improves the quality of healthcare but also facilitates lessening costs and growth efficiency in the clinical field. Generally, the IoMT is altering healthcare by enabling real-time monitoring, data-driven selections, and improved patient outcomes.

Keywords**:** Internet of Medical Things (IoMT), machine learning (ML), artificial intelligence (AI), data acquisition, data management

20.1 Introduction

Acquiring and managing biomedical data is crucial for contemporary healthcare systems, particularly as the usage of modern technology development [1]. Gathering clinical data from a variety of sources, such as clinics, hospitals, smart medical records, and patient's clinical records is referred to as data acquisition [2]. Managing the data effectively is also essential to assuring its application in enhancing healthcare outcomes. The Internet of Medical Things (IoMT) is the branch of the Internet of Things (IoT) system that comprises interconnected scientific equipment for healthcare tracking [3]. The IoT represents network-connected devices that continuously monitor, collect, as well as transmit medical data in real-time without human assistance. These gadgets include smart sensors, portable health monitors, and domestic activity monitors. The IoMT offers remote healthcare monitoring, which lowers costs, and prevents needless hospital stays [4]. The specialized area of artificial intelligence (AI) called computational intelligence (CI) improves biomedical data management. In the biomedical area, CI is essential in improving healthcare by making huge quantities of medical statistics [5]. When combined, the IoMT and CI provide effective, data-driven solutions for patient care and monitoring in the healthcare industry. The IoMT devices provide an enormous quantity of data, which CI swiftly addresses, analyzes, and processes for real-time perception [6]. This facilitates effective patient management, individualized treatment programs, and early identification of any health problem. Figure 20.1 displays the general layout of the IoMT mechanism.

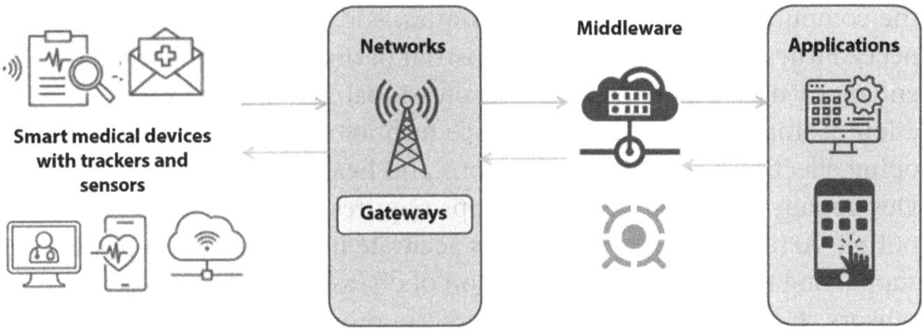

Figure 20.1 The overall design of the IoMT system. (Source: Own elaboration).

The aim of this review: The review's goal is to investigate how CI can be integrated into the IoMT to facilitate efficient biological data management and gathering.

20.2 Literature Review

In the healthcare sector, wearable technology is revolutionizing real-time monitoring of human body physiology. It was used to monitor everyday activities, chronic illnesses, and fitness. Through study and development, cutting-edge wearables are created for a variety of applications, including heart attack detection, high blood pressure monitoring, and diabetic foot monitoring. A study [7] discussed the development of hardware and machine learning (ML) algorithms, as well as case examples, such as stethoscope systems and smart insoles.

The ML techniques required a lot of labeled data to expedite the digitization of biological procedures by the author [8]. For algorithm training, data collecting and labeling were essential phases, however, scalability and security present difficulties. Terabytes of data are produced every day by high throughput operations, making data processing, aggregation, and transportation challenging. Because of immutability, trade secrets, and personal identity, data security must be maintained. Practicality and scalability were highlighted in the discussion of best practices for security and extracting useful information from gathered data. Recent uses of wearable technology were reviewed in the study [6], including sports applications, integrating wearables with the IoT, and medical diagnosis using unsupervised and supervised learning. Numerous AI approaches, including semi-supervised, supervised, unsupervised, and reinforcement learning, have been applied to a variety of tasks. It covers design and development difficulties, the computational load of AI techniques, and wearable technology prospects. Fitness, mental wellness, industrial performance enhancement, and enhanced user experience while professional gaming or exercising were a few examples. Artificial intelligence technology was essential for developing effective healthcare applications and healthcare prediction systems. Developing intelligent healthcare apps requires using ML and cloud computing. Artificial intelligence makes accurate illness detection possible by supporting the identity and prediction of diseases. Neural networks, frame sensors, and wireless wearable sensors can grow the efficacy of healthcare. With an emphasis on the effects of synthetic intelligence, ML, and wireless sensors on healthcare devices, the study [9] looks at how properly different technologies carry out healthcare prediction structures. A study [10] suggested classifying iron ore by the usage of an aggregate of system studying and laser-induced breakdown spectroscopy. The researchers utilized support vector machines, neural networks, and k-nearest neighbor fashions on 10 datasets. The findings revealed a high accuracy rate of 94.07%, 93.33%, and 82.96%, respectively. By combining laser-induced breakdown spectroscopy with gadget studying, iron ores can be quickly and appropriately categorized, beginning a brand-new choice technique for the metallurgical quarter.

The emergence of technologies, such as sensor technologies and the IoT that facilitate the collection and processing of records for healthcare choice-making, and scientific statistics processing has received significant interest in recent years. Wearables, chatbots, blockchain, allotted computing, system learning, and sample recognition could be useful resources in early detection and illness diagnosis. Deep learning was confronted with issues along with moral considerations, data accumulation, privacy protection, and the best warranty. The authors [11] tested cutting-edge investigations on applications of distributed computing systems, emphasizing on cloud computing, aspects, fog, the IoT, and hybrid structures. The capacity of huge statistics, analytics, and the IoT in biomedicine and healthcare was discussed in the article [12]. It discussed telemedicine with AI, telerobotic surgery, wearable technology for fitness prediction, and using IoT and big information in image database evaluation. From medication-centered delivery to personalized drug design, the bankruptcy also covers the improvement of these technologies inside the cutting-edge healthcare machine. Concepts that could be empirical, established, theoretical, and methodological were presented in this bankruptcy. With an incidence of 5–12% and an annual fee of $4 billion, temporomandibular joint (TMJ) issues were the second-most prevalent muscular skeletal disorder. The primary objective was to become aware of TMJ osteoarthritis before morphological deterioration takes place. Four fashions were tested by a study [13] for diagnostic performance using cutting-edge algorithms for system learning and data science. In terms of detecting TMJ osteoarthritis fame, the XGBoost integrated LightGBM version received accuracy, area under the curve, and F1-score. Using the Internet of Factors generation, a study [14] presented a wearable, low-strength, actual-time remote bio-alerts tracking gadget. The ineffectiveness of traditional bio-alert monitoring structures was addressed by using this generation, specifically for individuals with severe medical issues. Patients' body temperature, heart rate, oxygen saturation (SPO_2), and electrocardiogram (ECG) indicators were all remotely monitored by the gadget through a smartphone utility that serves as an IoT platform. An Arduino tool is based on a microcontroller and is used to technique the indicators. The primary contribution was the transmission of an ECG sign to a clever mobile tool for doctor tracking, which facilitates early heart sickness detection. Computers and clever phones display the outcome of the results.

20.3 Internet of Medical Things Technologies and Their Role in Biomedical Data Acquisition

A system of interrelated medical equipment and sensors that gather and send health-related data is known as the IoMT. These devices include wearable sensors, smart medical equipment, and remote monitoring tools that track vital signs like heart rate, blood pressure, and glucose levels. The IoMT performs an essential function in biomedical information acquisition by allowing real-time, continuous tracking of patients, making it less difficult for healthcare professionals to tune fitness situations remotely and provide timely interventions. This statistic can be used for analysis, treatment plans, and enhancing patient care.

20.4 The Internet of Medical Things Data Acquisition

20.4.1 Raw and Original Data

The term raw data is referred to as primary data. It generally refers to the original, unprocessed, or unmodified version of data that is gathered straight from its source. The initial information gathered from sensors, devices, or other data-collecting equipment should be raw data [15]. This data can take various forms depending on the type of data source, and it is often considered the initial stage in any data processing procedure. Raw data is information that has been observed or recorded exactly as it is without any changes, interpretations, manipulations, or transformations. To clean up valuable perceptions from this most detailed data, more processing could be necessary. Figure 20.2 displays the device gathering of raw data.

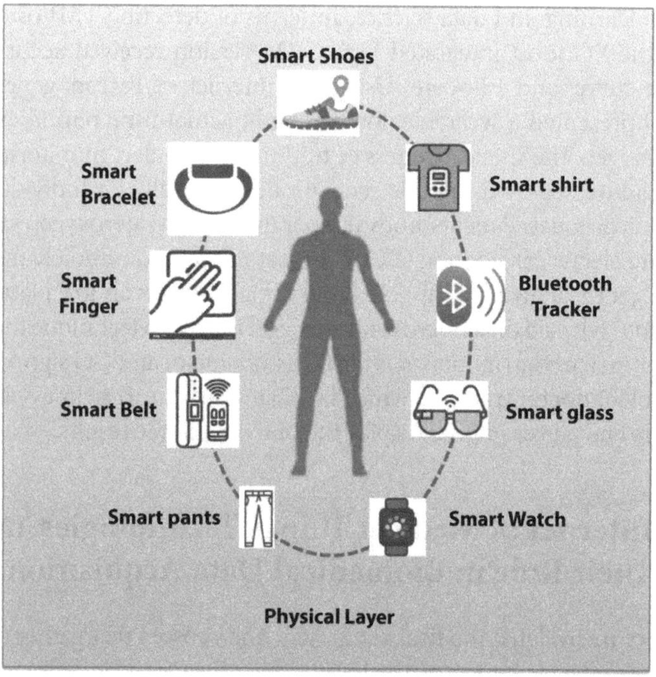

Figure 20.2 Collection of raw data sensors. (Source: https://www.researchgate.net/figure/Methods-of-objective-evaluation-of-fabric-comfort-a-Kawabata-evaluation-system-KES_fig8_355711865).

20.4.2 Role of Metadata

Raw data must be paired with the proper metadata to retrieve the most information possible. The extra information that gives context and characterizes the traits, qualities, and properties of raw data is referred to as metadata [16]. In a particular context or area, metadata offers important context, descriptions, and interpretations required for comprehending and correctly using the raw data. Metadata [17] can serve as a descriptive, structural, administrative, technological, contextual, and useful resource in facts governance, reproducibility, integration, interpretation, and pleasant evaluation. Effective data integration, discovery, sharing, collaboration, satisfactory evaluation, and repeatability are facilitated using metadata. Figure 20.3 illustrates the metadata types.

- **Descriptive metadata:** Descriptive metadata is essential for establishing study datasets or impacting personal data, as it provides the fundamental records needed to understand, search for, and retrieve biomedical statistics.

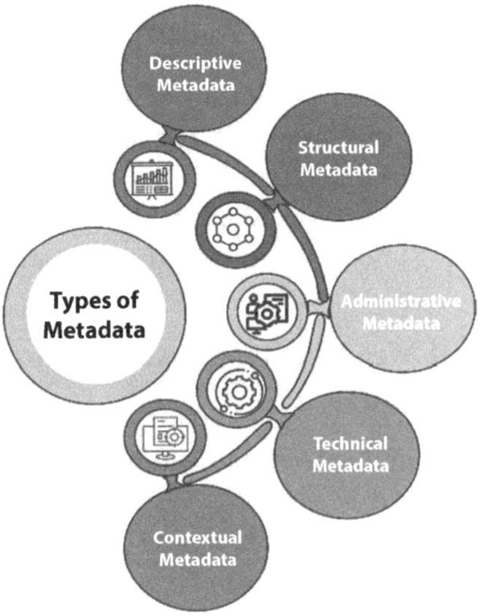

Figure 20.3 Types of metadata. (Source: Own elaboration).

- **Structural metadata:** Structural metadata allows users to navigate among associated files or data segments by defining relationships among additives inside a complex dataset.
- **Administrative metadata:** Information for controlling and regulating access to biomedical data is obscured in administrative metadata, which frequently focuses on lifecycle management, statistics protection, and privacy.
- **Technical metadata:** Technological metadata allows data processing, evaluation, and replication by presenting details about the technological traits of biological data.
- **Provenance metadata:** By monitoring the data's source and records, its validity is confirmed by the primary sources and assists in assessing the information's dependability.

20.4.3 Sensitive Data in Biomedical Study

Biomedical studies regularly deal with sensitive records, such as collecting, managing, or analyzing personalized data [18]. Clinical trials, genetic studies, and investigations utilizing human fluids, tissues, or cells are instances of circumstances where human topics are usually engaged. Protecting individual privacy and confidentiality must be the priority while handling sensitive data. Institutional rules and regulations, as well as ethical and legal obligations, are essential. To lessen any risks, protect an individual's privacy, and maintain the participants' trust and the community at large, sensitive data need to be handled cautiously. Protecting sensitive data during its transmission and storage requires the implementation of stringent safety precautions, which include encryption and authentication [19]. To reduce the risk of re-identification, identifiable records need to be removed wherever possible using anonymization and de-identification procedures.

20.4.4 Biomedical Measurement Systems Based on the Internet of Medical Things

In the physical layer, wearable technology (smartwatches, smart bracelets, glasses, and other gadgets) is primarily used by IoMT-based biomedical instruments for measuring systems to assess the vital signs of the subjects being monitored, such as blood pressure, oxygen concentration, heart rate, pulse rate, body temperature, blood sugar level, lung contraction volume, and respiration rate. Figure 20.4 illustrates the collection of raw data sensors. The received data is processed at the data integration layer before being forwarded to the layer of application services. The doctor analyzes the data at the framework's service layer, together with the individuals being observed.

20.4.5 Data Pre-Processing

Data in the healthcare industry exists in formats, including text, audio, voice, time series, signals, and images from many modalities. Therefore, to unlock the intricacies of healthcare data, effective data management and

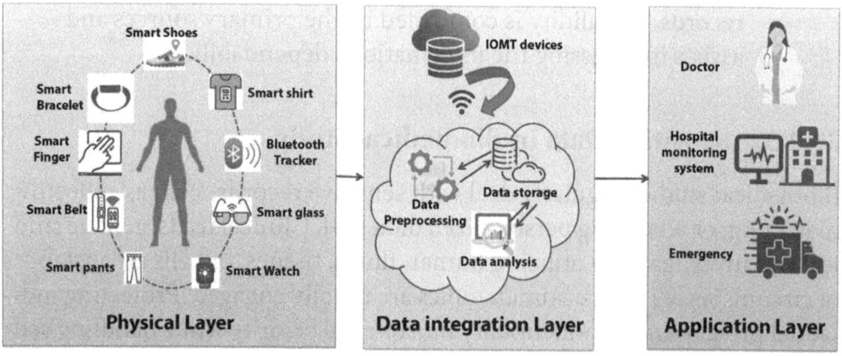

Figure 20.4 Collection of raw data sensors. (Source: Own elaboration).

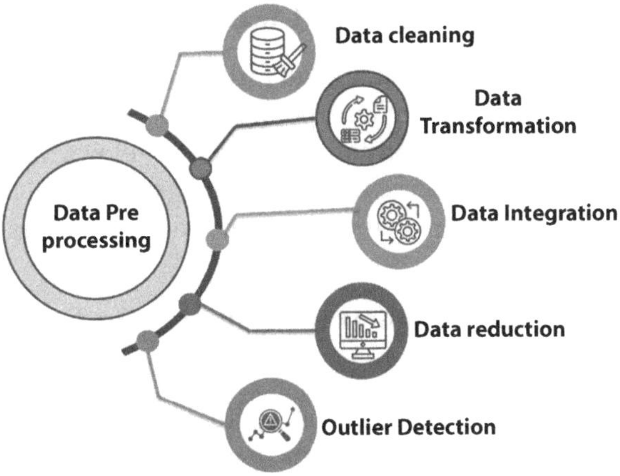

Figure 20.5 Data pre-processing procedures. (Source: https://www.geeksforgeeks.org/dbms/data-preprocessing-in-data-mining/).

processing approaches are needed. In ML, these procedures are known as feature engineering and data pre-processing [20]. The pre-processing methods are displayed in Figure 20.5.

Each offers distinct perspectives on the health and medical situations of people. In contrast, processed data have undergone a number of procedures, such as organization, cleaning, computations, transformations (such as normalization), filtering, aggregating, or summarizing the raw data to extract specific information or to improve their suitability for analysis or decision-making.

20.4.6 Data Cleaning and Its Impact on Quality

The purpose of data cleaning before further analysis is to eliminate redundant information, noise, and outliers.

- By locating and fixing mistakes, inconsistencies, missing numbers, and outliers, data cleaning increases the dataset's correctness and dependability.
- Standardizing formats, fixing variable discrepancies, and guaranteeing data compatibility are further benefits of data cleaning that assist in integration and analysis.

However, there are some disadvantages to data cleaning as well, such as the possibility of information loss and distortion.

20.4.7 Risk of Aggressive Data Cleaning

Excessive data cleaning can result in an insufficient or inaccurate underlying phenomenon by removing data points or introducing unconscious or conscious bias. To reduce information loss, which allows for the investigation of any biases, and preserve the dataset integrity, careful consideration and comprehension documentation of the cleaning processes are crucial.

20.4.8 Normalization and Transformation for Enhanced Analysis

Calculated metrics, derived functions, aggregated values, or transformed variables are examples of processed facts. It is organized to make evaluation, visualization, or modeling simpler. Aside from aggregated data arranged with specific categories or time intervals, processed facts contain computed averages, sums, or probabilities. Furthermore, to make comparisons between numerous variables or samples more equitable, normalization strategies are used to take into consideration differences in facts, sizes, and distributions. By enhancing the dependability, quality, and interpretability of the statistics, those numerous data processing phases also assist in enhancing the precision of ensuing evaluation and permit stronger scientific findings. However, an excessive amount of alteration additionally uploads biases or distorts the underlying patterns, it is critical to discover stability among records processing techniques and preserve the integrity of the original statistics. To ensure repeatability and permit others to assess how each degree influences the final result, the facts processing pipeline must be obvious and well documented.

20.4.9 Challenges in High and Low Throughput Datasets in Biomedical

Data gathering and processing differ considerably based on the experiment. Two primary categories distinguish datasets: low-throughput datasets and high-throughput datasets for omics and different high-throughput investigations. Understanding the differences among these types of datasets is essential for recognizing the unique challenges provided and the need for suitable experiment designs and reporting tactics.

20.4.10 High Throughput

High-throughput strategies typically generate large amounts of information. These databases contain a wealth of information about molecular components, their interactions, and their practical roles in organic structures. The organized nature of omics facts necessitates standardized statistics processing pipelines, stringent excellent manipulation protocols, and precise analytic techniques. Owing to their scale and complexity, omics datasets require superior computational and bioinformatics equipment for statistics processing and interpretation. Standardizing experimental strategies, record types, and metadata annotation is essential to ensure correct facts are integrated, evaluated, and transmitted across several studies and study enterprises.

20.4.11 Low Throughput

Smaller-scale investigations that focus on restrained biological strategies or molecular interactions often make up low-throughput biomedical studies. These analyses employ strategies along with cellular functional testing, flow cytometry, fluorescence microscopy, and immunostaining. Even though these inquiries could yield less data than high-throughput datasets, they require careful planning, trustworthy controls, and appropriate statistical analysis. Figure 20.6 displays biologically significant experimental signals, together with the raw and processed data types associated with interactions.

20.5 Biomedical Data Management

Biomedical data management is a versatile system that is specified as the gathering, processing, storage, and dissemination of biomedical information precisely and safely for study or clinical applications. The data management infrastructure is shown in Figure 20.7. Effective data management systems should have the following features and functionalities in a centralized data repository: data security/privacy, version control/data tracking, a template-based standard and consistent metadata, metadata annotation/tagging, integration with other data analysis tools, sharing and collaborating, documentation and provenance, compliance with rules and regulation, flexibility or scalability, easy operability, data backup, and disaster recovery.

20.5.1 Characteristics of the Data Management System

Centralized data source documentation and storage assure validity and accessibility for efficient biomedical data collection and management. Data is systematically organized using standardized formats, allowing

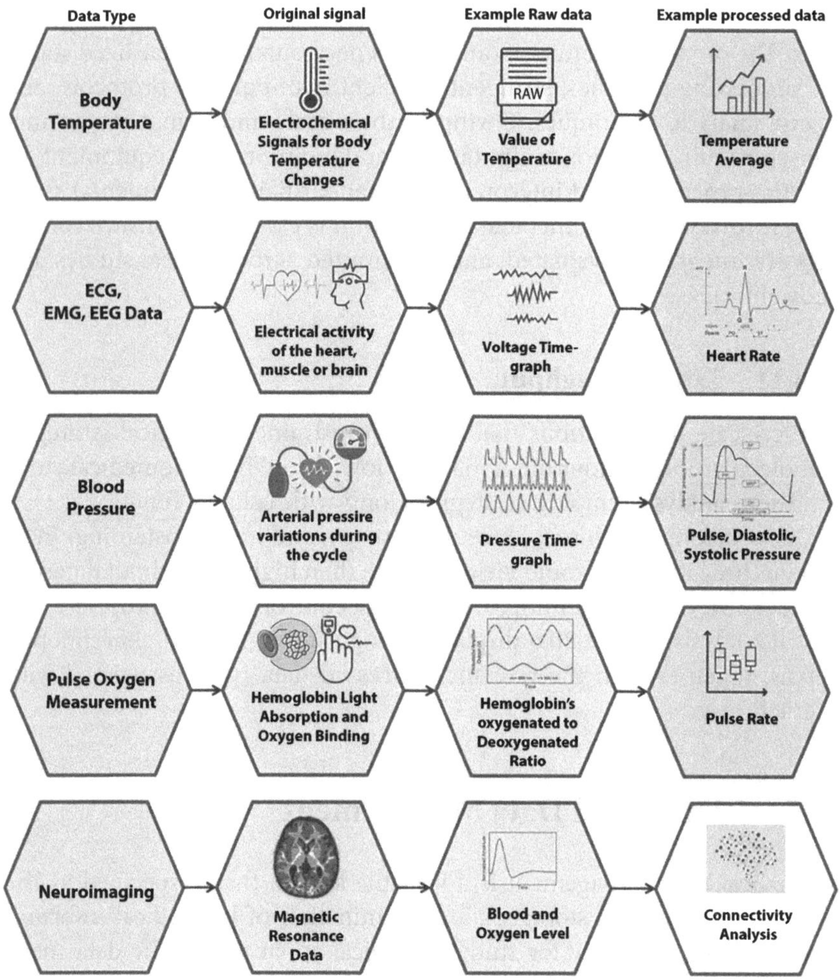

Figure 20.6 An illustration of unprocessed and processed data. (Source: Own elaboration).

researchers to access it through intuitive interfaces. Real-time monitoring is made possible by acquiring data *via* gadgets, such as the IoMT. Secure sharing facilitates collaboration, while version control ensures data accuracy [21]. Scalable systems integrate with analytical tools and adjust to expanding datasets. Sensitive information is protected by data security and adherence to legal requirements. Regular backups protect against loss, and tagging improves data discoverability, resulting in a dependable architecture for biomedical data management. Data management system characteristics are shown in Figure 20.8.

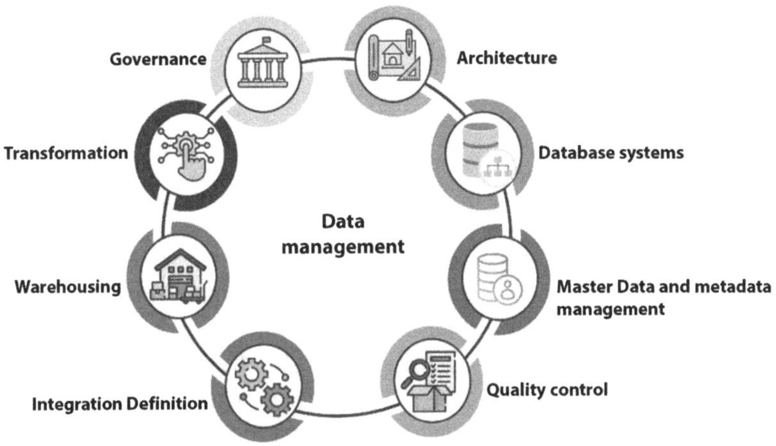

Figure 20.7 Data management architecture. (Source: https://medium.com/@lognoroy2000/what-is-data-management-fd3fc428c180).

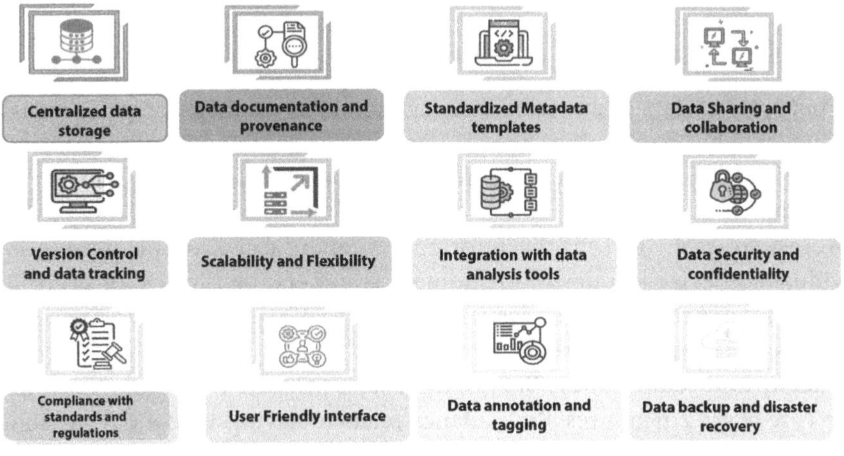

Figure 20.8 The data management system's characteristics. (Source: Own elaboration).

Medical data is gathered from a range of digital devices, such as wearables, sensors, medical equipment, and even electronic health records. Examples of such data are values like heart rates, temperature, blood pressure, glucose levels, and X-rays among others apart from the patients' records.

20.5.2 Data Storage and Security

Data storage and security are two critical components to protect patients' private data and ensure that data is stored safely and accessibly in biomedical studies and healthcare [22]. Biomedical data include medical records, imaging data, lab findings, and sensor data, among others requiring safe solutions for storage.

20.5.3 Storage Procedures

Cloud Storage and Local server: Many healthcare organizations use cloud services to store massive biological data. Data is stored remotely with the help of cloud storage, which allows access from numerous places, especially to academics and healthcare professionals. For securing data, cloud companies often employ robust security features like encryption and multi-factor authentication [23]. Other organizations have their data stored on local, in-house, or private servers installed in-house and on-site. These systems are locally hosted and are physically secured; however, their internal controls against physical damage, hacking, and loss of data are considerable.

20.5.4 Data Security Measures

Encryption: Data often receives encryption before either storage or transmission. This implies that even if unauthorized individuals get access to the information, without the correct decryption key, users are unable to read it.
Access control: The sensitive information can be accessed by a given individual authorized to do so, including researchers, physicians, or even IT specialists. Access control systems ensure that a person authorized can access or interact with the data.
Backup and redundancy: Biomedical data is protected by regular backups in case of system failures. Redundancy refers to having a secondary system or server that hosts data similar to the primary one in case the first one fails.
Firewalls and anti-virus protection: Anti-virus software locates and limits viruses that damage or corrupt data, while firewalls help to protect data systems from unauthorized access.

20.5.5 Data Analysis and Interpretation

In a biomedical study, useful information often comes only after processing and analyzing the collection of biological data. Here, AI, ML, and statistical tools are largely relevant.

Machine learning: ML enables researchers to analyze huge datasets automatically and identify hidden patterns leading to predictions without explicit programming. The ML algorithm predicts a disease based on a patient's medical record at a high risk.
Artificial intelligence: AI emulates human intellect, like the recognition of speech or medical images. Some applications of AI include the analysis of X-ray and CT scans and even diagnosing illnesses based on patient-reported symptoms.
Statistical tools: Statistical analysis utilizes the comparison of patient outcomes before and after therapy to evaluate the effectiveness of a treatment.

These methods facilitate the processing of raw biological data into valuable information that enable the detection of patterns, prediction of patient health, or even the enhancement of the accuracy in diagnosis. By using this in decision-making, medical professionals make informed decisions in the treatment and care of patients to ensure positive results.

20.5.6 Data Sharing and Interoperability in Biomedical Data Management

Data sharing and interoperability: It defines the degree of availability of medical information, which entails test results, patient records, and health statistics to different physicians, facilities, or groups at the same time [24]. This way, the individual is assured that the professionals caring for the patients are adequately prepared to offer the best care possible. Most medical systems or technologies in practice, such as mobile applications, medical equipment, or even hospital software, have interoperability. This makes doctors and hospital management utilize the same information about a patient, even if the patient uses different systems. This prevents confusion, error, and delays in treatments. Interoperability and data-sharing require that data be kept in a common format that is comprehensible by various systems. Furthermore, patient confidentiality and security are maintained during the data exchange procedure.

20.6 Assessment of Security

Security assures the safety of sensitive data information by ensuring confidentiality, integrity, availability, and defense against unwanted access along with possible breaches. In the assessment of security, encryption time (ms) is utilized to assess the effectiveness and resilience of encryption methods

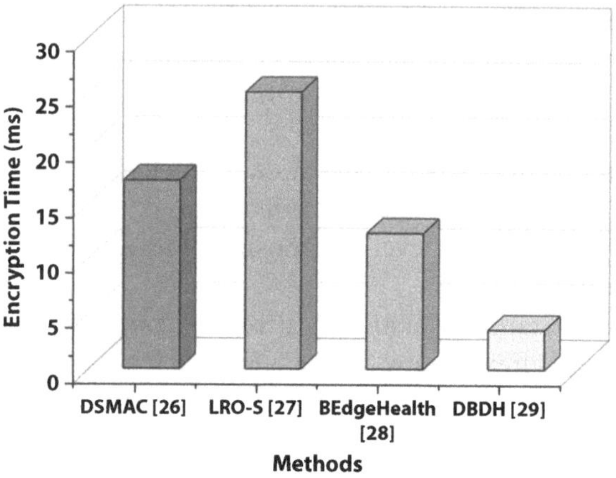

Figure 20.9 Graphical depiction of encryption time.

in protecting biomedical information data by assessing the amount of time required for encryption. The included methods of encryption time in security assessment are decentralized self-management of data access control (DSMAC) [25], lionized remora optimization-based serpent (LRO-S) [26], BEdgeHealth [27], and deep belief-based Diffie-Hellman (DBDH) [28]. Figure 20.9 illustrates the graphical representation of encryption time comparison.

Figure 20.9 compares the encryption time with various methods, and it emphasizes the efficiency in the data security applications. It indicates that

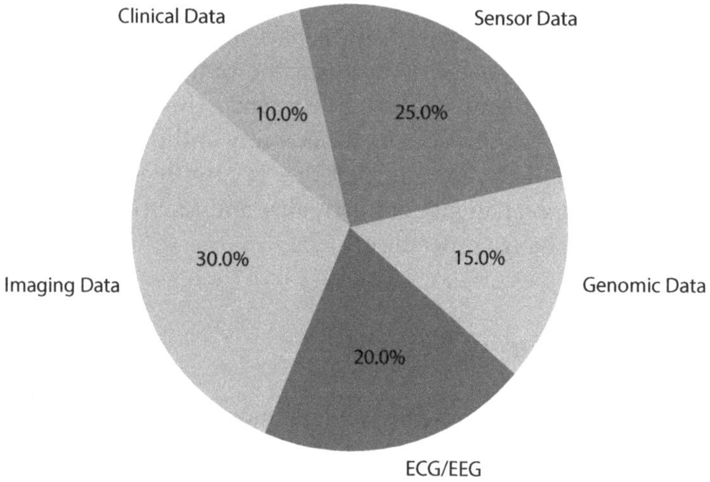

Figure 20.10 Data acquisition modalities.

BEdgeHealth offers the fastest encryption time, and DBDH provides the lowest time, which suggests the efficient solutions for secure data access management. Data acquisition modalities in biomedical systems are represented in Figure 20.10.

It offers an overview of the various kinds of data sources contributing to biomedical studies and healthcare applications. It categorizes biomedical data into five distinct modalities such as imaging data, sensor data, ECG/EEG, genomic data, and clinical data, and each segment indicates its proportional contribution. It illustrates the distribution of biomedical data acquisition modalities, highlighting five types are imaging data (30%), sensor data (25%), ECG/EEG (20%), genomic data (15%), and clinical data (10%). These modalities form a robust framework for biomedical systems, enabling advancements in diagnostics, personalized medicine, and healthcare delivery. Their combined utilization ensures a holistic approach to patient care and study.

20.7 Conclusion

In conclusion, the IoMT revolutionizes healthcare by permitting real-time tracking, stable statistics management, and record-driven selection-making. By connecting gadgets like wearables and scientific devices, the IoMT allows for frequent monitoring of patient's health metrics, enhancing the accuracy of diagnoses and facilitating early detection of illnesses. The use of superior technologies like AI and ML, in addition, complements this manner, supporting healthcare vendors to offer personalized care and make informed decisions. Overall, the IoMT not only improves patient results but also contributes to more performance, decreased healthcare expenses, and a more proactive method of health management.

References

1. Manickam, P., *et al.*, Artificial intelligence (AI) and internet of medical things (IoMT) assisted biomedical systems for intelligent healthcare. *Biosensors*, 12, 8, 562, 2022, https://doi.org/10.3390/bios12080562.
2. Ahmed, I., Balestrieri, E., Lamonaca, F., IoMT-based biomedical measurement systems for healthcare monitoring: A review. *Acta IMEKO*, 10, 2, 174–184, 2021, https://doi.org/10.21014/acta_imeko.v10i2.1080.
3. Mathkor, D.M., *et al.*, Multirole of the internet of medical things (IoMT) in biomedical systems for managing smart healthcare systems: An overview of

current and future innovative trends. *J. Infect. Public Health*, 17, 4, 559–572, 2024, https://doi.org/10.1016/j.jiph.2024.01.013.
4. Luo, H., *et al.*, Biomedical data and computational models for drug repositioning: a comprehensive review. *Briefings Bioinf.*, 22, 2, 1604–1619, 2021, https://doi.org/10.1093/bib/bbz176.
5. Oniani, S., *et al.*, Artificial intelligence for internet of things and enhanced medical systems, in: *Bio-inspired Neurocomputing*, pp. 43–59, 2021, https://doi.org/10.1007/978-981-15-5495-7_3.
6. Nahavandi, D., *et al.*, Application of artificial intelligence in wearable devices: Opportunities and challenges. *Comput. Methods Programs Biomed.*, 213, 106541, 2022, https://doi.org/10.1016/j.cmpb.2021.106541.
7. Chowdhury, M.E.H., *et al.*, Machine learning in wearable biomedical systems, in: *Sports Science and Human Health-Different Approaches*, London, UK, IntechOpen, 2020, https://doi.org/10.5772/intechopen.93228.
8. Fracchia, C., Secure and Scalable Collection of Biomedical Data for Machine Learning Applications, in: *Artificial Neural Networks*, pp. 317–336, Springer US, New York, NY, 2020, https://doi.org/10.1007/978-1-0716-0826-5_16.
9. Padma, A., Reddy, G.V., Ramachandran, G., Artificial Intelligence Techniques for the wireless wearable Smart Healthcare Prediction System Applications, in: *2023 Second International Conference on Electronics and Renewable Systems (ICEARS)*, IEEE, 2023, https://doi.org/10.1109/ICEARS56392.2023.10085051.
10. Yang, Y., *et al.*, Application of scikit and keras libraries for the classification of iron ore data acquired by laser-induced breakdown spectroscopy (LIBS). *Sensors*, 20, 5, 1393, 2020, https://doi.org/10.3390/s20051393.
11. Aminizadeh, S., *et al.*, The applications of machine learning techniques in medical data processing based on distributed computing and the Internet of Things. *Comput. Methods Programs Biomed.*, 241, 107745, 2023, https://doi.org/10.1016/j.cmpb.2023.107745.
12. Banerjee, A., *et al.*, Emerging trends in IoT and big data analytics for biomedical and health care technologies, in: *Handbook of Data Science Approaches for Biomedical Engineering*, pp. 121–152, 2020, https://doi.org/10.1016/B978-0-12-818318-2.00005-2.
13. Bianchi, J., *et al.*, Osteoarthritis of the temporomandibular joint can be diagnosed earlier using biomarkers and machine learning. *Sci. Rep.*, 10, 1, 8012, 2020, https://doi.org/10.1038/s41598-020-64942-0.
14. Al-Sheikh, M. A., *et al.*, Design of mobile healthcare monitoring system using IoTtechnology and cloud computing. *IOP Conf. Ser. Mater. Sci. Eng.*, 881, 1, 012113, 2020, https://doi.org/10. 1088/1757-899X/881/1/012113.
15. Shortliffe, E.H. and Chiang, M.F., Biomedical data: Their acquisition, storage, and use, in: *Biomedical Informatics: Computer Applications in Health care and Biomedicine*, pp. 45–75, Springer International Publishing, Cham, 2021, https://doi.org/10.1007/978-3-030-58721-5_2.

16. Ulrich, H., *et al.*, Understanding the nature of metadata: systematic review. *J. Med. Internet Study*, 24, 1, e25440, 2022, https://doi.org/10.2196/25440.
17. Meloni, V., *et al.*, Fairifying clinical studies metadata: a registry for the biomedical study, in: *Public Health and Informatics*, pp. 779–783, Amsterdam, Netherlands, IOS Press, 2021, https://doi.org/10.3233/SHTI210281.
18. Rujano, M.A., *et al.*, Sharing sensitive data in life sciences: an overview of centralized and federated approaches. *Briefings Bioinf.*, 25, 4, 2024, https://doi.org/10.1093/bib/bbae262.
19. Jaime, F.J., *et al.*, Strengthening privacy and data security in biomedical microelectromechanical systems by IoT communication security and protection in smart healthcare. *Sensors*, 23, 21, 8944, 2023, https://doi.org/10.3390/s23218944.
20. Martínez-García, M. and Hernández-Lemus, E., Data integration challenges for machine learning in precision medicine. *Front. Med.*, 8, 784455, 2022, https://doi.org/10.3389/fmed.2021.784455.
21. Bahmani, A., *et al.*, A scalable, secure, and interoperable platform for deep data-driven health management. *Nat. Commun.*, 12, 1, 5757, 2021, https://doi.org/10.1038/s41467-021-26040-1.
22. Thapa, C. and Camtepe, S., Precision health data: Requirements, challenges and existing techniques for data security and privacy. *Comput. Biol. Med.*, 129, 104130, 2021, https://doi.org/10.1016/j.compbiomed.2020.104130.
23. Zeydan, E., *et al.*, Managing Distributed Machine Learning Lifecycle for Healthcare Data in the Cloud. *IEEE Access*, 12, 115750–115774, 2024, https://doi.org/10.1109/ACCESS.2024.3443520.
24. Cunha-Oliveira, T., Ioannidis, J.P.A., Oliveira, P.J., Best practices for data management and sharing in experimental biomedical study. *Physiol. Rev.*, 104, 3, 1387–1408, 2024, https://doi.org/10.1152/physrev.00043.2023.
25. Saidi, H., *et al.*, DSMAC: Privacy-aware Decentralized Self-Management of data Access Control based on blockchain for health data. *IEEE Access*, 10, 101011–101028, 2022, https://doi.org/10.1109/ACCESS.2022.3207803.
26. Almalawi, A., *et al.*, Managing security of healthcare data for a modern healthcare system. *Sensors*, 23, 7, 3612, 2023, https://doi.org/10.3390/s23073612.
27. Nguyen, Dinh, C., *et al.*, BEdgeHealth: A decentralized architecture for edge-based IoMT networks using blockchain. *IEEE Internet Things J.*, 8, 14, 11743–11757, 2021, https://doi.org/10.1109/JIOT.2021.3058953.
28. Goel, A. and Neduncheliyan, S., An intelligent blockchain strategy for decentralised healthcare framework. *Peer-to-Peer Netw. Appl.*, 16, 2, 846–857, 2023, https://doi.org/10.1007/s12083-022-01429-x.

21

Biomedical Data Integration and Fusion

Smita Rath[1]*, Emalda Roslin S.[2], Rekha M.M.[3], Awakash Mishra[4], Gaurav Kumar Ameta[5] and Megha D. Bengalur[6]

[1]*Department of Computer Science and Information Technology, Siksha 'O' Anusandhan (Deemed to be University), Bhubaneswar, Odisha, India*
[2]*Department of Electronics and Communication Engineering, Sathyabama Institute of Science and Technology, Chennai, Tamil Nadu, India*
[3]*Department of Chemistry and Biochemistry, Jain (Deemed-to-be University), Bangalore, Karnataka, India*
[4]*Maharishi School of Engineering & Technology, Maharishi University of Information Technology, Uttar Pradesh, India*
[5]*Department of Computer Science & Engineering, Parul University, Vadodara, Gujarat, India*
[6]*Department of Computer Science and Engineering, Presidency University, Bangalore, Karnataka, India*

Abstract

Biomedical data integration and fusion involve combining various data types from different sources, such as clinical, omics, imaging, and wearable devices, to form a comprehensive understanding of health and disease. This research focuses on integrating and fusing biomedical data to improve disease prediction, personalize treatment strategies, and enhance overall healthcare insights. The OASIS Alzheimer's Detection and Alzheimer multiclass image data were obtained from open-source platforms like Kaggle. For the image data, the Wiener filter was used for preprocessing, while feature extraction was employed using the gray-level co-occurrence matrix (GLCM). The image data were then fused using feature-level fusion. To optimize the fusion process and improve prediction accuracy, a novel framework is proposed tabu search optimized dynamic random forest

**Corresponding author*: smitarath@soa.ac.in; ORCID: 0000-0003-0547-6609
Emalda Roslin S.: ORCID: 0000-0001-8699-9510
Rekha M.M.: ORCID: 0000-0002-7371-6478
Awakash Mishra: ORCID: 0009-0002-5447-7499
Gaurav Kumar Ameta: ORCID: 0000-0002-7463-2583

Satya Prakash Yadav, Abhay Bansal and Victor Hugo C. de Albuquerque (eds.) Computational Intelligence in Biomedical Internet of Medical Things, (365–382) © 2026 Scrivener Publishing LLC

(TSO-DRF). In this work, four classes of Alzheimer's disease, mild demented (MID), very mild demented (VMD), moderate demented (MOD), and non-moderate demented (NMD), are utilized for both binary class classification and multiclass classification tasks. In resulting with optimization, TSO-DRF outperformed in accuracy, such as MID (Vs) VMD -94.62%, MOD (Vs) NMD - 93.21%, MID (Vs) NMD -90.64%, VMD (Vs) MOD -91.29%, MID (Vs) MOD (Vs) VMD-95.64%, and NMD (Vs) MID (Vs) MOD-93.82%. Integrating diverse biomedical data sources significantly enhances predictive accuracy and allows for more personalized healthcare insights, providing a promising direction for advancing disease prediction and treatment strategies.

***Keywords*:** Biomedical data integration, data fusion, dynamic random forest (DRF), linear discriminant analysis (LDA), tabu search optimization (TSO), grey level co-occurrence matrix

21.1 Introduction

The growing difficulty of research and technological capabilities in the field of biomedicine science has catalyzed the generation of different amounts of data in different areas, focused on genomics, imaging, proteomics, and clinical diagnosis [1]. This enormous and complicated data referred to as 'big data' presents a revolutionizing opportunity in healthcare by facilitating care in medicine, constructive prospects on diseases, and improved clinical decisions. Data integration and data fusion in the biomedical domain are related to the existence of some international standard, which helps in the effective analysis and knowledge acquisition processes [2]. This process addresses the challenge posed by the different textures, shapes, and sources of information presented by electronic health records (EHR), e-health user reports, and molecular imaging profiling [3]. Through the integration and amalgamation of such data streams, patterns and relationships which were previously obscured, flash to researchers and health workers [4]. The integration and fusion of biomedical data also increase the use of machine learning (ML) and artificial intelligence (AI) in the health sector [5]. Multimodal data fusion and federated learning methods allow for data analysis without compromising data security and privacy. The method promotes predictive modeling, chances of accurate diagnosis, and personalized treatment development [6]. The importance of biomedical data integration and fusion is not an issue. Some of these issues include emphasis on data; interoperability, scalability, quality control, and privacy compliance [7]. The barrier also needs to be addressed through the development of novel computation techniques, the establishment of common frameworks, as well as cooperation among data scientists, practitioners, and policymakers [8]. Several issues exist with the integration and fusion of biomedical data, chiefly differences in data quality, problems with interconnectivity, and issues regarding data privacy. Standardized data structures, AI fused with other algorithms for data integration, and other set motor activities in different parts of the body movement and factors with a safe health system are advanced techniques that can help to facilitate these processes. The purpose of this research is to improve disease prediction, tailor treatment plans, and advance general healthcare insights by combining and integrating biomedical data.

21.1.1 Contributions

- The OASIS Alzheimer's Detection and Alzheimer multiclass image data were sourced from open platforms in Kaggle.
- A Wiener filter was applied for preprocessing the image data and gray level co-occurrence matrix (GLCM) was used for feature extraction, Image data were fused using feature-level fusion.
- A novel framework, tabu search optimized dynamic random forest (TSO-DRF), was proposed to optimize the fusion process and improve prediction accuracy.
- Four classes of Alzheimer's disease, mild demented (MID), very mild demented (VMD), moderate demented (MOD), and non-moderate demented (NMD), were utilized for both binary and multi-class classification tasks.

Structure of the paper: The studies are divided into sections, with Section 21.2 showing the literature reviews; Section 21.3 outlines the methodology; Sections 21.4 and 21.5 include the results and discussion, and Section 21.6 shows the conclusion.

21.2 Literature Reviews

The AI-driven framework for multi-class classification in colorectal cancer (CRC) diagnosis and classification [9] suggested the model makes use of a whale optimization method, feature extraction, and Gaussian filtering. It makes use of a deep support vector machine model, scale-invariant feature transform (SIFT), and Inception v4 deep features. In the simulation investigation, the model can identify and cure CRC with a maximum accuracy of 96.18%.

The additive manufacturing technique for producing intricate geometries with extreme precision, particularly in the creation of biomedical implants [10] fused deposition modeling. To use the Taguchi approach to optimize the fused deposition modeling process parameters to reduce surface roughness and circularity errors. Taguchi L9 orthogonal arrays were developed after factors influencing circularity were determined. The findings indicated that while layer thickness had the greatest impact, build orientation was the most important component for circularity error reduction.

Medical imaging has observed an increase in the usage of AI, which has potential uses throughout the imaging life cycle [11]. The obstacles include limited data access, a time-consuming and expensive data curation procedure, and the availability of vast, well-selected training data. The basic procedures must be discussed to get medical imaging data ready for the creation of AI algorithms and novel ideas.

Semantics were frequently absent from explainable AI, especially in the life sciences and healthcare industries [12]. Suggested data to ontologies and facilitated semantic similarity evaluations were the opportunities presented by the semantic web. Semantic annotation and the integration of diverse data into a shared semantic landscape were the biomedical explanation methodology, which enables *post-hoc* explanations regardless of the ML technique employed. The difficulties of diverse data sources and user competence were addressed by the method.

To enhance the connection between environmental and biomedical data, the National Academies of Sciences, Engineering, and Medicine organized a symposium on AI and ML. Researchers [13] suggested the recent advancements in AI and data-driven methodologies, promising uses in human health and illness, and the ethical, social, and policy ramifications of gathering and integrating health data were all covered in the workshop.

Electronic health records must incorporate pharmacogenomic data for better medication management [14] efforts are underway to tackle the issues of restricted scalability and standardization. Pharmacogenomics can be further adopted in clinics with the help of a vision of integrated informatics and data science, and additional clinical domains can benefit from the experiences of pioneering sites.

To integrate multi-omics data in cancer molecular biology studies, this outline looks at ML technologies [15] that evaluated accuracy, runtime efficiency, and accuracy in classifying cancer types by comparing five methods utilizing data from the Cancer Cell Line Encyclopedia. The evaluation promotes the creation of innovative data integration techniques for medication discovery and individualized therapies and offers suggestions for choosing appropriate approaches.

Progress in biomedical engineering by providing accurate, effective, affordable, and repeatable solutions Process, material, and application issues must be resolved, through [16] examined processes, post-processing methods, applications, and challenges associated with 3D printing in the biomedical sector. It examines these issues and makes recommendations for future developments. The growing significance of 3D printing in biomedical engineering, this review attempts to pinpoint potential research avenues and improve knowledge of biomedical engineering post-processing.

21.3 Methodology

The methodology begins with collecting biomedical data from various sources, followed by preprocessing using a standard scaler to standardize features. The GLCM is then applied for feature extraction and dimensionality reduction. The tabu search optimization (TSO) algorithm is used to optimize feature selection and improve model performance. The dynamic random forest (DRF) model is trained on the optimized data for accurate classification and prediction, with evaluation metrics used to assess its effectiveness. Figure 21.1 shows the overall flow for biomedical data integration and fusion.

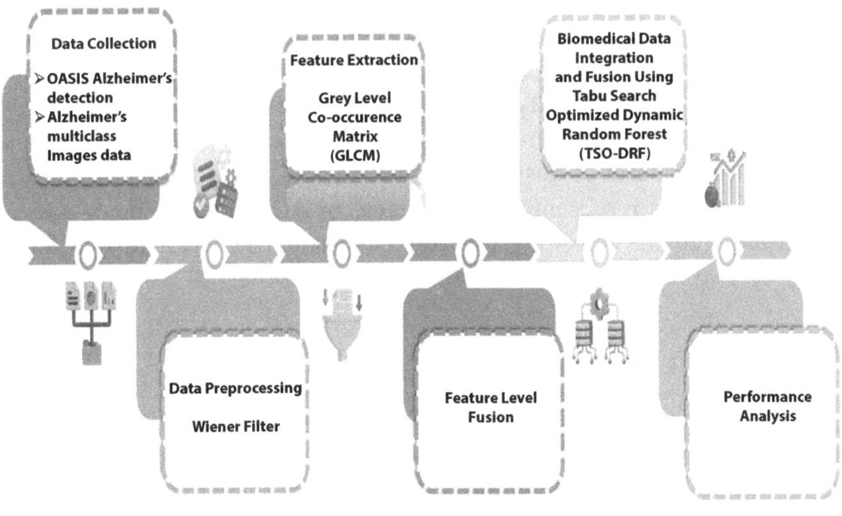

Figure 21.1 Overall flow for biomedical data integration and fusion. (Source: Own elaboration).

21.3.1 Data Collection

The research utilized open-source datasets, OASIS Alzheimer's Detection and Alzheimer multiclass image data, collected from Kaggle. These datasets include imaging and diagnostic information essential for Alzheimer's disease analysis and classification.

21.3.2 OASIS Alzheimer's Detection

The dataset was collected from the Kaggle website at https://www.kaggle.com/datasets/ninadaithal/imagesoasis/data. The 80,000 brain MRI images in the OASIS MRI dataset were used. Based on the course of Alzheimer's, the images have been categorized into four classes. To analyze and identify early indicators of Alzheimer's disease, the dataset attempts to offer a useful resource. The 3D MRI images that have been transformed into 2D slices of brain scans (in the NIfTI format, converted to JPG for training) are included in the OASIS MRI dataset. Based on the clinical dementia rating values and the given metadata, patients were classified into four classes: MOD, VMD, MID, and NMD. The many stages of Alzheimer's disease progression can be identified and studied due to these classes.

21.3.3 Alzheimer Multiclass Image Data

The dataset was obtained from the open-source Kaggle website: https://www.kaggle.com/datasets/aryansinghal10/alzheimers-multiclass-dataset-equal-and-augmented. The Alzheimer's disease Multiclass Dataset contains approximately 44,000 MRI images categorized into four distinct classes based on the severity of Alzheimer's disease. All images are skull-stripped and clean of non-brain tissue. Alzheimer's Disease Multiclass Dataset: This dataset consists of 2D MRI images (already converted into JPG format) that represent different stages of Alzheimer's. The dataset is organized into the following four directories, each representing a four-class MOD, VMD, MID, and NMD.

21.3.4 Data Preprocessing Using the Weiner Filter

The Weiner filter, which can be defined in the frequency or time domain, is one of the most basic techniques for noise reduction. By minimizing the image of interest and its evaluation, the time domain Weiner filter is obtained. In terms of minimal mean square error, the Wiener filter is perfect for recovering noisy images. This approach is particularly valuable in biomedical data integration and fusion, where accurate noise reduction is crucial for ensuring the reliability and clarity of biomedical data. The original images $e(w,z)$, and all the stationary noise $m(w,z)$ are assumed to be the cause of the detected image $h(w,z)$ shown in Equation 21.1.

$$h(w,z) = e(w,z) + m(w,z) \tag{21.1}$$

Where there is no mean or variance and the noise is spectrally white. According to the Weiner filter, the transfer function is in Equation 21.2.

$$G(v,u) = \frac{o_e(v,u)}{o_e(v,u) + \sigma^2} \tag{21.2}$$

The expression for noise-adaptive Wiener filtering in the context of image retrieval, essential for improving the quality of fused biomedical data, is provided in Equation 21.3.

$$e'(w,z) = n_e(w,z) + \frac{\sigma_e^2(w,z)}{\sigma_e^2(w,z) + \sigma_e^2(w,z)} \big(h(w,z) - n_e(w,z)\big) \tag{21.3}$$

By effectively addressing noise, the Wiener filter supports the integration and fusion of diverse biomedical data sources, ensuring enhanced data quality for downstream analyses and applications.

21.3.5 Feature Extraction Using Grey Level Co-Occurrence Matrix

In the context of biomedical data integration and fusion, the GLCM is particularly useful for extracting texture features from medical images. The spatial arrangement of pixel intensities can reveal important characteristics of the tissue or organ being studied. It is possible to specify the distance and direction of the spatial relationship between two adjacent pixels in a variety of ways; by default, it is between a pixel and its rightmost neighbor. Because different perspectives might emphasize particular traits or anomalies within the tissue structure, these four potential spatial correlations are essential for medical picture analysis. For a given image J of size $L \times L$, Equation 21.4 defines the components of a displacement vector's $\times H$ $GLCM$ $N_{CO}c = (= c_w, c_z)$.

$$N_{CO} = \sum_{w=1}^{L} \sum_{z=1}^{L} \begin{cases} 1, if\ J(w,z) = j\ and\ J(w + c_w, z + c_z) = i \\ 0, otherwise \end{cases} \quad (21.4)$$

This approach helps in the integration of texture features from multiple biomedical data sources, enabling a more comprehensive analysis and fusion of different image modalities for enhanced diagnostic accuracy.

21.3.6 Data Integration and Fusion Using Feature-Level Fusion

The performance of the recognition system is made more reliable and stable. This is particularly beneficial in biomedical data integration and fusion, where combining different types of biometric data enhances diagnostic capabilities by providing more comprehensive information. Some techniques are applied to biomedical datasets such as the OASIS Alzheimer's Detection dataset and the Alzheimer multiclass image data, which are used to test the fused biometric system in the context of health monitoring and disease detection. Following the extraction of each trait's features independently, the fusion technique is implemented using the sequential rule. By leveraging multiple feature extraction techniques, the system achieves a more robust and accurate classification, crucial for biomedical data fusion in health diagnostics feature extraction techniques, and the fused feature set is defined in Equation 21.5.

$$fusion_{EI} = \{W_{E2}, \ldots W_{Fq}, Z_{J1}, Z_{J2}, \ldots Z_{Jn}\} \quad (21.5)$$

In this case, W_{Fq} stands for the vector-size r facial features and Z_{Jn} for the vector-size n features, where n and r are are not equal. The fusion of these multimodal biometric features plays a key role in integrating and fusing diverse biomedical data, leading to improved accuracy and stability in diagnostic systems.

21.3.7 Biomedical Data Integration and Fusion Using Tabu Search Optimized Dynamic Random Forest

The TSO-DRF is a hybrid framework combining TSO and DRF for efficient classification tasks. Tabu search is employed to optimize features ensuring the most relevant features are used, while DRF dynamically adapts tree structures to handle varying data complexities. This integration enhances predictive accuracy and reduces computational overhead. The TSO-DRF model is particularly effective in multi-class classification and high-dimensional datasets, such as biomedical data integration and fusion.

21.3.8 Dynamic Random Forest

Dynamic random forest is a powerful ensemble learning approach that exhibits excellent performance in dealing with high-dimensional biomedical data. As it can perform both classification and regression tasks, it is crucial in health condition diagnosis using biomedical data for Alzheimer's disease. Its capability to handle noisy data, a common characteristic in Alzheimer's disease data processing, and its strong generalization ability make it ideal for early disease detection in population health settings. In biomedical data integration and fusion, the DRF approach is particularly beneficial for combining data from multiple sources or modalities. It can process images from various biomedical data, medical imaging, and patient health records, integrating to provide a more comprehensive diagnostic tool. The boosting technique in DRF adjusts the weight of each sample based on the corresponding error rate, increasing the weight for misclassified samples and reducing it for correctly classified ones. This adaptability enhances the robustness of the model when applied to biomedical data, where varying image quality and noise.

In the DRF for biomedical data analysis, a single sub-forest is generated, and all sample weights are altered through that sub-forest. However, this alteration excludes the contribution of previous rounds, creating a dynamic model that continuously adapts to new data. In the synthesis of image processing, all constructed trees are treated as a new DRF for subsequent rounds of tree construction, combining the boosting and bagging approaches to improve the handling of biomedical image data. This iterative process helps in adjusting the weight of each sample in the training set to 1N/where N is the total number of samples. Using the DRF technique, the first tree is built, and all sample weights are adjusted accordingly. The second tree is then constructed using the bootstrap procedure, with the weights of the samples updated through the first and second trees, forming a sub-forest. Subsequent trees are trained on the reweighted data, continuously improving the robustness of the model, which is essential for analyzing complex biomedical images from integrated data sources.

Dynamic random forest introduces a novel approach to feature selection, particularly useful in biomedical data fusion. The number of features at each node is randomly chosen based on the average inherent information of each feature, and random feature selection is used. In biological applications, this allows the model to focus on the most important features for image interpretation, enhancing overall diagnostic accuracy. In the context of biomedical data integration, this capability is crucial for synthesizing information from diverse data sources, such as genetic data measurements, and clinical history, to produce more accurate predictions. Given the current forest's ability to predict the class of a sample, Bernard applied the following method to adjust the sample weight, as described in Equation 21.6:

$$d(w,z) = \frac{1}{|g_{oob}|} \times \sum\nolimits_{g_j \in g_{oob}} J(g_j(w) = z) \tag{21.6}$$

The output of the jth classifier is represented by $g_j(w)$, the $g(w,\theta_j)$ equivalent symbol, where w is the input sample z is its actual class; and J is an instruction function. This mechanism makes the attention always on difficult samples, while well-classified cases play a minor role in the training of the other trees. The weight adjustment formula for a sample w is given by Equation 21.7.

$$X(d(w,z)) = 1 - d(w,z) \tag{21.7}$$

This adjustment formula helps refine the model's learning process by prioritizing more difficult samples, improving its overall accuracy in integrating and analyzing biomedical data for more reliable health predictions and diagnostics.

21.3.9 Tabu Search Optimization

The TSO algorithm to optimize parameters for the music emotion category focuses on optimizing biomedical disease data prediction, the methodology presented can also be applied to biomedical data integration and fusion. By optimizing hyperparameters for ML models, TSO can improve the handling of complex biomedical datasets, where various modalities of data need to be fused effectively for accurate health diagnosis.

This integration is particularly relevant in applications like disease prediction, where temporal dependencies in biomedical image data need to be captured and analyzed over time. Equations 21.8–21.14 can be extended to model biomedical data systems by applying similar principles to various biomedical image data types, improving the classification and prediction of health conditions:

$$R_K = \frac{Q_K}{Y_0}, Y_0 = \sqrt{\frac{K_{T_1}}{D_t}}, \omega_0 = \frac{1}{\sqrt{K_{T_1} D_t}} \tag{21.8}$$

$$\frac{Y_{in}(i\omega_m)}{Y_0} = \left((i\omega_m + \frac{1}{i\omega_m}\right) + \frac{\frac{i\omega_m}{K_o}\left(\frac{i\omega_m}{K_t} + R_K\right)}{\frac{i\omega_m}{K_o} + \frac{i\omega_m}{K_t} + R_K} \tag{21.9}$$

$$\left|J_{K_{T_1}}\right| = \frac{4U_{jm}}{\pi|Y_{jm}(i\omega_m|}, uBA_1(s) = \frac{4U_{jm}}{\pi} sin\omega_{t^s} \tag{21.10}$$

$$N_u = \left|\frac{i\omega_m RK^{K_T}}{RK^{K_m K_T} + i\omega_m(K_m + K_t)}\right| \frac{1}{|Y_{jm}(i\omega_m)|}$$

$$O_{core} = l_j|\Delta A|^{\beta-\alpha} e_t|2\Delta A|^{\alpha}\left(\frac{1}{2}\right)^{1-\alpha} \tag{21.11}$$

$$l_j = \frac{l_d}{2^{\beta-1}\pi^{\alpha-1}(1.1044 + \frac{6.8244}{\alpha + 1.354}}, \Delta A = \frac{U_{Sq,o}}{2M_o B_f e_t} \tag{21.12}$$

$$O_{Sq} = P_{core} + P_{cu}, P_{cu} = Q_o J_{o,rms}^2 + Q_T J_{S,rms}^2 \tag{21.13}$$

$$P_{rec} = 2U_E J_{O,rms} \tag{21.14}$$

By using advanced ML techniques such as the TSO-DRF method to accurately predict the biomedical data, combining TSO with DRF can be used to adaptively capture the temporal dependencies of biomedical image data. By identifying superior configurations, TSO enhances the DRF model's ability to analyze longitudinal medical data, improving the diagnostic performance for complex diseases.

The TSO-DRF focuses on hybrid methods for classification and prediction enhancement using optimization and ML, as well as the integration and fusion of biomedical data. The framework also improves feature selection and the fusion process using images. The TSO algorithm is used to alter the diversity of features to ensure pertinent data is made available for training the models. Many intricate and varied components of biomedical data prompted the need to adopt DRF because of its flexible and robust characteristics. When both types of data are integrated, the predictive accuracy of the Alzheimer's disease onset improves further. The above hybrid technique is an efficient medicine for the problem of multimodal biomedical data integration.

21.4 Results

The image integration techniques for Alzheimer's disease detection and classification, a set of improved and noisy image data, was created. Thereafter, to enhance the features of such image data and to clean the data from the surface noise, the Wiener filter was applied. This approach integrates TSO for the improvement of features and DRF to achieve effective classification. In this work, Alzheimer's disease is divided into four subclasses, namely MID, VMD, MOD, and NMD. These classes are used for assessing classification tasks in two ways: as a binary classification and as a multi-class classification. This way allows achieving the most thorough research of the dynamics within the disease. It also leads to enhanced clarity of diagnosis and individual treatment schemes. The evaluation of model performance was conducted by assessing performance metrics such as accuracy, precision, recall, and F1 score.

21.4.1 Comparison Between Binary Class Classification and Multi-Class Classification Using Stages of Alzheimer's Disease Data

Binary classification reduces the problem of classification into two classes – for example, distinguishing healthy people (NMD) from patients with Alzheimer's disease (MID, VMD, MOD). Such an approach aims at the larger separation and is simpler. However, it may miss the smaller one. Multi-class classification tackles the issue by classifying four different stages (NMD, MID, VMD, MOD), thus giving a clearer picture of the advancement of the disease. The ratio of occurrences accurately classified to instances in the data is known as accuracy, which is aimed to reveal model performance. Precision highlights the model's dependability in detecting pertinent outcomes by quantifying the ratio of real positive predictions to all anticipated positives. The ability to identify pertinent cases is highlighted by recall, also known as sensitivity, which computes the ratio of true positives to all actual positives. The F1 score is the harmonic mean of precision and recall, balancing both metrics to evaluate model performance under class imbalance.

Table 21.1 and Figure 21.2 indicates classification metrics for different stages of dementia. The MID (Vs) NMD stage achieves the highest precision (89.34%) and F1-score (90.43%), indicating robust performance. Conversely, MOD (Vs) NMD records lower accuracy (71.82%) and F1-score (68.46%), suggesting more challenging differentiation. The highest accuracy (95.82%) is achieved in MID (Vs) VMD.

Table 21.2 and Figure 21.3 highlights the performance of multi-class classification across dementia stages. The "NMD (Vs) MID (Vs) MOD" stage achieves the highest accuracy (94.26%) and precision (92.31%), indicating effective classification. Meanwhile, the "MID (Vs) MOD (Vs) VMD"

Table 21.1 Performance metrics for dementia stages for binary class classification.

Stages	Accuracy (%)	Precision (%)	Recall (%)	F1-score (%)
MID (Vs) VMD	95.82	73.45	81.82	72.24
MOD (Vs) NMD	71.82	69.23	73.42	68.46
MID (Vs) NMD	90.41	89.34	86.82	90.43
VMD (Vs) MOD	93.26	91.09	86.32	83.21

Note: Mild Demented (MID), Very Mild Demented (VMD), Moderate Demented (MOD), Non-Moderate Demented (NMD)

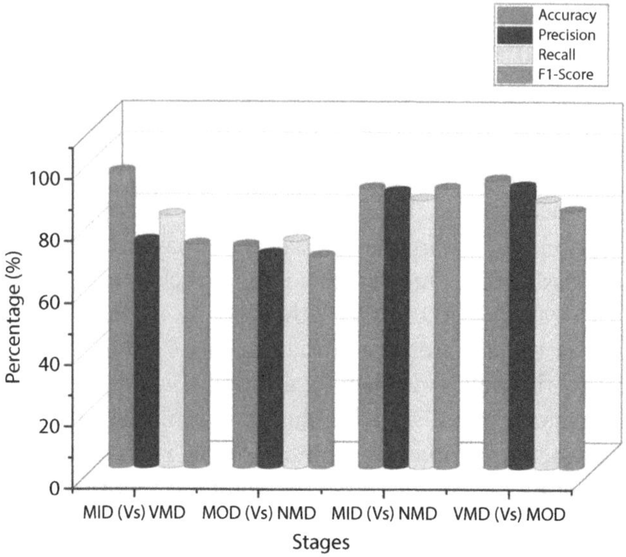

Figure 21.2 Comparison of binary class classification. (Source: Own elaboration).

Table 21.2 Multi-class classification metrics for dementia stages.

Stages	Accuracy (%)	Precision (%)	Recall (%)	F1-score (%)
MID (Vs) MOD (Vs) VMD	92.43	86.28	91.3	89.44
NMD (Vs) MID (Vs) MOD	94.26	92.31	89.34	91.6

stage shows a slightly lower accuracy (92.43%) but maintains better recall (91.30%) and F1-score (89.44%), demonstrating balanced performance.

21.4.2 Accuracy Comparison Between With and Without Optimization

The accuracy comparison between the TSO-DRF and the DRF highlights the effectiveness of optimization. The TSO-DRF demonstrates superior accuracy due to the tabu search algorithm's ability to fine-tune feature selection and parameter optimization during biomedical data integration and fusion. This ensures improved classification performance compared to the unoptimized DRF model.

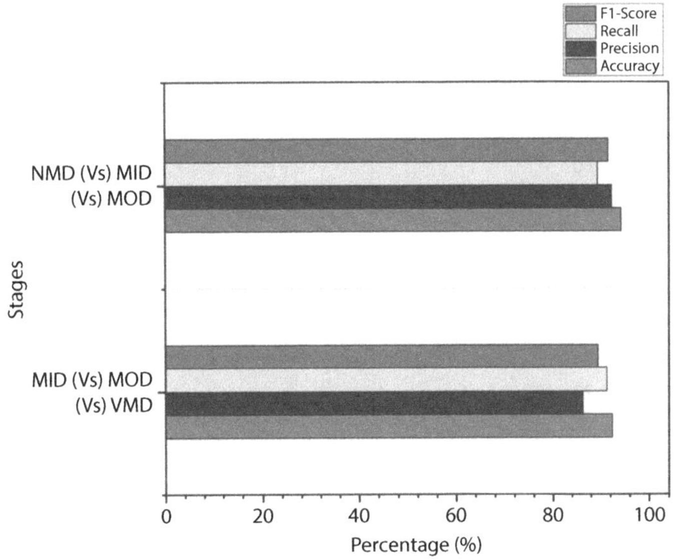

Figure 21.3 Comparison of stages in multi-class classification. (Source: Own elaboration).

Table 21.3 and Figure 21.4 compare the accuracy of the DRF model and the TSO-DRF model. The TSO-DRF model consistently outperforms the DRF model across all stages. For example, in the "MID (Vs) VMD" stage, the accuracy increases significantly from 83.62% to 94.62%. Similarly, for "NMD (Vs) MID (Vs) MOD," the accuracy improves from 83.41% to 95.64%, showcasing the effectiveness of the optimization technique in enhancing model performance.

Table 21.3 Accuracy comparison of DRF and TSO-DRF for dementia stages.

Stages	DRF (without optimization)	TSO-DRF (with optimization)
MID (Vs) VMD	83.62	94.62
MOD (Vs) NMD	80.42	93.21
MID (Vs) NMD	81.46	90.64
VMD (Vs) MOD	92.42	91.29
MID (Vs) MOD (Vs) VMD	83.41	95.64
NMD (Vs) MID(Vs) MOD	82.15	93.82

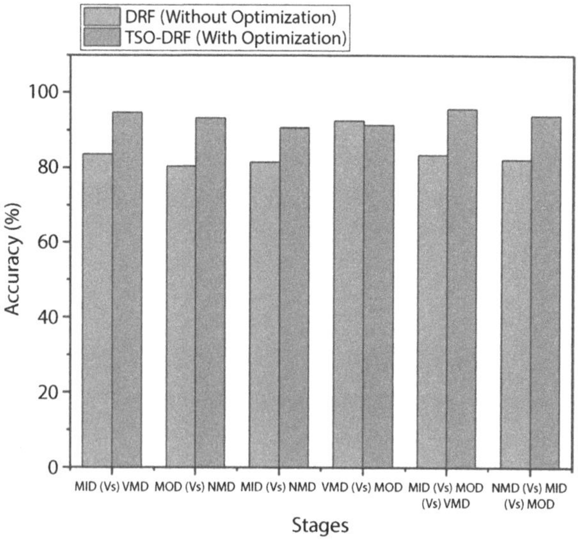

Figure 21.4 Accuracy for with and without optimization. (Source: Own elaboration).

21.5 Discussion

Comparing and categorizing the stages of cognitive impairment caused by Alzheimer's disease, the TSO-DRF model reliably outperformed the corresponding DRF non-optimized model, demonstrating strong improvements in both binary and multiclass classification tasks. In binary classification, the optimized method showed a better ability to discriminate stages than the non-optimized method particularly the extreme cases where the features were more overlapping and difficult to classify. Similarly, in the case of multiclass classification, the model was also able to deal with multiple stages and the small differences that come between quite well and stayed accurate, as well as balanced in all metrics. The model comparison with and without optimization describes the benefits of the optimization approach even more clearly. The TSO-DRF showed better accuracy, precision, recall, and F1 score, proving its efficiency in feature subset improvement and learning enhancement. The findings support the claim that the methodology of optimization can be useful in enhancing classification accuracy, especially in imaging of diseases such as Alzheimer's which are detailed and intricate.

21.6 Conclusion

Biomedical data integration and fusion involve combining diverse data sources to generate comprehensive insights and data coherence and support advanced analytics for improved decision-making in healthcare. It facilitates accurate disease diagnosis, personalized treatment, and biomedical research. The TSO-DRF method performs significantly better in the classification of various stages of Alzheimer's disease than the non-optimized version. High levels of accuracy were obtained by the model for binary and multi-class classifications indicating its strength in classifying different stages of dementia that are closely related. The optimization method involved the problem of feature selection and classification and the increase in accuracy observed its usefulness. Using an optimization method, TSO-DRF performed better than for the comparisons such as MID (Vs) VMD-94.62%, MOD (Vs) NMD – 93.21%, MID (Vs) NMD -90.64%, VMD (Vs) MOD -91.29%, MID (Vs) MOD (Vs) VMD-95.64%, and NMD (Vs) MID (Vs) MOD-93.82%. There are several difficulties in biomedical data integration such as the presence of several data types, data quality issues, and the problem of processing capacity in fused data where the amount of data is large. The presence of unclean and incomplete datasets can affect the performance of the model. To enhance the data fusion processes by creating new algorithms that would incorporate real-time data systems with different modalities and compressed quantum computing systems for processing. Improved interpretability of the fused systems would also facilitate clinical decisions.

References

1. Azghadi, Rahimi, M., *et al.*, Hardware implementation of deep network accelerators towards healthcare and biomedical applications. *IEEE Trans. Biomed. Circuits Syst.*, 14, 6, 1138–1159, 2020, https://doi.org/10.1109/TBCAS.2020.3013194.
2. Khanna, A., *et al.*, Internet of things and deep learning enabled healthcare disease diagnosis using biomedical electrocardiogram signals. *Expert Syst.*, 40, 4, e12864, 2023, https://doi.org/10.1111/exsy.12864.
3. Liu, Y., Chen, Y., Han, L., Bioinformatics: Advancing biomedical discovery and innovation in the era of big data and artificial intelligence. *Innov. Med.*, 1, 1, 100012, 2023, https://doi.org/10.59717/j.xinn-med.2023.100012.

4. Zhang, L., *et al.*, Analytics methods and tools for integration of biomedical data in medicine, in: *Artificial Intelligence in Medicine*, pp. 113–129, Academic Press, Cambridge, MA, 2021, https://doi.org/10.1016/B978-0-12-821259-2.00007-7.
5. Banerjee, A., *et al.*, Emerging trends in IoT and big data analytics for biomedical and health care technologies, in: *Handbook of data science approaches for biomedical engineering*, pp. 121–152, 2020, https://doi.org/10.1016/B978-0-12-818318-2.00005-2.
6. Su, C., *et al.*, Network embedding in biomedical data science. *Briefings Bioinf.*, 21, 1, 182–197, 2020, https://doi.org/10.1093/bib/bby117.
7. Manickam, P., *et al.*, Artificial intelligence (AI) and Internet of medical things (IoMT) assisted biomedical systems for intelligent healthcare. *Biosensors*, 12, 8, 562, 2022, https://doi.org/10.3390/bios12080562.
8. Wawale, S.G., *et al.*, Biomedical waste management using IoT tracked and fuzzy classified integrated technique. *Hum.-centric Comput. Inf. Sci.*, 12, 32, 32, 2022, https://doi.org/10.22967/HCIS.2022.12.032.
9. Mansour, R.F., *et al.*, Optimal deep learning based fusion model for biomedical image classification. *Expert Syst.*, 39, 3, e12764, 2022, https://doi.org/10.1111/exsy.12764.
10. Balasubramanian, Kumar, N., *et al.*, Optimization of process parameters to minimize circularity error and surface roughness in fused deposition modeling (FDM) using Taguchi method for biomedical implant fabrication. *Adv. Manuf. Polym. Compos. Sci.*, 10, 1, 2406156, 2024, https://doi.org/10.1080/20550340.2024.2406156.
11. Willemink, M.J., *et al.*, Preparing medical imaging data for machine learning. *Radiology*, 295, 1, 4–15, 2020, https://doi.org/10.1148/radiol.2020192224.
12. Pesquita, C., Towards Semantic Integration for Explainable Artificial Intelligence in the Biomedical Domain. *HEALTHINF*, 2021, https://doi.org/10.5220/0010389707470753.
13. National Academies of Sciences, Engineering, and Medicine, *Advances in Multimodal Artificial Intelligence to Enhance Environmental and Biomedical Data Integration: Proceedings of a Workshop–in Brief*, 2023, https://doi.org/10.17226/27202.
14. Hoffman, J.M., *et al.*, Biomedical data science and informatics challenges to implementing pharmacogenomics with electronic health records. *Annu. Rev. Biomed. Data Sci.*, 3, 1, 289–314, 2020, https://doi.org/10.1146/annurev-biodatasci-020320-093614.
15. Cai, Z., *et al.*, Machine learning for multi-omics data integration in cancer. *Iscience*, 25, 2, 2022, https://doi.org/10.1016/j.isci.2022.103769.
16. Ali, F., Kalva, S.N., Koc, M., Advancements in 3D printing techniques for biomedical applications: a comprehensive review of materials consideration, post-processing, applications, and challenges. *Discov. Mater.*, 4, 1, 53, 2024, https://doi.org/10.1007/s43939-024-00115-4.

22

Biomedical Robotics and Assistive Technologies

Prasad P. S.[1]*, Rourab Paul[2], Joany R. M.[3], G. Padma Priya[4], Sweta Jethava[5] and Ankita Thakur[6]

[1]*Department of Computer Science and Engineering, Presidency University, Bangalore, Karnataka, India*

[2]*Department of Computer Science and Engineering, Siksha 'O' Anusandhan (Deemed to be University), Bhubaneswar, Odisha, India*

[3]*Department of Electronics and Communication Engineering, Sathyabama Institute of Science and Technology, Chennai, Tamil Nadu, India*

[4]*Department of Chemistry and Biochemistry, Jain (Deemed-to-be University), Bangalore, Karnataka, India*

[5]*Department of MCA, Parul University, Vadodara, Gujarat, India*

[6]*Maharishi School of Engineering & Technology, Maharishi University of Information Technology, Uttar Pradesh, India*

Abstract

Integrating biomedical science and robotics has innovated healthcare by realizing precise interventions and enhancing patient care through assistive technologies. These systems involve advanced engineering, artificial intelligence (AI), and human-centric design to address the diverse needs of the medical field. Among these are assistive technologies, which empower people by enhancing mobility and rehabilitation and improving quality of life (QoL). This review explains four predominant types of biomedical robotics and assistive technologies: surgical robotics, rehabilitation robotics, assistive robotics, and wearable assistive devices. Surgical robotics aims at further precision and more minimally persistent procedures using systems such as the da Vinci Surgical System. Tools that can be used

**Corresponding author*: prasadps@presidencyuniversity.in
Rourab Paul: ORCID: 0000-0001-5322-281X
Joany R. M.: ORCID: https://orcid.org/0000-0002-2089-8503
G. Padma Priya: ORCID: 0000-0004911-1823
Sweta Jethava: ORCID: 0009-0005-7131-5610
Ankita Thakur: ORCID: 0009-0009-8301-5243

Satya Prakash Yadav, Abhay Bansal and Victor Hugo C. de Albuquerque (eds.) Computational Intelligence in Biomedical Internet of Medical Things, (383–400) © 2026 Scrivener Publishing LLC

for physical and neurological rehabilitation are being researched in rehabilitation robotics, such as exoskeletons and robotic arms used for training repetitive tasks. Devices that support people who have disabilities, from robotic wheelchairs to interactive humanoid companions, constitute the subject area of assistive robotics. Wearable assistive devices highlight innovations like hybrid exosuits and prosthetics, combining soft and rigid technologies for enhanced functionality and comfort. It delves into each type, emphasizing their applications, benefits, and challenges while exploring their potential to transform healthcare. The discussion underscores the importance of affordability and accessibility in ensuring widespread adoption and effective integration into healthcare systems.

***Keywords*:** Biomedical, artificial intelligence, technologies, wearable robotics

22.1 Introduction

The intelligent integration of perception and action is known as robotics [1]. Although traditionally it has meant that programmable robots can ensure locomotive tasks, robotics is now focusing on almost limitless fields of research, broadening its range of applications. Every industry uses robots, which provide an important function in everyday life. Generally speaking, robots have been used in the workforce to replace manual labor to improve process effectiveness. Robots are used extensively in a variety of industries, including healthcare, automotive, aviation, food manufacturing, and agriculture [2]. Robotic technology is rapidly being reassessed and applied to healthcare, logistics, and disinfection to stop the propagation of bacteria and viruses. Moreover, service robots are needed to help nurses and other healthcare professionals improve efficiency, reduce additional interpersonal contact, and make up for a large rise in healthcare worker losses brought on by the disease's highly contagious characteristics. Robotic applications could promise sustainable and cost-effective healthcare delivery without sacrificing treatment quality. While robot technology can be applied in a variety of contexts, it has the potential to significantly impact clinical care [3]. Surgical devices, assistive robotics, and robots that resemble the human body for instance prostheses, body-part simulators, and artificial organs are the three primary categories of medical robots, which are robotic equipment used in the health sciences for drug administration, diagnosis, and surgery [4].

Biomedical robotics and assistive technologies are revolutionizing the healthcare sector by merging engineering innovation with the intricacies of medical science. These technologies aim to improve the quality of life (QoL) for persons with cognitive and physical disabilities while advancing the efficiency and precision of healthcare delivery. The field encompasses a wide range of devices and systems, including robotic prosthetics, exoskeletons, surgical robots, rehabilitation technologies, and assistive devices for daily living. These tools are designed to augment human capabilities, restore lost functions, or assist healthcare professionals in diagnosing, treating, and managing various medical conditions. With advancements in artificial intelligence (AI), sensors, and human-robot interaction (HRI), biomedical robotics is becoming more adaptive and personalized, offering significant benefits to patients, clinicians, and society at large [5]. Soft, reasonably priced, low-profile, lightweight, and portable wearable assistive technology can considerably improve QoL and recovery pathways for people with disabilities of the upper body. Numerous rehabilitative and assistive gadgets have been created. To assist those who have difficulties in their upper bodies [6]. One of the key motivating factors behind the growing prominence of biomedical robotics is the increasing global aging population. As the elderly population rises, there is a greater need for assistive technologies that can enable older individuals to live independently for longer periods. Additionally, the prevalence of chronic conditions and disabilities, often resulting from accidents, aging, or congenital disorders, has created a strong demand for advanced medical devices that restore or augment lost functionality. In response to these needs, biomedical robotics has focused on designing systems that provide physical support, rehabilitation, and healthcare assistance to individuals with mobility impairments, as well as those recovering from surgeries or neurological events like strokes [7].

Aim and key contribution: This research aims to explore the transformative potential of biomedical robotics and assistive technologies in healthcare. It focuses on key innovations such as surgical robots, rehabilitation devices, assistive robotics, and wearable assistive technologies, emphasizing their applications in enhancing mobility, precision, and independent living. By highlighting advancements in AI, sensors, and human-centric design, it contributes to understanding how these technologies address critical healthcare needs, improve QoL, and adapt to a rapidly aging global population.

The organization of the paper: Section 22.2 explains surgical robotics; Section 22.3 explains rehabilitation robotics; Section 22.4 explains assistive robotics; Section 22.5 explains wearable assistive robotics; Section 22.6 gives the results; Sections 22.7 and 22.8 provide the discussion and conclusion.

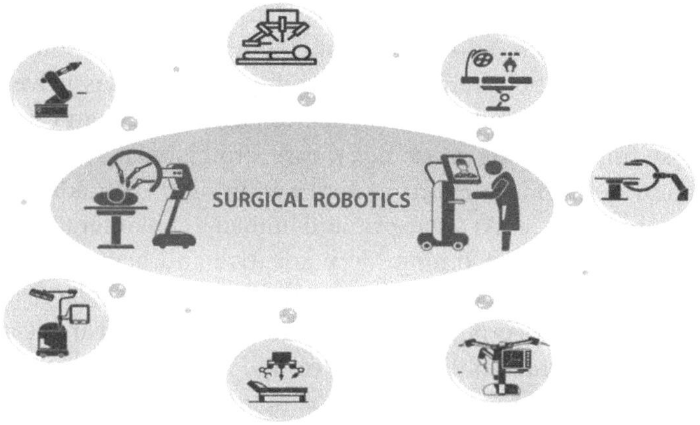

Figure 22.1 Surgical robotics illustration. (Source: Own elaboration).

22.2 Surgical Robotics

Surgical robotics is an innovative field that integrates robotic systems into medical procedures, enhancing precision, dexterity, and visualization. These systems enable minimally invasive surgeries (MIS) with smaller incisions, reduced recovery times, and fewer complications. Technologies like MAKO Robotic-Arm Assisted Surgery and da Vinci Surgical System are widely used for urology, orthopedics, and general surgery, offering unparalleled control and access to complex surgical sites. Applications extend to ophthalmology, urology, neurosurgery, cardiothoracic surgery, gynecology, etc., where robotic systems ensure precise and targeted interventions [8]. Despite challenges like high costs and the need for specialized training, advancements in AI, telepresence surgery, and augmented reality are driving the future of surgical robotics, making healthcare safer and more efficient. Figure 22.1 illustrates surgical robotics.

22.2.1 Human-Robot Interaction

Minimally invasive surgery aims to improve surgical treatment by focusing on smaller, fewer incisions, safer, more effective, faster procedures, and user-friendly manipulation. However, its development faces challenges, particularly in the core surgical instruments, such as endoscopes. The next generation of medical informatics, MIS surgical mechanism, will become more precise, flexible, and multifunctional to improve surgical performance.

In addition to increasing their workload and psychological strain, this will make it challenging for surgeons to operate hand-held devices. The development of intelligent robot-assisted platforms is a significant MIS trend. The two components of HRI in MIS are the surgeon-robot structure contact and the patient-robot system interaction. The former prioritizes gathering all available patient-side data, whereas the latter focuses on reliable and quick information transfer among robot-assisted and surgeon's platforms. Sensors are essential to MIS because they give these platforms thorough and precise information. Environmental discernment, proprioception, and interactive insight are the three categories into which it can be separated. Since information from a single type of sensor is typically less valuable or meaningless, data fusion of various sensor types is essential. The perfectly incorporated sensing elements must meet several necessities, including compatibility, elasticity, and avoiding stress concentrators. Interface matching involving sensors and surgical instruments is also essential [9].

22.2.2 Haptics

The creation and application of suitable instrumentation, such as the placement and selection of sensors on or inside surgical instruments to monitor multidimensional forces acting on the instruments, are essential to haptics in surgical robots. This procedure is complicated by space constraints and clinical limitations. To regulate the needle's gripping force during procedures like suturing, the surgeon must rely on shear force, skin stretch, and felt normal force. The intricacy of instrumenting surgical instruments for force sensing is highlighted by the fact that no one sensor technology can offer all these details during surgical procedures. Two approaches to the development of sensorized tools are as follows adding sensors to already-existing surgical instruments, such as those found in da Vinci surgical robotic systems, and creating new instruments with sensors built in. Existing tools can be sensorized by altering their design and constructing to enable force sensing. To enable sensitive force records, the Deutsches Zentrum für Luft- und Raumfahrt surgical system, for instance, features a fastening mechanism close to the tip that flexes slightly during tool-tissue engagement. Capacitive pressure sensors for force distribution maps are one type of specialized instrument made for determining force as the primary function, primarily for soft tissue palpation. Additional examples include wireless palpation and disposable, inexpensive, and customized systems [10].

22.2.3 Leading Surgical Robotic System

Robot-assisted MIS (RAMIS) provides a high-resolution video stream from the surgery site using real-time imaging with an endoscopic camera. Using a surgical console and a human-machine interface (HMI) that depends on the video stream, the surgeon manipulates robotically articulated equipment. With the da Vinci Surgical System being the most widely utilized, robotic assistance has grown because of the collaboration across minimally invasive paradigms. Advanced technological features, safety, and ergonomics, robust evidence of better patient outcomes, focus on procedures that improve QoL, robust training programs, a lack of high-level autonomy, extensive marketing and promotion, and a solution-selling business model are some of the key elements that have contributed to its success [11].

Table 22.1 Key aspects of surgical robotics and leading systems.

Aspect	Details
Overview of surgical robotics	Robotic systems improve precision in MIS, offering reduced recovery times. Examples include da Vinci and MAKO.
Interaction between humans and robots	Emphasizes the collaboration between patients, surgeons, and robotic systems through sensors for enhanced surgical performance.
Role of haptic feedback	Integration of sensors in surgical tools provides tactile feedback, essential for tasks like suturing. Examples include da Vinci's flexing mechanism and capacitive sensors.
Leading robotic systems	Systems like RAMIS and da Vinci use real-time imaging and remote controls to enhance surgical precision and patient outcomes.
da Vinci surgical platform	A widely used Food and Drug Administration-approved robotic system for various surgeries, offering a stereoscopic view and remote control through a console.

da Vinci Surgical System: The most extensively utilized robotic platform in human surgery now is the Food and Drug Administration-approved da Vinci Surgical System. It is frequently utilized in specialties like cardiac surgery, gynecology, urology, and general surgery. With this approach, the surgeon controls three robotic slave arms from a distance *via* a remote console. One arm has a dual-channeled endoscope for taking pictures, while the remote console has a binocular viewfinder for stereoscopic viewing [12]. Table 22.1 provides a summary of the surgical robotic section.

22.3 Rehabilitation Robotics

Rehabilitation robotics leverages advanced robotic systems to assist in the recovery of motor functions for individuals with physical or neurological impairments, promoting neural plasticity and improving QoL. These systems provide task-oriented, repetitive therapy for upper limb, pediatric, and neurological rehabilitation, enhancing therapy precision and engagement.

22.3.1 Advancing Rehabilitation Through Robotics

People with a variety of conditions, including cerebral palsy, diplegia, hemiparesis, and paraplegia, can benefit greatly from robotics technology in lower and upper limb rehabilitation. Patients' involvement in the healthcare process and the efficacy of integrated care pathways are important areas to research. When patients stay cognitively engaged, the extremely repetitive tasks required for robotic treatment can improve. Robotics can stimulate brain plasticity for functional rehabilitation, and robotic games can improve kids' engagement in therapy. Healthcare robotics is a new field that requires further research and assistance to successfully incorporate robotic systems into the lives of patients and the work of physiotherapists. The assessment, rehabilitation, and replacement of lost and irreparable functions are being carried out by new high-tech gadgets, such as wearable robotic exoskeletons. The success of both robotic therapy and conventional therapies depends on assessing the expectations of patients, the attitudes of parents, and the impact on the workplace. Working circumstances and workload should be carefully considered, especially in high-tech systems, to prevent anomalous reactions that can risk patient care and results [13].

- **Upper limb rehabilitation:** Upper limb rehabilitation using robotics focuses on restoring the functional movement of arms and hands for individuals recovering from conditions such as stroke, traumatic brain injuries, or neurological disorders. Robotic devices like the ArmeoSpring [14] or MIT-MANUS (Interactive Motion Technologies) assist patients in performing repetitive, task-oriented exercises that promote neural plasticity and motor recovery. These systems are equipped with sensors to monitor performance, provide real-time feedback, and adjust the difficulty of exercises based on the patient's capabilities. By ensuring exact and consistent movements, robotic rehabilitation enhances the effectiveness of therapy, motivates patients through interactive tasks, and allows for detailed progress tracking. This technology is particularly beneficial in addressing fine motor skills and improving the ability to perform daily activities, such as grasping, lifting, and writing [15].
- **Pediatric rehabilitation:** Pediatric rehabilitation focuses on enhancing the functional abilities and QoL of children with physical, cognitive, or developmental challenges. It encompasses a multidisciplinary approach involving physical therapy, occupational therapy, language therapy, speech, and sometimes psychological support to address a wide range of conditions, such as cerebral palsy, muscular dystrophy, traumatic brain injuries, or developmental delays. The goal is to help children achieve their maximum potential in mobility, communication, self-care, and social participation. Pediatric rehabilitation often integrates individualized treatment plans, family involvement, and adaptive equipment to ensure a supportive environment that fosters growth, independence, and inclusion in daily activities [16, 17].
- **Neurological rehabilitation:** It focuses on restoring function and improving QoL for individuals with neurological conditions such as traumatic brain injury, stroke, Parkinson's disease, or multiple sclerosis. Rehabilitation robotics plays a crucial role in this domain by providing repetitive, task-oriented therapy that promotes neural plasticity the brain's capability to rearrange and adapt following injury. These robotic systems assist in retraining motor skills by guiding precise, controlled movements of affected limbs, often

incorporating real-time feedback and performance tracking. Advanced technologies like brain-computer interfaces facilitate straight communication between the brain and robotic devices, permitting patients with brutal impairments to regain some control over their movements. By integrating AI and adaptive algorithms, these systems personalize therapy to the patient's progress, optimizing recovery outcomes. Neurological rehabilitation robots not only enhance the intensity and consistency of therapy but also reduce the physical strain on therapists, fostering more efficient and effective recovery pathways [18]. Table 22.2 provides a summary of rehabilitation robotics and their benefits.

Table 22.2 Key areas of rehabilitation robotics and their benefits for patients.

Focus area	Robotic technology	Key benefits for patients	Conditions treated
Upper limb rehabilitation	ArmeoSpring, MIT-MANUS	Restores movement, promotes brain plasticity, improves fine motor skills, and enhances daily activities	Stroke, traumatic brain injuries, neurological disorders
Pediatric rehabilitation	Adaptive devices, exoskeletons	Improves mobility, communication, and self-care; fosters independence and inclusion	Cerebral palsy, muscular dystrophy, developmental delays
Neurological rehabilitation	Robotic exoskeletons, brain-computer interfaces	Provides task-oriented therapy, enhances neural plasticity, reduces therapist strain, personalized therapy	Traumatic brain injury, stroke, multiple sclerosis, Parkinson's disease

22.4 Assistive Robotics

Assistive robotics refers to the development and use of robotic systems designed to support individuals with physical, cognitive, or sensory impairments, improving their QoL and promoting independence. These robots assist with daily tasks such as mobility, communication, and personal care, with examples including robotic wheelchairs [19], exoskeletons [20], and robotic arms [21] that help users perform physical tasks. Additionally, assistive robots provide emotional and social support, such as Pepper [22], a humanoid robot designed to engage with users by recognizing emotions and holding conversations, often used to combat loneliness among the elderly. Other examples include therapy robots for individuals with autism. With advancements in HRI, AI, and safety features, these robots are becoming increasingly adaptable, personalized, and capable of integrating with other healthcare technologies. The goal is to enhance the autonomy of individuals, reduce caregiver burden, and improve rehabilitation outcomes, though challenges remain in terms of affordability, accessibility, and ethical considerations.

22.4.1 Advancements and Challenges in Human-Robot Collaboration for Assistive Robotics

In biomedical applications, machine learning (ML) models have been used to solve robotic problems, especially in service robots. Complex biosignals are interpreted by these models, which is very helpful for service robotics. Over the past decade, assistive robots that help humans with tasks have proliferated in the workplace to achieve greater automation through a division of labor between humans and robots. Nonetheless, human-robot collaboration must continue to focus on HRIs. Robots require input from their environment, which can be obtained from location sensors, thermal imaging data, and visual data. Kinematic data can also be recorded by wearable technology to facilitate human-robot cooperation. In addition, assistive robots can help humans with household or medical duties including meal service in hospitals and assisted living facilities and robot monitoring for people who require round-the-clock care. In complicated situations, speech recognition is a crucial component of HRI because it gives robots additional reference data for autonomous task execution and possibly improves decision-making. Integrating voice recognition software with service robots is still difficult, though. In some circumstances, nonverbal communication techniques like gestures and facial expressions may be more effective. Although surface electromyography sensors can record muscle electrical activity, some users, especially those with disabilities, may refrain from using their extremities to request assistance from robots [23].

22.5 Wearable Assistive Robotics

Wearable assistive robots are made to help people with physical disabilities, with particular emphasis on the joints and lower and upper limbs. Rigid, soft, or hybrid materials can be used to construct these robots. Advanced wearable sensors for human body monitoring and helpful robots have been developed as a result of developments in flexible electronics and materials. Numerous factors, including limb position, motion, heart function, sleep apnea, brain activity, Parkinson's disease, and chemical and electrochemical sensors, can be tracked using these sensors. Soft wearable gloves, ankle-foot robot orthotics, hand exoskeletons, and exosuits are just a few of the products that use wearable sensors to help with everyday tasks and rehabilitation. Figure 22.2 illustrates some examples of wearable assistive robotics.

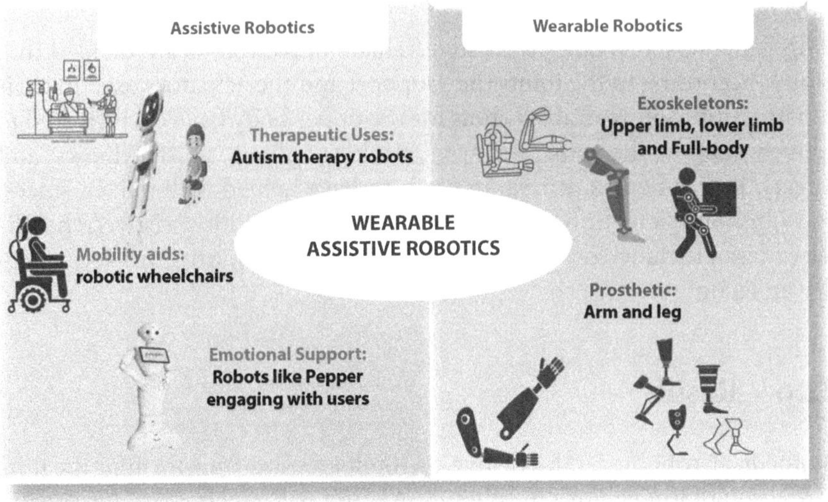

Figure 22.2 Some example robotics of wearable assistive robotics. (Source: Own elaboration).

22.5.1 Hybrid Wearable Assistive Robotics: Advancing Adaptability and Intelligence

To improve the trade-off for assistive robot design, hybrid wearable assistive systems are being created. These systems are made of soft and hard materials that are flexible, lightweight and do not impede the human body's natural motion. This strategy expands the range of sensing modalities and skills that can be included in the hybrid arrangement, offering larger and more diverse datasets that could expand the range of possibilities for learning new ML and control techniques for determining and adjusting the kind and degree of help that is needed. Two essential elements for creating safe and effective assistive robots are their capacity to learn and adjust to their users over time. Present-day wearable assistive robots are made to help people in certain, regulated situations, but it frequently malfunctions when put to the test outside or when the test parameters are slightly altered. Wearable assistive robot architectures can incorporate new ML and control techniques as well as advanced intelligent robot architectures, which encompass modules like data fusion, sensing, perception, decision-making, and control. To develop new robots in an ethical manner and with the necessary regulations, datasets, and standards is essential. The creation of intelligent, effective, and pleasant wearable assistive robotics for patients' everyday use requires a mixture of human factors, ML, sensors, materials, and clinical feedback [24].

In general, soft wearable assistive/rehabilitative robots are divided into groups according to the joints they support and the actuators used in their construction. Soft wearable robots for the upper body have been created to actively support the spine, forearms, neck, shoulders, wrists, elbows, and fingers. Lower-body soft wearable robots have helped with ankles, knees, and hips. Soft actuation techniques frequently used for assistive/rehabilitative tasks include soft pneumatic actuators (SPAs), origami, and cable-driven techniques [25].

22.6 Result

Biomedical robotics and assistive technologies are transforming healthcare through innovations in robotics, AI, and natural language processing (NLP). Robotics aids in rehabilitation, prosthetics, and surgery, offering precision and improving patient outcomes. Assistive technologies, like BERT-based medical Chatbots, enhance communication by understanding patient queries through natural language understanding. Text messaging-based medical diagnosis uses NLP and Fuzzy Logic for real-time diagnosis *via* SMS, increasing accessibility. Additionally, smart ubiquitous chatbots with deep learning sentiment analysis have been crucial during COVID-19, providing support and answering health-related questions. These technologies together improve patient care, making healthcare more efficient and accessible. The outcomes with metrics were given in Table 22.3 and Figure 22.3.

Biomedical robotics and assistive technologies leverage advanced systems like chatbots and AI to enhance healthcare delivery. Using NLP, these systems, such as the CUDoctor chatbot, can interpret user inputs (e.g., symptoms), predict diseases *via* fuzzy logic and support vector machines (SVM), and provide personalized feedback. The chatbot integrates with messaging platforms like Telegram and Twilio for communication. These technologies increase accessibility, allowing patients to receive real-time,

Table 22.3 Summary of AI-based chatbot applications in healthcare with performance metrics.

Reference	AI	Application	Metrics
[26]	BERT-based medical chatbot	Provides personalized healthcare, improves diagnosis, and predicts diseases, addressing chatbot limitations	Accuracy (98%), precision (97%), recall (96%), f1-score (98%)
[27]	COVID chatbot using NLP and deep learning for sentiment analysis	Provides reassurance, increases awareness, and helps manage stress during and after quarantine, potentially slowing the spread of COVID-19	Model-based long short-term memory: precision (86.62%), recall (75.70%), accuracy: (92%), f1-score (80.78%) model-based gated recurrent unit: precision (86.74%), recall (70.46%), accuracy (90%), f1 score (77.75%)

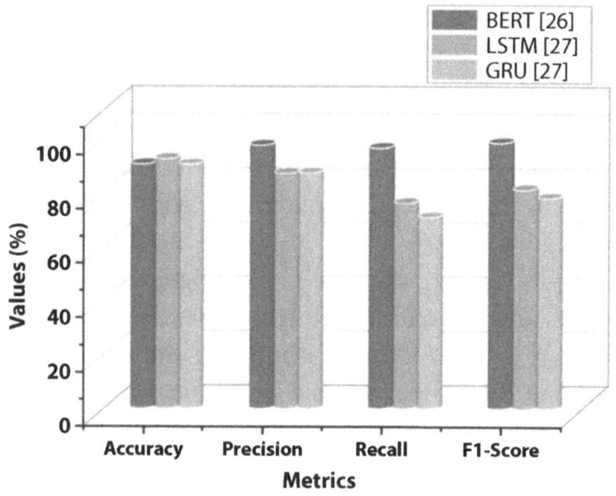

Figure 22.3 Comparison of models across various evaluation metrics.

accurate medical advice and diagnoses, making healthcare more efficient and user-friendly. The system usability scale (SUS) is a widely used tool to measure the usability of products or systems, with scores indicating user satisfaction. In the graph, each question (Q1-Q10) represents a specific aspect of the CUDoctor system, with scores reflecting user feedback on factors like complexity and integration [28], the results are presented in Figure 22.4.

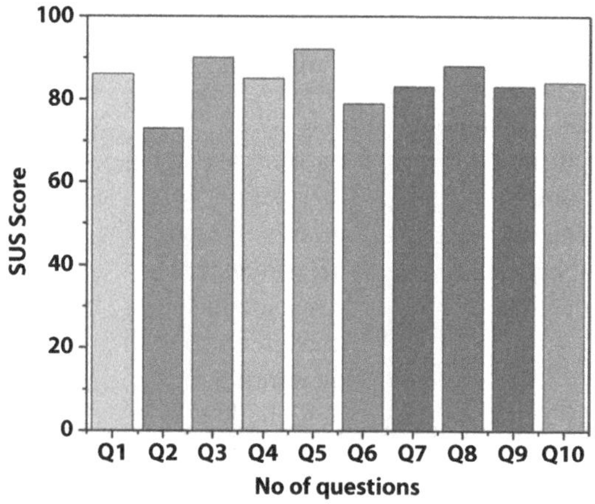

Figure 22.4 Findings from the SUS usability test of CUDoctor.

22.7 Discussion

An in-depth exploration of the integration of robotics is provided in both surgical and assistive technologies, highlighting the transformative impact on patient care and rehabilitation. In surgical robotics, systems like the da Vinci Surgical System are revolutionizing MIS, enhancing precision, and reducing recovery times. It discusses the main developments for HRI, including sensor integration to improve surgeon-robot communication, and the challenges in adapting instruments toward the improvement of force sensing in surgical tools. It also addresses leading systems developed for robotic surgery and points out key aspects like how technologies like RAMIS and da Vinci can improve surgical outcomes. Rehabilitation robotics works look at the use of systems that consist of robots used in the upper limb, pediatric, and neurological rehabilitation, showing how these systems promote neural plasticity and aid in motor recovery. Further, it has discussed assistive robotics and its examples such as robotic wheelchairs and humanoid robots to support people who are either cognitively or physically handicapped. Further, it indicates the importance of wearable assistive robots, particularly for mobility and for rehabilitation with the power of advanced sensors, and ML. In general, the integration of robotics within healthcare is portrayed as a promising field with avenues for improvement in patient outcomes, though affordability and accessibility remain some of the most pressing challenges.

22.8 Conclusion

Biomedical robotics and assistive technologies are changing healthcare, integrating engineering innovation with medical science to meet critical challenges in clinical care, rehabilitation, and independent living. Such technologies are promising avenues for the development of the QoL of people with disabilities, chronic conditions, and the rising healthcare demands of an aging population. The innovations associated with robotic systems, including surgical devices, prosthetics, and wearable assistive technologies, call for personalized and adaptive care. Additionally, AI and sophisticated sensors improve precision, efficiency, and user-friendliness, thus integrating the tools into modern healthcare. This work underlines the great contributions of biomedical robotics in offering revolutionized healthcare delivery aspects with cost-effectiveness and sustainability. There remain, however, the restrictions of high development costs, limited accessibility for underserved populations, and the necessity of rigorous clinical validation. Future work will be to decrease the cost, improve the ability to use these systems, and increase functionality to allow broader accessibility. Advancements in HRI, data security, and ethical considerations will determine the future course of biomedical robotics. These technologies can help redefine healthcare practices by fostering interdisciplinary research and innovation, thus bringing closer the human needs and medical possibilities.

References

1. Hann, *et al.*, 4D printing soft robotics for biomedical applications. *Addit. Manuf.*, 36, 101567, 2020, https://doi.org/10.1016/j.addma.2020.101567.
2. Ashuri, *et al.*, Biomedical soft robots: current status and perspective. *Biomed. Eng. Lett.*, 10, 369–385, 2020, https://doi.org/10.1007/s13534-020-00157-6.
3. Holland, *et al.*, Service robots in the healthcare sector. *Robotics*, 10, 1, 47, 2021, https://doi.org/10.3390/robotics10010047.
4. Boubaker, O., Medical robotics, in: *Control Theory in Biomedical Engineering*, pp. 153–204, 2020, https://doi.org/10.1016/B978-0-12-821350-6.00007-X.
5. Brunete, *et al.*, Smart assistive architecture for the integration of IoT devices, robotic systems, and multimodal interfaces in healthcare environments. *Sensors*, 21, 6, 2212, 2021, https://doi.org/10.3390/s21062212.
6. Shveda, *et al.*, A wearable textile-based pneumatic energy harvesting system for assistive robotics. *Sci. Adv.*, 8, 34, eabo2418, 2022, https://doi.org/10.1126/sciadv.abo2418.
7. Yang, *et al.*, Homecare robotic systems for healthcare 4.0: Visions and enabling technologies. *IEEE J. Biomed. Health Inf.*, 24, 9, 2535–2549, 2020, https://doi.org/10.1109/JBHI.2020.2990529.
8. Huang, *et al.*, A High-Precision Robotic System Design for Microsurgical Applications. *Eng. Proc.*, 58, 1, 66, 2023, https://doi.org/10.3390/ecsa-10-16221.
9. Zhu, *et al.*, Intelligent soft surgical robots for next-generation minimally invasive surgery. *Adv. Intell. Syst.*, 3, 5, 2100011, 2021, https://doi.org/10.1002/aisy.202100011.
10. Patel, *et al.*, Haptic feedback and force-based teleoperation in surgical robotics. *Proc. IEEE*, 110, 7, 1012–1027, 2022, https://doi.org/10.1109/JPROC.2022.3180052.
11. Haidegger, *et al.*, Robot-assisted minimally invasive surgery—Surgical robotics in the data age. *Proc. IEEE*, 110, 7, 835–846, 2022, https://doi.org/10.1109/JPROC.2022.3180350.
12. Tsui, *et al.*, Robotic surgery in ophthalmology, in: *Robot Surgery*, pp. 149–164, INTECH, Croatia, 2010, https://doi.org/10.5772/6902.

13. Gilardi, *et al.*, Robotic technology in pediatric neurorehabilitation. A pilot study of human factors in an italian pediatric hospital. *Int. J. Environ. Res. Public Health*, 17, 10, 3503, 2020, https://doi.org/10.3390/ijerph17103503.
14. Rose, *et al.*, The road forward for upper-extremity rehabilitation robotics. *Curr. Opin. Biomed. Eng.*, 19, 100291, 2021, https://doi.org/10.1016/j.cobme.2021.100291.
15. Nam, *et al.*, An exoneuromusculoskeleton for self-help upper limb rehabilitation after stroke. *Soft Rob.*, 9, 1, 14–35, 2022, https://doi.org/10.1089/soro.2020.0090.
16. Butchart, *et al.*, Child and parent perceptions of acceptability and therapeutic value of a socially assistive robot used during pediatric rehabilitation. *Disabil. Rehabil.*, 43, 2, 163–170, 2021, https://doi.org/10.1080/09638288.2019.1617357.
17. Kokkoni, *et al.*, GEARing smart environments for pediatric motor rehabilitation. *J. NeuroEng. Rehabil.*, 17, 1–15, 2020, https://doi.org/10.1186/s12984-020-0647-0.
18. Morbidi, *et al.*, Assistive robotic technologies for next-generation smart wheelchairs: Codesign and modularity to improve users' quality of life. *IEEE Rob. Autom. Mag.*, 30, 1, 24–35, 2022, https://doi.org/10.1109/MRA.2022.3178965.
19. Hramov, *et al.*, Physical principles of brain–computer interfaces and their applications for rehabilitation, robotics and control of human brain states. *Phys. Rep.*, 918, 1–133, 2021, https://doi.org/10.1016/j.physrep.2021.03.002.
20. Foroutannia, *et al.*, A deep learning strategy for EMG-based joint position prediction in hip exoskeleton assistive robots. *Biomed. Signal Process. Control*, 75, 103557, 2022, https://doi.org/10.1016/j.bspc.2022.103557.
21. Procter, S., *et al.*, Design of a biomimetic BLDC driven robotic arm for teleoperation & biomedical applications. *J. Hum. Earth Future*, 2, 4, ISSN, 2785–2997, 2022, http://dx.doi.org/10. 28991/HEF-2021-02-04-03.
22. Pande, A. and Mishra, D., Assessment of Pepper Robot's Speech Recognition System through the Lens of Machine Learning. *Biomimetics*, 9, 7, 391, 2024, https://doi.org/10.3390/biomimetics9070391.
23. Mahmood, *et al.*, Prospects of robots in assisted living environment. *Electronics*, 10, 17, 2062, 2021, https://doi.org/10.3390/electronics10172062.
24. Martinez-Hernandez, *et al.*, Wearable assistive robotics: A perspective on current challenges and future trends. *Sensors*, 21, 20, 6751, 2021, https://doi.org/10.3390/s21206751.
25. Nguyen, P.H. and Zhang, W., Design and computational modeling of fabric soft pneumatic actuators for wearable assistive devices. *Sci. Rep.*, 10, 1, 9638, 2020, https://doi.org/10.1038/s41598-020-65003-2.
26. Babu, A. and Boddu, S.B., BERT-Based Medical Chatbot: Enhancing Healthcare Communication through Natural Language Understanding. *Explor. Res. Clin. Social Pharm.*, 13, 100419, 2024, https://doi.org/10.1016/j.rcsop.2024.100419.

27. Ouerhani, N., *et al.*, Smart ubiquitous chatbot for COVID-19 assistance with deep learning sentiment analysis model during and after quarantine, 2020, https://doi.org/10.21203/rs.3.rs-33343/v1.
28. Omoregbe, N.A.I., *et al.*, Text Messaging-Based Medical Diagnosis Using Natural Language Processing and Fuzzy Logic. *J. Healthc. Eng.*, 2020, 1, 8839524, 2020, https://doi.org/10.1155/2020/8839524.

23

Predictive Modeling in Healthcare

Trapty Agarwal[1]*, Lambodar Jena[2], Tabrej Mulla[3], Megalan Leo L.[4] and Subbulakshmi Ganesan[5]

[1]Department Computer Science, Maharishi School of Engineering & Technology, Maharishi University of Information Technology, Uttar Pradesh, India
[2]Centre for Data Science, Siksha 'O' Anusandhan (Deemed to be University), Bhubaneswar, Odisha, India
[3]Arihant Institute of Business Management, India
[4]Department of Electronics and Communication Engineering, Sathyabama Institute of Science and Technology, Chennai, Tamil Nadu, India
[5]Department of Chemistry and Biochemistry, Jain (Deemed-to-be University), Bangalore, Karnataka, India

Abstract

Predictive modeling in healthcare aims to improve patient outcomes and disease diagnosis using advanced machine learning (ML) techniques. The limitations such as data quality, missing values, and model interpretability pose challenges. The research focuses on developing a predictive modeling framework to enhance decision-making in healthcare applications. The primary aim is to leverage advanced ML techniques called Refined Golden Jackal fine-tuned Random Forest (RGJ-RF) for predictive modeling in healthcare. The proposed method RGJ-RF integrates the optimization capabilities of the RGJ with the robustness of the RF classifier. The dataset utilized for the research comprises healthcare data analysis and predictive modeling. Data preprocessing is performed using z-score normalization to standardize the dataset, ensuring consistency across features. Feature extraction is carried out through principal component analysis (PCA), which reduces dimensionality while preserving the essential variance in the data, thus improving model efficiency and performance. The model is fine-tuned to achieve

**Corresponding author*: trapty@muit.in; ORCID: 0009-0007-4081-4999
Lambodar Jena: ORCID: 0000-0003-0052-3330
Tabrej Mulla: ORCID: https://orcid.org/0009-0009-7281-4146
Megalan Leo L.: ORCID: https://orcid.org/0000-0002-6179-1411
Subbulakshmi Ganesan: ORCID: 0000-0002-8345-116X

Satya Prakash Yadav, Abhay Bansal and Victor Hugo C. de Albuquerque (eds.) Computational Intelligence in Biomedical Internet of Medical Things, (401–416) © 2026 Scrivener Publishing LLC

optimal performance, enhancing its predictive accuracy. Accuracy (89%), precision (87.5%), recall (87%), and F1-score (88.4%) are utilized to assess the effectiveness of the model. Experimental results demonstrate the efficacy of the RGJ-RF method, achieving competitive results in healthcare predictions, with significant improvements in all evaluation metrics, indicating its potential for practical application in medical decision support systems.

Keywords: Predictive modeling in healthcare, refined Golden Jackal fine-tuned Random Forest (RGJ-RF)

23.1 Introduction

In medical treatment research and practice, models of prediction play a significant role. While prognosis forecasting algorithms calculate the likelihood of an upcoming health consequence, diagnostic predictor models forecast a patient's present state of health [1]. It works with big data. These models find a correlation that helps in estimating the risks of diseases, complications, or treatment outcomes [2]. This makes it easy for healthcare providers to make various decisions, thus changing from treatment-based care to prevention-oriented, patient-specific care [3]. Many people have conjectured about the possible uses of deep learning (DL) for medical purposes, particularly in precise medicine, which focuses on timely and individualized preventive health detection, diagnosis, and therapy. It is feasible to determine the causality and compute alternatives if one has domain comprehension of every factor involved in proposed linkages and route and sufficient data produced at random to cover all potential path arrangements [4]. The neural networks, decision trees, and ensemble methods are especially good for working with large, multivariate healthcare data. Electronic health records, genomic information, and arable device outputs also form part of the input model for improving prognosis and applicability [5].

As an application, predictive modeling has its drawbacks that accompany its future in healthcare; data privacy issues, biases in datasets, and the necessity of interpretability in clinical settings [6]. To forecast health risks, seek to directly combine organized data and unorganized text using DL methods, which have advanced significantly in a variety of fields, including imaging, speech recognition, and processing of natural languages [8]. It could also support operational decisions such as staff scheduling, patient traffic forecasting, and minimizing the length of stay [7]. It helps in predicting the number of patients likely to arrive so that an appropriate number of personnel and other resources can be arranged and avoid putting pressure on human resources.

Long short-term memory or convolution neural networks are used to simulate temporal data and sequential clinical notes, while used to represent static information. The suggested fusion models also use document embeddings to represent lengthy clinical note documents [8]. Increased population testing for hazards and education initiatives are examples of such mitigation initiatives. It has been shown that the best ways to prevent the condition from getting worse with the least amount of expense are through changes in habits, such as losing weight, eating better, exercising more, drinking less alcohol, quitting smoking, getting a renal specialist early, taking treatment as prescribed, and controlling other risk variables. Establishing adequate dialysis treatment facilities and staff training are other mitigation measures [9]. Close monitoring of individuals at risk, early chronic kidney disease detection, improved resource allocation, and patient-centered management were all made possible by the models.

The potential of probabilistic machine learning (ML) to improve healthcare was investigated [10]. It looks at issues like missing data and calibration in the predictive model development process where probabilistic models might be useful and probabilistic ML models' use in reinforcement learning, generative models for therapeutic use cases, and phenotyping. The Minimum Information for Medical AI Reporting concept outlines the minimal amount of data required to comprehend target populations, intended forecasts, hidden biases, and the capacity to generalize these new technologies has been proposed [11]. Managing issues about bias and accuracy makes it easier to create and execute these models and encourage the creation and application of related clinical decision support systems.

The transformational potential of big data analytics in healthcare was examined [12]. An essential component of electrical service providers is the prediction of load. Those making decisions in the utility industry must project future consumption of electricity with an accurate proportion to give consumers load-shedding-free and continuous electricity. Energy providers can save thousands of dollars by using load forecasting with a lower rate of inaccuracy [13]. These numerical results highlight the revolutionary contribution of ML to the development of precision treatment for individuals with diabetes. The methods for multiple illness prediction were examined, focusing on four primary health issues, diabetes, heart disease, breast cancer, and lung cancer [14]. The result indicated that predictive capabilities hold promise for assisting in early diagnosis and tailored interventions for better patient outcomes in healthcare analytics.

The research aims to leverage advanced ML techniques using refined Golden Jackal fine-tuned Random Forest (RGJ-RF) for predictive modeling in healthcare. In Section 23.2, the method is explained. Section 23.3 includes the results. Section 23.4 is the conclusion.

23.2 Methodology

The methodology for predictive modeling in healthcare involves using a healthcare dataset with healthcare data analysis and predictive modeling. Data preprocessing is performed using z-score normalization to standardize the features, ensuring comparability. Feature extraction is carried out through principal component analysis (PCA) to reduce dimensionality and retain essential patterns. The predictive model utilizes the RGJ-RF, which enhances the Random Forest algorithm's performance by optimizing hyperparameters with the Golden Jackal approach, improving prediction accuracy in healthcare applications. Figure 23.1 shows an overview of the process.

23.2.1 Dataset

The 10,000 artificial patient medical records in this collection include information about the patient's demographics, health problems, admissions, and other characteristics. Real patient data is not provided because it is intended for educational and non-commercial purposes. The dataset is appropriate for use in healthcare-related research, analysis, and education applications due to its synthetic nature. Information gathered

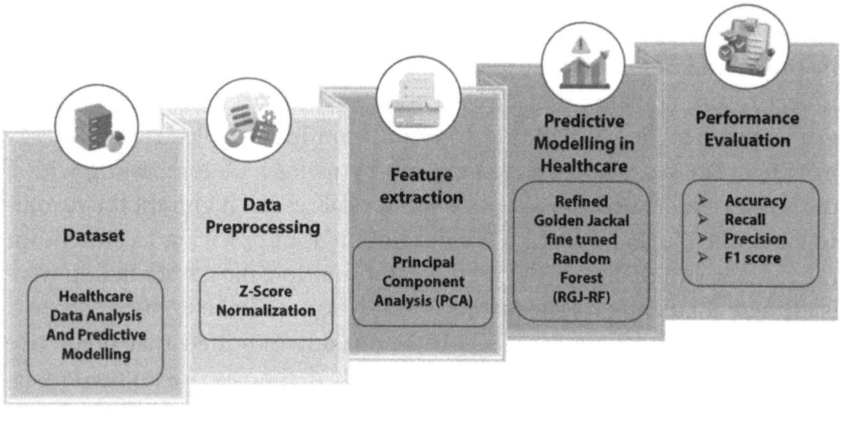

Figure 23.1 Overview of the process.

in this dataset are from Kaggle: https://www.kaggle.com/code/devraai/healthcare-data-analysis-and-predictive-modeling/input.

23.2.2 Data Preprocessing Using z-Score Normalization

In the z-score normalization, data is broken down into numerical attributes that has been used to convert data values into a particular range. The z-score normalization converts a u_j value obtained from the attribute F to u into a previously unidentified range in Equation 23.1.

$$u' = \frac{u_j - F_j}{std(F)} \tag{23.1}$$

Described:
u'= The normalization value's outcome
u = Value of the attribute to be normalized
F_j =The mean value of the attribute
The standard deviation characteristic F is equal to $std(F)$.

23.2.3 Feature Extraction Using Principal Component Analysis

The PCA reduces high-dimensional healthcare data into key components, preserving variance while eliminating redundancy. It extracts features like vital signs or lab results, enhancing predictive modeling for diseases like diabetes or heart failure, ensuring computational efficiency and interpretability.

Consider a collection of $N \times M2$-D training predictions. Each row is concatenated to create a lengthy vector, where $1 \leq j \leq$ min an NM-dimensional space. Each healthcare predictive is represented as a 1-D column vector J_j. The set's mean face is determined in Equation 23.2.

$$n = \frac{1}{m} \sum_{j=1}^{m} J_j \tag{23.2}$$

Every face deviates from the mean by vector $w_j = J_j - n$, where $j = 1, \ldots.., m$. The shifted faces are put on a $NM \times m$ matrix, $W = [w_1 w_2 \ldots. w_m]$. The training predictive healthcare set's covariance matrix D_W is determined in Equation 23.3.

$$D_W = WW^S \tag{23.3}$$

The *eigenvalue* problem needs to be resolved in Equation 23.4.

$$D_W V = V\Lambda \tag{23.4}$$

Where V is the related *eigenvectors* of λ and Λ has a diagonal matrix determined by the matrix of $D_W eigenvalues\lambda$ were $\Lambda = diag[\lambda_1, \lambda_2, \ldots., \lambda_{NM}]$. The new face space is now represented by these eigenvectors.

The image vector w can be projected in NM a multitude of ways in Equation 23.5.

$$z_i = v_i^S w \quad , i = 1, \ldots\ldots, NM \tag{23.5}$$

Where z_i are the projections of w and are referred to as the principal components (sometimes called *eigenfaces*), and v_i are the eigenvectors in the covariance matrix D_w.

The projections z_i allow for an exact reconstruction of the predictive modeling vector w, as Equations 23.6 and 23.7.

$$z = [z_1, z_2, \ldots., z_{NM}] \tag{23.6}$$

$$w = Vz = \sum_{i=1}^{NM} v_i z_i \tag{23.7}$$

By choosing the first $m'(\ll NM)$ eigenvectors with big variances and eliminating the others with minor variances, the dimensionality can be decreased. The expansion of Equation 23.8 can be truncated after m terms in the following manner to approximate the predictive modeling vector w:

$$w = \sum_{i=1}^{m'} v_i z_i \tag{23.8}$$

Thus, for predictive coding and healthcare identification, a small number of eigenvectors offer enough information.

23.2.4 Refined Golden Jackal Fine-Tuned Random Forest

The RGJ-RF hybrid model combines the strengths of RGJ and RF for predictive modeling in healthcare. Golden Jackal Optimization, inspired by the golden jackal's adaptability and hunting strategies, is used to optimize the hyperparameters of the RF algorithm, which is known for its ability to handle large datasets and provide accurate classifications. This is a hybrid approach enhancing the RF model's efficiency by adjusting decision trees for specific predictions to healthcare subjects, including disease diagnosis, patient outcome prognosis, or medical image analysis. The RGJ-RF model improves precision and minimizes the possibility of overfitting by increasing its robustness to healthcare datasets. The presented high efficiency in terms of both nonlinear relationships and variant features make them significant for predictive healthcare analytics.

23.2.5 Random Forest

The RF split selection is used to create a random forest, which is based on bagging decision trees. A random training set is used to build each tree in the forest, and an input variable subset selected at random is used to produce every split inside every tree. The variety of trees increases when this randomness is introduced. The forest's trees are all fully-grown binary trees.

Random Forest naturally produces variable importance measures. The fundamental idea behind variable importance measures is that if an input variable, w_i affects the response, the prediction accuracy drops as the values of variable w_i change. The new model's prediction accuracy is assessed when the values of the variables are permuted one at a time; the stronger the correlation between the permuted variable and the response, the larger the prediction accuracy loss. The evaluation index has often been the decrease in mean squared error (*MSE*). To keep new forests from being trained in RF, the out-of-bag (*OOB*) samples are permuted to measure variable importance [1, 2]. The used to determine the *MSE* decrease for variable w_i and j tree in Equation 23.9.

$$Imp_i^j = MSE\left(S_{C(r_j)}\right) - MSE\left(S_{C_{OOB}^i(r_j)}\right) \tag{23.9}$$

Where $C_{OOB}^i\left(r_j\right)$ represents variable w_i in the *OOB* samples in $C\left(r_j\right)$ that is permuted; Imp_i^j is the decrease in *MSE* of variable w_i in tree $j; S_{C(r_j)}$ is the jth tree predictor relying on $C\left(r_j\right)$, which indicates both bagged samples and random splits in tree j. The ultimate *MSE* reduction of variable w_j is obtained by averaging the output of each of the forest's L tree predictors in Equation 23.10.

$$Imp_i = \frac{1}{L}\Sigma_{j=1}^{L} Imp_i^j \quad (23.10)$$

The relative MSE reduction of each variable was chosen to gauge variable relevance more clearly. The following is the expression for variable w_i and RMR in Equation 23.11.

$$RMR_i = \frac{Imp_i}{\Sigma_{j=1}^{N} Imp_j} \quad (23.11)$$

23.2.6 Refined Golden Jackal

The basic RGJ incorporates the simplex technique and the elite opposition-based learning method to address the limitations of prediction modeling in the healthcare industry. This prevents search stagnation and achieves additional superiority, which accelerates the rate of convergence and improves computation precision.

23.2.7 Elite Opposition-Based Method of Instruction

An effective and reliable method that intensifies global search, expands the search zone, prevents premature convergence, and increases population variation is the elite opposition-based learning methodology. The search method sorts the best person to finish the iteration by using the reverse solution to determine the prey's prediction. The healthcare is calculated as follows, assuming that the search agent with the highest prediction modeling is considered a healthcare individual as the feasible solution, $w_f = \left(w_{f,1}, w_{f,2},.., w_{f,C}\right)$ is calculated as follows $w_j = \left(w_{j,1}, w_{j,2},.., w_{j,C}\right)$ and the opposite solution, $w_j' = \left(w_{j,1}', w_{j,2}',\ldots, w_{j,C}'\right)$. The formula is calculated in Equation 23.12.

$$w_{j,i}' = l.(db_i + da_i) - w_{f,i}, j = 1,2,..,m; i = 1,2,\ldots,C \quad (23.12)$$

Where C is the issue dimension, m is the population size, l was an arbitrary value such that $\in (0,1)$, db_i and da_i are the decision variables has dynamic limits of the ith, respectively, in Equation 23.13.

$$db_i = \min\left(w_{j,i}\right), da_i = \max\left(w_{j,i}\right) \quad (23.13)$$

The healthcare prediction has an inverse solution's search zone and stores the best solution. The search agent's $w'_{j,i}$ are calculated in Equation 23.14.

$$w'_{j,i} = rand(db_i, da_i), if\ w'_{j,i} < db_i\ or\ w'_{j,i} < da_i \qquad (23.14)$$

23.2.8 The Simplex Method

The simplex technique is an important and useful technique that strengthens local search, increases optimization depth, boosts computational precision, and speeds up the search process.

Through the evaluation of the feasible response to the initial solution, the simplex technique preserves the optimal option.

Step 1: Estimate each prey's fitness value. To evaluate the prediction values $e(W_h)$, $e(W_a)$, and $e(W_t)$. W_h represents the ideal value, W_a the below optimal value, and W_t the refreshing value.

Step 2: Determine the approximate center of W_d between W_h and Wa in Equation 23.15.

$$W_d = \frac{W_h + W_a}{2} \qquad (23.15)$$

Step 3: Calculate the fitness value $e(W_q), W$ by estimating and obtaining the reflection point W_q based on W_d *and* W_t in Equation 23.16.

$$W_q = W_d + \alpha(W_d - W_t) \qquad (23.16)$$

Where the reflectivity is expressed by α, which has a value of 1.

Step 4: The existing response is extended further if $e(W_h) > e(W_q)$ in Equation 23.17.

$$W_c = W_d + \gamma(W_q - W_d) \qquad (23.17)$$

Where the fitness value $e(W_f)$ is evaluated, W_c represents the point of extension, and γ reflects the 1.5 value of the extension coefficient. Change W_t *to* W_f ife$(W_h) > e(W_f)$; change W_t *to* W_q otherwise.

Step 5: A compression operation is carried out to get the optimal solution if $e(W_t) > e(W_q)$ in Equation 23.18.

$$W_s = W_d + \beta(W_t - W_d) \quad (23.18)$$

Where 0.5 represents the β compression coefficient and W_s represents the compression point. Change $W_t\ to\ W_q ife(W_t) > e(W_s);$ otherwise, it changes $W_t\ to\ W_s$.

Step 6: To acquire a contraction point W_x, more compression operation is needed if $e(W_t) > e(W_q) > e(W_h)$ in Equation 23.19.

$$W_x = W_d - \beta(W_t - W_d) \quad (23.19)$$

When the contraction coefficient, denoted by β, has a value of 0.5. Change $W_t\ to\ W_x ife(W_t) > e(W_x);$ change $W_t\ to\ W_q$, otherwise.

23.3 Result

The methodology proposed was tested using a Windows 11 laptop equipped with an Intel i7 9th Gen CPU, 32 GB of RAM, and a Python 3.10.1 environment. Using the concepts presented in this section, multi-layer perceptron (MLP) was used to analyze and compare [15]. Table 23.1 shows the overall performance.

23.3.1 Accuracy

The healthcare predictive model takes into consideration patient records and other health-related data together with ML-configured algorithms to predict patient health. From identifying patterns and risk factors,

Table 23.1 Overall performance.

Method	Accuracy	Precision	Recall	F1-score
MLP [15]	75.1%	69.2%	62.6%	64.7%
RGJ-RF [Proposed]	89%	87.5%	87%	88.4%

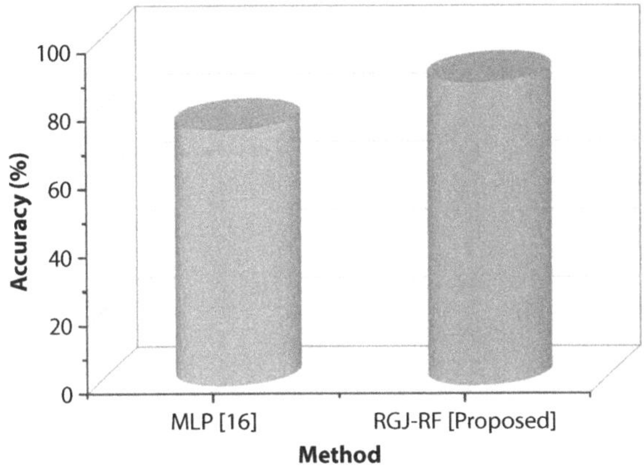

Figure 23.2 Result of accuracy.

treatment, and progress of diseases, these models make predictions based on the course, effectiveness of treatment, and needs of patients. This allows for early prevention and treatment, individual treatment, and the best possible decisions for patients, which in the end improves the patient's status and makes proper use of available resources in the delivery of proper healthcare. Figure 23.2 shows the result of the accuracy.

The suggested RGJ-RF model performed better than MLP, according to the accuracy findings. The RGJ-RF achieves an accuracy of 89%, surpassing MLP at 75.1%. This indicates that the RGJ-RF model provides a more reliable and accurate performance compared to traditional ML models, demonstrating its potential for improved classification tasks.

23.3.2 Precision

Healthcare predictive modeling is a process of data mining, statistics, or ML to forecast future healthcare conditions based on historical patient records. Such an approach makes it easier to detect high-risk patients, tailor interventions, and hence enhance patient care. It depends on the correctness of the data, features used, and model's test to make predictions that are useful in the healthcare facilities. Figure 23.3 shows the result of the precision.

The MLP reached 69.2%, and the proposed RGJ-RF model achieved the highest precision at 87.5%. This indicates that the RGJ-RF model is the most accurate in identifying true positive instances among the predicted positives, surpassing the other models.

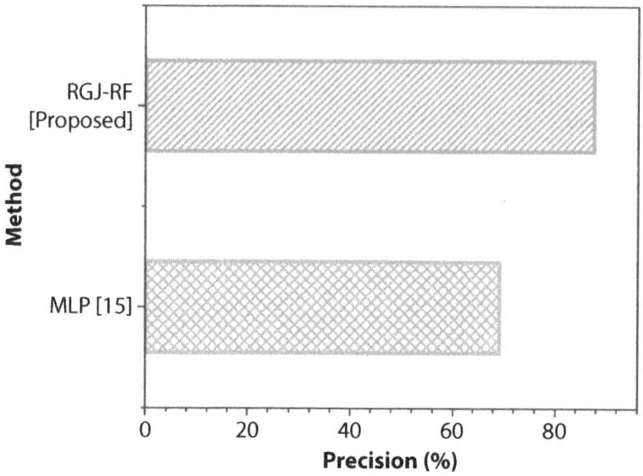

Figure 23.3 Result of precision.

23.3.3 Recall

Healthcare predictive modeling estimates patient behavior and risk factors to generate treatment protocols and strategies. Using historical data, such models can indicate disease trajectories, risk of readmissions, and effectiveness of the applied treatment, contributing to better decision-making, increasing the quality of patient care, and, therefore, decreasing the overall healthcare costs due to preventive and personalized measures. Figure 23.4 shows the result of the recall.

The recall values for the models indicate their ability to correctly identify true positives. The MLP performed less effectively with a recall of 62.6%,

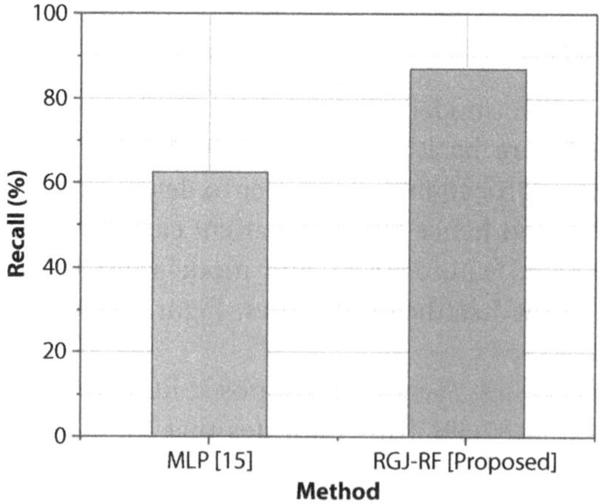

Figure 23.4 Result of recall.

highlighting its lower accuracy in detecting positives. The proposed RGJ-RF model demonstrated the highest recall at 87%, reflecting its strong performance in correctly identifying positive cases in predictive healthcare.

23.3.4 F1-Score

The F1-score is a measure in healthcare predictive modeling; this involves integrating the measure of precision and recall. It is especially valuable in medicine because both false positive or failed diagnoses can be as detrimental as false negative or missed diagnoses. The F1-score demonstrates the highest convergence area in decision-making to confront the real health challenges. Figure 23.5 shows the result of the F1-score.

The F1-score results for the models show varying performance levels. The MLP model has a lower F1-score of 64.7%, reflecting less effectiveness in both precision and recall. In contrast, the proposed RGJ-RF model outperforms the others with an F1-score of 88.4%, demonstrating superior accuracy in balancing both precision and recall.

23.4 Discussion

The training of MLPs demands a great deal of data pre-processing and big data corpora to avoid overfitting. It may require a long time for training because of the biomechanical complex structures and many parameters. Furthermore, the black-box nature of MLPs is concomitant of high opacity,

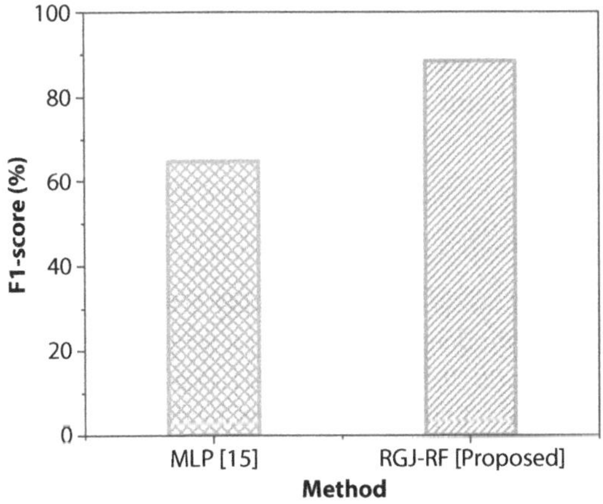

Figure 23.5 Result of the F1-score.

which becomes cumbersome for healthcare professionals who require easily understandable predictions. Both optimizing hyperparameters and selecting an operational system with satisfactory processing power are very important but challenging. To overcome these issues, the proposed RGJ-RF method is used for predictive modeling in healthcare.

23.5 Conclusion

In conclusion, the research introduces the development and evaluation of the presented RGJ-RF model for predictive healthcare applications. The dataset utilized for the research involves healthcare data and was specifically created for computational modeling used in healthcare decision-making. To make features comparable and improve the quality of model training, data preprocessing included features normalization, where z-score normalization was applied. Before classification, feature extraction was performed using PCA, which had the effect of decreasing the dimensionality of the data and decreasing the quantity of inessential variance while simultaneously improving model speed and performance. Experimental results established that the proposed RGJ-RF model achieved an accuracy of 89%, precision of 87.5%, recall of 87% and, an F1-score of 88.4%. These results demonstrate that applying this model can enhance the decision and prediction of different healthcare areas. Challenges of predictive modeling in healthcare include data quality problems, model interpretability, patient privacy issues, model generalization, and issues of dataset biases; these lead to reduced accuracy and reliability of the models. Application of predictive modeling in healthcare increases the speed of early diagnosis of diseases, improves the accurate treatment plan, and increases the rate of patient satisfaction and outcome besides averting extra and unnecessary utilization of resources with medicine.

References

1. De Hond, L., *et al.*, Guidelines and quality criteria for artificial intelligence-based prediction models in healthcare: a scoping. *npj Digital Med.*, 5, 1, 2, 2022, https://doi.org/10.1038/s41746-021-00549-7.
2. Saraswat, D., *et al.*, Explainable AI for healthcare 5.0: opportunities and challenges. *IEEE Access*, 10, 84486–845175, 2022, https://doi.org/10.1109/ACCESS.2022.3197671.

3. Nancy, A.A., *et al.*, IoT-cloud-based smart healthcare monitoring system for heart disease prediction *via* deep learning. *Electronics*, 11, 15, 2292, 2022, https://doi.org/10.3390/electronics11152292.
4. Prosperi, G., *et al.*, Causal inference and counterfactual prediction in machine learning for actionable healthcare. *Nat. Mach. Intell.*, 2, 7, 369–375, 2020, https://doi.org/10.1038/s42256-020-0197-y.
5. Van Smeden, M., *et al.*, Clinical prediction models: diagnosis versus prognosis. *J. Clin. Epidemiol.*, 132, 142–1455, 2021, https://doi.org/10.1016/j.jclinepi.2021.01.009.
6. Goh, K.H., *et al.*, Artificial intelligence in sepsis early prediction and diagnosis using unstructured data in healthcare. *Nat. Commun.*, 12, 1, 711, 2021, https://doi.org/10.1038/s41467-021-20910-4.
7. Ramesh, J., Aburukba, R., Sagahyroon, A., A remote healthcare monitoring framework for diabetes prediction using ML. *Healthc. Technol. Lett.*, 8, 3, 45–57, 2021, https://doi.org/10.1049/htl2.12010.
8. Zhang, D., *et al.*, Combining structured and unstructured data for predictive models: a deep learning approach. *BMC Med. Inf. Decis. Making*, 20, 1–11, 2020, https://doi.org/10.1186/s12911-020-01297-6.
9. Krishnamurthy, *et al.*, ML Prediction Models for Chronic Kidney Disease Using National Health Insurance Claim Data in Taiwan. *Healthcare*, 9, 546, 2021, https://doi.org/10.3390/healthcare9050546.
10. Chen, I.Y., *et al.*, Probabilistic ML for healthcare. *Annu. Rev. Biomed. Data Sci.*, 4, 1, 393–415, 2021, https://doi.org/10.1146/annurev-biodatasci-092820-033938.
11. Hernandez-Boussard, T., *et al.*, MINIMAR (MINimum Information for Medical AI Reporting): Developing reporting standards for artificial intelligence in health care. *J. Am. Med. Inf. Assoc.*, 27, 12, 2011–2015, 2020, https://doi.org/10.1093/jamia/ocaa088.
12. Sunny, Md.N., *et al.*, Optimizing Healthcare Outcomes through Data-Driven Predictive Modeling. *J. Intell. Learn. Syst. Appl.*, 16, 4, 384–402, 2024, https://doi.org/10.4236/jilsa.2024.164019.
13. Al Mamun, A., Sohel, M., *et al.*, A comprehensive of the load forecasting techniques using single and hybrid predictive models. *IEEE Access*, 8, 134911–134939, 2022, https://doi.org/10.1109/ACCESS.2020.3010702.
14. Naik, S., *et al.*, Predictive Healthcare Analytics: A Multidisease Approach using Logistic Regression. *2024 15th International Conference on Computing Communication and Networking Technologies (ICCCNT)*, IEEE, 2024, https://doi.org/10.1109/ICCCNT61001.2024.10725194.
15. Kim, B.J., ML Applications in Diabetes Diagnosis: Optimizing Predictive Models. *Nanotechnol. Percept.*, 611–626, 2024, https://doi.org/10.62441/nano-ntp.v20iS3.46.

24

Blockchain for Secure and Equitable Health Data Management

Ravindra Pandey[1]*, Arun Khatri[2], Amrutanshu Panigrahi[3], Malathi H.[4], Intekhab Alam[5] and Akshatha Y.[6]

[1]*Department of Management, Hult International Business School, Cambridge, USA*
[2]*Mittal School of Business, Lovely Professional University, India*
[3]*Department of Computer Science and Engineering, Siksha 'O' Anusandhan (Deemed to be University), Bhubaneswar, Odisha, India*
[4]*Department of Biotechnology and Genetics, Jain (Deemed-to-be University), Bangalore, Karnataka, India*
[5]*Maharishi School of Engineering & Technology, Maharishi University of Information Technology, Uttar Pradesh, India*
[6]*Department of Computer Science and Engineering, Presidency University, Bangalore, Karnataka, India*

Abstract

Blockchain technologies have a decentralized and secure approach toward managing sensitive healthcare data to enhance interoperability among healthcare providers while ensuring improved privacy. It provides, in practice, patient-controlled data access so that data integrity can be ensured. It can change how healthcare data management systems are operated. This study looks into the transformative potential of blockchain technology in healthcare, especially regarding its capacity for protecting sensitive patient data, enhancing privacy, and transparency across different healthcare systems. This decentralized and tamper-resistant structure presented by blockchain gives a new way to manage health data, minimizing risks in unauthorized access, data breaches, and interoperability failures. This review

**Corresponding author*: pandey.ravindra@gmail.com; ORCID: https://orcid.org/0000-0002-1137-8506
Arun Khatri: ORCID: 0000-0002-5895-7951
Amrutanshu Panigrahi: ORCID: 0000-0002-1077-8532
Malathi H.: ORCID: 0000-0001-6198-8428
Intekhab Alam: ORCID: 0000-0001-5473-2408

Satya Prakash Yadav, Abhay Bansal and Victor Hugo C. de Albuquerque (eds.) Computational Intelligence in Biomedical Internet of Medical Things, (417–438) © 2026 Scrivener Publishing LLC

has focused on the types and features of blockchain technology, layered architecture, and relevant protocols to healthcare applications. The analysis includes crucial application areas, such as the protection of patient records, feasible sharing of data for healthcare studies, and automatic access through permitted patients. This review focuses on permissioned blockchain models, offering controlled access designed to scale and fit the regulatory landscape of healthcare. While blockchain promises tremendous benefits in creating an equitable health data ecosystem, it also offers challenges, such as scalability, strict compliance with privacy laws, and standardized protocols in adoption. It refers to blockchain technology as an emerging technology that can transform the health data management space, discussing opportunities and problems relating to its use in future healthcare. The opportunities and problems associated with the usage of blockchain in future healthcare are discussed.

Keywords: Blockchain, healthcare data management, patient privacy, data security, patient-controlled access, medical study, blockchain protocols, healthcare challenges

24.1 Introduction

Healthcare is the process of prevention, diagnosis, treatment, and management of diseases to maintain good health in patients. The sector has challenges in areas including data security, privacy, and interoperability of systems and thus requires innovative solutions, such as blockchain, to significantly tackle the problems [1]. Health data management is the organized collection, storage, and sharing of patient information across healthcare providers to provide accurate, timely, and efficient care. This includes electronic health records (EHRs), patient privacy laws, and secure data exchange systems. With better healthcare data management, clinical results improve decision-making-aligned care coordination. However, issues such as data breaches, lack of interoperability, and privacy concerns remind the administrators of a need for safe and innovative solutions in managing health information [2]. This requires a revolutionary approach, which can enhance patient satisfaction by improving data management without compromising the privacy and security of medical information [3]. Blockchain is a distributed ledger technology. Blockchain technology has several interconnected nodes. Because of this, data is guaranteed to have integrity, security, and transparency. Decentralization of the storage and the validation process makes tampering and unauthorized changes difficult. All transactions on the blockchain are grouped into blocks; this creates a chain of records known as an immutable chain, bonded to the previous block [4]. Primarily, it is a base for cryptocurrencies. Interest in blockchain technology has emerged due to the feasibility of complete revolution in several industries. The health industry has reached a crucial point in the digital transformation era with such an opportunity, as an unprecedented volume of healthcare data has been generated over the past years due to digital imaging, wearable health technologies, electronic health records, and other breakthroughs [5]. Blockchain is so far a decentralized, tamper-resistant solution where the requirement for protection of data integrity and security is of primary importance in the health industry. Initially conceptualized as a reliable form of cryptocurrency for monetary transactions, it was realized that the uses extended far beyond the financial world into other industries like healthcare, finance, and supply chain [6]. Its significant benefits include security, integrity of data, and clear access, thus promising as a tool in managing sensitive information, especially in environments requiring robust data protection along with controlled sharing. Information is safeguarded through cryptographic encryption, decentralization, and immutability; data in a single location reduces the complexity of managing multiple access points, thereby minimizing the vulnerability of hacking and enhancing security measures [7]. Each record is connected to the preceding one through a cryptographic hash, and transforming it makes it difficult to modify or change easily. Enabling change in every subsequent one, with every block containing an assignment that might involve controlling the majority of the network. This distributed, tamper-resistant design means that the data is secure, verifiable, and protected against unauthorized access [8]. Blockchain has three types: private, consortium, and public. Public blockchains are available to anyone, viewable and decentralized, with Bitcoin and Ethereum representing examples. Private blockchain is controlled by one organization, offering better privacy and higher speed, and are applied primarily in enterprise applications. Consortium blockchains are managed by a consortium of organizations that strike a balance between the control issue and transparency requirement and are utilized in industries like banking and supply chain management [9]. While each provides distinct advantages for a specific case, the level of decentralized systems, privacy, and control varies between types. There are critical problems with administration costs and the modern healthcare systems face high maintenance. It contains so many sectors, such as doctors, practitioners, support staff, patients, and management personnel, and the healthcare system is particularly complex [10]. Health data management includes the safe handling, processing, and sharing of confidential patient information among various health service providers in compliance with regulations and privacy, like the General Data Protection

Regulation and the Health Insurance Portability and Accountability Act [11]. Traditionally, health data is kept on centralized systems exposed to intrusions and lack interoperability between different platforms. Efficient management demands secure access controls, encryption, as well as procedures for data sharing to permit the updates of the data. Also, when combining technologies such as transparency, and electronic health records, blockchain improves the accuracy of information, as well as patient control, for better and more integrated healthcare delivery [12]. The objective is to investigate how blockchain technology enhances patient empowerment, privacy, and healthcare data security. It aims to assess blockchain's potential for efficient data management, patient-controlled access, and enhanced transparency while addressing associated challenges.

24.2 Methodology

This study investigates the blockchain role in healthcare, focusing on its types, key features, and protocols for securing patient records and enabling data sharing. It also reviews the potential of permissioned blockchains and patient-controlled access while addressing challenges such as scalability and regulatory concerns.

24.3 Blockchain

Decentralized blockchain makes it easier to track assets in an organization network and record transactions with an immutable database. A blockchain is composed of a growing set of documents that are secured and linked to each other by encryption. Transaction information, cryptographic hash, and timestamp of the preceding block are included in each block [13]. That transaction information was present when the record was created, as indicated by the timestamp. Since each block is interconnected and contains information about the one before it, the blocks work together to build a chain. Blockchain transactions are therefore irreversible, as they cannot be reversed once they have been recorded without also reversing all subsequent blocks [14].

24.3.1 Blockchain Types and Key Features

The main characteristic of blockchain technology is distribution. The blockchain operates without a central authority, relying on a decentralized network and various agreement minimization procedures to regulate and validate the material uploaded to the blockchain. The primary blockchain transaction is information security. There is virtually unplanned data manipulation since information is sent over the blockchain without the participation of external parties [15]. Another important aspect of the blockchain is durability. Due to a blockchain that is maintained across numerous nodes, submissions on the blockchain cannot be removed once they have been identified. The aspect of blockchain is that it is utilized by numerous blockchains, enhancing privacy and security. Figure 24.1 shows the key features of blockchain.

Blockchains can generally be categorized into four types: public, consortium, private, and hybrid, each offering distinct features based on the ability to create, access, and read data, with varying levels of permission and control over the blockchain's operations [16]. Everyone can see the chain data on a public blockchain, and anybody can join, contribute, or alter the original software. Public blockchains have been used in several locations. It observes a slight increase in its usage in cryptocurrency. Bitcoin and Ethereum are the leading cryptocurrencies with Bitcoin as a decentralized digital currency and Ethereum enabling smart contracts and decentralized applications [17]. A consortium blockchain restricts access and participation to a small number of groups. Private blockchain technology prevents access to or participation in the network by anyone from outside; it can only be done from a central location. The definition and categorization of blockchain types are still up for debate. Figure 24.2 represents the blockchain types.

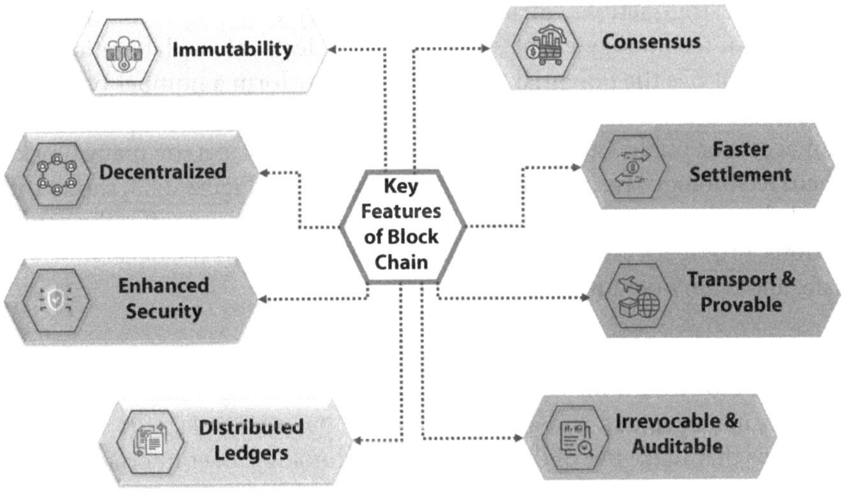

Figure 24.1 Key features of blockchain. (Source: https://www.mdpi.com/2079-8954/11/1/38).

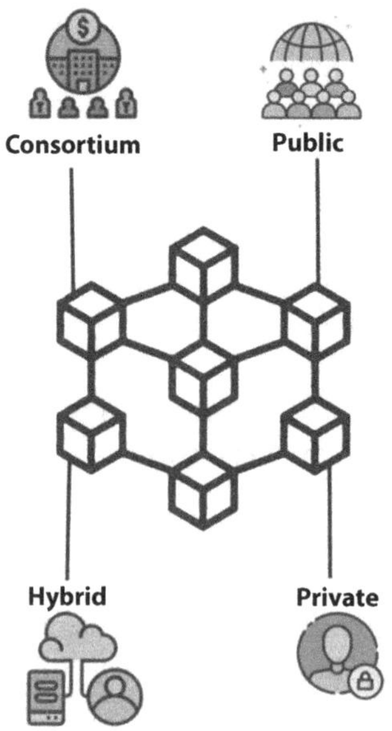

Figure 24.2 Types of blockchain. (Source: https://www.nature.com/articles/s41598-024-68529-x).

24.3.2 Blockchain Layers and Protocols

A blockchain's node network collaborates to validate new transactions and to keep the ledger up to date. Advanced cryptographic methods are used to validate transactions, guaranteeing integrity and immutability. Since blockchain technology enables new kinds of electronic collaboration and creativity, it has the potential to completely transform a number of industries [18]. Blockchains can be private, meaning only authorized entities can access or public (anybody can). This section explains the many blockchain technology layers, each of which, as shown in Figure 24.3, shows the blockchain layers and protocols [19]. Together, these layers offer the applications, protocols, and infrastructure needed to support the decentralized, safe, and open operations of the blockchain.

Application layer: This layer enables developers and consumers to interact with the blockchain for certain applications, including financial services, identity management, and asset monitoring. It consists of smart contracts and apps that make use of the blockchain technology. User interfaces, such

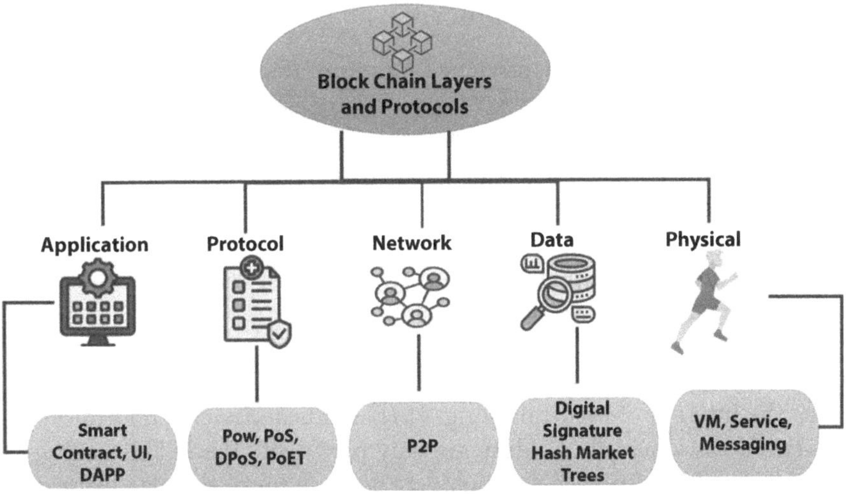

Figure 24.3 Layers of blockchain. (Source: https://www.geeksforgeeks.org/ethical-hacking/layered-architecture-of-blockchain-ecosystem/).

as browsers and wallets, make it possible to engage with the blockchain network intuitively.

Protocol layer: This layer specifies the guidelines that control how the blockchain network operates. It includes the fundamental software of the blockchain, which uses consensus techniques to validate transactions and carry out smart contracts. Interfaces for developers and APIs to create decentralized apps are also included in the protocol layer.

Data layer: This layer, which is in charge of managing and storing data on the blockchain, secures transaction data using cryptographic methods and data structures like Merkle trees. It is distinct from the network layer function in general network management since it exclusively oversees the consensus techniques necessary for transaction validation.

Network layer: It controls connectivity and communication between nodes in the blockchain network. This layer makes use of techniques and protocols that supports decentralized communication without requiring middlemen. It is used for both blockchain-specific peer-to-peer protocols and common protocols like TCP/IP and HTTP.

Physical layer: This layer consists of the servers, data centers, and hardware that make up the actual infrastructure that supports the blockchain network. This layer, split through several blockchain agents, offers the necessary resources such as processing power, storage space, and network bandwidth.

24.3.3 Blockchain in Healthcare

The healthcare industry has stretched for more effective and safe data management solutions due to its extensive databases of private patient information and complex operating networks. Blockchain is a technology that has the potential to completely alter established paradigms [20]. The applications of potential blockchain in healthcare data management are significant and revolutionary, reaching from guaranteeing unchangeable patient records to promoting open study partnerships [21]. Figure 24.4 represents the healthcare advantages of blockchain.

At the same time, new ideas presented in the literature, like references, provide creative approaches to make user information sharing easy and safe. The Internet of Medical Things (IoT) medical devices and healthcare are two areas where these ideas are very pertinent. The IoT's tracking of patient's health with medical tools has become more popular in healthcare environments [22]. These gadgets assess a person's health since data concerning physiological markers can be transmitted in real time. Some examples include temperature, heart rate, oxygen saturation, and internal body temperature.

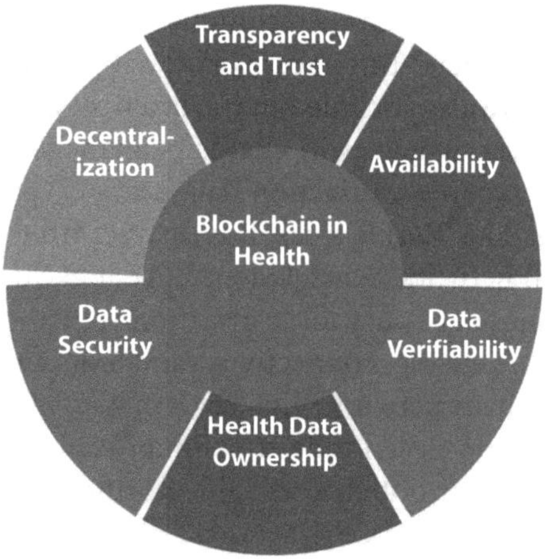

Figure 24.4 Advantages of blockchain in healthcare. (Source: https://assets.cureus.com/uploads/review_article/pdf/255674/20240718-23291-15xr7x0.pdf).

24.3.4 Securing Patient Records

The growing deployment of digitization by healthcare organizations around the world has also brought both an urgent security issue, as well as its concomitant challenge: safeguarding the patient record. Another problem is to prove that it is impossible to make undetectable changes to patient records. The impossibility of performing undetectable changes to a record after it has been written into the system provides an elementary level of security in an evolving digital landscape [23]. This integrity of the data maintains its immutability, meaning that every entry, from histories of treatment to results of diagnosis, is held constant and impenetrable. Figure 24.5 shows blockchain in a healthcare application.

Simple data capture in an unalterable form, however, is not enough; keeping these records also requires caution. Data storage through encryption refers to the process of converting uncoded patient data into information that can only be decoded using a correct cryptographic key [24]. Advanced encryption algorithms, therefore protecting patient data, ensure its security as unintelligible and unusable to hackers. Except for keeping the data safe from external threats, this form of encryption protects the data from internal threats as well, meaning that only people authorized to access and understand the data inside an organization can access it.

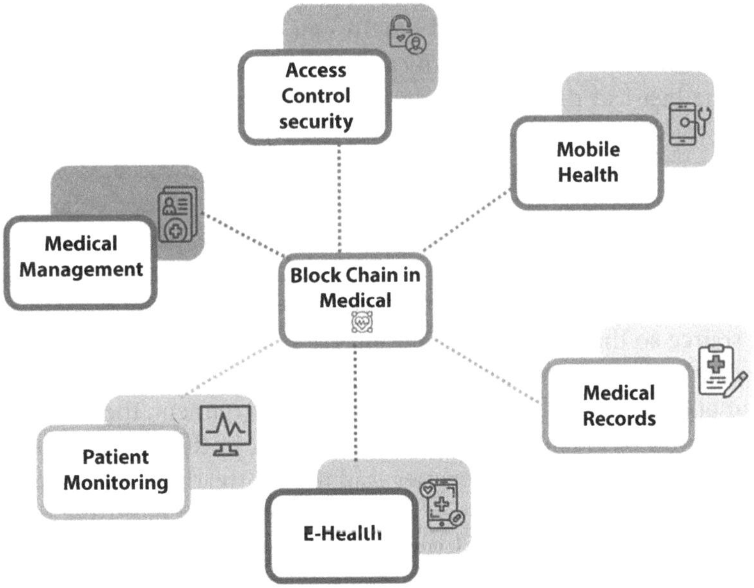

Figure 24.5 Blockchain in a healthcare application. (Source: https://www.nature.com/articles/s41598-024-68529-x).

In healthcare, flexibility is important for managing access to documents while ensuring security. Blockchain technology helps to achieve this through smart contracts, which are automated agreements that enforce access rules autonomously by coding the terms of the agreement. The system creates a smart contract that grants only the history of everything a patient has ever done inside a healthcare center for a primary care provider yet only enables a specialist or any other doctor to read parts of the information as it applies to a specialty [25]. Only the billing information would be available to the insurance providers. Such fine detail of access control undertaken automatically and uniformly by smart contracts would then lead to the healthcare system under which patient data would not only be safely preserved but also efficiently and morally shared.

In a world where data breaches are increasingly common, such patient record security measures can only add to the strengthening of technical defenses while also serving to preserve and restore that very real sacred trust that patients have in medical organizations [26].

24.3.5 Medical Study Data Sharing

The persistent pursuit of new understandings of health and illness conditions to be produced by medical studies produce enormous amounts of data. Data leads to a revolution in healthcare, but finding this delight has its own set of problems and requires an overarching strategy for data exchange that can balance security with accessibility [27].

At the heart of the new paradigm of study, medicine is the desire for greater traceability and transparency. When procedures are transparent, the work of colleagues around the world can be reproduced, verified, and extended. Datasets and methods are opened to encourage collaboration and facilitate peer evaluation, improvement, and expansion of findings [28]. Traceability enables careful tracking of sources, changes, and uses of data. A clearly defined lineage helps to trace back every data point to a specific source so that the validity and integrity of data are ensured at a time when authenticity becomes highly critical.

But once data travels across a networked environment, the critical issue of protection of intellectual property comes up. In the competitive world of medical study, where discoveries lead to new treatment paradigms, the protection of intellectual property is important [29]. It necessitates strong systems that authenticate and timestamp original contributions but also provides a means of claiming inventions, whereby the diffusion of information would ensure the rightful authors get appropriate credit and any benefits arising from the information.

It is about finding the right balance between transparent cooperation and cautious attention to detail for the future of medical study [30], precisely creating a future where data-driven insights improve healthcare while respecting the rights of those providing the data and maintaining the integrity of that data.

24.3.6 Management Data

It is evident from reading the articles that the management of medical records and information has been given the highest priority. Blockchain has been suggested by previous studies as an efficient way to manage electronic private information and medical data. Blockchain manages data ecosystems in an efficient manner. A personal health record (PHR) integrates vast quantities of medical data, as well as data from many sources [31]. In these three key elements, Figure 24.6 shows the most often studied areas. This subject is covered in more detail in the following section.

Information privacy: Prior studies on blockchain technology in the healthcare industry have focused on protecting data confidentiality following access to medical records. The management of user authentication has been the subject of extensive study. The challenge in the healthcare business is made more difficult by the need to safeguard the secrecy of sensory medical information through improved responsiveness, constancy, and verification [32]. To enable qualified, user-oriented, and controllable ways

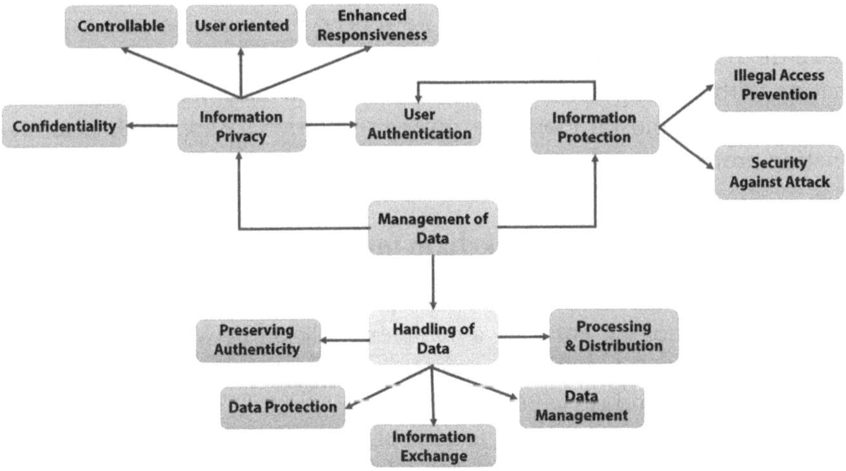

Figure 24.6 Management of data. (Source: https://www.mdpi.com/2079-8954/11/1/38).

to use PHRs and other medical information, prior studies have developed blockchain-based architectures.

Protection of information: Studying healthcare issues in blockchain information systems focuses on data security and preventing unauthorized access. But almost every study that was examined concentrated on protecting against disguise and stopping unauthorized access. The employment of numerous identities, biometric authentication, effective authenticity, and user identification are some of the strategies that are proposed to achieve this objective [33]. However, avoiding external attacks, including conspiracy attacks, transactional attacks, and sensor data attacks, was not given much attention.

Handling of data: While some studies have been done to process, disseminate, and oversee ethical compliance, other studies have legally guaranteed the handling of healthcare data. According to analysis, some studies acknowledged the need for compliance with the guidelines and goals. However, maintaining the accuracy of the information has received a lot of attention. Legitimate information gathering, information theft prevention, dual storage cost prevention, and information permanently preserved are a few examples of topics covered in previous studies [34]. It focused on health assurance and data protection from medical equipment as blockchain usage grew across institutions. Studies have also been conducted on enabling the transmission of information between institutions and data transport as capacities increase.

24.3.7 Enhancing Privacy with Blockchain

Blockchain shows promise in the digital age, where privacy issues and data breaches have become all too regular. The fundamental features of this ground-breaking technology, which powers cryptocurrencies like Bitcoin, have the potential to significantly improve data privacy. Its decentralized nature with cryptographic security, especially in healthcare, where data integrity is of utmost importance, gives a revolutionary approach to information protection [35].

24.3.8 Permissioned Blockchain for Healthcare

Healthcare permissioned blockchains represent an interesting mix of judgment and technology, entailing a complex trade-off between information exchange and security, with the requirements of data sensitivity paramount in the healthcare industry [36].

Public blockchains have the feature of transparency, since all transactions are visible. However, the health industry cannot be treated as openly as it deals with patient reports, study data, and other sensitive information.

In such a scenario, selective transparency can be valuable in permissioned blockchains. It allows validation only of block transactions from particular companies as against public counterparts. Such a systematic approach results in the fact that although data is accessible on the blockchain, it can be accessed by those who have proper permission [37]. In this manner, appropriate information can be shared between trusted organizations such as hospitals, insurance companies, or institutes without the confidentiality and integrity of the information being compromised. The level of detailed control helps to prevent security breaches, ensures data integrity, and creates a structured data flow that aligns with the complexities of the healthcare industry. In simple words, permissioned blockchains for healthcare offer far more than just a technical fix are imbued with the basic tenets of privacy, trust, and responsible information sharing [38].

24.3.9 Patient-Controlled Data Access

Patient-controlled data access is a conceptual change to look at healthcare as it is a technological advance. The patient is seen as both a recipient of care and the keeper of medical records [39].

Over the years, medical experts have been in the space of medical data. Though patients are subjects of the data, they have felt disconnected from the elaborate data management processes. When digital innovation finally started invading the healthcare sector, this dream of having personal control over one's data caught more decisive eyes [40]. The most illustrative example of this shift is patient-controlled data access, which allows people to maintain control over health data.

However, the system has elevated itself to the domain of access permissions that can be withdrawn. Access must be granted, but it must also, independently, be revoked. A patient allows for a certain diagnosis by a professional; however, after treatment, they can withdraw such permission, thus ensuring that data is secured properly. This dynamism ensures that access to data is a dynamic, changing choice, among others, which reflects the dynamics of health, medical interventions, and personal choices.

Patient-controlled access to data marks a significant milestone in empowering individuals, allowing them to have greater control over personal information in the digital age. It certainly represents a fundamental shift in the healthcare narrative from passive acceptance towards proactive involvement while also respecting the inviolable rights of individuals over data. Patients are no longer passive recipients of care; they are currently active participants in shaping healthcare by engaging in meaningful and informed discussions about individual needs and treatment options.

24.3.10 Blockchain Potential in Healthcare

Blockchain in healthcare enhances data security and interoperability, ensuring tamper-proof records and seamless data sharing across providers. It also empowers patients with greater control over health data, promoting transparency and trust. There is a growing issue in healthcare that needs attention where data and staff-intensive domains are accessible from any location; this work is criticized and edited for reliable operations across all industries. The healthcare industry's activities can be broken down into a number of categories, including triage, evaluation, clinical decision-making, knowledge-based care perception, and health problem solutions. A method for involving the medical staff to improve outcomes is demonstrated. The most advanced experience, technology, and knowledge should be offered to patients based on the type of care [41]. When working with educational institutions, this must give patients access to the training facilities and medical department so that the students acquire the skills required. Consequently, educational institutions can produce competent personnel. When a corporation and an organization collaborate on a study, the health organization helps with professionals, informants, samples, and test takers. Healthcare organizations can help with planning, developing, conducting, and reporting clinical trials by taking part in the organization. Rather, study institutions provide methods and tools to the healthcare industry. Health workers' education and biomedical studies are conducted by health organizations. Consent, patient data supporting documentation, and payment procedures must all be shared for this to happen, which is the responsibility of data exchange. Health organizations are required by law to safeguard patient information. Blockchain in healthcare can streamline administrative processes by reducing fraud and minimizing the need for intermediaries, improving efficiency.

24.3.11 Challenges and Limitations of Blockchain in Healthcare

It is indisputable that the healthcare industry has the potential to transform blockchain technology. Many are interested as it has the potential to make patient information safe, compatible, and available to everyone. However, as blockchain is incorporated into the healthcare system, several complications and obstacles appear that make it difficult for this technology to coexist peacefully with an established industry.

The scaling issues are among the most significant obstacles. Healthcare is unique among industries in that it generates and disseminates data on an enormous scale. The flow of data from test findings to patient histories, from medication prescriptions to therapy notes, is constant. Blockchains have historically shown restrictions on transactional throughput, particularly the ones that rely on techniques like proof-of-work. The sheer volume of transactions that are made by patients, physicians, and health plans daily requires a resilient yet scalable blockchain infrastructure [42]. There is a conflict in the need for data immutability compared to the fact that speed and scalability work against each other.

Healthcare is not a monolithic entity. Rather, it is a patchwork of organizations, with some as small as individual practitioners, others as large as global pharmaceutical giants, and everything in between primary-care clinics and vast hospital systems. Therefore, for blockchain to become that sharing platform, an agreement needs to be reached on protocols, data structures, security measures, and dozens of other factors [43]. This is not just technology; various goals, interests, and visions need to be balanced.

24.3.12 Future Prospects

The bold acceptance of blockchain technology in health, however still at the infancy stage, promises to be bright. Equally remarkable is the fact that blockchain has tweaked the gross goal of a more excellent and productive healthcare industry, patient-focused and secure [44].

Custom development of blockchain technology is required to suit the healthcare sector. Decentralization, immutability, and transparency are the core principles of blockchain technology, but these technologies must be tweaked to fit the peculiar needs of the health industry. From granular data for patient privacy to instant access to critical medical data in a real emergency, this custom development can provide for it all [45]. To improve scalability in large-scale settings, the blockchain-enabled auditing with optimal multi-key homomorphic encryption approach in cloud computing entails additional optimization of the encryption and key generation procedures. The auditing system's adaptive capabilities can be enhanced by integrating algorithms, enabling dynamic threat identification and response [46]. Probably many more startups sprout up as technology matures and picks up speed, bringing closer the possibility of a safe and patient-centered health environment.

24.4 Assessment of Healthcare Management

Healthcare management assessment aids in determining how well blockchain works to enhance data security, privacy, and accessibility. It guarantees that healthcare systems are more effective, transparent, and impervious to fraud or illegal access. Furthermore, it promotes fair data exchange by giving people more authority over medical records. For the assessment of healthcare management, this section discusses the parameters used in the EHR [47] and the computation complexity used in medical cyber-physical systems (MCPS) based on blockchain [32], EHR [32], smart EHR based on blockchain [49], and universal serial bus- mass storage devices (USB-MSD) [50].

24.4.1 Parameters of Electronic Health Records

A patient's height, weight, disease symptoms, and past medical history are all included in healthcare data. As the amount grows, it might be difficult to handle the simple data included in EHRs. A number of stakeholders have created, saved, and altered this record to ensure appropriate patient care and the efficient use of medical records. Whenever these stakeholders require the data, they are granted authorization. The parameters that comprise the EHR are displayed in Figure 24.7.

Figure 24.7 shows that clinical notes (17.3%), order prescriptions (17.0%), patient listings (16.8%), and lab results (13.9%) represent the majority of EHR features. Other features include imaging results (9.1%), integration with patient management systems (8.6%), hospital data feeds (7.3%),

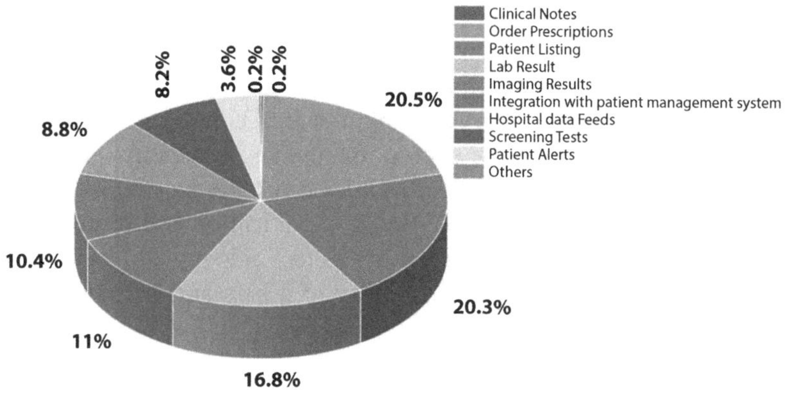

Figure 24.7 Electronic health records' parameters.

screening tests (6.8%), patient alerts (3.0%), and others (0.2%), demonstrating EHRs' complete ability to manage different healthcare data.

24.4.2 Computation Complexity

The term computational complexity describes the quantity of computing resources (such as time and memory) needed to solve a problem, where computation time is the amount of time an algorithm really needs to complete a task. To assess how well blockchain algorithms handle and validate transactions including health data while maintaining security and scalability, several ideas are essential. To sustain blockchain performance in extensive healthcare systems, it is imperative to minimize computational complexity and optimize computation time. Furthermore, Figure 24.8 shows how computing cost is evaluated using correlated procedures.

Figure 24.8 shows the calculation time of several systems for exchanging and authenticating healthcare data with a growing number of verifiers. The program that took the longest to compute, MCPS [32], used a lot of resources. The performances of EHR [48] and smart EHR [49] were mediocre; they demonstrated linear scalability but were less efficient than MCPS. By comparison, the USB-MSD [50] demonstrated greater efficiency and scalability, achieving the lowest calculation time. The USB-MSD technique outperformed alternative approaches as the number of verifiers increased while maintaining a steady performance with little computational cost. This demonstrated how effectively and practically it might be applied in safe healthcare systems.

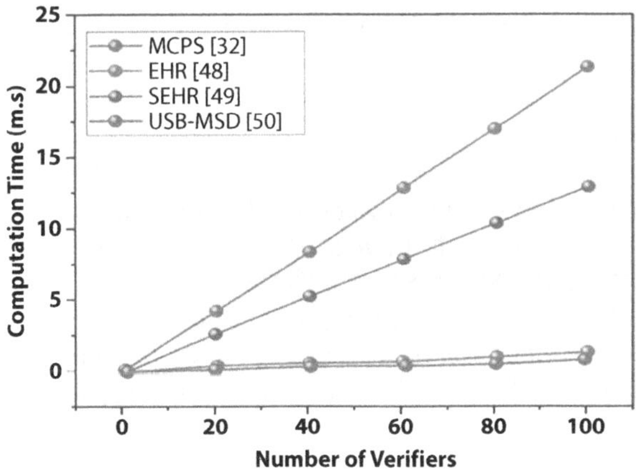

Figure 24.8 Computational complexity.

24.5 Conclusion

Blockchain could potentially alter the paradigm of health data management. Blockchain provides a safe, clear, and decentralized path that enables patients to have more integrity in data. Its security features could be robust enough to address and combat critical challenges such as breaches and lack of interoperability in healthcare. A fundamental knowledge of how decentralization can enhance and streamline data is provided by this examination of blockchain, including its key features and types. An emphasis on Blockchain in healthcare and securing patient records considers the probability of enhancing data security, interoperability among providers, and preventing unauthorized access. A study on medical study data sharing and management data considers how blockchain fosters collaborative studies and transparent handling of data. Lastly, topics such as enhancing privacy, permissioned blockchain, and patient-controlled data access demonstrate blockchain's ability to allow patients to be in control of who gets information and hence improve privacy and patient-centered care. This review highlighted the blockchain's transformative potential in healthcare, from securing patient records to enabling patient-controlled data access and enhancing data transparency. While blockchain offers significant privacy and data management benefits, overcoming technical and regulatory challenges remains essential for widespread adoption. The future scope is scalability in the management of health data through blockchain. It needs to develop new scalable solutions for wide adoption, in addition to fortifying patient-centered data ownership and fostering interoperability across healthcare systems. Therefore, as technology and legal frameworks advance, blockchain can serve as the cornerstone for creating safe, effective, and just healthcare data ecosystems.

References

1. Namasudra, S., *et al.*, The revolution of blockchain: State-of-the-art and research challenges. *Arch. Comput. Methods Eng.*, 28, 1497–15155, 2021, https://doi.org/10.1007/s11831-020-09426-0.
2. Ameur, M.A.A., *et al.*, Advancing healthcare through intelligent human-robot collaboration: overview, challenges, and opportunities, in: *The 29th International Conference on Automation and Computing (ICAC 2024)*, pp. 1–6, 2024, https://doi.org/10.1109/icac61394.2024.10718809.

3. Tyagi, A.K. and Seranmadevi, Blockchain for Enhancing Security and Privacy in the Smart Healthcare, in: *Digital Twin and Blockchain for Smart Cities*, pp. 343–370, 2024, https://doi.org/10.1002/9781394303564.ch16.
4. ALmasoodi, M.F., *et al.*, Leveraging Digital Transformation to Enhance Quality Tourism Services in Babylon City, Iraq. *Int. J. Sustain. Dev. Plann.*, 18, 10, 3195–3211, 2023, https://doi.org/10.18280/ijsdp.181020.
5. Thapa, C. and Camtepe, S., Precision health data: Requirements, challenges and existing techniques for data security and privacy. *Comput. Biol. Med.*, 129, 1041305, 2021, https://doi.org/10.1016/j.compbiomed.2020.104130.
6. Haleem, A., Javaid, M., *et al.*, Blockchain technology applications in healthcare: An overview. *Int. J. Intell. Netw.*, 2, 130–1395, 2021, https://doi.org/10.1016/j.ijin.2021.09.005.
7. Velmurugadass, D., *et al.*, Enhancing Blockchain security in cloud computing with IoT environment using ECIES and cryptography hash algorithm. *Mater. Today Proc.*, 37, 2653–26595, 2021.
8. Jacobetty, P. and Orton-Johnson, K., Blockchain imaginaries and their metaphors: Organising principles in decentralized digital technologies. *Soc. Epistemol.*, 37, 1, 1–14, 2023, https://doi.org/10.1080/02691728.2022.2086086.
9. Elbialy, M., *et al.*, A Logical Framework for Scientific Research Projects based on Blockchain Technology. *Int. J.*, 10, 5, 3028–3036, 2021, https://doi.org/10.30534/ijatcse/2021/151052021.
10. Shaikh, Z.A., *et al.*, BIoMT modular infrastructure: the recent challenges, issues, and limitations in blockchain hyperledger-enabled e-healthcare application. *Wirel. Commun. Mobile Comput.*, 1, 3813841, 2022, https://doi.org/10.1155/2022/3813841.
11. Bafghi, F. and Aldin, H., Leveraging Blockchain Technology for Sustainable, Transparent and Efficient Supply Chain Management: An Integrative Exploration from an Engineering Management Perspective, 2024, https://doi.org/10.34726/hss.2024.114644.
12. Ahmed, S.F., *et al.*, Insights into the Internet of Medical Things (IoMT): Data fusion, security issues and potential solutions. *Inf. Fusion*, 102, 1020605, 2024, https://doi.org/10.1016/j.inffus.2023.102060.
13. Abbas, A., *et al.*, Blockchain-assisted secured data management framework for health information analysis based on Internet of Medical Things. *Pers. Ubiquitous Comput.*, 28, 1, 59–72, 2024, https://doi.org/10.1007/s00779-021-01583-8.
14. Ye, G., Chen, Z., *et al.*, Adaptive reversible image-data hiding algorithm based on blockchain and zero watermarking. *Opt. Laser Technol.*, 179, 1113805, 2024, https://doi.org/10.1016/j.optlastec.2024.111380.
15. Pradeep, A.S.E., *et al.*, Blockchain aided information exchange records for design liability control and improved security. *Autom. Constr.*, 126, 1036675, 2021, https://doi.org/10.1016/j.autcon.2021.103667.

16. Ghadi, Y.Y., *et al.*, The role of blockchain to secure internet of medical things. *Sci. Rep.*, 14, 1, 18422, 2024, https://doi.org/10.1038/s41598-024-68529-x.
17. Avula, R., Addressing barriers in data collection, transmission, and security to optimize data availability in healthcare systems for improved clinical decision-making and analytics. *Appl. Res. Artif. Intell. Cloud Comput.*, 4, 1, 78–93, 2021, https://orcid.org/0009-0006-8476-8544.
18. Koh, L., Dolgui, A., *et al.*, Blockchain in transport and logistics–paradigms and transitions. *Int. J. Prod. Res.*, 58, 7, 2054–2062, 2020, https://doi.org/10.1080/00207543.2020.1736428.
19. Majnarić, L.T., *et al.*, AI and big data in healthcare: towards a more comprehensive research framework for multimorbidity. *J. Clin. Med.*, 10, 4, 766, 2021, https://doi.org/10.3390/jcm10040766.
20. Kohane, I., *et al.*, What every reader should know about studies using electronic health record data but may be afraid to ask. *J. Med. Internet Res.*, 23, 3, e22219, 2021, https://doi.org/10.2196/22219.
21. Sarode, R., *et al.*, Blockchain for committing peer-to-peer transactions using distributed ledger technologies. *Int. J. Comput. Sci. Eng.*, 24, 3, 215–227, 2021, https://doi.org/10.1504/IJCSE.2021.115651.
22. Chavan, D.S., *et al.*, Blockchain and Cybersecurity Revolutionizing Healthcare in the Digital Era, in: *Ensuring Security and End-to-End Visibility Through Blockchain and Digital Twins*, pp. 72–101, 2024, https://doi.org/10.4018/979-8-3693-3494-2.ch005.
23. Shi, D., Wang, X., *et al.*, Ress: A reliable and effcient storage scheme for bitcoin blockchain based on raptor code. *Chin. J. Electron.*, 32, 3, 577–586, 2023, https://doi.org/10.23919/cje.2022.00.343.
24. Chakraborty, C., *et al.*, *Implementation of Smart Healthcare Systems Using AI, IoT, and Blockchain*, Cambridge, MA, USA, Academic Press, 2022, https://doi.org/10.1016/C2021-0-00057-2.
25. Tertulino, R., *et al.*, Privacy in electronic health records: a systematic mapping study. *J. Public Health*, 32, 3, 435–454, 2024, https://doi.org/10.1007/s10389-022-01795-z.
26. Odeh, A., Keshta, I., *et al.*, Analysis of blockchain in the healthcare sector: application and issues. *Symmetry*, 14, 9, 1760, 2022, https://doi.org/10.3390/sym14091760.
27. Pravallika, K., Nadiya Sk, Poojitha, T., Greeshma, K., Block chain technology in healthcare: challenges and opportunities. *Int. J. Health Care Biol. Sci.*, 3, 3, 51–55, 2022, https://doi.org/10.46795/ijhcbs.v3i3.334.
28. Andreoulaki, I., *et al.*, Evaluating the Barriers to Blockchain Adoption in the Energy Sector: A Multicriteria Approach Using the Analytical Hierarchy Process for Group Decision Making. *Energies*, 17, 6, 1278, 2024, https://doi.org/10.3390/en17061278.
29. Kumar, A., Kumar, R., Sodhi, S.S., A novel privacy preserving blockchain based secure storage framework for electronic health records. *J. Inf. Optim. Sci.*, 43, 3, 549–570, 2022, https://doi.org/10.1080/025226 67.2022.2042092.

30. Ghiro, L., Restuccia, F., *et al.*, What is a Blockchain? A Definition to Clarify the Role of the Blockchain in the Internet of Things. *arXiv preprint arXiv:2102.03750*. https://doi.org/10.48550/arXiv.2102.03750, 2021.
31. Attaran, and Mohsen, Blockchain technology in healthcare: Challenges and opportunities. *Int. J. Healthc. Manage.*, 15, 1, 70–83, 2022, https://doi.org/10.1080/20479700.2020.1843887.
32. Cheng, X., *et al.*, Design of a secure medical data sharing scheme based on blockchain. *J. Med. Syst.*, 44, 2, 52, 2020, https://link.springer.com/article/10.1007/s10916-019-1468-1.
33. Galetsi, P., Katsaliaki, K., *et al.*, Exploring benefits and ethical challenges in the rise of mHealth (mobile healthcare) technology for the common good: An analysis of mobile applications for health specialists. *Technovation*, 121, 1025985, 2023, https://doi.org/10.1016/j.technovation.2022.102598.
34. Tedeschi, E., Predictive Modeling for Fair and Efficient Transaction Inclusion in Proof-of-Work Blockchain Systems. https://doi.org/10.18710/8IKVEU, 2023.
35. Laroiya, C., *et al.*, Applications of blockchain technology, in: *Handbook of Research on Blockchain Technology*, pp. 213–243, Cambridge, MA, USA, Academic Press, 2020, https://doi.org/10.1016/B978-0-12-819816-2.00009-5.
36. Zhang, L., *et al.*, Overview of the integration of communications, sensing, computing, and storage as enabling technologies for the metaverse over 6G networks. *Electronics*, 12, 17, 3651, 2023, https://doi.org/10.3390/electronics12173651.
37. Abdul, M. and Saleem, S., Navigating Blockchain's Twin Challenges: Scalability and Regulatory Compliance. *Blockchains*, 2, 3, 265–298, 2024, https://doi.org/10.3390/blockchains2030013.
38. Velmovitsky, P.E., *et al.*, Blockchain applications in health care and public health: increased transparency. *JMIR Med. Inf.*, 9, 6, e20713, 2021, https://doi.org/10.2196/20713.
39. Zuboff, S., Surveillance capitalism or democracy? The death match of institutional orders and the politics of knowledge in our information civilization. *Organ. Theory*, 3, 3, 26317877221129290, 2022, https://doi.org/10.1177/26317877221129290.
40. Nasseef, O.A., *et al.*, Artificial intelligence-based public healthcare systems: G2G knowledge-based exchange to enhance the decision-making process. *Gov. Inf. Q.*, 39, 4, 101618, 2022, https://doi.org/10.1016/j.giq.2021.101618.
41. Malakhov, I., *et al.*, On the use of proof-of-work in permissioned blockchains: Security and fairness. *IEEE Access*, 10, 1305–13165, 2021, https://doi.org/10.1109/ACCESS.2021.3138528.
42. Perera, S., *et al.*, Blockchain technology: Is it hype or real in the construction industry? *J. Ind. Inf. Integr.*, 17, 1001255, 2020, https://doi.org/10.1016/j.jii.2020.100125.

43. Ramzan, S., *et al.*, Healthcare applications using blockchain technology: Motivations and challenges. *IEEE Trans. Eng. Manage.*, 70, 8, 2874–2890, 2022, https://doi.org/10.1109/TEM.2022.3189734.
44. Kaur, J., Decentralized Finance (DeFi) and Blockchain Technology in Healthcare: A Promising Confluence for Enhanced Security, Data Interoperability, and Patient, in: *Harnessing Technology for Knowledge Transfer in Accountancy, Auditing, and Finance*, pp. 126–149, 2024, https://doi.org/10.4018/979-8-3693-1331-2.ch006.
45. Chenthara, S., *et al.*, Healthchain: A novel framework on privacy preservation of electronic health records using blockchain technology. *PLoS One*, 15, 12, e0243043, 2020, https://doi.org/10.1371/journal.pone.0243043.
46. Bandaru, V.N.R. and Visalakshi, P., Block chain enabled auditing with optimal multi-key homomorphic encryption technique for public cloud computing environment. *Concurrency Comput. Pract. Exper.*, 34, 22, e7128, 2022, https://doi.org/10.1002/cpe.7128.
47. Taloba, A.I., *et al.*, A framework for secure healthcare data management using blockchain technology. *Int. J. Adv. Comput. Sci. Appl.*, 12, 12, 639–646, 2021, http://dx.doi.org/10.14569/IJACSA.2021.0121280.
48. Shamshad, S., *et al.*, A secure blockchain-based e-health records storage and sharing scheme. *J. Inf. Secur. Appl.*, 55, 102590, 2020, https://doi.org/10.1016/j.jisa.2020.102590.
49. Feng, Q., *et al.*, Lightweight collaborative authentication with key protection for smart electronic health record system. *IEEE Sens. J.*, 20, 4, 2181–2196, 2019, https://doi.org/10.1109/JSEN.2019.2949717.
50. Renuka, K., Kumari, S., Li, X., Design of a secure three-factor authentication scheme for smart healthcare. *J. Med. Syst.*, 43, 5, 133, 2019, https://doi.org/10.1007/s10916-019-1251-3.

25

Quantum Computing in Biomedical Intelligence

Indraah Kolandaisamy[1], Renuka Jyothi S.[2], Muthiah M.A.[3*], Bharat Jyoti Ranjan Sahoo[4], Sharath Kumar A.J.[5] and Deeksha Choudhary[6]

[1]Department of BBA, School of Business Management, Universiti Utara Malaysia, Sintok, Kedah Darul Aman, Malaysia
[2]Department of Biotechnology and Genetics, Jain (Deemed-to-be University), Bangalore, Karnataka, India
[3]Department of Electronics and Communication Engineering, Sathyabama Institute of Science and Technology, Chennai, Tamil Nadu, India
[4]Department of Computer Science and Engineering, Siksha 'O' Anusandhan (Deemed to be University), Bhubaneswar, Odisha, India
[5]Department of Electronics and Communication Engineering, Vidyavardhaka College of Engineering, Mysuru, Karnataka, India
[6]Maharishi School of Engineering & Technology, Maharishi University of Information Technology, Uttar Pradesh, India

Abstract
The medical field is essential in developing models for predictions, and there is an extensive amount of information on numerous diseases globally. Machine learning (ML) is critical for discovering and utilizing these data in healthcare. The development of secure healthcare information systems is an emerging issue, with quantum computing (QC) serving as an essential resource for handling health-related information. This information can be utilized to determine the fastest drug-forming procedures and safe mechanisms of drugs for diseases, thus improving healthcare effectiveness. It examines the usage of QC along with ML to improve prediction

**Corresponding author*: muthiah.ece@sathyabama.ac.in; ORCID: https://orcid.org/0000-0001-8007-7937
Renuka Jyothi S.: ORCID: 0000-0003-3248-337X
Bharat Jyoti Ranjan Sahoo: ORCID: https://orcid.org/0000-0002-3487-2822
Sharath Kumar A.J.: ORCID: https://orcid.org/0000-0002-1694-8205
Deeksha Choudhary: ORCID: https://orcid.org/0009-0001-8298-6082

Satya Prakash Yadav, Abhay Bansal and Victor Hugo C. de Albuquerque (eds.) Computational Intelligence in Biomedical Internet of Medical Things, (439–456) © 2026 Scrivener Publishing LLC

models for disease diagnosis and drug discovery. Quantum computing can speed up the development of drugs by optimizing simulations of molecules and lowering study time and expenses. It demonstrates QC's potential to transform biomedical studies and healthcare, providing considerable increases in diagnostic accuracy, medication modification, and overall outcomes for patients. By demonstrating its capacity to manage enormous, complicated datasets, provide quicker and more accurate evaluation, and transform personalized medicine and early detection of diseases, to demonstrate the possibilities of QC in healthcare investigation.

Keywords: Machine learning (ML), diagnosis of the disease, drug discovery, patient healthcare, quantum mechanisms

25.1 Introduction

A new generation of biomedical programs has been made possible with the aid of quantum computing (QC) technology, which offers previously unheard-of sensitivity and backbone in tissue imaging, bio-molecules detection, and physiological parameter monitoring [1]. These technologies use quantum physics ideas like quantum superposition and quantum entanglement to attain sensitivity and accuracy levels that have been formerly not possible with traditional sensing strategies [2]. Although not as considerably studied, the intersection of QC and biomedical studies has sizable brief-time period capacity [3]. This includes information on human health, mental and bodily issues and illnesses, and a simple study of biological and molecular mechanisms, in addition to making selections from clinical statistics [4]. The hastily developing subject of the quantum era holds promise for accelerating computation across several medical and technological domains. Quantum computing employs a completely distinct technique from traditional computing and is based on the concepts of quantum mechanics [5]. Because of this, QC devices may be able to perform intricate computations more quickly than conventional computers, which can cause an interesting use in biomedical study and healthcare [6]. For medicinal demanding situations with high computational needs, QC may provide numerous benefits over traditional computing. For instance, simulating interactions among molecules and protein folding are two difficult troubles with an underlying quantum shape that may be optimized with QC [7]. Likewise, quantum algorithms are superior to their classical equivalents at searching unstructured datasets, allowing for the extra efficient optimization of challenging troubles in biomedical studies and healthcare [8]. With an extensive range of excessive-stage languages for programming, easily available systems, and cloud-hosted resources, which include simulators based on CPUs known as important processing gadgets and quantum processing units denoted as QPUs, the accessibility of quantum competencies has hastily improved [9]. Despite those advancements, it is still difficult to apply QC realistically to unique obligations, and there are few examples accessible for practitioners who will not have plenty of knowledge of low-stage programming or quantum concepts [10].

Objective: The goal of the project is to explore the application of QC with the help of machine learning (QML) to enhance forecasting algorithms for identifying diseases and drug discovery. It aims to illustrate the potential of QC in improving medical results by optimizing computational models of molecules and speeding up medication discovery.
Organization of the study: Section 25.2 explains QC; Section 25.3 illustrates the difference between QC and classical computing; Section 25.4 describes QC with ML; Section 25.5 explains healthcare in QC; Section 25.6 defines the existing study method efficiently; disease diagnosis in QC is well explained in Section 25.7, and the impact of QC in drug discovery is explained in Section 25.8; results are presented in Section 25.9; following the result section, the discussion is represented in Section 25.10, and finally Section 25.11 shows the conclusion.

25.2 Quantum Computing

An innovative method for computation, QC leverages the theory of quantum mechanics to resolve intricate issues more quickly than conventional computers. To make consumption of the particular characteristics of quantum physics, like superposition and entanglement, quantum computers employ specific hardware.

Qubits: A quantum bit, also known as a qubit, is similar to a conservative bit yet distinct from it. The matrices that describe qubits are $b\begin{pmatrix}1\\0\end{pmatrix}+a\begin{pmatrix}0\\1\end{pmatrix}$, where $\begin{pmatrix}1\\0\end{pmatrix}$ denotes the $|0\rangle$ qubit and $\begin{pmatrix}0\\1\end{pmatrix}$, the $|1\rangle$ qubit. Alternatively, the matrix's rows can be numbered, with the first row receiving a 0. Ones have ones in the one-row and zeros have ones in the zero-row. $||b||^2+||a||^2=1$ is satisfied by the complex integers b and a. Qubits can have a value between 0 and 1 according to this criterion, provided that the total length of their vectors equals 1. This makes it possible for qubits to be in superposition. Because $\begin{pmatrix}1\\0\end{pmatrix}$ and $\begin{pmatrix}0\\1\end{pmatrix}$, meet inside this definition, it is important to understand that traditional bits are simply specific examples of qubits. In conclusion, the tensor combination of each qubit's corresponding matrix presents two or more quantum bits. Equation 25.1 represents the qubits $|0\rangle$, for instance [11].

$$|0\rangle = \begin{pmatrix} 0 \\ 1 \end{pmatrix} \otimes \begin{pmatrix} 1 \\ 0 \end{pmatrix} = \begin{pmatrix} 0 \\ 0 \\ 1 \\ 0 \end{pmatrix} \tag{25.1}$$

Quantum gates: Quantum gates, which resemble Boolean operation gates in classical computing, are used in QC. One significant difference between quantum and classical gates is that each one is reversible. This indicates that each QC gate and operator has an inverse. Some of the more popular quantum gates are included in it, including the Pauli X, Pauli Z, Hadamard, and Controlled NOT-gate.

Quantum entanglement: An entanglement state of two qubits is possible in QC. If two qubits' product states cannot be decomposed into two distinct bits, they are considered to be entangled. Equation 25.2 illustrates such an entanglement [11].

$$\begin{pmatrix} \frac{1}{\sqrt{2}} \\ 0 \\ 0 \\ \frac{1}{\sqrt{2}} \end{pmatrix} = \begin{pmatrix} b \\ a \end{pmatrix} \otimes \begin{pmatrix} d \\ c \end{pmatrix} bd = \frac{1}{\sqrt{2}}, bc = 0, ad = 0, ac = \frac{1}{\sqrt{2}} \tag{25.2}$$

25.3 Difference Between Classical and Quantum Computing

The following Table 25.1 and Figure 25.1 illustrate the differences between QC compared to classical computing (CC).

Table 25.1 Quantum computing vs classical computing.

Features	CC	QC
A) Error rates and environment	• Able to function at room temperature • Low rates of error	• High rates of error • Certain quantum systems require extremely cold temperatures
B) Suitability	• Appropriate for routine processing	• Adequate for complex processing
C) Computing units	• Uses transistors for calculations, which have two levels: 0 and 1.	• Uses qubits for calculations, which can simultaneously represent 0 and 1
D) Computing capacity	• The number of transistors enhanced capability in a linear (1:1) ratio	• As the number of qubits increased, capability expanded rapidly

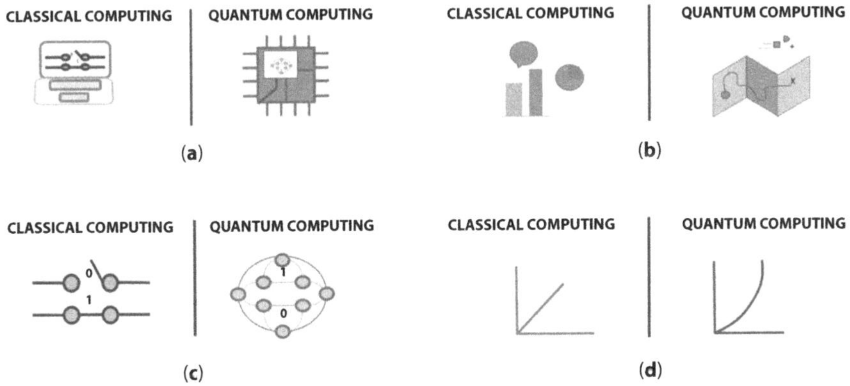

Figure 25.1 Visual representation of (a) error rates and environment, (b) suitability, (c) computing units, and (d) computing capacity. Source: (https://xypro.com/enterprise-identity-access-management/xypros-2023-cybersecurity-predictions-what-to-expect-in-the-coming-year/).

25.4 Quantum Computing in Machine Learning

Biomedical evaluation, computer vision, the processing of natural languages, mining data, and machine learning (ML), a component of artificial intelligence (AI), have been widely used in numerous other studies and industrial domains. In a few decades, QC will be considered one of the most potentially useful human innovations. To receive more advantages, researchers have suggested combining ML and QC. The result is QML, a new integrative subject [12].

25.5 Quantum Computing in Healthcare

By providing novel approaches to difficult problems that conventional computers are incapable of handling, QC has the potential to completely transform medical studies. This novel innovation has the potential to greatly speed up biomedical studies, from bettering public health monitoring systems to comprehending the causes of diseases. The need to comprehend intricate biological processes involving enormous volumes of information stands at the core of biomedical studies. Computational processes including the folding of proteins, genome sequencing, and modeling of molecular dynamics can be completed faster by QC [13]. The article presents an in-depth examination of disease diagnosis and the discovery of drugs. Figure 25.2 illustrates the healthcare performance of QC.

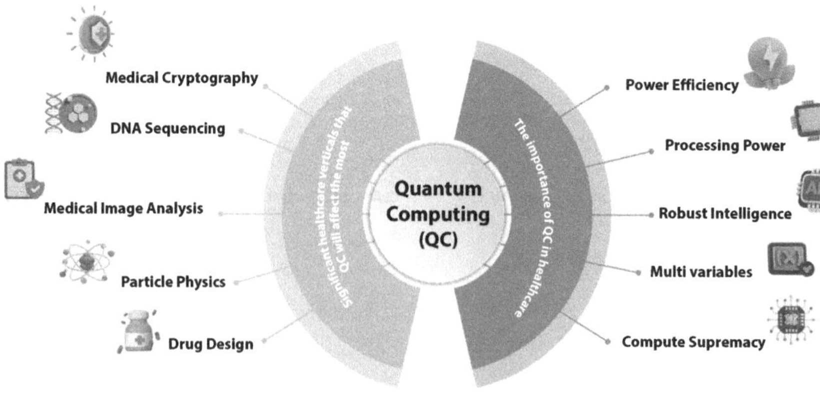

Figure 25.2 Quantum computing in biomedical components. Source: (https://assets.cureus.com/uploads/review_article/pdf/278342/20240921-407091-d5ch7h.pdf).

25.6 Methodology

This section explains how well QC performs in disease diagnosis and drug discovery. It also shows the dataset of disease predictions.

25.6.1 Dataset

Numerous diseases require diagnosis, for example, heart disease and lung disease. These are two commonly used open-source datasets from the Kaggle platform. It has been preprocessed and extracted. The prediction was made employing QC along with ML technologies, and the outcome measures were recommended, as demonstrated in Figure 25.3.

Lung disease: The Lung X-Ray Image Dataset is a detailed collection of 3,475 X-ray images organized into three distinct groups: normal (1250 images), lung opacity (1125 images), and viral pneumonia (1100 images). These images show healthy lung functioning, provide an array of study cases, and help with the identification, categorization, and comprehension of lung illnesses. The dataset is critical in the healthcare industry since it advances respiratory medicine and improves patient outcomes by offering a comprehensive and established collection of X-ray images [14]. Figure 25.3 shows the sample image of lung disease.

Heart disease: The four databases that make up this information collection date back to 1988. There are 76 attributes in total, including the expected trait; however, only 14 are used in all reported tests. The target field specifies whether the patient has heart problems. A number of 0 denotes no illness, while a value of 1 denotes disease [15]. Below Figure 25.4 demonstrates the flow of the method.

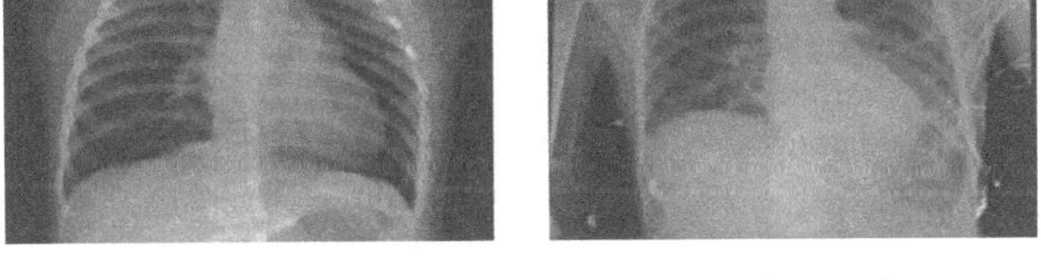

Figure 25.3 Sample image. Source: (Kaggle: https://www.kaggle.com/datasets/fatemehmehrparvar/lung-disease?select=Lung+X-Ray+Image).

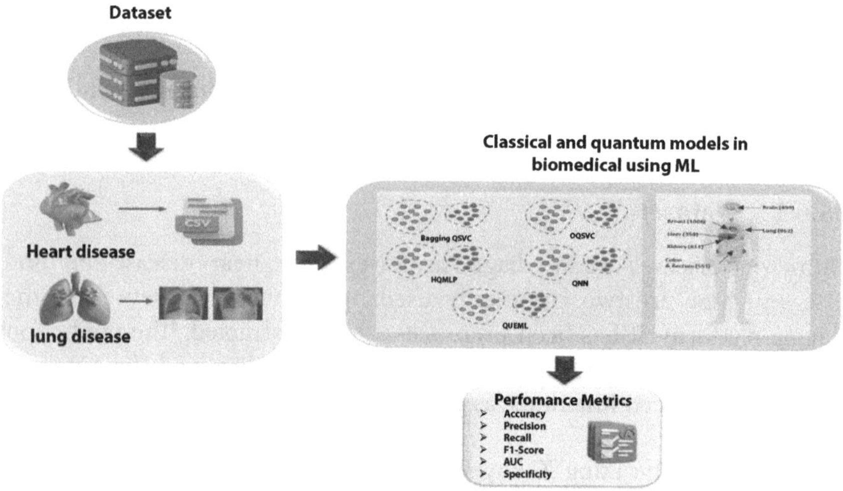

Figure 25.4 Flow for study methodology. Source: (Own elaboration).

25.7 Diagnosing Disease Using Quantum Computing

Table 25.2 illustrates the use of QC in disease diagnosis across multiple datasets. Quantum techniques are investigated to increase diagnostic accuracy and detect patterns within complicated medical data. The study shows the promise of QC in improving healthcare analytics.

Table 25.2 Disease diagnosis in employing QC.

References	Data collection	Method	Result
[16]	The Cleveland dataset	The Bagging-Quantum Support Vector Classifier	Precision (pre) - 90% Accuracy (acc) - 90.16% Recall (rec) - 90% F1-score (F1) - 90%
[17]	The real-time cardiovascular dataset	Optimized quantum support vector machine and hybrid quantum multi-layer perceptron	acc - 94% for both F1- 93% and 92%

(*Continued*)

Table 25.2 Disease diagnosis in employing QC. (*Continued*)

References	Data collection	Method	Result
[18]	A thyroid disease dataset	Quantum support vector machine (QSVM)	acc - 98.77% pre - 99% rec - 99% F1 - 99%
[19]	The Kaggle heart disease dataset	Quantum-enhanced ML	acc - 96.1% pre - 97.1% rec - 95.5% Specificity - 96.8% F1- 96.3%
[20]		Quantum Neural Network (QNN)	acc - 97.31% pre - 97.41% rec - 97.31% F1 - 97.30%
[21]	ADNI 1 and ADNI 2 datasets	VGGNet + ResNet + QSVM	acc - 99.89 % pre - 99.25 % rec - 99.23 % F1 - 99.13% Area under the curve - 99.99%
[22]	PIMA Indian Diabetes dataset	QML and deep learning	acc - 95% pre - 90% rec - 95% F1 - 93%
[23]	Dataset of 14 attributes	Quantum-enhanced machine learning	acc - 89% F1 - 88% rec - 93% pre - 89%
[24]	The diabetes dataset	QML	All performance metrics achieve 69%
[25]	The Cleveland Heart Disease dataset	Bagging QSVM method	The evaluation metrics achieve 100%

25.8 Impact of Quantum Computing on Drug Discovery

Table 25.3 emphasizes the transformational power of QC in the development of drugs. It investigates its potential for accelerating study processes, optimizing molecular simulations, and integrating with existing computational approaches. The study emphasizes obstacles, novel approaches, and potential applications for furthering pharmaceutical development.

25.9 Result

In this phase, the performance measures for QC in biomedical expertise are thoroughly described in Equations 25.3 to 25.7 with a focus on efficiency, accuracy, and the ability to address difficult biomedical problems. These indicators assist in determining the efficacy of QC in promoting medical services.

Accuracy: In healthcare prediction using QC, accuracy refers to the percentage of accurate predictions compared to total estimates.

$$Accuracy = \frac{Accurate\ positive\,(AP) + Accurate\ negative(AN)}{AP + AN + Inaccurate\ positive\,(IP) + Inaccurate\ negative\,(IN)} \tag{25.3}$$

Precision: In biomedical data, precision refers to the proportion of accurate positives compared to the total number of positives.

$$Precision = \frac{AP}{AP + IP} \tag{25.4}$$

Recall: Recalling the method used correctly shows accurate positives. Individuals who suffered from the medical conditions recollect how many were true.

$$Recall = \frac{AP}{AP + IN} \tag{25.5}$$

Table 25.3 Medication development in QC.

References	Background	Uses	Result
[26]	Machine learning and AI technologies have transformed the development of drugs and life sciences.	Quantum computation is expected to revolutionize technology, with early practical applications including quantum chemical simulation.	It explores the possible integration of QC in generative science, highlighting its benefits and problems, as well as the incorporation of quantum technologies into existing AI systems.
[27]	Innovative medicine creation is a laborious and expensive multistage process. Recent technological advances have significantly reduced timescales, complexity, and expense.	The study examines the use of QC in drug studies, emphasizing its potential to solve a variety of drug discovery challenges using AI and ML algorithms.	This article presents the principles of QC, Hamiltonians, their use in drug development, and the drawbacks of noisy intermediate-scale quantum approaches.
[28]	A wealth of information crucial to drug development is provided by the growing number of private and public datasets dedicated to tiny compounds assessed against living substrates or whole cells.	Machine learning algorithms such as SVM and deep neural network are computationally costly for big datasets. Quantum computing techniques aim to speed up QML; however, it has limits, particularly in drug discovery, due to the requirement for substantial molecular description reduction.	The article demonstrates the processes required to be quantum computer-ready for employing QC to drug development and lay a foundation for future study in this area.
[29]	The focus of their study is on quantum chemistry computations, which they believe will have the most significant impact on medication design.	The article compares the computational demands of computer-aided drug development to quantum chemistry challenges where quantum machines can provide faster results than traditional approaches.	To discover potential study areas to make QC an invaluable resource in the drug industry.

(*Continued*)

Table 25.3 Medication development in QC. (*Continued*)

References	Background	Uses	Result
[30]	The QML concept requires shortening the Study and Development phase of developing medications from three to six months, thus lowering expenditure by fifty dollars to eighty thousand dollars.	Machine learning molecule generation establishes hits based on the protein of interest structure, while quantum simulations filter compounds based on response and binding efficacy, resulting in MLMV for optimization of leads.	To establish pre-clinical-trial-ready medications, optimized compounds are subjected to many rounds of quantum simulations filtering to ensure superior safety and efficacy.
[31]	Quantum computing has potential benefits, but it is constrained in hardware. Using near-term QC in CARD necessitates careful separation of classical and QC.	HypaCADD is a hybrid approach that employs both conventional docking and quantum ML to create medications that consider genetic mutations, as well as a mutation-impact predictor.	To discover that QML models can perform on level with or better than traditional baselines. In conclusion, HypaCADD offers an effective method for applying QC in CADD.
[32]	Quantum computing techniques are predicted to dramatically speed up the complex process of medication discovery and development.	To investigate the possible applications of quantum technology in a variety of domains, including computer-aided drug design, quantum modeling, quantum biology, and clinical studies.	It addresses a number of basic quantum concepts to provide a complete grasp of this breakthrough technology.
[33]	From traditional studies, it creates a complex process aimed at real-world drug development difficulties.	This approach to drug discovery relies on quantum computing, with a focus on accurate Gibbs free energy levels and accurate modeling of covalent bond interaction.	The results obtained show the possibility of a QC pipeline for inclusion in actual drug design operations.

F1-score: The F1-score can be determined using the mathematical mean of both recall and precision.

$$F1 - Score = \frac{2(Precision \times Recall)}{Precision + Recall} \tag{25.6}$$

Specificity: Specificity refers to when a forecasting diagnostic is negative and the individual is healthy.

$$Specificity = \frac{True\ negative}{True\ negative + False\ Positive} \times 100\% \tag{25.7}$$

Area under the curve (AUC): The receiving operator characteristic (ROC) graph analyzes the performance of models by comparing the true positive rate and false positive rate of ML classifiers. The AUC measures the model's ROC. A high AUC score indicates that the model is performing well. Figure 25.5 illustrate the parameters' efficiency in disease diagnosis with QC.

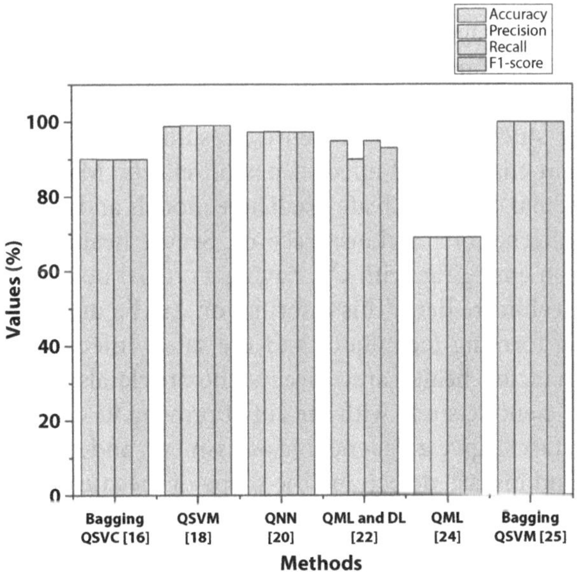

Figure 25.5 Performance evaluation of existing methods using metrics.

25.10 Discussion

Quantum computing has enormous promise to transform healthcare technology by addressing complicated challenges that traditional computers struggle with. It speeds up processing in biological domains, such as disease detection, drug development, and molecular simulation, by utilizing quantum mechanics principles such as superposition and entanglement. Machine learning approaches combined with QC, known as QML, improve the accuracy of predictive models in medical care, as proven in datasets such as heart disease and lung illness. The capability of the best control to drastically grow diagnostic accuracy, as measured by means of overall performance metrics like acc, pre, rec, and F1, bodes agreeably for the future of precision medical care. Furthermore, QC speeds up the improvement of medication by optimizing biochemical simulations, potentially lowering study timetables and costs. The increasing study into quantum-primarily based technologies highlights their revolutionary opportunities in medical studies and patient consequences. However, problems like hardware constraints and mistakes prices persist, necessitating ongoing innovation for practical software.

25.11 Conclusion

Research on the usage of QC and ML was shown to improve disease models for prediction and drug discovery. It highlights how QC might accelerate the advent of medicine *via* optimizing molecular simulations and lowering study time and expenses, resulting in advanced prognosis, medication change, and affected person effects. Machine learning is used in medicinal drugs to create predictive models and access substantial amounts of international sickness records. Secure healthcare systems for facts have been emerging, with QC having a crucial position in the management of healthcare data. This information can be used to discover the quickest drug-forming techniques and the safest infection mechanisms, therefore enhancing healthcare efficacy. The article also highlights QC's capability in scientific study with the aid of proving its capacity to manipulate large datasets, give a dependable assessment, and change treatments for persons and disease detection. The scope of the study is restrained by using the modern-day state of QC technological advances, which will not be fully suitable for massive-scale biology applications. Furthermore, the combination of QC with device-gaining knowledge for clinical purposes remains in its experimental grade, with few realistic uses. Future studies would possibly give attention to enhancing quantum algorithms for real-time scientific applications and growing the capability of QC structures for biomedical information. Furthermore, combining QC with AI-pushed custom-designed medicine has the potential to transform infection evaluation and treatment innovation.

References

1. Marchetti, L., *et al.*, Quantum computing algorithms: getting closer to critical problems in computational biology. *Briefings Bioinf.*, 23, 6, bbac437, 2022, https://doi.org/10.1093/bib/bbac437.
2. McWeeney, S., *et al.*, Quantum Computing for Biomedical Computational and Data Sciences: A Joint DOE-NIH Roundtable, USDOE Office of Science (SC), United States, 2023, https://doi.org/10.2172/2228574.
3. Davids, J., *et al.*, Artificial intelligence in medicine using quantum computing in the future of healthcare, in: *Artificial Intelligence in Medicine*, pp. 423–446, Springer International Publishing, Cham, 2022, https://doi.org/10.1007/978-3-030-64573-1_338.
4. Flöther, F.F., The state of quantum computing applications in health and medicine. *Study Dir. Quantum Technol.*, 1, e10, 2023, https://doi.org/10.1017/qut.2023.4.
5. Jayanthi, P., Rai, B.K., Muralikrishna, I., The potential of quantum computing in healthcare, in: *Technology Road Mappings for Quantum Computing and Engineering*, pp. 81–101, Hershey, PA, IGI Global, 2022, https://doi.org/10.4018/978-1-7998-9183-3.ch006.
6. Giang, V., Quantum Computing and its Applications in Healthcare. *OUR J.: ODU Undergrad. Study J.*, 10, 1, 5, 2023, https://doi.org/10.1038/s42254-023-00558-3.
7. Laxminarayana, N., *et al.*, Quantum-assisted activation for supervised learning in healthcare-based intrusion detection systems. *IEEE Trans. Artif. Intell.*, 5, 3, 977–984, 2022, https://doi.org/10.1002/wcms.1481.
8. Khan, H.U., *et al.*, Multi-criterial based feature selection for health care system. *Mobile Netw. Appl.*, 1–14, 2023, https://doi.org/10.1109/AISC56616.2023.10085380.
9. Aggarwal, L., *et al.*, Quantum healthcare computing using precision based granular approach. *Appl. Soft Comput.*, 144, 1104585, 2023, https://doi.org/10.1016/j.asoc.2023.110458.
10. Durant, T.J.S., *et al.*, Young, L.O.-M., Schulz, W.L., A primer for quantum computing and its applications to healthcare and biomedical study. *J. Am. Med. Inf. Assoc.*, 31, 8, 1774–1784, 2024, https://doi.org/10.1093/jamia/ocae149.

11. van der Kerk, C., *et al.*, Quantum Computing in the Biomedical Sciences; A Brief Introduction into Concepts and Applications. *Comput. Inf. Sci.*, 12, 3, 104–116, 2019, https://doi.org/10.5539/cis.v12n3p104.
12. Zhang, Y. and Ni, Q., Recent advances in quantum machine learning. *Quantum Eng.*, 2, 1, e34, 2020, https://doi.org/10.1002/que2.34.
13. Jeyaraman, N., *et al.*, Revolutionizing Healthcare: The Emerging Role of Quantum Computing in Enhancing Medical Technology and Treatment. *Cureus*, 16, 8, e67486, 2024, https://doi.org/10.7759/cureus.67486.
14. https://www.kaggle.com/datasets/fatemehmehrparvar/lung-disease?select=Lung+X-Ray+Image.
15. https://www.kaggle.com/datasets/johnsmith88/heart-disease-dataset.
16. Abdulsalam, G., Meshoul, S., Shaiba, H., Explainable heart disease prediction using ensemble-quantum machine learning approach. *Intell. Autom. Soft Comput.*, 36, 1, 761–779, 2023, https://doi.org/10.32604/iasc.2023.032262.
17. Maheshwari, D., *et al.*, Quantum machine learning applied to electronic healthcare records for ischemic heart disease classification. *Hum.-Cent. Comput. Inf. Sci.*, 1, 06, 2023, https://doi.org/10.22967/HCIS.2023.13.006.
18. Sha, M., Quantum intelligence in medicine: Empowering thyroid disease prediction through advanced machine learning. *IET Quantum Commun.*, 5, 2, 123–139, 2024, https://doi.org/10.1049/qtc2.12078.
19. Babu, S.V., Ramya, P., Gracewell, J., Revolutionizing heart disease prediction with quantum-enhanced machine learning. *Sci. Rep.*, 14, 1, 7453, 2024, https://doi.org/10.1038/s41598-024-55991-w.
20. Prabhu, S., *et al.*, QuCardio: Application of Quantum Machine Learning for Detection of Cardiovascular Diseases. *IEEE Access*, 11, 136122–1361355, 2023, https://doi.org/10.1109/ACCESS.2023.3338145.
21. Jeber Belay, A., *et al.*, Deep Ensemble learning and quantum machine learning approach for Alzheimer's disease detection. *Sci. Rep.*, 14, 1, 14196, 2024, https://doi.org/10.1038/s41598-024-61452-1.
22. Gupta, H., *et al.*, Comparative performance analysis of quantum machine learning with deep learning for diabetes prediction. *Complex Intell. Syst.*, 8, 4, 3073–3087, 2022, https://doi.org/10.1007/s40747-021-00398-7.
23. Kumar, Y., *et al.*, Heart failure detection using quantum-enhanced machine learning and traditional machine learning techniques for internet of artificially intelligent medical things. *Wirel. Commun. Mobile Comput.*, 2021, 1, 1616725, 2021, https://doi.org/10.1155/2021/1616725.
24. Maheshwari, D., *et al.*, Machine learning applied to diabetes dataset using Quantum versus Classical computation, in: *2020 IEEE international symposium on signal processing and information technology (ISSPIT)*, IEEE, pp. 1–6, 2020, https://doi.org/10.1109/ISSPIT51521.2020.9408944.
25. Enad, H.G. and Mohammed, M.A., Cloud computing-based framework for heart disease classification using quantum machine learning approach. *J. Intell. Syst.*, 33, 1, 20230261, 2024, https://doi.org/10.1515/jisys-2023-0261.

26. Pyrkov, A., *et al.*, Quantum computing for near-term applications in generative chemistry and drug discovery. *Drug Discov. Today*, 28, 8, 103675, 2023, https://doi.org/10.1016/j.drudis.2023.103675.
27. Bonde, B., *et al.*, *High Performance Computing for Drug Discovery and Biomedicine*, pp. 153–179, New York, Springer Nature, 2023, https://doi.org/10.1007/978-1-0716-3449-3_7.
28. Batra, K., *et al.*, Quantum machine learning algorithms for drug discovery applications. *J. Chem. Inf. Model.*, 61, 6, 2641–2647, 2021, https://doi. org/10.1021/acs.jcim.1c00166.
29. Santagati, R., Aspuru-Guzik, A., Babbush, R., Degroote, M., Gonzalez, L., Kyoseva, E., Moll, N., *et al.*, Drug design on quantum computers. *Nat. Phys.*, 20, 4, 549–557, 2024, https://doi.org/10.1038/s41567-024-02411-5.
30. Zhou, Y., *et al.*, Implementation of The Future of Drug Discovery: Quantum Based Machine Learning Simulation (QMLS). *arXiv preprint arXiv:2308.08561*. https://doi.org/10.5281/zenodo.7983561, 2023.
31. Lau, B., *et al.*, Insights from incorporating quantum computing into drug design workflows. *Bioinformatics*, 39, 1, btac789, 2023, https://doi.org/10.1093/bioinformatics/btac789.
32. Kumar, G., *et al.*, Recent Advances in Quantum Computing for Drug Discovery and Development. *IEEE Access*, 12, 64491–64509, 2024, https://doi.org/10.1109/ACCESS.2024.3376408.
33. Li, W., Yin, Z., *et al.*, A Quantum Computing Pipeline for Real World Drug Discovery: From Algorithm to Quantum Hardware. *bioRxiv*, 2024–01, 2024, https://doi.org/10.1101/2024.01.08.574600.

Index

Printed in the USA/Agawam, MA
September 16, 2026

910661.150